HART CRANE

Hart Crane

COMPLETE POEMS
AND SELECTED LETTERS

THE LIBRARY OF AMERICA

The paper used in this publication meets the
minimum requirements of the American National Standard for
Information Sciences—Permanence of Paper for Printed
Library Materials, ANSI Z39.48—1984.

Distributed to the trade in the United States
by Penguin Putnam Inc.
and in Canada by Penguin Books Canada Ltd.

Library of Congress Catalog Number: 2006040922
For cataloging information, see end of Notes.
ISBN 978–1–931082–99–0
ISBN 1–931082–99–5

———

First Printing
The Library of America—168

Manufactured in the United States of America

Contents

Poems Published in Magazines

WHITE BUILDINGS

Ce ne peut être que la fin du monde, en avançant.
—RIMBAUD

Legend

As silent as a mirror is believed
Realities plunge in silence by . . .

I am not ready for repentance;
Nor to match regrets. For the moth
Bends no more than the still
Imploring flame. And tremorous
In the white falling flakes
Kisses are,—
The only worth all granting.

It is to be learned—
This cleaving and this burning,
But only by the one who
Spends out himself again.

Twice and twice
(Again the smoking souvenir,
Bleeding eidolon!) and yet again.
Until the bright logic is won
Unwhispering as a mirror
Is believed.

Then, drop by caustic drop, a perfect cry
Shall string some constant harmony,—
Relentless caper for all those who step
The legend of their youth into the noon.

Black Tambourine

The interests of a black man in a cellar
Mark tardy judgment on the world's closed door.
Gnats toss in the shadow of a bottle,
And a roach spans a crevice in the floor.

Aesop, driven to pondering, found
Heaven with the tortoise and the hare;
Fox brush and sow ear top his grave
And mingling incantations on the air.

The black man, forlorn in the cellar,
Wanders in some mid-kingdom, dark, that lies,
Between his tambourine, stuck on the wall,
And, in Africa, a carcass quick with flies.

Emblems of Conduct

By a peninsula the wanderer sat and sketched
The uneven valley graves. While the apostle gave
Alms to the meek the volcano burst
With sulphur and aureate rocks . . .
For joy rides in stupendous coverings
Luring the living into spiritual gates.

Orators follow the universe
And radio the complete laws to the people.
The apostle conveys thought through discipline.
Bowls and cups fill historians with adorations,—
Dull lips commemorating spiritual gates.

The wanderer later chose this spot of rest
Where marble clouds support the sea
And where was finally borne a chosen hero.
By that time summer and smoke were past.
Dolphins still played, arching the horizons,
But only to build memories of spiritual gates.

My Grandmother's Love Letters

There are no stars tonight
But those of memory.
Yet how much room for memory there is
In the loose girdle of soft rain.

There is even room enough
For the letters of my mother's mother,
Elizabeth,
That have been pressed so long
Into a corner of the roof
That they are brown and soft,
And liable to melt as snow.

Over the greatness of such space
Steps must be gentle.
It is all hung by an invisible white hair.
It trembles as birch limbs webbing the air.

And I ask myself:

"Are your fingers long enough to play
Old keys that are but echoes:
Is the silence strong enough
To carry back the music to its source
And back to you again
As though to her?"

Yet I would lead my grandmother by the hand
Through much of what she would not understand;
And so I stumble. And the rain continues on the roof
With such a sound of gently pitying laughter.

Sunday Morning Apples

To William Sommer

The leaves will fall again sometime and fill
The fleece of nature with those purposes
That are your rich and faithful strength of line.

But now there are challenges to spring
In that ripe nude with head
                reared
Into a realm of swords, her purple shadow
Bursting on the winter of the world
From whiteness that cries defiance to the snow.

A boy runs with a dog before the sun, straddling
Spontaneities that form their independent orbits,
Their own perennials of light
In the valley where you live
              (called Brandywine).

I have seen the apples there that toss you secrets,—
Beloved apples of seasonable madness
That feed your inquiries with aerial wine.
Put them again beside a pitcher with a knife,
And poise them full and ready for explosion—
The apples, Bill, the apples!

Praise for an Urn

In Memoriam: Ernest Nelson

It was a kind and northern face
That mingled in such exile guise
The everlasting eyes of Pierrot
And, of Gargantua, the laughter.

His thoughts, delivered to me
From the white coverlet and pillow,
I see now, were inheritances—
Delicate riders of the storm.

The slant moon on the slanting hill
Once moved us toward presentiments
Of what the dead keep, living still,
And such assessments of the soul

As, perched in the crematory lobby,
The insistent clock commented on,
Touching as well upon our praise
Of glories proper to the time.

Still, having in mind gold hair,
I cannot see that broken brow
And miss the dry sound of bees
Stretching across a lucid space.

Scatter these well-meant idioms
Into the smoky spring that fills
The suburbs, where they will be lost.
They are no trophies of the sun.

Garden Abstract

The apple on its bough is her desire,—
Shining suspension, mimic of the sun.
The bough has caught her breath up, and her voice,
Dumbly articulate in the slant and rise
Of branch on branch above her, blurs her eyes.
She is prisoner of the tree and its green fingers.

And so she comes to dream herself the tree,
The wind possessing her, weaving her young veins,
Holding her to the sky and its quick blue,
Drowning the fever of her hands in sunlight.
She has no memory, nor fear, nor hope
Beyond the grass and shadows at her feet.

Stark Major

The lover's death, how regular
With lifting spring and starker
Vestiges of the sun that somehow
Filter in to us before we waken.

Not yet is there that heat and sober
Vivisection of more clamant air
That hands joined in the dark will answer
After the daily circuits of its glare.

It is the time of sundering . . .
Beneath the green silk counterpane
Her mound of undelivered life
Lies cool upon her—not yet pain.

And she will wake before you pass,
Scarcely aloud, beyond her door,
And every third step down the stair
Until you reach the muffled floor—

Will laugh and call your name; while you,
Still answering her faint good-byes,
Will find the street, only to look
At doors and stone with broken eyes.

Walk now, and note the lover's death.
Henceforth her memory is more
Than yours, in cries, in ecstasies
You cannot ever reach to share.

Chaplinesque

We make our meek adjustments,
Contented with such random consolations
As the wind deposits
In slithered and too ample pockets.

For we can still love the world, who find
A famished kitten on the step, and know
Recesses for it from the fury of the street,
Or warm torn elbow coverts.

We will sidestep, and to the final smirk
Dally the doom of that inevitable thumb
That slowly chafes its puckered index toward us,
Facing the dull squint with what innocence
And what surprise!

And yet these fine collapses are not lies
More than the pirouettes of any pliant cane;
Our obsequies are, in a way, no enterprise.
We can evade you, and all else but the heart:
What blame to us if the heart live on.

The game enforces smirks; but we have seen
The moon in lonely alleys make
A grail of laughter of an empty ash can,
And through all sound of gaiety and quest
Have heard a kitten in the wilderness.

Pastorale

No more violets,
And the year
Broken into smoky panels.
What woods remember now
Her calls, her enthusiasms.

That ritual of sap and leaves
The sun drew out,
Ends in this latter muffled
Bronze and brass. The wind
Takes rein.

If, dusty, I bear
An image beyond this
Already fallen harvest,
I can only query, "Fool—
Have you remembered too long;

Or was there too little said
For ease or resolution—
Summer scarcely begun
And violets,
A few picked, the rest dead?"

In Shadow

Out in the late amber afternoon,
Confused among chrysanthemums,
Her parasol, a pale balloon,
Like a waiting moon, in shadow swims.

Her furtive lace and misty hair
Over the garden dial distill
The sunlight,—then withdrawing, wear
Again the shadows at her will.

Gently yet suddenly, the sheen
Of stars inwraps her parasol.
She hears my step behind the green
Twilight, stiller than shadows, fall.

"Come, it is too late,—too late
To risk alone the light's decline:
Nor has the evening long to wait,"—
But her own words are night's and mine.

The Fernery

The lights that travel on her spectacles
Seldom, now, meet a mirror in her eyes.
But turning, as you may chance to lift a shade
Beside her and her fernery, is to follow
The zigzags fast around dry lips composed
To darkness through a wreath of sudden pain.

—So, while fresh sunlight splinters humid green
I have known myself a nephew to confusions
That sometimes take up residence and reign
In crowns less grey—O merciless tidy hair!

North Labrador

A land of leaning ice
Hugged by plaster-grey arches of sky,
Flings itself silently
Into eternity.

"Has no one come here to win you,
Or left you with the faintest blush
Upon your glittering breasts?
Have you no memories, O Darkly Bright?"

Cold-hushed, there is only the shifting of moments
That journey toward no Spring—
No birth, no death, no time nor sun
In answer.

Repose of Rivers

The willows carried a slow sound,
A sarabande the wind mowed on the mead.
I could never remember
That seething, steady leveling of the marshes
Till age had brought me to the sea.

Flags, weeds. And remembrance of steep alcoves
Where cypresses shared the noon's
Tyranny; they drew me into hades almost.
And mammoth turtles climbing sulphur dreams
Yielded, while sun-silt rippled them
Asunder . . .

How much I would have bartered! the black gorge
And all the singular nestings in the hills
Where beavers learn stitch and tooth.
The pond I entered once and quickly fled—
I remember now its singing willow rim.

And finally, in that memory all things nurse;
After the city that I finally passed
With scalding unguents spread and smoking darts
The monsoon cut across the delta
At gulf gates . . .   There, beyond the dykes

I heard wind flaking sapphire, like this summer,
And willows could not hold more steady sound.

Paraphrase

Of a steady winking beat between
Systole, diastole spokes-of-a-wheel
One rushing from the bed at night
May find the record wedged in his soul.

Above the feet the clever sheets
Lie guard upon the integers of life:
For what skims in between uncurls the toe,
Involves the hands in purposeless repose.

But from its bracket how can the tongue tell
When systematic morn shall sometime flood
The pillow—how desperate is the light
That shall not rouse, how faint the crow's cavil

As, when stunned in that antarctic blaze,
Your head, unrocking to a pulse, already
Hollowed by air, posts a white paraphrase
Among bruised roses on the papered wall.

Possessions

Witness now this trust! the rain
That steals softly direction
And the key, ready to hand—sifting
One moment in sacrifice (the direst)
Through a thousand nights the flesh
Assaults outright for bolts that linger
Hidden,—O undirected as the sky
That through its black foam has no eyes
For this fixed stone of lust . . .

Accumulate such moments to an hour:
Account the total of this trembling tabulation.
I know the screen, the distant flying taps
And stabbing medley that sways—
And the mercy, feminine, that stays
As though prepared.

And I, entering, take up the stone
As quiet as you can make a man . . .
In Bleecker Street, still trenchant in a void,
Wounded by apprehensions out of speech,
I hold it up against a disk of light—
I, turning, turning on smoked forking spires,
The city's stubborn lives, desires.

Tossed on these horns, who bleeding dies,
Lacks all but piteous admissions to be spilt
Upon the page whose blind sum finally burns
Record of rage and partial appetites.
The pure possession, the inclusive cloud
Whose heart is fire shall come,—the white wind rase
All but bright stones wherein our smiling plays.

Lachrymae Christi

Whitely, while benzine
Rinsings from the moon
Dissolve all but the windows of the mills
(Inside the sure machinery
Is still
And curdled only where a sill
Sluices its one unyielding smile)

Immaculate venom binds
The fox's teeth, and swart
Thorns freshen on the year's
First blood. From flanks unfended,
Twanged red perfidies of spring
Are trillion on the hill.

And the nights opening
Chant pyramids,—
Anoint with innocence,—recall
To music and retrieve what perjuries
Had galvanized the eyes.

                While chime
Beneath and all around
Distilling clemencies,—worms'
Inaudible whistle, tunneling
Not penitence
But song, as these
Perpetual fountains, vines,—

Thy Nazarene and tinder eyes.

(Let sphinxes from the ripe
Borage of death have cleared my tongue
Once and again; vermin and rod
No longer bind. Some sentient cloud
Of tears flocks through the tendoned loam:
Betrayed stones slowly speak.)

Names peeling from Thine eyes
And their undimming lattices of flame,
Spell out in palm and pain
Compulsion of the year, O Nazarene.

Lean long from sable, slender boughs,
Unstanched and luminous. And as the nights
Strike from Thee perfect spheres,
Lift up in lilac-emerald breath the grail
Of earth again—

                    Thy face
From charred and riven stakes, O
Dionysus, Thy
Unmangled target smile.

Passage

Where the cedar leaf divides the sky
I heard the sea.
In sapphire arenas of the hills
I was promised an improved infancy.

Sulking, sanctioning the sun,
My memory I left in a ravine,—
Casual louse that tissues the buckwheat,
Aprons rocks, congregates pears
In moonlit bushels
And wakens alleys with a hidden cough.

Dangerously the summer burned
(I had joined the entrainments of the wind).
The shadows of boulders lengthened my back:
In the bronze gongs of my cheeks
The rain dried without odour.

"It is not long, it is not long;
See where the red and black
Vine-stanchioned valleys—": but the wind
Died speaking through the ages that you know
And hug, chimney-sooted heart of man!
So was I turned about and back, much as your smoke
Compiles a too well known biography.

The evening was a spear in the ravine
That throve through very oak. And had I walked
The dozen particular decimals of time?
Touching an opening laurel, I found
A thief beneath, my stolen book in hand.

"Why are you back here—smiling an iron coffin?"
"To argue with the laurel," I replied:
"Am justified in transience, fleeing
Under the constant wonder of your eyes—."

He closed the book. And from the Ptolemies
Sand troughed us in a glittering abyss.
A serpent swam a vertex to the sun
—On unpaced beaches leaned its tongue and drummed.
What fountains did I hear? what icy speeches?
Memory, committed to the page, had broke.

The Wine Menagerie

Invariably when wine redeems the sight,
Narrowing the mustard scansions of the eyes,
A leopard ranging always in the brow
Asserts a vision in the slumbering gaze.

Then glozening decanters that reflect the street
Wear me in crescents on their bellies. Slow
Applause flows into liquid cynosures:
—I am conscripted to their shadows' glow.

Against the imitation onyx wainscoting
(Painted emulsion of snow, eggs, yarn, coal, manure)
Regard the forceps of the smile that takes her.
Percussive sweat is spreading to his hair. Mallets,
Her eyes, unmake an instant of the world . . .

What is it in this heap the serpent pries—
Whose skin, facsimile of time, unskeins
Octagon, sapphire transepts round the eyes;
—From whom some whispered carillon assures
Speed to the arrow into feathered skies?

Sharp to the windowpane guile drags a face,
And as the alcove of her jealousy recedes
An urchin who has left the snow
Nudges a cannister across the bar
While August meadows somewhere clasp his brow.

Each chamber, transept, coins some squint,
Remorseless line, minting their separate wills—
Poor streaked bodies wreathing up and out,
Unwitting the stigma that each turn repeals:
Between black tusks the roses shine!

New thresholds, new anatomies! Wine talons
Build freedom up about me and distill
This competence—to travel in a tear
Sparkling alone, within another's will.

Until my blood dreams a receptive smile
Wherein new purities are snared; where chimes
Before some flame of gaunt repose a shell
Tolled once, perhaps, by every tongue in hell.
—Anguished, the wit that cries out of me:

"Alas,—these frozen billows of your skill!
Invent new dominoes of love and bile . . .
Ruddy, the tooth implicit of the world
Has followed you. Though in the end you know
And count some dim inheritance of sand,
How much yet meets the treason of the snow.

"Rise from the dates and crumbs. And walk away,
Stepping over Holofernes' shins—
Beyond the wall, whose severed head floats by
With Baptist John's. Their whispering begins.

"—And fold your exile on your back again;
Petrushka's valentine pivots on its pin."

Recitative

Regard the capture here, O Janus-faced,
As double as the hands that twist this glass.
Such eyes at search or rest you cannot see;
Reciting pain or glee, how can you bear!

Twin shadowed halves: the breaking second holds
In each the skin alone, and so it is
I crust a plate of vibrant mercury
Borne cleft to you, and brother in the half.

Inquire this much-exacting fragment smile,
Its drums and darkest blowing leaves ignore,—
Defer though, revocation of the tears
That yield attendance to one crucial sign.

Look steadily—how the wind feasts and spins
The brain's disk shivered against lust. Then watch
While darkness, like an ape's face, falls away,
And gradually white buildings answer day.

Let the same nameless gulf beleaguer us—
Alike suspend us from atrocious sums
Built floor by floor on shafts of steel that grant
The plummet heart, like Absalom, no stream.

The highest tower,—let her ribs palisade
Wrenched gold of Nineveh;—yet leave the tower.
The bridge swings over salvage, beyond wharves;
A wind abides the ensign of your will . . .

In alternating bells have you not heard
All hours clapped dense into a single stride?
Forgive me for an echo of these things,
And let us walk through time with equal pride.

For the Marriage of Faustus and Helen

*"And so we may arrive by Talmud skill
And profane Greek to raise the building up
Of Helen's house against the Ismaelite,
King of Thogarma, and his habergeons
Brimstony, blue and fiery; and the force
Of King Abaddon, and the beast of Cittim;
Which Rabbi David Kimchi, Onkelos,
And Aben Ezra do interpret Rome."*
—THE ALCHEMIST.

I

The mind has shown itself at times
Too much the baked and labeled dough
Divided by accepted multitudes.
Across the stacked partitions of the day—
Across the memoranda, baseball scores,
The stenographic smiles and stock quotations
Smutty wings flash out equivocations.

The mind is brushed by sparrow wings;
Numbers, rebuffed by asphalt, crowd
The margins of the day, accent the curbs,

Convoying divers dawns on every corner
To druggist, barber and tobacconist,
Until the graduate opacities of evening
Take them away as suddenly to somewhere
Virginal perhaps, less fragmentary, cool.

*There is the world dimensional for
those untwisted by the love of things
irreconcilable . . .*

And yet, suppose some evening I forgot
The fare and transfer, yet got by that way
Without recall,—lost yet poised in traffic.
Then I might find your eyes across an aisle,
Still flickering with those prefigurations—
Prodigal, yet uncontested now,
Half-riant before the jerky window frame.

There is some way, I think, to touch
Those hands of yours that count the nights
Stippled with pink and green advertisements.
And now, before its arteries turn dark
I would have you meet this bartered blood.
Imminent in his dream, none better knows
The white wafer cheek of love, or offers words
Lightly as moonlight on the eaves meets snow.

Reflective conversion of all things
At your deep blush, when ecstasies thread
The limbs and belly, when rainbows spread
Impinging on the throat and sides . . .
Inevitable, the body of the world
Weeps in inventive dust for the hiatus
That winks above it, bluet in your breasts.

The earth may glide diaphanous to death;
But if I lift my arms it is to bend
To you who turned away once, Helen, knowing
The press of troubled hands, too alternate
With steel and soil to hold you endlessly.

I meet you, therefore, in that eventual flame
You found in final chains, no captive then—
Beyond their million brittle, bloodshot eyes;
White, through white cities passed on to assume
That world which comes to each of us alone.

Accept a lone eye riveted to your plane,
Bent axle of devotion along companion ways
That beat, continuous, to hourless days—
One inconspicuous, glowing orb of praise.

II

Brazen hypnotics glitter here;
Glee shifts from foot to foot,
Magnetic to their tremulo.
This crashing opéra bouffe,
Blest excursion! this ricochet
From roof to roof—
Know, Olympians, we are breathless
While nigger cupids scour the stars!

A thousand light shrugs balance us
Through snarling hails of melody.
White shadows slip across the floor
Splayed like cards from a loose hand;
Rhythmic ellipses lead into canters
Until somewhere a rooster banters.

Greet naïvely—yet intrepidly
New soothings, new amazements
That cornets introduce at every turn—
And you may fall downstairs with me
With perfect grace and equanimity.
Or, plaintively scud past shores
Where, by strange harmonic laws
All relatives, serene and cool,
Sit rocked in patent armchairs.

O, I have known metallic paradises
Where cuckoos clucked to finches
Above the deft catastrophes of drums.
While titters hailed the groans of death
Beneath gyrating awnings I have seen
The incunabula of the divine grotesque.
This music has a reassuring way.

The siren of the springs of guilty song—
Let us take her on the incandescent wax
Striated with nuances, nervosities
That we are heir to: she is still so young,
We cannot frown upon her as she smiles,
Dipping here in this cultivated storm
Among slim skaters of the gardened skies.

III

Capped arbiter of beauty in this street
That narrows darkly into motor dawn,—
You, here beside me, delicate ambassador
Of intricate slain numbers that arise
In whispers, naked of steel;
                          religious gunman!
Who faithfully, yourself, will fall too soon,
And in other ways than as the wind settles
On the sixteen thrifty bridges of the city:
Let us unbind our throats of fear and pity.

                    We even,
Who drove speediest destruction
In corymbulous formations of mechanics,—
Who hurried the hill breezes, spouting malice
Plangent over meadows, and looked down
On rifts of torn and empty houses
Like old women with teeth unjubilant
That waited faintly, briefly and in vain:

We know, eternal gunman, our flesh remembers
The tensile boughs, the nimble blue plateaus,
The mounted, yielding cities of the air!

That saddled sky that shook down vertical
Repeated play of fire—no hypogeum
Of wave or rock was good against one hour.
We did not ask for that, but have survived,
And will persist to speak again before
All stubble streets that have not curved
To memory, or known the ominous lifted arm
That lowers down the arc of Helen's brow
To saturate with blessing and dismay.

A goose, tobacco and cologne—
Three winged and gold-shod prophecies of heaven,
The lavish heart shall always have to leaven
And spread with bells and voices, and atone
The abating shadows of our conscript dust.

Anchises' navel, dripping of the sea,—
The hands Erasmus dipped in gleaming tides,
Gathered the voltage of blown blood and vine;
Delve upward for the new and scattered wine,
O brother-thief of time, that we recall.
Laugh out the meager penance of their days
Who dare not share with us the breath released,
The substance drilled and spent beyond repair
For golden, or the shadow of gold hair.

Distinctly praise the years, whose volatile
Blamed bleeding hands extend and thresh the height
The imagination spans beyond despair,
Outpacing bargain, vocable and prayer.

At Melville's Tomb

Often beneath the wave, wide from this ledge
The dice of drowned men's bones he saw bequeath
An embassy. Their numbers as he watched,
Beat on the dusty shore and were obscured.

And wrecks passed without sound of bells,
The calyx of death's bounty giving back
A scattered chapter, livid hieroglyph,
The portent wound in corridors of shells.

Then in the circuit calm of one vast coil,
Its lashings charmed and malice reconciled,
Frosted eyes there were that lifted altars;
And silent answers crept across the stars.

Compass, quadrant and sextant contrive
No farther tides . . . High in the azure steeps
Monody shall not wake the mariner.
This fabulous shadow only the sea keeps.

Voyages

I

Above the fresh ruffles of the surf
Bright striped urchins flay each other with sand.
They have contrived a conquest for shell shucks,
And their fingers crumble fragments of baked weed
Gaily digging and scattering.

And in answer to their treble interjections
The sun beats lightning on the waves,
The waves fold thunder on the sand;
And could they hear me I would tell them:

O brilliant kids, frisk with your dog,
Fondle your shells and sticks, bleached
By time and the elements; but there is a line
You must not cross nor ever trust beyond it
Spry cordage of your bodies to caresses
Too lichen-faithful from too wide a breast.
The bottom of the sea is cruel.

II

—And yet this great wink of eternity,
Of rimless floods, unfettered leewardings,
Samite sheeted and processioned where
Her undinal vast belly moonward bends,
Laughing the wrapt inflections of our love;

Take this Sea, whose diapason knells
On scrolls of silver snowy sentences,
The sceptred terror of whose sessions rends
As her demeanors motion well or ill,
All but the pieties of lovers' hands.

And onward, as bells off San Salvador
Salute the crocus lustres of the stars,
In these poinsettia meadows of her tides,—
Adagios of islands, O my Prodigal,
Complete the dark confessions her veins spell.

Mark how her turning shoulders wind the hours,
And hasten while her penniless rich palms
Pass superscription of bent foam and wave,—
Hasten, while they are true,—sleep, death, desire,
Close round one instant in one floating flower.

Bind us in time, O Seasons clear, and awe.
O minstrel galleons of Carib fire,
Bequeath us to no earthly shore until
Is answered in the vortex of our grave
The seal's wide spindrift gaze toward paradise.

III

Infinite consanguinity it bears—
This tendered theme of you that light
Retrieves from sea plains where the sky
Resigns a breast that every wave enthrones;
While ribboned water lanes I wind
Are laved and scattered with no stroke
Wide from your side, whereto this hour
The sea lifts, also, reliquary hands.

And so, admitted through black swollen gates
That must arrest all distance otherwise,—
Past whirling pillars and lithe pediments,
Light wrestling there incessantly with light,
Star kissing star through wave on wave unto
Your body rocking!
                and where death, if shed,
Presumes no carnage, but this single change,—
Upon the steep floor flung from dawn to dawn
The silken skilled transmemberment of song;

Permit me voyage, love, into your hands . . .

IV

Whose counted smile of hours and days, suppose
I know as spectrum of the sea and pledge
Vastly now parting gulf on gulf of wings
Whose circles bridge, I know, (from palms to the severe
Chilled albatross's white immutability)
No stream of greater love advancing now
Than, singing, this mortality alone
Through clay aflow immortally to you.

All fragrance irrefragably, and claim
Madly meeting logically in this hour
And region that is ours to wreathe again,
Portending eyes and lips and making told
The chancel port and portion of our June—

Shall they not stem and close in our own steps
Bright staves of flowers and quills today as I
Must first be lost in fatal tides to tell?

In signature of the incarnate word
The harbor shoulders to resign in mingling
Mutual blood, transpiring as foreknown
And widening noon within your breast for gathering
All bright insinuations that my years have caught
For islands where must lead inviolably
Blue latitudes and levels of your eyes,—

In this expectant, still exclaim receive
The secret oar and petals of all love.

v

Meticulous, past midnight in clear rime,
Infrangible and lonely, smooth as though cast
Together in one merciless white blade—
The bay estuaries fleck the hard sky limits.

—As if too brittle or too clear to touch!
The cables of our sleep so swiftly filed,
Already hang, shred ends from remembered stars.
One frozen trackless smile . . . What words
Can strangle this deaf moonlight? For we

Are overtaken. Now no cry, no sword
Can fasten or deflect this tidal wedge,
Slow tyranny of moonlight, moonlight loved
And changed . . . "There's

Nothing like this in the world," you say,
Knowing I cannot touch your hand and look
Too, into that godless cleft of sky
Where nothing turns but dead sands flashing.

"—And never to quite understand!" No,
In all the argosy of your bright hair I dreamed
Nothing so flagless as this piracy.

But now
Draw in your head, alone and too tall here.
Your eyes already in the slant of drifting foam;
Your breath sealed by the ghosts I do not know:
Draw in your head and sleep the long way home.

VI

Where icy and bright dungeons lift
Of swimmers their lost morning eyes,
And ocean rivers, churning, shift
Green borders under stranger skies,

Steadily as a shell secretes
Its beating leagues of monotone,
Or as many waters trough the sun's
Red kelson past the cape's wet stone;

O rivers mingling toward the sky
And harbor of the phoenix' breast—
My eyes pressed black against the prow,
—Thy derelict and blinded guest

Waiting, afire, what name, unspoke,
I cannot claim: let thy waves rear
More savage than the death of kings,
Some splintered garland for the seer.

Beyond siroccos harvesting
The solstice thunders, crept away,
Like a cliff swinging or a sail
Flung into April's inmost day—

Creation's blithe and petalled word
To the lounged goddess when she rose
Conceding dialogue with eyes
That smile unsearchable repose—

Still fervid covenant, Belle Isle,
—Unfolded floating dais before
Which rainbows twine continual hair—
Belle Isle, white echo of the oar!

The imaged Word, it is, that holds
Hushed willows anchored in its glow.
It is the unbetrayable reply
Whose accent no farewell can know.

THE BRIDGE

From going to and fro in the earth,
and from walking up and down in it.
THE BOOK OF JOB

To
Brooklyn Bridge

How many dawns, chill from his rippling rest
The seagull's wings shall dip and pivot him,
Shedding white rings of tumult, building high
Over the chained bay waters Liberty—

Then, with inviolate curve, forsake our eyes
As apparitional as sails that cross
Some page of figures to be filed away;
—Till elevators drop us from our day . . .

I think of cinemas, panoramic sleights
With multitudes bent toward some flashing scene
Never disclosed, but hastened to again,
Foretold to other eyes on the same screen;

And Thee, across the harbor, silver-paced
As though the sun took step of thee, yet left
Some motion ever unspent in thy stride,—
Implicitly thy freedom staying thee!

Out of some subway scuttle, cell or loft
A bedlamite speeds to thy parapets,
Tilting there momently, shrill shirt ballooning,
A jest falls from the speechless caravan.

Down Wall, from girder into street noon leaks,
A rip-tooth of the sky's acetylene;
All afternoon the cloud-flown derricks turn . . .
Thy cables breathe the North Atlantic still.

And obscure as that heaven of the Jews,
Thy guerdon . . . Accolade thou dost bestow
Of anonymity time cannot raise:
Vibrant reprieve and pardon thou dost show.

O harp and altar, of the fury fused,
(How could mere toil align thy choiring strings!)
Terrific threshold of the prophet's pledge,
Prayer of pariah, and the lover's cry,—

Again the traffic lights that skim thy swift
Unfractioned idiom, immaculate sigh of stars,
Beading thy path—condense eternity:
And we have seen night lifted in thine arms.

Under thy shadow by the piers I waited;
Only in darkness is thy shadow clear.
The City's fiery parcels all undone,
Already snow submerges an iron year . . .

O Sleepless as the river under thee,
Vaulting the sea, the prairies' dreaming sod,
Unto us lowliest sometime sweep, descend
And of the curveship lend a myth to God.

I
Ave Maria

Venient annis, saecula seris,
Quibus Oceanus vincula rerum
Laxet et ingens pateat tellus
Tethysque novos detegat orbes
Nec sit terris ultima Thule.

—SENECA

Be with me, Luis de San Angel, now—
Witness before the tides can wrest away
The word I bring, O you who reined my suit
Into the Queen's great heart that doubtful day;
For I have seen now what no perjured breath
Of clown nor sage can riddle or gainsay;—
To you, too, Juan Perez, whose counsel fear
And greed adjourned,—I bring you back Cathay!

Here waves climb into dusk on gleaming mail;
Invisible valves of the sea,—locks, tendons
Crested and creeping, troughing corridors
That fall back yawning to another plunge.
Slowly the sun's red caravel drops light
Once more behind us. . . . It is morning there—
O where our Indian emperies lie revealed,
Yet lost, all, let this keel one instant yield!

I thought of Genoa; and this truth, now proved,
That made me exile in her streets, stood me
More absolute than ever—biding the moon
Till dawn should clear that dim frontier, first seen
—The Chan's great continent. . . . Then faith, not fear
Nigh surged me witless. . . . Hearing the surf near—
I, wonder-breathing, kept the watch,—saw
The first palm chevron the first lighted hill.

And lowered. And they came out to us crying,
"The Great White Birds!" (O Madre Maria, still
One ship of these thou grantest safe returning;

Columbus,
alone, gazing
toward Spain,
invokes the
presence of
two faithful
partisans of
his quest . . .

Assure us through thy mantle's ageless blue!)
And record of more, floating in a casque,
Was tumbled from us under bare poles scudding;
And later hurricanes may claim more pawn. . . .
For here between two worlds, another, harsh,

This third, of water, tests the word; lo, here
Bewilderment and mutiny heap whelming
Laughter, and shadow cuts sleep from the heart
Almost as though the Moor's flung scimitar
Found more than flesh to fathom in its fall.
Yet under tempest-lash and surfeitings
Some inmost sob, half-heard, dissuades the abyss,
Merges the wind in measure to the waves,

Series on series, infinite,—till eyes
Starved wide on blackened tides, accrete—enclose
This turning rondure whole, this crescent ring
Sun-cusped and zoned with modulated fire
Like pearls that whisper through the Doge's hands
—Yet no delirium of jewels! O Fernando,
Take of that eastern shore, this western sea,
Yet yield thy God's, thy Virgin's charity!

—Rush down the plenitude, and you shall see
Isaiah counting famine on this lee!
                    .   .   .

An herb, a stray branch among salty teeth,
The jellied weeds that drag the shore,—perhaps
Tomorrow's moon will grant us Saltes Bar—
Palos again,—a land cleared of long war.
Some Angelus environs the cordage tree;
Dark waters onward shake the dark prow free.
                    .   .   .

O Thou who sleepest on Thyself, apart
Like ocean athwart lanes of death and birth,
And all the eddying breath between dost search
Cruelly with love thy parable of man,—
Inquisitor! incognizable Word
Of Eden and the enchained Sepulchre,

Into thy steep savannahs, burning blue,
Utter to loneliness the sail is true.

Who grindest oar, and arguing the mast
Subscribest holocaust of ships, O Thou
Within whose primal scan consummately
The glistening seignories of Ganges swim;—
Who sendest greeting by the corposant,
And Teneriffe's garnet—flamed it in a cloud,
Urging through night our passage to the Chan;—
Te Deum laudamus, for thy teeming span!

Of all that amplitude that time explores,
A needle in the sight, suspended north,—
Yielding by inference and discard, faith
And true appointment from the hidden shoal:
This disposition that thy night relates
From Moon to Saturn in one sapphire wheel:
The orbic wake of thy once whirling feet,
Elohim, still I hear thy sounding heel!

White toil of heaven's cordons, mustering
In holy rings all sails charged to the far
Hushed gleaming fields and pendant seething wheat
Of knowledge,—round thy brows unhooded now
—The kindled Crown! acceded of the poles
And biassed by full sails, meridians reel
Thy purpose—still one shore beyond desire!
The sea's green crying towers a-sway, Beyond

And kingdoms
                    naked in the
                                trembling heart—
        Te Deum laudamus
                                O Thou Hand of Fire

II
Powhatan's Daughter

"—Pocahuntus, a well-featured but wanton yong girle . . .
of the age of eleven or twelve years, get the boyes forth with her
into the market place, and make them wheele, falling on their
hands, turning their heels upwards, whom she would followe,
and wheele so herself, naked as she was, all the fort over."

The Harbor Dawn

Insistently through sleep—a tide of voices—
They meet you listening midway in your dream,
The long, tired sounds, fog-insulated noises:
Gongs in white surplices, beshrouded wails,
Far strum of fog horns . . . signals dispersed in
    veils.

400 years and
more . . . or is
it from the
soundless shore
of sleep that time

And then a truck will lumber past the wharves
As winch engines begin throbbing on some deck;
Or a drunken stevedore's howl and thud below
Comes echoing alley-upward through dim snow.

And if they take your sleep away sometimes
They give it back again. Soft sleeves of sound
Attend the darkling harbor, the pillowed bay;
Somewhere out there in blankness steam

Spills into steam, and wanders, washed away
—Flurried by keen fifings, eddied
Among distant chiming buoys—adrift. The sky,

Cool feathery fold, suspends, distills
This wavering slumber. . . . Slowly—
Immemorially the window, the half-covered chair
Ask nothing but this sheath of pallid air.

recalls you to
your love,
there in a
waking dream
to merge
your seed

And you beside me, blessèd now while sirens
Sing to us, stealthily weave us into day—
Serenely now, before day claims our eyes
Your cool arms murmurously about me lay.

38

While myriad snowy hands are clustering at the panes—

> *your hands within my hands are deeds;*
> *my tongue upon your throat—singing*
> *arms close; eyes wide, undoubtful*
> >   *dark*
> >   *drink the dawn—*
> *a forest shudders in your hair!*

—with whom?

The window goes blond slowly. Frostily clears.
From Cyclopean towers across Manhattan waters
—Two—three bright window-eyes aglitter, disk
The sun, released—aloft with cold gulls hither.

Who is the
woman with
us in the
dawn? . . .
whose is the
flesh our feet
have moved
upon?

The fog leans one last moment on the sill.
Under the mistletoe of dreams, a star—
As though to join us at some distant hill—
Turns in the waking west and goes to sleep.

Van Winkle

Macadam, gun-grey as the tunny's belt,
Leaps from Far Rockaway to Golden Gate:
Listen! the miles a hurdy-gurdy grinds—
Down gold arpeggios mile on mile unwinds.

Streets spread
past store and
factory—sped
by sunlight
and her
smile . . .

Times earlier, when you hurried off to school,
—It is the same hour though a later day—
You walked with Pizarro in a copybook,
And Cortes rode up, reining tautly in—
Firmly as coffee grips the taste,—and away!

There was Priscilla's cheek close in the wind,
And Captain Smith, all beard and certainty,

And Rip Van Winkle bowing by the way,—
"Is this Sleepy Hollow, friend—?" And he—

Like Memory,
she is time's
truant, shall
take you by the
hand . . .

And Rip forgot the office hours,
*   and he forgot the pay;*
*   Van Winkle sweeps a tenement*
*   way down on Avenue A,—*

The grind-organ says . . . Remember, remember
The cinder pile at the end of the backyard
Where we stoned the family of young
Garter snakes under . . . And the monoplanes
We launched—with paper wings and twisted
Rubber bands . . . Recall—recall

                              the rapid tongues
That flittered from under the ash heap day
After day whenever your stick discovered
Some sunning inch of unsuspecting fibre—
It flashed back at your thrust, as clean as fire.

And Rip was slowly made aware
*   that he, Van Winkle, was not here*
*   nor there. He woke and swore he'd seen Broadway*
*   a Catskill daisy chain in May—*

So memory, that strikes a rhyme out of a box,
Or splits a random smell of flowers through glass—
Is it the whip stripped from the lilac tree
One day in spring my father took to me,
Or is it the Sabbatical, unconscious smile
My mother almost brought me once from church
And once only, as I recall—?

It flickered through the snow screen, blindly
It forsook her at the doorway, it was gone
Before I had left the window. It
Did not return with the kiss in the hall.

Macadam, gun-grey as the tunny's belt,
Leaps from Far Rockaway to Golden Gate. . . .
Keep hold of that nickel for car-change, Rip,—
Have you got your "*Times*"—?
And hurry along, Van Winkle—it's getting late!

The River

Stick your patent name on a signboard
brother—all over—going west—young man
Tintex—Japalac—Certain-teed Overalls ads
and lands sakes! under the new playbill ripped
in the guaranteed corner—see Bert Williams
   what?
Minstrels when you steal a chicken just
save me the wing for if it isn't
Erie it ain't for miles around a
Mazda—and the telegraphic night coming on Thomas

*. . . and past
the din and
slogans of
the year—*

a Ediford—and whistling down the tracks
a headlight rushing with the sound—can you
imagine—while an EXPRESS makes time like
SCIENCE — COMMERCE and the HOLYGHOST
RADIO ROARS IN EVERY HOME WE HAVE THE NORTHPOLE
WALLSTREET AND VIRGINBIRTH WITHOUT STONES OR
WIRES OR EVEN RUNning brooks connecting ears
and no more sermons windows flashing roar
breathtaking—as you like it . . . eh?

      So the 20th Century—so
whizzed the Limited—roared by and left
three men, still hungry on the tracks, ploddingly
watching the tail lights wizen and converge, slip-
ping gimleted and neatly out of sight.

    .   .   .   .   .   .

The last bear, shot drinking in the Dakotas
Loped under wires that span the mountain stream.
Keen instruments, strung to a vast precision

Bind town to town and dream to ticking dream.   *to those*
But some men take their liquor slow—and count   *whose*
—Though they'll confess no rosary nor clue—   *addresses*
The river's minute by the far brook's year.   *are never near*
Under a world of whistles, wires and steam
Caboose-like they go ruminating through
Ohio, Indiana—blind baggage—
To Cheyenne tagging . . . Maybe Kalamazoo.

Time's rendings, time's blendings they construe
As final reckonings of fire and snow;
Strange bird-wit, like the elemental gist
Of unwalled winds they offer, singing low
My Old Kentucky Home and *Casey Jones,*
Some Sunny Day. I heard a road-gang chanting so.
And afterwards, who had a colt's eyes—one said,
"Jesus! Oh I remember watermelon days!" And sped
High in a cloud of merriment, recalled
"—And when my Aunt Sally Simpson smiled," he drawled—
"It was almost Louisiana, long ago."
"There's no place like Booneville though, Buddy,"
One said, excising a last burr from his vest,
"—For early trouting." Then peering in the can,
"—But I kept on the tracks." Possessed, resigned,
He trod the fire down pensively and grinned,
Spreading dry shingles of a beard. . . .

                                  Behind
My father's cannery works I used to see
Rail-squatters ranged in nomad raillery,
The ancient men—wifeless or runaway
Hobo-trekkers that forever search
An empire wilderness of freight and rails.
Each seemed a child, like me, on a loose perch,
Holding to childhood like some termless play.
John, Jake or Charley, hopping the slow freight
—Memphis to Tallahassee—riding the rods,
Blind fists of nothing, humpty-dumpty clods.

Yet they touch something like a key perhaps.
From pole to pole across the hills, the states
—They know a body under the wide rain;   *but who have*
Youngsters with eyes like fjords, old reprobates   *touched her,*
With racetrack jargon,—dotting immensity   *knowing her*
They lurk across her, knowing her yonder breast   *without name*
Snow-silvered, sumac-stained or smoky blue—
Is past the valley-sleepers, south or west.
—As I have trod the rumorous midnights, too,

And past the circuit of the lamp's thin flame
(O Nights that brought me to her body bare!)
Have dreamed beyond the print that bound her name.
Trains sounding the long blizzards out—I heard
Wail into distances I knew were hers.
Papooses crying on the wind's long mane
Screamed redskin dynasties that fled the brain,
—Dead echoes! But I knew her body there,
Time like a serpent down her shoulder, dark,
And space, an eaglet's wing, laid on her hair.

Under the Ozarks, domed by Iron Mountain,
The old gods of the rain lie wrapped in pools
Where eyeless fish curvet a sunken fountain   *nor the*
And re-descend with corn from querulous crows.   *myths of her*
Such pilferings make up their timeless eatage,   *fathers . . .*
Propitiate them for their timber torn
By iron, iron—always the iron dealt cleavage!
They doze now, below axe and powder horn.

And Pullman breakfasters glide glistening steel
From tunnel into field—iron strides the dew—
Straddles the hill, a dance of wheel on wheel.
You have a half-hour's wait at Siskiyou,
Or stay the night and take the next train through.
Southward, near Cairo passing, you can see
The Ohio merging,—borne down Tennessee;
And if it's summer and the sun's in dusk
Maybe the breeze will lift the River's musk
—As though the waters breathed that you might know

Memphis Johnny, Steamboat Bill, Missouri Joe.
Oh, lean from the window, if the train slows down,
As though you touched hands with some ancient clown,
—A little while gaze absently below
And hum *Deep River* with them while they go.

Yes, turn again and sniff once more—look see,
O Sheriff, Brakeman and Authority—
Hitch up your pants and crunch another quid,
For you, too, feed the River timelessly.
And few evade full measure of their fate;
Always they smile out eerily what they seem.
I could believe he joked at heaven's gate—
Dan Midland—jolted from the cold brake-beam.

Down, down—born pioneers in time's despite,
Grimed tributaries to an ancient flow—
They win no frontier by their wayward plight,
But drift in stillness, as from Jordan's brow.

You will not hear it as the sea; even stone
Is not more hushed by gravity . . . But slow,
As loth to take more tribute—sliding prone
Like one whose eyes were buried long ago

The River, spreading, flows—and spends your dream.
What are you, lost within this tideless spell?
You are your father's father, and the stream—
A liquid theme that floating niggers swell.

Damp tonnage and alluvial march of days—
Nights turbid, vascular with silted shale
And roots surrendered down of moraine clays:
The Mississippi drinks the farthest dale.

O quarrying passion, undertowed sunlight!
The basalt surface drags a jungle grace
Ochreous and lynx-barred in lengthening might;
Patience! and you shall reach the biding place!

Over De Soto's bones the freighted floors
Throb past the City storied of three thrones.
Down two more turns the Mississippi pours
(Anon tall ironsides up from salt lagoons)

And flows within itself, heaps itself free.
All fades but one thin skyline 'round . . . Ahead
No embrace opens but the stinging sea;
The River lifts itself from its long bed,

Poised wholly on its dream, a mustard glow
Tortured with history, its one will—flow!
—The Passion spreads in wide tongues, choked and slow,
Meeting the Gulf, hosannas silently below.

The Dance

The swift red flesh, a winter king—
Who squired the glacier woman down the sky?   *Then you shall*
She ran the neighing canyons all the spring;   *see her truly*
She spouted arms; she rose with maize—to die.   *—your blood*
                                                      remembering
                                                      its first
And in the autumn drouth, whose burnished   *invasion of*
        hands   *her secrecy,*
With mineral wariness found out the stone   *its first*
Where prayers, forgotten, streamed the mesa   *encounters*
        sands?   *with her kin,*
He holds the twilight's dim, perpetual throne.   *her chieftain*
                                                      lover . . . his
                                                      shade that
Mythical brows we saw retiring—loth,   *haunts the*
Disturbed and destined, into denser green.   *lakes and hills*
Greeting they sped us, on the arrow's oath:
Now lie incorrigibly what years between . . .

There was a bed of leaves, and broken play;
There was a veil upon you, Pocahontas, bride—
O Princess whose brown lap was virgin May;
And bridal flanks and eyes hid tawny pride.

I left the village for dogwood. By the canoe
Tugging below the mill-race, I could see
Your hair's keen crescent running, and the blue
First moth of evening take wing stealthily.

What laughing chains the water wove and threw!
I learned to catch the trout's moon whisper; I
Drifted how many hours I never knew,
But, watching, saw that fleet young crescent die,—

And one star, swinging, take its place, alone,
Cupped in the larches of the mountain pass—
Until, immortally, it bled into the dawn.
I left my sleek boat nibbling margin grass . . .

I took the portage climb, then chose
A further valley-shed; I could not stop.
Feet nozzled wat'ry webs of upper flows;
One white veil gusted from the very top.

O Appalachian Spring! I gained the ledge;
Steep, inaccessible smile that eastward bends
And northward reaches in that violet wedge
Of Adirondacks!—wisped of azure wands,

Over how many bluffs, tarns, streams I sped!
—And knew myself within some boding shade:—
Grey tepees tufting the blue knolls ahead,
Smoke swirling through the yellow chestnut glade . . .

A distant cloud, a thunder-bud—it grew,
That blanket of the skies: the padded foot
Within,—I heard it; 'til its rhythm drew,
—Siphoned the black pool from the heart's hot root!

A cyclone threshes in the turbine crest,
Swooping in eagle feathers down your back;
Know, Maquokeeta, greeting; know death's best;
—Fall, Sachem, strictly as the tamarack!

A birch kneels. All her whistling fingers fly.
The oak grove circles in a crash of leaves;
The long moan of a dance is in the sky.
Dance, Maquokeeta: Pocahontas grieves . . .

And every tendon scurries toward the twangs
Of lightning deltaed down your saber hair.
Now snaps the flint in every tooth; red fangs
And splay tongues thinly busy the blue air . . .

Dance, Maquokeeta! snake that lives before,
That casts his pelt, and lives beyond! Sprout, horn!
Spark, tooth! Medicine-man, relent, restore—
Lie to us,—dance us back the tribal morn!

Spears and assemblies: black drums thrusting on—
O yelling battlements,—I, too, was liege
To rainbows currying each pulsant bone:
Surpassed the circumstance, danced out the siege!

And buzzard-circleted, screamed from the stake;
I could not pick the arrows from my side.
Wrapped in that fire, I saw more escorts wake—
Flickering, sprint up the hill groins like a tide.

I heard the hush of lava wrestling your arms,
And stag teeth foam about the raven throat;
Flame cataracts of heaven in seething swarms
Fed down your anklets to the sunset's moat.

O, like the lizard in the furious noon,
That drops his legs and colors in the sun,
—And laughs, pure serpent, Time itself, and moon
Of his own fate, I saw thy change begun!

And saw thee dive to kiss that destiny
Like one white meteor, sacrosanct and blent
At last with all that's consummate and free
There, where the first and last gods keep thy tent.

.   .   .   .

Thewed of the levin, thunder-shod and lean,
Lo, through what infinite seasons dost thou gaze—
Across what bivouacs of thine angered slain,
And see'st thy bride immortal in the maize!

Totem and fire-gall, slumbering pyramid—
Though other calendars now stack the sky,
Thy freedom is her largesse, Prince, and hid
On paths thou knewest best to claim her by.

High unto Labrador the sun strikes free
Her speechless dream of snow, and stirred again,
She is the torrent and the singing tree;
And she is virgin to the last of men . . .

West, west and south! winds over Cumberland
And winds across the llano grass resume
Her hair's warm sibilance. Her breasts are fanned
O stream by slope and vineyard—into bloom!

And when the caribou slant down for salt
Do arrows thirst and leap? Do antlers shine
Alert, star-triggered in the listening vault
Of dusk?—And are her perfect brows to thine?

We danced, O Brave, we danced beyond their farms,
In cobalt desert closures made our vows . . .
Now is the strong prayer folded in thine arms,
The serpent with the eagle in the boughs.

Indiana

The morning glory, climbing the morning long   *. . . and read*
   Over the lintel on its wiry vine,   *her in a*
Closes before the dusk, furls in its song   *mother's*
       As I close mine . . .   *farewell gaze.*

And bison thunder rends my dreams no more
  As once my womb was torn, my boy, when you
Yielded your first cry at the prairie's door . . .
            Your father knew

Then, though we'd buried him behind us, far
  Back on the gold trail—then his lost bones stirred . . .
But you who drop the scythe to grasp the oar
            Knew not, nor heard

How we, too, Prodigal, once rode off, too—
  Waved Seminary Hill a gay good-bye . . .
We found God lavish there in Colorado
            But passing sly.

The pebbles sang, the firecat slunk away
  And glistening through the sluggard freshets came
In golden syllables loosed from the clay
            His gleaming name.

A dream called Eldorado was his town,
  It rose up shambling in the nuggets' wake,
It had no charter but a promised crown
            Of claims to stake.

But we,—too late, too early, howsoever—
  Won nothing out of fifty-nine—those years—
But gilded promise, yielded to us never,
            And barren tears . . .

The long trail back! I huddled in the shade
  Of wagon-tenting looked out once and saw
Bent westward, passing on a stumbling jade
            A homeless squaw—

Perhaps a halfbreed. On her slender back
  She cradled a babe's body, riding without rein.
Her eyes, strange for an Indian's, were not black
            But sharp with pain

And like twin stars. They seemed to shun the gaze
   Of all our silent men—the long team line—
Until she saw me—when their violet haze
         Lit with love shine . . .

I held you up—I suddenly the bolder,
   Knew that mere words could not have brought us nearer.
She nodded—and that smile across her shoulder
         Will still endear her

As long as Jim, your father's memory, is warm.
   Yes, Larry, now you're going to sea, remember
You were the first—before Ned and this farm,—
         First-born, remember—

And since then—all that's left to me of Jim
   Whose folks, like mine, came out of Arrowhead.
And you're the only one with eyes like him—
         Kentucky bred!

I'm standing still, I'm old, I'm half of stone!
   Oh, hold me in those eyes' engaging blue;
There's where the stubborn years gleam and atone,—
         Where gold is true!

Down the dim turnpike to the river's edge—
   Perhaps I'll hear the mare's hoofs to the ford . . .
Write me from Rio . . . and you'll keep your pledge;
         I know your word!

Come back to Indiana—not too late!
   (Or will you be a ranger to the end?)
Good-bye . . . Good-bye . . . oh, I shall always wait
   You, Larry, traveller—
                  stranger,
                      son,
                         —my friend—

III
Cutty Sark

O, the navies old and oaken,
O, the Temeraire no more!
    —MELVILLE

I met a man in South Street, tall—
a nervous shark tooth swung on his chain.
His eyes pressed through green glass
—green glasses, or bar lights made them
so—
    shine—
           GREEN—
                    eyes—
stepped out—forgot to look at you
or left you several blocks away—

in the nickel-in-the-slot piano jogged
"Stamboul Nights"—weaving somebody's nickel—sang—

    O Stamboul Rose—dreams weave the rose!

        Murmurs of Leviathan he spoke,
        and rum was Plato in our heads . . .

"It's *S.S. Ala*—Antwerp—now remember kid
to put me out at three she sails on time.
I'm not much good at time any more keep
weakeyed watches sometimes snooze—" his bony hands
got to beating time . . . "A whaler once—
I ought to keep time and get over it—I'm a
Democrat—I know what time it is—No
I don't want to know what time it is—that
damned white Arctic killed my time . . ."

    O Stamboul Rose—drums weave—

"I ran a donkey engine down there on the Canal
in Panama—got tired of that—

then Yucatan selling kitchenware—beads—
have you seen Popocatepetl—birdless mouth
with ashes sifting down—?
                              and then the coast again . . ."

  Rose of Stamboul O coral Queen—
  teased remnants of the skeletons of cities—
  and galleries, galleries of watergutted lava
  snarling stone—green—drums—drown—

Sing!
"—that spiracle!" he shot a finger out the door . . .
"O life's a geyser—beautiful—my lungs—
No—I can't live on land—!"

I saw the frontiers gleaming of his mind;
or are there frontiers—running sands sometimes
running sands—somewhere—sands running . . .
Or they may start some white machine that sings.
Then you may laugh and dance the axletree—
steel—silver—kick the traces—and know—

  ATLANTIS ROSE drums wreathe the rose,
  the star floats burning in a gulf of tears
  and sleep another thousand—

                              interminably
long since somebody's nickel—stopped—
playing—

A wind worried those wicker-neat lapels, the
swinging summer entrances to cooler hells . . .
Outside a wharf truck nearly ran him down
—he lunged up Bowery way while the dawn
was putting the Statue of Liberty out—that
torch of hers you know—

I started walking home across the Bridge . . .
> .   .   .   .   .

Blithe Yankee vanities, turreted sprites, winged
British repartees, skil-
ful savage sea-girls
that bloomed in the spring—Heave, weave
those bright designs the trade winds drive . . .

> *Sweet opium and tea, Yo-ho!*
> *Pennies for porpoises that bank the keel!*
> *Fins whip the breeze around Japan!*

Bright skysails ticketing the Line, wink round the Horn
to Frisco, Melbourne . . .
Pennants, parabolas—
clipper dreams indelible and ranging,
baronial white on lucky blue!

> Perennial-*Cutty*-trophied-*Sark*!

Thermopylae, Black Prince, Flying Cloud through Sunda
—scarfed of foam, their bellies veered green esplanades,
locked in wind-humors, ran their eastings down;

> *at Java Head freshened the nip*
> *(sweet opium and tea!)*
> *and turned and left us on the lee* . . .

Buntlines tusseling (91 days, 20 hours and anchored!)
Rainbow, Leander
(last trip a tragedy)—where can you be
Nimbus? and you rivals two—

> a long tack keeping—
> *Taeping?*
> *Ariel?*

IV
Cape Hatteras

The seas all crossed,
weathered the capes, the voyage done . . .
—WALT WHITMAN

Imponderable the dinosaur
          sinks slow,
               the mammoth saurian
                    ghoul, the eastern
                        Cape . . .
While rises in the west the coastwise range,
               slowly the hushed land—
Combustion at the astral core—the dorsal change
Of energy—convulsive shift of sand . . .
But we, who round the capes, the promontories
Where strange tongues vary messages of surf
Below grey citadels, repeating to the stars
The ancient names—return home to our own
Hearths, there to eat an apple and recall
The songs that gypsies dealt us at Marseille
Or how the priests walked—slowly through Bombay—
Or to read you, Walt,—knowing us in thrall

To that deep wonderment, our native clay
Whose depth of red, eternal flesh of Pocahontas—
Those continental folded aeons, surcharged
With sweetness below derricks, chimneys, tunnels—
Is veined by all that time has really pledged us . . .
And from above, thin squeaks of radio static,
The captured fume of space foams in our ears—
What whisperings of far watches on the main
Relapsing into silence, while time clears
Our lenses, lifts a focus, resurrects
A periscope to glimpse what joys or pain
Our eyes can share or answer—then deflects
Us, shunting to a labyrinth submersed
Where each sees only his dim past reversed . . .

But that star-glistered salver of infinity,
The circle, blind crucible of endless space,
Is sluiced by motion,—subjugated never.
Adam and Adam's answer in the forest
Left Hesperus mirrored in the lucid pool.
Now the eagle dominates our days, is jurist
Of the ambiguous cloud. We know the strident rule
Of wings imperious . . . Space, instantaneous,
Flickers a moment, consumes us in its smile:
A flash over the horizon—shifting gears—
And we have laughter, or more sudden tears.
Dream cancels dream in this new realm of fact
From which we wake into the dream of act;
Seeing himself an atom in a shroud—
Man hears himself an engine in a cloud!

"—Recorders ages hence"—ah, syllables of faith!
Walt, tell me, Walt Whitman, if infinity
Be still the same as when you walked the beach
Near Paumanok—your lone patrol—and heard the wraith
Through surf, its bird note there a long time falling . . .
For you, the panoramas and this breed of towers,
Of you—the theme that's statured in the cliff,
O Saunterer on free ways still ahead!
Not this our empire yet, but labyrinth
Wherein your eyes, like the Great Navigator's without ship,
Gleam from the great stones of each prison crypt
Of canyoned traffic . . . Confronting the Exchange,
Surviving in a world of stocks,—they also range
Across the hills where second timber strays
Back over Connecticut farms, abandoned pastures,—
Sea eyes and tidal, undenying, bright with myth!

The nasal whine of power whips a new universe . . .
Where spouting pillars spoor the evening sky,
Under the looming stacks of the gigantic power house
Stars prick the eyes with sharp ammoniac proverbs,
New verities, new inklings in the velvet hummed
Of dynamos, where hearing's leash is strummed . . .
Power's script,—wound, bobbin-bound, refined—

Is stropped to the slap of belts on booming spools, spurred
Into the bulging bouillon, harnessed jelly of the stars.
Towards what? The forked crash of split thunder parts
Our hearing momentwise; but fast in whirling armatures,
As bright as frogs' eyes, giggling in the girth
Of steely gizzards—axle-bound, confined
In coiled precision, bunched in mutual glee
The bearings glint,—O murmurless and shined
In oilrinsed circles of blind ecstasy!

Stars scribble on our eyes the frosty sagas,
The gleaming cantos of unvanquished space . . .
O sinewy silver biplane, nudging the wind's withers!
There, from Kill Devils Hill at Kitty Hawk
Two brothers in their twinship left the dune;
Warping the gale, the Wright windwrestlers veered
Capeward, then blading the wind's flank, banked and spun
What ciphers risen from prophetic script,
What marathons new-set between the stars!
The soul, by naphtha fledged into new reaches
Already knows the closer clasp of Mars,—
New latitudes, unknotting, soon give place
To what fierce schedules, rife of doom apace!

Behold the dragon's covey—amphibian, ubiquitous
To hedge the seaboard, wrap the headland, ride
The blue's cloud-templed districts unto ether . . .
While Iliads glimmer through eyes raised in pride
Hell's belt springs wider into heaven's plumed side.
O bright circumferences, heights employed to fly
War's fiery kennel masked in downy offings,—
This tournament of space, the threshed and chiselled height,
Is baited by marauding circles, bludgeon flail
Of rancorous grenades whose screaming petals carve us
Wounds that we wrap with theorems sharp as hail!

Wheeled swiftly, wings emerge from larval-silver hangars.
Taut motors surge, space-gnawing, into flight;
Through sparkling visibility, outspread, unsleeping,
Wings clip the last peripheries of light . . .

Tellurian wind-sleuths on dawn patrol,
Each plane a hurtling javelin of winged ordnance,
Bristle the heights above a screeching gale to hover;
Surely no eye that Sunward Escadrille can cover!
There, meaningful, fledged as the Pleiades
With razor sheen they zoom each rapid helix!
Up-chartered choristers of their own speeding
They, cavalcade on escapade, shear Cumulus—
Lay siege and hurdle Cirrus down the skies!
While Cetus-like, O thou Dirigible, enormous Lounger
Of pendulous auroral beaches,—satellited wide
By convoy planes, moonferrets that rejoin thee
On fleeing balconies as thou dost glide,
—Hast splintered space!

                Low, shadowed of the Cape,
Regard the moving turrets! From grey decks
See scouting griffons rise through gaseous crepe
Hung low . . . until a conch of thunder answers
Cloud-belfries, banging, while searchlights, like fencers,
Slit the sky's pancreas of foaming anthracite
Toward thee, O Corsair of the typhoon,—pilot, hear!
Thine eyes bicarbonated white by speed, O Skygak, see
How from thy path above the levin's lance
Thou sowest doom thou hast nor time nor chance
To reckon—as thy stilly eyes partake
What alcohol of space . . ! Remember, Falcon-Ace,
Thou hast there in thy wrist a Sanskrit charge
To conjugate infinity's dim marge—
Anew . . !

                But first, here at this height receive
The benediction of the shell's deep, sure reprieve!
Lead-perforated fuselage, escutcheoned wings
Lift agonized quittance, tilting from the invisible brink
Now eagle-bright, now
                    quarry-hid, twist-
                            -ing, sink with
Enormous repercussive list-
                    -ings down

Giddily spiralled
    gauntlets, upturned, unlooping
In guerrilla sleights, trapped in combustion gyr-
Ing, dance the curdled depth
      down whizzing
Zodiacs, dashed
     (now nearing fast the Cape!)
       down gravitation's
        vortex into crashed
. . . . dispersion . . . into mashed and shapeless debris. . . .
By Hatteras bunched the beached heap of high bravery!
   . . . . . .

The stars have grooved our eyes with old persuasions
Of love and hatred, birth,—surcease of nations . . .
But who has held the heights more sure than thou,
O Walt!—Ascensions of thee hover in me now
As thou at junctions elegiac, there, of speed
With vast eternity, dost wield the rebound seed!
The competent loam, the probable grass,—travail
Of tides awash the pedestal of Everest, fail
Not less than thou in pure impulse inbred
To answer deepest soundings! O, upward from the dead
Thou bringest tally, and a pact, new bound
Of living brotherhood!

     Thou, there beyond—
Glacial sierras and the flight of ravens,
Hermetically past condor zones, through zenith havens
Past where the albatross has offered up
His last wing-pulse, and downcast as a cup
That's drained, is shivered back to earth—thy wand
Has beat a song, O Walt,—there and beyond!
And this, thine other hand, upon my heart
Is plummet ushered of those tears that start
What memories of vigils, bloody, by that Cape,—
Ghoul-mound of man's perversity at balk
And fraternal massacre! Thou, pallid there as chalk
Hast kept of wounds, O Mourner, all that sum
That then from Appomattox stretched to Somme!

Cowslip and shad-blow, flaked like tethered foam
Around bared teeth of stallions, bloomed that spring
When first I read thy lines, rife as the loam
Of prairies, yet like breakers cliffward leaping!
O, early following thee, I searched the hill
Blue-writ and odor-firm with violets, 'til
With June the mountain laurel broke through green
And filled the forest with what clustrous sheen!
Potomac lilies,—then the Pontiac rose,
And Klondike edelweiss of occult snows!
White banks of moonlight came descending valleys—
How speechful on oak-vizored palisades,
As vibrantly I following down Sequoia alleys
Heard thunder's eloquence through green arcades
Set trumpets breathing in each clump and grass tuft—'til
Gold autumn, captured, crowned the trembling hill!

Panis Angelicus! Eyes tranquil with the blaze
Of love's own diametric gaze, of love's amaze!
Not greatest, thou,—not first, nor last,—but near
And onward yielding past my utmost year.
Familiar, thou, as mendicants in public places;
Evasive—too—as dayspring's spreading arc to trace is:—
Our Meistersinger, thou set breath in steel;
And it was thou who on the boldest heel
Stood up and flung the span on even wing
Of that great Bridge, our Myth, whereof I sing!

Years of the Modern! Propulsions toward what capes?
But thou, *Panis Angelicus*, hast thou not seen
And passed that Barrier that none escapes—
But knows it leastwise as death-strife?—O, something green,
Beyond all sesames of science was thy choice
Wherewith to bind us throbbing with one voice,
New integers of Roman, Viking, Celt—
Thou, Vedic Caesar, to the greensward knelt!

And now, as launched in abysmal cupolas of space,
Toward endless terminals, Easters of speeding light—
Vast engines outward veering with seraphic grace

On clarion cylinders pass out of sight
To course that span of consciousness thou'st named
The Open Road—thy vision is reclaimed!
What heritage thou'st signalled to our hands!

And see! the rainbow's arch—how shimmeringly stands
Above the Cape's ghoul-mound, O joyous seer!
Recorders ages hence, yes, they shall hear
In their own veins uncancelled thy sure tread
And read thee by the aureole 'round thy head
Of pasture-shine, *Panis Angelicus!*

                            yes, Walt,
Afoot again, and onward without halt,—
Not soon, nor suddenly,—no, never to let go
    My hand
           in yours,
                Walt Whitman—
                         so—

V
Three Songs

The one Sestos, the other Abydos hight.
—MARLOWE

Southern Cross

I wanted you, nameless Woman of the South,
No wraith, but utterly—as still more alone
The Southern Cross takes night
And lifts her girdles from her, one by one—
High, cool,
          wide from the slowly smoldering fire
Of lower heavens,—
              vaporous scars!

Eve! Magdalene!
        or Mary, you?

Whatever call—falls vainly on the wave.
O simian Venus, homeless Eve,
Unwedded, stumbling gardenless to grieve
Windswept guitars on lonely decks forever;
Finally to answer all within one grave!

And this long wake of phosphor,
                    iridescent
Furrow of all our travel—trailed derision!
Eyes crumble at its kiss. Its long-drawn spell
Incites a yell. Slid on that backward vision
The mind is churned to spittle, whispering hell.

I wanted you . . . The embers of the Cross
Climbed by aslant and huddling aromatically.
It is blood to remember; it is fire
To stammer back . . . It is
God—your namelessness. And the wash—

All night the water combed you with black
Insolence. You crept out simmering, accomplished.

61

Water rattled that stinging coil, your
Rehearsed hair—docile, alas, from many arms.
Yes, Eve—wraith of my unloved seed!

The Cross, a phantom, buckled—dropped below the dawn.
Light drowned the lithic trillions of your spawn.

National Winter Garden

Outspoken buttocks in pink beads
Invite the necessary cloudy clinch
Of bandy eyes. . . . No extra mufflings here:
The world's one flagrant, sweating cinch.

And while legs waken salads in the brain
You pick your blonde out neatly through the smoke.
Always you wait for someone else though, always—
(Then rush the nearest exit through the smoke).

Always and last, before the final ring
When all the fireworks blare, begins
A tom-tom scrimmage with a somewhere violin,
Some cheapest echo of them all—begins.

And shall we call her whiter than the snow?
Sprayed first with ruby, then with emerald sheen—
Least tearful and least glad (who knows her smile?)
A caught slide shows her sandstone grey between.

Her eyes exist in swivellings of her teats,
Pearls whip her hips, a drench of whirling strands.
Her silly snake rings begin to mount, surmount
Each other—turquoise fakes on tinselled hands.

We wait that writhing pool, her pearls collapsed,
—All but her belly buried in the floor;
And the lewd trounce of a final muted beat!
We flee her spasm through a fleshless door. . . .

Yet, to the empty trapeze of your flesh,
O Magdalene, each comes back to die alone.
Then you, the burlesque of our lust—and faith,
Lug us back lifeward—bone by infant bone.

Virginia

O rain at seven,
Pay-check at eleven—
Keep smiling the boss away,
Mary (what are you going to do?)
Gone seven—gone eleven,
And I'm still waiting you—

O blue-eyed Mary with the claret scarf,
Saturday Mary, mine!

It's high carillon
From the popcorn bells!
Pigeons by the million—
And Spring in Prince Street
Where green figs gleam
By oyster shells!

O Mary, leaning from the high wheat tower,
Let down your golden hair!

High in the noon of May
On cornices of daffodils
The slender violets stray.
Crap-shooting gangs in Bleecker reign,
Peonies with pony manes—
Forget-me-nots at windowpanes:

Out of the way-up nickel-dime tower shine,
Cathedral Mary,
shine!—

VI

Quaker Hill

I see only the ideal. But no ideals
have ever been fully successful on
this earth.

—ISADORA DUNCAN

The gentian weaves her fringes,
The maple's loom is red.

—EMILY DICKINSON

Perspective never withers from their eyes;
They keep that docile edict of the Spring
That blends March with August Antarctic skies:
These are but cows that see no other thing
Than grass and snow, and their own inner being
Through the rich halo that they do not trouble
Even to cast upon the seasons fleeting
Though they should thin and die on last year's stubble.

And they are awkward, ponderous and uncoy . . .
While we who press the cider mill, regarding them—
We, who with pledges taste the bright annoy
Of friendship's acid wine, retarding phlegm,
Shifting reprisals ('til who shall tell us when
The jest is too sharp to be kindly?) boast
Much of our store of faith in other men
Who would, ourselves, stalk down the merriest ghost.

Above them old Mizzentop, palatial white
Hostelry—floor by floor to cinquefoil dormer
Portholes the ceilings stack their stoic height.
Long tiers of windows staring out toward former
Faces—loose panes crown the hill and gleam
At sunset with a silent, cobwebbed patience . . .
See them, like eyes that still uphold some dream
Through mapled vistas, cancelled reservations!

High from the central cupola, they say
One's glance could cross the borders of three states;
But I have seen death's stare in slow survey
From four horizons that no one relates . . .
Weekenders avid of their turf-won scores,
Here three hours from the semaphores, the Czars
Of golf, by twos and threes in plaid plusfours
Alight with sticks abristle and cigars.

This was the Promised Land, and still it is
To the persuasive suburban land agent
In bootleg roadhouses where the gin fizz
Bubbles in time to Hollywood's new love-nest pageant.
Fresh from the radio in the old Meeting House
(Now the New Avalon Hotel) volcanoes roar
A welcome to highsteppers that no mouse
Who saw the Friends there ever heard before.

What cunning neighbors history has in fine!
The woodlouse mortgages the ancient deal
Table that Powitzky buys for only nine-
Ty-five at Adams' auction,—eats the seal,
The spinster polish of antiquity . . .
Who holds the lease on time and on disgrace?
What eats the pattern with ubiquity?
Where are my kinsmen and the patriarch race?

The resigned factions of the dead preside.
Dead rangers bled their comfort on the snow;
But I must ask slain Iroquois to guide
Me farther than scalped Yankees knew to go:
Shoulder the curse of sundered parentage,
Wait for the postman driving from Birch Hill
With birthright by blackmail, the arrant page
That unfolds a new destiny to fill. . . .

So, must we from the hawk's far stemming view,
Must we descend as worm's eye to construe
Our love of all we touch, and take it to the Gate
As humbly as a guest who knows himself too late,

His news already told? Yes, while the heart is wrung,
Arise—yes, take this sheaf of dust upon your tongue!
In one last angelus lift throbbing throat—
Listen, transmuting silence with that stilly note

Of pain that Emily, that Isadora knew!
While high from dim elm-chancels hung with dew,
That triple-noted clause of moonlight—
Yes, whip-poor-will, unhusks the heart of fright,
Breaks us and saves, yes, breaks the heart, yet yields
That patience that is armour and that shields
Love from despair—when love foresees the end—
Leaf after autumnal leaf
                    break off,
                            descend—
                                    descend—

VII
The Tunnel

To Find the Western path
Right thro' the Gates of Wrath.
            —BLAKE

Performances, assortments, résumés—
Up Times Square to Columbus Circle lights
Channel the congresses, nightly sessions,
Refractions of the thousand theatres, faces—
Mysterious kitchens. . . . You shall search them all.
Someday by heart you'll learn each famous sight
And watch the curtain lift in hell's despite;
You'll find the garden in the third act dead,
Finger your knees—and wish yourself in bed
With tabloid crime-sheets perched in easy sight.

> Then let you reach your hat
> and go.
> As usual, let you—also
> walking down—exclaim
> to twelve upward leaving
> a subscription praise
> for what time slays.

Or can't you quite make up your mind to ride;
A walk is better underneath the L a brisk
Ten blocks or so before? But you find yourself
Preparing penguin flexions of the arms,—
As usual you will meet the scuttle yawn:
The subway yawns the quickest promise home.

Be minimum, then, to swim the hiving swarms
Out of the Square, the Circle burning bright—
Avoid the glass doors gyring at your right,
Where boxed alone a second, eyes take fright
—Quite unprepared rush naked back to light:
And down beside the turnstile press the coin
Into the slot. The gongs already rattle.

67

And so
of cities you bespeak
subways, rivered under streets
and rivers. . . . In the car
the overtone of motion
underground, the monotone
of motion is the sound
of other faces, also underground—

"Let's have a pencil Jimmy—living now
at Floral Park
Flatbush—on the fourth of July—
like a pigeon's muddy dream—potatoes
to dig in the field—travlin the town—too—
night after night—the Culver line—the
girls all shaping up—it used to be—"

Our tongues recant like beaten weather vanes.
This answer lives like verdigris, like hair
Beyond extinction, surcease of the bone;
And repetition freezes—"What

"what do you want? getting weak on the links?
fandaddle daddy don't ask for change—IS THIS
FOURTEENTH? it's half past six she said—if
you don't like my gate why did you
swing on it, why *didja*
swing on it
anyhow—"

And somehow anyhow swing—

The phonographs of hades in the brain
Are tunnels that re-wind themselves, and love
A burnt match skating in a urinal—
Somewhere above Fourteenth TAKE THE EXPRESS
To brush some new presentiment of pain—-

"But I want service in this office SERVICE
I said—after
the show she cried a little afterwards but—"

Whose head is swinging from the swollen strap?
Whose body smokes along the bitten rails,
Bursts from a smoldering bundle far behind
In back forks of the chasms of the brain,—
Puffs from a riven stump far out behind
In interborough fissures of the mind . . . ?

And why do I often meet your visage here,
Your eyes like agate lanterns—on and on
Below the toothpaste and the dandruff ads?
—And did their riding eyes right through your side,
And did their eyes like unwashed platters ride?
And Death, aloft,—gigantically down
Probing through you—toward me, O evermore!
And when they dragged your retching flesh,
Your trembling hands that night through Baltimore—
That last night on the ballot rounds, did you,
Shaking, did you deny the ticket, Poe?

For Gravesend Manor change at Chambers Street.
The platform hurries along to a dead stop.

The intent escalator lifts a serenade
Stilly
Of shoes, umbrellas, each eye attending its shoe, then
Bolting outright somewhere above where streets
Burst suddenly in rain. . . . The gongs recur:
Elbows and levers, guard and hissing door.
Thunder is galvothermic here below. . . . The car
Wheels off. The train rounds, bending to a scream,
Taking the final level for the dive
Under the river—
And somewhat emptier than before,
Demented, for a hitching second, humps; then

Lets go. . . . Toward corners of the floor
Newspapers wing, revolve and wing.
Blank windows gargle signals through the roar.

And does the Daemon take you home, also,
Wop washerwoman, with the bandaged hair?
After the corridors are swept, the cuspidors—
The gaunt sky-barracks cleanly now, and bare,
O Genoese, do you bring mother eyes and hands
Back home to children and to golden hair?

Daemon, demurring and eventful yawn!
Whose hideous laughter is a bellows mirth
—Or the muffled slaughter of a day in birth—
O cruelly to inoculate the brinking dawn
With antennae toward worlds that glow and sink;—
To spoon us out more liquid than the dim
Locution of the eldest star, and pack
The conscience navelled in the plunging wind,
Umbilical to call—and straightway die!

O caught like pennies beneath soot and steam,
Kiss of our agony thou gatherest;
Condensed, thou takest all—shrill ganglia
Impassioned with some song we fail to keep.
And yet, like Lazarus, to feel the slope,
The sod and billow breaking,—lifting ground,
—A sound of waters bending astride the sky
Unceasing with some Word that will not die . . . !
                  .   .   .   .   .

A tugboat, wheezing wreaths of steam,
Lunged past, with one galvanic blare stove up the River.
I counted the echoes assembling, one after one,
Searching, thumbing the midnight on the piers.
Lights, coasting, left the oily tympanum of waters;
The blackness somewhere gouged glass on a sky.
And this thy harbor, O my City, I have driven under,
Tossed from the coil of ticking towers. . . . Tomorrow,
And to be. . . . Here by the River that is East—
Here at the waters' edge the hands drop memory;

Shadowless in that abyss they unaccounting lie.
How far away the star has pooled the sea—
Or shall the hands be drawn away, to die?

Kiss of our agony Thou gatherest,
                    O Hand of Fire
                              gatherest—

VIII
Atlantis

*Music is then the knowledge of that which
relates to love in harmony and system.*

—PLATO

Through the bound cable strands, the arching path
Upward, veering with light, the flight of strings,—
Taut miles of shuttling moonlight syncopate
The whispered rush, telepathy of wires.
Up the index of night, granite and steel—
Transparent meshes—fleckless the gleaming staves—
Sibylline voices flicker, waveringly stream
As though a god were issue of the strings. . . .

And through that cordage, threading with its call
One arc synoptic of all tides below—
Their labyrinthine mouths of history
Pouring reply as though all ships at sea
Complighted in one vibrant breath made cry,—
"Make thy love sure—to weave whose song we ply!"
—From black embankments, moveless soundings hailed,
So seven oceans answer from their dream.

And on, obliquely up bright carrier bars
New octaves trestle the twin monoliths
Beyond whose frosted capes the moon bequeaths
Two worlds of sleep (O arching strands of song!)—
Onward and up the crystal-flooded aisle
White tempest nets file upward, upward ring
With silver terraces the humming spars,
The loft of vision, palladium helm of stars.

Sheerly the eyes, like seagulls stung with rime—
Slit and propelled by glistening fins of light—
Pick biting way up towering looms that press
Sidelong with flight of blade on tendon blade
—Tomorrows into yesteryear—and link

What cipher-script of time no traveller reads
But who, through smoking pyres of love and death,
Searches the timeless laugh of mythic spears.

Like hails, farewells—up planet-sequined heights
Some trillion whispering hammers glimmer Tyre:
Serenely, sharply up the long anvil cry
Of inchling aeons silence rivets Troy.
And you, aloft there—Jason! hesting Shout!
Still wrapping harness to the swarming air!
Silvery the rushing wake, surpassing call,
Beams yelling Acolus! splintered in the straits!

From gulfs unfolding, terrible of drums,
Tall Vision-of-the-Voyage, tensely spare—
Bridge, lifting night to cycloramic crest
Of deepest day—O Choir, translating time
Into what multitudinous Verb the suns
And synergy of waters ever fuse, recast
In myriad syllables,—Psalm of Cathay!
O Love, thy white, pervasive Paradigm . . . !

We left the haven hanging in the night—
Sheened harbor lanterns backward fled the keel.
Pacific here at time's end, bearing corn,—
Eyes stammer through the pangs of dust and steel.
And still the circular, indubitable frieze
Of heaven's meditation, yoking wave
To kneeling wave, one song devoutly binds—
The vernal strophe chimes from deathless strings!

O Thou steeled Cognizance whose leap commits
The agile precincts of the lark's return;
Within whose lariat sweep encinctured sing
In single chrysalis the many twain,—
Of stars Thou art the stitch and stallion glow
And like an organ, Thou, with sound of doom—
Sight, sound and flesh Thou leadest from time's realm
As love strikes clear direction for the helm.

Swift peal of secular light, intrinsic Myth
Whose fell unshadow is death's utter wound,—
O River-throated—iridescently unborne
Through the bright drench and fabric of our veins;
With white escarpments swinging into light,
Sustained in tears the cities are endowed
And justified conclamant with ripe fields
Revolving through their harvests in sweet torment.

Forever Deity's glittering Pledge, O Thou
Whose canticle fresh chemistry assigns
To wrapt inception and beatitude,—
Always through blinding cables, to our joy,
Of thy white seizure springs the prophecy:
Always through spiring cordage, pyramids
Of silver sequel, Deity's young name
Kinetic of white choiring wings . . . ascends.

Migrations that must needs void memory,
Inventions that cobblestone the heart,—
Unspeakable Thou Bridge to Thee, O Love.
Thy pardon for this history, whitest Flower,
O Answerer of all,—Anemone,—
Now while thy petals spend the suns about us, hold—
(O Thou whose radiance doth inherit me)
Atlantis,—hold thy floating singer late!

So to thine Everpresence, beyond time,
Like spears ensanguined of one tolling star
That bleeds infinity—the orphic strings,
Sidereal phalanxes, leap and converge:
—One Song, one Bridge of Fire! Is it Cathay,
Now pity steeps the grass and rainbows ring
The serpent with the eagle in the leaves . . . ?
Whispers antiphonal in azure swing.

KEY WEST

AN ISLAND SHEAF

The starry floor,
The wat'ry shore,
Is given thee 'til the break of day.
            —BLAKE

O Carib Isle!

The tarantula rattling at the lily's foot
Across the feet of the dead, laid in white sand
Near the coral beach—nor zigzag fiddle crabs
Side-stilting from the path (that shift, subvert
And anagrammatize your name)—No, nothing here
Below the palsy that one eucalyptus lifts
In wrinkled shadows—mourns.

                    And yet suppose
I count these nacreous frames of tropic death,
Brutal necklaces of shells around each grave
Squared off so carefully. Then

To the white sand I may speak a name, fertile
Albeit in a stranger tongue. Tree names, flower names
Deliberate, gainsay death's brittle crypt. Meanwhile
The wind that knots itself in one great death—
Coils and withdraws. So syllables want breath.

But where is the Captain of this doubloon isle
Without a turnstile? Who but catchword crabs
Patrols the dry groins of the underbrush?
What man, or What
Is Commissioner of mildew throughout the ambushed senses?
His Carib mathematics web the eyes' baked lenses!

Under the poinciana, of a noon or afternoon
Let fiery blossoms clot the light, render my ghost
Sieved upward, white and black along the air
Until it meets the blue's comedian host.

Let not the pilgrim see himself again
For slow evisceration bound like those huge terrapin
Each daybreak on the wharf, their brine caked eyes;
—Spiked, overturned; such thunder in their strain!
And clenched beaks coughing for the surge again!

Slagged of the hurricane—I, cast within its flow,
Congeal by afternoons here, satin and vacant.
You have given me the shell, Satan,—carbonic amulet
Sere of the sun exploded in the sea.

The Mermen

And if
Thy banished trunk be found in our dominions—
KING LEAR

Buddhas and engines serve us undersea;
Though why they bide here, only hell that's sacked
Of every blight and ingenuity—
Can solve.

       The Cross alone has flown the wave.
But since the Cross sank, much that's warped and cracked
Has followed in its name, has heaped its grave.
                     Oh—

Gallows and guillotines to hail the sun
And smoking wracks for penance when day's done!
                     No—

Leave us, you idols of Futurity—alone,
Here where we finger moidores of spent grace
And ponder the bright stains that starred this Throne

—This Cross, agleam still with a human Face!

To the Cloud Juggler

In Memoriam: Harry Crosby

What you may cluster 'round the knees of space
We hold in vision only, asking trace
Of districts where cliff, sea and palm advance
The falling wonder of a rainbow's trance.

Your light lifts whiteness into virgin azure . . .
Disclose your lips, O Sun, nor long demure
With snore of thunder, crowding us to bleed
The green preëmption of the deep seaweed.

You, the rum-giver to that slide-by-night,—
The moon's best lover,—guide us by a sleight
Of quarts to faithfuls—surely smuggled home—
As you raise temples fresh from basking foam.

Expose vaunted validities that yawn
Past pleasantries . . . Assert the ripened dawn
As you have yielded balcony and room
Or tempests—in a silver, floating plume.

Wrap us and lift us; drop us then, returned
Like water, undestroyed,—like mist, unburned . . .
But do not claim a friend like him again,
Whose arrow must have pierced you beyond pain.

The Mango Tree

Let them return, saying you blush again for the great
Great-grandmother. It's all like Christmas.

When you sprouted Paradise a discard of chewing-gum
took place. Up jug to musical, hanging jug just gay spiders
yoked you first,—silking of shadows good underdrawers for
owls.

First-plucked before and since the Flood, old hypnotisms

wrench the golden boughs. Leaves spatter dawn from emerald
cloud-sprockets. Fat final prophets with lean bandits crouch:
and dusk is close

under your noon,
you Sun-heap, whose

ripe apple-lanterns gush history, recondite lightnings, irised.

O mister Señor
missus Miss
Mademoiselle
with baskets

Maggy, come on

Island Quarry

Square sheets—they saw the marble only into
Flat prison slabs there at the marble quarry
At the turning of the road around the roots of the mountain
Where the straight road would seem to ply below the stone,
    that fierce
Profile of marble spiked with yonder
Palms against the sunset's towering sea, and maybe
Against mankind. It is at times—

In dusk, as though this island lifted, floated
In Indian baths. At Cuban dusk the eyes
Walking the straight road toward thunder—
This dry road silvering toward the shadow of the quarry
—It is at times as though the eyes burned hard and glad
And did not take the goat path quivering to the right,
Wide of the mountain—thence to tears and sleep—
But went on into marble that does not weep.

Old Song

Thy absence overflows the rose,—
    From every petal gleam
Such words as it were vain to close,
    Such tears as crowd the dream.

So eyes that mind thee fair and gone,
    Bemused at waking, spend
On skies that gild thy remote dawn
    More hopes than here attend.

The burden of the rose will fade
    Sped in the spectrum's kiss.
But here the thorn in sharpened shade
    Weathers all loneliness.

The Idiot

Sheer over to the other side,—for see—
The boy straggling under those mimosas, daft
With squint lanterns in his head, and it's likely
Fumbling his sex. That's why those children laughed

In such infernal circles round his door
Once when he shouted, stretched in ghastly shape.
I hurried by. But back from the hot shore
Passed him again . . . He was alone, agape;

One hand dealt out a kite string, a tin can
The other tilted, peeled end clamped to eye.
That kite aloft—you should have watched him scan
Its course, though he'd clapped midnight to noon sky!

And since, through these hot barricades of green,
A Dios gracias, grac—I've heard his song
Above all reason lifting, halt serene—
My trespass vision shrinks to face his wrong.

A Name for All

Moonmoth and grasshopper that flee our page
And still wing on, untarnished of the name
We pinion to your bodies to assuage
Our envy of your freedom—we must maim

Because we are usurpers, and chagrined—
And take the wing and scar it in the hand.
Names we have, even, to clap on the wind;
But we must die, as you, to understand.

I dreamed that all men dropped their names, and sang
As only they can praise, who build their days
With fin and hoof, with wing and sweetened fang
Struck free and holy in one Name always.

Bacardi Spreads the Eagle's Wing

"Pablo and Pedro, and black Serafin
Bought a launch last week. It might as well
Have been made of—well, say paraffin,—
That thin and blistered . . . just a rotten shell.

"Hell! out there among the barracudas
Their engine stalled. No oars, and leaks
Oozing a-plenty. They sat like baking Buddhas.
Luckily the Cayman schooner streaks

"By just in time, and lifts 'em high and dry . . .
They're back now on that mulching job at Pepper's.
—Yes, patent-leather shoes hot enough to fry
Anyone but these native high-steppers!"

Imperator Victus

Big guns again.
No speakee well
But plain.

Again, again—
And they shall tell
The Spanish Main

The Dollar from the Cross.

Big guns again.
But peace to thee,
Andean brain.

Again, again—
Peace from his Mystery
The King of Spain,

That defunct boss.

Big guns again,
Atahualpa,
Imperator Inca—

Slain.

Royal Palm

For Grace Hart Crane

Green rustlings, more-than-regal charities
Drift coolly from that tower of whispered light.
Amid the noontide's blazed asperities
I watched the sun's most gracious anchorite

Climb up as by communings, year on year
Uneaten of the earth or aught earth holds,
And the grey trunk, that's elephantine, rear
Its frondings sighing in aetherial folds.

Forever fruitless, and beyond that yield
Of sweat the jungle presses with hot love
And tendril till our deathward breath is sealed—
It grazes the horizons, launched above

Mortality—ascending emerald-bright,
A fountain at salute, a crown in view—
Unshackled, casual of its azured height
As though it soared suchwise through heaven too.

The Air Plant

Grand Cayman

This tuft that thrives on saline nothingness,
Inverted octopus with heavenward arms
Thrust parching from a palm-bole hard by the cove—
A bird almost—of almost bird alarms,

Is pulmonary to the wind that jars
Its tentacles, horrific in their lurch.
The lizard's throat, held bloated for a fly,
Balloons but warily from this throbbing perch.

The needles and hack-saws of cactus bleed
A milk of earth when stricken off the stalk;
But this,—defenseless, thornless, sheds no blood,
Almost no shadow—but the air's thin talk.

Angelic Dynamo! Ventriloquist of the Blue!
While beachward creeps the shark-swept Spanish Main
By what conjunctions do the winds appoint
Its apotheosis, at last—the hurricane!

The Hurricane

Lo, Lord, Thou ridest!
Lord, Lord, Thy swifting heart

Naught stayeth, naught now bideth
But's smithereened apart!

Ay! Scripture flee'th stone!
Milk-bright, Thy chisel wind

Rescindeth flesh from bone
To quivering whittlings thinned—

Swept—whistling straw! Battered,
Lord, e'en boulders now out-leap

Rock sockets, levin-lathered!
Nor, Lord, may worm out-creep

Thy drum's gambade, its plunge abscond!
Lord God, while summits crashing

Whip sea-kelp screaming on blond
Sky-seethe, high heaven dashing—

Thou ridest to the door, Lord!
Thou bidest wall nor floor, Lord!

Key West

Here has my salient faith annealed me.
Out of the valley, past the ample crib
To skies impartial, that do not disown me
Nor claim me, either, by Adam's spine—nor rib.

The oar plash, and the meteorite's white arch
Concur with wrist and bicep. In the moon
That now has sunk I strike a single march
To heaven or hades—to an equally frugal noon.

Because these millions reap a dead conclusion
Need I presume the same fruit of my bone
As draws them towards a doubly mocked confusion
Of apish nightmares into steel-strung stone?

O, steel and stone! But gold was, scarcity before.
And here is water, and a little wind. . . .
There is no breath of friends and no more shore
Where gold has not been sold and conscience tinned.

—And Bees of Paradise

I had come all the way here from the sea,
Yet met the wave again between your arms
Where cliff and citadel—all verily
Dissolved within a sky of beacon forms—

Sea gardens lifted rainbow-wise through eyes
I found.

                Yes, tall, inseparably our days
Pass sunward. We have walked the kindled skies
Inexorable and girded with your praise,

By the dove filled, and bees of Paradise.

To Emily Dickinson

You who desired so much—in vain to ask—
Yet fed your hunger like an endless task,
Dared dignify the labor, bless the quest—
Achieved that stillness ultimately best,

Being, of all, least sought for: Emily, hear!
O sweet, dead Silencer, most suddenly clear
When singing that Eternity possessed
And plundered momently in every breast;

—Truly no flower yet withers in your hand.
The harvest you descried and understand
Needs more than wit to gather, love to bind.
Some reconcilement of remotest mind—

Leaves Ormus rubyless, and Ophir chill.
Else tears heap all within one clay-cold hill.

Moment Fugue

The syphillitic selling violets calmly
        and daisies
By the subway news-stand knows
                how hyacinths

This April morning offers
        hurriedly
In bunches sorted freshly—
                and bestows
On every purchaser
                    (of heaven perhaps)

His eyes—
                like crutches hurtled against glass
Fall mute and sudden (dealing change
        for lilies)
Beyond the roses that no flesh can pass.

By Nilus Once I Knew . . .

Some old Egyptian joke is in the air,
Dear lady—the poet said—release your hair;
Come, search the marshes for a friendly bed
Or let us bump heads in some lowly shed.

An old Egyptian jest has cramped the tape.
The keyboard no more offers an escape
From the sweet jeopardy of Anthony's plight:
You've overruled my typewriter tonight.

Decisive grammar given unto queens,—
An able text, more motion than machines
Have levers for,—stampede it with fresh type
From twenty alphabets—we're still unripe!

This hieroglyph is no dumb, deaf mistake.
It knows its way through India—tropic shake!
It's Titicaca till we've trod it through,
And then it pleads again, "I wish I knew".

To Shakespeare

Through torrid entrances, past icy poles
    A hand moves on the page! Who shall again
Engrave such hazards as thy might controls—
    Conflicting, purposeful yet outcry vain
Of all our days, being pilot,—tempest, too!
    Sheets that mock lust and thorns that scribble hate
Are lifted from torn flesh with human rue,
    And laughter, burnished brighter than our fate
Thou wieldest with such tears that every faction
    Swears high in Hamlet's throat, and devils throng
Where angels beg for doom in ghast distraction
    —And fail, both! Yet thine Ariel holds his song:
    And that serenity that Prospero gains
    Is justice that has cancelled earthly chains.

POEMS PUBLISHED
IN MAGAZINES

C 33

He has woven rose-vines
About the empty heart of night,
And vented his long mellowed wines
Of dreaming on the desert white
With searing sophistry.
And he tented with far truths he would form
The transient bosoms from the thorny tree.

O Materna! to enrich thy gold head
And wavering shoulders with a new light shed

From penitence, must needs bring pain,
And with it song of minor, broken strain.
But you who hear the lamp whisper through night
Can trace paths tear-wet, and forget all blight.

1916

October–November

Indian-summer-sun
With crimson feathers whips away the mists;
Dives through the filter of trellises
And gilds the silver on the blotched arbor-seats.

Now gold and purple scintillate
On trees that seem dancing
In delirium;
Then the moon
In a mad orange flare
Floods the grape-hung night.

1916

Carmen de Boheme

Sinuously winding through the room
On smokey tongues of sweetened cigarettes,—
Plaintive yet proud the cello tones resume
The andante of smooth hopes and lost regrets.

Bright peacocks drink from flame-pots by the wall,
Just as absinthe-sipping women shiver through
With shimmering blue from the bowl in Circe's hall.
Their brown eyes blacken, and the blue drop hue.

The andante quivers with crescendo's start,
And dies on fire's birth in each man's heart.
The tapestry betrays a finger through
The slit, soft-pulling:—and music follows cue.

There is a sweep,—a shattering,—a choir
Disquieting of barbarous fantasy.
The pulse is in the ears, the heart is higher,
And stretches up through mortal eyes to see.

Carmen! Akimbo arms and smouldering eyes;—
Carmen! Bestirring hope and lipping eyes;—
Carmen whirls, and music swirls and dips.
"Carmen!" comes awed from wine-hot lips.

Finale leaves in silence to replume
Bent wings, and Carmen with her flaunts through the gloom
Of whispering tapestry, brown with old fringe:—
The winers leave too, and the small lamps twinge.

Morning: and through the foggy city gate
A gypsy wagon wiggles, striving straight.
And some dream still of Carmen's mystic face,—
Yellow, pallid, like ancient lace.

1916

The Hive

Up the chasm-walls of my bleeding heart
Humanity pecks, claws, sobs, and climbs;
Up the inside, and over every part
Of the hive of the world that is my heart.

And of all the sowing, and all the tear-tendering,
And reaping, have mercy and love issued forth.
Mercy, white milk, and honey, gold love—
And I watch, and say, "These the anguish are worth."

1917

Fear

The host, he says that all is well,
And the fire-wood glow is bright;
The food has a warm and tempting smell,—
But on the window licks the night.

Pile on the logs. . . . Give me your hands,
Friends! No,—it is not fright. . . .
But hold me . . . somewhere I heard demands . . .
And on the window licks the night.

1917

Annunciations

The anxious milk-blood in the veins of the earth,
That strives long and quiet to sever the girth
Of greenery. . . . Below the roots, a quickening quiver
Aroused by some light that had sensed,—ere the shiver
Of the first moth's descent,—day's predestiny. . . .
The sound of a dove's flight waved over the lawn. . . .
The moans of travail of one dearest beside me. . . .
Then high cries from great chasms of chaos outdrawn. . . .
Hush! these things were all heard before dawn.

1917

Echoes

1

Slivers of rain upon the pane,
Jade-green with sunlight, melt and flow
Upward again:—they leave no stain
Of all the storm an hour ago.

2

Over the hill a last cloud dips
And disappears, and I should go
As silently but that your lips
Are warmer with a redder glow.

3

Fresh and fragile, your arms now
Are circles of cool roses,—so. . . .
In opal pools beneath your brow
I dream we quarreled long, long ago.

1917

The Bathers

Two ivory women by a milky sea;—
The dawn, a shell's pale lining restlessly
Shimmering over a black mountain-spear:—
A dreamer might see these, and wake to hear,
But there is no sound,—not even a bird-note;
Only simple ripples flaunt, and stroke, and float,—
Flat lily petals to the sea's white throat.

They say that Venus shot through foam to light,
But they are wrong . . . . Ere man was given sight
She came in such still water, and so nursed
In silence, beauty blessed and beauty cursed.

1917

Modern Craft

Though I have touched her flesh of moons,
Still she sits gestureless and mute,
Drowning cool pearls in alcohol.
O blameless shyness;—innocence dissolute!

She hazards jet; wears tiger-lilies;—
And bolts herself within a jewelled belt.
Too many palms have grazed her shoulders:
Surely she must have felt.

Ophelia had such eyes; but she
Even, sank in love and choked with flowers.
This burns and is not burnt . . . . My modern love were
Charred at a stake in younger times than ours.

1917

Exile

(after the Chinese)

My hands have not touched pleasure since your hands,—
No,—nor my lips freed laughter since 'farewell',
And with the day, distance again expands
Voiceless between us, as an uncoiled shell.

Yet love endures, though starving and alone.
A dove's wings cling about my heart each night
With surging gentleness, and the blue stone
Set in the tryst-ring has but worn more bright.

1918

Postscript

Though now but marble are the marble urns,
Though fountains droop in waning light and pain
Glitters on the edges of wet ferns,
I should not dare to let you in again.

Mine is a world foregone though not yet ended,—
An imagined garden grey with sundered boughs
And broken branches, wistful and unmended,
And mist that is more constant than all vows.

1918

Forgetfulness

Forgetfulness is like a song
That, freed from beat and measure, wanders.
Forgetfulness is like a bird whose wings are reconciled,
Outspread and motionless,—
A bird that coasts the wind unwearyingly.

Forgetfulness is rain at night,
Or an old house in a forest,—or a child.
Forgetfulness is white,—white as a blasted tree,
And it may stun the sybil into prophecy,
Or bury the Gods.

I can remember much forgetfulness.

1918

To Portapovitch

(du Ballet Russe)

Vault on the opal carpet of the sun,
Barbaric Prince Igor:—or, blind Pierrot,
Despair until the moon by tears be won:—
Or, Daphnis, move among the bees with Chloe.

Release,—dismiss the passion from your arms.
More real than life, the gestures you have spun
Haunt the blank stage with lingering alarms,
Though silent as your sandals, danced undone.

c. 1917–19

Legende

The tossing loneliness of many nights
Rounds off my memory of her.
Like a shell surrendered to evening sands,
Yet called adrift again at every dawn,
She has become a pathos,—
Waif of the tides.

The sand and sea have had their way,
And moons of spring and autumn,—
All, save I.
And even my vision will be erased
As a cameo the waves claim again.

c. 1918–19

Interior

It sheds a shy solemnity,
This lamp in our poor room.
O grey and gold amenity,—
Silence and gentle gloom!

Wide from the world, a stolen hour
We claim, and none may know
How love blooms like a tardy flower
Here in the day's after-glow.

And even should the world break in
With jealous threat and guile,
The world, at last, must bow and win
Our pity and a smile.

c. 1918–19

Porphyro in Akron

I

Greeting the dawn,
A shift of rubber workers presses down
South Main.
With the stubbornness of muddy water
It dwindles at each cross-line
Until you feel the weight of many cars
North-bound, and East and West,
Absorbing and conveying weariness,—
Rumbling over the hills.

Akron, "high place",—
A bunch of smoke-ridden hills
Among rolling Ohio hills.

The dark-skinned Greeks grin at each other
In the streets and alleys.
The Greek grins and fights with the Swede,—
And the Fjords and the Aegean are remembered.

The plough, the sword,
The trowel,—and the monkey wrench!
O City, your axles need not the oil of song.
I will whisper words to myself
And put them in my pockets.
I will go and pitch quoits with old men
In the dust of a road.

II

And some of them "will be Americans",
Using the latest ice-box and buying Fords;
And others,—

          I remember one Sunday noon,
Harry and I, "the gentlemen",—seated around
A table of raisin-jack and wine, our host
Setting down a glass and saying,—

          "One month,—I go back rich.
I ride black horse. . . . Have many sheep."
And his wife, like a mountain, coming in
With four tiny black-eyed girls around her
Twinkling like little Christmas trees.

And some Sunday fiddlers,
Roumanian business men,
Played ragtime and dances before the door,
And we overpayed them because we felt like it.

III

Pull down the hotel counterpane
And hitch yourself up to your book.

"Full on this casement shone the wintry moon,
And threw warm gules on Madeleine's fair breast,
As down she knelt for heaven's grace and boon . . ."

"Connais tu le pays . . . ?"

Your mother sang that in a stuffy parlour
One summer day in a little town
Where you had started to grow.
And you were outside as soon as you
Could get away from the company
To find the only rose on the bush
In the front yard. . . . . . .

But look up, Porphyro,—your toes
Are ridiculously tapping
The spindles at the foot of the bed.

The stars are drowned in a slow rain,
And a hash of noises is slung up from the street.
You ought, really, to try to sleep,
Even though, in this town, poetry's a
Bedroom occupation.

1920–21

A Persuasion

If she waits late at night
Hearing the wind,
It is to gather kindnesses
No world can offer.

She has drawn her hands away.
The wind plays andantes
Of lost hopes and regrets,—
And yet is kind.

Below the wind,
Waiting for morning
The hills lie curved and blent
As now her heart and mind.

1921

Three Locutions des Pierrots

from the French of Jules Laforgue

I

Your eyes, those pools with soft rushes,
O prodigal and wholly dilatory lady,
Come now, when will they restore me
The orient moon of my dapper affections?

For imminent is that moment when,
Because of your perverse austerities,
My crisp soul will be flooded by a languor
Bland as the wide gaze of a Newfoundland.

Ah, madame! truly it's not right
When one isn't the real Gioconda,
To adaptate her methods and deportment
For snaring the poor world in a blue funk.

II

Ah! the divine infatuation
That I nurse for Cydalise
Now that she has fled the capture
Of my lunar sensibility!

True, I nibble at despondencies
Among the flowers of her domain
To the sole end of discovering
What is her unique propensity!

—Which is to be mine, you say?
Alas, you know how much I oppose
A stiff denial to postures
That seem too much impromptu.

III

Ah! without the moon, what white nights,
What nightmares rich with ingenuity!
Don't I see your white swans there?
Doesn't someone come to turn the knob?

And it's your fault that I'm this way.
That my conscience sees double,
And my heart fishes in troubled water
For Eve, Gioconda, and Dalila.

Oh, by the infinite circumflex
Of the archbeam of my cross-legged labours,
Come now,—appease me just a little
With the why-and-wherefore of Your Sex!

1922

The Great Western Plains

The little voices of prairie dogs
are tireless . . .
They will give three hurrahs
alike to stage, equestrian, and pullman,
and all unstintingly as to the moon.

And Fifi's bows and poodle ease
whirl by them centred in the lap
of Lottie Honeydew, movie queen,
toward lawyers and Nevada.

And how much more they cannot see!
Alas, there is so little time,
the world moves by so fast these days!
Burrowing in silk is not their way—
and yet they know the tomahawk.

Indeed, old memories come back to life;
pathetic yelps have sometimes greeted
noses pressed against the glass.

1922

America's Plutonic Ecstasies

with homage to E. E. Cummings

preferring laxatives to wine
all america is saying
"how are my bowels today?" and
feeling them in every way and
peering
for the one goat (unsqueezable)
that kicked out long ago—

or, even thinking
of something—Oh!
unbelievably—Oh!
HEADY!—those aromatic LEMONS!
that make your colored syrup fairly
PULSE!—yes, PULSE!

the nation's lips are thin and fast
with righteousness. Yet if
memory serves there is still
catharsis from gin-daisies as well as
maiden-hair ferns, and the BRONX
doesn't stink at all

                    These
and other natural grammarians are ab-
so-loot-lee necessary
for a FREE-ER PASSAGE—(NOT
to india, o ye faithful,
but a little BACK DOOR DIGNITY)

1923

Interludium

To "La Montagne" by Lachaise

Thy time is thee to wend
with languor such as gains
immensity in gathered grace; the arms
to spread; the hands to yield their shells

and fostering
thyself, bestow to thee
illimitable and unresigned
(no instinct flattering vainly now)

Thyself
that heavens climb to measure, thus
unfurling thee untried,—until
from sleep forbidden now and wide
partitions in thee—goes

communicant and speeding new
the cup again wide from thy throat to spend
those streams and slopes untenanted thou
hast known . . . . And blithe

Madonna, natal to thy yielding
still subsist I, wondrous as
from thine open dugs shall still the sun
again round one more fairest day.

c. 1923–24

March

Awake to the cold light
of wet wind running
twigs in tremors. Walls
are naked. Twilights raw—
and when the sun taps steeples
their glistenings dwindle
upward . . .

March
slips along the ground
like a mouse under pussy-
willows, a little hungry.

The vagrant ghost of winter,
is it this that keeps the chimney
busy still? For something still
nudges shingles and windows:

but waveringly,—this ghost,
this slate-eyed saintly wraith
of winter wanes
and knows its waning.

1927

The Broken Tower

The bell-rope that gathers God at dawn
Dispatches me as though I dropped down the knell
Of a spent day—to wander the cathedral lawn
From pit to crucifix, feet chill on steps from hell.

Have you not heard, have you not seen that corps
Of shadows in the tower, whose shoulders sway
Antiphonal carillons launched before
The stars are caught and hived in the sun's ray?

The bells, I say, the bells break down their tower;
And swing I know not where. Their tongues engrave
Membrane through marrow, my long-scattered score
Of broken intervals . . . And I, their sexton slave!

Oval encyclicals in canyons heaping
The impasse high with choir. Banked voices slain!
Pagodas, campaniles with reveilles outleaping—
O terraced echoes prostrate on the plain! . . .

And so it was I entered the broken world
To trace the visionary company of love, its voice
An instant in the wind (I know not whither hurled)
But not for long to hold each desperate choice.

My word I poured. But was it cognate, scored
Of that tribunal monarch of the air
Whose thigh embronzes earth, strikes crystal Word
In wounds pledged once to hope,—cleft to despair?

The steep encroachments of my blood left me
No answer (could blood hold such a lofty tower
As flings the question true?)—or is it she
Whose sweet mortality stirs latent power?—

And through whose pulse I hear, counting the strokes
My veins recall and add, revived and sure
The angelus of wars my chest evokes:
What I hold healed, original now, and pure . . .

And builds, within, a tower that is not stone
(Not stone can jacket heaven)—but slip
Of pebbles,—visible wings of silence sown
In azure circles, widening as they dip

The matrix of the heart, lift down the eye
That shrines the quiet lake and swells a tower . . .
The commodious, tall decorum of that sky
Unseals her earth, and lifts love in its shower.

1932

UNPUBLISHED POEMS
AND FRAGMENTS

A Song for Happy Feast Days

A song for happy feast days,
A song for fortune's spurns,
In merry and consoling lays—
The cheery songs of Bobbie Burns.

1914

Sonnet

Ere elfish Night shall sift another day
Hope-broken 'neath her ebon scepter's keep,
Or the fainting soul's last flames all trembling creep
White-taper-like, and paler, pulse away,
Then shalt thou come, O Saint, in magic sway
Of midnight's purple organ-breath, and sweep
Brave echoes from the spooming coast to steep,
Blue heights where cone-wood calls near summits spray
Frost-fringes through thine octaves. . . . And from shades
Of moon-fled valleys, there shall rise a rift,
The supplication of all earth, mute serenades,
Whispering, "Cecilia, Saint, leave us thy gift."
And sleep shalt thou bestow, the final song,
And Time shall set the morning stars adrift.

c. 1915–16

The Moth That God Made Blind

Among cocoa-nut palms of a far oasis,
Conceived in the light of Arabian moons,
There are butterflies born in mosaic date-vases,
That emerge black and vermeil from yellow cocoons.

Some say that for sweetness they cannot see far,—
That their land is too gorgeous to free their eyes wide
To horizons which knife-like would only mar
Their joy with a barren and steely tide—

That they only can see when their moon limits vision,
Their mother, the Moon, marks a halo of light
On their own small oasis, ray-cut, an incision,
Where are set all the myriad jewelleries of night.

So they sleep in the shade of black palm-bark at noon,
Blind only in day, but remembering that soon
She will flush their hid wings in the evening to blaze
Countless rubies and tapers in the oasis' blue haze.

But over one moth's eyes were tissues at birth
Too multiplied even to center his gaze
On that circle of paradise cool in the night;—
Never came light through that honey-thick glaze.

And had not his pinions with signs mystical
And rings macrocosmic won envy as thrall,
They had scorned him, so humbly low, bound there and tied
At night like a grain of sand, futile and dried.

But once though, he learned of that span of his wings,—
The florescence, the power he felt bud at the time
When the others were blinded by all waking things;
And he ventured the desert,—his wings took the climb.

And lo, in that dawn he was pierroting over,—
Swinging in spirals round the fresh breasts of day.
The moat of the desert was melting from clover
To yellow,—to crystal,—a sea of white spray—

Till the sun, he still gyrating, shot out all white,—
Though a black god to him in a dizzying night;—
And without one cloud-car in that wide meshless blue
The sun saw a ruby brightening ever, that flew.

Seething and rounding in long streams of light
The heat led the moth up in octopus arms:
The honey-wax eyes could find no alarms,
But they burned thinly blind like an orange peeled white.

And the torrid hum of great wings was his song
When below him he saw what his whole race had shunned—
Great horizons and systems and shores all along
Which blue tides of cool moons were slow shaken and
    sunned.

A little time only, for sight burned as deep
As his blindness before had frozen in Hell,
And his wings atom-withered,—gone,—left but a leap:—
To the desert,—back,—down,—still lonely he fell.

I have hunted long years for a spark in the sand;—
My eyes have hugged beauty and winged life's brief spell.
These things I have:—a withered hand;—
Dim eyes;—a tongue that cannot tell.

c. 1915–17

To Earth

Be earnest, Earth,—and kind.
This flower that opened in the storm
Has fallen with the after-hush.
Be earnest, Earth,—and kind.

c. 1916–18

Medusa

"Fall with me
  Through the frigid stars:
  Fall with me
  Through the raving light:—
  Sink
  Where is no song
  But only the white hair of aged winds.

Follow
Into utterness,
Into dizzying chaos,—
The eternal boiling chaos
Of my locks!

Behold thy lover,—
Stone!"

c. 1916–18

Meditation

I have drawn my hands away
Toward peace and the grey margins of the day.
The andante of vain hopes and lost regret
Falls like slow rain that whispers to forget,—
Like a song that neither questions nor replies
It laves with coolness tarnished lips and eyes.

I have drawn my hands away
At last to touch the ungathered rose. O stay,
Moment of dissolving happiness! Astir
Already in the sky, night's chorister
Has brushed a petal from the jasmine moon,
And the heron has passed by, alas, how soon!

I have drawn my hands away
Like ships for guidance in the lift and spray
Of stars that urge them toward an unknown goal.
Drift, O wakeful one, O restless soul,
Until the glittering white open hand
Of heaven thou shalt read and understand.

c. 1916–18

Episode of Hands

The unexpected interest made him flush.
Suddenly he seemed to forget the pain,—
Consented,—and held out
One finger from the others.

The gash was bleeding, and a shaft of sun
That glittered in and out among the wheels,
Fell lightly, warmly, down into the wound.

And as the fingers of the factory owner's son,
That knew a grip for books and tennis
As well as one for iron and leather,—
As his taut, spare fingers wound the gauze
Around the thick bed of the wound,
His own hands seemed to him
Like wings of butterflies
Flickering in sunlight over summer fields.

The knots and notches,—many in the wide
Deep hand that lay in his,—seemed beautiful.
They were like the marks of wild ponies' play,—
Bunches of new green breaking a hard turf.

And factory sounds and factory thoughts
Were banished from him by that larger, quieter hand
That lay in his with the sun upon it.
And as the bandage knot was tightened
The two men smiled into each other's eyes.

1920

The Bridge of Estador

An Impromptu,
Aesthetic
TIRADE

Walk high on the bridge of Estador,
No one has ever walked there before.
There is a lake, perhaps, with the sun
Lapped under it,—or the dun
Bellies and estuaries of warehouses,
Tied bundle-wise with cords of smoke.

Do not think too deeply, and you'll find
A soul, an element in it all.

How can you tell where beauty's to be found?
I have heard hands praised for what they made;
I have heard hands praised for line on line;
Yet a gash with sunlight jerking through
A mesh of belts down into it, made me think
I had never seen a hand before.
And the hand was thick and heavily warted.

High on the bridge of Estador
Where no one has ever been before,—
I do not know what you'll see,—your vision
May slumber yet in the moon, awaiting
Far consummations of the tides to throw
Clean on the shore some wreck of dreams. . . .

But some are twisted with the love
Of things irreconcilable,—
The slant moon with the slanting hill:
O Beauty's fool, though you have never
Seen them again, you won't forget.
Nor the Gods that danced before you
When your fingers spread among stars.

And you others,—follow your arches
To what corners of the sky they pull you to,—
The everlasting eyes of Pierrot,
    Or, of Gargantua, the laughter.

c. 1920–1921

After Jonah

In my beginning was the memory, somehow
contradicting Jonah, that essential babe
of unbaptised digestion, being a nugget
to call pity on Jerusalem and on Nature, too.

We have his travels in the snare so widely
ruminated,—of how he stuck there, was reformed,
forgiven, also—
and belched back like a word to grace us all.

There is no settling tank in God. It must be borne
that even His bowels are too delicate to board
a sniping thief that has a pious beard.
We must hail back the lamb that went unsheared.

O sweet deep whale as ever reamed the sky
with high white gulfs of vapor, castigate
our sins, but be hospitable as Hell.
And keep me to the death like ambergris,
sealed up, and unforgiven in my cell.

c. 1922–26

Euclid Avenue

To be or not to be—?

But so to be the denizen stingaree—
As stertorous as nations romanized may throw
Surveys by Maytimes slow. . . . Hexameters
Suspending jockstraps for gangsters while the pil-

Bland (grim)aces Plutarch's perch. And angles
Break in folds of crêpe that blackly drape
The broken door . . . Crouch so. Amend

Then; and clinch.

Sweep. . . .
Clean is that cloven Hoof. Then reap
Strain, clasp oblivion as though Chance
Could absent all answer save the chosen rant.

Stop now, as never, never. Speak

As telegrams continue, write, strike
Your scholarship (stop) through broken ribs; jail
(Stripe) answers Euclid. Einstein curves, but does not
Quail. Does Newton take the Eucharist on rail
Nor any boulevard no more? I say . . .

For there are statues, shapes your use
Repeals. Youse use. You're prevalent,—prevail!
Youse
Food once more and souse, like all me under sail.
My friends, I never thought we'd fail.

That dirty peacock's pride, once gory God's own story:
It didn't belong no more; no, never did glory
Walk on Euclid Avenue, as didn't Wm.
Bleached or blacked, whichever 'twas. What milk
We've put in blasted pigs! I says . . . O, well—

But I say, what a swell chance, boys. No more
Cancers, jealousy, tenements or giblets! Death, my boys,
Nor blinkers either—

Four shots at who-knows-how—how

Many-it-was unsupervised

Grabbed right outa my mouth that final chew—
Right there on Euclid Avenue.

c. 1922–26

To Buddha

You are quite outside of such issues,
The polished bottom of your sound font
Is taught to ride in heaven, and you know
The tangents of desire the other quells

c. 1923–24

———

Where gables pack the rainless
fulsome sky
permit a song as comes into the street

permit a song that swings with ropes
and skipping feet
above the laughter that rebounds below.

1923

Well/Well/Not-At-All

Yakka-hoola-hikki-doola
Pico-della-miran-dohhh-la
leonarda-della-itchy-vinci
es braust ein Ruf wie
　　DONNERHALL

pffffff !

1923

———

OF AN EVENING
PULLING OFF A LITTLE EXPERIENCE
(with the english language)

by

NIGHTS
EEEEEECCCUUUMMMMMMIIINNNGGGSSS (for short)　69

wrists web rythms
and the poke-
　　　,dot smile;
of Genevive

talks

back

i KNew,kneW my feet
?go on) were an applesauce
　　　　　　part
of yoU belching POCHETTEkeepit
upyou s,uede
ballbearing

celery = grin

remind of-of la guerre

UM
Trimvirate (creamed dancing bitches)

corking with Helene, (exactly you make)
my perpendicularly crowdedPOCKets

       smilepoke

,,besides: which
April has
a
word to say: classy)eh(!
while blundering fumbiguts gather   accu
rate little, O-SO masturbations in/
                    to
fractions of heaven. Hold   tight   bless
worms trilling rimple flock to
sad iron

              goats of
         love-
            semi-colon
            piping (dash)

                          1923

What Nots ?

to chorus of: "O bury me not
*   In the lone prairie-ee,*
*   Where the wild coyotes*
*   Will how-ow-owl at me!"*

What is a What Not
if what is not negates
what is not what
you thought it was   ?

O berenberg not
in Laocoön trot —

No;   what is not
esperanto may well be

Lessing to what
not Guthries
plus pot shot double-
double-you Williams:

so   clams open not
to the naughty What Not   !

What a lot of rot, not what
grandma was hot about,   you
say: so
wot I too.   But

what knots and dots
remind *you* of forget-
me-nots   ?

1923

In a Court

His hand changed in the kitchen
by the fire: she moved a little,
like wax against his gaze
that followed flame and transfusion,—
every spark meshed white, a part
of his most solemn appetite.

I looked into the kitchen where
they sat.
Breathless I was that peace should come
where fat is to be grasped and lean
is clenched,
and fingers are a teeth that taste
and smell.

1924

With a Photograph to Zell, Now Bound for Spain

From Brooklyn Heights one sees the bay:
And, anchored at my window sill,
I've often sat and watched all day
The boats stream by against the shrill
Manhattan skyline,—endlessly
Their mastheads filing out to sea.

And just so, as you see me here
(Though kodaked somewhat out of focus,
My eyes have still the proper locus)
I'm flashing greetings to your pier,
Your ship, your auto-bus in France—
All things on which you glide or prance
Down into sunny Spain, dear Zell.
Good berths, good food and wine as well!

I hope to know these wishes a true
Forecasting. Let me hear from you.
Enclose some petals from a wall
Of roses in Castile, or maybe garden stall;
While I'll be waiting at this old address,
Dear Aunt, God-mother, Editress!

1924

————

This way where November takes the leaf
to sow only disfigurement in early snow
mist gained upon the night I delved, surely
as the city took us who can meet and go
(who might have parted, keen beyond any sea,
in words which no wings can engender now).

For this there is a beam across my head;
its weight not arched like heaven full, its edge
not bevelled, and its bulk that I accept,
triumphing not easily upon the brow . . .

And, margined so, the sun may rise aware
(I must have waited for so devised a day)
of the old woman whistling in her tubs,
and a labyrinth of laundry in the courted sky;
while inside, downward passing steps
anon not to white buildings I have seen,
leave me to whispering an answer here
to nothing but this beam that crops my hair.

Vaulted in the welter of the east be read,
"These are thy misused deeds."—
And the arms, torn white and mild away, be bled.

1924

———

You are that frail decision that devised
Their lowest common multiple of human need,
And on that bleak assumption risked the prize
Forgetfulness of all you bait for greed . . .

c. 1924–26

———

Thou canst read nothing except through appetite
And here we join eyes in that sanctity
Where brother passes brother without sight,
But finally knows conviviality . . .

Go then, unto thy turning and thy blame.
Seek bliss then, brother, in my moment's shame.
All this that baulks delivery through words
Shall come to you through wounds prescribed by swords:

That hate is but the vengeance of a long caress,
And fame is pivotal to shame with every sun
That rises on eternity's long willingness . . .
So sleep, dear brother, in my fame, my shame undone.

c. 1924–26

To Liberty

Out of the seagull cries and wind
On this strange shore I build
The virgin. They laugh to hear
How I endow her, standing
Hair mocked by the sea, her lover
A dead sailor that knew
Not even Helen's fame.

Light the last torch in the wall,
The sea wall. Bring her no robes yet.
They have not seen her in this harbor;
Eyes widely planted, clear, yet small.
And must they overcome the fog,
Or must we rend our dream?

Provide these manners, this salute
The brows feed on, anticipate this sanction.
Things become separate, final—
While I become more whole
Infinite—the gradual all
Which is a laugh at last
Struggles

c. 1924–27

Mirror of Narcissus

They judge, whose strictures of their sight
Preclude the evidence I speak. And how
Shall I of their dead conscience build the proof
Unto themselves, whereof their birth was God?
Who will but laugh, and lengthily defer
Their heritage, and sneer down all the pain,
And vomit back the incense breathed in vain!
—O minute elegy, pantouffle pain,
O mirror of Narcissus, when is your wane?

His perfect image dies upon the stage
Or gains, it is no matter for the gods.
The water flows, divides his gain—
Loving the Styx, he sees the rain
Speak otherwise in his own tones
Upon the land he lends such dirges to.

Thy repetition freezes thus my pain . . .

c. 1924–27

The Masters

Their brains are smooth machines that colonize
The sun,—their eyes are atoms of a split hereafter.
They must explain away all moan and laughter,
Then ticket, subdivide and overrule
Each former entity *****
I saw them turn old Demos from the stage
And mock their hearts because their hearts spoke better,
Elaborate all, divided school by school

c. 1924–27

———

Her eyes had the blue of desperate days,
Freezingly bright; I saw her hair unfurl,
Unsanctioned, finally, by anything left her to know
She had learned that Paradise is not a question of eggs
If anything, it was her privilege to undress
Quietly in a glass she had guarded
Always with correcting states before.

It was this, when I asked her how she died,
That asked me why her final happy cry
Should not have found an echo somewhere, and I stand

Before her finally, as beside a wall, listening as though
I heard the breath of Holofernes toast
Judith's cold bosom through her righteous years.

1925

———

O moon, thou cool sibilance of the sun, we utmost love
A Quaker in the sky the clouds resign—
For that ye yield one answer, one above
All else of midnight—that we shall not
I begged a mediator in thy sign
                    thy free industry
Thy leap and petal over the stiff edge
Where no one else dare set the wedge
O the moon crops weather on the spine
Of every buckwheat that the bee takes in in his prime
Your mother, sibilance of the sun, is the vine

c. 1925–29

Lenses

In the focus of the evening there is this island with the buzz of
saw mills, the crunch and blast of quarries; furnaces, chisels
and ploughs.

And the idiot boy by the road, with carbonated eyes, laughing
or extending a phallus through the grating,—talking to a kite
high in the afternoon, or in the twilight scanning pebbles
among cinders in the road through a twice-opened tomato
can.

And there is work, blood, suet and sweat,—the rigamarole
of wine and mandolines. Midnight; and maybe love . . .

And there is, as Mr. Budge explained before his
chorea took him away—there is the Nine of
three-times-three, the hopeful plasm,
the vigilance of the ape, the repe-
tition of the parrot. Locks on
doors and lips of agony to
dance upon. And there is

time for these; time for all these, as cattle and birds
know, Mr.
Budge—
why did
you
die
so
soon
?

There is
this gate of
wrath

c. 1926–27

To the Empress Josephine's Statue

Martinique

Image of Constancy

You, who contain augmented tears, explosions
Have kissed, caressed the model of the hurricane
Gathered and made musical in feathered fronds
The slit eclipse of moon in palm-lit bonds
Deny me not in this sweet Caribbean dawn

You, who have looked back to Leda, who have seen
   the Swan
In swirling rushes, urged the appointed charge,
Outdid our spies and hoodwink sputum,
Now you may compute your lecheries—
As well as I, but not with her,—

I own it still—that sure deliberation—
Leave, leave that Caribbean praise to me
Who claims a devout concentration
To wage you surely out of memory—
Your generosity dispose relinquishment and care.
Thy death be sacred to all those who share
Love and the breath of faith, momentous bride
You did not die for conquerors at your side
Nor for that fruit of mating that is widowed pride

c. 1926–27

Supplication to the Muses on a Trying Day

"How many dawns, chill from his rippling rest,
The seagull's wings shall—"

Hold it in a high wind. The fender curving over the breast-
plate, and all in high gear. I watched to see the river rise. The
forests had all given out their streams and tributaries. When
would the bones of De Soto come down in the wild rinse? And
when would Ponce de Leon remember Hammerfest? . . .
There were periods when the salt-rising bread broke out all
over me in heinous sores. If you can't abuse a machine, why
have it! Machines are made for abuse. . . . Fool-proof! Human
beings were never jetted, conceived, articulated, ejected,
nursed, spanked, corrected, educated, harangued, married,
divorced, petted, emasculated, loved and damned, jailed and
liberated, besides being plastered, frightened and mangled,
pickled and strangled—THEY were never meant to be abused!
Thou art no more than Chinese to me, O Moon! A simian
chorus to you, and let your balls be nibbled by the flirtatious

hauchinango. The tide would rise—and did. I held the crupper by a lasso conscripted from white mice tails spliced to the fore-top gallant. Old Mizzentop rose, but all in vain. It was a wild night among the breakers and the smooth racoons. All the pistols came dressed in white lattice, winking as never before; but the prawns held out till nearly daybreak,—simpering, simpering and equivocating. By the time I reached Berlin—or was it Shanghai?—there were no more stitches for wounds, nor tortoises for telescopes. "What a waste of eternity!" I exclaimed into the ear of the most celebrated microphone you ever smashed. Then the wind rose, and I strangled in the embraces of a derelict aigrette.

These dermatologists of Mozambique have got hold of me since. They say my digits fidget, that I'm but a follicle of my former fratricide. . . . What shall I do? I masticate firmly and bite off all my nails. I practise invention / to the brink of intelligibility. I insult all my friends and ride ostriches furiously across the Yukon, while parrots berate me to the accompaniment of the most chaste reticules. By all the mystery of Gomorrha, I ask, what can a gaping gastronomist gather in such a gulch of simulation?!!

c. 1926–27

————

The sea raised up a campanile . . . The wind I heard
Of brine partaking, whirling into shower
Of column that breakers sheared in shower
Back into bosom,—me—her, into natal power . . .

c. 1926–27

Eternity

September—remember!
October—all over.
BARBADIAN ADAGE

After it was over, though still gusting balefully,
The old woman and I foraged some drier clothes
And left the house, or what was left of it;
Parts of the roof reached Yucatan, I suppose.
She almost—even then—got blown across lots
At the base of the mountain. But the town, the town!

Wires in the streets and Chinamen up and down
With arms in slings, plaster strewn dense with tiles,
And Cuban doctors, troopers, trucks, loose hens . . .
The only building not sagging on its knees,
Fernandez' Hotel, was requisitioned into pens
For cotted negroes, bandaged to be taken
To Havana on the first boat through. They groaned.

But was there a boat? By the wharf's old site you saw
Two decks unsandwiched, split sixty feet apart
And a funnel high and dry up near the park
Where a frantic peacock rummaged amid heaped cans.
No one seemed to be able to get a spark
From the world outside, but some rumor blew
That Havana, not to mention poor Batabanó,
Was halfway under water with fires
For some hours since—all wireless down
Of course, there too.

                    Back at the erstwhile house
We shoveled and sweated; watched the ogre sun
Blister the mountain, stripped now, bare of palm,
Everything—and lick the grass, as black as patent
Leather, which the rimed white wind had glazed.
Everything gone—or strewn in riddled grace—
Long tropic roots high in the air, like lace.
And somebody's mule steamed, swaying right by the pump,

Good God! as though his sinking carcass there
Were death predestined! You held your nose already
Along the roads, begging for buzzards, vultures . . .
The mule stumbled, staggered. I somehow couldn't budge
To lift a stick for pity of his stupor.

                          For I
Remember still that strange gratuity of horses
—One ours, and one, a stranger, creeping up with dawn
Out of the bamboo brake through howling, sheeted light
When the storm was dying. And Sarah saw them, too—
Sobbed, Yes, now—it's almost over. For they know;
The weather's in their noses. There's Don—but that one,
          white
—I can't account for him! And true, he stood
Like a vast phantom maned by all that memoried night
Of screaming rain—Eternity!

                          Yet water, water!
I beat the dazed mule toward the road. He got that far
And fell dead or dying, but it didn't so much matter.

The morrow's dawn was dense with carrion hazes
Sliding everywhere. Bodies were rushed into graves
Without ceremony, while hammers pattered in town.
The roads were being cleared, injured brought in
And treated, it seemed. In due time
The President sent down a battleship that baked
Something like two thousand loaves on the way.
Doctors shot ahead from the deck in planes.
The fever was checked. I stood a long time in Mack's talking
New York with the gobs, Guantanamo, Norfolk,—
Drinking Bacardi and talking U.S.A.

                                        c. 1926–27

                    ———

So dream thy sails, O phantom bark
That I thy drownèd men may speak again
Perhaps as once Will Collins spoke the lark,
And leave me half adream upon the main.

For who shall lift head up to funnel smoke,
And who trick back the leisured winds again
As they were fought—and wooed? They now but stoke
Their vanity, and dream no land in vain.

Of old there was a promise, and thy sails
Have kept no faith but wind, the cold stream
—The hot fickle wind, the breath of males
Imprisoned never, no not soot and steam.

c. 1926–28

A Postscript

Friendship agony! words came to me
at last shyly. My only final friends—
the wren and thrush, made solid print for me
across dawn's broken arc. No; yes . . . or were they
the audible ransom, ensign of my faith
toward something far, now farther than ever away?

Remember the lavender lilies of that dawn,
their ribbon miles, beside the railroad ties
as one nears New Orleans, sweet trenches by the train
after the western desert, and the later cattle country;
and other gratuities, like porters, jokes, roses . . .

Dawn's broken arc! and noon's more furbished room!
Yet seldom was there faith in the heart's right kindness.
There were tickets and alarm clocks. There were counters
        and schedules;
and a paralytic woman on an island of the Indies,
Antillean fingers counting my pulse, my love forever.

c. 1926–28

The Sad Indian

Sad heart, the gymnast of inertia, does not count
Hours, days—and scarcely sun and moon—
The warp is in the woof—and his keen vision
Spells what his tongue has had—and only that—
How more?—but the lash, lost vantage—and the prison
His fathers took for granted ages since—and so he looms

Farther than his sun-shadow—farther than wings
—Their shadows even—now can't carry him.
He does not know the new hum in the sky
And—backwards—is it thus the eagles fly?

c. 1926–30

———

I have that sure enclitic to my act
Which shall insure no dissonance to fact.
Then Agamemnon's locks grow to shape
Without my forebear's priceless model of the ape . . . .
Gorillas die—and so do humanists—who keep
Comparisons clear for evolution's non-escape
And man the deathless target, of his own weak sheep . . .

c. 1926–29

The Pillar and the Post

What you may yank up *readiest* Yank—
May not so well serve your purpose as your plaint
When you have no one but the devil—to thank
And you wretched with your clean-limbed taint—

Of strangling the Argives of the palms—
        Midas of motion—love those lingering
instants that bespeak a careful manure for all
your progeny—and ask the sun what time it

is before your fingers lose their ten—in biological
and betrothèd answer to the ambitious monkey synthesis
    that you adore.

c. 1926–29

The Visible the Untrue

to E. O.

Yes, I being
the terrible puppet of my dreams, shall
lavish this on you—
the dense mine of the orchid, split in two.
And the fingernails that cinch such
environs?
And what about the staunch neighbor tabulations,
with all their zest for doom?

I'm wearing badges
that cancel all your kindness. Forthright
I watch the silver Zeppelin
destroy the sky. To
stir your confidence?
To rouse what sanctions—? toothaches?

The silver strophe . . . the canto
bright with myth . . . Such
distances leap landward without
evil smile. And, as for me . . .

The window weight throbs in its blind
partition. To extinguish what I have of faith.
Yes, light. And it is always
always, always the eternal rainbow
And it is always the day, the farewell day unkind.

c. 1927–29

Shall I subsume the shadow of the world—
The sun-spot that absolves us all? In fine
There is the wisp, there is the phantom,
"Fantisticon", in the comedy where we meet.
The interlude without circumvention
This, between the speech of shells and battle gases.
I know this effort by the slant of the obdurate moon.
She, at worst, is the chancel—of our worst reflection

Immeasurable scope of veins, imprisoned within mood
Whereon the distance thrives—O jealousy of space!
I, these cameos, carve—thy caverns limitless achieve—
These arteries explore. What is the extent of the sod?
And where is the clod blown up with

c. 1927–29

———

Tenderness and resolution
What is our life without a sudden pillow—
What is death without a ditch?

The harvest laugh of bright Apollo
And the flint tooth of Sagittarius
Rhyme from the same jaw—(closing cinch by cinch)
And pocket us who, somehow, do not follow,
As though we knew those who are variants—
Charms—that each by each refuse the clinch

With desperate propriety, whose name is writ
In wider letters than the alphabet,—
Who is now left to vary the Sanscrit
Pillowed by

My wrist in the vestibule of time—who
Will hold it—wear the keepsake, dear, of time—
Return the mirage on a coin that spells
Something of sand and sun the Nile defends. . . .

c. 1927–29

———

Time cannot be worn strapped to the supple wrist
Like any buckled jewel or bangle; no,
Lady, though fingers that attach it twist
The oyster from its shell, may guide the bow
Across cool strings that lift a lasting claim
Upon Eternity. No, Lady,

c. 1927–29

———

I rob my breast to reach those altitudes—
To meet the meaningless concussion of
Pure heights—Infinity resides below. . . .
The obelisk of plain infinity founders below
My vision is a grandiose dilemma—

Place de la Concorde! Across that crowded plain—
I fought to see the stricken bones, the noble
Carcass of a general, dead Foch, proceed
To the defunct pit of Napoleon—in honor
Defender, not usurper.

My countrymen,—give form and edict—
To the marrow. You shall know
The harvest as you have known the spring
But I believe that such "wreckage" as I find
Remaining presents evidence of considerably more
Significance than do the cog-walk gestures
Of a beetle in a sand pit.

1929

———

Enrich my resignation as I usurp those far
Feints of control—hear rifles blown out on the stag
Below the aeroplane—and see the fox's brush
Whisk silently beneath the red hill's crag
—Extinction stirred on either side
Because love wonders, keeps a certain mirth—
Die, Oh, centuries, die, as Dionysius said,
Yet live in all my resignation—
It is the moment, now, when all—
The heartstrings spring, unlaced—Oh thou fiend and

Here is the peace of the fathers

1929

———

All this—and the housekeeper—
Written on a blotter, Hartford, Bridgeport—
The weekend at Holyoke
His daughters act like kings
Pauline and I, the Harvard game
—A brand new platform
Way on Stutzing up to Spring
—Not a cent, not a cent, wish we'd known beforehand.

And the last of the Romanoffs
Translated the International Code
Tea and toast across radios
Swung into lullabies.
His father gave him the store outright
—All sorts of money, Standard Oil
And his two sons, their fourth or fifth cousins
How well he carried himself
And a stick all the time

1929

A Traveller Born

Of sailors—those two Corsicans at Marseille,—
The Dane at Paris and the Spanish abbé
With distance, lizard-like, green as Pernod;
Its cargo drench, its wet inferno
Condenses memory. The abbey colonnade, the vesperal
    fountain—
Oh, sudden apple-math of ripe night fallen!
Concluding handclasp, cider, summer-swollen
Folds, and is folden in the echoing mountain. . . .

Yields and is shielded, wrapt in traffic flame,
The One, this crucifix that bears a name
Like Science, and the Pasteur Institute . . .
That home for serums keeps the student mute
Until the Fourteenth of July—
(Contain the Paternosters and waive the West wind by)

When midnight to lamp bruised black
That nuisance silhouette unhands me
On the ceiling—the midnight clasp extends
(My shadow to myself)
To all the courtesies of foreign friends—

I read it clear of anything that bows
Less of the midnight than that midnight shows
Into intrinsic skeletal sincerity—
Less than the stoker or the pilot knows
More than the statesman or the plowman shows. . . .

This rhetoric sincere that blinds its flame
To yield it without smoke, intense and sure
The flower's unwithered in vase with name
And so the traveller's home's a foreign cure

c. 1926–31

———

The alert pillow, the hayseed spreads
And mountains wasting carpet—
O willows, drooping forecast—tears?
That demiurge, turf earns the station
Whereby candles are bought and hymns
Sparkle alone in wastebaskets and whereto
Scythes, those seldom spears—by
Poets urged—so their sunset crescents
Swiftly and like iron sweep acceptance

1930

———

There are the local orchard boughs
With apples—August boughs—their unspilled spines
Inter-wrenched and flocking with gold spousal wine
Like hummocks drifting in the autumn shine

1930

———

Dust now is the old-fashioned house
Where Jacob dreamed his ladder climb,—
Thankfully fed both hog and mouse
And mounted rung on rung of rhyme

1930

———

They were there falling;
And they fell. And their habitat
Left them. And they fell.
And what they remembered was—
Dismembered. But they fell.
And now they dispel
Those wonders that posterity constructs,
By such a mystery as time obstructs;

And all the missions and votaries
And old maids with their chronic coteries
Dispense in the old, old lorgnette views
What should have kept them straight in pews.
But doesn't confuse
These Indians, who scan more news
On the hind end of their flocks each day
Than all these tourists bring their way.

c. 1931–32

Havana Rose

Let us strip the desk for action—now we have a horse in Mexico. . . . That night in Vera Cruz—verily for me "the True Cross"—let us remember the Doctor and my thoughts, my humble, fond remembrances of the great bacteriologist. . . .

The wind, that night, the clamour of incessant shutters, trundle doors—and the cheroot watchman—tiptoeing the successive patio balconies with a typical pistol—trying to muffle doors—and the pharos shine—the mid-wind midnight stroke of it, its milk-light regularity above my bath partition through the lofty, dusty glass—*Cortez—Cortez*—his crumbled palace in the square—the typhus in a trap, the Doctor's rat trap. Where? Somewhere in Vera Cruz—to bring—to take—to mix—to ransom—to deduct—*to cure*. . . . The rats played ring around the rosy (in their basement basinette)—the Doctor slept supposedly in #35—thus in my wakeful watch at least— the lighthouse flashed . . . whirled . . . delayed, and struck —*again, again*. Only the Mayans surely slept— whose references to typhus and whose records spurred the Doctor into something nigh those metaphysics that are typhoid plus—and had engaged him once before to death's beyond and back again—antagonistic wills—into immunity. Tact, horsemanship, courage were germicides to him. . . . Poets may not be doctors, but doctors are rare poets when roses leap like rats—and too, when rats make rose nozzles of pink death around white teeth. . . .

And during the wait over dinner at La Diana, the Doctor
had said—who was American also—"You cannot heed the
negative—, so might go on to undeserved doom . . . must
therefore loose yourself within a pattern's mastery that you can
conceive, that you can yield to—by which also you win and
gain that mastery and happiness which is your own from
birth."

1931

Purgatorio

My country, O my land, my friends—
Am I apart,—here from you in a land
Where all your gas lights—faces,—sputum gleam
Like something left, forsaken,—here am I—
And are these stars—the high plateau—the scents
Of Eden—and the dangerous tree—are these
The landscape of confession—and if confession
So absolution? Wake pines—but pines wake here.
I dream the too-keen cider—the too-soft snow.
Where are the bayonets that the scorpion may not grow?
Here quakes of earth make houses fall—
And all my countrymen I see rush toward one stall.
Exile is thus a purgatory—not such as Dante built

But rather like a blanket than a quilt
And I have no decision—is it green or brown
That I prefer to country or to town?
I am unraveled, umbilical anew,
So ring the church bells here in Mexico—
(They ring too obdurately here to need my call)
And what hours they forget to chime I'll know
As one whose altitude at one time was not

c. 1931–32

The Circumstance

To Xochipilli

The anointed stone, the coruscated crown—
The drastic throne, the
Desperate sweet eyepit-basins of a bloody foreign clown—
Couched on bloody basins floating bone
Of a dismounted people. . . .

If you could buy the stones,
Display the stumbling bones
Urging your unsuspecting
Shins, sus-
Taining nothing in time but more and more of Time,
Mercurially might add but would
Subtract and concentrate. . . . If you
Could drink the sun as did and does
Xochipilli,—as they who've
Gone have done, as they
Who've done. . . . A god of flowers in statued
Stone . . . of love—

If you could die, then starve, who live
Thereafter, stronger than death smiles in flowering stone;—
You could stop time, give florescent
Time a longer answer back (shave lightning,
Possess in halo full the winds of time)
A longer answer force, more enduring answer
As they did—and have done. . . .

c. 1931–32

Hieroglyphic

Did one look at what one saw
Or did one see what one looked at?

1932

To Conquer Variety

I have seen my ghost broken
My body blessed
And Eden
Scraped from my mother's breast
When the charge was spoken
Love dispossessed
And the seal broken . . . . .

c. 1931–32

SELECTED PROSE

The Case Against Nietzsche

Before the war, Nietzsche's writings were moderately popular in France, where he was hailed by the Sorbonne long before Oxford awoke to his dimensions. But now the French call him the herald of modern Prussianism.

How paradoxical their accusation seems, when we know that Nietzsche was drawn to the French temperament more than to any other. His favorite novelists were French; Pascal and Montaigne were sources which he frequently mentions as potent influences in his development. Goethe and Schopenhauer were the only Germans for whom he had philosophic ears; and these, as he declares, were fundamentally un-German.

And yet again, how can he be called the spokesman of a nation which always affected him with disgust,—if not with hatred? His epithets on characteristic "Germania" at times approach the unprintable. He even denied his German origin, and declared himself a Pole in all his views and sympathies. Anyone who can picture him as an inspired leader of legions of "the pig-headed," as he called them, has indeed capacities for self-delusion.

I might refer to Par. 320 in *Menschliches, Allzumenschliches* for a direct arraignment of Prussianism, although no names are mentioned in it. Here the autocratic machine is coolly exposed. He cites the direct control by the state over all educational institutions; the inaccessibility to all personal distinction except through some service, sooner or later, to the state; compulsory military training; the supremacy of the army; and at the end he ironically observes,—"Then nothing more is wanted but an opportunity for great wars. These are provided from professional reasons (and so in all innocence) by diplomats, aided by newspapers and Stock Exchanges. For the 'nation,' as a nation of soldiers, need never be supplied with a good conscience in war,—it has one already."

Nietzsche, Zeppelins, and poisoned-gas go ill together. But Great Indra! one may envy Nietzsche a little; think of being so elusive,—so mercurial, as to be first swallowed whole, then coughed up, and still remain a mystery!

1918

147

Joyce and Ethics

The Los Angeles critic who commented on Joyce in the last issue was adequately answered, I realize,—but the temptation to emphasize such illiteracy, indiscrimination, and poverty still pulls a little too strongly for resistance.

I noticed that Wilde, Baudelaire, and Swinburne are "stacked up" beside Joyce as rivals in "decadence" and "intellect." I am not yet aware that Swinburne ever possessed much beyond his "art ears," although these were long enough, and adequate to all his beautiful, though often meaningless mouthings. His instability in criticism and every form of literature that did not depend almost exclusively on sound for effect and his irrelevant metaphors are notorious. And as to Wilde,—after his bundle of paradoxes has been sorted and conned,—very little evidence of intellect remains. "Decadence" is something much talked about, and sufficiently misconstrued to arouse interest in the works of any fool. Any change in form, viewpoint, or mannerism can be so abused by the offending party. Sterility is the only "decadence" I recognize. An abortion in art takes the same place as it does in society,—it deserves no recognition whatever,—it is simply outside. A piece of work is art, or it isn't: there is no neutral judgment.

However,—let Baudelaire and Joyce stand together, as much as any such thing in literary comparison will allow. The principal eccentricity evinced by both is a penetration into life common to only the greatest. If people resent a thrust which discovers some of their entrails to themselves, I can see no reason for resorting to indiscriminate comparisons, naming colours of the rainbow, or advertising the fact that they have recently been forced to recognize a few of their personal qualities. Those who are capable of being only mildly "shocked" very naturally term the cost a penny, but were they capable of paying a few pounds for the same thinking, experience and realization by and in themselves, they could reserve their pennies for work minor to Joyce's.

The most nauseating complaint against his work is that of immorality and obscenity. The character of Stephen Dedalus is all too good for this world. It takes a little experience,—a few reactions on his part to understand it, and could this have been accomplished in a detached hermitage, high above the mud, he would no doubt have preferred that residence. *A Portrait of the Artist as a Young Man*, aside from Dante, is spiritually the most inspiring book I have ever read. It is Bunyan raised to art, and then raised to the ninth power.

1918

Review of The Ghetto and Other Poems

Extremities in the modern world clash in a close proximity, so that there is a finer, harder line than usual to divide them. There is a cruelty in this,—a kind of desperation that is dramatic. Science, grown uncontrollable, has assumed a grin that has more than threatened the supposed civilization that fed it; science has brought light,—but it threatens to destroy the idea of reverence, the source of all light. Its despotism recognizes no limits. In one sense it has become a gargoyle.

Lola Ridge's volume is eloquent with a dramatic "awareness," or a kind of sharp recognition, of these dominating aspects of her time.

Her poems are always vivid:

> "Life thunders on. . . .
>
> > Over the black bridge
> > The line of lighted cars
> > Creeps like a monstrous serpent
> > Spooring gold. . . .
> >
> > Watchman, what of the track?
> >
> > Night. . . . silence. . . . stars. . . .
> > All's well!"

She is seldom immersed in herself,—she never seems to lose consciousness of surroundings. Quite naturally this treatment gives a dramatic quality to even such a personal utterance as, —"Submerged"—

> "I have known only my own shallows—
> Safe, plumber places,
> Where I was wont to preen myself.
>
> But for the abyss
> I wanted a plank beneath
> And horizons. . . .
>
> I was afraid of the silence
> And the slipping toe-hold. . . ."

The essential to all real poetry is in Miss Ridge's work,—sincerity. Sometimes the "macabre intensity" of her words suggests a slight theatricality. Sometimes a figure or construction is so amazingly brilliant, that one suspicions it has been used for itself alone, and that Miss Ridge has been tempted toward a barren cleverness. That she has decided capacities for it is certain. I hope only, that if her course swerves still further that way, she will utilize the novel, or some such form, other than poetry.

"The Ghetto" is representative of the best of Miss Ridge's endowments. In some aspects it is like a miniature "Comédie humaine," with the dominant note of sadness that runs through Balzac's narratives so insistently.

I have spoken more of the social significance of Miss Ridge's work than strictly aesthetic canons would probably admit, because I have felt the interpretive aspects of her work to be its most brilliant facet. When work is so widely and minutely reflective of its time, then, certainly, other than questions of pure *aesthétique* must be considered.

1919

Review of Minna and Myself

I think that many of these poems will endure though they will probably not be widely popular for the principal reason that they are too distinguished,—too peculiar. They will be classed as "minor poetry," which designation, by the way, is beginning to assume a far from depreciative connotation in these days of attempted epics in "the grand style" like Miss Amy Lowell's very journalistic *Can Grande's Castle*.

Bodenheim cultivates a more limited field. His poems are often little heaps of images in which the verbal element is subordinated, making for an essentially static and decorative quality. There are, however, a few that make me think of the swaying plume of tiny bubbles that an effervescent pill, dissolving in a glass of water, will make. For example:—

"Grey, drooping-shouldered bushes scrape the edges
 Of bending swirls of yellow-white flowers.
 So do my thoughts meet the wind-scattered color of you."
        etc.

But the static element generally predominates, as here:—

"An old silver church in a forest
 Is my love for you.
 The trees around it
 Are words that I have stolen from your heart.
 An old silver bell, the last smile you gave
 Hangs at the top of my church.
 It rings only when you come through the forest
 And stand beside it . . ." etc.

Bodenheim believes that "pure poetry is the vibrant expression of everything clearly delicate and unattached with surface sentiment in the emotions of men toward themselves and nature . . . True poetry is the entering of delicately imaginative plateaus, unconnected with human beliefs or fundamental human feelings." I quote from his article in *The New Republic* of December 22nd, 1917. Now this definition seems to me inordinately precious. Fortunately for all he has not "lived up" to it, except in rare instances. A reaction to the general abuse of his art as a vehicle for all kinds of propaganda is responsible for this extremity of statement, I am sure.

In regard to the plays . . . I should prefer to call them tapestries, scenic rather than dramatic, in interest. Bodenheim is not a dramatist in the real sense of the term, and I question his possibilities in this field. But if he is to insist on incorporating such fine lines as are included in the conversation in *The Master Poisoner*, I think I should easily be won to listening. The most dramatic piece in the book, to my thinking, is the one called *Soldiers*, and that is so by virtue of arrangement,—a painful focus of realities.

1919

Review of
Winesburg, Ohio

Beyond an expression of intense gratitude to the author, it is hard to say a word in regard to a book such as Sherwood Anderson's *Winesburg, Ohio*. The entire paraphernalia of criticism is insignificant, erected against the walls of such a living monument as this book, so that defense and explanation are soon evident as its only office.

First of all, the book is Sherwood Anderson; then humanity, then a certain period in the development of America's "Middle West," so called, and finally, art. It is a great heart, in company with a strong hand, that can elicit the sympathy, or at least, the understanding of his auditor toward each and every one of the characters of his book; and it is in the nature of Sherwood Anderson, as it often was in Balzac, to accomplish it.

The spark that Edgar Lee Masters struck with his *Spoon River Anthology* was a mighty seedling of dynamite, cold and intense,—but I might say sporadic, in comparison with the dignity, the "power in repose," and the sustained inner illumination and bloom of this book. There is the same infinite pathos here, but it seems curbed to a finer reticence that is more genuine than many of the portraits by the elder poet, which at times almost touch the melodramatic. However, there is no need to diminish the proportions of the adventurous discoverer in order to sufficiently praise the richness of the settler, for this, to me, seems the relationship in outlook, time, and performance, of these two Americans.

The Puritan that stalks through the swamps of "Spoon River" is manifest also in "Winesburg," but he is here a little less gaunt; I will not say more or less historically "true," although I do maintain that Sherwood Anderson, while typifying him

strongly in local garments and habits, has nevertheless some-
what modified him with a certain beauty and suggestiveness of
his universal recurrence in many ages. He is alive in a tale called
"Godliness," but the beauty and innocence of youth escape
him in terror. He plays parts in other episodes, but is by no
means a preoccupation of the author. The windows, alleys, and
lanes of the village are open to us to find what epics, tragedies,
and idylls we may. There is everlasting beauty in a scene called
"Mother." The ironic humor and richness of "An Awakening"
are unmatched in anything I know of. "Queer" is a story that
carries De Maupassant into an anti-climax of grating cogs; and
"Paper Pills," perhaps the finest and most exquisite thing in
the book, is so utterly new, that I know nothing with which to
compare it, except, perhaps, an idyll of Lucretius.

To end with aesthetic considerations, the style is flawless. I
know of no finer selection of "significant material," combined
with proper treatment and economy of detail. America should
read this book on her knees. It constitutes an important chap-
ter in the Bible of her consciousness.

1919

A Note on Minns

An ignorance of the professional, technical "elements" of
photography, it seems to me, should very slightly, if at all, in-
validate one's claim to the appreciation of such work as that of
H. W. Minns. In his case, my appreciation can begin only
where the fundamental pedagogics of the camera leave off,—at
the point where the craftsman merges into the artist,—where
the creative element becomes distinct. Some combination of
eye and sympathy and hand are subtly responsible for the qual-
ity in his work. His "arrangements" are not the empty, obvious
contortions of so many modern photographers. He plainly
could not content himself with that. There is, in his faces, the
urge of an ethical curiosity and sympathy as strongly evident as
in the novels of Henry James. Undoubtedly his portraits are
deeper, more vivid, than the daily repetitions of his sitters in

their mirrors give back to any but themselves, but this is only to mention again the creative element that gives to his portraits such a sense of dramatic revelations.

Mr. Minns has often exhibited in Europe, and has received extensive recognition at Dresden, Vienna, and Copenhagen exhibitions. He began taking pictures when he was considerably beyond thirty, and has since spent some twenty years working in the rather limited and unresponsive locality of Akron, Ohio.

1920

Sherwood Anderson

We have come a long way from the pattern-making preoccupations of a Henry James when we can welcome a statement from an artist with as bold a contrasting simplicity as the answer that Sherwood Anderson once gave me to an analysis I had attempted of one of his short stories. "I am in truth mighty little interested in any discussions of art or life, or what a man's place in the scheme of things may be. It has to be done, I suppose, but after all there is the *fact* of life. Its story wants telling and singing. That's what I want,—the tale and the song of it." And it is that Anderson has so pre-eminently captured the "tale and the song of it" that I find his words so acceptable—at least in so far as they relate to his own work.

I spoke of an "attempted" analysis because of being since satisfied that beyond the possibility of a certain uneven surface penetration, Anderson's stories possess a too defiant and timeless solidity,—too much a share of life and clay itself,—to be tagged and listed with mechanical precisions. And what a satisfaction this is, to read stories over and again without a bundle of dry bones and cogwheels of "situations" and "plots" spilling out into one's lap. It must have been because of a surfeit of such disappointments that *Winesburg, Ohio*, when it first appeared, kept me up a whole night in a steady crescendo of emotions. Here was "stark realism," but a realism simplified and strangely sophisticated by the inscrutable soil. And by "soil" I mean something much more than a kind of local colour. There is plenty of that quite wonderfully applied, both in *Winesburg* and in *Poor White*, but there is also something more important and rare than this,—a contact with animal and earthy life so indefinably yet powerfully used as a very foundation to the stories that it might be compared to the sap that pervades the tree-trunk, branches, and twigs. Let me quote an instance of what I mean from *Poor White*.

Clara Butterworth, merging into womanhood, is musing in the shadows of her father's barn. . . .

Clara jumped quickly out of the hammock and walked about under the trees in the orchard. Her thoughts of Jim Priest's youth startled her. It was as though she had walked suddenly into a room where a man and woman were making love. Her cheeks burned and her hands trembled. As she walked slowly through the clumps of grass and weeds that grew between the trees where the sunlight struggled through, bees coming home to the hives heavily laden with honey flew in droves about her head. There was something heady and purposeful about the song of labor that arose out of the beehives. It got into her blood and her step quickened. The words of Jim Priest that kept running through her head seemed a part of the same song the bees were singing. "The sap has begun to run up the tree," she repeated aloud. How significant and strange the words seemed! They were the kind of words a lover might use in speaking to his beloved. She had read many novels, but they contained no such words. It was better so. It was better to hear them from human lips.

This is but one of many remembered paragraphs and pages from which arises a lyricism, deliberate and light, as a curl of milkweed seeds drawn toward the sun. It is his love for rows of corn on flat lands, fields bending over rolling Ohio hills, and the smell of barns under the warm hours of noon, that has given Anderson's descriptions of modern city life, with its mechanical distortions of humanity, such thrust and bite.

In *Poor White* there is the "machine" of modern existence, —the monster that is upon us all. No one who treats however slightly of the lives of the poor or middle classes can escape the issues of its present hold on us. It has seduced the strongest from the land to the cities, and in most cases made empty and meaningless their lives. It has cheapened the worth of all human commodities and even the value of human lives. It has destroyed the pride and pleasure of the craftsman in his work.

"Hugh McVey," the son of a tramp of sordid Missouri River life, becomes a "dreamer of the machines" who invents one after another typical practical improvements such as harvesters, potato-planters, etc., which enrich the speculating manufacturers who grasp at them, bow down before them, and wrangle about them. McVey goes on inventing and himself making money, but finds himself in time becoming more and more indifferent and disappointed. Most of all he is bewildered by the ever greater rush of the new industrialism with its "becoming" towns, its smoke and squalor. He has found no satisfactory foothold. His own machines have robbed him of something and left nothing in its place. He cannot be satisfied with himself as a machine producing machines. Unconsciously he is being urged by more natural impulses that he has perhaps denied too long. Like so many others he is lost among cogs and complicated springs. One sees all through this book how character is bent, blunted, regulated, diverted, or lacerated by the "machine." There is the perfect episode of a harness-maker whose love for manual perfection of craft finally drives him to the murder of an upstart apprentice who had insisted in overruling him by adopting machine-made saddles as substitutes for the carefully wrought saddles of the old man.

Looking back at two earlier books, *Windy McPherson's Son* and *Marching Men*, one can see a great advance in *Poor White*. There has always been the propagandist threatening the artist in Anderson; and in these first two books the propagandist comes out too dangerously near a victory to satisfy us despite the much brilliant description these books contain. Since then he has freed himself from much of this. Not that he has chosen to ignore any facts or problems, but rather that he has succeeded in treating them more impersonally, incorporating them, less obviously, in character and action. To appreciate this advance from the seductive stagnations of sentimentality to a clear acceptance and description of our life to-day for what it be worth, is to realize how few other Americans have had the courage, let alone the vision, to do anything like it. Norris and Dreiser, and one or two others of native birth, have been the only ones. In Anderson there has been some great sincerity, perhaps the element of the "soil" itself personified in him, that has made him refuse to turn aside to offer the crowds those profitable "lollypops" that have "made" and ruined so many other of our writers.

Of course it is patent that people do not like to be told the truth. Especially our Puritans! *Winesburg* was the first book to tell the truth about our small midwestern towns. And what a fury it threw some people into! It seemed to be so much easier for those people to fling back,—"Neuroticism!" "Obscenity!" and "Exaggeration!" than to recognize themselves and others there. I could understand it perfectly myself, having lived for a while in a small town of similar location and colour. But my real point for admiring it was not because it merely told the truth; it was that *Winesburg* represented a work of distinct aesthetic achievement, an example of synthetic form,—not merely a medley of a thousand exterior details such as Lewis's *Main Street*. It takes more than the recognition of facts as facts to move us in fiction. There must be some beauty wrung from them to hold us long. We can recognize this quality without having it pointed out to us if our hearts are not too deadened, our sensibilities too dulled. In *Winesburg*, the windows, alleys, and lanes of the place are opened to us to find what we may. There is an exalting pathos in the episode called "Mother." The ironic humor and richness of "An Awakening" has the vivid and unbroken vitality of a silhouette. "Paper Pills," to me the finest thing in the book, has an idyllic beauty that sets it beside the old legend of "Daphnis and Chloe," and there are other chapters and episodes unmatched anywhere.

During the last two years there have been some short stories published in various magazines, such as "I Want to Know Why," "The Triumph of the Egg," "The New Englander," and "The Other Woman," that I look forward to seeing collected into a volume. I would like to see Anderson handle the negro in fiction. So far it has not been done by anyone without sentimentality or cruelty, but the directness of his vision would produce something new and deep in this direction. In the winter and spring of '20 Anderson was in southern Alabama near the sea finishing *Poor White*, and his interest in the black man became so aroused that he wrote me,—"The negroes are the living wonder of this place. What a tale if someone could penetrate into the home and the life of the Southern negro and not taint it in the ordinary superficial way."

The time has already arrived when Anderson is beginning to be recognized as among the few first recorders of the life of a people coming to some state of self-consciousness. He is without sentimentality; and he makes no pretense of offering solutions. He has a humanity and simplicity that is quite baffling in depth and suggestiveness, and his steady and deliberate growth is proving right along the promise it gives of finer work. A verse from his "A New Testament" has an oddly personal tone to it:

My mind is the mind of a little man with thin legs who sells cigars in a store. My mind is the mind of a cripple who died in an alleyway at Cleveland, Ohio. My mind is the mind of a child who fell into a well, the mind of one who cleans the streets of a city, of an actor who walks up and down on a stage.

1921

Review of
Eight More Harvard Poets

The main bulk of this collection credits Harvard with little more than an even gait with recent Oxford and Cambridge anthologies of similar intention, and helps to prove that there are as many incipient "Georgians" in America as in England. The fact would hardly warrant mention if beyond this margin of quietude there were not the more animated gestures of two poets who have at least convincing manners. The attenuated Woodberrian echoes still haunt the banks of the Charles, but beside the fresher reactions of Malcolm Cowley and John Brooks Wheelwright even the disguise of vers libre fails to rescue their notes from the embrace of familiar nostalgias and worn allusions.

In this well-bred and predominating group (whose tradition certainly needs no present defense), Royall Snow is the only one to approach an interesting idiom. He has a rather true sense for classic diction, though he fails to carry his expression through to the point of valor. Like the others, he gives scattered couplets that are pleasant and all-too-quotable, but there is scarcely a poem from any of the six poets of this group which is satisfying as a completed statement.

A genial pedestrianism, however, in several of Malcolm Cowley's poems indicates the possibility of a 20th century "pastoral" form. A faculty for fresh record, city and road panorama, and ironic nuance, all make Cowley's experiments quite valuable. For one who can so well afford to stick closer to home, he deliberately allows French and 18th century influences to intrude too notably in several instances; yet practically all of his poems achieve consistent form. I think that its austerity and sense of timelessness make "Mountain Valley" his best accomplished poem. Its intonation is suave and deeper than the graded accents of his other poems; its rhythm is accumulative of something less amiable, yet rarer and more abstract than his usual "Chaucerian" method of observation includes. Cowley seems to be civilized in the same sense as the older Chinamen. His alertness is a steady reassurance against crudities or bathos wherever his technical facilities may lead him.

John Brooks Wheelwright has little of Cowley's refinement, but the stertorous drive in several of his poems carries with it real emotional significance. The Hamilton poem, which best exemplifies this quality, is certainly one of the three best poems in the anthology, and the last verse of "Closing Gesture" is a statement so imaginative and balanced that it should be quoted:—

> Myself,
> stand against the black drift of storms,
> trustful as the appealing brave, praying with his arms,
> invincible as Hamilton in granite,
> firm as a colossal crucifix upon a mountain trail
> forever changeless against a changing sky.

It is good to find a poet with the power of fusing ideas with such subjective intensity that the result is poetry. Wheelwright's stringency is a rare quality in American poetry. We have had it in Robinson; but, unless I am mistaken, Wheelwright is emotionally more generously endowed, and, in spite of several second-rate poems, he offers interesting conjectures.

A detailed record of the Muses' bouts at Cambridge is included in Dorian Abbott's able preface. Turning poets loose is a natural privilege of universities, but it will never become, at least in our America, a popular inter-collegiate sport. The Fates are kind in this, even though the idea of the undergraduate anthology seldom gets as much encouragement as it really deserves.

1923

General Aims and Theories

When I started writing "Faustus & Helen" it was my intention to embody in modern terms (words, symbols, metaphors) a contemporary approximation to an ancient human culture or mythology that seems to have been obscured rather than illumined with the frequency of poetic allusions made to it during the last century. The name of Helen, for instance, has become an all-too-easily employed crutch for evocation whenever a poet felt a stitch in his side. The real evocation of this (to me) very real and absolute conception of beauty seemed to consist in a reconstruction in these modern terms of the basic emotional attitude toward beauty that the Greeks had. And in so doing I found that I was really building a bridge between so-called classic experience and many divergent realities of our seething, confused cosmos of today, which has no formulated mythology yet for classic poetic reference or for religious exploitation.

So I found "Helen" sitting in a street car; the Dionysian revels of her court and her seduction were transferred to a Metropolitan roof garden with a jazz orchestra; and the *katharsis* of the fall of Troy I saw approximated in the recent World War. The importance of this scaffolding may easily be exaggerated, but it gave me a series of correspondences between two widely separated worlds on which to sound some major themes of human speculation—love, beauty, death, renascence. It was a kind of grafting process that I shall doubtless not be interested in repeating, but which is consistent with subsequent theories of mine on the relation of tradition to the contemporary creating imagination.

It is a terrific problem that faces the poet today—a world

that is so in transition from a decayed culture toward a reorganization of human evaluations that there are few common terms, general denominators of speech that are solid enough or that ring with any vibration or spiritual conviction. The great mythologies of the past (including the Church) are deprived of enough façade to even launch good raillery against. Yet much of their traditions are operative still—in millions of chance combinations of related and unrelated detail, psychological reference, figures of speech, precepts, etc. These are all a part of our common experience and the terms, at least partially, of that very experience when it defines or extends itself.

The deliberate program, then, of a "break" with the past or tradition seems to me to be a sentimental fallacy. . . . The poet has a right to draw on whatever practical resources he finds in books or otherwise about him. He must tax his sensibility and his touchstone of experience for the proper selections of these themes and details, however,—and that is where he either stands, or falls into useless archeology.

I put no particular value on the simple objective of "modernity." The element of the temporal location of an artist's creation is of very secondary importance; it can be left to the impressionist or historian just as well. It seems to me that a poet will accidentally define his time well enough simply by reacting honestly and to the full extent of his sensibilities to the states of passion, experience and rumination that fate forces on him, first hand. He must, of course, have a sufficiently universal basis of experience to make his imagination selective and valuable. His picture of the "period," then, will simply be a by-product of his curiosity and the relation of his experience to a postulated "eternity."

I am concerned with the future of America, but not because I think that America has any so-called par value as a state or as a group of people. . . . It is only because I feel persuaded that here are destined to be discovered certain as yet undefined spiritual quantities, perhaps a new hierarchy of faith not to be developed so completely elsewhere. And in this process I like to feel myself as a potential factor; certainly I must speak in its terms and what discoveries I may make are situated in its experience.

But to fool one's self that definitions are being reached by merely referring frequently to skyscrapers, radio antennae, steam whistles, or other surface phenomena of our time is merely to paint a photograph. I think that what is interesting and significant will emerge only under the conditions of our submission to, and examination and assimilation of the organic effects on us of these and other fundamental factors of our experience. It can certainly not be an organic expression otherwise. And the expression of such values may often be as well accomplished with the vocabulary and blank verse of the Elizabethans as with the calligraphic tricks and slang used so brilliantly at times by an impressionist like Cummings.

It may not be possible to say that there is, strictly speaking, any "absolute" experience. But it seems evident that certain aesthetic experience (and this may for a time engross the total faculties of the spectator) can be called absolute, inasmuch as it approximates a formally convincing statement of a conception or apprehension of life that gains our unquestioning assent, and under the conditions of which our imagination is unable to suggest a further detail consistent with the design of the aesthetic whole.

I have been called an "absolutist" in poetry, and if I am to welcome such a label it should be under the terms of the above definition. It is really only a *modus operandi*, however, and as such has been used organically before by at least a dozen poets such as Donne, Blake, Baudelaire, Rimbaud, etc. I may succeed in defining it better by contrasting it with the impressionistic method. The impressionist is interesting as far as he goes—but his goal has been reached when he has succeeded in projecting certain selected factual details into his reader's consciousness. He is really not interested in the *causes* (metaphysical) of his materials, their emotional derivations or their utmost spiritual consequences. A kind of retinal registration is enough, along with a certain psychological stimulation. And this is also true of your realist (of the Zola type), and to a certain extent of the classicist, like Horace, Ovid, Pope, etc.

Blake meant these differences when he wrote:

> We are led to believe in a lie
> When we see *with* not *through* the eye.

The impressionist creates only with the eye and for the readiest surface of the consciousness, at least relatively so. If the effect has been harmonious or even stimulating, he can stop there, relinquishing entirely to his audience the problematic synthesis of the details into terms of their own personal consciousness.

It is my hope to go *through* the combined materials of the poem, using our "real" world somewhat as a spring-board, and to give the poem *as a whole* an orbit or predetermined direction of its own. I would like to establish it as free from my own personality as from any chance evaluation on the reader's part. (This is, of course, an impossibility, but it is a characteristic worth mentioning.) Such a poem is at least a stab at a truth, and to such an extent may be differentiated from other kinds of poetry and called "absolute." Its evocation will not be toward decoration or amusement, but rather toward a state of consciousness, an "innocence" (Blake) or absolute beauty. In this condition there may be discoverable under new forms certain spiritual illuminations, shining with a morality essentialized from experience directly, and not from previous precepts or preconceptions. It is as though a poem gave the reader as he left it a single, new *word*, never before spoken and impossible to actually enunciate, but self-evident as an active principle in the reader's consciousness henceforward.

As to technical considerations: the motivation of the poem must be derived from the implicit emotional dynamics of the materials used, and the terms of expression employed are often selected less for their logical (literal) significance than for their associational meanings. Via this and their metaphorical interrelationships, the entire construction of the poem is raised on the organic principle of a "logic of metaphor," which antedates our so-called pure logic, and which is the genetic basis of all speech, hence consciousness and thought-extension.

These dynamics often result, I'm told, in certain initial difficulties in understanding my poems. But on the other hand I find them at times the only means possible for expressing certain concepts in any forceful or direct way whatever. To cite two examples:—when, in "Voyages" (II), I speak of "adagios of islands," the reference is to the motion of a boat through islands clustered thickly, the rhythm of the motion, etc. And it seems a much more direct and creative statement than any more logical employment of words such as "coasting slowly through the islands," besides ushering in a whole world of music. Similarly in "Faustus and Helen" (III) the speed and tense altitude of an aeroplane are much better suggested by the idea of "nimble blue plateaus"—*implying* the aeroplane and its speed against a contrast of stationary elevated earth. Although the statement is pseudo in relation to formal logic—it *is* completely logical in relation to the truth of the imagination, and there is expressed a concept of speed and space that could not be handled so well in other terms.

In manipulating the more imponderable phenomena of psychic motives, pure emotional crystallizations, etc., I have had to rely even more on these dynamics of inferential mention, and I am doubtless still very unconscious of having committed myself to what seems nothing but obscurities to some minds. A poem like "Possessions" really cannot be technically explained. It must rely (even to a large extent with myself) on its organic impact on the imagination to successfully imply its meaning. This seems to me to present an exceptionally difficult problem, however, considering the real clarity and consistent logic of many of the other poems.

I know that I run the risk of much criticism by defending such theories as I have, but as it is part of a poet's business to risk not only criticism—but folly—in the conquest of consciousness I can only say that I attach no intrinsic value to what means I use beyond their practical service in giving form to the living stuff of the imagination.

New conditions of life germinate new forms of spiritual articulation. And while I feel that my work includes a more consistent extension of traditional literary elements than many contemporary poets are capable of appraising, I realize that I am utilizing the gifts of the past as instruments principally; and that the voice of the present, if it is to be known, must be caught at the risk of speaking in idioms and circumlocutions sometimes shocking to the scholar and historians of logic. Language has built towers and bridges, but itself is inevitably as fluid as always.

1925

A Letter to Harriet Monroe

Your good nature and manifest interest in writing me about the obscurities apparent in my Melville poem certainly prompt a wish to clarify my intentions in that poem as much as possible. But I realize that my explanations will not be very convincing. For a paraphrase is generally a poor substitute for any organized conception that one has fancied he has put into the more essentialized form of the poem itself.

At any rate, and though I imagine us to have considerable differences of opinion regarding the relationship of poetic metaphor to ordinary logic (I judge this from the angle of approach you use toward portions of the poem), I hope my answers will not be taken as a defense of merely certain faulty lines. I am really much more interested in certain theories of metaphor and technique involved generally in poetics, than I am concerned in vindicating any particular perpetrations of my own.

My poem may well be elliptical and actually obscure in the ordering of its content, but in your criticism of this very possible deficiency you have stated your objections in terms that allow me, at least for the moment, the privilege of claiming your ideas and ideals as theoretically, at least, quite outside the issues of my own aspirations. To put it more plainly, as a poet I may very possibly be more interested in the so-called illogical impingements of the connotations of words on the consciousness (and their combinations and interplay in metaphor on this basis) than I am interested in the preservation of their logically rigid significations at the cost of limiting my subject matter and perceptions involved in the poem.

This may sound as though I merely fancied juggling words and images until I found something novel, or esoteric; but the process is much more predetermined and objectified than that. The nuances of feeling and observation in a poem may well call for certain liberties which you claim the poet has no right to take. I am simply making the claim that the poet does have that authority, and that to deny it is to limit the scope of the medium so considerably as to outlaw some of the richest genius of the past.

This argument over the dynamics of metaphor promises as active a future as has been evinced in the past. Partaking so extensively as it does of the issues involved in the propriety or non-propriety of certain attitudes toward subject matter, etc., it enters the critical distinctions usually made between "romantic" and "classic" as an organic factor. It is a problem that would require many pages to state adequately—merely from my own limited standpoint on the issues. Even this limited statement may prove onerous reading, and I hope you will pardon me if my own interest in the matter carries me to the point of presumption.

Its paradox, of course, is that its apparent illogic operates so logically in conjunction with its context in the poem as to establish its claim to another logic, quite independent of the original definition of the word or phrase or image thus employed. It implies (this *inflection* of language) a previous or prepared receptivity to its stimulus on the part of the reader. The reader's sensibility simply responds by identifying this inflection of experience with some event in his own history or perceptions—or rejects it altogether. The logic of metaphor is so organically entrenched in pure sensibility that it can't be thoroughly traced or explained outside of historical sciences, like philology and anthropology. This "pseudo-statement," as I. A. Richards calls it in an admirable essay touching our contentions in last July's *Criterion*, demands completely other faculties of recognition than the pure rationalistic associations permit. Much fine poetry may be completely rationalistic in its use of symbols, but there is much great poetry of another order which will yield the reader very little when inspected under the limitation of such arbitrary concerns as are manifested in your judgment of the Melville poem, especially when you constitute such requirements of ordinary logical relationship between word and word as irreducible.

I don't wish to enter here defense of the particular symbols employed in my own poem, because, as I said, I may well have failed to supply the necessary emotional connectives to the content featured. But I would like to counter a question or so of yours with a similar question. Here the poem is less dubious in quality than my own, and as far as the abstract pertinacity of question and its immediate consequences are concerned the point I'm arguing about can be better demonstrated. Both quotations are familiar to you, I'm sure.

You ask me how a *portent* can possibly be wound in a *shell.* Without attempting to answer this for the moment, I ask you how Blake could possibly say that "a *sigh* is a *sword* of an Angel King." You ask me how *compass, quadrant and sextant "contrive"* tides. I ask you how Eliot can possibly believe that "Every street *lamp* that I pass *beats* like a fatalistic *drum!*" Both of my metaphors may fall down completely. I'm not defending their actual value in themselves; but your criticism of them in each case was leveled at an illogicality of relationship between symbols, which similar fault you must have either overlooked in case you have ever admired the Blake and Eliot lines, or have there condoned them on account of some more ultimate convictions pressed on you by the impact of the poems in their entirety.

It all comes to the recognition that emotional dynamics are not to be confused with any absolute order of rationalized definitions; ergo, in poetry the *rationale* of metaphor belongs to another order of experience than science, and is not to be limited by a scientific and arbitrary code of relationships either in verbal inflections or concepts.

There are plenty of people who have never accumulated a sufficient series of reflections (and these of a rather special nature) to perceive the relation between a *drum* and a *street lamp* —*via* the *unmentioned* throbbing of the heart and nerves in a distraught man which *tacitly* creates the reason and "logic" of the Eliot metaphor. They will always have a perfect justification for ignoring those lines and to claim them obscure, excessive, etc., until by some experience of their own the words accumulate the necessary connotations to complete their connection. It is the same with the "patient etherized upon a table," isn't it? Surely that line must lack all eloquence to many people who, for instance, would delight in agreeing that the sky was like a dome of many-colored glass.

If one can't count on some such bases in the reader now and then, I don't see how the poet has any chance to ever get beyond the simplest conceptions of emotion and thought, of sensation and lyrical sequence. If the poet is to be held completely to the already evolved and exploited sequences of

imagery and logic—what field of added consciousness and in-
creased perceptions (the actual province of poetry, if not lulla-
bies) can be expected when one has to relatively return to the
alphabet every breath or so? In the minds of people who have
sensitively read, seen, and experienced a great deal, isn't there
a terminology something like short-hand as compared to usual
description and dialectics, which the artist ought to be right in
trusting as a reasonable connective agent toward fresh con-
cepts, more inclusive evaluations? The question is more impor-
tant to me than it perhaps ought to be, but as long as poetry is
written, an audience, however small, is implied, and there re-
mains the question of an active or an inactive imagination as its
characteristic.

It is of course understood that a street-lamp simply can't
beat with a sound like a drum; but it often happens that im-
ages, themselves totally dissociated, when joined in the circuit
of a particular emotion located with specific relation to both of
them, conduce to great vividness and accuracy of statement in
defining that emotion.

Not to rant on forever, I'll beg your indulgence and come at
once to the explanations you requested on the Melville poem:

> "The dice of drowned men's bones he saw bequeath
>   An embassy."

Dice bequeath an embassy, in the first place, by being ground
(in this connection only, of course) in little cubes from the
bones of drowned men by the action of the sea, and are finally
thrown up on the sand, having "numbers" but no identifica-
tion. These being the bones of dead men who never com-
pleted their voyage, it seems legitimate to refer to them as the
only surviving evidence of certain messages undelivered, mute
evidence of certain things, experiences that the dead mariners
might have had to deliver. Dice as a symbol of chance and cir-
cumstance is also implied.

> "The calyx of death's bounty giving back," etc.

This calyx refers in a double ironic sense both to a cornu-
copia and the vortex made by a sinking vessel. As soon as the
water has closed over a ship, this whirlpool sends up broken

spars, wreckage, etc., which can be alluded to as livid *hiero-glyphs*, making a *scattered chapter* so far as any complete record of the recent ship and her crew is concerned. In fact, about as much definite knowledge might come from all this as anyone might gain from the roar of his own veins, which is easily heard (haven't you ever done it?) by holding a shell close to one's ear.

> "Frosted eyes lift altars."

Refers simply to a conviction that a man, not knowing per-haps a definite god yet being endowed with a reverence for deity—such a man naturally postulates a deity somehow, and the altar of that deity by the very *action* of the eyes *lifted* in searching.

> "Compass, quadrant and sextant contrive no farther tides."

Hasn't it often occurred that instruments originally in-vented for record and computation have inadvertently so extended the concepts of the entity they were invented to measure (concepts of space, etc.) in the mind and imagination that employed them, that they may metaphorically be said to have extended the original boundaries of the entity measured? This little bit of "relativity" ought not to be discredited in poetry now that scientists are proceeding to measure the uni-verse on principles of pure *ratio*, quite as metaphorical, so far as previous standards of scientific methods extended, as some of the axioms in Job.

I may have completely failed to provide any clear interpreta-tion of these symbols in their context. And you will no doubt feel that I have rather heatedly explained them for anyone who professes no claims for their particular value. I hope, at any rate, that I have clarified them enough to suppress any suspi-cion that their obscurity derives from a lack of definite inten-tions in the subject-matter of the poem. The execution is another matter, and you must be accorded a superior judg-ment to mine in that regard.

1926

Modern Poetry

Modern poetry has long since passed the crest of its rebellion against many of the so-called classical strictures. Indeed the primary departures of the early intransigeants were often more in a classic direction, with respect to certain neglected early European traditions, than were many of the Victorian regulations that formed the immediate butt of attack.

Revolution flourishes still, but rather as a contemporary tradition in which the original obstacles to freedom have been, if not always eradicated, at least obscured by floods of later experimentation. Indeed, to the serious artist, revolution as an all-engrossing program no longer exists. It persists at a rapid momentum in certain groups or movements, but often in forms which are more constricting than liberating, in view of a generous choice of subject matter.

The poet's concern must be, as always, self-discipline toward a formal integration of experience. For poetry is an architectural art, based not on Evolution or the idea of progress, but on the articulation of the contemporary human consciousness *sub specie æternitatis*, and inclusive of all readjustments incident to science and other shifting factors related to that consciousness. The key to the process of free creative activity which Coleridge gave us in his *Lectures on Shakespeare* exposes the responsibilities of every poet, modem or ancient, and cannot be improved upon. "No work of true genius," he says, "dares want its appropriate form, neither indeed is there any danger of this. As it must not, so genius can not, be lawless: for it is even this that constitutes its genius—*the power of acting creatively under laws of its own origination.*"

Poetry has at once a greater intimacy and a wider, more exact scope of implication than painting or any of the other arts. It is therefore more apt to be indicative of impending changes in other media such as painting or music. This is a logical deduction that facts do not always favor, as in the case of some modern composers such as Stravinsky, the full purport of whose inspiration seems to lie beyond the reach of current literary expression. Literature has a more tangible relationship to painting; and it is highly probable that the Symbolist movement in French poetry was a considerable factor in the instigation first, of Impressionism, and later, of Cubism. Both arts have had parallel and somewhat analogous tendencies toward abstract statement and metaphysical representation. In this recent preoccupation it is certain that both media were responding to the shifting emphasis of the Western World away from religion toward science. Analysis and discovery, the two basic concerns of science, became conscious objectives of both painter and poet. A great deal of modern painting is as independent of any representational motive as a mathematical equation; while some of the most intense and eloquent current verse derives sheerly from acute psychological analysis, quite independent of any dramatic motivation.

The function of poetry in a Machine Age is identical to its function in any other age; and its capacities for presenting the most complete synthesis of human values remain essentially immune from any of the so-called inroads of science. The emotional stimulus of machinery is on an entirely different psychic plane from that of poetry. Its only menace lies in its capacities for facile entertainment, so easily accessible as to arrest the development of any but the most negligible esthetic responses. The ultimate influence of machinery in this respect remains to be seen, but its firm entrenchment in our lives has already produced a series of challenging new responsibilities for the poet.

For unless poetry can absorb the machine, i.e., *acclimatize* it as naturally and casually as trees, cattle, galleons, castles and all other human associations of the past, then poetry has failed of its full contemporary function. This process does not infer any program of lyrical pandering to the taste of those obsessed by the importance of machinery; nor does it essentially involve even the specific mention of a single mechanical contrivance. It demands, however, along with the traditional qualifications of the poet, an extraordinary capacity for surrender, at least temporarily, to the sensations of urban life. This presupposes, of course, that the poet possesses sufficient spontaneity and gusto to convert this experience into positive terms. Machinery will tend to lose its sensational glamour and appear in its true subsidiary order in human life as use and continual poetic allusion subdue its novelty. For, contrary to general prejudice, the wonderment experienced in watching nose dives is of less immediate creative promise to poetry than the familiar gesture of a motorist in the modest act of shifting gears. I mean to say that mere romantic speculation on the power and beauty of machinery keeps it at a continual remove; it can not act creatively in our lives until, like the unconscious nervous responses of our bodies, its connotations emanate from within—forming as spontaneous a terminology of poetic reference as the bucolic world of pasture, plow, and barn.

The familiar contention that science is inimical to poetry is no more tenable than the kindred notion that theology has been proverbially hostile—with the *Commedia* of Dante to prove the contrary. That "truth" which science pursues is radically different from the metaphorical, extra-logical "truth" of the poet. When Blake wrote that "a tear is an intellectual thing, And a sigh is the sword of an Angel King"—he was not in any logical conflict with the principles of the Newtonian Universe. Similarly, poetic prophecy in the case of the seer has nothing to do with factual prediction or with futurity. It is a peculiar type of perception, capable of apprehending some absolute and timeless concept of the imagination with astounding clarity and conviction.

That the modern poet can profitably assume the roles of philosopher or theologian is questionable at best. Science, the uncanonized Deity of the times, seems to have automatically displaced the hierarchies of both Academy and Church. It is pertinent to cite the authors of the *Commedia* and *Paradise Lost* as poets whose verse survives the religious dogmas and philosophies of their respective periods, but it is fallacious to assume that either of these poets could have written important religious verse without the fully developed and articulated religious dogmas that each was heir to.

The future of American poetry is too complicated a speculation to be more than approached in this limited space. Involved in it are the host of considerations relative to the comparative influences of science, machinery, and other factors which I have merely touched upon;—besides those influential traditions of early English prosody which form points of departure, at least, for any indigenous rhythms and forms which may emerge. The most typical and valid expression of the American *psychosis* seems to me still to be found in Whitman. His faults as a technician and his clumsy and indiscriminate enthusiasm are somewhat beside the point. He, better than any other, was able to coördinate those forces in America which seem most intractable, fusing them into a universal vision which takes on additional significance as time goes on. He was a revolutionist beyond the strict meaning of Coleridge's definition of genius, but his bequest is still to be realized in all its implications.

1930

Note on the Paintings of David Siqueiros

With equal vigour and refinement of technique, David Siqueiros has brought to modern painting a coordinated human content and a spiritual axis which have long been obscured in Continental painting. Siqueiros is not the only contemporary Mexican of deserved renown to have undergone a spiritual rebirth on his own soil after a novitiate in the schools of European experimentalism. Perhaps the abstract preoccupations of Picasso, Braque and others taught him considerably; but it is quite certain that they can have contributed but little to his own essential vision and ultimate mastery.

Siqueiros' painting has the restraint and inherent eloquence of all great painting. It is classic in its grounding on those persistent earth-problems that both challenge and nourish the man who is strong enough to invite and incorporate them as major elements in his own cosmos of design. Pure abstractionism becomes a species of mechanics, even with the powerful infusions of metaphysics that so fine a painter as Chirico is capable of adding.

I admire the boldness with which Siqueiros publicly announced his discontent with such limited preoccupations several years ago. Painting need not become mere illustration, he said practically, in order to convey a rich and human concept in direct and natural forms, terms and arrangements. Nor by incorporating these "documentary" elements consistently need any of the underlying abstract beauty of design be relinquished. Siqueiros is organic enough to convey them both in a single impact. And some ideas besides.

Throughout his murals, portraits, aquarelles and lithographs there speaks the same prophetic sense of humanity—the Mexican masses—in permanent and elemental relationship to their mountains, burros, misery, their elation and resignation . . . And all this implicitly; not in a pictorial way. Soil mingles with expression in the pigment of their skins. The contour of a cheek, though only the head need be shown, can adequately imply the flexions and natural movements of the body they surmount. A very elusive and difficult feat, but one that particularly distinquishes Siqueiros. It is hard to explain all the inferences of latent drama that Siqueiros' brush can indicate beneath the closed eyelids of a sleeping Indian mother, painted withal in colors so suave and sombre and against a background so dark that such dramatic contexts would seem anything but obviously proffered.

But the profound commentaries that emerge from these unspectactular madonnas, miners, workmen and pensive children of Siqueiros' are real emanations, deeply racial, rockbound in the past of Mexico and "shadowed forth" into the future, far beyond the mere superfices of ordinary action. Reticence amplifies accent in the magnificent plastic control and finesse of a hand and eye that seem to create statically, certainly sculpturally, —but with this presumable advantage—that the brush permits a greater play of dynamic inference within the confines of a rigidly defined design than stone does. At least a thorough consideration of this great painter's work draws one toward that somewhat novel conjecture.

Mexico City, Oct. '31.

From Haunts of Proserpine

To write adequate biography is one task, but to convey that record convincingly in terms of heroic couplets is a far more delicate achievement. It involves a closer identification of the author with the intimate aspirations of his subject—an even finer apprehension of his very pulse and successive subconscious motivations than most matter-of-fact accounts take into consideration. James Whaler, inspired by the noble vision and tragic frustrations of the Sicilian-American naturalist, Constantine Rafinesque, has taken a life that is all but forgotten, and so illumined it with the intrinsic light of its own Shelleyan pantheism and purity of motive that this long dramatic monologue, in which the aging botanist pours out his recollections, penetrates and transcends the bare recorded facts of his career. And if this results in a characterization imposing enough to take on some of the outlines of a myth, it is all to Mr. Whaler's credit as a poet. In so doing he has been but the more faithful to his subject, whose scientific obsessions were the active manifestations of a poetic imagination.

A beautiful and adulterous wife robbed Rafinesque of his native Sicily and all further hope of earthly love. His courtship of this daughter of a Greek innkeeper, his subsequent struggle between the claims of science and matrimony, and his desperate and lonely departure for the unpoisoned wildernesses of the New World form the theme of the first half of *Green River*. But still more disastrous was the storm which foundered his ship in Long Island Sound, swallowing within call of shore his fifty boxes of scientific equipment and his books, manuscripts and funds, the results of years of devoted labor. Later on, while working in a Philadelphia counting-house, he was to hear how his wife—whom he constantly envisages as "Proserpine"—was squandering what remained of his once ample fortune in frolic with an island lover. But the final blow came with the death of John Clifford, his friend and benefactor, for whose sake he had gone west into Kentucky.

It is easy to conceive how this series of calamities could confuse the vision of the staunchest spirit. Rafinesque died, a half-insane pauper in a garret on lower Race Street, Philadelphia, in 1840. During his twenty-five years in America, however, he had been a lecturer—received and remembered with honor—at Transylvania University; had crossed the Alleghenies five times on foot rather than by horse, in order to neglect no possible discoveries of uncharted forms of natural life; and had consistently held the respect, if not always the unbiased understanding, of Audubon and other more fortunate representative scientists of his period. The cave region along the Green River in Kentucky still has mementoes of his wanderings; and it is in his monologue relating his presumable discovery of what is actually named Rafinesque's Cave that his high moral conscience and lyric phantasy unite in a scene (*Section II*) which forms the poem's dramatic apex. There, amidst "Babylons of stalactite"—

> Where pearl-boughs blossoming in bursts of stars
> Show me a jeweled heaven of dead czars,
> And moon-tailed orioles roost wing to wing
> With mocking-birds that only dream they sing—

as this nacreous Plutonian palace unfolds before him, his ecstasy conceives an idealistic prehistoric race of river-men about him, stone-frozen, "paired lovers all, in a dominion where beauty is omnipotent with death." Before him also looms the mummy-phantasy of his wife, his "Proserpine" of bitter memory, whose beautiful image he there commits to flames, burning her imprint forever from his heart.

The curtain falls on Rafinesque before the tragic breakup of his faculties, but already in his Race Street garret over-looking the shipping on the Delaware. In a stoic refrain he is left in contemplation of the world about him:

> With masts and mariners before
> Your window, street-cries in your ears,
> There lay your bed, there nail your desk,
> There leaven all you know with tears.

Green River contains few of those psychological nuances and moral casuistries abounding in the narrative verse of Mr. Robinson, Mr. Aiken, and others. Though it often features nature, society, and the individual at odds, they are like the more elemental odds that have occupied such themes as Masefield's. *Green River* is often melodramatic with expletives, rhapsodic flights of fancy, and bitter invocations. Perhaps any extended monologue must be so rhetorically energized in order to sustain the burden of so long a narrative. But here one occasionally feels a strain in the otherwise vigorous and tough texture of the verse, so felicitously inlaid with a thousand names from field and stream. Rafinesque speaks in this multitudinous world of flowers, birds, and fish as intensely as an astronomer breathes among the stars. Mr. Whaler's fresh evocation of this natural background (so prettified and sterile in most hands) is almost as fine an achievement as his resurrection of a forgotten hero.

1932

———

A pure approach to any art or creative endeavor must involve the elimination of extraneous elements that through confusion, prejudice or inertia have gained a bastard identification with the ideal subject as determined by its special tendencies. Equally commonplace is the corollary that persistent respect for such a method of precedure leads not only to an ever deeper comprehension of the *medium* of that art and its potentials—it finally forces the subject to yield surprising illuminations and assertions new to our experience, additions to the total of our sensibilities.

As such, the approach to certain irreducible common denominators, called Truth, is evident as a perpetually creative principle. Paradoxically, when seeming most to narrow and confine the subject (to itself) it proceeds to open and extend it by this purification. It may not be until the distinct florescence has been already in large degree achieved that we begin to gather any assurance of a harvest at all, for there are no guide posts or tracks to answer us, seldom even a terminology to follow us. An inward synthesis of past recognitions may apprehend the logic of our pursuit, but it is only when that moving factor in this process, a really scientific honesty, has already connected a new link of realizations to our perceptions that the proper order of relationships is evident. Simultaneously, then, occurs a creation and its recognition and the proof of a deeper logic in the medium and subject than could have been located or perhaps even guessed at before.

undated

SELECTED LETTERS

To Clarence Arthur Crane

Cleveland, O.
My dear Father:—   June 2 1910
    I had written to Mother so many times that I thought I would write to you this time. It is raining very hard out doors. I just came home from the Library with a new book called Mr. Wind and Madm. Rain   The day before yesterday I had my test in Spelling, and stood 100. I got your little note the other day and Mothers letter this morning and I am expecting you home Sunday morning to eat breakfast with us. It will seem good to have you back again. Tell Mother I am brushing my teeth every day. With much love to you and Mother.

Sincerely your son

Harold

To Grace Hart Crane

Cleveland O
My dear Mother—   Nov. 5, 1910
    I have been going to write you for a long time but I have been so busy with my home work that I have not had time.
    This afternoon we all went to the Hipp. and I never saw a better show   Eva Tangua was the princepul feature of the show. She was even better than I thought she would be. She had seven new gowns and they were beautiful just the kind I like.
    I got your letter and we were glad to get it.
    Tuesday night Grandpa and Grandma invited me to supper and after supper we all went to here Elmensdorfs lecture on the Art Galliers in Europe   He told us when all the pictures were painted and showed us the exact picture on canvass and told us much more and I enjoyed it very much. That night I stayed at Grandpas, and went to school in the morning.
    Father has written two or three letters.
    We are all well and happy.

With much love

Harold Crane

To Elizabeth Belden Hart

My dear Grandmother: Jan. 26, 1916
    Examination time is *on* now and I am kept completely occu-
pied in the preparation for them. We had *English* today and
Latin and Geometry are due tomorrow. They are my hoo-
dooes and so I am not a little worried tonight about the out-
come. I am invited over to G. Cranes for supper tonight as
Aunt Bess is to be there on about a day's visit so Dora can go
out early. As you already know, Father and Mother are in New
York and I am running things now. The store was doing sur-
prisingly well today when I was there owing perhaps to the
balmy weather (almost summer) which we are having. Alice
has been *very sick* and in response to my gift of some roses she
sent me a beautiful note as soon as she was able to sit up. Your
letters would augur a fairly favorable winter and good condi-
tions on the island. So you rest as much as you can and enjoy
the care-free feelings while you can whirl around with the
Wilcoxs in the machine. It is fine that you have found a group
of such sympathetic thinkers and be sure and carry the *science*
as far as you can. I know of few better places to get a foothold
in the faith than in the quiet and beauty of the island.
    Mother left feeling fine for New York and suppose, tho busy,
she is enjoying a splendid time. They will be back Sat. morn.
With the exception of a little sore throat I have felt fine myself
lately. I think it is unnecessary to go to Mr. Ely. My writing has
suffered neglect lately due to study for examinations, but I am
intensely, grippingly interested in a new balled I am writing of
six hundred lines. I have resolved to become a *good* student
even if I have to sit up all night to become one. You will un-
doubtly wink when you read this stale declaration so often
made but his time it is in earnest.
                                        Yours affectionately—
                                        Harold Crane

To Clarence Arthur Crane

308 East 15th Street
New York City

My Dear Father,   December 31, 1916

I have just been out for a long ride up Fifth Ave. on an omnibus. It is very cold but clear, and the marble facades of the marvelous mansions shone like crystal in the sun. Carl has been very good to me, giving hours of his time to me, advising, helping me get a room, etc. The room I have now is a bit too small, so after my week is up, I shall seek out another place near here, for I like the neighborhood. The houses are so different here, that it seems most interesting, for a while at least, to live in one.

It is a great shock, but a good tonic, to come down here as I have and view the countless multitudes. It seems sometimes almost as though you had lost yourself, and were trying vainly to find somewhere in this sea of humanity, your lost identity.

Today, and the remainder of the week, I shall devote to serious efforts in my writing. If you will help me to the necessities, I think that within six months I shall be fairly able to stand on my own feet. Work is much easier here where I can concentrate. My full love to you, dear father. Write me often and soon.

Harold

To Clarence Arthur Crane

308 East 15th Street
New York City

My dear father;—   January 5, 1917

Your letter informing me of the arrival of Mildred and Erwin has just come; and I shall go up town this afternoon to see them. It does me a great deal of good to hear from you often, and I hope you will continue to write me as often as you have lately done. While I am not home-sick, I yet am far from comfortable without letters, and often, from you.

Nearly every evening since my advent, has been spent in the companionship of Carl. Last night we unpacked some furniture of his which had arrived from his home, and afterward talked until twelve, or after, behind our pipes. He has some very splendid ideas about artistic, and phsychic balance, analysis, etc. I realize more entirely every day, that I am preparing for a fine life: that I have powers, which, if correctly balanced, will enable me to mount to extraordinary latitudes. There is constantly an inward struggle, but the time to worry is only when there is no inward debate, and consequently there is smooth sliding to the devil. There is only one harmony, that is the equelibrium maintained by two opposite forces, equally strong. When I perceive one emotion growing overpowering to a fact, or statement of reason, then the only manly, worthy, sensible thing to do, is to build up the logical side, and attain balance, and in art,—formal expression.

I intend this week to begin my studying,—Latin, German, and philosophy, right here in my room. They will balance my emotional nature, and lead me to more exact expression.

I have had only one letter from Mother, so far, but I hear from Grandma, this morning, that she is in Chicago and feeling much better.

Hazel has been fine to me, tho I haven't seen her often, as she has been out nearly every time I have been into the office. Miss Bohn, tho, is a dandy, and I have enjoyed talking to her. She has a very sweet way, sincere, and earnest way.

I do most of my bathing and dumping over at Carl's, as these rooming-house privys, and bath-tubs are frightful. Sometime later I expect to be able to afford a small bath-room of my own. Bedbugs, too, have been an awful trial; but never you fear, I am having some fine experiences. In spite of all, tho, I insist on a fair amount of bodily cleanliness for health. Bunshop food has really made me quite magnificent and fat.

Love always from sonny, Harold

To Grace Hart Crane

54 West 10th Street
New York City
(Phone: Stuyvesant 5155)

My Dear Mother:—   February 22, 1917

Your good letter I have just read, and it cheered me up a good deal. You know, I am working hard and see very few people and even now haven't had more than a half-hour's talk with anyone for over a week. My work, though, is coming along finely, and I shall be published both in *Others*—and again in the *Pagan* this next month. Yesterday was a day of tremendous work. I turned out in some ways, the finest piece of work yet, beside writing a shorter poem also.

Mother, you do not appreciate how much I love you. I can tell by your letters that there exists a slight undercurrent of doubt, and I do not want it there. If you could know how I long to see you perhaps that might make some difference.

Now everything is in truth going splendidly, only I get terribly lonesome often when I am through working. A man *must* wag his tongue a little, or he'll lose his voice. Hurry, so that we can both wag!

Harold

To Clarence Arthur Crane

54 West 10th Street
New York City

My Dear Father:—   Sunday, April 1, 1917

It is such a beautiful day that I can hardly find it tolerable to remain indoors and study. I hope it was this fine in Cleveland. The city seems like a pageant.

I got your good letter yesterday, and I tell that there was a long sigh of relief escaped me when I saw that you approved my action in the matter of studies. It was really the only thing to do. And by this arrangement only, can I be prepared to enter Columbia by next Fall. The lessons cost two dollars apiece, and three a week are at least necessary. I paid my tutor yesterday, and only have a quarter to pay for "eats" today, so I hope you will send me a small check soon.

Lessons are keeping me humping now, and will probably do so all summer. My poetry is being accepted right and left now. You will find one piece in the *Pagan* if you care to take the trouble to go into Laukhuff's Bookstore in the Taylor Arcade. But any writing has got to stop now, when I am so occupied in studies. Of course algebra doesn't help any in versifying, but I realize that I have plenty of time in the future for the latter.

I hope you returned home less nervous than when you left for the West. As for me, I have forgotten the word. It signifies nothing whatsoever for me now. I am really quite healthy.

I hear there is some chance of your coming here. If you do, there will be a chance to tell you many interesting experiences I have had which are too lengthy to tell interestingly in letters.

The tape on this typewriter is so clumsy today that I will give up writing much more.

My expenses are about the same in board, and room, only that I would like to enlarge a little on the board, and not have to eat in some of the sloppy places, which, Lord knows why, I felt necessitated in resorting to, when I first came. I guess I had some romantic notion, or felt tempted to try some of the places of the poor. The expenses of the past few weeks of course, do not indicate any such things, but I thought you would surely not object to me taking Mother around to a few theaters, and I had to have a new trunk, as the old one has come all to pieces, that little one, you know.

I shall write often now, and we must keep in better touch with each other.

Unreserved love to you, Harold

To Clarence Arthur Crane

54 West 10 St., N.Y.C.

My dear Father:—   April 7, 1917

Your check came in good time. Many thanks! I am working about six hours a day on my studies now, applying myself rather closely. My existence at present, aside from general troubles which you know all about, is very pleasant. When I get any time from my prescribed work, it is generally filled with reading and poetry. I shall really without doubt be one of the foremost poets in America if I am enabled to devote enough time to my art. This prediction has come from more than one writer of established merit, whom I have met since my arrival. I am sure you shall have every reason to feel very proud of me some day. I am keeping my promise to you, and intend to keep a far more difficult promise to myself, that is, to accomplish what I am sure is my life-work.

Within a year I am pretty sure to be published in either Scribner's or Harper's or the Century. After that, you know, one's reputation is on the rise. I wrote a splendid poem yesterday. Carl puts great trust in me, and if you knew him better, you would soon discover that he is a good critic. You will excuse this somewhat pompous optimism, I am sure, for it is silly for a man to disguise the very breath of his confidence, without which he could do but little.

I think 25 dollars a week will cover everything pretty well. The tutoring comes to 6 dollars; the board 6 dollars; food that is decent amounts to nearly eleven dollars; laundry comes to about 1.50, and then there is carfare, paper, stamps and a hundred lesser things. Of course clothes vary. I havent bought a dud since arriving, and shall need a summer suit soon. Do you want to send money extra at the times when I shall need these things? I think it would be a good way of doing to send a weekly allowance of the twenty-five dollars, and then I can ask you for clothing when I need the money.

I have just made friends with a graduate of Christ's Church Oxford, who is a very cultured fellow, and who is going to introduce me to Frank Harris, the editor of Pearson's Magazine. Did you see my work in the "Pagan"? The editor was around the other evening, and accepted three more poems which will appear soon.

I often see the office people, and they are very nice to me indeed.

My love to you —
Harold

To Clarence Arthur Crane

54 West 10th St., N.Y.C.
My dear Father:—   May 5, 1917
We certainly have had bum weather since Mother arrived. This was on last Tuesday, and it has rained ever since.

I am sorry not to have answered you before this, but there has been a great deal to do, and there is the studying to be done besides, you know.

How is business? The war seems to put the blink on everything in the confectionary line, but you will have to suffer no worse than the rest. They are all getting out patriotic packages now, and you had better do the same. Pictures of Lincoln and Washington seem to be on all the boxes here, and they are tying them with red-white-and-blue ribbons. If the candy-makers are to live at all now, they have GOT to be patriotic.

We hope to find some place to live soon, and believe me it is some job to find anything at all decent just now.

Love from sonny,
Harold

To Clarence Arthur Crane

44 Gramercy Park, N.Y.C.
My dear Father:—   May 19, 1917
Your letter of the 16th arrived and explained some of the things about which I had been uncertain for a time. I need not mention that its tone wounded Mother a good deal, for that was probably planned anyway, but do ask you to be a little considerate of me, and realize that I have suffered a good deal—more than anyone of my age whom I know, and I think that I deserve to have a little consideration and allowance in the measurement, estimation and treatment, which perhaps would be rightfully denied to others who have had a little happiness during their younger years. You know, poverty and obligations thrust on the shoulders of a child are not the only hardships which may warp and deform and sadden. I do not

want you to do for me anymore than you have planned, but I do want you to remember that I have suffered terribly, and am an old man before twenty. So please do not regard everything that you do for me as unprecedented, and "unheard-of." If it is "unheard-of", it has been caused by things almost as rarely heard of.

The last few days have been very warm. Some of the old residenters on the square here are leaving for the summer, and I would like to go myself, were it not for my student plans.

Straw hats have come in, and as I knew I should have to have one soon, I went up to the office this morning and drew out ten dollars for a hat, a cap, and some low shoes.

Mother has had to pay the May rent in advance, and asks that you pay my share now. I must thank you for all you are doing for me, and I trust I shall not dissappoint you.

Mr. and Mrs. Charles Brooks from Cleveland are living here in the apartment (the same building) with us, and have been very kind to Mother and I. If ever you can manage to come to New York, I shall be very, very glad to see you, and show you where we are situated now. Mother is surely doing a great deal to make me happy, and I hope, in time, to compensate her for her past troubles.

Your son,
Harold Crane

To Clarence Arthur Crane

44 Gramercy Park
New York City

My dear Father:—   August 8, 1917

I am very, very sorry that things are going so badly with Mother. I guess there is nothing for her to do but to get back here as soon as is possible and try to re-instate herself in poise and health. I look for her this week. At least I see no reason why she should linger longer. But I have received no word from her and am uncertain as to much of the true state of affairs with her. I only hope you are avoiding any meetings as much as possible, for as I said, it is now too early,—she is not yet established well enough to endure the strain which you know any contact causes.

The picture is to go this morning. Its name is "Olga," and I am sure you will like her very well. Carl is thinking of returning to Warren and Youngstown for a month to fulfil some portrait contracts, but you have pulled him out of a very serious difficulty. He is a little bashful about sending you his doggerel on so slight an acquaintance so maybe I can get it and send it later. I hope that when he comes west you may be able to spend a day together. I assure you an entertaining time.

I have been diabolically nervous ever since that shock out at the house, but Sunday Carl, Potapovitch and I went out to long beach, and lying in the sun did me some good. If you could shake responsibilities like this for a week or so, it would work inestimable good upon you. You cannot worry on such a beautiful beach with the sound of waves in your ears. We all get to thinking that our heads are really our bodies, and most of the time go floating around with only our brain conscious, forgetting that our bodies have requirements also.

I feel so near to you now that I do hope that nothing can ever again break the foundation of sincerity that has been established beneath our relations. Never has anyone been kinder than you were when I was last home. I want you to know that I appreciate it, and also your two fine letters.

Much love,—Hart Crane

To Clarence Arthur Crane

My dear Father:—   Sept. 18, '17

Your good letter rec'd yesterday. From what Hazel says I presume this will find you back in Cleveland, and busy looking over what has happened while you have been away. I haven't written more because, as you can readily perceive, I haven't known your address most of the time, but once again you may expect regular letters.

This one thing though, I am going to ask of you. If, when you write me, you are thinking of Mother in a distasteful way, please conceal it, remaining silent on the subject. And if, in thinking of her, one kind thought should occur (as I know it does) express it. You remember that when I last was home, I said that I "was through."—That was possible with me for but one hour. My heart is still as responsive to both your loves, and more so, than ever. I have seen more tears than I ever expected in this world, and I have shed them through others' eyes, to say nothing of my own sorrow. And now, when I hear nothing but forgiveness, tenderness, mercy, and love from one side, how can I bear resentment and caustic words coming from the other without great pain? Happiness may some time come to me, I am sure it will. But please, my dear Father, do not make the present too hard,—too painful for one whose fatal weakness is to love two unfortunate people, by writing barbed words.

I don't know how long we three shall dwell in purgatory. We may rise above, or sink below, but either way it may be, the third shall and must follow the others, and I leave myself in your hands.

Write soon, I do hope you come to New York.

Affectionately,
Harold

To Grace Hart Crane

My dear sweet Mother:—   Friday—Sept. 28, '17

I have just read your letter and find it hard to express my rage and disgust at what you say concerning C. A. Crane's conduct. "Forget him," is all I can say. He is too low for consideration. I am only quietly waiting,—stifling my feelings in the realization that I might as well get as much money as possible out of him. Why be scrupulous in one's dealings with unscrupulous people, any way?

I breakfasted an hour ago with the Brooks'. Mrs Brooks had attempted to call on you at the Waldorf two days ago, and was not surprised when I told her of your absence. They ended by inviting me to a *home* dinner tonight at six-thirty, which I shall of course accept.

Maxwell Bodenheim called the other evening, complimented my poetry excessively, and has taken several pieces to the editor of the "Seven Arts," a personal friend of his.

Bodenheim is at the top of American poetry today, and he says that after four years of absolute obscurity, he succeeding in getting publication only through the adverse channels of flattery, friendships and "pull." It is all a strange business. Editors are generally disappointed writers who stifle any genius or originality as soon as it is found. They seldom even trouble to read over the manuscript of a "new man". Bodenheim is a first-class critic though, and I am proud to have his admiration and encouragement. As soon as "Others" begins again this winter, he says I shall have an organ for all of my melodies, as he is one of the editors. Success seems imminent now more than ever. I am very encouraged, poetically, at least.

This ought to reach for Sunday. It is more considerably than has reached C.A. for I don't intend him to hear much about me in the future. You have all my love, and if I *am* a little reckless, you shall find in the end, some wisdom. Forget all the past and leave C.A. to that bastard, T——. You have lived too long in a house of shadows, ignoring the pulse and vivacity of life around you, and it is time to forget. Your letter sounded good, and I am so glad to hear of your work in the house. It will be looking finely when I come home for Christmas.

Give my love to Molly and dear Grandma. Of course I am well—

Hart

To Grace Hart Crane

My dear Mother:—   Monday evening

Perhaps, if my last letter arrived on Saturday as it should certainly have done, you will forgive the lack of a "Sunday Special" from me. That day I spent with Anna and Stan. We ferried to Staten Island and back, had dinner, and then I took Anna to the Strand, as Stan is dancing every evening from six until two at Healy's Restaurant. (100 dollars per week). Surely, you will say, he *has* earned it. What a diabolical proffession! And yet he likes it. I suppose that the occaissional opportunity for expression is the scant reward.

O if you knew how much I am learning! The realization of

true freedom is slowly coming to me, and with it a sense of poise which is of inestimable value. My life, however it shall continue, shall have expression and form. Believe me when I tell you that I am fearless that I am determined on a valorous future and something of a realization of life. The smallness of hitherto large things, and the largness of hitherto small things is dawning. I am beginning to see the hope of standing entirely alone and to fathom Ibsen's statement that translated is, "The strongest man in the world is he who stands entirely alone."

I have now let M. Tardy go as he could only tutor me at the inconvenient hour of seven P.M. and have arranged with a French teacher here in the house who teaches at the Scudder School, to give me lessons at the same price and at convenient hours.

The news of the repairs pleases me. Especially in this, that you are to be more comfortable. Your facials too, sound encouraging.

Now about my books. Please do send them. They might just as well be here, and needless to say, I need them. It wont cost too much, I am sure, to send them.

As to father, I am thinking almost nothing at all about him. I have ceased to respect him, and dislike is dominent anyway. Please forget about him, and master yourself as decidedly as you once did. Someday, all the remaining Crane's will creep around and disappear. Their opinions as to myself are not of the least consequence to me, and I would prefer to have them as ignorant as possible as to my conditions, life, intentions and whereabouts. You and Grandma are the only ones who matter a snap of the finger. No, I am not malicious nor "blue" as this might possibly deceive you into thinking. I have never felt as encouraged, as free or as clean. Think of me often as such or not at all, for I hope you will understand me.

Goodbye for now, dear Mother. Love to Grandma.

                                                        Hart.

To Clarence Arthur Crane

25 East 11 St. N.Y.

My dear Father:—   Monday—Oct. 8, 1917

My typewriter has overworked and broken down. So I must beg you to excuse this handwritten epistle.

I am now, as you see by the above, in my new room, quite near the old neighborhood of last winter. It is a much cleaner house and I am well contented. Mr. and Mrs. Charles Brooks live quite near and this often makes it pleasant at mealtimes to have their company at the little French café around the corner. Mr. Brook's new book, "There's Pippins and Cheese to Come", is to be issued this autumn and when it arrives in Cleveland you must read it during some lonely evening for it is very funny. When I went up to the office this morning I noticed a large consignment had just arrived (eleven hundred lbs. I think) so I see that occasionally the express co. relieves you. Hazel says that the dealers here are making a terrible fuss about the raise you have put on the candy. I dont of course appreciate half the extent of your difficulties, but Hazel at any rate, seems to be having a miserable time. She says she doesn't dare approach half the customers.

Now for a winter coat and hat you are owing Mother fifty-one dollars. And the last two months rent on the apartment, eighty-dollars, you also owe her. If I am to buy my clothes out the twenty-five dollars a week allowance, I can't have any at all. My room-rent is eleven dollars, food is expensive, at least 1.50 to 2:00 a day, and the only tutoring which I have possibly managed to wedge in costs 2:00 per week. Add to that 1:50 for laundry, 1:80 for carfare, paper, stamps, shoeshines, haircuts, and clothes-pressing, and what remains for clothes? I haven't a single winter suit, nor shoes and am in debt seven dollars already on next week's allowance. Living is steadily rising, not only here, but all over the country, as you cannot have escaped noticing.

I do wish you could make your son a visit, and then see perhaps the true state of affairs here in New York.

Yours sincerely,

Harold

To Clarence Arthur Crane

25 East 11th St., N.Y.C.

My dear Father:—   Sunday evening: Oct. 14, '17

Whether you or myself were mistaken as to my account of clothing expenses in my last letter, I hasten to correct it now. When Mother was here, or rather, just as she was leaving to return to Cleveland, seeing that I had no overcoat suitable for fall wear, and that I needed a new hat badly, she forwarded the money for them, amounting to fifty-one dollars. I do not remember mentioning anything about her buying me a suit. Perhaps I may have done so though, and the words escaped my notice in re-reading the letter. I have no fall or winter suit, and am still in my summer one. While it still looks well, and is suitable for everyday wear, it is much out of place at this time of year for wear on Sundays or any "occasions". So, with the further mention of a new pair of shoes, I think this clears the confusion.

I do not see why you seem to think it strange or inconvenient for me to be living here in New York. Whatever I may be doing it is obviously no more expensive, nor as much so, as it would be for me to live in Cleveland. Things are just as expensive there, and it would be necessary for me to return favors in the matter of dinners, theaters etc, from friends, that are entirely obviated here. And then too, I should be more or less miserable in Cleveland. I dont intend to ever live there again if I can help, and I am sure I can help it. Every sundown finds me more determined on my manner of work too. I am writing and reading most of the time, and when you caution me in your last letter, "life is earnest", I feel like saying that I, above all people I know, have found it so. Of all people to accuse of superficiality, I think I am the least deserving. However, I am gaining from much suffering a certain steady confidence and optimism. I am not afraid of a great many things which a year ago might have caused a slight quaking, and as the slowness and enduring of four years is at my back,—four years of sorrow, the potency of which I am sure I shall never have to meet again,—any changes that the future may bring will doubtless be more acceptable. Whether I accomplish my purpose in life with assistance, or without it, will make little difference in the determination or the effort. I have no doubts but that within a year I shall be able to provide myself with money for amusements occaisionally, but as I am at present far less an expense to you than I was a year ago this time, I feel utterly no qualms or any consciousness of weakness in accepting this allowance from you. Very soon you will probably be able to feel entirely free from any obligations even in the mercenary way,—to the woman who gave you the best of her life during the twenty years of her youth and womanhood, who,—as you mentioned yourself,—had been the inspiration and the helper to a large extent in the certain amount of success that you have achieved. The remaining responsibility, namely the provision of a certain amount of money for my wants, can be waived at about the same time as the former. These next four or five years mean a great deal to me. During this time I must master a technique of writing;—read a tremendous amount,—for these are the years when I must have time for that, and must survey a great deal of the work of the masters;—and thirdly must I be in a fair way to establish a market for my own wares. I am not asking you for those years, because I know I have a right to them in more ways than one. But this I would like, and this I ask for:— that you do not assume the attitude of your Father, that is, the outlook on all questions of money that he seems to have held all his life. I am not, and never expect to be informed, as to the state of my Father's finances, but I do realize that I am in no way exorbitant in my demands for a living. I do not ask you for any more than I am getting at present. This, with a certain economy will manage to keep me within the bounds of admirable austerity, and the dissipations of life I am more than content to postpone until I have earned them. Please though, do not confuse yourself into thinking that my expenses are "unheard-of", for they are less, considering your financial station, than a great many sons I know of.

I hope sincerely to see you walk into my room some morning soon and surprise me. We can talk these things so much better than they can be written. Meanwhile, if possible, please write me.

Sincerely,—your son,

Harold

To George B. Bryan

78 Washington Place

Dear George:—   April 23, 1918

You just caught your train and I just caught the rain. I had a regular cloud-burst to return in after I left the ferry.—Now don't remonstrate against this ink,—I tell you it is spring and green is the only proper color.—To go on with the story, I must tell you I missed you the rest of the day and must exhort you to plan before you come (ten days hence) to stay *over* Sunday this time. I got a letter from home yesterday as doleful as usual. In fact I have had "the blues" nearly all day as a result of reading it last night just before sleeping.—

Another concert to criticize this afternoon which jerked me out of the mood. Also a young lady I took for company was largely responsible.—

But I have saved the big event. I must inform you that I have bought a Liberty Bond,—at a "dollar down," etc. I shan't ever be able to pay it but one must be patriotic at all hazards. The editor of the *Pagan* hasn't returned yet, and I am beginning to feel annoyed with all the unanswered mail that lies around the office.—And worse,—the old Hebrew hasn't kept me posted as to where he is, so that he may be in Nova Scotia for all I know, or he may even be back here in town.

You surely are planning to come in again a week from Saturday last, aren't you, George?

I haven't had as much pleasure and happiness in two years as was crammed into those few hours you were here. I am sure you cannot say as much, but you must remember, George, I have been practically starved for any happiness whatever for a long, long time.

Write soon, George, because you are the *one* person who brings me some sense of restfulness and satisfaction.

Yours as always, Harold

To William Wright

Dear William:—   Aug 12, '18

Your letter freshly "arriven." Your reference to ambulance service arouses me to protest . . . You will *not* be drafted—this year anyway, and I hope you won't become agitated so much as to rush into any kind of service. A word in the ear;—I tried to enlist this morning and was not permitted even to enter the office. The guard at the door said to "look in the paper", which I did, and found that all minors are to be excluded from "volunteering" and, if drafted at all, will be apprenticed in machine shops etc. during the war period. Anyhow, I think by the way things look at present, ambulance service, after the time necessary for training, transportation etc. would be a little superfluous. (Some would call me a demon of the Huns for whispering this in your ear) I really believe the war isn't to last much longer.

Being destined, as you are, for Yale, you won't be drafted for anything. But you will have to undergo some discipline, as Mother, who visited no less than twelve eastern colleges in her last expedition, states.

Let me clear myself. Heat and conditions at home (both of which you comprehend, I'm sure) drove me to the deed from which I was frustrated this morning. I take no credit for patriotism nor bravery. Neither is it an attempt to get into a uniform before the war is over for certain effects with the ladies. I am really sorry I couldn't get in, principally, I suppose, because I had made my mind up, and disposed of so many seductive distractions, such as, (well—) love, poetry, career etc. Now the damned things come back again, sporting about me with all too much familiarity.

I may go to N. York,—I may remain here, I may explode, Lord knows. Thank your stars that you have a settled course to follow, and write soon.

                                    Harold Hart Crane

To the Rev. Charles C. Bubb

1709 East 115th Street
Cleveland, Ohio
Dear Mr. Bubb:—   November 13, 1918

I hope I am not guilty of an officious presumption in approaching you with this meagre sheaf of poems. I am merely offering them to your consideration as being perhaps of enough interest for you to publish them at The Church Head Press. As you have published, much to the gratification of the few really interested in poetry, some recent war-poems of Mr. Aldington, I know your critical judgment to be of the highest standard, and while I am certain that you will be the first to detect any flaws and abberations in these lyrics, I know that you will also be alive to whatever beauty they may contain.

These few poems are "gleanings," as it were, from my work of the last two years, representing the best that I have done so far.—There is still hope, as I am yet under twenty. They have been published mostly in *The Pagan*, one in *The Little Review* of December last, and while they are few in number, I thought they might possibly be equal to the boundaries of a modest pamphlet. *Six Lyrics*, or some such title might be used for the booklet. But anon for such matters . . .

I am at present engaged on the *Plain Dealer* as a junior reporter, and am too much occupied there for much of any personal "business." So, in lieu of a real call on you at your residence, I am leaving these with Mr. Laukhuff, as he says that you are a frequent visitor to his establishment.

May I again express my hope that I have not infringed upon your generosity, and assure you that I shall welcome any opinion that you might express regarding the poems themselves, or my suggestions.

Very truly yours, Hart Crane

To George B. Bryan

Dear George:—   Saturday, December 28, 1918
   If you plan to come home New Year's please let me know
beforehand or while here. I incline to think that you won't
have the opportunity but, hope so of course.
   One night of happiness,—that was Christmas night! I was
tired next day until about six o'clock, but after that I began to
revive somewhat, and by midnight I never felt finer in my life.
I believe we can think so much about being tired and that we
ought to be tired after only 1 hour's sleep, etc. etc, that we *are*
tired, whereas, if we are so busy as to not have any time to
think about ourselves at all we soon feel as fresh as ever.
   I suppose you went back on the midnight sleeper.
   I'm off to work now.—

                              With love, Harold
                              Write soon and often!!

To Carl Zigrosser

                              1709 East 115th Street
                              Cleveland, Ohio
Dear Sir: December 30, 1918
   The illustration crowning the Stevens poem in the Decem-
ber issue of *The Modern School* tempts me to submit the en-
closed lyric of mine as a possible subject of like treatment. I
hope to hear from you soon regarding this, and venture my
praise of the recent numbers of your magazine.

                              Very truly yours, Hart Crane

To George B. Bryan

Dear George:—
   No, I'm not planning to go to New York until April or May.
By that time I hope to have saved enough money to launch

forth upon the venture. When I go this time, it will probably be permanently, and when we meet it will be upon Broadway. The nearest possible time I can plan on seeing you, that is, coming to Pittsburgh,—is a week from this next Friday, and that seems to me altogether too near the time you plan to be home for a few days to excuse my journey. If your plan shouldn't materialize, I would probably attempt to console you by coming, but I really hope you do get home, as we can have a better time here. The work has been rather stupid in the office for the last few days, and I can't help longing for the time when I shall be out of it. Keep up writing me, as I would be quite lost without word from you occasionally.

As ever,—Hart Crane

To Carl Zigrosser

1709 East 115th Street
Cleveland, Ohio
February 12, 1919

Dear Mr. Zigrosser:—

Perhaps it is my fault that the poem I sent you about eight weeks ago is not included in the February issue of the *Modern School* as I had rather expected it would be. You will remember that I suggested an illustration for it by Mr. Kent, and your reply to this was that you "should be glad to use the poem, 'To Potapovitch,' tho I don't know whether the artist who illustrated Wallace Stevens 'Apostrophe to Vincentine' will be able to make a drawing for it, as he has gone up to Alaska for an extended period." Thinking that you may have felt a hesitancy about publishing the poem under those conditions and without hearing further from me in reply, I am bothering you now with this letter of reassurance. Illustration or not, I shall feel it a real pleasure to see the poem in your magazine, though I presume that a woodcut by Kent could not but enhance a poem which seems particularly suitable for accompanying illustration.

I have yet to see a better-printed magazine in this country than yours, and as soon as I can spare the amount I intend to send for the complete *1918* file. I enjoyed your article on

Bourne, and though only slightly acquainted with him myself, I think you "place" him more exactly than Floyd Dell and several other of his friends have done in recent monographs of the man. Would you be interested in seeing any further examples of my poetry? I have no very strict prejudices regarding vers libre or the established conventional.

If you have time and the inclination, please let me hear from you soon,

Very truly yours, Hart Crane

To Carl Zigrosser

119 West 76th Street
Dear Mr. Zigrosser:—   New York City

Your very generous response to my last letter has been forwarded to me here in New York where I hope to subsist for a while by whatever wits I may have,—at least for a short period. It has been some time since I have any time whatever for poetical preoccupations, but I am in hopes to send you a few other of my productions as soon as I can get them together.

When here before the war I resided in the village, but at last have made the break, and really like my new location, out a ways, much better.

Your appreciation of the Potapovitch poem warms the cockles of my heart. Floyd Dell was on the point of taking it last year, but failed to get the other members of the *Liberator* staff to aggree sufficiently on the matter. Again, I tried the *Pagan*, but Kling, the editor, has mysterious aesthetic touchstones. Then, the *Little Review* rejected it, on account, I presume, of Mr. Pound's rabid dislike of my things. I don't "deal extensively in verse," and am quite particular about where I put in an appearance, and when I chanced on *The Modern School* with its fine typography and woodcuts, I couldn't rest until I had sent the poem to you, although it had to be swiftly and covertly done in that Cleveland newspaper office where poetry of any other sort than the Walt Mason, Edgar Guest, or Robert Service brands is regarded rather superstitiously.

When you are in town I hope you will afford me the opportunity of meeting you. I am much in, and the phone number is Schuyler 5352.

Very truly yours,—Hart Crane

To Grace Hart Crane

Dear Mother:—   Wednesday, Feb. 25, '19

Your letter yesterday was a real pleasure. You certainly must be used to my abscence by this time. At any rate, you can have no "fault to complain" about my writing you often.

Yesterday I helped Mrs. Spencer move some of Claire's things from her rooms to the bridal suite on Madison Ave. Their new place is decorated quite lavishly, and will be a wonderful place for them to live in. We shall probably go to church together tonight. This afternoon I have asked her to go to the bank with me to identify me in cashing the draft.

I was much pleased by that letter from the editor of "The Modern School", and hope you will send me the file of his magazine that he promises to send under seperate cover. I am going to send my moving picture scenario around to some other companies instead of waiting to hear from those people until the story has become stale in interest. In this morning's "Times" there is a report of just such an impending strike in the Hog Island shipyards as I had included in the story.

I had a wonderful lunch and talk with Mr. Brooks yesterday at the Yale Club. I certainly have been on the go ever since arriving, but I expect to begin to refuse invitations for a few days now,—get my typewriter,—and get a little business done. The Browns will be here in a week and I expect some excitement then. I wrote Mrs. Brown yesterday and thanked her for her remuneration. All the Cranes have been attended to with postal cards, and, added to that, the due attention to several friends, you see I have been busy writing.

Love to Grandma, too.—

Hart

(over)

I enclose pictures of Claire and "Hal" which you are to return at an early date. They were taken on the "weddin day" up near Hartford.

To George B. Bryan

119 West 76th Street
New York City
Dear Georgie:—   March 2, 1919

A four or five days visit here about the twenty-first of this month sounds mighty good to me. You will find it very comfortable staying with me, as I have a much better room than when you made your last visit. I only hope I sell a scenario before your arrival so that we can have a spree from the proceeds. I have two of them going the rounds now and I may hear from them most any time. I am busy enough now thinking up new stories. Hope in time to have a kind of fleet going around from office to office. Really, George, there's loads of money in writing movie stories. A writer friend of mine has just been offered $2000 for a scenario that won't take him over a day to write.

You speak in your last letter as though you were going back to a job something like the one you had before—a road job. How does it happen that you are coming to New York? This town isn't included in Southern territory, is it? Don't think me curious or impertinent,—I'm principally interested in knowing whether or not your work will be apt to bring you to New York often, seldom, or never. If you haven't already found something why don't you try for some position with the Thos. Cusack Co. right here in town. It ought not to be very hard for you to manage something like that. By the way, the new Cusack Bldg. on Fifth Ave. and Broadway, is a beauty. If I find, after considerable effort and trial, that I am not a success at scenario writing, I expect to enter the advertising writing game. I should like it much better than newspaper work, and I have always had a hunch that I could write interesting adds,—and,—there is a lot of money waiting for the man who can write good adds.

Haven't been to very many shows, nor leading much of any

gay life. I'm too busy and too poor to think about it. No,—
I'm not in want, in fact I'm very comfortable, but I haven't
the cash for extras just now.

Write me soon, old boy,—Your loving Harold

To George B. Bryan

307 West 70th Street
New York City
Dear Georgie:—   March 17, 1919

Don't give up your job until you have to, is my advice these
days to almost everybody. The situation of employment here
in New York is quite critical at present. There have been so
many thousands of soldiers landed here from overseas that
have deceided to settle here in preference to returning to their
home towns in the west that the place is choke-full, and I am
having a devil of a time to find anything at all to do. It's
damned lucky for me that I have a dependable allowance these
days. Why you cannot even get a job as a waiter or street-
cleaner. This isn't saying that I have applied for these elevated
positions as yet, but you can see that the situation is pretty bad
when such conditions are existant.

You will see by the above address that I have moved. The
landlady in the old place was crazy as a lune, and I had to
almost call the police to assist in getting my baggage out of the
hellish place, as it was. One of the other roomers in the house
and I deceided to take this place together. It makes our rent
only $3.50 apiece per week, and we have practically three rooms,
—one of them immense. Baltzly is a lieutenant just out of the
army, a Harvard grad. and a champion tennis player. I think
we'll get along very well. This arrangement will not make any
difference in your staying with me when you come to town.
We have a double bed and a smaller one in use, and as a matter
of fact, you will like this new place better, much better, than
you would have liked the old one.

I often long to see you, old boy,—wish you were here
tonight for a long pleasant stroll down Broadway with me.
Whenever you chance to remember a confession I told you

one night last summer when we were together, remember that it still holds good, and will,—for a long, long time.

Glad you went in to see my Mother and Grandparent when you were last home. They are fond of you, and it was a real complement to me on your part, I think, to have done it.

Lovingly yours, Harold H. Crane

To Grace Hart Crane

307 West 70th Street,
New York City
April 2nd, '19

My dearest Mother:—   Telephone: Columbus 2037

Your letter just came. Evidently you had not received my telegram before writing it:— I wanted you to be assured that I had not forgotten the date.

Yes, you do seem to be qyuite occupied with various engagements, pleasant and painful, as in the case of the dentistry, although I am very glad to hear of your having that duty performed as you have needed work and attention expended on your teeth for a long while back. I think you are holding the wrong and un-Scientific thought concerning me and my attitude toward Science. The fact that I do not talk and write about it continually is no sort of testimony that I am not as much interested as ever in it. You know that I am not and probably never will be one of those who make the matter a complete obsession, reducing every subject and thought and description to the technical language of the textbooks. I have met a number of Scientists who by such proceedure managed not only to bore me and others quite dreadfully, but also to leave one with the impression that they were scared to death about everything and found it necessary to maintain a continual combat against every aspect and manifestation of life in general. Perhaps it may serve as sufficient testimony to the efficacy of right thought, etc. that I am finding far less problems and fears that demand denial. I certainly have not felt quite so well or quite so clear-headed for several years, and that is, or ought to be enough to reassure you and alterate your somewhat morbidly anxious fears for me which have leaked into your last few letters. I again beg you to relax from such fears, etc. which seem to have you in their power enough to prompt you to such seemingly strenuous conflicts of resistance and denials. Your letters seem to be prompted by some fear (I mean certain references in them) that seems to me entirely un-Scientific. Please do not mistake me and become hurt or offended. I only feel that you have not overcome, not quite, what might be called "the fear of fear" which is an ultimate Scientific triumph.

It is very nice to think of Mrs. Zucker's calling on me. I certainly hope that she does it. My room-mate is due to return from Mass. today. I guess I told you that we get along very well and have many tastes in common.

I am considering a plan which might work out very well. The editors of The Little Review have offered to let me take over the advertising and subscription department of the magazine on a commission basis. If once started up well along this line, the wrk would prove to be reasonably remunerative for me,—affording me at least as much per week even from the start, as I got working in the Plain Dealer office. To a certain extent I would be my own boss with unrestricted initiative freedom to develope my department systematically and along my own lines. I am just about ready to assent to the proposition for the summer months anyway. Three months trial would be quite justified, and the work interests me. There is no reason why The Little Review could not be developed into as paying a periodical as The New Republic, The Nation, or The Dial. All it has lacked from its inception has been someone with business initiative ability to develope the advertising and subscription departments of the magazine. I am going to talk the matter over again with the editors, however, before deceiding definitely. One good thing about it will be the advantage it will give me of association with influential people who have to do with The Little Review and also a certain amount of personal freedom to develope my own talents along with the other work.

Will you do something for me? I wish you would send me via parcel post these volumes which you will find up in my room on front shelves:—"Lustra, poems" by Ezra Pound, "Complete Poetical Works of Swinburne", and the "Portrait of the Artist as a Young Man", by James Joyce.

I am glad to hear of your connection with the Playhouse. It ought to afford you many a good time to get in touch with the crowd that supports it, in my mind, the most interesting set in Cleveland. I dined with Kreymborg one night, as I guess I wrote you, and he said that he had been especially invited to stay with Mr. O'Neil when in town. I was glad to hear this because I anticipated the season of house-cleaning in which he would have found you at present had he accepted our invitation. I understand that he is having great successes in Chicago and throughout the middle west. He is a member of poets' lecture bureau recently started here and to which belong our most distinguished 'moderns'. I may join and lecture myself, —you never can tell.

Haven't been to see Hazel yet, in spite of your report of what she said about my conduct. I don't think I shall go, either, unless conditions alter my reasons which prevent such, and which you know,—deceidely. Please send my new check by next Monday, as my expenses have been slightly heavier lately than the preceeding weeks were. As soon as time enough has elapsed to warrant a report on C.A.'s response to our present arrangement of allowance, I hope you will let me know about it. It seems to me that you ought to have received recompense for your first month's advancement to me by this time. I was glad to hear that his conduct toward you on the street, etc. had suffered a change for the better. I hope that in addition his courtesy will have been not only a superficial compromise, but, better, a voluntary expression from deeper, (under the skin,) and will extend to the more fundamental obligations of a contract faithfully fulfilled.

I certainly hope that it will warm up a bit for a few hours at least. I have been rarely colder than during the last few days. The sun is out now, however, and the papers predict 'fair and warmer' for tomorrow. It will interest you to know that I met by accident M. Tardy, the bookseller and my old tutor in the subway on the way to a meeting of the Poetry Society a few evenings ago. He inquired very anxiously about you, and was glad to know that you were quite well again.

That man, Charley Bubb, is going to make you a call if ever he gets any time, so he informs me in his last letter. He has been very kind in presenting Colum with some of his de luxe books in answer to an order I gave him for them, but for which he refuses to accept payment. William Wright is in Cleveland now, and if you would like to warm up a little with remembrances of last summer, you could probably reach him with a dinner invitation at the home of Wheeler Lovell, which is somewhere on East 84th, 85th or thereabouts. The phone-book would locate it exactly.

I have told you all the gossip, etc. that I could think of at the moment, and only hope that I'll have something interesting enough to supply matter for your Sunday letter. Please discount misspelled words, etc., this machine is at times quite balky and at others quite exuberant.

Lovingly, your son,

Hart

Thank you for your letter, Grandma,—I'll write you personally quite soon

To William Wright

24 West 16th Street
New York City

Dear William:—   May 2, 1919

Your letter came this morning, so you can't deny my promptitude. Dash haberdashery! I hope you have more free-dom in writing your next letter,—the note of pain caused by the watchful eye of the floor-walker was too evident. It was like a hurried lunch, I felt your situation and rushed from line to line in trepidation of the next moment. And then you asked such very vital questions that you have set me thinking a good deal. No:—at present I am not a Christian Scientist. I try to make my Mother think so because she seems to depend on that hypocrisy as an additional support for her own faith in it. So,—mums the word to her. If it weren't very evident how very much good it has done her I should not persist in such conduct,—lying to both Lord and Devil is no pleasure,—but as I frankly was very much interested in Christian Science at the time of my own exit from home, I have not made any distinct denial of it to her since, and for the aforementioned reasons.

However, Bill, I have unbounded faith in its efficacy. Not that a normal optimism will not accomplish the same wonders,—it is a psychological attitude which will prevail over almost anything, but as a religeon, there is where I balk. I recommend it to you if you are nervous etc. though, as a cure, and the best and only one to my knowledge. What it says in regard to mental and nervous ailments is absolutely true. It is only the total denial of the animal and organic world which I cannot swallow.

I don't quite understand your criticism toward my "attitude of mind," and sincerely wish you would particularize more in detail. We have had so many good talks that I wish you were here right now to tell me. But when you come to New York next autumn we shall have an opportunity. I am laying many plans for your coming, and you will enjoy meeting some of my friends here, I am sure. My advertising work for *The Little Review* is coming a little slower than I expected. You have no idea how hard it is to even break into some of these huge and ominous mechanisms, New York Offices. It ought to toughen me a little and perhaps that is what I need. It is a very different matter when one approaches with the intent of selling, and selling the appealing article,—space. However, *The Little Review* has the possibility of affording me over four thousand per year on commissions if I can fill up the allowable space, and perhaps I am not wasting my time after all.

My plans for this summer are very uncertain. Probably the only contact I will have with the West is a visit from my Mother who will probably motor here or something like that. Otherwise a few seashore weekends at friends of mine will be my only diversions. Perhaps you will accompany your father here on some business trip, and if so, I can guarantee you comfortable accommodations. I have an extra room beside my office here all fitted up for guests, and it's yours whenever you care to come.

I don't plan to take up any journalistic course anywhere. I understand that the course at Columbia demands two previous years of college anyway, so it looks as though that were out of the question. Mother has often talked about that plan, but I cannot seem to convince her of the attendant impossibilities.

Suppose you received the Columbia Varsity Play program, and am sending you also a poem of mine which appeared last month. You've read it before, but you may be interested in seeing it in print. Write soon, please, and tell me what is the matter with your old and affectionate rhymester,—

Hart Crane

To William Wright

24 West 16th Street

My dear William:—   Tuesday, June 17, 1919

I've just returned from several days in the country with Hal Smith and wife (Claire). They rent a little cottage out in New Jersey that is perfection itself and we go canoeing and play tennis and eat amazingly every time we go out there. I am, unfortunately, badly sunburned today,—rather a sight,—and am remaining in my room rather than shock my friends and enemies by exposing myself. It is fine, (though) to get out of this crowded metropolis once in a while, and see the moon and stars and hear the frogs croak. We intend to go out again next Friday and stay until Monday, living in our bathing suits most of the time.

From your last letter, you're in for quite a pleasant summer. I wish I could be in Cleveland when you are there. Hope you'll go out and see my mother if you get time,—she likes you very much and always asks about you in her letters. We have had some differences of late, but my fundamental feelings toward her are not in the least altered. If I can get enough money together I intend to take a short course in business advertising out at Columbia this summer,—which might possibly be continued next fall when you will be there. I aggree with you that for such as ourselves business life is not to be scorned. The commercial aspect is the most prominent characteristic of America—and we all must bow to it sooner or later. I do not think, though, that this of necessity, involves our complete surrender of everything else nobler and better in our aspirations. (Illusions are falling away from everything I look at lately. At present the world takes on the look of a desert,—a devastation to my eyes, and I am finding it rather hard at best. Still, there is something of a satisfaction in the developement of one's consciousness even though it is painful.) There is a certain freedom gained.—A lot of things pass out of one's concern that before had mattered a great deal. One feels more freedom and the result is not by any means predominantly negative. To one in my situation (N.Y. is a series of exposures intense and rather savage which never would be quite as available in Cleveland etc.) New York handles one roughly but presents also more remedial recess,—more entrancing vistas than any other American location I know of. When you come to Columbia you will not be apt to feel it because any college (less Col. than any other) enforces its own cloistral limitations which are the best things in the world while one is there. It will only be after you have left the place, and lived and worked in the city (should you do so) that you will begin to feel what I mentioned. May I venture a personal criticism in your last letter? It's out of my habit to do so, and if I didn't care for you so much I wouldn't. Your remarks "about the ladies" really hurt me with a kind of ragtime vulgarity. It's hard to say in the limitations of a letter what I mean. You know I am very free from Puritanical preoccupations—as much as from excessive elegance. What I lament is that gross attitude of the crowd that is really degrading and which is so easily forced upon us before we know it. You are far too sensitive to harbour it long, I know. It is only because I hate to see the slightest tarnish at all in you that I run the risk of offending you. I do hope you won't resent it.

Please write soon, and tell me what you think is wrong with me. You didn't in the last letter and I was really disappointed.

Yours,—Hart Crane

To Grace Hart Crane

Brookhaven, L.I.
July 30th, '19

My dear Mother:—

Your letter dated the 28th has just come, and in answer, I of course will not need to repeat the contents of yesterday's note. At best I think your words are a little unkind and very inconsiderate. I will not attempt again to reckon with your misunderstanding, etc. of the part you and I together, and as individuals, have played in relation to C.A. You either have a very poor memory, or are very confused when you think you have a right to accuse me of either a wrong or a right attitude toward him,—an unfriendly or unfriendly one,—after the continually opposite statements and accusations you have made to me for the last four years yourself. At one time you recommended a course of diplomacy toward a veritable devil, and five minutes later a blow in the face and scorn of any relationship whatever. And now you suggest a wiley and conniving attitude toward a character which you claim as fundamentally good. With such inconsistences in memory I fail to see how you have adequate reasons for 'accusing' me of a 'wrong' attitude toward him, whatever position I might have taken. It has all been very hard, I know. Probably the truth consists more moderately in the estimate of him as a person of as many good inclinanations as bad ones. Your feelings as a woman lover were bound to be dangerous in diverting you from an impersonal justice, and, however much I may have been blinded by my own relationship with him, I cannot deny having been influenced by your sufferings and outcries. There are reasons for acts and prejudices which cannot always be justified at the turn of the moment, but look hard enough, and substantial roots will be found.

I returned to Brookhaven last night after a very satisfactory interview with Mr. Reinthal, of the firm of Reinthal and Newman, which handles the Parrish prints. I shall begin work there in the order department early in September, until which time I'll be out here with Hal and Claire. My note of yesterday was expressive enough of the satisfaction I am feeling about the matter without repetition here. Everything is pointing toward very friendly relations with C.A. in the future, which good turn is greatly due to the interest of the New York office. People change in their attitude either from enlighiment of the understanding or change of impulse. In the case of father toward me I think a revival of interest was seconded by a more adequate understanding of my motives, interests, character and position which the office supplied. Also, a certain pride, (now that his wealth begins to assume rather large dimensions) in the position of his only son, was equally responsible. Again, yesterday's note supplies you with conjectural details regarding the possibilities for the future, to spoil which, as you see, will only demand more floundering about of a kind which has confused greatly the course of the last year or two. I am not building many air castles, as I have learned too much already for that,— but it is hopeful, at least, with present relationships prevailing.

Of course you will understand that the advertising project is off under present situation. However, don't think that I fail to be grateful for your interest, and that you always retain my affection and love.

Best regards to Grandma, too,—

Hart

To Gorham Munson

My dear Gorham:—   November 13, 1919

It begins to look as though my work is to be confined to the hours between midnight and dawn,—that is, in writing. I go to Akron, O. next week to take up a position in my father's new store there and my own hours are to be from six in the morning until eleven at night. I was down there with him yesterday, and find that he has a wonderful establishment,— better than anything of its kind in New York. It's too bad to waste it all on Akron, but there seems to be a lot of money there that the rubber tire people have made. The place is burgeoning with fresh growth. A hell of a place. The streets are full of the debris from old buildings that are being torn down to replace factories etc. It looks, I imagine, something like the western scenes of some of Bret Harte's stories. I saw about as many Slavs and jews on the streets as on Sixth Ave. Indeed the main and show street of the place looks something like Sixth ave. without the elevated.

The size of my father's business has surprized me much. Things are whizzing, and I don't know how many millions he will be worth before he gets through growing. If I work hard enough I suppose I am due to get a goodly share of it, and as I told you, it seems to me the wisest thing to do just now to join him. He is much pleasanter than I expected him to be, and perhaps will get around after while to be truly magnanimous.

You evidently were not consulted about the Josephson mss. as I saw one of them returned the day I left N.Y. I haven't been able to locate a single copy of *The Modernist* anywhere in Cleveland, and I suggest that Richard Laukhuff, 40 Taylor Arcade would be a good one to send it to. He handles most of the radical stuff, and the *Pagan,* he tells me, is getting too tame. He also says that the *Little Review* has suffered neglect since the last Baroness contribution. The B. is a little strong for Cleveland.

I don't know when I shall get time or the proper mood to work more on the Grandame poem. Contact with the dear lady, as I told you I feared, has made all progress in it at present impossible.

Rec'd a letter from Sherwood Anderson this morning in which he tells me about early business experiences in Cleveland and Elyria. The latter is about as unpleasant as Akron, so I guess I needn't despair. My mother and grandmother are going to Cuba this winter and close up the house, so I fear that our visiting plans will have to be postponed a while. I won't be in Akron long. After that it may be Kansas City, Frisco, or even New York. The business is simply enormous now and growing so that I expect I will have a real job in time. I like to think that I can keep on writing a little, at least, of good quality, until,— someday when I shall start up a magazine that will be an eye-opener. I feel in a Billy Sunday mood this evening, and am very much in haste, so I hope you will not consider this letter as anything other than a scrap-heap of petty news. But I do hope to hear from you soon.

Warmly yours,—Hart Crane

To Gorham Munson

Hotel Akron
My dear Gorham:—   November 22
This is the first moment I have had since Monday to give your letter my response. My typewriter is still in Cleveland, so you will have to "bear with me" in my writing. If business were to continue as slow behind my counter at the drug store

as it has thus far, I would get a good deal of reading done. As it *has* been, *Pavannes & Divisions*, T. S. Eliot, Maupassant and the *L.R.* have been my steady companions. I have to be on the job about 14 hours every day, and when the Christmas rush begins I fancy I will be indeed "well tired out at night." However, I don't expect to remain here very long after that date on account of a probable promotion, when my evenings, at least, will be free and, after all, that is about all I ask for.

Josephson wrote me a fascinating letter last week, enclosing a poem of his own and two translations from Jules Romains. If you two continue to keep me warm, I am not at all pessimistic about my interest waning in les arts. Josephson's opinions of the *Modernist* will more than match your own, I think,— Fawcett sent me a copy of the *Modernist*, and having time to peruse it, I was quite astonished by the amount of literary rubbish he had managed to get into its confines. There was hardly a gleam of promise through it all. Your three poems were practically the best things in it; and I am not complimenting you thereby. For a time I was sorry for you and for me. I wanted to write a letter withdrawing my contributions. But a certain resignation to fatality dissuaded me from the effort. . . . Fawcett is a poor ignorant bastard of some kind. His comments on history and government are not even in a class with the *Evening Journal*. The rest of the sheet seems like a confused, indiscriminate, jelly-like mass. . . . But ah, well-a-day, the time must come when we can do more than "groan and hoot."

I have thought for some time that your connection with it resulted in a waste of time. I may send them more stuff simply to have it published and also on account of a kind of dumb-animal affection that I have for Waldo. How furious he would be to hear this!!

I am liable to break forth in song most any time, but nothing has happened as yet. I wrote a short affair last night that I may hammer into shape. Grandma and her love letters, are too steep climbing for hurried moments, so I don't know when I shall work on that again. As it is, I have a good beginning and I don't want any anti climax effect. If I cannot carry it out any further, I may simply add a few finishing lines and leave it simply as a mood touched upon. New theories are filling my head every day. —Have you given the poems of

Wallace Stevens in the Oct. *Poetry* any attention. There is a man whose work makes most of the rest of us quail. His technical subtleties alone provide a great amount of interest. Note the novel rhyme and rhythm effects.

Josephson gives me a list of names for reading that you might be interested in. Marlowe is one of his favorites, John Webster, and Donne, the last is a wonder speaking from my own experience. I've got to rush back to work now, so this is all. Please write again and send me samples of what you are writing that you value. I promise to do likewise.

Faithfully, Hart

To Gorham Munson

Hotel Akron
Dear Gorham:—   Friday

Have been up to Cleveland for over Thanksgiving, and rushed back again at dawn today and spent the day as usual. I enjoyed your letter with its encouragement to Grandma and am sending you a record of her behaviour to date. She would get very fretful and peevish at times, and at other times, hysterical and sentimental, and I have been obliged to handle her in the rather discouraging way my words attest. However, I think that something has been said, after all, although the poem hasn't turned out as long as I had expected. Tell me, pray, how you like it.

Have you read *The Young Visitors* by Daisy Ashford (alias Sir James Barrie) yet? I don't know when I have been more delighted. Subtle satire par excellence!

I shall try to get hold of your article in the *Smart Set* and see how you have got up in the world, according to Joe Kling.

I hear a little gossip even here in Akron. There is a bookseller here who is well known far and wide as a character. I had known him years ago in Cleveland, but our acquaintance has recently come to more ripeness here. I just missed dining with Alfred Knopf who came here to see him the other day. Knopf tells him that Mencken is about to publish a book with him of which the title I forget, but the last scene is laid in the Sultan's bed. The S. having a very large and luxurious one. This book seller also gave me the enclosed booklet which was written by Mark Twain in one of his ribald moments. You will enjoy it, I know, and it gives me a stronger light on some of Mencken's enthusiasm for the writer. The grand ejaculatory climacteric of Queen Bess is magnificent. You will regard the book as quite a treasure. I don't know where else on earth it could be published.

I have little personal to relate except that I have a sore throat and hope to have the grippe long enough soon to have a vacation and time to read and "work" a little more.

Yours faithfully, Hart

To Gorham Munson

Hotel Akron

My dear Gorham:—   December 13, 1919

I think you are wrong about "1601." The bookseller friend who gave me the book you have, informs me that that is just another name for the same piece. So you see it is even more scarce and valuable than you thought. Will you ever forget that sentence of Raleigh's where he says he was but clearing his nether throat!? I must get another one and send it to Josephson, who, by the way, has just written me about my "Grandmother." He has some of the same complaints to make of her as yourself and many others, but he ends up by calling it the best thing I have written, and, what is more flattering, begs to keep the copy I sent him. He says he has had a falling out with Amy Lowell, but a falling in with T. S. Eliot by way of compensation. His letters are charming with a peculiar and very definite flavor to them, and buck me up a good deal. I have lately begun to feel some wear from my surroundings and work, and to make it worse, have embarked on a love affair, (of all places unexpected, here in Akron!) that keeps me broken in pieces most of the time, so that my interest in the arts has sunk to a rather low station. Now that Christmas is coming in with its usual inhuman rush in candy selling, I shall not have a moment for anything but business and sleep. My life is quite barbarous and the only thing to do is recognize the situation and temporarily bow to it.

Waldo Frank's book IS a pessimistic analysis! The worst of it is, he has hit on the truth so many times. I am glad to see such justice done to Sherwood Anderson, but this extreme national consciousness troubles me. I cannot make myself think that these men like Dreiser, Anderson, Frost, etc. could have gone so far creatively had they read this book in their early days. After all, has not their success been achieved more through natural unconsciousness combined with great sensitiveness than with a mind so thoroughly logical or propogandistic (is the word right?) as Frank's? But Frank has done a wonderful thing to limn the characters of Lincoln and Mark Twain as he has,—the first satisfactory words I have heard about either of them. The book will never be allowed to get dusty on the library shelves unless he has failed to give us the darkest shadows in his book,—and I don't think he has. I notice that Marsden Hartley is mentioned, but how does it come that "our Caesar" is omitted!?

This last makes me think of the *Little Review*, and how terrible their last issue, November's, is. I have sent them my poem, but have heard no answer as yet. If the *Dial* goes on as you announced in your last letter perhaps they would care to print it. I am thoroughly confident about the thing itself since it has got by the particular, hierarchic Josephson, and I won't blush to show it to almost anyone now.

If the *Modernist* is not already in the mails for me, please do not forget that I am anxious for a copy. I wrote Fawcett a long time ago, but he hasn't responded. My last letter from Anderson urges me to make him a visit, and I am hoping that sometime next summer such a thing will be possible. He calls the poem beautiful, but says that it is not as much poetry to him as "the flesh and bone" of my letters. He and Josephson are opposite poles. J., classic, hard and glossy,—Anderson, crowdbound, with a smell of the sod about him, uncouth. Somewhere between them is Hart Crane with a kind of indetermination, still much puzzled.

As ever,—Hart

To Gorham Munson

My dear Gorham:—   December 27, 1919

Before I forget it,—the next time you write me you had better address the letter to 1709 East 115th St., as I am going up to Cleveland next Wednesday for an indefinite period with some work, probably, in the factory. My stand in the drug store has not proved exactly a success, although my father is good enough to admit that I am not to blame in any way. The principal reason that it will be discontinued is that no one can be found to work there without a quite exorbitant salary, and the location is too poor to afford that. So many things have happened lately with the rush of Christmas, etc. that I am tired out and very much depressed today. This 'affair' that I have been having, has been the most intense and satisfactory one of my whole life, and I am all broken up at the thought of leaving him. Yes, the last word will jolt you. I have never had devotion returned before like this, nor ever found a soul, mind, and body so worthy of devotion. Probably I never shall again. Perhaps we can meet occasionally in Cleveland, if I am not sent miles away from there, but everything is so damned dubious as far as such conjectures lead. You, of course, will consider my mention of this as unmentionable to any one else.

Sherwood Anderson is coming to N.Y. this week, he writes, and perhaps it would be possible for you to meet him. Vide the *Little Review* for information as to his whereabouts. He says that Van Wyke Brooks has given in Doran's hands for publication a book well named,—*The Ordeal of Mark Twain,* which, I imagine, will follow on something the same line of direction that Waldo Frank suggests in his book. Hackett's review of the latter is a bit severe, although he touches the weak points in every instance. The work *is* too rhapsodical, and I noticed frequent lapses in plain grammer, not to mention diction. But the meat is there anyway, and the book is stimulating, even though a bit pathetic. Anderson says he respects the mind of Brooks more. Brooks and Hackett belong, both, to a harder and more formal species. Therefore Hackett's critique is quite consistent with his characteristics.

I have been reading Edgar Lee Masters' latest, "Starved

Rock," and must mention to you my enthusiasm for "Spring Lake," the best thing he has written since the "Spoon River" elegies. "The Dream of Tasso" has a few splendid passages free from rhetoric, and there are others, a few, that satisfy. More and more am I turning toward Pound and Eliot and the minor Elizabethans for values. I have not written anything for a month, but I feel, somehow or other, as though progress were being made. Your estimates of Djuna Barnes and Ida Rauh are interesting and true. I have been instructed recently not to read behind my counter and so, working twelve hours per day, have not had time to do much reading. I want to get at your *New Republic* reviews, if possible, tomorrow. The booklet, "1601," is your own to keep. I can get another, I think, any day for the asking. My write up in the paper was silly enough, but forced upon me, and misquotations as well. However, I took it as an aggreeable joke and an anachronism in Akron. But the pater was furious, at the headlines in particular, and I spent a nervous day yesterday with him in explanations etc. Sic semper. Akron has afforded me one purple evening, however. I got dreadfully drunk on dreadful raisin brew, smoked one of the cigars made especially for the Czar, defunct, of Russia, and puked all over a boarding house. You will believe me an ox when I tell you that I was on the job again next morning, and carried the day through with flying colours. I enclose an opus by Eugene Field,—very exclusive,—which you will copy if you wish, and then return. Do not let Burleson or your father see it, as it is quite strong. I think you will more than smile.

Yours,—H.H. Crane

Yes, Edgar Saltus *is* gone. I remember reading him a rare and wonderfully complete edition of Catallus on the night of the debauch. However,—I hope you will not think that my companion on that occasion was the one I mention early in the letter. This fellow of the raisin brew is another poor soul, like myself, in Akron exile from N.Y. A very sophisticated and erudite fellow to whom I was introduced by my bookseller.

To Gorham Munson

My dear Gorham:—   January 9th, 1920
   What a good job Somerset Maugham does in his *Moon and Sixpence*! Have just finished reading it at a single sitting. Pray take the time to read it if you haven't already. How far it follows the facts biographical to Gauguin, I am not able to say, but from what little I do know, it touches his case at many angles. Your letter coming this morning calls echoes in my ears of many such moods familiar to me during my times in N.Y. and I know how you feel. The mentioned book, I suggest as a tonic for hardness,—we all need how much more of it!
   Complaining of a headache this morning I was excused from my duties for the day, and so have had time for reading, etc. I have not had to serve at the soda fountain as yet, and as a matter of fact, have not had much of anything to do,—my duty seeming to be a kind of marking time until I shall be occupied in the addition to the store,—a restaurant,—or am sent up to Cleveland to fly about in a Dodge car, selling. I have a kind of tacit quarrel with everyone at the store, in spite of smiles, etc., but am becoming accustomed to the atmosphere, and suffer considerably less. Akron has, after all, afforded me more than N.Y. would under present circumstances and times, and, odd as it may seem, I have almost no desire for an immeadiate return there. Of course, I suppose my "affair" may have a good deal to do with my attitide. And I have also made two very delightful friendships, one,—the fellow I mentioned as my companion in the raisin brew debauch (Candee), and a more recent acquaintance with a filthy old man,—a marvelous photographer, the only one in this country to hold the Dresden and Munich awards, and who has several times been "written up" in the International Studio. Authorities rank him with Coburn and Hoppé of London, and there is no one in New York who compares with him. He used to read the *Little Review,* knows Marsden Hartley,—and lives in a tumble down old house in the center of the city. I expect the pictures of me that he takes to be wonders. He refused to take the "rubber-king," F. H. Seiberling, for love nor money, simply because he thought his face without interest. He confided to me yesterday

that he was an anarchist, and I picture with some pain the contrast in his circumstances here with what acclaim he would achieve in place like London. He has always been afraid of N.Y.—and wisely,—for probably he would have long since starved there.

I was suddenly surprised last evening (Candee and I have been in the habit of talking until two and three in the morning) to hear him mention the Baroness. It seems he knows her very well. Knew her before she came to the village and Margaret Anderson got hold of her at all, and believe me he had some surprising tales to tell. He goes on for hours telling of exotic friends of his and strange experiences. He knows Europe well, English country house parties, and Washington society,— prizefighters, cardinals, poets and sculptors, etc. etc., and the wonderful thing is to find him here in Akron, forced to earn his living as secretary for some wheezing philanthropist.

Your anecdote of New Year's Eve was interesting,—who knows,—perhaps someday you will fall too. Prenez garde!

Hart Crane

To Gorham Munson

11431 Euclid Avenue

Dear Gorham:— Cleveland, Ohio

Your play presents simple difficulties of criticism as far as particular details. Of course you cannot take it seriously as a work of art after the first page. It is stark propaganda, however much in the right direction it may be. For types like ourselves it should hold no deep interest, as it begins and ends with the universally obvious understanding between the artist and what is supposed to be his "audience." The Comstock raps are good but not well enough,—humorously enough, placed to be sufficiently amusing or effective. Humour is the artist's only weapon against the proletariat; Mark Twain knew this, and used it effectively enough, take "1601," for example. Mencken knows it too. And so did Rabelais. I think that *The Liberator* would be likely to take it, but I cannot imagine it presented on a stage. You have a sense of humor and I cannot see how you allowed some lines of it to pass your pencil. I have marked a few. You're too damned serious. You victimize your hero. Your aristocrat is much more vital and admirable than the polyphonic God, chosen to symbolize the artist. And anyway,—it's sentimentality to talk the way he does. The modern artist has got to harden himself, and the walls of an ivory tower are too delicate and brittle a coat of mail for substitute. The keen and most sensitive edges will result from this "hardening" process. If you will pardon a more personal approach, I think that you would do better to think less about aesthetics in the abstract, —in fact, forget all about aesthetics, and apply yourself closely to a conscious observation of the details of existence, plain psychology, etc. If you ARE an artist then, you will create spontaneously. But I pray for both of us,—let us be keen and humorous scientists anyway. And I would rather act my little tradgedy without tears. Although I would insist upon a tortured countenance and all sleekness pared off the muscles.

My love affair is affording me new treasures all the time. Our holidays are spent together here in Cleveland, and I have discovered new satisfactions at each occasion. The terrible old grind at the factory is much relieved by this. I live from Saturday to Saturday. Gold and purple. Antinous at Yale. So the wind blows, and whatever might happen, I am sure of a wonderful pool of memories. Perhaps this is the romance of my life,—it is wonderful to find the realization of one's dreams in flesh, form, laughter and intelligence,—all in one person. I am not giddy or blind, but steadier and keener than I've ever been before. The daily grind prevents me from doing anything productive. Here is something enclosed on which I would like your opinion, as frank and unmerciful as mine has been of your play. Write soon. Josephson has a volume going the rounds of the pubs and a lucrative job as translator of French works.

Yours,— Hart

To Gorham Munson

1709 East 115th Street
My dear Gorham:—   March 6, 1920
    Well,—my mother is at length returned and the house open again. At present, however, the domestic vista appears a deso-

late prospect to me,—a violent contrast to the warm pictures that the former rooming-house room had conjured up as anticipations. I wrote you a while ago that I had gotten 'round to enjoy my mother's companionship. That illusion, at least for the present, seems to be dispelled. She left here two months ago, a rather (for her) ductile and seductive woman with a certain aura about her. She comes back now, satisfied, shallow, unemotional, insistent on talking food receipts and household details during meals. The weight of this terrible Christian Science satisfaction I feel growing heavier and heavier on my neck. Tonight I am distraught after a two-hour's effort at camaraderie and amusement with her. "Dutiful son," "sage parent" —that's nice,—and a pat on the back and the habitual "goodnight kiss." I give my evenings to her to hear advice about details in business affairs which she knows nothing about. Mon Dieu!!! And there is Grandmother in a loud background to add to the confusion. Exhausted as one may be from an inhuman day, one must beam out the dinner and evening in proper style or there are exclamations culminating in excruciating tears. However, I mind it most when I am alive, like tonight, —not tired, stupid, mild, as on "week nights."

Well, anyway, last night was made enjoyable by the spectacle of a good prize-fight. I have been to a number lately as guest of a newspaperman who lived over at the rooming house. Of course, many matches are boresome, but provide two sublime machines of human muscle-play in the vivid light of a "ring," —stark darkness all around with yells from all sides and countless eyes gleaming, centered on the circle,—and I get a real satisfaction and stimulant. I get very heated, and shout loudly, jump up from my seat etc. and get more interested every time I go. Really, you must attend a bout or two in N.Y. where a real knock-out is permitted. Along with liquor, that aristocratic assertion has disappeared here. There is something about the atmosphere of a ring show that I have for long wanted to capture into the snares of a poem. I shall not rest easy until I do, I fear. To describe it to you,—what I mean,—would be to accomplish my purpose. A kind of patent leather gloss, an extreme freshness that has nothing to do with the traditional "dew-on-the-grass" variety conveys something suggestive of my aim. T. S. Eliot does it often,—once merely with the name

"Sweeney" and Sherwood Anderson, though with quite different method in a story of his in *The Smart Set,* some time ago, called "I Want to Know Why," one of the greatest stories I ever expect to read,—better even than most of the *Winesburg* chapters. This brings me to your story in the *Ploughshare.* What there was of it was well done. But it seems to me that the humor and satire of this kind of theme depends on a continued heaping-up and heaping-up of absurd detail, etc. until a climacteric of either bitterness or farce is reached. For example, have you read Gogol's, "The Cloak," ever? I don't know what Hervey White did to it—but I would distrust him of any improvements on it after reading his comments on Frank's *Our America.*

(The rest of this you will have to bother to painfully decipher from the pen, as Mother has gone to bed and objects to my use of the typewriter.) I am as anti-semitic as they make 'em, but Frank's comments cannot afford to be ignored merely because of race prejudice. White is just an ordinary ass, though, and can easily be disposed of. I don't understand, though, how you can consent to such "operations" on your mss.

I'm very glad you sent the poem. It begins well,—dramatically, and maintains itself well until the last two lines. They are an appendix which I'd remove,—merely repetition of better phrases in the beginning. Why not divide up the second verse into two equal parts and have three quartet line verses? Another thing,—the "shoot-the-chutes" image jars,—one wants to laugh,—and one shouldn't,—something else there would be better. Also,—why use a French title? I know it's "done in the best families," but there seems a touch of servility,—inadequacy about it to me. I'd send it to the *Dial* if I had it, and be quite proud of it, whether taken or not.

Josephson writes me that the *Dial* is causing a great stir, but that clique favoritism, the old familiar and usual magazine button, is beginning to become evident. J's letters are charming, and a recent love affair of his, a disappointment, has added seasoning to his observations. I only hope that you, he, and Anderson continue to keep me awake with occasional mail.

I had a long and hypocritical conference with my father today, and succeeded to the extent of a five dollars per week raise in salary,—this makes existence at least possible.

I don't know, G., whether I'm strong and hardened or not. I know that I am forced to be very flexible to get along at all under present conditions. I contrive to humanize my work to some extent by much cameraderie with the other employees and this is my salvation there. Of course I am utterly alone,— want to be,—and am beginning to rather enjoy the slippery scales-of-the-fish, continual escape, attitude. The few people that I can give myself to are out of physical reach, and so I can only write where I would like to talk, gesture, and dine. The most revolting sensation I experience is the feeling of having placed myself in a position of quiescence or momentary sur- render to the contact & possession of the insensitive fingers of my neighbors here. I am learning, just beginning to learn,— the technique of escape, and too often yet, I betray myself by some enthusiasm or other.

My Akron friend has not been able to see me for some five weeks, and I am in need of a balm, spiritual and fleshly. I hope next Sunday something can be arranged.

Glad to hear of your friendship with Powys. Write me more about him.

As ever, Hart

To Matthew Josephson

1709 East 115th Street
Dear Matty:—   March 15, 1920

Your praise of *Parsifal* reminded me to buy a certain Vic- trola reproduction,—"The Processional,"—that I have long wanted, and I have found it an incessant pleasure ever since. I read the *Times* often enough to realize that music is the only extra stimulus that N.Y. has to offer above Cleveland in these dry days. As I've said before, I don't especially long for N.Y. as of yore, except once in a while when an overwhelming disgust with my work afflicts me and I want to lose myself in the chill vastness of the old place. (I should better have said "find myself," for I play a business part so much and so painfully, that the effort wears.) The little "iridescent bubbles" of poems that you suggest as fortnightly events simply refuse to come to the surface, and as I get so much of regularity in my daily routine,—time-clock ringing, etc. and rushing,—I won't even worry about it. I cannot commit the old atrocities,—and I have not time at present for new adventures. At any rate, in the slow silence my taste is not suffering. There are still Rabelais, Villon, Apulius, and Eliot to snatch at occasionally,. In my limited surroundings I grow to derive exceptional pleasures from little things such as a small Gaugiun I have on the wall, Japanese prints, and Russian records on the Victrola, in fact, the seclusion of my room. My mother is able to offer me only the usual "comforts of home" combined with stolid, bourgeois ultimatums and judgments which I am learning how to accept gracefully. So, if you are bored and spleenful, we have much in common, though you are less impulsive and emotional than myself, and take, I am sure, more lightly. Your suggestion of a flight to the walks of Chelsea or the Mediterranean tempts me exceedingly. I should like to be rash. I assure you that if I were in your position I should do just such a thing, but I feel too much bound by responsibilities in connection with my Mother's fate, to more than dream of it. However, I wish we could get together for a while next summer. Perhaps you could make me a visit here. I will be badly in need of your conversation for a tonic by that time, and perhaps you will consider it. I can offer you no woodland retreat or metropolitan carnival, —only a very middle-class house and dull conversation,—but the time we had to ourselves would be very interesting to me, at least.

The last *Dial* was interesting, mainly on account of a story of Anderson's and "Mrs. Maecenas." Burke can write at least very cleverly. I was entertained. The hero, I cannot help remarking, touches resemblance to you in several intellectual instances. Physically,—I never saw you broken out with a rash, or gawky,—but Burke has known you longer,—Is there an understanding between you about it?. . . . My opus comes out in the April issue, and you will remark a couple of salutary changes,—omissions.

It's late, and those who arise at five must get sleep, so I'll bar-

barically acquiesce. My poem, the phallic theme, was a highly concentrated piece of symbolism, image wound within image. You were only too right in your judgment of it. When I get some time I'll work more on it. What you saw was fresh and unshodden enough.

Yours,—HART

To Gorham Munson

1709 East 115th Street
Cleveland, Ohio
April 14, 1920

My dear Gorham:—

Escuse me,—but I am tired, peevish, and impulsive, and shall write you but a disordered record at best. I feel like committing what is left of me after the day's end, to paper, and you shall have the bones of the feast anyway.

Your letter I found waiting for me, and have just read it. I am glad you wrote, as I was just beginning to think that you might be ill, or something worse. I don't mean "dead," but married, or such. I was just on the point of writing one of those tiresome epistles confined to inquiries on such points etc. which would have annoyed you.

Yes,—the "Grandmother" poem came out very nicely. You notice, of course, that I cut it in several places, which improved it, I am sure. It is the only thing I've done that satisfies me at all now,—whether I can even equal it in the future remains to be seen. I've recently been at work on something that I enclose for your verdict. As usual I am much at sea about qualities and faults. It is interesting to me,—but do I succeed in making it of interest to others? Please slam and bang your best about it,—pro or con. I have much faith in your critical powers. Much remains to be done on it yet,—but enough is done with it at present to detect the main current of it, which is principally all that worries me. My daily routine tends to benumb my faculties so much that at times I feel an infantile awe before any attempt whatever, critical or creative. This piece was simply a mood which rose and spilled over in a slightly cruder form than what you see. It happens to be autobiographic, which makes any personal estimate of it all the more dangerous.

I like Marion Moore in a certain way. She is so prosaic that the extremity of her detachment touches, or seems to touch, a kind of inspiration. But she is too much of a precieuse for my adulation. Of this latter class even give me Wallace Stevens, and the fastidious Williams in preference. Is there anything more fastidious in poetry than these lines of his in a recent *Little Review.*—?

> You know that that is not much
> That I desire, a few crysanthemums
> half lying on the grass, yellow
> and brown and white, the talk
> of a few people, the trees,
> an expanse of dry leaves perhaps
> with ditches among them.—

The Bynner poems and translations were fine. Vildrac is the one who set me on the track of the Grandmother mood, and it is odd that our poems should have come out in the same issue.

Have not heard from Josephson for some time. His last letter told of splenetic days following his post-graduation from Columbia, and an urge to ramble toward the continent via a stewardship on some vessel. Perhaps, for all I know, he has left our shores. Anderson writes me often from his Alabama bower. He is enthusiastic about the negroes and their life, and will probably write something, sooner or later, on the subject.

The prospect of Easter spent at home was too much for me, and so I went to visit my Akron friend armed with two bottles of dago red. That didn't seem to suffice after we got started, and a quart of raisin jack was divided between us with the result that the day proper (after the night before) was spent very quietly, watered and Bromo-Seltzered, with amusing anecdotes occasionally sprouting from towelled head to towelled head. The bath in the unconscious did me good, though, and was much better than the stilted parade and heavy dinner that my home neighborhood offered. Since then I have been beset by two terrible occasions,—a Crane-grandparent-golden-wedding celebration, and a collegiate ball. The terrors of the first were alleviated by some real champagne, but the second was aggravated by auto trouble on the way home with two hysterical, extremely young and innocent females under my care at three in the morning. I am just getting over it.

Well this is all for tonight. I have no youths to put to bed,— otherwise my correspondence might suffer. I'm afraid I wouldn't do in your position at all. But enough! I read in the paper that John Barrymore is going to appear before the movie public in *Dorian Grey*!! Mercy me! Poor Oscar's ghost upon the screen!! I wonder what will be done with the part.

Yours as ever,—Hart

To Gorham Munson

Dear Gorham:—   Monday, April 26, 1920

Thank you 'muchly' for your speedy response to the plea for a critique. I was very anxious for your words, and they proved very valuable. You are right in every particular, except in so far as the understanding of my personal motives of interest in the poem. I realize that it is only my failure in the realization (concretely) which has permitted you this possibility. The poem fails, not because of questions, propagandistic and economic, which you mentioned, but because of that synthetic conviction of form & creation, which it lacks. It is all too complicated an explanation to attempt leastwise on paper at this time of the night,—but perhaps you will miraculously be able to penetrate through to my meaning. As it stands, there are only a few fragments scattered thru it to build on,—but I may make something of it in time. However,—if it does evolve into something,—it will be too elusive for you to attach sociological arguments to, at least in the matter of most of the details you have mentioned. At present,—I feel apathetic about it,—but there is, of course, no telling when I will take it up again. The "Garden Abstract" has got hold of me now,—and I venture that you would not recognize it. It is carrying me on with all the adventuresome interest that "Grandmother's Love-Letters" did, and I am very hopeful. Later, when I am further advanced with it and surer, I'll send it to you. Also,—I am "working up" the "Aunty Climax" which you will remember,—and a new piece in conventional form about a child hearing his parents quarrelling in the next room at midnight,—a rather Blake-ian theme, I fear.

I have gone through a great deal lately,—seen love go down through lust to indifference etc. and am also, not very well. This I blame mostly to overwork. In fact the most of last week I spent at home minding an incipient rupture caused by the incessant heavy lifting at the factory. The possibility of such a thing made me furious with all those concerned in the circumstances of its cause. But I am quieter, now that the affair has not been as serious as I at first suspected. I am back at it again today,—but shall in the future take more precautions against strenuosity. Your letter breathed an equanimity which it seems is more possible in your late surroundings. The change must be doing you good.

As ever, Hart

To Gorham Munson

1310 L Street N.W.
Dear Gorham:—   September 24, 1920

Your letter has just been read and as I feel like answering you right now I'm at it. I've been running around talking talking, talking and waiting for the proper persons to arrive at their offices etc. etc. etc. all week, and have succeeded to the mild extent of inaugurating two new accounts for the firm. Fortunately, people here don't seem to arrive at their offices until after ten, and so I have the opportunity to sleep more than I did in Cleveland where the requirements commanded my resurrection at five A.M. My Akron friend, Mr. Candee, gave me an introduction to a poet friend of his who has charge of all the official communications etc. that come into the state department. He has proved a charming person, and has introduced me to several other interesting people. He is one of the few who is thoroughly cognizant of what is going on abroad, knows some things weeks in advance of the newspapers and, of course, a great many things that never come out. His opinion of most of Europe, especially some of the freshly hatched nationalitics, is below cynicism.

I have not yet heard from the *Dial* about Porphyro, or at any rate he has not been redirected to me. I am beginning to feel that he is my lost soul, and will be a long time in returning. This simply means that I haven't had a creative impulse for so long that I am even getting not to miss it. I am not in the type of Washington life that offers material or incentive for writing. The diplomatic circles have all kinds of scandals waving around which I generally hear a whisper of from the fringes, but there is really no cafe life here or factory or shop life worth mentioning. Thousands of clerks pour out of government offices at night and eat and go to the movies. The streets are beautiful with many parks etc. but it is all rather dead. I am really more interested in the soldiers and sailors that one meets than in anything else. They have a strange psychology of their own that is new to me. This sounds bad, and perhaps it is so,—but what should one do with the reported example of our new VICE-president, Franklin Roosevelt, scenting the air as it does. From what I'm hearing, about every other person in the government service and diplomatic service are enlarged editions of Lord Douglas. Amusing Household! as Rimbaud would say.

I shall look for *The Rainbow* in Brentanoe's here, and hope that it may be interesting. Are all of your critiques in the *Freeman* signed? I've been looking for you there and haven't found that Pollard article yet. Cheer up there in your country retreat. You are about as well off as I am anyway. I don't even get a sip of academic tea nor advice from President Wilson. Excuse my type and spelling mistakes and don't forget to write at once.

Yours as always,—Hart

To Gorham Munson

1310 L Street N.W.
Washington, D.C.
October 20, 1920

Dear Gorham:

I am going to return to Cleveland about a week from the above date, so when you write again you had better write me at the house in C. (1709 East 115th St.)

Your letter that arrived this morning had the true rage of the celibate unwilling in it. I sympathize with you. . . . My nights

are uneasy also. But you ought to pity me more than yourself,
—my satisfactions are far more remote and dangerous than
your's, and my temptations frequent, alas!

I have just been reading your Pollard article, and on bringing
it to the attention of my friend Wilbur Underwood here, was
delighted to find that U. knew Pollard very well, the latter
having been enthusiastic about the two vols. of verse that
Underwood brought out in England a long time ago. What
pathos there is in these sudden flashes on forgotten people,
forgotten achievements and encounters! Here is this man,
Underwood, with the beauty and promise of his life all dried
and withered by the daily grind he has had to go through year
after year in the State Dept. with a meagre salary. A better critic
and more interesting person one seldom meets, yet the routine
of uninteresting work has probably killed forever his creative
predispositions. A very few friends is all that his life holds for
him. Yes, Pound is right in what he says in his "The Rest,"—
"O helpless few in my country, O remnant enslaved! . . . You
who cannot wear yourselves out by persisting to successes."

U. has a very fine collection of rare translations etc. from an-
tiquity, and I have just been enjoying to the full his copy of the
Satyricon of Petronius (Arbiter), a rare completely unexpur-
gated Paris edition, purported to have been translated by
Oscar Wilde, although it seems to me too fine a job for what I
imagine Wilde's scholarship to have been. Also, I am enjoying
The Golden Asse of Apuleius, and some Saltus vols. that he has.

I went to see Hampden in *The Merchant of Venice* recently
here. The way it was done, setting, costumes, speech, gesture,
—everything was sickening. Hampden, in one scene only,—
the tantrum with Tubal,—was good, everywhere else his
acting was indifferent. I cannot understand how a man of his
intelligence,—for I remember his Hamlet as being quite good,
—will venture forth with such a cast of burlesque queens, (his
Portia!!!) and bitches. The worst examples of antiquated the-
atricality, and mouthing of words! And the audience was ample
and enthusiastic,—a true barometer of the American stage at
present.

I must mention that I have recently heard from Josephson
and Sherwood Anderson. The former is now financial editor!
for the *Newark Ledger*, and Anderson, who has been working

for a month in Chicago has earned enough money to settle down in a cabin at Palos park, near Chicago, for a winter of painting and writing. *Poor White* will be out from Huebsch this month, and A. says he has a new novel very nearly completed. There is a bookseller and his wife here who know A. and I have been interested in their recountal of some of his early experiences. Josephson had a poem in the last (Oct) *Poetry* which is amusing, but no more. So far as I can see, American poetry is on a slump or vacation at present. I suppose I am not the only one who feels the stultifying influence of the times.

I shall be glad to get back to Cleveland for a while, if only to see the copies of Vildrac, Rimbaud, and Laforgue that have arrived from Paris since my leaving. I expect to return to W. later, in Jan. when the "season" here is on. I find aggreement from my father that my lack of results here has not been so much a matter of personal inadequacy as the weather and general slowness of business here at this particular time. I shall certainly be in an ungodly rush, though, all the time I am at the factory, as the holiday season orders will be coming in and things become perfectly maddening there for two months. However, anything will be better than the maddening experience I have been having here of clawing the air day after day without getting any but the most meagre results.

This is all for now,—and I hope it to be more satisfactory to you than my last offering.

As always,—Hart

To Gorham Munson

My dear Gorham:—   November 23, 1920

Your letter has just come, and I'm sorry to know you are having such an ordeal of "nerves." Of course, being thrown back violently again on celibacy after your Woodstock freedom would naturally tend to being about such a result, and it is only a pity that you cannot find anything near you of sufficient temporary interest to relieve your situation. Of course, I realize, that the puritanical taboos of a typical boys' school are what stands in the way most of all, and then you might possibly resent and refuse sheer sensuality after having experienced what I imagine has been offered you. I don't believe in the "sublimation" theory at all so far as it applies to my own experience. Beauty has most often appeared to me in moments of penitence and even sometimes, distraction and worry. Lately my continence has brought me nothing in the creative way,— it has only tended to create a confidence in me along lines of action,—business, execution, etc. There is not love enough in me at present to do a thing. This sounds romantic and silly,— you understand that I mean and refer to the strongest incentive to the imagination, or, at least, the strongest in my particular case. So I have nothing to offer you for reading and judgement. Mart Anderson writes me that the next *L.R.* will be out the twenty-fifth,—96 pgs. and will contain my poem, etc. and a publication of the J. Joyce trial and proceedings which she says are interesting. It ought to be a rich number with John Quinn and Burleson throwing epithets at each other. I stopped in the middle of *The Possessed* to read *Poor White*, but am again on the Russian trail. What marvelous psychology!!! A careful reading of "Dosty" ought to prepare one's mind to handle any human situation comfortably that ever might arise. . . . You will like the Anderson book. It fascinated me as much as *Winesburg* and this in spite of a great fear of disappointment. There is a woman in it something like jh although too removed to do anything but suggest her. I wish, after you have read it, that we could have a fireside hour over the book. We might aggree perhaps on the exquisite work of such scenes as the description of the murderer-saddlemaker sitting by the pond and rocking gently to and fro (the simplicity of A's great power of suggestion is most mocking to the analyst)—and the scene where the sex-awakening girl hears the men in the barn in speaking of her, say,—"the sap is mounting into the tree." Nature is so strong in all the work of Anderson, and he describes it as one so willingly and happily surrendered to it, that it colors his work with the most surprising grasp of what "innocence" and intuition ought to mean. Also, his uncanny intuition into the feelings of women (a number of women have remarked to me about this) is very unusual. I have an absurd prejudice against Frank's *Dark Mother* merely on account of what I read of it in a copy of the *Dial*. There it seemed to me too exclamatory, Semetic, and too much in the style of David Pinski, whose stuff I somehow am terribly bored with. So I probably shall never read it, as I probably shall never read more than the three pages of W. D. Howells that I once attempted. Frankly, you see, I admit to a taste for certain affectations and ornamental commissions. I wish I could follow your finger guide to the advice of Brooks in the *Freeman* about "outside interests" for the fallow seasons between poems. I had read the article and aggree with it in many ways. But with me, there are no poems for "doldrums" to lag between, and no time, literally, for poems, to say nothing of energy. The fact is last week I ran gait at the factory at the rate of fourteen hours straight per day of rushed and heavy and confusing labor, and as it is will probably continue that way until very near Christmas, I have all I can do to think of getting enough sleep to begin the rush again next day. Of course I am becoming very morose and irritable under this pressure of exertion, not to mention disgust and boredom, and yesterday, my first day of a chance to sit down and think a minute, I found myself in a rather serious state of indigestion and neurotic fever. So it goes. Our age tries hard enough to kill us, but I begin to feel a pleasure in sheer stubborness, and will possibly turn in time into some sort of a beautiful crank.

Pax vobiscum!!!! as ever Hart

To Sherwood Anderson

Dear Anderson:—   December 8, 1920

Your mention of a possible trip East soon makes me hope very much that you will care to stop off at Cleveland here (a few hours at least) and see me. I shall not be living at home at the time as my mother expects to leave for her place in Cuba very soon, closing the house, but if you come down I can accommodate you at my room where ever it may be. I want very much to talk with you and hope you can "make it" this time. Better look me up at the factory at 208 St. Clair Ave. if you arrive between 8 A.M. and 5 P.M. You don't know how much I appreciate the encouragement your letters give me. Although I am not at present doing anything creatively, I have not sunk too much into despair or indifference to hope.

Do come,—won't you! Hart Crane

To Wilbur Underwood

Dear Wilbur:—

NEWS!News!NEWS! —The "golden halo" has widened,— descended upon me (or "us") and I've been blind with happiness and beauty for the last full week. Joking aside, I am too happy not to fear a great deal, but I believe in, or have found God again. It seems vulgar to rush out with my feelings to anyone so, but you know by this time whether I am vulgar or not (I don't) and it may please you, as it often might have helped me so, to know that something beautiful can be found or can "occur" once in awhile, and so unexpectedly. Not the brief and limited sensual thing alone, but something infinitely more thrilling and inclusive. I foolishly keep wondering,— "How can this be?—How did it occur?" How my life might be changed could this continue, but I scarcely dare to hope. I feel like weeping most of the time, and I have become reconciled, strangely reconciled, to many aggravations. Of course it is the return of devotion astounds me so, and the real certainty that, at least for the time, it is perfectly honest. It makes me feel very unworthy,—and yet what pleasure the emotion under such circumstances provides. I have so much now to reverence, discovering more and more beauty every day,—beauty of character, manner, and body, that I am for the time, completely changed.—But why aren't you here to talk with me about it! How I wish you were.

I have written you this way (typewriter) because, as you have discovered, my writing is hard deciphering. I have given up trying to improve it, and don't try any more. You have probably got the candy and hymn by this time,—neither amount to much, but I wanted to send them. I don't understand Harry's silence,—but certainly hope that I have not been relinquished as one of Akron's temporary "makeshifts" or "reliefs." It would really hurt. I have told you all that has happened. This rest would merely be to mention details of ungodly strain and hours of "Christmas rush" at the factory,—seventeen hours at a stretch sometimes. When I have had time I have spent it with Dostoievsky's *Les Freres Karamazov* which I like even better than *The Possessed*. The beautiful young Alyosha, and Father Zosimma! Dostoievsky seems to me to represent the nearest type to the "return of Christ" that there is record of,—I think the greatest of novelists. But I am forgetting Frank Harris, who, you know, comes second to the "woman taken in adultery."

My mother leaves for her southern island in ten days, and I am taking a room for the rest of the winter. Write me here for the present, anyway, and it will be faithfully forwarded with the "seal secure." I wish you would care to send me some of your poetry which I can't understand how I missed reading in Washington. You must have some extra copies somewhere. My regards to Mme. C.

> And much love to you, from H. H. C.

To Wilbur Underwood

> The Del Prado Apts.
> 40th Street and Euclid Avenue
> Cleveland, Ohio
> January 2, 1921

Dear Wilbur:—

My mother left last Tuesday for her winter quarters in the West Indies and I am installed here with a room and bath for a few weeks anyway. A hint dropped from the pater the other day, makes me think that I may soon be sent on the road again (perhaps Chicago this time) so my plans for a winter of relative ease and time for a little writing seem to be fated. I was exhausted completely after the rush at the factory, and am just beginning to pick up a normal attitude again. Your poems are much appreciated. "Cujus Aninam Gememtem" is one of the finest poems I've ever read, and there is much charm and beauty in all the others,— "Poison" in particular. And I like the dread beauty of "The Sword." You MUST continue to write, Wilbur,—if for no other audience than myself. Make a

New Year's resolution. I have finally heard from Harry,—a beautiful letter that filled me with warmth and memories. It is pleasant to be missed, and Harry avows such feelings toward Akron and myself. Well,—hell may be turned into Paradise with the proper company. I have my poem "out" in the *Little Review* at last,—it will not be a new one to you,—but what do you think of the Minns photographs? Do write me soon. I am still within the "halo" influence. Your poems are particularly appropriate to the subject. The head and eyes of Pierrot,—a beautiful grace with a certain sadness, and every movement of the body a poem. Mon Dieu! How I shall hate to depart.

Always yours,—H

To Matthew Josephson

The Del Prado Apts.
Cleveland, Ohio
January 14, 1921

Dear Matty:—

It's taken me a long time to get you an answer, but I have had to go through the hellish rush of the Christmas season at the factory, get moved from the house to rooms here (my mother left for the south and the house is closed up) and then go through with inventory and general clean-up at the factory, and I have had no time nor energy.

What you say about the Akron suite is very true. I have only one point of disagreement with you,—crudeness of form. This was deliberate, and you have got to convince me that such a treatment of such a mood and subject is inconsistent before we can pick asphodels together again on the slopes of Parnassus. By the way,—do you care for my "Garden Abstract" in its final form in the *L.R.*? I think that the version I sent you was an earlier and poorer experiment. I must bestir myself and write something new. My main difficulty is at present a kind of critical structure that won't permit me the expression of the old asininities, *and* (as you say) the poverty of society in these "provinces." Your suggestion about the trade paper work is alluring. However, I am bound not to break away from my father's concern until spring, when there may be a little striving and stirring up of the dust,—I hope.

Are you still planning on Italy? Why not the island of Capri? I hear there is interesting company about there,—D. H. Lawrence and Mackensie musing and moping around the baths and arcades of Tiberius. . . . I don't long so much for change of surroundings as time, TIME which I never seem to get to read or write or amuse myself. I hear that "New York" has gone mad about "Dada" and that a most exotic and worthless review is being concocted by Man Ray and Duchamp, billets in a bag printed backwards, on rubber deluxe, etc. What next! This is worse than the Baroness. By the way I like the way the discovery has suddenly been made that she has all along been, unconsciously, a Dadaist. I cannot figure out just what Dadaism is beyond an insane jumble of the four winds, the six senses, and plum pudding. But if the Baroness is to be a keystone for it,—then I think I can possibly know when it is coming and avoid it.

Write me soon. HART

To Gorham Munson

The Del Prado Apts.
Cleveland, Ohio
January 28, 1921

Dear Gorham:

Your N.Y. bulletin interested me immensely. Last Sunday I went down to Akron to see Minns after a four months' separation. I read him the opinions of Man Ray, whereat he flew into a holy rage. "There is no sense in the theory of interesting 'accidents.'" And I am with Minns in that. There is little to be gained in any art, so far as I can see, except with much *conscious* effort. If he doesn't watch his cards, M. Ray will allow the Dada theories and other flamdoodle of his section to run him off the track. He seems to have done much good work so far, but it has been in spite of his "ideas." If he is just recently infected it is too bad, because there is less chance of him sustaining his qualities under such theories.—But so much for photography—

I am feeling better already since I've made up my mind about my interest in regard to the factory. And this without as yet having really, *physically,* broken away. Don't expect too much of me. The times are terrible and there is literally nothing to grasp hold of here in *any* line, so I'll have to wait a while. I recently ran across a couple of men here in town who make interesting talking. This delights me, as I have, as you know, always found little better than starvation dieting here. One of them is a partner in a large advertising house here and there may be room for me in a couple of months to work into a place as a copywriter. It was an odd experience for me to find a "successful business man" who was interesting as a reader of Scarron, Brantome, France, Cabell, Anderson, etc. etc.

When I get "Dosty" more cleared out of the way I intend to get more poetry reading again, but just now he is all-absorbing, and somehow his offering is such a distinct type of itself that one doesn't want to mix any other kind of reading with it. Here is my sum poetic output for the last three months,—two lines—

> "The everlasting eyes of Pierrot
> And of Gargantua,—the laughter."

Maybe it is my epitaph,—it is contradictory and wide enough to be. But I hope soon to make it into a poem, and thereby, like Lazarus, return.

ti Salute! Hart

To Wilbur Underwood

The Del Prado Apts.
Cleveland, Ohio

Dear Wilbur:— January 31, 1921

I am grateful and satisfied in many ways. The love and devotion of Pierrot still continues,—but there are things I often long for, and you may think them strange companions,—my desires. But I would like a walk again with you among the ghostly facades of Washington,—and I would like an evening again at Cooke's with the delicious and potent home-brew that his housekeeper makes him,—and I am always longing for the beautiful gay laughter of Harry. All these are, it seems to me, a long way off. I shall undoubtedly not return to Washington again, at least as a salesman in my father's employ. And N.Y. & Harry are remote, though I hear from him often. He wrote me of two visits he had made to Washington after my exit, and I wish I could have been there. They may not have meant much to you, but our nuits au balcon in (as Harry calls it) "Hel"-L it will always be a pleasant memory to me,—the falling stars that punctuated our comments on "Under the Hill" and shameless anecdotes and half-sad and half-gay expressions. I was too worried by all the sickly and trivial preoccupations I was then forced into of commercial conquests (a flattering title for them) to have shown you much of my real self and so I am allowing myself at this late hour, a better sign of appreciation than was given me then.

Your last letter dealing with the "baboon's" late conquests and "floral" tributes thrilled me by the abject enormity of the situation. Something terrible must in time happen in those "parlours,"—you must guard the aged enchantress with Palmer vigilance. Her tender flesh, nourished from the flesh of a thousand lovers, and her over-refined sensibilities (think of the degradation of those maritime breakfasts!) must not be allowed to fall into unsympathetic hands! The roving eyes and suffering hands.—There is something desperate, pitiful and grotesque in the spectacle. No wonder we could not keep many,—and gobs may come and gobs may go,—but *Smith* comes on forever!

Have you been to any concerts of interest. This is the best musical "season" that Cleveland has ever been offered, and while I have not been to very many concerts, I heard Ernest Bloch conduct his Symphony in C# Minor here and was shaken with such effects as I had never heard before. The man is a genius, and living here in Cleveland! Pecuniary circumstances (I can imagine no others) have captured him as the head of an institute of music here.

Just finished the *Brothers Karamazov* yesterday. Dostoevsky leaves his mark upon you forever. As a friend of mine writes:— "Flaubert one can say a great deal about, but Dostoevsky,— what more can you say than that his novels each give one an experience which leaves its mark till death? The reading of most books is the living through of a series of incidents. But you can't escape *suffering* an experience at the hands of old

'Dosty.'" I think you would be very much interested in a book I have just got—*Kora in Hell: Improvisations* by Wm. Carlos Williams; Four Seas Co, Boston ($2.00). It's a book for poets alone, as I see,—meaningless to a large extent to most people, but very suggestive and, to me, stimulating.

I am just getting 'round to a writing mood again. I don't want to move out of here for a long time,—I'm so tired of moving, moving uncertainly from place to place these last six years. I expect to leave my father & strike out for myself in some less commercial work in town here as soon as there is an opportunity.—But I won't bore you more to-night. Write me here, and, I hope soon. And I wish you as much true love as I have lately had given me.

Yours, Hart

To Gorham Munson

Dear Gorham:—   February 11, 1921
Yes my writing is quite Dada,—very Dada (I like the term as applied) and yet you must put up with it again as my machine has suffered another relapse.

I was very much amused and interested by the "Contact" that arrived about a week ago. Thank you, as always, dear old bean, for being so thoughtful. You are always sending me something to make my eyes blink delightedly and arouse me from the general stupor of these parts. How fine the Wallace Stevens were! And some of Williams' talk was good,—but how horrid that the room had to be splashed with the wet-dream explosions of Virgil Jordan and McAlmon. Their talk is all right,—but what is true of it has been said adequately before, —and all they can seem to add is a putrid remnant or two. Perhaps I am on the downward grade, but when I come to such stuff I can only say, "Excuse me." I will be glad to receive stimulation from the sky or a foetid chamber or maybe a piss-pot, but as far as I can make out they have wound their PHALLI in a frantic and vain effort to squeeze out an idea. In fact they seem very "Dada" in more sense than one. But enough!!!

Don't disown me,—but I have done literally no writing to

give you. The fact is that I am entirely engrossed in personal erotic experience lately that nothing seems possible in that way. O if you had ever seen the very Soul of Pierrot (in soul and incarnate) you would at least admire. Never, though, has such beauty and happy-pain be given me before—which is to say that my love is at least somewhat requited. You and one other are the only ones to know now or later of this, so do not think me silly or vulgar to tell you. Well, you have felt the fire somewhat yourself so you may appreciate my mood. Never have I supposed so, or reached such moods of ecstasy.—

What do you think of "Poor White"? It certainly has made Anderson one of the most talked-of artists there are. I wrote you my opinion some time past. I'm still on "Dosty"—a very fine biography and estimate and analysis by J. Middleton Murry. You will please forgive this letter. I have been perhaps a little too personal;—perhaps vulgar. But if anything's to blame it's the Subconscious rioting out through gates that only alchahol has the power to open.

Yours, H.H.C.

Del Prado

I have recently had my position somewhat changed. I'm now keeper of a warehouse which handles bulk supplies for my father's various Cleveland stores. My own boss, and not rushed, and even have time for occasional half-hours of reading. At present, then, I'm somewhat more satisfied.

To Gorham Munson

The Del Prado Apts.
Cleveland, Ohio
April 10

Dear Gorham:—

No word from you for ever so long. I do hope you aren't ill or anything like that.

For me here—the same old jog-trot except that I have lately run across an artist here whose work seems to carry the most astonishing marks of genius that have passed before my eyes in original form—that is—I mean present-day work and I am saying much I think when I say that I prefer *Sommers'* work to

most of Brzeska and Boardman Robinson. A man of 55 or so—
works in a lithograph factory—spent most of his life until the
last seven years in the rut of conventional forms—liberated
suddenly by sparks from Gauguin, Von Gogh, Picasso and
Wyndham Lewis etc. I have taken it upon myself to send out
some of his work for publication, an idea that seems, oddly,
never to have occurred to him. An exhibition of his work in
N.Y. would bring him in something and I wish I could only be
there to do something for him. Have sent Joe Kling several
minor sketches and fragments, but doubt his capacity of ap-
preciation. If you are in N.Y. soon he may still have them to
show you so drop in if you care to. If I ever get time I want to
send some of his better things to the *Dial* and give them some
real material for reproduction. They have, so far, brought out
only a few worthwhile things in drawings. What a damned pity
there are so few channels for such work to get to people here.
What *has* happened to Margaret Anderson and the *L.R.* I
wrote them but got no answer—and worse—no new issue has
appeared now for three months! I'll weep many tears if the
L.R. has gone overboard.

How are your plans for Europe? Sherwood Anderson writes
me that he is going next month—Paris & London—they all
are—alas—but me. The medical journal art are interesting. I
enclose an incipient effort of mine of recent date.

Write soon, Hart

To Gorham Munson

1709 East 115th Street
Dear Gorham: April 20

Your letter did me good, and has left a good hangover for
me for the last few ungenerous days. I left my father's employ
yesterday *for good*—nothing, I think, will ever bring me back.
The last insult was too much. I've been treated like a dog now
for two years,—and only am sorry it took me so long to find
out the simple impossibility of ever doing anything with him
or for him. It will take me many months, I fear, to erase from
memory the image of his overbearing head leaning over me
like a gargoyle. I think he had got to think I couldn't live with-

out his aid. At least he was, I am told, furious at my departure. Whatever comes now is surely better than the past. I shall learn to be somewhere near free again,—at least free from the hatred that has corroded me into illness.

Of course I won't be able to get to N.Y. now for any summer vacation. You know what a privation that means to me. I have nothing in sight in the way of employment,—and as times are bad,—I don't know when I shall. A job as copy-writer for an advertising agency will probably be open to me about June 1st. And there is a newspaper opening out here soon,—perhaps that may yield me something. I have a roof over my head and food anyway—here at home—and maybe I shall write something. The best thing is that the cloud of my father is beginning to move from the horizon now. You have never known me when it has not been there—and in time we *both* may discover some new things in me. *Bridges burn't behind!*

Glad you like "Estador". I'm beginning to myself. I cannot quite accept your word changes although I'm far from satisfied with it. But the more I work over it the less I seem likely to be,—so I'm going to try it on the *Dial.*—Anything for some money now.

Write soon Hart

To Wilbur Underwood

1709 East 115th Street
Cleveland, Ohio
Dear Wilbur:—   May 14

Your Calvert Sonnet only brings me to lament again that you do not write more. How perfect a thing it is! I am very glad to have it. No doubt there are more things of yours in rich, out-of-the-way corners, and let me ask you to tell me about them—where to look etc. Do, I pray you, take up a broken thread again—you really have much to give.

Yes,—I keep on reading the *Dial.* Occasionally, also, the *Freeman.* The new New Orleans attempt called the *Double-Dealer* has some good poems in it this month by Padraic Colum. Has a copy of Carlos Williams' *Contact* strayed into

Washington yet? They started printing it on the multigraph but now, I hear, have graduated to the printers,—and are also giving reproductions of paintings etc. Some really good things in it. Address *G.P.O 89. N.Y.C.* $.25 per copy.

I wish my days and *nights* were as exciting as yours. I can not wish for riches commensurate with Mme. Cooke's appetites,— but the descriptions of your inamoratas almost, nay really,— moves me to envy. I am tempted to spring to a Washington train & rush into your office with "vine leaves in my hair" as dear old Hedda would say. About all the excitement offered me now is a person of ravenous appetites who entertains me with wines and we get drunk and silly about once a week. During these lapses I still rhapsodize over "Ibsen"—whose name you will remember from similar evocative circumstances when I was with you in Wash. We had a wonderful week together about a month ago—but he is now out of town and I don't know when he'll be back—and the curtain is down. Mme. X, of the liquors, tells me that Cleveland is a very rich place—but so far I have not been made to feel it. So,—I repeat—you are fortunate.

We are both in the same boat as regards Harry. About a month ago I had a tiny scribble from him saying that he was leaving N.Y. again to stay a week at Brown's Physical Training Farm, on the Hudson—with Harold Matthews, who had been so impressed by Harry's previous benefits from the regime there that he had decided to try the training himself on condition that Harry went with him. He also added that his Mother & nephew were quite ill with influenza and that everything was in an uproar. That is my last. Of course there may have been many reasons for not writing in case his relatives got worse. But I am always afraid of Harry's disposition to take desperate chances—and so am worried.

He goes at such a pace I am often sure that he can not last long. It would be good if he could live in a disgusting slough of smugness for awhile and recover more reserve forces for the lists. How fond we both are of him!

Mes regards à Mme Cooke et a vous—

vôtre ♡

I venture to force 2 poems on you that have been done recently.

To Gorham Munson

Cleveland, Ohio

Dear Gorham:—   Friday

It will be all right for you to take your second drawing at the 10.00 discount, which will make it only necessary to remail me the check. But before you do this—that is, make your second choice,—I wish you would go to the *Little Review* office and take a look over what they have there. They have some exceptionally fine ones there, and I also wish you would please find out if they intend using any of them for reproduction or not. Again I am worried about them and can't seem to get a word from them about anything. Don't even know if they are in New York or not. I think it's the last time I send them any other work but my own. If they don't want any of the drawings, will you please take it upon yourself to send them back to me with the others you mention for signing etc.?

I wrote a careful letter to De Zayas with prices etc. and am hoping to hear from him soon. I am glad your enthusiasm has been aroused by this second bunch, so much more diversified in subject and medium than the others. I got a postal from Anderson (Paris) this morning in which he enthuses over the churches and old streets, etc.

More later. HART

P.S.—Excuse my apparent evasion of your request for an explanation about "Black Tambourine." The Word "midkingdom" is perhaps the key word to what ideas there are in it. The poem is a description and bundle of insinuations, suggestions bearing on the negro's place somewhere between man and beast. That is why Aesop is brought in, etc.—the popular conception of negro romance, the tambourine on the wall. The value of the poem is only, to me, in what a painter would call its "tactile" quality,—an entirely aesthetic feature. A propagandist for either side of the negro question could find anything he wanted to in it. My only declaration in it is that I find the negro (in the popular mind) sentimentally or brutally "placed" in this midkingdom. etc. Tell me if I have made it plain or not to you. H. C.

To Gorham Munson

Cleveland, Ohio
Dear Gorham:—   October 1, 1921

My terrible hay fever days are over, and the fine autumn weather that I like the best of the year has arrived to console me. My mood is neither happy nor desperately sad. It will best be conveyed to you by the quotation of a new poem, "Chaplinesque"—only started (if I can help it) as yet:

> Contented with such random consolations
> as the wind deposits
> in slithered and too ample pockets,
> we make our meek adjustments.
> For we can still love the world, who find
> a famished kitten on the step, and know
> recesses for it from the fury of the street,
> or warm torn elbow coverts.
>
> We will side-step, and to the final smirk,
> daily the doom
> of that inevitable thumb
> that slowly chafes toward us the puckered index,
> facing the dull squint with what innocence
> and what surprise!
>   (etc.etc.—perhaps—)

And I must tell you that my greatest dramatic treat since seeing Garden in *The Love of Three Kings* two winters ago, was recently enjoyed when Charlie Chaplin's *The Kid* was shown here. Comedy, I may say, has never reached a higher level in this country before. We have (I cannot be too sure of this for my own satisfaction) in Chaplin a dramatic genius that truly approaches the fabulous sort. I could write pages on the overtones and brilliant subtleties of this picture, for which nobody but Chaplin can be responsible, as he wrote it, directed it,— and I am quite sure had much to do with the settings which are unusually fine. If you have not already seen it in N.Y., it may now be in Paris. It was a year late in arriving in Cleveland, I understand, on account of objections from the state board of censors!!!! What they could possibly have objected to, I cannot imagine. It must have been some superstition aroused against good acting! But they will always release any sickening and false melodrama of high life and sex, lost virginities, etc. at the first glance. Well, I am thankful to get even what their paws have mawled of the Chaplin and Caligari sort. My poem is a sympathetic attempt to put into words some of the Chaplin pantomime, so beautiful, and so full of eloquence, and so modern.

My poem is on the stands now (Oct. *Dial*) and is in the good company of Anatole France, Santayana, and D. H. Lawrence. It gratifies me to be paid for it, but a better satisfaction is company. I may (softly now!) send them a really good futuristic picture of mine (pastel-watercolour) so much would it delight me to "pull off" some such stunt. I sent them a poem two weeks ago which I have not heard from yet, I quote it on the back. It is always such a pity that when I do get three things out on the stands in a month, as now, I have exhausted myself, and have temporarily nothing to send to other editors who might be moved at the apparent potency of popularity, to take me better than otherwise. I am doing a trans. of de Gourmont's "Marginalia on Poe and Baudelaire" for the *Double Dealer*.

"The Bottom of the Sea Is Cruel"

Above the fresh ruffles of the surf
bright striped urchins flay each other with sand.
They have contrived a conquest for shell shucks,
and their fingers crumble fragments of baked weed,
gaily digging and scattering.

And in answer to their treble interjections
the sun beats lightening on the waves,
the waves fold thunder on the sand;
and could they hear, I would tell them:

"O brilliant kids, frisk with your dog,
fondle your shells and sticks, bleached
with the time and the elements, but there is a line
you must not cross. Your hands will find beyond it
no golden fringe to fling upon the wind.
—The Bottom of the sea is cruel."

This is not nearly so good, to my mind, as my start on Chaplin, but has a certain crispness to recommend it.

You seem to be having a fine time, and I realize that you have only begun. I loved your description of Brest, something a la Morand in style! I keep looking in the *Freeman* every so often to see if you haven't sent them something. It will be time for me to raise my voice in praise of Anderson soon, as his new book *The Triumph of the Egg,* and other stories, is on the market. This also includes the serial "Out of Nowhere into Nothing" recently completed in the *Dial.* I would lay a bet on it that long after Zona Gale, Lewis etc. are forgotten Sherwood will hold his own. There are lots of things I want to read but haven't the money to buy like Hecht's first novel, a great success they say, *Erik Dorn,* recently out. I guess I wrote you how much I enjoyed Shaw's *Back to Methuselah,* a review of which I wrote for the *D.D.*

I am taking a course in advertising two nights of every week until next May which is very good and ought to help me to get started. It has the advantage, at any rate, of giving one a diploma which, I understand, has a real value. I am now pretty sure of making advertising my real route to bread and butter, and have a strong notion that as a copy writer I will eventually make a "whiz". Next week I start out on a job bossing four men distributing hand-bills from house to house. This is only a temporary affair, as I want something much better when I can get it. Naturally I will not care to work long at 2.50 per day. If anything, this is a symbol of my need for cash. Write soon and complete, dear old Boy.

your affectionate, Hart

To Gorham Munson

Cleveland, Ohio
Dear Gorham:—　　　　　　　　　　　　October 6, 1921

Here you are with the rest of the Chaplin poem. I know not if you will like it,—but to me it has a real appeal. I have made that "infinitely gentle, infinitely suffering thing" of Eliot's into the symbol of the kitten. I feel that, from my standpoint, the pantomime of Charlie represents fairly well the futile gesture of the poet in U.S.A. today, perhaps elsewhere too. And yet, the heart lives on. . . .

Maybe this is because I myself feel so particularly futile just now that I feel this pathos, (or is it bathos?). Je ne sais pas.

Yesterday I worked my first day foremaning three men on a distribution job, and walked untold miles of city blocks. I am stiff,—but the exercise did me much good. No work today— perhaps tomorrow. At this work the most I can hope to get before spring is $30.00 per week. Yesterday brought me $2.00. Needless to say, I will look for something better as soon as I can get hands on it.

A new light and friend of my friend, the Swiss-French painter, Willy Lescaze, has arrived in town,—Jean Binet, teacher of Eurythmics in our very alive Cleveland School of Music which Ernest Bloch heads. I am to meet him tonight and with some anticipations, as I am told he is a remarkable and inspired amateur pianist, playing Erik Satie, Ravel, etc. to perfection. Lescaze has proved an inspiration to me. Knowing intimately the work of Marcel Proust, Salmon, Gide, and a host of other French moderns, he is able to see so much better than anyone else around here, the aims I have in my own work. We have great times discussing the merits of mutual favorites like Joyce, Donne, Eliot, Pound, de Gourmont, Gordon Craig, Nietzsche etc ad infinitum. After this it goes without saying that I never found a more stimulating individual in N.Y. Sommer has been too busy looking for a house in the city to be seen for several weeks.

Thanks for the Breton peasants! And send me all the "views" you can, your own predominating. Please give my regards to Liza.

As always, HART

"Chaplinesque"
To Charles Chaplin

We make our meek adjustments,
contented with such random consolations
as the wind deposits
in slithered and too ample pockets

For we can still love the world, who find
a famished kitten on the step, and know

recesses for it from the fury of the street,
or warm torn elbow coverts.

We will side-step, and to the final smirk,
daily the doom of that inevitable thumb
that slowly chafes toward us its puckered index,
facing the dull squint with what innocence
and what surprise!

And yet these fine collapses are not lies
more than the pirouettes of any pliant cane;
our obsequies are, in a way, no enterprise.
We can evade you, and all else but the heart:
what blame to us if the heart live on.

The game enforces jerks; but we have seen
the moon in lonely alleys make
a grail of laughter of an empty ash can,
and through all sound of gaiety and quest
we heard a kitten in the wilderness.

To William Wright

Cleveland, Ohio
Dear William:—   October 17, 1921

I can come half way with you about Edna Millay,—but I fear
not much further. She really has genius in a limited sense, and
is much better than Sara Teasdale, Marguerite Wilkinson, Lady
Speyer, etc. to mention a few drops in the bucket of feminine
lushness that forms a kind of milky way in the poetic firma-
ment of the time (likewise all times); indeed I think she is
every bit as good as Elizabeth Browning. And here it will be
probably evident that most of her most earnest devotees could
not ask for more. I can only say that I also do not greatly care
for Mme. Browning. And on top of my dislike for this lady,
Tennyson, Thompson, Chatterton, Byron, Moore, Milton,
and several more, I have the apparent brassiness to call myself
a person of rather catholic admirations. But you will also
notice that I *do* run joyfully towards Messrs. Poe, Whitman,
Shakespeare, Keats, Shelley, Coleridge, John Donne!!!, John

Webster!!!, Marlowe, Baudelaire, Laforgue, Dante, Cavalcanti, Li Po, and a host of others. Oh I wish we had an evening to talk over poetic creeds,—it is ridiculous to attempt it in a letter. I can only apologize by saying that if my work seems needlessly sophisticated it is because I am only interested in adding what seems to me something really *new* to what *has* been written. Unless one has some new, intensely personal viewpoint to record, say on the eternal feelings of love, and the suitable personal idiom to employ in the act, I say, why write about it? Nine chances out of ten, if you know where in the past to look, you will find words already written in the more-or-less exact tongue of your soul. And the complaint to be made against nine out of ten poets is just this,—that you are apt to find their sentiments much better expressed perhaps four hundred years past. And it is not that Miss Millay fails entirely, but that I often am made to hear too many echoes in her things, that I cannot like her as well as you do. With her equipment Miss Millay is bound to succeed to the appreciative applause of a fairly large audience. And for you, who I rather suppose have not gone into this branch of literature with as much enthusiasm as myself, she is a creditable heroine.

I admit to a slight leaning toward the esoteric, and am perhaps not to be taken seriously. I am fond of things of great fragility, and also and especially of the kind of poetry John Donne represents, a dark musky, brooding, speculative vintage, at once sensual and spiritual, and singing rather the beauty of experience than innocence.

As you did not "get" my idiom in "Chaplinesque," I feel rather like doing my best to explain myself. I am moved to put Chaplin with the poets (of today); hence the "we". In other words, he, especially in *The Kid* made me feel myself, as a poet, as being "in the same boat with" him. Poetry, the human feelings, "the kitten", is so crowded out of the humdrum, rushing, mechanical scramble of today that the man who would preserve them must duck and camouflage for dear life to keep them or keep himself from annihilation. I have since learned that I am by no means alone in seeing these things in the buffooneries of the tragedian, Chaplin, (if you want to read the opinions of the London and Paris presses, see *Literary Digest*, Oct. 8th) and in the poem I have tried to express these "social sympathies" in words corresponding somewhat to the antics of the actor. I may have failed, as only a small number of those I have shown it to have responded with any clear answer,—but on the other hand, I realize that the audience for my work will always be quite small. I freely admit to a liking for the thing, myself,—in fact I have to like something of my own once in awhile being so hard to please anyway.

The job I mentioned lasted just one day. I took the men out and carried the thing through to success, sore feet, and numb limbses,—but,—there was no work for the next day, nor the next,—and I got tired of trailing around hoping for only 2.50 for a fortune, and don't care whether there is little or much awaiting me there now, having hit the employment trail again toward other fields. When I get pastured again, I'll praise even Miss Millay—may even buy her *Second April* (if it is in Season) and not bore you so much with long diatribes on Poetry. Just now, though, that is all I have. Can't even buy the books I long to read, like *Three Soldiers, Erik Dorn,* and the new *Little Review* (Quarterly-AND $2.00). Write soon and cheer me up. Just for fun, look up the poems of Donne in the Library and read some of the short lyrics like "The Apparition", "A Jet Ring Sent", "The Prohibition", "The Ecstasy", and some of the longer things like "The Progress of the Soul", etc. if you feel intrigued.

Affectionately, Hart

To Gorham Munson

Cleveland, Ohio
Dear Gorham:— November 26, 1921

How you do ricochet about, tour a tour, and I here, biting and munching my nails with envy! I would like to see the Lewis hotel decors, perhaps more charming even than the rustic kitchen in Sommer's house where flamboyant roosters chase flies about the ceiling. I imagine you have found London already a temptation against Paris, that is, for a certain mood. At least I have heard there is a kind of atavism attacks the American in London that he is suddenly introduced to on arrival.

I've been having a wonderful time diving into Ben Johnson, so you see I haven't been so far off, after all. After one has read *Bartholomew Fair* it can't be so hard to see where Synge got his start,—a start toward a husky folk-element in the drama. I can see myself from now rapidly joining Josephson in a kind of Elizabethan fanaticism. You have doubtless known my long-standing friendship with Donne, Webster, and Marlowe. Now I have another Mermaid 'conjugal' to strengthen the tie. The fact is, I can find nothing in modern work to come up to the verbal richness, irony and emotion of these folks, and I would like to let them influence me as much as they can in the inter-pretation of modern moods,—somewhat as Eliot has so beau-tifully done. There are parts of his "Gerontion" that you can find almost bodily in Webster and Johnson. Certain Eliza-bethans and Laforgue have played a tremendous part in Eliot's work, and you can catch hints of his great study of these writers in his "Sacred Grove". I don't want to imitate Eliot, of course,—but I have come to the stage now where I want to carefully choose my most congenial influences and, in a way, "cultivate" their influence. I can say with J that the problem of form becomes harder and harder for me every day. I am not at all satisfied with anything I have thus far done, mere win-nowings, and too slight to satisfy me. I have never, so far, been able to present a vital, living and tangible,—a positive emotion to my satisfaction. For as soon as I attempt such an act I either grow obvious or ordinary, and abandon the thing at the second line. Oh! it is hard! One must be drenched in words, literally soaked with them to have the right ones form them-selves into the proper pattern at the right moment. When they come, as they did in "Pastorale" (thin, but rather good) they come as things in themselves; it is a matter of felicitous jug-gling!; and no amount of will or emotion can help the thing a bit. So you see I believe with Sommer that the "Ding an Sich" method is ultimately the only satisfactory creative principle to follow. But I also find that J stirred up a hornet's nest in me this summer with his words about getting away from current for-mulae, from Heine to Wallace Stevens, by experimentation in original models etc. and my reaction to this stimulation is to work away from the current impressionism as much as possible. I mean such "impressionism" as the Cocteau poem (trans.) in the *Little Review,* which you have probably seen. Dada (maybe I am wrong but you will correct me), is nothing more than the dying agonies of this movement, maladie moderne. I may even be carried back into "rime and rhythm" before I get through provided I can carry these encumbrances as deftly and un-self-consciously as, say Edward Thomas sometimes did. I grow to like my "Black Tambourine" more, for this reason, than before. It becomes in my mind a kind of diminutive model of ambition, simply pointing a direction. S'much for this endless tirade, but write as usual and keep me cheered and momentarily thrilled.

Maybe J. has already started his novel, burlesquing the Americans in the Quartier that he intended. Tell him to send me some poetry, anything he is writing. It's sure to be better than anything the magazines offer here.

Vale, HART

To Gorham Munson

Cleveland, Ohio
Dear Gorham:—   December 10

Your letter in French (which innovation I like) reached me yesterday; a welcome evening stimulant after the day's work. For I am, in a way, very glad to announce that I've been busy for the last two weeks at selling books in a store here during the seasonal "rush." This is, in all probability, entirely a temporary tent for me,—but it has enabled me, though intensely occupied, to get free of the money-complex that had simply reduced me to ashes. This item added to a total lack of my sex life for a long period had left me so empty that I gave up insulting you with a mere heap of bones for a letter, and though I haven't more to offer you now, I have sufficient interest again in the activity of writing to make my meagreness seem less obvious. Erotic experience is stumbled upon occasionally by accident, and the other evening I was quite nicely entertained in my usual way, of course. And thus the spell is broken! I can't help remarking also that this "breaker of the spell" is one very familiar with your present haunts, "La Rotonde" etc. etc. only of a few years back. You see, then, that one may enjoy a few Parisian sophistications even in Cleveland!

The *Ulysses* situation is terrible to think on. I shall be eternally grateful to you if you can manage to smuggle my already-subscribed-for copy home with you. If this will in any chance be possible, please let me send you the cash for purchase etc. at the proper time. I *must* have this book!

De Gourmont's *Une Coeur Virginal* has just been published here, (trans. by Aldous Huxley) and I have snatched it up against its imminent suppression along with *Jurgen* and other masterpieces. If this is a fair sample of its author and it's supposed to be, I cannot see how his *Physique d'Amour* translated by Pound and to be published by Boni & Liveright, will ever get beyond the printers' hands. Yet how mellow and kindly is the light from de Gourmont! One hates to see him on the tables with Zane Grey and Rex Beach. Maybe, after all, (and since I have procured my volumes), it will not be so heart-rending to see the "destruction" of the jealous Puritan at work again. Two weeks of book-service to the "demands of the public" in a store have bred curious changes of attitude toward the value of popularity (of the slightest sort) in my mind. The curious "unread" that slumber lengthily on the shelves, and whose names are never called, are much nearer my envy than I had once thought they might be from the mere standpoint of neglect. This pawing over of gift-book classics in tooled leather bindings etc. etc, is a sight to never forget. Poor dear Emerson must slumber badly. Aristocratic is Whitman though, —no one ever calls for that "democrat" any more than for Landor or Donne. Edgar Guest and Service, death's heads both, are rampant.

Of course you have heard of Anderson's winning of the *Dial* prize. I was quite certain of it anyway, but intensely gratified at the fact nonetheless. He will probably go to Mexico now as money was all he needed. He wrote me an answer recently to my criticism of *Erik Dorn,* praising parts of it much and slamming others. The book still puzzles me, which makes me dislike it a little more than ever. As a whole it is deficient, but I have always admitted certain parts good. But when one compares it with such a book as Anderson's *Triumph of the*

Egg it fades out terribly. This latter is an anthology of recent short stories of Anderson, and re-reading them together I get the most violent reaction. He has written of ghastly desolations which are only too evident in my own experience and on every hand. I am more enthusiastic than ever in my praise for him although I feel, in an odd way, that he has, like a diver, touched bottom in a certain sense, and that his future work must manifest certain changes of a more positive character than the bare statement of reality, or conclude his promise.

I am extremely urgent to know some of your impressions of the author of *Tarr* and await your letter with great expectations.

As always, Hart

To Gorham Munson

Dear Gorham:— December 25, 1921

Your letter arriving a few days ago, of the 5th, and the note of the seventh announcing my presence on the boulevards (in Chaplinesque attire) have provided me with rich materials for a kind of Christmas tree, at least as thrilling as any of remotest childhood memories. Names and presences glitter and fascinate with all kinds of exotic suggestions on the branches. I can be grateful to you for the best of Christmas donations, as I can thank you for the main part of my mental and imaginative sustenance of the last six months, weary and tormented as they have been. And now things seem, at least, to look a little better for me. I have been asked to remain on for a brief period in the capacity of book-clerk, and there is a possibility in sight of my gaining a very promising position in a very high-class advertising house here that has the attraction of the best connections with the largest agencies in New York and elsewhere. At least my interview with the "authorities" there today proved favorable to me, and if I can only manage to write them the proper kind of letter and "sell myself" as they ridiculously put it, I may secure myself something profitable. Leastwise, however, I have paid off an obligation that worried me and had a little change to spend during the last few weeks which has worked unbelievable miracles on my spirit. My work has been so hectic during the last month that I have not had time to write you, much less poems, but I have a feeling that now that the rush is over and the New Year started, I shall again do something. You see I am promising again.

You cannot imagine how interesting to me have been your opinions of the personalities you have come in contact with. Your opportunities in this direction have far exceeded my happiest anticipations for you. It strikes me that you have met about all the personalities in the younger left-wing at all worth while. It must indeed have been hard for you to have torn yourself from that scintillating metropolis of the world, and I have doubts about your finding Italy as actively stimulating. Of course there is all the (almost, I imagine) oppressing congregation of concrete and exterior magnificence, but the ideas, les idees, are far less in evidence there. That may make it the place of all Europe now for you to assimilate what you have gobbled in Paris, and perhaps an ideal resort for the pouring forth of the creative broth so richly agitated already in you. I hope to see more soon of what you have been writing, and maybe this will give you time to copy off a thing or two and send me.

It has been very gratifying, also, to hear of your amiable progress with Josephson. His "tightening and hardening" effect on one is exactly the compliment I owe to him. In a way he is as cold as ice, having a most astonishing faculty for depersonization,—and on the other hand, you have no doubt found a certain affectionate propensity in his nature that is doubly pleasant against the rather frigidly intellectual relief of the rest of him. He likes you much, and wrote me so, also sending me some poems to submit to the *D.D.* which I cannot fancy as having a ghost of a show in such an uneven corner. But he needs money, and I shall be glad to do anything in my power to help him along,—not worrying, however, very, very much, as he has a flexibility and resourcefulness that I envy.

The Dec. *Gargoyle* has not reached me yet, but probably will next week. If you have not sent more than one copy, could you possibly have three or four more sent soon? The table of contents you wrote sounds very appetising. I may get together some things of Bill Sommer's and Lescaze, things not too large to suffer too much in transit, and submit them. Sommer is burgeoning every day the more with the wonderful genius he has, and Lescaze is doing, so far as I can judge, work as good as any of the sophisticated Parisians. Of course he is really one of them, a year in America not being quite sufficient to dilute his natural acquirements there. He has recently gone to New York for a few days and expects to meet Paul Rosenfeld, who has seen some of his work recently and is reported to have liked it. This in the light of Rosenfeld's growing prestige, may mean a good deal to him. If I were only in N.Y.C. I should see to it that S's work were given its due,—but that time will have to wait. Meanwhile he shows not the slightest inclination to wilt. As I said, his achievements present one gorgeous surprise after another. A mutual friend of our's here recently died, a Nietzschian and thorough appreciator of all the best, who has pursued his lonely way in America since the age of fifteen when he left his family in Norway on account of religious differences. Bill and I were among the pall-bearers at this funeral, where were only a few others present, although all appreciative of what the man was. I can't go into detail, but the affair was tremendous, especially the finale at the crematorium. It was beautiful, but left me emotionally bankrupt last Sunday, the day following. That funeral was one of the few beautiful things that have happened to me in Cleveland.

Now for a brief resumé of American literature. It is, in a way, hopefully significant that Anderson's *Winesburg* has been issued by Boni and Liveright in their Modern Library with a very fine introduction by Ernest Boyd which gives much praise to the *L.R.* for having had the acumen to introduce Anderson to the world. I think I wrote you my impressions from a second reading of the stories included in the *Triumph of the Egg* book. Brown has recently issued an Aldous Huxley trans. of De Gourmont's *Une Coeur Virginale* that I have enjoyed, but which stands every chance of being suppressed on account of the signs of life in it.

The *Dial* for December has a fine article in it on American painting by Rosenfeld, singling out Hartley for extra and very intelligent praise. It also includes a very good poem by Malcolm Cowley, a rather disappointing article on Flaubert by Middleton Murry, and an atrocious piece of dull nonsense by Bodenheim. The new *Shadowland* is far from thrilling as those tepid baths it did offer last summer, and the *Ladies Home Journal* and the *Atlantic* are as bouncing as ever.

This all for tonight. We have a houseful of indiscriminate relatives and it has been hard to collect myself for even this pot-pourri, but I have more to say when I can get to it. I need time (a natural requirement with me for all writing or thought) to sit Bhudda-like for a couple of hours every day and let things sift themselves into some semblance of order in my brain. But I haven't had the opportunity for such operations for weeks, and may never,—until which time I pray you be contented as you can by such thrusts in haste as this letter.

Your figure haunts me like a kind of affectionate caress through all sorts of difficulties. You are always my final and satisfactory "court of appeal," and it is useless to attempt to tell you how much this means to me. So believe me when I tell you that I love you, and plan and plan for that glorious day when we shall get knees together under the table and talk, and talk, and talk. The inefficacy of my letters to you always troubles me.

As ever, your HART

To Sherwood Anderson

1709 East 115th Street
Cleveland, Ohio
January 10

Dear Anderson:—

Waiting on shoppers in a book store during the holiday hurricane deferred my answer to your letter. I was glad to get any kind of work, however, after my empty-pocketed summer and fall. Now I am working as a copywriter for the Corday and Gross Co., here which you may have heard of. I like this better than any bread-and-butter work I've ever done. You were right about the real estate job. Ogling poor people for small investments against their will didn't appeal to me very long. I had given it up before you wrote.

If I can satisfy the requirements of my position here, I shall feel a little hope returning for the satisfaction of a few aims again. I mean, of course, to turn out a little verse or prose this winter. When out of work I am not able to rid myself of worries enough to accomplish anything. Some pecuniary assurances seem necessary to me to any opening of the creative channels. Now things begin to look a little better for me.

I saw your story "The Contract" in the last *Broom,* and would like to offer a criticism. It may be an infraction, but if it is I want to ask your forgiveness. This story in some ways strikes me as inferior to the intensity and beauty of your other recent work, and I have an idea that it is something you wrote quite a while ago. Coming from anyone else, I would think, "This is good; but this fellow is trying to imitate Anderson and can't quite do it."

I wouldn't attempt any suggestions nor try to point out any places. Your work is always too much a composite whole for that critical sort of prodding to yield anything. I only felt this story as somehow an anti-climax to the amazing sense of beauty I recently got in re-reading the short stories you have done during the last few years that are collected together in the *Egg* volume. Please pardon me for this doubtless unnecessary comment. It is only in light of my own desires and feelings in such circumstances that I have ventured it.

In my own work I find the problem of style and form becoming more and more difficult as time goes on. I imagine that I am interested in this style of writing much more than you are. Perhaps, though, we include the same features under different terms. In verse this feature can become a preoccupation, to be enjoyed for its own sake. I do not think you will sympathize with me very strongly on this point, but, of course, if you got as much pleasure out of finding instances of it in other writers as I do, you would see what I mean. For instance, when I come to such a line as the following from John Donne,—I am thrilled—

> "Thou shallt not peep through lattices of eyes,
>   Nor hear through labyrinths of ears, nor learn
>   By circuit or collections to discern; etc."

Or take another, called "The Expiration"

> "So, so break off this last lamenting kiss,
>   Which sucks too souls and vapours both away:

Turn thou, ghost, that way, and let me turn this,
   And let ourselves benight our happiest day;
We ask none leave to love; nor will we owe
   Any so cheap a death, as saying, go.

Go; and if that word have not quite killed thee,
   Ease me with death by bidding me go too;
Or if it have, let my word work on me,
   And a just office on a murderer do;
Except it be too late to kill me so,
   Being double dead, going, and bidding go."

What I want to get is just what is so beautifully done in this poem, an "interior" form, a form that is so thorough and intense as to dye the words themselves with a peculiarity of meaning, slightly different maybe from the ordinary definition of them separate from the poem. If you remember my "Black Tambourine" you will perhaps aggree with me that I have at least accomplished this idea once. My aims make writing slow for me, and so far I have done practically nothing,—but I can wait for slow improvements rather more easily than I can let a lot of stuff loose that doesn't satisfy me. There is plenty of that in the publishing houses and magazines every day to amuse the folks that like it. This may very well be a tiresome ranting for you, but I think you will like the quotations anyway.

What are you going to do this winter: go to Mexico as you had thought of? I was all ready to scrape around for money enough to start for Europe when this job came along, and I thought I had better take it. Two friends of mine, however, have been in Paris for some time, writing me letters that made me foam at my moorings, and the desire to break loose has been strong.

If you aren't too busy write me. A friend of mine, Lescaze, was in N.Y. over Christmas and says he had a very pleasant talk with you one evening at Paul Rosenfeld's.

                          Your's, Hart Crane

To Gorham Munson

Dear Gorham:—   January 23, 1922

I come to my first evening, free and alone, in some time, and recognize quite plainly that I have neglected you. There are so many rather interesting people around this winter that there is always something or other doing. A concert to go to, a soiree, —and then since I have been writing ads a certain amount of hangover work to be done evenings sometimes,—that altogether I don't like it. But I like my work and am wonderfully treated at the office. Never guessed a commercial institution could be organized on such a decent basis. And they actually will come of their own accord and tell you that they are pleased with the work you are doing for them!!!!!!!!!!! I pass my goggle-eyed father on the street now without a tremor! I go on mad carrouses with Bill Sommer wherein we begin with pig's feet and sauercraut and end with Debussy's "Gradus ad Parnassum" in the "ivory tower". Around Ernest Bloch at the Institute of Music here are gathered some interesting folks from all over everywhere. There is even a french restaurant here where the proprietress stands at the cashier's desk reading *La Nouvelle Revue Francaise* and where wonderful steaks with mushrooms are served—alas, everything, including real garcons, except vin. The place looks like a sentence without any punctuation, or, if you prefer, this letter.

And now, mon cher, willy-nilly as it all may be, we come to your magazine. I don't want to hurt you at all, but I must confess to little or no enthusiasm at the prospect of another small magazine, full of compressed dynamite as your's might well be. Unless one has half a million or so, what's the use of adding to the other little repercussions that dwindle out after a few issues!? Don't waste your time with it all, is my advice. Much better sit down and pound on your typewriter, or go toting mss around to stolid editors. Listen,—there is now *some* kind of magazine that will print one's work however bad or good it is. The "arty" book stores bulge and sob with them all. I pray you invest your hard-earned money in neckties, theatre tickets or something else good for the belly or the soul,—but don't throw it away in paper and inffiecient typography.

Don't come home three months sooner for the prospects of that rainbow.

No one will especially appreciate it and it will sour your mouth after all the vin rouge you have been drinking. By all this you must not think that I have joined the Right Wing to such an extent that I am rollicking in F. Scott Fitzgerald. No, —but by the straight and narrow path swinging to the south of the village DADA I have arrived at a somewhat and abashed posture of reverence before the statues of Ben Jonson, Michael Drayton, Chaucer, sundry others already mentioned. The precious rages of dear Matty somehow don't seem to swerve me from this position. He is, it strikes me, altogether unsteady. Of course, since Mallarme and Huysmans were elegant weepers it is up to the following generation to haw-haw gloriously! Even dear old Bhudda-face de Gourmont is passé. Well, I suppose it is up to one in Paris to do as the Romans do, but it all looks too easy to me from Cleveland, Cuyahoga County, God's Country. But Matty will always glitter when he walks provided the man in front of him has not sparkled,—which we hope he never does, of course,—and so I am happy to hear from him always about his latest change of mind. Quite seriously Matty is thrilling, in prose especially. His performance is always aggreeable despite my inability to sympathize with his theories. Paris seems to be a good place for him to work and I suppose he will stay there at least until his contes are published.

This is all for now, I've got some work to do. When you get back here I want you to come to Cleveland for a fortnight's visit. Also, I may come to New York on my vacation this summer; I expect to have one, you know.

Write me soon, and never mind about the Joyce. I am not anxious enough to have it strain my pocketbook this week, and it can be procured later anyway.

As ever, HART

To William H. Wright

Dear Bill: Saturday, February 11, 1922
    Don't let me keep on worrying. Your visit was a great pleasure to me, resulting in the renewal of old contacts and the

discoveries of many new ones. I am so much interested in you now, that I am in danger of pestering you with all kinds of advice and admonitions. One of these is not to let the caprices of any unmellow ladies result in your unbalance or extreme discomfiture. Even the best of them, at times, know not and care not what they do. They have the faculty of producing very debilitating and thoroughly unprofitable effects on gentlemen who put themselves too much in their hands. Woman was not meant to occupy this position. It was only the Roman Catholic Church who gave it to her. Greeks, Romans, and Egyptians knew better how to handle her. I suggest your reading De Gourmont's *Virgin Heart* for a delicate dissection of this kind of problem. De Gourmont was something more than a purely "literary critic," you know. He was one of the most thorough students of physiology and psychology of the modern world. He was an adept scientist of the emotions. Stendhal was another, but less clear.

All this suffering is quite romantic and beautiful, you know, but you pay a stupid price for it. I can't help saying these things because of my interest and because I saw you go away in ominous style. I hope you haven't been ill, and that you have merely forgotten to write me.

I have been through two or three of these cataclysms myself, harder than your's because of their unusual and unsympathetic situations. Maybe I have gained something by them, I don't know,—but it is certain that I lost a great deal too.

Anyway, let me hear from you soon.

Yours, HART

To William Wright

Jamestown

Dear Bill: March 2, 1922

This is my second excursion to this place, no doubt somewhat familiar to you,—having been here part of last week. It's a matter of business for the Co. ("investigation of the product", in ad. lingo) and I rather enjoy getting out of Cleveland for a day or so. I've been getting out a catalog for the Art

Metal folks here and puzzling my head over blue prints and figures until I have become somewhat dull. I hope to get back home in time to listen to the concert Saturday when Ernest Block conducts for several of his new compositions. This would be enough to brighten even the following Sunday!

By this time I suppose you are back again and full tilt in your customary carousels. I was glad to know that the trouble with you was only "physiological". By this time you have probably read some of De Gourmont's observations on that sort of thing, and, wise man!, were fully experienced to appreciate them. What an awful lot of novel forms there are! The novel is the most flexible literary form there is. It permits the freest and completest expression. Have you read Louis Hemon's "Maria Chapdelaine" yet? The young French emmigrant who wrote it died shortly afterward, but for what it intends it is one of the most finished things one could hope for. Human emotion in it is like delicate pastel tinted flowers on a background of midnight black. The black terrific power of the forest and winter threatens continually behind every word in the action. But I am no where near so enthused about this book as I am about Gogol's "Taras Bulba" that I read on the train recently. I think someone has called it the Russian "Iliad". It is certainly not secondary to the Iliad in many ways. That sting and tang of those Cossack adventures are something I won't forget, and the hero, old Taras, is altogether memorable. This is something you *must* read.

I don't want to go any further without thanking you for your Ballade. I find so much that is good in it that I am tempted beyond the proper respect for your very degage gesture of presentation in your letter, and want to risk the impropriety of some criticism of it. The main faults of it are faults inherent with the form you used. I do not, as you know, insist by any means on vers libre forms. But it is just when I see such a thing as your ballade with the (unavoidable) tiresome repetitions of sound or rhyme, that I am most moved to applaud even the slouchy vers libre work that seems to "get over" its meaning or lack of meaning at least without that mechanical insistence of certain formal patterns that can sometimes enfuriate me. For instance, after "sweet, feet, deceit, conceit, and fleet" have all successively pecked at the ear, along comes "discreet retreat"!!

giving the whole poem at the point a tone of the neatest mean-
ness. And that sort of tone is exactly what you do not want,—
at least not along with some of your quite exquisite imagery
that speaks in largeness of a full heart.

The first verse, the first four lines especially, is fine, and the
idea behind that "discreet retreat behind sophistications of
bread and meat" is good. It would be improved by using an-
other and richer word than sophistications just to *improve* the
sophistication a little, however. I feel this way,—that however
you wrote this poem,—in jest, literary exercise, or emotionally,
—it proves distinct poetic possibilities in you, which, whether
you care to follow or not, are still there. Why don't you work
this poem into an easier form or perhaps into a vers libre form?
I could do it to show you what I mean, but that would take all
the fun out of it for you. Forms as strict as the ballade, can, in
my opinion, be used satisfactorily for only very artificial sub-
jects, or abstract themes.

I've been doing something myself, but don't feel satisfied
enough with it yet to send it. Write me soon, won't you?

Hart

To Gorham Munson

Dear Gorham: April 19—'22
Your letter dated Vienna, April 3rd, has just come,—
announcing among other things your reception of "Praise for
an Urn." Since writing this I hope you have somehow or other
read my letter withdrawing this poem on account of its being
taken by the Dial. If you haven't, I must blush with chagrin.
My letter explains that at the time of sending you the "opus"
the same was still in the hands of the Dial, although it had
been there so long that I assumed their rejection. A thousand
apologies, dear Gorham, your present and awfully fine letter
will serve to make me more careful in the future. And now I
breathe easier!

The two copies of "Secession" reached me yesterday. Of
course they were immediately and doubly devoured. But
right here I ought to stop—I have so many things to say about

it. If it would serve as an inducement I should certainly bolt dead and refuse to write you a word more beyond a violent invitation to Cleveland. But I know that you will come if you can—anyway,—and so I will let myself off—though rather sketchily.

I find I have many, at least several disagreements with you. I can't say nearly so much for Matty's poem as you do—I mean the Café phallicus. The Tzara poem is perfectly flat. The Cowley poem is encouraging, although dreadfully like something he had published in one of the last L.Rs. The Aragon prose is, in its odd way, a quite beautiful thing. But what has happened to Matty!?! And,—just *why* is Appolinaire so portentous a god? Will radios, flying machines, and cinemas have such a great effect on poetry in the end? All this talk of Matty's is quite stimulating, but it's like coffee,—twenty-four hours afterward not much remains to work with. It is metallic and pointillistic—not derogatory terms to my mind at all, but somehow thin,—a little too slender and "smart"—after all.

O Matty *must* be amusing himself perfectly in Paris. And so he took you to be a real, honest-to-God disreputable and commercial editor! Serve you right, you bad boy, following the primrose path of the magazines!

But please don't misunderstand my antics. The greatest and the highest truth is that I am very anxious to see you. Can't you come at once for a two weeks visit—ample accommodations, ivory tower. Back to Raoul and Pizetti, Bill Sommer, Lescaze, Cadillac light, etc, etc. I'm expecting you. Wire me the hour you arrive.

Hart

To Gorham Munson

May 16, 1922

Hooray! Whoop La! that little note on the back of the envelope meant a lot to me. And I somehow feel good that you are once more with me on the same stretch of land! Jump right on the train, old dear, and I'll meet you at the station. I'm very anxious to see you. I want you to meet this *great* Bill Sommer

—and tell me all about all you have done and seen. I have the assurance now that you'll come as soon as you can get the money, and it makes me quite happy.

Your rough & tedious transition back to the States gave you a good chance to prepare for the surprises of New York—there must have been some new aspects of the place awaiting you. I know that even a few months in the West Indies and Canada open your eyes to new things on your return. Of course there will be only too evident all the old aggravations,—but from occasional references in your letters I judge that you have more than once been touched by these same things during the last six months. The world is becoming fast standardized,— and who knows but what our American scene will be the most intricate and absorbing one in fifty years or so?

Something is happening. Some kind of aristocracy of taste is being established—there is more of it evidenced every year. People like you, Matty and I belong here. Especially Matty, who was doing better work last summer before he got in with the Paris crowd than I suspect since. I'm just wondering lately if one ought to consider the semitic element in him. Your comment in your letter aggrees with that characteristic as well,— and Jews are so damned adaptable. Matty has often boasted of that qualification. His present crazes are, frankly, beyond my understanding. They are so much so that I share a great deal of confidence that no matter how wild and eccentric he becomes, it's just a phase which will be a practical benefit in the end. But, on the other hand, if one denies all emotional suffering the result is a rather frigid (however "gay") type of work. Let us watch & pray!

I haven't half answered your letter or said all I want to,—but I have some advertising work to do at home this evening—a damned hot water heater campaign that has hung around for months—so I'll urge your visit again and promise a better answer to your next.

                                          Heartily, Hart

I got a charming note from Charlie Chaplin last week in response to the "Chaplinesque" that I sent him. How do you like my portrait?

To Gorham Munson

Dear Gorham:—   Same evening
   I forgot to mention that the art books reached me and how
pleased I am. Derain is one of my favorites—more even than
Matisse and Picasso—and Vlaminck I have long admired.
Marie Laurencin is amusing—but no more than any other
febrile female. Have you seen the amazing satires of (Georg?)
Grosz and the beautiful metaphysics of Chirico. My friend
Lescaze has put me in touch with a lot of moderns that I fear,
off here in Cleveland, I should otherwise never have heard of.
   I'm at work on a metaphysical attempt of my own—again I
mention the familiar "Faustus & Helen" affair which has re-
ceived a little stimulus lately. The trouble is,—I get so little *ex-
panse* of time undisturbed for it, that it's hopelessly
fragmentary so far.—Here is a tentative beginning:—

> "The mind has shown itself at times
>   Too much the baked & twisted dough,
>   Food for the accepted multitude.
>   The mind is brushed by sparrow wings;
>   Rebuffed by asphalt, numbers crowd
>   The margins of the day, accent the curbs,
>   Convoying diverse dawns on every corner
>   To druggist, barber, and tobacconist." etc.

   I wish you would tell me how you like my translations from
Laforgue's "Locutions des Pierrots" in the current *Double
Dealer.*
   You will notice below them a very interesting poem by Allen
Tate. This poem interested me so much that I wrote him a let-
ter and his answer reached me along with yours' today. He
lives at 2019 Broad St. Nashville, Tenn.—and he might he in-
terested in submitting something to *Secession.* I shall take the
liberty of urging him in that direction when I answer him. If
you are interested it might be good for you to write him too.
   Well—I must get at that "copy".
                                                        Hart

To Allen Tate

Cleveland, Ohio

Dear Allen Tate: May 16, 1922

Being born in '99, I too, have a little toe-nail in the last century. You are not alone in all your youth and disgrace! But perhaps the umbilical cord made a clean margin of it with you, for I am reminded that it is 1922 and there is a chance of that. I popped on the scene shortly after Independence Day! and consequently have always had a dread of firecrackers.

Despite all this desperate imminence, I want to thank you for your answer to my letter. It has thrown me clear off the advertising copy work I brought home with me (yes, I'm one of the band!) as I feel more like putting that off until tomorrow, than this. But on the other hand there are so many things I want to say that I don't know where to begin. Letters are sometimes worse than nothing, especially for introductions, so if I am chatty and autobiographical you must pardon it.

Certain educated friends of mine have lamented my scant education, not in the academic sense, but as regards my acceptance and enthusiasm about some modern french work without having placed it in relation to most of the older "classics," which I haven't read. I have offered apologies, but continued to accept fate, which seems to limit me continually in some directions. Nevertheless, my affection for Laforgue is none the less genuine for being lead to him through Pound and T. S. Eliot than it would have been through Baudelaire. There are always people to class one's admirations and enthusiasms illigitimate, and though I still have the dictionary close by when I take up a french book, a certain sympathy with Laforgue's attitude made me an easier translator of the three poems in the *D.D.* than perhaps an accomplished linguist might have been. However, no one ought to be particularly happy about a successful translation. I did them for fun, and it finally occurred to me that I might as well be paid for them.

As I said before, it is because your poem seemed so much in line with the kind of thing I am wanting to do, that I felt almost compelled to write to you. While I am always interested in the latest developements in poetry I am inveterately devoted to certain English old fellows that are a constant challenge. I refer to Donne, Webster, Jonson, Marlowe, Vaughan, Blake, etc. More "modernly", have you read and admired Yeats (later poems), Ezra Pound, T. S. Eliot, Edward Thomas, Wallace Stevens? I am missing a few, but I like all these people.

I am interested greatly in seeing your poems in the *Fugitive*. It occurs to me that my friend, Gorham Munson, editor of *Secession*, would possibly be interested in publishing some of your things, although he can't pay anything yet for mss. Notice and N.Y. address of his magazine are in the back pages of the current *D.D.* I am trying to give him something myself, but I write so little that I simply haven't anything. The last went to the *Dial* and ought to be out next month.

Don't tell me you like the enclosed poems unless you really do. You may have seen them in different places, but I'm in the dark as to that.

Fraternally, Hart Crane

P. S. Robinson is very interesting—his work is real and permanent, yet it also is a tragedy—one of the tragedies of Puritanism, materialism, America and the last century. Wm Vaughn Moody's beautiful tonality suffered in a kind of vacuum, too. We are more fortunate today despite Amy Lowell!

The poetry of negation is beautiful—alas, too dangerously so for one of my mind. But I am trying to break away from it. Perhaps this is useless, perhaps it is silly—but one *does* have joys. The vocabulary of damnations and prostrations has been developed at the expense of these other moods, however, so that it is hard to dance in proper measure. Let us invent an idiom for the proper transposition of jazz into words! Something clean, sparkling, elusive!

To Gorham Munson

Dear Gorham:—   May 25

Since writing you last a letter has come from Matty on the eve of his departure for Rome on his way to the Tyrol with Slater Brown for the summer. This is the first I have heard from Matty for several months, due, as he admits, to his sullenness.

Matty is easily piqued—all of which is quite delightful if you are depending on him for nothing. His letters are always amusing and stimulating—but I find myself so little in aggreement with him that I expect another breach of several months before the mood induced by my answer will leave him.

In this last he speaks in praiseful & very hopeful tones of *Secession* (which includes you, of course) so I assume that you are reinstated in his affections. He plans a series of wild stories,—"each getting wilder than the next" to be conceived, spawned, or otherwise produced in the Hungarian Mts. Some kind of "Peregrination" story has been taken by the *D.D.* he says,—and it is doubtless very good. Everything within certain bounds that M. has written has been good.

This reminds me that a *Gargoyle* reached me yesterday containing your account of Vienna. Cowley's poem is somewhat obvious it strikes me. The rest of the magazine is certainly not worth 35¢. What an ineffectual slap on the wrist they administer *Secession!*

I took the *Secessions* down to Laukhuff and I hope they are being sold. I may not go in for a considerable period as Laukhuff has acted so strangely and unpleasantly to me several times lately that I have more-or-less made up my mind to keep away from him. His address is,—Richard Laukhuff, 40 Taylor Arcade, Cleveland.

I am glad you like my Lescaze "portrait." Three oils by L. are now on exhibition at the Montross gallery, if you care to look at them.

I have a bone to pick with you, or a misunderstanding to unravel. I am hoping you come to Cleveland soon,—it can't be too soon for me. All this talk from Matty on Appolinaire—about being gay and *so* distressingly and painfully delighted about the telegraph, the locomotive, the automat, the wireless, the street cars and electric lamp post, annoy me. There is no reason for *not* using them—but why is it so important to stick them in. I am interested in possibilities. Appollinaire lived in Paris, I live in Cleveland, Ohio. These quotidian conveniences so dear to him are not of especial pleasure to me here. I am not going to pity myself—but on the other hand, why should I stretch my face continually into a kind of "glad" expression.

Besides—sadness (you will shrink in horror at this) has a real and lasting appeal to me.

I am stubborn—and grow indifferent at times about all this mad struggle for advance in the arts. Every kind of conceivable work is being turned out today. Period styles of every description. Isn't it, after all, legitimate for me to write something the way I like to (for my own pleasure) without considering what school it harmonizes with?

I'm afraid I don't fit in your group, or any group, for all that. But there are so many things I want to talk over with you, I hope you'll come. Stay a month or so if possible.

As ever, Hart

To Gorham Munson

Dear Gorham: June 4, 1922

I cannot at the moment locate your last letter, so I may be omitting an answer to something in it. There is otherwise so little to offer except the quotidian complaints that I probably should not be here at the Corona were it not that I want you to see the new coin from the mint enclosed herewith.

I have been at it for the last 24 hours and it may be subjected to a few changes and additions, but as I see it now in the red light of the womb it seems to me like a work of youth and magic.

At any rate, it is something entirely new in English poetry, so far as I know. The jazz rhythms in that first verse are something I have been impotently wishing to "do" for many a day. It is the second part of the (three section) "Marriage of Faustus and Helen" that I must have tired you with mentioning. The other parts are entirely unlike it, and God knows when they will be done. The first part is just begun. However, I have considerable ambitions in this opus, as I have told you. Please let me know your sentiments regarding the enclosed.

The reassurance of your projected visit here makes me happy in spite of rose-fever cyclones. What talks we shall have! and there are three others here who have heard so much about you that they are anxious to meet you too. Bill Sommer has moved to his country place where the charming schoolhouse-studio is located. We shall have to spend a week-end there among the gay canvasses that line its walls.

Your affectionate HART

To Allen Tate

1709 East 115th Street
Cleveland, Ohio
June 12

Dear Allen:

So you are in love with the dear Duchess of Malfi also! How lovely she speaks in that one matchless passage:—

"Doth not the colour of my hair 'gin to change?
When I wax grey, I shall have all the court
Powder their hair with arras, to be like me.
You have cause to love me; I entered you into my heart
Before you would vouchsafe to call for the keys."

Exquisite pride surrendering to love! And it was this that faced all the brutality of circumstance in those hideous and gorgeous final scenes of the play! The old betrayals of life, and yet they are worth something—from a distance, afterward.

What you say about Eliot does not surprise me,—but you will recover from the shock. No one ever says the last word, and it is a good thing for you, (notice I congratulate myself!) to have been faced with him as early as possible. I have been facing him for *four* years,—and while I haven't discovered a weak spot yet in his armour,—I flatter myself a little lately that I have discovered a safe tangent to strike which, if I can possibly explain the position,—goes *through* him toward a *different* goal. You see it is such a fearful temptation to imitate him that at times I have been almost distracted. He is, you have now discovered, far more profound than Huxley (whom I like) or any others obviously under his influence. You will profit by reading him again and again. I must have read "Prufrock" twenty-five times and things like the "Preludes" more often. His work will lead you back to some of the Elizabethans and point out the best in them. And there is Henry James, Laforgue, Blake and a dozen others in his work. He wrote most of this verse between 22 and 25, and is now, I understand, dying piecemeal as a clerk in a London bank. In his own realm Eliot presents us with an absolute *impasse*, yet oddly enough, he can be utilized to lead us to, intelligently point to, other positions and "pastures new." Having absorbed him enough we can trust ourselves as never before, in the air or on the sea. I, for instance, would like to leave a few of his "negations" behind me, risk the realm of the obvious more, in quest of new sensations, *humeurs*. These theories and manoeuvres are consolatory,—but of course, when it comes right down to the act itself,—I have to depend on intuition, "inspiration" or what you will to fill up the page. Let us not be too much disturbed, antagonized or influenced by the fait accompli. For in the words of our divine object of "envy" ("Reflections on Contemporary Poetry," *Egoist*, London, '19)—"Admiration leads most often to imitation; we can seldome long remain unconscious of our imitating another, and the awareness of our imitation naturally leads us to hatred of the object imitated. If we stand toward a writer in this other relation of which I speak we do not imitate him, and though we are quite as

To Wilbur Underwood

1709 East 115th Street
Cleveland, Ohio

Dear Wilbur: June 15

This is written at the office, so you will have to excuse "mistic" language, paper, and haste. I can't seem to get anything done at home in the way of correspondence, so I'm taking a moment at noon.

My affairs, after a hectic few weeks, are at a low ebb, everybody being apparently determined to leave town either for vacations or permanently. Consequently it looks as though I were destined for several walks in the parks during the warm evenings coming.

Your letter was a most pleasant surprise, as usual replete with those delightful tid-bits touching on the simian favorite. I really feel flattered that she thinks and speaks of me often. Harry wrote me two wonderful letters about his "doings" when he was with you before his departure for Europe. I have had three letters since then,—one was an amazingly eloquent revelation of present-day, war-ridden London and his reactions to it. But I don't know what stamp his next letter will bear. He spoke of the cold weather in London, and mentioned Spain as an escape.

I am getting ready for a week's vacation the first week in August. That is the limit to my time this year with this company. But I hope to get down to New York to see some old friends, and if I have money enough, would like to run down to Washington for a day to see you and Mme. C——. I will let you know when to prepare!

Do you like my poem in the June *Dial*? I presume you have seen it by this time. I am trying hard to write a few worthwhile things, and at present am very much interested in a kind of metaphysical-quotidian combination called "Three Poems for the Marriage of Faustus and Helen", the second part of which, a jazz roof garden description in amazing language, is already completed.

I shall get *Memoirs of a Midget* on your recommendation. It must be very good. Otherwise I have lately enjoyed Aldous Huxley's *Crome Yellow* very much. Also Pound's trans. of de Gourmont's *Physique d'Amour* and that delightful *Moby Dick* of Melville's including the memorable and half-exciting erotic suggestions of dear Queequeg. Melville is probably an old story to you,—but until the recent craze about him, I never had heard of him.

Life is awful in Cleveland. . . . I must write a play or something that will give me enough for a place on Long Island or in the Jersey woods. The only real bright spot ahead this summer is a possible visit from Gorham Munson who has just got back from a year in Europe and brings me a copy (smuggled in) of Joyce's *Ulysses* that I ordered and paid for over a year ago.

As ever, Hart

To Gorham Munson

Apologies Later!

Dear Gorham!—   Sunday midnight

I have been in a house up in "Little Italy," a section of Secil-
ian immigrants very near our house where one can get good
three-year Chianti,— and incidentally am feeling very fine as
Sunday evenings go. *There* is the place to enjoy oneself in the
family parlour of a pickslinger's family with chromos on the
walls that are right in style of Derain and Vlaminck. Bitch dogs
and the rest of the family wander in while the bottle is still half
empty and some of the family offspring. *Tristram Shandy* read
to a friend with a Spanish "Bolero" going on the Victrola
sounds good in such a milieu! I never should live without
wine! When you come here we shall make many visits to this
charming family. You will like my classic, puritan, inhibited
friend, Sam Loveman who translates Baudelaire charmingly! It
is hard to get him to do anything outside the imagination,—
but he is charming, and has just given me a most charming
work on Greek Vases (made in Deutschland) in which Satyrs
with great erections prance to the ceremonies of Dionysios with
all the fervour of de Gourmont's descriptions of sexual sacri-
fices in *Physique d L'Amour* which I am lately reading in trans.

I am glad you like Lescaze's "portrait" of me. He *has* an ath-
letic style. Your criticism of painting et al strikes me as very
exact and appreciative—at least, as far as I am able to justly
criticize it. He hates Cleveland with all the awareness of the re-
cent description of this place accorded in the last *Masses* or *Lib-
erator*, as I understand. Just now I am in too banal a mood to
give sympathy to anything. At times dear Gorham, I feel an
enormous power in me—that seems almost supernatural. If this
power is not too dissipated in aggravation and discouragement
I may amount to something sometime. I can say this now with
perfect equanimity because I am notoriously drunk and the
Victrola is still going with that glorious "Bolero." Did I tell
you of that thrilling experience this last winter in the dentist's
chair when under the influence of aether and *amnesia* my
mind spiraled to a kind of seventh heaven of consciousness and

egoistic dance among the seven spheres—and something like an objective voice kept saying to me—"You have the higher consciousness—you have the higher consciousness. This is something that very few have. This is what is called genius"? A happiness, ecstatic such as I have known only twice in "inspirations" came over me. I felt the two worlds. And at once. As the bore went into my tooth I was able to follow its long revolution as detached as a spectator at a funeral. O Gorham, I have known moments in eternity. I tell you this as one who is a brother. I want you to know me as I feel myself to be sometimes. I don't want you to feel that I am conceited. But since this adventure in the dentist's chair, I feel a new confidence in myself. At least I had none of the ordinary hallucinations common to this operation. Even that means something. You know I live for work,—for poetry. I shall do my best work later on when I am about 35 or 40. The imagination is the only thing worth a damn. Lately I have grown terribly isolated, and very egoist. One has to do it Cleveland. I rush home from work to my room, hung with the creations of Sommer and Lescaze— and fiddle through the evenings. If I could afford wine *every* evening I might do more. But I am slow anyway. However, to-day I have made a good start on the first part of "Faustus & Helen". I am, needless to say, delighted that you like the second part so well. The other two parts are to be quite different. But, as yet, I am dubious about the successful eventuation of the poem as a *whole*. Certainly it is the most ambitious thing I have ever attempted and in it I am attempting to evolve a conscious pseudo-symphonic construction toward an abstract beauty that has not been done before in English—at least directly. If I can get this done in the way I hope—I might get some consideration for the *Dial* prize. Perhaps I'm a fool for such hopes—sooner or later I expect to get that yearly donation.

I can't give you any encouragement for a position in *my* own Co. for a position for the summer, but you might find a good place somewhere else here as—on a new Cleveland paper that has just started up—or why not work in a factory here this summer? It's only a few weeks. Certainly, somehow or other, dear Gorham, you must come. I will pay your way back—no need to worry about that! In the meantime don't let me languish too long!

Yours, Hart

Allen Tate's address is: 2019 Broad St, Nashville, Tenn. Please write him and send a copy of *Secession*—the poor boy has T.B. and genius, and is isolated from all the world we know. He has done wonders considering his handicaps. His letters to me of the past month prove this.   H. C.

I am not going to read this over in the clear sober light of the dawn. Take it for what it is worth tonight when I seal the envelope—*if* you can read it!

To Wilbur Underwood

Dear Wilbur: 4th of July WHOOPS!

I must get *Mortal Coils*. All of Huxley's stuff is worth reading. My memory serves me better than yours on *Crome Yellow*—I shall never forget that ornamental tower of the bowels nor the wonderful romance of the dwarves with their ponies. Nor Barbecue Smith, for all that. The younger generation in England today seems very tame beside the younger French and American crowd. So far as my ken swims it strikes me that Huxley has the field pretty much to himself in England,—and of course, he has been very much influenced by such people as Laforgue, de Gourmont, André Gide, etc. I often wish we could get together and read aloud,—there are so few people who like that mutual pastime any more, and beautiful prose should be read aloud to truly appreciate it.

I am afraid my trip to New York and Washington is as good as cancelled for this year. Sherwood Anderson is coming for a visit soon and Gorham Munson is coming on a little later to spend the rest of the summer here probably. As the first week in August is my only time away from the office you can see how it stands. I am, in a way, disappointed, but of course one can't expect to have everything. I should have liked to have seen you, drunk delicious brew at Mme. C——'s and seen her fly her fanny about in those new empire gowns you mention.

I have been driven at last to the parks. The first night brought me a most strenuous wooing and the largest instrument I have handled. Europa and the Bull are now entirely passé. As this happened only two nights ago, I am modest and satisfied. Still, I am uneasy. I fear for all the anti-climaxes that are surely now in store for me. Like Alec, I yearn for new worlds to conquer, and I fear that there are only a few insignificant peninsulas and archipelagoes left.

I am sorry to disappoint you about my "Praise". There were no accouchements there at all. Not even temptations in that direction. It is, or was, entirely "platonic". Nelson was a Norwegian who rebelled against the religious restrictions of home and came to America when a mere kid. Went to art school in Washington and won some kind of distinguished medal there. As soon as he was through school, an aunt of his in America who had been paying his tuition abruptly withdrew all her help and forced him into the prostitution of all his ideas and a cheap lithographic work that he was never able to pull out of afterward. He wrote several good poems published in *Scribners* and *Century* a long time ago, got married, and I finally met him here in Cleveland where he had been living in seclusion for a number of years. One of the best read people I ever met, wonderful kindliness and tolerance and a true Nietzschean. He was one of many broken against the stupidity of American life in such places as here. I think he has had a lasting influence on me.

To end in true Roman fashion—I am enclosing a letter from a former truck driver of my father's who left about the same time I did. We had great times together. I probably would not have continued as long there had it not been for his genial company. He was a pleasure to educate. The letter has references to his successor in the organization who is still in jail for getting drunk and shooting all over town.

By all means send me the papers. But don't let it become an effort.

As ever, H

Please return enclosed letter at your convenience.

To Allen Tate

Wednesday
Dear Allen: July 19, 1922

Just a word before I dive into the day's work,—and then more before the week is ended, when I will have more time. . . .

Let me salute you again. "Bored to Choresis" is as good as "Euthanasia",—if not better. You do the trick here. Your vocabulary is exceedingly interesting—you have a way of meticulously accenting certain things in a quiet, yet withal so sharp a note, that the effect is greater than as though you roared. "Tribal library", "Her rhythms are reptilian and religious", etc. are excellent. And then, of course, I like your lunge at the bourgeois literary biographical interests. No one has ever put it better than you have.

You see what is good about this poem of yours is over and above the merely personal sketches and digs that Robinson has been getting you into. Here you come into something larger, as you did in "Euthanasia", where you hit all humanity a few slaps, but in so interesting a way! In other words,—this poem is *creative* where the ordinary "character" portrait is merely analytic and, generally, unimportant (at least in poetry). You needn't be afraid of running too squarely into Eliot with work like this.

I would like to see you follow out the directions indicated in this poem—not their downward slant (interesting enough), but (if you get what I mean) their upward slant into something broadly human. Launch into praise. *You* are one who can give praise an edge and beauty, Allen. You have done so well in a couple of damnations, that I feel confident in you.

I must close. Bosses brush near my shoulder, and poetry isn't exactly encouraged around here. Munson is strong for you with this new poem. I think he would like it for *Secession* if the *Dial* does not take it. He asks me to inform you that no particular "jargon" is necessary for *Secession* contributors. Be your own language—in so pure a way that it will be noticeable, and you will do well enough.

My hay fever temporarily passes. I peer again on the world with subsiding eyes. It's a pleasure to think of you down in the clear valleys, and feeling so top-spinning! Marriage! well, it sounds ominous. Think well, beforehand. Are you easily satisfied? That's the main danger.

Affectionately, Hart

To Wilbur Underwood

1709 East 115th Street
Dear Wilbur: July 27, 1922

I suppose you have heard from Harry by this time, but in case you haven't don't worry about any "crash". A postal and yesterday a letter, have recently reassured me, although, for a while, I was worried, too. Harry seems to have gone mad about the English. I know they are an old love of his, but I would prefer to have him give a little more about himself in his letters and less description of lords and ladies. The school exercises at Eton and Harrow were the praiseful burden of his last song. But I suppose I ought to be glad to be given a "look in", whether I am so thrilled or not. Harry is so damned romantic about everything,—that is his charm in one way, but it sometimes is disappointing in others.

I feel like shouting *EUREKA!* When Munson went yesterday after a two weeks visit, he left my copy of *Ulysses*, a huge tome printed on Verge d'Arche paper. But do you know—since reading it partially, I do not think I will care to trust it to any bookbinder I know of. It sounds ridiculous, but the book is so strong in its marvelous oaths and blasphemies, that I know I wouldn't have an easy moment while it was out of the house. You will pardon my strength of opinion on the thing, but it appears to me easily the epic of the age. It's as great a thing as Goethe's *Faust* to which it has a distant resemblance in many ways. The sharp beauty and sensitivity of the thing! The matchless details! I DO HOPE you get a copy, but from what Munson says there is little hope unless you can get some friend of yours in Europe to smuggle it in his trunk. It has been barred from England. It is quite likely I have one of two or three copies west of New York. The *Dial* ordered six and has only been able to get one so far, etc. etc. Munson, who met Joyce several times in Paris last summer, tells me that the Man

Ray photo of J. in the recent *Vanity Fair* is really not a good resemblance. The face is not so puffy looking, nor the odd ocular expression. Man Ray, you know, has his own individual temperament to express! Ah, these interesting photographers. Joyce dresses quietly and neatly. Is very quiet in manner, and Anderson says, does not seem to have read anything contemporary for years. His book is steeped in the Elizabethans, his early love, and Latin Church, and some Greek,—but the man rarely talks about books. His oldest son, about 18, threatens to beat him up sometimes when he comes home drunk, which is quite frequently,—at least McAlmon (Frank Harris' definition of the b.b. here) his latest concubine, says.

Joyce is still very poor. Recently some french writers headed by Valery Larbaud, gave a dinner and reading for his benefit. It is my opinion that some fanatic will kill Joyce sometime soon for the wonderful things said in *Ulysses.* Joyce is too big for chit-chat, so I hope I haven't offended you with the above details about him. He is the one above all others I should like to talk to.

I have been very quiet while Munson has been here. Tonight, however, I break out into fresh violences. Write me about some of your summer perturbations;—and Mme. C? How did the legal proceedings anent the ex-marine come out. I have a wonderful selection from a small funny magazine to send you. Watch for it. And thanks, dear Wilbur, for the newspaper bundle. In the *Times* I enjoyed Colum's account of Joyce's early Dublin days, although he told me the story of the Yeats encounter several years ago.

How much of the Joyce book did you read in the *Little Review?* Maybe I can find you some interesting passages to quote you if you haven't read them.

Write soon, Hart

To Gorham Munson

Dear Gorham: Friday night
    Let me explain why I don't feel like writing you at length at this moment—though I may do so, possibly, within the next few days. My enthusiasms, the hot weather, the onset of hay

fever, the infinite and distasteful work I have been doing at the office, and the suspense of finding another position, etc. etc, have brought me very near the ground. In fact, for several days this week I have been unable to retain food and have thought that at any moment something would snap and I would go into a million pieces. I haven't felt as "dangerously" for several years. But I am picking up today—since I have got the job matter settled and informed the office that I shall not be with them after the first of September. This bit of news I had the wonderful pleasure of delivering to them just as my boss was starting in on a series of gentle reprimands etc. and so instead of ever hearing the end of that rigamarole—I was begged to remain at a higher salary. Where I am going, however, I shall have complete charge of the copy work and shall receive ten dollars a week more to start with and a considerable raise within sixty days. I was literally urged to come with them—a new agency—which was a unique pleasure for me!

Well,—we heard from Anderson! Rosenfeld's remarks along with those of several other artists present at the time of the "trial" were quoted in effect that S. was not a notable man at all—had no personal vision—his work a mixture of halfdozen modern influences—and *couldn't draw a head on man, woman or animal!* Anderson was very sorry he had had anything to do with any adverse criticism, etc, etc. So much for that. Dear G. let us create our own little vicious circle! Let us erect it on the remains of such as Paul Rosenfeld. But enough of this for now.

Of course I'm enthusiastic about "Faustus and Helen" now! Who wouldn't be after your comments. However,—when it comes to the last section—I think I shall not attempt to make it the paragon of SPEED that I thought of. I think it needs more sheer weight than such a motive would provide. Beyond this I have only the surety that it is, of course, to include a comment on the world war—and be Promethean in mood. What made the first part of my poem so good was the extreme amount of time, work and thought put on it. The following is my beginning of the last part—at present:

> Their windows staring intermittent testimony
> While corymbulous formations of mechanics
> Hurried the breezes, spouted malice

Plangent over meadows, chipping
Delicate recesses into death—
Like old women with teeth unjubilant
Viewing a civic fireworks in July
The openmouthed and empty houses waited
Faintly for faces and new words again.

How neatly here is violence clothed in pathos!

I enclose a recent attempt to improve the poem you thought of using in *Secession*. Let me know what you think of it,—and don't use it unless you feel enthusiastic about it. Perhaps I am in no mood to judge capably the last week,—during which the enclosed and the above were written. But you know me—I'm hard as nails when it comes to taking critiques!

Sec #2 is *great*. I am now an enthusiast. But I can't go into critical details now. Liked your *Broom* article—"Limbo of Am. Lit"—although it is not completely representative of you now. *Enormous Room* a permanently beautiful thing. Haven't finished Joyce yet nor got into *Rahab*. Oi-Yoi—my omissions are terrible. But I have explained that already. O yes,—heard from Matty—waterplace, high cultured life and everything! Such a dear!

Sans breath! Hart

Lescaze was enraged and disgusted at the Rosenfeld judgement. Is going to see him when in N.Y. on his way to Paris soon and tell him his opinion of such faux pas. How about having Sommer do a cover for *Secession*? The man is so dejected lately that it hurts me. I wish you would write him a letter and send him a copy of #2 sometime soon. His family seem to have turned against him lately, or rather, perhaps I am just finding out (since last weekend out there) how difficult his wife is and the son you met. The old fellow has been in town most all week—dreading to go home nights at any rate.

To Gorham Munson

Dear Gorham: Thursday

More than anything else my eyes were to blame for the strained state under which I last wrote you. This was augmented by the ungodly work I had been doing at the office on that campaign for the company. Now that I have been away for almost a week I am back on my feet. The day after I wrote you they let me go—not wishing they said, to keep me up to the "last moment" as I was going to a strong competitors' etc. So—I have had this week for a little vacation. I shall start in with my new job next Monday probably as they have had a lot of rush work to be done. I shall be less hampered there and have complete charge of the copy—with the prospect of "bossing" some other writer within a few weeks if the swell of their business continues.

My vacation has given me the time to read *Rahab* and finish *Ulysses*. *Rahab* is a beautiful book. It has a synthetic beauty that is more evident than the lyric note behind *Ulysses*. It contains beautiful language—Frank is a real artist—no doubt about that and of course way beyond Anderson when it comes to craft. My only doubt about *Rahab* comes in with the question, as yet undecided, as to whether or not there isn't a slight touch of sentimentality attached to Frank's "mysticism". Certainly the man is not a *realist*—certainly he is sincere. There is also this question—Fanny's later developement, so far as I can see, does not put her far enough beyond her initial appreciation of life at the time she is deserted by her husband to warrant the stress on that thesis which Frank evidently intends as the *motif* of the book. As a picture of crucifixion the book is superb— but, after all, what tangible gain has Fanny got out of it except an attitude that Butler outlines in some such words as I believe I have repeated to you: "No one has ever begun to really appreciate life, or lived, until he has recognized the background of life as essentially Tragedy." It is from this platform of perception that I conceive every artist as beginning his work. Does Frank consider Fanny's course as complete where he leaves her at the end of *Rahab*—or isn't there still something more to be said? The reason I pose this question is because Stephen Daedalus has already gone as far as Fanny before *Ulysses* begins. The *Portrait* took him beyond where Fanny sits at the end of *Rahab*. Of course it would stretch reality a great deal, probably, to take Fanny Dirk any further—but, in my mind, it is just this stubborn impossibility (however irresponsible Frank may be) that makes my judgement of *Rahab* suffer in the light of *Ulysses*. Perhaps I am unfair and "all off". Both books, however, have a strong ethical and Nietschzian basis and reading them at the same time as I have, I am irresistably drawn into comparisons. Frank is so young that he has lots of time to benefit by Joyce and even go further—although I doubt if such will be done for a hundred years or more. The point is—after all—I am interested in Frank and thank you for putting me out of predjudice. As an American today he is certainly in the front line—no doubt about that at all.

Have you seen the new *Gargoyle* yet? My portrait came out quite well along with Cowley's and Wright's both of whom I was glad to get glimpses of. For a number of reasons, all of which you would appreciate, I should like to meet Wright sometime. Moss sends me & with apologies a $1 check for the *Western Plains* and invites me to send photographs of Bill Sommer's work for reproduction. I think I shall have some made at once—sending one or two to *Broom* also. Thank you for your interest in the cover idea. I'll get in touch with Sommer about that right away. Your array against Rosenfeld fills me with glee. I imagine Seldes is a very different sort of person at least in some ways. I feel I would enjoy talking to him anyway. You, my dear fellow, seem to be getting a great deal of attention lately in the metropolis. I should certainly like to be there.

Matty's last letter to me bore as much advice as possible—but I noticed a certain admiring reference to my idols,—Jonson, Marlowe, Donne etc via admonishing me, despite my success, not to "waste" more time on the trans. of the minor tonalities of Laforgue. At 30—Matty will be a dyed-in-the-wool conservative, wait and see. But I am full of interest in him—and his fib about Moss apropos my mention of the poem in the last no. was delightful. He said that Moss finally bothered him so that he had to knock him down on the floor in a cafe! Bravo—Matthew! I think it was quite beautiful the way Stevens came around to eat out of your hands again after your rejection of him once.

I am glad you are showing my poetry to Frank and that, so far, he has liked it. Show him "Faustus" I & II if you like—and get his reaction from them. He ought to get the best out of "Black Tambourine."

Well—my writing is bad enough before my hand gets stiff It's impossible now. The family greatly wishes to be remembered to you. You made a great "hit" here, you know. When do you make for the woods? My hay fever continues mightily and exhaustingly. But Europe is the only cure for that. Wish I were going with Lescaze who sails Sept. 5th for Geneva, via Berlin etc. He is going to bring back a raft of *Ulysses* for frantic Clevelanders including our friend Loveman who often speaks of you.

Lights out! Hart

To Wilbur Underwood

Dear Wilbur: Saturday, September 2

Doubly desolate does my ivory tower seem tonight since your letter with its fruit-cake richness and the one I got from Harry yesterday. Having cast my nets on the telephone wires in vain and wasted totally the first half of the morning, I have "compromised with the public taste" to the extent of a quiet midnight over late correspondence. But how I am stalked by lust these dog days! And how many "shadowy" temptations beset me at every turn! Were I free from my family responsibilities I would give myself to passion to the final cinder. After all—that and poetry are the only things life holds for me.

Harry's letter is redolent with the affection and love he found in the heart of some golden boy. He mentions four days of glorious abandon when they drank, sang and loved, careening from Buckingham Palace to the lanes of Limehouse. His glorious outburst after 18 months of celibacy! He claims that he thereby regained his power of commanding affection again—not mere passion. But he has probably written you all about it so I won't repeat more. Dear Harry!

As long as you are in Washington I shall think often of that gold & white city when the leaves turn. God knows why—I was, or thought I was supremely miserable when I was there, and most of the time I was. But that was my fault. I should never have tried to sell candy or work for my father. I would like to come back for a few more evenings on that narrow balcony off that dreadful room and talk with you as we did then, about Beardsley, Rabelais, aphrodisiacs, poetry and lust. But often now I wonder that I even enjoy my memories. I have to pump up enthusiasms every day for various products from thermometers to gas ranges and turn out written arguments in their praise as fast as possible. In a way I like copywriting, but it enslaves the imagination. I find routine work and figures even worse, however, so I ought not to howl, I suppose.

Can't you stop off here on your vacation? I offer the prime inducement of a reading of *Ulysses*. You will be well fortified against my routine absence during the day with this book in your hands.

I'm too dead tired of the typewriter to make any transcriptions tonight. My intentions are better than anything else about me. I palpitate with dark expectations for our Mme. Keep me posted of her Nubian adventures.

Affectionately Hart

To William Carlos Williams

Dear Williams: Friday, September 14
The day before your letter came one from Munson telling me about the picture, etc. Munson said that he had quoted the price of 25.00 on the picture and that you had bought it with that understanding. I told Sommer about it and he said 25 bucks was alright. Your letter of day before yesterday quotes your price as $20.00. I'm not mercenary and besides, have nothing whatever to gain by the sale of Sommer's pictures. On the other hand I'm going to turn this price adjustment over directly to you and Sommer, yourselves,—that is if you want to try to get it from him for $20.00. I dislike going to him with a lower price after he has accepted something else. You will see what I mean, I'm sure. You can get him at care; the Otis Lithograph Co., Cleveland.

He likes your poetry and felt flattered at the interest of a man who could appreciate painting as well as your Matisse poem showed in *Contact*. Sommer will advise you directly about the framing.

Hastily, Hart Crane

I'm sending Sommer your letter today with the hope that he'll write you about the price at once. He's terribly slow about such things, however, so you'd better write him yourself in the meantime, I s'pose.

To William Carlos Williams

Dear Williams: Wednesday

Thanks for you letter of last Monday. Now I can write you better than before, as I had lunch with Sommer today.

He says to frame it close (no mat whatever) with a narrow white band, not more than an inch wide. I saw it here on exhibition that way, and must say that it struck me as the right trick. I'm prejudiced against gold frames to some extent anyway.

Ye Gods! don't ask me to tell you what price to make on it. Sommer himself can't be made to care very much since it is going to a fellow artist. He's baulky as hell about letters, simply gets the d.t.s at the thought, but, between ourselves and whether he writes you or not, I wish you would make it $25.00 if you can. Considering the current prices of most work infinitely inferior to his, it's certainly worth it, and he needs the money for canvass. It's too bad that much of his best oil work has had to be done on mere beaver board. You will, of course, send the check direct to him at Macedonia when convenient.

I wish you could meet old Sommer. We want to get him out of that union labour hell-hole lithograph factory before it's too late. Make any noise you can about your picture to the right people, *please*, and let me know of any friends of your's that might care to see more of his work, either to talk or buy.

There's nobody in this country that's got certain line qualities that Sommer has. I wish you could see some of his things around the walls of my room! But their practically buried here.

Let me thank *you*, my dear Williams, for *your* interest, and of course Sommer feels (silently perhaps, but more visually!) even

stronger. I'm glad to hear that you are a *Secession* enthusiast—
for *Secession*'s sake.

Faithfully yours, Hart Crane

To Wilbur Underwood

Dear Wilbur:—   Monday evening
   In a *Wave* advertisement in the last *Double-Dealer* I notice
the announcement of a poem or so from you. I'm going to
make an effort to get a copy. Is it out yet?
   I'm not going to empty my purse for that Ben Hecht novel.
Ben is like a hawker of a circus. He has no real finesse, just
enough to stir the docile bovine American public to fits and
shocks. I'd rather have Beardsley, Joyce or Rabelais! (Ye Gods!
I almost left out Petronius!)
   I'm getting so I can't bear the sight of newspapers. I'll bet
you know a few real facts anent this Turkish situation. Did you
read Cuthbert Wright's recent defense of the Turk in the
Nation?
   Yesterday night I at last was taken into the arms of love
again! Seldom have I had such affection offered me. An athlete
—very strong—20 only—dark haired—distantly Bohemian. I
hope it will last a while—I deserve a little kindness and he *was*
so kind!
   You must write Harry—he was very peeved in his last to me
about it—about a week ago.

(insignia in futureo) ♡

To Gorham Munson

Dear Gorham: September 29, 1922
   What would you think of my using the first part of "F and
H" alone? Calling it just "For the Marriage of" etc. This would
seem rather disappointing, I know, but I feel that it is fate.
This conviction comes after much thought and especially after
writing one added verse (originally intended for part 3) to be

inserted as the next-last, coming just before the "eye motif". I feel that with this added the first part becomes an intensity that is definitely developed and closed,—and that further additions such as part 2 are irrelevant,—at least anti-climactic by position. And as for the third part, I am interested enough in the aeroplane, war—speed idea but I think it would be better developed under a different sky. Let me know what you think of the idea;—what you think of the additional verse also.

"The Springs of Guilty Song," or former part 2, would do very well, I think, to send to *Broom*. Of course, I want to try *Dial* on "F and H," before it goes anywhere else. It's present length will slightly overlap two pages.

I am glad to have the *Secession* program in advance. You're travelling right along it seems. I wish I could spare an erection, as suggested, but I have to save them all for Seiberling Tires, Furnaces, etc. I have a widening interest, you see, in filling the public mind with my ideas of excellence. Frankly, I'm tired to death. The new job has been beyond expectations in many ways, but it simply keeps my imagination tied down more than ever. I have so much to do.

Allen Tate is in Cincinnati visiting his brother and may come up here for a couple of days. I really enjoy admonishing him— Matty is not the only one who has "disciples". By the way,—I guess that latter gent got peeved again at my last letter. I preface every letter now, you know, with the prediction that its contents will absolutely disgust him beyond the desire to answer—someday, perhaps already, that prophecy will be fulfilled.

I can't spare the money to put into reproductions of Bill's pictures for some time. It will cost twenty dollars just for six. It will be two months before I even break clear from the dentist and hay fever bills of the year,—so I guess we can't send Loeb anything yet. If I could get more help from Bill I could do more,—but you see what a state he is in when he can't keep his family from opening his mail. He asked me to write Williams again the other day to tell him to send his check to the Company for such reasons. Too much family! By God I wouldn't have any acquisitive bitch opening my mail!!! Williams wrote me a very nice letter accepting the $25.00 price with remittance as soon as a poem provided it. I blew off steam on Bill. So that's ended.

Write soon, Hart

To Wilbur Underwood

Dear Wilbur: October 30, 1922

Have just seen Harry. Got up at five and had an hour and a half with him at the station en route to Chicago. Of course I was highly excited as I hadn't seen him for three years,—and won't again for another year. I think he is looking exceptionally well. Well—the station rang with our noises!

Of course I am more pleased at your Joyce purchase, even though it broke you flat, than I would have been at your New York vacation without it. You are probably there by this time anyway, but you were right in grabbing up the book first. I read it through without a moment of boredom, and cannot understand those people of considerable literary pretensions who have mentioned the "effort" it took to reach the end. The "Night-Town" episodes are the most thrilling things intellectually that I ever read. And the pure prose style of the first chapter is unmatched.

Your mention of Mme. C's attempts at an assignation threw me into fits of hysteria. Your prose style is perfectly adapted to set her off in the brilliant greens of sarcasm that her adventures provoke. Certainly I have no rival friend of equal picturesque actions to amuse me in Cleveland. The best I can offer is a lady with shredded wheat biscuit hair who more than coughs at the slightest provocation. I am waiting for her return to town next month for a wild scenario.

♡

It may be too late to suggest it, but I wish you would look up my friend, Gorham Munson, if possible. He lives at 378 Nostrand Avenue, Brooklyn. You would find him interesting company and of perfect understanding.

To Gorham Munson

Dear Gorham: November 20, 1922

I am immersed totally in a rush job and will be for a week or so more. These campaigns are taxing affairs and very confining, so I can't write much. But I do want to assure you of my enthusiastic desire to both write the jacket for your Frank Study and also write a communication to the *Double Skull* (delightful name) about it. As regards the latter,—it will necessarily be very short, as they once returned a reasonably sized review I had written on Shaw's *Back to Methuselah* on the argument that it was too long for the comparative importance of the book! Please send me the proofs as soon as they are out and I'll begin.

I hope you enjoyed Underwood. I took the liberty of writing him to look you up because you had once mentioned a certain interest in him incurred in Pollard's *Their Day in Court.* Wilbur is delightful company, whether he goes in for post-Beardlsey attitudes or not. The episodes of the *Satyricon* are mild as compared to his usual exploits in N.Y. during vacations.

God knows where Tate is. I haven't heard anything for two weeks or more, but he will probably blow in here sometime soon if he comes at all. I confess myself snowed under, temporarily, with all of my office work. It would take something like one of your Tuesday Nights to revive me from the malaises of Cleveland. Just now I am looking rather yearningly for #3 *Sec.*

Are you continuing with the advertising instruction? What do you think of Eliot's *The Wastelands*? I was rather disappointed. It was good, of course, but so damned dead. Neither does it, in my opinion, add anything important to Eliot's achievement.

I like the admonitions you offered on Macy etc. in the *New Republic.* You are developing a tightened hold on criticism that is a favorable opposite to mr. rosenfeld's raputurous Turner-sunset technique.

As ever, HART

To Gorham Munson

Dear Gorham: Thanksgiving Day 1922
    I am sending you along with this and also special delivery—
six photos, including some of Sommer's best achievements on
paper. This rush is due to the good news contained in your
letter which I got last night along with *Sec.* #3. I hope they ar-
rive in time to show to Fischer, as well as to Stieglitz. In the
case of the former they are in one sense better than the origi-
nals because they give him an opportunity to see them as they
would look in a monograph. If Stieglitz becomes interested,
please assure him that I shall be glad to send him originals, etc.
    I am not any too well satisfied with these photos. Several are
very good, but the ox or bull (which is it?!) has not come out
with the pure white background as it should and there appear
to be some minor scratches over the nude. However, I paid
twenty $ for them, so don't lose them. Keep them as long as
you want and show them anywhere you think advisable. I had
it in mind to send them to Loeb. Would you care to do so at
the proper time? You mentioned such a plan once, but your
present feelings may interfere. If they do, I'll be glad to send
them over when you get through with them.
    I ventured titles in one or two cases as being a better dis-
tinction for them as separate pieces, but they are open to criti-
cism, and your change if such occurs to you. It is lucky, in a
sense, that these photos are ready at this time. I have not seen
Sommer for weeks and weeks. He is very peculiar, never looks
you up, never phones or manifests the slightest interest. I have
got tired of ever-lastingly tagging after him and shall wait until
I have some important news for him before I crash into his
cosmos again. I don't think he ever so much as replied with a
note of thanks to Williams for his purchase and beautiful, gen-
erous tribute of praise. I can't understand it. But it is perhaps
good to become impersonal in the admiration of art.
    Poor Underwood! I feared you would not like him very
much. My affection for him is based on a certain community of
taste and pursuit which you will understand. Because he has
been mewed up so long with unpleasant work in a government
office in a city where conversation and letters never existed—he

has, out of sheer ennui, been forced to find entertainment in ways which have taken the best of him to feed what has become a sort of obsession. His creative impulse was never very strong, but in his letters and on his favorite topic you get as strong a satire as Petronius'. Life has tamed him terribly,—yet he has lived a great deal if the senses mean anything.

I haven't had time to read all of #3. But I can well understand your dismay at Matty. With all his boasted time and leisure he ought to have made a better job of it. And that silly slant at Joyce—putting him along with Cabell! Matty's "gay intellectualism" will eventually expose him to the jibes of a psychoanalyst if he continues in such loose estimates as his article in *Broom* on advertising displays. Some things he says may be true,—but how damned vulgar his rhapsodies become! I would rather be on the side of "sacred art" with Underwood than admit that a great art is inherent in the tinsel of the billboards. Technique there is, of course, but such gross materialism has nothing to do with art. Artistry and fancy will be Matty's limit as long as he is not willing to admit the power and beauty of emotional intensity—which he has proven he hasn't got.

Burke has an Egyptian quality of hard and solid speculation. Egyptian literature is, of course, not my comparison,— but in looking at the sculpture of that nation one gets the same impression, the same austerity. I have decided, perhaps I repeat myself, that no advance in sculpture has been made since the Egyptians as essential plastique is concerned. This after looking at the 200 or so photographs in a modern German book on the subject.

Sam Loveman didn't like your Saltus review. Said it was scattered, etc. I haven't read it. His book on the man and his works is progressing, he says. I think it will probably be very bad. He is the kind of "critic" that feels it needful to damn every one else in order to praise. He made the terrible assertion that "while Saltus was steadily working, neglected in obscurity, Henry James was applauded in two countries for his *puking.*" James never did that, whatever else you may say about him. Ridiculous. Of course I don't take Sam seriously in any criticism. The man *Ryctarik* and his wife are really the best company I have now. (Note the spelling of his name, correct this time.) His initials are W. R. I mention this because it would be sad to get his name wrong for that cover. He was pleased greatly by your acceptance and praise.

This is a scattered enough letter. Rushed, as usual. I'll be glad when I say the last word on Pittsburgh Water Heaters, my present campaign. If you are jagging so much, write me during one of them as a kind of return insult for my past revelations. One needs some kind of excitement here!

Hart

To Waldo Frank

Dear Waldo Frank: November 30, 1922

I have heard through Munson that you care for some of my poems. Let me take the occasion of *Secession* #3 to tell you how powerfully I think you can write in such a story or episode as "Hope". This is so fine that I cannot help writing you.

I never read prose before that flowed with such lyricism and intensity. I suppose there are sure to be some shocked cries, but the beautiful manipulation of symbolism in the thing has made your daring (if it took any) infinitely worth while. Writing like this is a real legacy, and nothing could be cleaner!

You may be interested in seeing six reproductions of work by Wm. Sommer that I sent Gorham today. In that case, anyway, this outburst may have served some purpose.

Faithfully yours, Hart Crane

To William H. Wright

Dear William: December 4, 1922

However much boredom you may find in Warren—I assure you, it will not be as strenuous as the hot water I am stewing in. The Pittsburg Water Heater surely has been on my mind the last three weeks, and the burden is still unshifted. I am growing bald trying to scratch up new ideas in housekeeping and personal hygiene—to tell people WHY they need more and quicker hot water. Last night I got drunk on some sherry. Even in that wild orgy my mind was still enchained by the hot water complex—and I sat down and reeled off the best lines written so far in my handling of the campaign. All of my poems in the future will attest this sterilizing influence of HOT WATER!

Nothing happens here, either. I am grateful only for wine. I have neither women or song. Cleveland street car rides twice a day take out all hope of these latter elements. I think of New York and next summer when the present is too sharp (or is it dull!). But the main faults are not of our city, alone. They are of the age. A period that is loose at all ends, without apparent direction of any sort. In some ways the most amazing age there ever was. Appalling and dull at the same time.

You have my pulse. I wish I had something more inspiring to offer. But not today. Thanks for the cheque, and write me when you feel like it.

                                                    Merrily, Hart

To Wilbur Underwood

                                        1709 East 115th Street
                                        Cleveland, Ohio
My dear Wilbur: December 10, 1922

My mother will not tolerate wine at the house—so I am rebelling. I am thinking seriously of moving into permanent private quarters where one need not be questioned about every detail of life and where one can be free of the description of one's food and its contents and manner of preparation while it is eaten at the table. To this end I am at present staying for a few days at a hotel. Maybe I shall move out as above indicated, or maybe I shall go back; it all depends on the course she takes. Because I dread to leave her on account of the position it puts her in I hope she will be more lenient with me. I don't ask much, and the little wine I succeed in getting has never resulted in embarrassing her. I never "carry on" at the house or annoy her. The fact of wine, alone, is what infuriates her puritanical instincts. All this is tedious and maudlin stuff to write, but that very fact makes it in some measure an excuse for my present dull outlook on things. Life is hard enough, God knows, without having to put up with a hundred extra restrictions in order to just have a room and a bed!

My affair with L'Afrique failed to culminate. My anticipations were so strong and my desire to give you a shock was so gleeful that I announced it as a fait accompli when, in reality, it was only dependent on the promise of another person to arrange an assignation. I am sorry to relate that it never came to pass. I am still limited to the experiences of a single race. The dark and warm embrace is yet to come!

How *do* you manage such exquisite delights every time you journey to the Metropolis? Your letter was superb. I can understand, also, how you failed to "mix" with Munson and his friends. You are so much of the nineties that it was scarcely to be expect. You had the same reactions as Harry would have had to such a meeting. I am not saying that there is any single attitude toward art that is final. I do contend, however, that Munson, Burke, Cummings and Waldo Frank all have something new and fine to offer. And whether or not you aggree with their critical "lingo" you will nevertheless find their creative results interesting and vital. In last week's *New Republic* there was an article on the group by Louis Untermeyer, noncommittal but intelligent, on *Secession* and its contributors in which I was mentioned casually. We are all of us quite different. Our differences from the attitude of the present generation-in-power are in each case individual. I shall probably never amount to anything—but the others that I have just mentioned will do things of considerable importance. Frank, in *Rahab*, and Burke in his criticisms and in a number of short ideographic stories, have already established places in contemporary letters. I don't know whether or not you saw #3 *Secession* while you were in New York. It had probably not arrived from Vienna. But it would be worth more than it's cost, 20¢, to send to Munson for a copy and read the beautiful episode by Waldo Frank, not included in his *City Block* for fear of the censors, and the Romanesque essay-story-dialogue by Kenneth Burke. On second thought I shall send you one from here, so you'll not need to bother about it.

I am quite disrupted. Family affairs and "fusses" have been my destruction since I was eight years old when my father and mother began to quarrel. That phase only ended recently, and the slightest disturbance now tends to recall with consummate force all the past and its horrid memories on pretext of the

slightest derangement of equilibrium. As I write I am en-
sconced at my office. Everybody else is away, for it is Sunday.
Yet, in forgetfulness someone was very kind in leaving a gallon
of delicious sherry. I have already had two good glasses of it
without permission. I shall probably have two more before I
go to see Isadora Duncan this evening and go back to the un-
interesting room at the hotel. For without my books around
me and my pictures and my Victrola with its Ravel, Debussy,
Strauss and Wagner records—I am desolate, I find. I have
grown accustomed to an "ivory tower" sort of existence. I am
succeeding very well in my advertising writing. Salary raised
and promises of more and decent people to work with who en-
joy Joyce, Cabell, Pater and the best things of life. Yet, even
so—Life is meagre with me. I am unsatisfied and left always
begging for beauty. I am tied to the stake—a little more waste-
fully burnt every day of my life while all America is saying,
"every day I am growing better and better in every way", and
Dr. Coúe makes his millions!

I am just enough filled with wine at the time of this letter to
make confessions that will bore you. Yet, oddly enough, it is at
such times that I feel most like writing you and Harry. He is
floating under the shades of bamboos up the rivers of China
under the dragon stars. You and I are in offices—seeking the
same things—but my gift of humor has left me today. Forgive
it and write me soon.

Hart

A friend of mine is mad about your *Book of Masks*. Could you
send me one to give to him? Whatever the price is he'll be glad
to pay.

To Gorham Munson

Dear Gorham: Tuesday, December 12
You, as well as some of my local friends must share in my ex-
citement at seeing Isadora Duncan dance on Sunday night.
She gave the same program (All Tschaikowsky) that she gave
in Moscow for the Soviet celebration and, I think, you saw it
in New York recently. It was glorious beyond words, and sad

beyond words, too, from the rude and careless reception she got here. It was like a wave of life, a flaming gale that passed over the heads of the nine thousand in the audience without evoking response other than silence and some maddening cat-calls. After the first movement of the "Pathetique" she came to the fore of the stage, her hands extended. Silence,—the most awful silence! I started clapping furiously until she disappeared behind the draperies. At least one tiny sound should follow her from all that audience. She continued through the perform-ance with utter indifference for the audience and with such in-tensity of posture and such plastique grace as I have never seen, although the music was sometimes almost drowned out by the noises from the hall. I felt like rushing to the stage, but I was stimulated almost beyond the power to walk straight. When it was all over she came to the fore-stage again in the little red dress that had so shocked Boston, as she stated, and among other things, told the people to go home and take from the bookshelf the works of Walt Whitman, and turn to the section called, "Calamus". Ninety-nine percent of them had never heard of Whitman, of course, but that was part of the beauty of her gesture. Glorious to see her there with her right breast and nipple quite exposed, telling the audience that the truth was not pretty, that it was really indecent and telling them (boobs!) about Beethoven, Tschaikowsky and Scriabine! She is now on her way back to Moscow, so I understand, where someone will give her some roses for her pains.

I am in great ferment, and have been staying at a hotel for several days until I talk to my mother about some things that will determine whether or not I shall continue to live out at the house any more. They are little things, mostly, but such little things accumulate almost into a complex that is too much for me to work under. There is no use in discussing them here, but just the constant restraint necessary in living with others, you may appreciate, is a deadening thing. Unless something happens to release me from such annoyances I give up hope of doing any satisfactory writing. This isn't a letter, it is a "state of mind". I await news from you in order to have something de-cent to say.

Yours as ever, Hart

Write me at 1709—

To Gorham Munson

Dear Gorham: January 5, 1923
   I cannot remember a more hectic month than the last unless
I recall some of the old bivouacs of New York days, when I
ricochet-ed "from roof to roof" without intermission. Two
rush campaigns to write, gifts and remembrances to buy and
send to far too many people—suppers, parties and evenings—
much tossing of the pot,—"prison, palace and reverberation"!
That is why I've been so slow in writing.
   At present I'm flabbergasted and dull. But my carousing on
New Year's Eve had one good outcome; it started the third
part of "Faustus and Helen" with more gusto than before.
When I catch my next breath I hope to carry it on to the end.
   Your explanation of *Secession* and its aims in the last *S4N* was
especially good. Paul R. with his "premature ejaculations" was
especially apt. I imagine the magazine reaches a select sort of
crowd where such comment will arouse a question at least.
What is the meaning of *S4N*? A silly question to ask you, but
I'm puzzled sometimes for an answer when questioned. Sam
Loveman and Kathryn Kenney have both mentioned receiving
copies, so I guess you supplied Fitts with their names.
   By the way, has Laukhuff paid you anything yet? He has, to
my best knowledge, sold all the copies of #2 and #3 *S*. About
#1 I don't know. He is good pay and strictly honest, but his
personal indifference to *Secession* makes me doubt his memory
a little in remitting. When you get around to it, I'd like another
copy of #3. Someone ran off with mine.
   Waldo Frank wrote me a very cordial letter in answer to my
written praise of "Hope". I should like to be in New York and
hear his lectures at the Rand School. I am hoping to make my
visit along in May or June when the weather is mild and some
of the shows are still going. I shall appear with a new cane that
was given me for Christmas. Despite my objections to cane-
carrying of last summer, I find it very pleasant. Pucecolored-
gloves complete the proper touch.
   I notice that *Broom* has been consistently weak in poetry.
Cowley's things have been by far the best—but (with all due

modesty) I think that my "F. and H." will be an improvement over their past offerings. Matty appears to rest in clover and periwinkles, what with the Guggenheim millions and the international sweep of editorial authority. (In accepting my poems he merely mentioned that he thought Loeb also liked them)! What do you think of his *Broom* ad. in the Dec. number? He asked my opinion on the grounds that literary ads were generally the flattest in the world. It seems attractive enough to me —but the prize-subscription offer I balk at as a matter of policy in such a type of magazine.

Stieglitz voiced an old feeling of mine about Bill's work— the lack of finish evident in so much of it. This has always pained me. As a whole, his comments seem very just. But I tend to differ with him on one point in common with other critics who are so obsessed with the importance of current developements in art that they fail to recognize certain positive and timeless qualities.

I refer to the quality of line in Sommer's work. That has, in particular, nothing more to do with modern work than the draughtsmanship of Michelangelo. It is something that may not distinguish a man as a great innovator or personality—but it is, for all that, a rare and wondrous quality. From what you write Stieglitz has the sense to recognize this quality and to value it. But a person like Georgia O'Keeffe, who has so distinctly her own horn to play, is scornful of everything short of evolution and revolution.

It is a relief once in awhile to detach one's judgement from such considerations as her's, and to look at a piece of work as totally detached from time and fashion, and then judge it entirely on its individual appeal. I think that in Sommer's case, you, Williams and myself are appreciators of this kind. I can enjoy Bill's things regardless of their descent, evident or otherwise, from French or German artists of the last generation. He has certain perfections which many of the most lauded were lacking in. God DAMN this constant nostalgia for something always "new". This disdain for anything with a trace of the past in it!! This kind of criticism is like a newspaper, always with its dernier cri. It breeds its own swift decay because its whole theory is built on an hysterical sort of evolution theory. I shall probably always enjoy El Greco and Goya. I still like to look at the things Sommer makes, because many of them are filled with a solid and clear beauty.

I have frequently wondered why you were so laggard in your interest in Eliot. Your recent announcement brings me much pleasure of anticipation. Please let know what you find in Eliot. With your head knocked against Burke's over such a topic there ought to be some fine illuminations. You already know, I think, that my work for the past two years (those meagre drops!) has been more influenced by Eliot than any other modern. He has been a very good counter-balance to Matty's shifting morale and violent urgings. My amusement at Matty's acceptance of "F and H" considerably heightened by the memory of several sly hints against Eliot which some of his more recent letters had contained.

There is no one writing in English who can command so much respect, to my mind, as Eliot. However, I take Eliot as a point of departure toward an almost complete reverse of direction. His pessimism is amply justified, in his own case. But I would apply as much of his erudition and technique as I can absorb and assemble toward a more positive, or (if must put it so in a sceptical age) ecstatic goal. I should not think of this if a kind of rhythm and ecstacy were not (at odd moments, and rare!) a very real thing to me. I feel that Eliot ignores certain spiritual events and possibilities as real and powerful now as, say in the time of Blake. Certainly the man has dug the ground and buried hope as deep and direfully as it can ever be done. He has outclassed Baudelaire with a devastating humor that the earlier poet lacked.

After this perfection of death—nothing is possible in motion but a resurrection of some kind. Or else, as everyone persists in announcing in the deep and dirgeful *Dial*, the fruits of civilization are entirely harvested. Everyone, of course wants to die as soon and as painlessly as possible! Now is the time for humor, and the "Dance of Death." All I know through very much suffering and dullness (somehow I seem to twinge more all the time) is that it interests me to still affirm certain things. That will be the persisting theme of the last part of my "F and H" as it has been all along.

I have probably forgotten some items, but s'nuff said now.

Belated greetings and wishes for the new year are included here from mother and my grandmother along with mine.

Affectionately, Hart

Allen Tate writes me rather touching letters from Asheville, Kentucky, where he is working in the office of a coal mine, owned by an older brother. He couldn't make either a visit to Cleveland or New York after all.

I am looking forward to the proofs of your *Study*. Please send them on whenever they're ready.

To Gorham Munson

Dear Gorham: Sunday, January 14, 1923

This (enclosed) may, or may not yet be finished. Anyway, I think it is rounded enough as it is to be somewhat enjoyed.

Some things about it surprise and satisfy me. It has a bit of Dionysian splendor, perhaps an overtone of some of our evenings together last summer. It is so packed with tangential slants, interwoven symbolisms, that I'm not sure whether it will be understood. However, I am sure that it perfectly consorts with the other two parts of the poem as I intend them.

> Part I   Meditation, Evocation, Love, Beauty
> Part II   Dance, Humor, Satisfaction
> Part III Tragedy, War (the eternal soldier)
>   Resumé, Ecstacy, Final Declaration

There is an organization and symphonic rhythm to III that I did not think I could do. The last three evenings! have been wonderful for me, anyway! A kind of ecstacy and power for WORK.

Write soon, Hart

III doesn't seem half long enough to me now—but I'm too much "with and in it" to know.

To Louis Untermeyer

1709 East 115th Street
Cleveland, Ohio
Dear Mr. Untermeyer: January 19, 1923

I know I am running the risk of the conventional accusation of impetuosity always accorded poets,—but I am rather willing, that is, in view of your article in the current *Freeman* regarding T. S. Eliot's *The Waste Land*. This, and your recent mention of me along with the "new patricians" may perhaps excuse my present infringement of the ordinary rules of the mail—that of sending poems about in mss. to comparative strangers.

While my genuine and deep admiration for Mr. Eliot's work continuing since his first poems in the *Little Review*, makes me feel that you have miscalculated him in several ways, I so solidly agree with you on many points of your article that whether or not my enclosed poem has reached its final form in every detail, I feel that you will be interested in it as a close agreement with your ideas, and perhaps as even an answer to something that apparently both of us have been demanding for some time.

You may possibly read the first two sections of this "Marriage of Faustus and Helen" poem when they appear in the *Broom* in Feb. or March. While these three poems are conceived as a single structure, each one is nevertheless possible of isolated reading. Combined, they are designed to erect an almost antithetical spiritual attitude to the pessimism of *The Waste Land*, although the poem was well finished before *The Wasteland* appeared.

It has been my conviction, based on personal experience (whether my poems prove it or not) that ecstacy and beauty are as possible to the active imagination now as ever. (What did Blake have from "the outside" to excite him?) My "Three Poems for the Marriage of Faustus and Helen" aims at a synthetic statement of this fact. Practically all of the current images used have their counter equivalents "of ancient days", yet at the same time they retain their current colour in the fusion process. This mystical fusion of beauty is my religion. Simply, then, I regard my poem as a kind of bridge that is, to my way of thinking, a more creative and stimulating thing than the settled formula of Mr. Eliot, superior technician that he is!

If my poem bores you, don't finish it. If it happens, in any degree, to answer some of the stipulations voiced in your article, I'd appreciate knowing it. In any case I hope you will pardon my impulsiveness provoked by what you say. Such sincerity as mine may be banal, but it *may* succeed in entertaining sometimes. In closing may I ask you to regard the enclosed version as very possibly incomplete, and as confidential to ourselves for the immeadiate present. As I said before, I am very impulsive.

Sincerely yours, Hart Crane

On second thought I have decided to send you enclosed the first and second parts, also. This will enable a reading in just sequence.

To Charmion von Wiegand

My dear Charmion: January 20, 1923

It didn't take me long to decide that Buschour's *Griechische Vasenmalerei* is a book that I shall always carry about with me, even though it has taken me an unforgivably long time to tell you so. You and Hermann have my sincerest gratitude for such an unexpected and beautiful holiday present.

With a few exceptions I prefer Egyptian sculpture to the Greek, and this book makes me feel that the Greeks had more to express in line & design than they had in the third dimension. In pottery you get the less ambitious and less "cosmopolitan" ambition and expression of these people. There is an intimacy and rusticity to the pottery which especially appeals to the literary instinct. The famous Nike of Samothrace craze always left me somewhat cool. Lady Milo is a bit imposing (Jove is too much around the corner) and these idealized human dolls all stand too much on their dignity. O I know how they prostrated Heine and Pater et al, and I do respect them— but give me those lovely vase intaglios and arabesques, and maids and naughty satyrs with their rank lustful lives and leaves and brine and wine!

And the next thankful mention concerns your leisurely long letter which came just before Christmas. *S4 N* has naught to do with the Ku Klux Klan. Nobody seems to be certain what it does mean—perhaps the insignia of a war-time mosquito fleet, which I like to imagine, anyway, as it is so àpropos. I gave your name to Munson along with other friends' names to send *Secession* manifestos' out to, etc. So he probably gave the *S4 N* editor the same list to send that particular issue of the latter to, as it contained Munson's article. I think it is a credit to Munson's platform and writing that so much attention has already been proffered *Secession*. I was very lukewarm in the beginning and urged him not to "waste his time" on any magazine project. But after his visit here last summer I quickly switched about, especially as *S* has contained such new and suggestive material as the last 2 numbers included. *Secession* gets away from the "temperamental" editorial attitude of the *Little Review* (good in many ways as this has been) and bases its judgement on more tradition while at the same time being far more daring in its experiments than such magazines as the *Dial*. It has been discouraging to see how very "safe" the *Dial* plays sometimes, despite its protests to the contrary.

I find that I have derived considerable stimulation from *Secession*. Without it there would be only the vague hope that the steady pessimism which pervades the *Dial* since Eliot and others have announced that happiness and beauty dwell only in memory—might sometime lift. I cry for a positive attitude! When you see the first two parts of my "Faustus & Helen" that comes out in *Broom* in Feb. or March, you will see better what I mean. I've about finished the third and last part now— and am pleased at the finale.

Your experience with Farrar (the *Bookman*) accords perfectly with my conceptions of him and his magazine. The *Bookman* has a distinct place, I think, although I never read it any more. It seems to me I've heard that it pays quite liberally. As to the *Double Dealer*—it is at present very tremulous. I haven't yet been payed for my Laforgue Translations of last June. They're decent and generous as possible, but seem to be going through that dreadful trial of "the second year" that, like the first million, the *Dial* announces as "the hardest."

I'm rather worn out with the incessant activities of the last two weeks,—last *month* in fact. I can't stand much "society" even with interesting people, and my acquaintance in Cleveland has somehow increased so extensively during the last two years that with work, reading, writing etc. things are becoming entirely too febrile. You'll excuse my mention of such "ailments" I hope, as part of my excuse for delay in writing. But I have already probably exhausted you beyond "resentments" of such nature by this lengthy gust.

Please remember me to every one, which includes Hermann, Norman and Alec (I roar at his conversation!) and remember to write me soon.

Faithfully, Hart

To Gorham Munson

Dear Gorham: February 6, 1923

Everyone writes me such encouraging notes about "F and H" that I am doubly sorry that I ever sent any to *Broom* for publication. Frank wrote me a very shrewd appreciation of Part II which he probably repeated to you. Untermeyer's mention of me among the New Patricians prompted me to send him a copy after reading his article on Eliot in a recent *Freeman*. I disagreed with him openly on many points, but the substance of his last paragraph made me think he would be interested in reading the poem. I was rather foolish to follow such an impulse, but his answer was quite decent. He made the charge of a new type of a "rhetoric" however, which is just what Frank took pains to mention as fully absent. Untermeyer comes here for a lecture on March 11th and says he wants to have a talk with me if possible. This is all right, but I am not keen about argument. Allen Tate writes me the most glowing praises possible, calls me the greatest contemporary American poet, etc. etc. so I feel about ready to deliver myself of my memoirs and expire in roses. And then, your appreciation has especially been enjoyed. You "get" the form and arrangement of the "Stark Major" poem much better than Frank does, but he is right about the second paragraph being too complicated and vague and you are wrong about the last verse being redundant.

When I get the second verse worked out to suit me I'll send you another copy. In the meantime I am ruminating on a new longish poem under the title of *The Bridge* which carries on further the tendencies manifest in "F and H." It will be extremely difficult to accomplish it as I see it now, so much time will be wasted in thinking about it. Your news about *Broom* is discouraging in view of the fact that I had just sent part III of "F and H" to Matty last week. Everything has been bungled all the way through. I hope I can get enough material together for a small volume whose things are arranged in proper order. I am so deadly sick of manipulating things with magazines, the *Dial* included. This latter refuses my "F and H" and then takes such a silly thing as that Apleton or what's'rname woman contained this month in its covers. I have been so rushed around with too much society that I have not yet got at the review for your study, but it will be done within two weeks anyway. It was much easier to rap out this enclosed review for Fitts. Let me know what you like or don't like about it. I am very awkward at reviews, mainly, I suppose, because the procedure is strange to me. I am through doing things for Sommer until he cooperates better. He has received notice and photographs from the *Dial.* I learn from second hand. Ten days ago this was. I had especially asked him to phone me as soon as he heard anything definite from them, certainly a small task, but he never peeps or comes near. I shall not send back the photographs to you to show to anyone until he returns them to me. He knows I paid twenty dollars for them and that I want to keep them circulating, etc. He knew that I would be the one to write to the *Dial* and blow 'em up if they failed to keep their word on the reproductions, and naturally want to know the facts of the situation, yet he keeps his stolid distance. What's the use? It's too much trouble with all the rest I have to do, thought I'd be only too glad to keep it up indefinitely if he'd show a little interest. This has been a terrible lump, hastily written. Please pardon it all. I shall have a final and complete version of "F and H" for you within a few days, so don't bother to copy out yourself. I'll send a complete version to Frank, also, in answering his last letter. S'much for now.

Hart

To Allen Tate

Dear Allen: February 6, 1923

I can't seem to get around to write you a decent considera-
tion of your recent poems, "Yellow River" etc. When I get time
to write, as now at the office, they are not by me, and you have
already had evidence of my state of mind at other odd mo-
ments. Meanwhile, do not think me indifferent, please.

I'm afraid you will have to postpone your kind proclama-
tions in regard to "F and H" until the three parts appear in
book form and in proper sequence. The inadvertency of "The
Springs of Guilty Song" in the *Broom* is too complicated to ex-
plain fully. Josephson is most unscrupulous in his editorship,
and it takes so long to get word back and forth that I shall
probably not send anything more to *Broom* even if they finish
"F and H" with the other two parts. This is quite unlikely as
Munson writes me doleful presages about its financial straits.
Two more issues and it will probably expire. However, in case
they do print the third part which I sent about two weeks ago,
it will include a note at the bottom of the page explaining the
sequence, etc. and correcting the misnomer "The Springs of
Guilty Song". In regard to this latter I had a very fine appreci-
ation from Waldo Frank who was quite astonished at it. Then
with your fine praise and Munson's I feel more encouraged
than ever about my work. I'm already started on a new poem,
The Bridge which continues the tendencies that are evident in
"Faustus and Helen", but it's too vague and nebulous yet to
talk about.

In the next S4N I have an amusing parody of Cummings
and have asked Fitts, the editor, to send you a copy. Don't be
puzzled by the name of this magazine, it's taken from the in-
signia of a mosquito fleet during the war, I think. I wish I
could partake of the genuine Tatian Theory, but it's not so
universal in its application, I fear, as it used to be. Sherry and
bad Port are all one succeeds in safely absorbing around here.
When am I to expect that promised portrait of you?

                                        Hastily, Hart

To Waldo Frank

1709 East 115 Street
Cleveland, Ohio
February 7, 1923

Dear Waldo Frank:

I have not been so stimulated for a long time as I was with your letter and its exact appreciation of the very things I wanted to put into the second part of "For the Marriage of Faustus and Helen" or its misnomer, "The Springs of Guilty Song". The fact that its intention was completely evident to you without any explanations or "notes" from me, has renewed my confidence and made me quite happy. It has also made me doubly anxious that you should have a copy of the entire poem to read. This is enclosed, and, of course, is your's to keep if you want it. It has been very discouraging the way *Broom* has handled the publication of this poem. The mails are slow and unreliable, and Josephson is hasty, to say the least, in his methods. At best now, it will come out in broken sequence, and a final Note with part III cannot much repair the situation. I want at least a few of my friends to have the thing in decent shape.

A few planks of the scaffolding may interest you, so I'll roughly indicate a few of my intentions. Part I starts out from the quotidian, rises to evocation, ecstasy and statement. The whole poem is a kind of fusion of our own time with the past. Almost every symbol of current significance is matched by a correlative, suggested or actually stated, "of ancient days". Helen, the symbol of this abstract "sense of beauty", Faustus the symbol of myself, the poetic or imaginative man of all times. The street car device is the most concrete symbol I could find for the transition of the imagination from quotidian details to the universal consideration of beauty,—the body still "centered in traffic", the imagination eluding its daily nets and self consciousness. Symbolically, also, and in relation to Homer, this first part has significance of the rape of Helen by Paris. In one word, however, Part I stands simply for the EVOCATION of beauty.

Part II is, of course, the DANCE and sensual culmination. It is also an acceleration to the ecstasy of Part III. This last part begins with *catharsis*, the acceptance of tragedy through de-struction (The Fall of Troy, etc. also in it). It is Dionysian in its attitude, the creator and the eternal destroyer dance arm in arm, etc. all ending in a restatement of the imagination as in Part I. You would probably get all these things without my crude and hasty mention of them, but to me, the entire poem is so packed with cross-currents and multiple suggestions that I am anxious that you should see the thing as I do, even though I have perhaps not succeeded in "putting over" all the points which I think I have. If you feel like severe criticism in any cases I shall certainly welcome it. Certainly I was not "hurt" by the very accurate criticisms you offered in your last letter.

"Nuances" in Part II takes the American pronunciation, that is, the "es" is voiced. You were quite right about the sec-ond verse in "Stark Major". I have never been satisfied with it as to clarity, and it will undergo revision before publication anywhere.

I am looking forward to meeting you along in June, when it is quite possible that I shall have two weeks vacation in N.Y. Thanks for your generous interest.

Hastily, Hart Crane

To Gorham Munson

Excuse bum type, etc. Corona has measles

Dear Gorham: February 9, 1923

You don't deserve my pains in copying these two charming things of Allen Tate's until you send back that much belabored poem of Harris's, but these being yours to keep or throw away, I submit them casually, as possible material for *Secession*. Tate sent them to me this week and seems to have written them in a mood of amusement with no idea of their publication any-where. I shall not say anything at all to him about above con-siderations unless you should happen to want one or both of them. Tate has a whole lot to offer when he finds his way out of the Eliot idiom, which as you know, is natural to him, and was before he ever heard of Eliot. These things are certainly not imitative of anyone to noticeable extent. They certainly beat Gerty Stein on her own ground—that is from the stand-point of her announced desire to break up poetry into an idiom corresponding to cubism, etc. Tate has much more precision, while giving the broken effect. Not that I care a damn about such theories beyond their being merely interesting, but that may be because from now on I feel that personal problems of my own, extenuating from the experience in writing "F and H", will be enough to interest myself.

I am in a very unfavorable mood, and just after having con-gratulated myself strongly on security against future outbreaks of the affections. You see, for two or three years I have not been attacked in this way. A recent evening at a concert some glances of such a very stirring response and beauty threw me into such an hour of agony as I supposed I was beyond feeling ever again. The mere senses can be handled without such ef-fects, but I discover I am as powerless as ever against those higher and certainly hopeless manifestations of the flesh. O God that I should have to live within these American restric-tions forever, where one cannot whisper a word, not at least exchange a few words! In such cases they almost suffice, you know. Passions of this kind completely derail me from any-thing creative for days,—and that's the worst of it.

Tate wrote me a charming old fashioned sonnet on my pic-ture that I recently sent him. Because, in a loose way, it is so clairvoyant, I confide it to you, an act which would be almost immodest in other circumstances.

Write me soon, Hart

To Allen Tate

Dear Allen: February 12, 1923

Let me congratulate you on the "Tercets of the Triad" how-ever mockingly intended. It is among your very best results, as is, also, the "Pins and Needles". O I shall not soon forget "grandfather's knees", etc. etc. The interweaving of the lines is very cunning. I think you display a great amount of cleverness also in the "Pins and Needles"—although I'm not sure I ap-plaud the name for this. There might be others more apropos. To my mind you beat "Gerty" Stein on her own race track.

That is, you succeed much better than she in accomplishing what is her avowed aim—to split up lyrical or picture-word sequences into pieces in the same way the Cubists do in painting. She is entertaining only at the expense of all coherence, whereas you break things up into sharp impressions and also preserve the outlines of the shattered pieces. This comparison, now that I see it written, is aimless, because your directions and temperaments are so entirely different. Yet its record here may amuse you as an idea that immeadiately came to my mind when I read your poem.

Odd paradoxes occur. These things which you claim to have written for amusement only, seem to carry through so far as completeness of form is concerned better than "Yellow River" and "Quality of Mercy" where your "seriousness" was, if anything, too evident. You won't misunderstand me on this, I hope. I simply mean that your satirical leanings are very strong. . . . That their astringency frequently breaks up your lyrical passages and at other times overloads them to the point of obscurity. In an indifferent or gay mood you escape these encumbrances, as well slight tendency that such endowments always carry with them—the danger of occasional lapses into sentimentality. Do not be abashed. The same was true of no less a man than Jules Laforgue, who was like you in many ways and who naturally had far less temptations in Paris and Berlin than you and I, Allen and Hart in Kentucky and Ohio (U.S.A.) respectively. If I can find it I'll send you a scrap of De Gourmont's essay on Laforgue that I translated last summer. This is more illuminating than anything I could offer.

I think you need to cultivate greater simplicity of statement in your more emotional things,—however well your present facility suits the more ornamented and artificial incongruities of satire or brilliant impressionism. In "Yellow River" there are many lines that are too noble to be wasted,—some of great penetration and beauty. So all this makes me wish you would devote some extra effort into perfecting this poem, willfully extracting the more obvious echoes of Eliot. You are certainly rich enough to get along without them. Don't let your interest in the *Fugitive* woo too many things into too sudden print. Forgive my pedantic bass and lifted finger, but I think you are inclined to too hasty mss. dispatches sometimes.

The ads are calling, so Addios. I feel like quoting the first verse of *The Bridge* for a snappy close:—

> Macadam, gun grey as the tunny's pelt,
> Leaps from Far Rockaway to Golden Gate,
> For first it was the road, the road only
> We heeded in joint piracy and pushed.

La-La, Hart

To Allen Tate

Dear Allen: February 15, 1923

I'm laid up with la grippe, so excuse my brevity. Since finding your letter with your *specific* Nashville address it occurs to me that you may not have received the two notes I sent you some time ago,—especially as I have not heard anything from you for so long. My notes were addressed just "Nashville", so it may be that they were undelivered. Nothing to worry about missing, of course, only that I don't want to bother you by inflicting a recent poem of mine on you twice. (One of the notes contained a copy of "Belle Isle", a lyric that I think you will like.)

I enclose a note from James Daly, whose poetry you may have sampled in *Broom*. He was here last Fall visiting a mutual friend, and I think I showed him some of your verse. After you have seen what "some others" think of you, please return the enclosed. *Broom*, by the way, has busted, N.Y. office closed last Saturday, March issue, the last, to be distributed from Berlin while the tent-stakes are being pulled up. I rejoice in a way. At least they won't get a chance to murder my "F and H" any more. *Secession* will publish the three parts together probably sometime next summer. (There is no use in my sending anything more to the *Dial*; they just rejected my "Stark Major," and it is plain that their interest in helping American letters is very incidental. Note the predominance given to translations of the older generation of Germans, etc. who have absolutely nothing to give us but a certain ante-bellum "refinement". They aren't printing the younger crowd of any country.) All this should convince you, as well as myself, of the real place and necessity for *Secession*. Of course I'm sorry now that I fooled around sending "F and H" anywhere else at all. *Dial* had a chance at that, too, you know.

You may be indisposed to Waldo Frank, but I must recommend to you *City Block* as the richest in content of any "fiction" that has appeared in the American 20th century. Frank has the real mystic's vision. I have also enjoyed reading Ouspensky's *Tertium Organum* lately. Its corroboration of several experiences in consciousness that I have had gave it particular interest.

Write soon, please, Hart

To Gorham Munson

Dear Gorham: February 18, 1923
Pardon this "billet-doux" stationery—I bought too much for Christmas greetings and am now forcing it upon my intimates until it's used up.

Your summary of praises for "F and H" was such a fine tribute that it might account for my backache and confinement to the bed yesterday. But the more probable cause for *that*, however, is liquor and the cogitations and cerebral excitements it threw me into regarding my new enterprise, *The Bridge*, on the evening precedent. I am too much interested in this *Bridge* thing lately to write letters, ads, or anything. It is just beginning to take the least outline,—and the more outline the conception of the thing takes,—the more its final difficulties appall me. All this preliminary thought has to result, of course, in some channel forms or mould into which I throw myself at white heat. Very roughly, it concerns a mystical synthesis of "America". History and fact, location, etc. all have to be transfigured into abstract form that would almost function independently of its subject matter. The initial impulses of "our people" will have to be gathered up toward the climax of the bridge, symbol of our constructive future, our unique identity, in which is included also our scientific hopes and achievements of the future. The mystic portent of all this is already flickering through my mind (when I say this I should say "the mystic possibilities," but that is all that's worth announcing, anyway) but the actual statement of the thing, the marshalling of the forces, will take me months, at best; and I may have to give it up entirely before that; it may be too impossible an ambition. But if I do succeed, such a waving of banners, such ascent of towers, such dancing etc, will never before have been put down on paper! The form will be symphonic, something like "F and H" with its treatment of varied content, and it will probably approximate the same length in lines. It is perhaps rather silly to go on this way before more than a dozen lines have been written, but at any rate it serves to excuse my possible deficiencies in correspondence in the near future, should the obsession carry me much further. I hate to have to go work every day!

When I get *The Bridge* done, or something of equal length, I think it will be time to try Liveright or Huebsch or Knopf for a collected publication. Just now I have hardly enough of even quality and tone to satisfy me. Of course I'm glad to know that Wheeler and Wescott are interested in me, especially as I am led to respect their standards, but I might as well relinquish my mss to the desk drawer as to offer its publication to Wheeler, at least so far as I know. Did he publish Turbyfill in Chicago? or was it Berlin? You will naturally see my reasons for at least attempting the more standard publishers first, I'm sure. And until I have the extra and necessary amount to add, there is no use committing myself to any arrangements at all. In passing I do want to thank you, Gorham, for your constant interest in interpreting me to others whose added interest all makes me confident that I have more to offer than I once supposed. And I am even more grateful for your very rich suggestions best stated in your Frank study on the treatment of mechanical manifestations of today as subject for lyrical, dramatic, and even epic poetry. You must already notice that influence in "F & H". It is to figure even larger in *The Bridge*. The field of possibilities literally glitters all around one with the perception and vocabulary to pick out significant details and digest them into something emotional.

Your visit to Amy Lowell was a characteristic literary experience in American letters of the day, a baptism, as it were, from the Episcopal font, endowing you with the proper blessing and chastisement necessary for the younger generation. All hail to Amy's poetry propaganda! but I should not enjoy talking to her.

I think you discovered the weak points in my review pretty well. However, I think that Wheelwright's recent letter about *Secession* in the *Freeman* displayed very little evidence of prose workmanship, even of the most fundamental nature. He certainly sustained himself much better as "Dorian Abbott". In the latter his parti pris emotionalism was too evident to convince his readers properly. In this sense, a course in advertising would be good for him, which reminds me that I'll soon send you one of my campaigns that not only "went over big" but is theoretically a good piece of work. Are you still studying this modern science?

It must be rather hellish reading through so many books every week that your eyes pop out. Truly, you must look for some editorial post, copy-writing job, or something that will relieve you of such strains. I think you will probably find things much smoother in your new apartment which I'm delighted to think of. Is it in the Village? I can't quite place it. When I come down in June, I'll probably plan on staying with you and Elizabeth.

Just now, it's Vulcan back to the Furnace! The "bowels" poem comes out in the next S4N, which bunch Tate writes that he has just joined through my communications. He has submitted "Pins and Needles", which I imagine Fitts will use. I'm waiting now for the *Dial* to send back my "Stark Major". Just sent a caricature of Paul Rosenfeld to the *Little Review*, telling them to publish it, if they cared to, "along with the rest of my inadvertent correspondence". It is called "Anointment of Our Well Dressed Critic", or "Why Waste the Eggs?"— Three-dimensional Vista, by Hart Crane. Allons!

                                                              Hart

To Wilbur Underwood

Dear Wilbur: February 20, 1923
    Those who have wept in the darkness sometimes are rewarded with stray leaves blown inadvertently. Since your last I

have one of those few experiences that come,—ever, but which are almost sufficient in their very incompleteness. This was only last evening in a vaudeville show with a cousin of mine who goes to college here. Joe has manifested charming traits before, but there has always been an older brother around. Last night—it sounds silly enough to tell (but not in view of his real beauty)—O, it was only a matter of light affectionate stray touches—and half-hinted speech. But these were genuine and in that sense among the few things I can remember happily. With Joe you must think of someone mildly sober, with a face not too thin, but with faun precision of line and feature. Crisp ears, a little pointed, fine and docile hair almost golden, yet darker,—eyes that are a little heavy—but wide apart and usually a little narrowed,—aristocratic (English) jaws, and a mouth that is just mobile enough to suggest voluptuousness. A strong rather slender figure, negligently carried, that is perfect from flanks that hold an easy persistence to shoulders that are soft yet full and hard. A smooth and rather olive skin that is cool—at first.

Excuse this long catalog—I admit it as mainly for my own satisfaction, and I am drunk now and in such state my satisfactions are always lengthy. When I see you ask me to tell you more about him for he is worth more and better words I assure you. O yes, I shall see him again soon. The climax will be all too easily reached,—But my gratitude is enduring—if only for that *once*, at least, something beautiful approached me and as though it were the most natural thing in the world, enclosed me in his arm and pulled me to him without my slightest bid.

And we who create must endure—must hold to spirit not by the mind, the intellect alone. These have no mystic possibilities. O flesh damned to hate and scorn! I have felt my cheek pressed on the desert these days and months too much. How old I am! Yet, oddly now this sense of age—not at all in my senses—is gaining me altogether unique love and happiness. I feel I have been thru much of this again and again before. I long to go to India and stay always. Meditation on the sun is all there is. Not that this isn't enough! I mean I find my imagination more sufficient all the time. The work of the workaday world is what I dislike. I spend my evenings in music and sometimes ecstasy. I've been writing a lot lately. Did you see my poem in *Broom* for Jan? It is misnamed, and is properly the second part of "For the Marriage of Faustus & Helen", the first part of which comes out in the Feb. number. The third and last part is sent to *Broom* but when it will appear I don't know. I'm bringing much into contemporary verse that is new. I'm on a synthesis of America and its structural identity now, called *The Bridge*. I quote the last lines—

> And midway on that structure I would stand
> One moment, not as diver, but with arms
> That open to project a disk's resilience
> Winding the sun and planets in its face.
> Water should not stem that disk, nor weigh
> What holds its speed in vantage of all things
> That tarnish, creep, or wane; and in like laughter,
> Mobile, yet posited beyond even that time
> The Pyramids shall falter, slough into sand,—
> And smooth and fierce above the claim of wings,
> And figured in that radiant field that rings
> The Universe:—I'd have us hold one consonance
> Kinetic to its poised and deathless dance.

Thanks for Harry's letter. He wrote me about the same, with addition that he was coming back after Indo-China. So I shan't write more. Yes, it must be great to be in China, and above all, with Harry's capacity for fun.

Write soon, oZ

To Gorham Munson

Dear Gorham: February 27

Your book came today. It's a beautiful job all the way through. You certainly are to be congratulated.

Frank wrote me most inspiring series of tributes on "F. & H." last week, and your reference to the "content" of my poetry—all this makes me glow with a new kind of happiness.

Hastily, Hart

To Waldo Frank

1709 East 115th Street
Cleveland, Ohio
February 27, 1923

Dear Waldo Frank:

Such major criticism as both you and Gorham have given my "Faustus and Helen" is the most sensitizing influence I have ever encountered. It is a new feeling, and a glorious one, to have one's inmost delicate intentions so fully recognized as your last letter to me attested. I can feel a calmness on the sidewalk—where before I felt a defiance only. And better than all —I am certain that a number of us at last have some kind of community of interest. And with this communion will come something better than a mere clique. It is a consciousness of something more vital than stylistic questions and "taste," it is vision, and a vision alone that not only America needs, but the whole world. We are not sure where this will lead, but after the complete renunciation symbolised in *The Wasteland* and, though less, in *Ulysses* we have sensed some new vitality. Whether I am in that current remains to be seen,—but I am enough in it at least to be sure that you are definitely in it already. What delights me almost beyond words is that my natural idiom (which I have unavoidably stuck to in spite of nearly everybody's nodding, querulous head) has reached and carried to you so completely the very blood and bone of me. There is only one way of saying what comes to one in ecstasy. One works and works over it to finish and organize it perfectly— but fundamentally that doesn't affect one's *way* of saying it. The enclosed poem will evidence enough meaning of that, I fear, in certain flaws and weaknesses that, so far, I've not had the grace to change. The norm of accuracy in such things is, however, at best so far from second-reader penetration, that bad as it is, I can't resist sending it to you now.

Please do not feel it necessary to answer me until you are perfectly free from other preoccupations. I know what such things cost, and knew before your last letter exactly why you delayed. (Now that I see this written, it sounds all-too presumptuous, however, my appreciation was "prematurely ripe", for that idea did occur.)

Munson's *Study* came to me today. I think Liveright did a very good job, better than I expected. The photograph seconded an impression I remembered of you several years ago in New York. I may be repeating myself when I mention that you came into Brown's Chop House one evening and greeted some friends near a table where Harrison Smith and myself were dining;—only, of course this Stieglitz portrait gives me a much deeper impression.

I intend to write a review of the study for insertion in the *Double Dealer*. The only difficulty is, that when I begin to think about the abbreviations I must commit in order to qualify it for their niggard editorial limitations, I almost despair. This has occasioned the useless delay that I am still in regarding this matter which could really have been just as well done weeks ago when Gorham sent me the proofs. But I won't keep you longer with such details. But keep in mind above the other possible futilities of this letter my lasting joy and thanks, dear Waldo Frank, for your appreciation!

Prosit! Hart Crane

To Gorham Munson

Dear Gorham: March 2, 1923

For some odd reason I feel a great desire to write you although I have nothing to offer, or little anyway, beyond the reflection of a most annoying week. There is, however, a paradoxical qualification to add to the statement in the mention that the last several days have been equally among the most intense in my life. The annoyance comes in only on the scoring of a repressive *fate*. To be stimulated to the nth degree with your head burgeoning with ideas and conceptions of the most baffling interest and lure—and then to have to munch ideas on water heaters (I am writing another book for house fraus!) has been a real cruelty this time, however temporary. The more I think about my *Bridge* poem the more thrilling its symbolical possibilities become, and since my reading of you and Frank (I recently bought *City Block*) I begin to feel myself directly connected with Whitman. I feel myself in currents that are positively awesome in their extent and possibilities. "Faustus and Helen" was only a beginning—but in it I struck new *timbres* that suggest dozens more, all unique, yet poignant and expressive of our epoch. I went to hear D'Indy's II Symphony last night and my hair stood on end at its revelations. To get those, and others of men like Strauss, Ravel, Scriabine, and Block into *words* one needs to *ransack* the vocabularies of Shakespeare, Jonson, Webster (for theirs were the richest) and add our scientific, street and counter, and psychological terms, etc. Yet, I claim that such things can be done! The modern artist needs gigantic assimilative capacities, emotion,—and the greatest of *all—vision*. "Striated with nuances, nervosities, that we are heir to"—is more than a casual observation for me. And then—structure! What pleased me greatly about Frank's comment was the notice of great structural evidence in "F. and H." Potentially I feel myself quite fit to become a suitable *Pindar* for the dawn of the machine age, so called. I have lost the last shreds of philosophical pessimism during the last few months. O yes, the "background of life"—and all that is still there, but that is only three-dimensional. It is to the pulse of a greater dynamism that my work must revolve. Something terribly fierce and yet gentle.

You have no doubt wondered why I have behaved so strangely about the review for your *Study*. It is coming sometime. At present I have developed a chronic hesitation against it which must seem almost pathological. I am so enthused about it that I can't seem to adopt a level-headed, conventionally critical attitude about it. Also, the space for such considerations as I would like to get into is too restricted in the *Double-Skull* to permit much more than either a screed, ineffective or broken, or mere jacket type of advertisement. I hope you won't misinterpret my delay at any rate. As I said in my last note the typography, paper, cover, photograph—everything in fact, is of the best taste and distinction. This book is bound to do you as much good as Frank. The latter is shown by Stieglitz's picture to be an extremely mystic type. Don't think me silly when I call the head and the eyes extremely beautiful. Frank has done me a world of good by his last letter (which promised another soon including further points on "F. and H.") and, as I wrote him, now I feel I can walk calmly along the sidewalk whereas before I felt only defiance. He gripped the mystical content of the poem so thoroughly that I despair of ever finding a more satisfying enthusiast.

And now to your question about passing the good word along. I discover that I have been all-too easy all along in letting out announcements of my sexual predilections. Not that anything unpleasant has happened or is imminent. But it does put me into obligatory relations to a certain extent with "those who are in the know", and this irks me to think of sometimes. After all, when you're dead it doesn't matter, and this statement proves my immunity from any "shame" about it. But I find the ordinary business of "earning a living" entirely too stringent to want to add any prejudices against me *of that nature* in the minds of any publicans and sinners. Such things have such a wholesale way of leaking out! Everyone knows now about Bynner, Hartley and others—the list too long to bother with. I am all-too free with my tongue and doubtless always shall be—but I'm going to ask you to advise and work me better with a more discreet behavior.

I enclose a note to Matty which I hope you will return me with your next. It describes my attitude and opinion of him without my needing to write it out again. I think I am "through" with that skipping snipe.

As ever, Hart

To Charlotte and Richard Rychtarik

New York City
Dear Lotte and Richard: Sunday

Did you see the name of the car I rode here in? It was called "The High Bridge"! What do you think of that??!!??!! Wonderful??!!??!!

Your cakes are all gone. Both Gorham and Eliza think they are *great*. Richard's pictures, too!

I am quite happy. A long walk this afternoon in salt air and clear sunlight. Everyone carrying canes and wearing bright clothes. Lunch tomorrow with Waldo Frank. Munson is enthusiastic about my staying with them. They have a fresh and charming apartment with room enough for me, so everything is FINE.

I sat a long while thinking about how beautiful you both were when I left you last night. Yes,—of course, Life is very beautiful when there are such people to meet and love as I love you both. Be very happy. Along with me. I never felt better before.

I'll write again soon,

hastily, Hart

To Waldo Frank

New York City
Easter

Dear Waldo:

I couldn't seem to get time before this hour to thank you for your letter of introduction. I called on Mr. Michaels last week, but he will not return from his trip until tomorrow, so I am yet to see him.

I don't need to mention that it was great to shake hands and talk with you. This I must mention, however,—that we have not yet had a real meeting. My mind has been packed with things that must be talked over with you when conditions are opportune. I am not intending mysterious words. But I am looking forward to the time—perhaps the times—that we shall get together and (in the wonderful slang phrase) "spark." Since reading *City Block* I have not wavered in an enthusiastic conviction that yours is the most vital consciousness in America, and that potentially I have responses which might prove interesting, even valuable to us both. My statements are awkward, and I really do not know how to proceed about such conversations: they "usually", as you know, "just happen". All this leads to a very simple suggestion, however,—and that is that I hope you will let me know when you are next in town when we can lunch or dine together.—

Gorham sends his regards also.

Faithfully, Hart

To Alfred Stieglitz

4 Grove Street
Dear great and good man, Alfred Stieglitz: April 15, 1923

I don't know whether or not I mentioned to you yesterday that I intend to include my short verbal definition of your work and aims in a fairly comprehensive essay on your work. I had not thought of doing this until you so thoroughly confirmed my conjectures as being the only absolutely correct statement that you had thus far heard concerning your photographs. That moment was a tremendous one in my life because I was able to share all the truth toward which I am working in my own medium, poetry, with another man who had manifestly taken many steps in that same direction in *his* work. Since we seem, then, already so well acquainted I have a request to make of you regarding the kernel of my essay, which I am quoting below as you requested. Until I can get the rest of my essay on your work into form, I would prefer that you keep my statement in strict confidence. I would like to give it a fresh presentation with other amplifications and details concerning what I consider your position as a scientist, philosopher or whatever wonder you are. You know the world better than I do, but we probably would agree on certain reticences and their safeguarding from inaccurate hands. I shall be up to see you probably very soon, and we can talk again. The reason for my not accompanying Mr. Munson this afternoon, however, is that I want to get into certain explanations of your photographs about which, now, I feel a certain proud responsibility.

Yours faithfully, Hart Crane

"The camera has been well proved the instrument of personal perception in a number of living hands, but in the hands of Alfred Stieglitz it becomes the instrument of something more specially vital—apprehension. The eerie speed of the shutter is more adequate than the human eye to remember, catching even the transition of the mist-mote into the cloud, the thought that is jetted from the eye to leave it instantly forever. Speed is at the bottom of it all—the hundredth of a second caught so precisely that the motion is continued from the picture infinitely: the moment made eternal.

"This baffling capture is an end in itself. It even seems to get at the motion and emotion of so-called inanimate life. It is the passivity of the camera coupled with the unbounded respect of this photographer for its mechanical perfectibility which permits nature and all life to mirror itself so intimately and so unexpectedly that we are thrown into ultimate harmonies by looking at these stationary, yet strangely moving pictures.

"If the essences of things were in their mass and bulk we should not need the clairvoyance of Stieglitz's photography to arrest them for examination and appreciation. But they are suspended on the invisible dimension whose vibrance has been denied the human eye at all times save in the intuition of ecstasy. Alfred Stieglitz can say to us today what William Blake said to as baffled a world more than a hundred years ago in his 'To the Christians:'

> 'I give you the end of a golden string:
> Only wind it into a ball,—
> It will lead you in at Heaven's gate,
> Built in Jerusalem's wall.' "

To William Sommer

New York City
Dear Bill: May 9, 1923

At LAST! a letter from you!!! And let me mention that it was one of the most beautiful I ever got from anyone. AND I am expecting more. I read it the second and third times during my meal last night down in one of the Italian restaurants on the lower East Side. There you get a bottle of wine (fine, too!) and a good meal (that delights the eyes as well as the stomach) for about $1. And such service! The waiters all beam and are really interested in pleasing you. As Rychtarik said when he was here last week, it's just like Europe. I don't know where I should have been by this time, however, had it not been for three or four fine people,—Gorham and his wife, and Slater Brown (the friend of Cummings, "B" in *The Enormous Room*) who, in spite of knowing me only a couple of weeks, has put me up nights in his room during the recent spell of grippe in the Munson household, and who has kept me in funds, poured wine into me, and taken me to the greatest burlesque shows down on the lower east side that you ever imagined. We went to one last night, and I so wished you were along. (They do everything but the ACT itself right on the stage, marvelous jazz songs, jokes, etc. and really the best entertainment there is in N.Y. at present). I have bids in for jobs at two very good agencies. The thing is a farce, however, the way you are kept waiting to know the outcome of one interview after another with various executives. J. Walter Thompson have had me on the string for three weeks, and a letter this morning tells me that within the next few days I must drag myself up there again for another interview with one more Thompson executive. It is the same way at Batten's. I shall have to cast about for anything available from stevedoring to table-waiting pretty soon if they don't get a move on.

Of course I have been rushing around to a lot of other agencies, too, but the ones I just mentioned are the only ones who have anything to offer me at the present time. I am very glad that you reminded me about the cost of the photographs as I certainly can use as much of that money as you can afford to send me at the present time. Hill charged me $20.00 for the six reproductions. I can't cash any check here, so if you can send me whatever portion of this amount in currency through the mail (I enclose an addressed envelope) I'll be immensely grateful. There is, you realize, no use whatever in my thinking about returning to Cleveland. I should simply have to go through the same process there of looking around for work, and under embarrassing conditions. You need me HERE, now, more than *there*, too, Bill, as I want to do everything I can to get your pictures shown around and maybe bought. And also, in almost every way, N.Y. is getting to be a really stupendous place. It is the center of the world today, as Alexandria became the nucleus of another older civilization. The wealthier and upper parts of the city have their own beauty, but I prefer as a steady thing the wonderful streets of this lower section, crowded with life, packed with movement and drama, children, kind and drab looking women, elbows braced on window ledges, and rows of vegetables lining the streets that you would love to paint. Life is possible here at greater intensity than probably any other place in the world today, and I hope and pray that you will be able to slip down here for a week or so during the summer. You must plan on it. Later on I shall probably take a small apartment with Brown, and then there will be plenty of room for you to stay with us at no expense at all.

What you say about Mart worries me. Is she ill? or what does your reference mean? If you can manage it please send a part of my money quite soon, and please don't tell anyone but Mart and Sam that I am in such a predicament. It won't last much longer, I'm sure. My love to you, Bill, and also to Mart, the boys, and Sambo.

As ever, Hart

To Wilbur Underwood

4 Grove Street
New York City
Dear Wilbur: Wednesday

No, even I at this time cannot quite curse the world. While the great abstract entity, mass, (or what you will) of life has exerted its utmost cruelties upon me again, those few worthies called friends, have somehow alleviated it all with attentions, spiritual and otherwise, and I can still be glad of living. When your letter and its contents came I had not a sou, but you and others are helping to pull me through quite beautifully. I shall get something to do now fairly soon. Gratitude is something that I really enjoy as a privilege, so please accept a thanks which is doubly felt.

You must have guessed by now that I'm in love. I told you about "B" in my last letter. This is a quite unsensual and peculiar case, for B's physical propensies are quite in the opposite direction. This real affection is, however, sufficient in other ways. I feel a real reciprocation, and the man's beauty of manner, face, body and attitude has made me a most willing slave. How it will end doesn't matter. At least not in my present mind. We are going to take an apartment together when I get a job, and I'm sure of a certain stimulation from the fine companionship. I saw Harry off on the boat, and just got a boat letter from Southampton. He won't be back until next spring, I guess. Summer in England and then China and Japan again. I have to rush everything now,—this letter included, so please forgive its ill writing and worse-assembled contents.

Write me soon.

As always, Hart

To Grace Hart Crane and Elizabeth Belden Hart

Dear Grace and Grandma: Friday evening

All week I've been trying to get a chance to write you, and you will never understand *all* the complications that have prevented me—simply because they are beyond description.

I got hired by J. Walter Thompson Tuesday morning at the same time that the other job with the trade journal, "Machinery" broke through also. It was a matter of choosing the better one,—which wasn't hard to do. This agency is either the first or second largest in the world and provides a maximum of opportunities. They liked my copy from the first, and so much so that they have practically made a place for me in the dept. of statistics and investigation until they need me in my real field. I work in a beautiful building on Madison Ave near where the Noyes school used to be, and just a block from *5th* Ave. Thompson occupies four whole floors of the building and you get a fine series of views from the windows. They have started me in at 35.00, but most of their copy writers get 75.00 to 100.00 a week. I think I have, all considered, made a big jump in the last 2 months, though it would astonish you to know the many sleepless nights and dreary days it has cost me. I haven't talked about *that* and I won't begin to now when things are on the mend, but suffice it to say that it is very hard living with two people who don't know anything about housekeeping in a tiny apartment,—and then to have them both get sick and necessitate your moving around from one place to another, clothes here, there and everywhere and not knowing where the next meal was coming from.

I don't know what I should have done had it not been for
Slater Brown who has done all kinds of gracious things for me.
Given me money, the key to his room and slept on the floor
(insisted on it) that I might be comfortable. I'm not feeling
anything but love and gratitude toward Gorham, but had it
not been for Brown I should certainly have given up long
before my job. Gorham and Liza live on the edge of things all
the time, and so—I could accept only so much and no more
from them when my funds gave out.

As Gorham is entertaining a writer from the South at pres-
ent I am staying again with Brown until the first of the month
when my pay comes and I can afford a room. About 2 weeks
ago I asked Bill Sommer if he could pay me the $20.00 I in-
vested for him in the photos (you know how long ago that
was) and after all this time he comes back with a letter con-
taining $5.00! That's thoughtfulness for you. The only pictures
he has ever sold have been sold through my efforts, and their
total returns alone amount to nearly $100.00. I'm through
trying to help such people out. If I hadn't been damned tough
I couldn't have got through this ordeal without sickness, but I
guess I've pulled through very well. I nearly died for awhile
with hemmoroids and extreme constipation, but have finally
found a very satisfactory cure for that. Now that it's all over I
feel free to tell you some of my past troubles, and mainly by
way of assurance that I've done my best all the time to keep
you free from worries (they wouldn't have done any good,
after all) and write as often as I could.

It's very fine, I think, that I should have accomplished all I
have recently instead of waisting for two more years in Cleve-
land. My samples wouldn't have proved any more effective in
convincing a N.Y. agency then than they have been lately, and
I am where its best for me to be in every sense now—just so
much sooner!

Today was lovely on the Ave. I enjoy my walks at lunch hour
when every body is out and the streets just blaze with life and
colour. N.Y. has never been so gay before—it certainly is the
only place to live in this country.

This has been a very sloppy letter, rushed off at a great rate
and full of unpleasant details. I just felt like getting rid of some
confidences inasmuch as they are so much on my mind that I

can't settle down to write a gayer letter until relieved of them. You can imagine how busy I am—working all day, and bustling around for food and lodging until bed time. The details of the decent toilette, alone, under such erratic circumstances, take a lot of extra time. But it's all going to be cleared up now very soon, and I'll settle back to a steady gait, plenty of sleep and more peace and quiet.

I *must* get to bed. Write me soon, and mention as casually as you wish that I'm connected with J. Walter Thompson. *To those who know* it is a very flattering connection.

Good night!/Hart

Write me at 4 Grove until further notice

To Grace Hart Crane

45 Grove Street

Dear Grace: Sunday, June 10, 1923

This is really the first moment this week I have had to write you. There is always someone who wants you to dine with him and then it is quite usually difficult to get away before bedtime. I have been getting to sleep more, however, and today, after a regular home cooked dinner with Brown & his lady (who is a fine cook) I feel "as usual" for Sunday. Really, I'm having the finest time in my life. There's no use trying to describe the people I go round with. Not that there are so many —there could easily be, but I'm always cutting down on all but the few I like the most. Last night marketing with Sue and Bill Brown, down in the Italian section (where every one looks so happy!) was a perfect circus. We carried pots and pans, spinach, asparagus etc. etc. from place to place—only buying one kind of thing in each store—jostling with the crowds etc. I've never been with young people I enjoyed so much, and they, of course, have had real lives. Then there is Kenneth Burke up at the *Dial* office, Matty Josephson (who has suddenly been moved to value me highly), Edward Nagle, Gaston Lachaise, Malcolm Cowley—but what's the use going on with so many mere names. You can see how much fun I am having—and all the more because I have a job and a totally different world to live in half the time. Did I write you that I am getting quite a reputation with my "Faustus & Helen" poem? Although it is only now being printed in Florence, those critics and writers who have seen it are acclaiming me with real gusto. Waldo Frank asked me to luncheon with him recently and said I was the greatest contemporary American poet with that piece alone. And John Cowper Powys, whose *Suspended Judgement* and *Visions & Revisions* you have read, is very enthusiastic. Since I got presented with my Victrola I am all ready to start again on *The Bridge*. Waldo Frank is very anxious for me to have that finished, as he intends to take me up to his publisher, (Boni & Liveright) and have me published in volume form. But, of course, such things *can't* be rushed as he understands.

I have not seen or heard from Miss Spencer since I made her my initial bow. She spoke of finding me something but evidently didn't sprain herself in the attempt. That's alright, however. There was little reason why she should have. I didn't *ask* her, anyway. I shan't see her again, as she is your friend and we have nothing special in common any way. Waldo Frank, Alys Gregory & others used some influence in getting me my job with *J. Walter Thompson* (get the name right this time!) but I never would have got it if my samples and conversation had not convinced them. I begin to see N.Y. very much more intimately since I've been working. It makes living here far more pleasant than ever before. Such color and style (on men, too) I've never seen before—no two alike. That's what is so interesting—the perfect freedom of wearing what you want to, walking the gait you like (I have a much less hurried gait than you're familiar with) and nobody bothering you.

I don't know many at the office yet. It's too immense and I'm confined to a highly specialized dept. but I've already been invited out to tea by the personnel secretary. They employ a lot of real writers as copy writers at Thompson's and have an entirely different feeling about art & business than you encounter any place west of N.Y. In fact its a feather in your cap if you know a little more than you're "supposed to" here. I think I've gained immeasureably by coming here now instead of dragging along in Cleveland month after month.

Willy bounced into the office the other day and quite surprised me. I expect to see him some evening this week and hear more of his plans. He is staying with some friends at Rye, (N.Y.) at present. Charlotte lives just around the corner from me. I found her card in the mail box this morning saying that she was back from her visit to her mother in Rayland, Ohio, where she has been for three weeks or so. She is more cheerful here than I've ever seen her before. Is making good money & has plenty of company. I didn't know anything about Binet's operation. He'll probably settle in Paris, however, if Bloch stays on in Cleveland. Frank cannot understand why I didn't know Bloch in Cleveland and is going to introduce us soon when Bloch comes here for a month's vacation.

You asked about Mrs. Walton. She looks as uncanny as ever, and more severe as she gets older. Mme Lebeque is almost a mystery. But Mrs. Walton knows she went back to France two summers ago and never came back, and *thinks* she is staying with her husband again from a hint on a postal card she sent.

The Smiths move out on Long Island tomorrow for the summer. The Habicht's whom I have had time for only one visit with, will probably also go soon. I look forward to a swim or two at Long Beach soon. I haven't had a touch of rose fever—that is great to escape and alone would be reason enough for my living here.

I'm glad to hear about the C.A. trouble. I think we are to be envied as compared to *that* family. I want to congratulate you on your gift from J. Taylor, Esq! I can see you speeding around in a perfect frenzy of excitement and elation. Willy mentioned your great kindness in driving him to the station and your pulchritude & style as well.

God, but what a long letter, but you *would* have it!

Love to Grandma, Hart

To Alfred Stieglitz

45 Grove Street
Dear STIEGLITZ: Fourth of July
    Your letter was the most welcome thing that has come to me in these last two weeks since you left, however late and partial my response may seem to be. You should have heard from me

much before this if I hadn't been neck high in writing some climacterics for my *Bridge* poem. That simply carried me out of myself and all personal interests from the dot of five until two in the morning sometimes—for several days during which I was extremely happy. Those were also the very days when I wanted most to write you,—paradoxically as it sounds, I *was*, of course, for you and I meet on the same platform in our best and most impersonal moods,—SO, I've been with you very much. The thing which hurts me now that I have the time to write letters, is that I not only have left the creative currents that would have prompted me to better statements than I am usually equal to,—but also that I'm in a low state of reactions towards everything, following an evening with Mr. Josephson. Malice seems to settle inertly but very positively in some people, and as he is somehow attached to several really fine friends of mine whose company I would hate to forego on such account, I suppose I must learn to face this little clown with better results. So far, I can only say that wine is no ally against such odds. It even turns to vinegar! and that is much less pleasing than pure water. I don't need to say any more to you about this man, his vacant mind, vague eyes and empty hands. We've given that enough attention. I rant here merely because I have been cheated (willy-nilly) of pouring out a clearer cup today, as I had planned. I, in the end, am really the one to blame.

When I say that I welcomed your letter it doesn't mean that I was unconcerned enough with its testament of pain and accident not to think about you and your situation many hours. What the details of those matters were certainly would not help me to realize any the better that you have been going through a very tumultuous period and that it has been very fortunate that you should arrive in the country when you did, not that you escaped them,—but that you were able to *see* them more tranquilly. The city is a place of "broken-ness", of drama; but when a certain development in this intensity is reached a new stage is created, or must be, arbitrarily, or there is a foreshortening, a loss and a premature disintegration of experience. You are setting the keynote now for a higher tranquillity than ever. It is an even wider intensity, also. You see, I am writing to you perhaps very egoistically, but you will understand that I am always seeing your life and experience very solidly as a part of my own because I feel our identities so much alike in spiritual direction. When it comes to action we diverge in several ways,—but I'm sure we center in common devotions, in a kind of timeless vision.

In the above sense I feel you as entering very strongly into certain developements in *The Bridge*. May I say it, and not seem absurd, that you are the first, or rather the purest living indice of a new order of consciousness that I have met? We are accomplices in many ways that we don't yet fully understand. "What is now proved was once only imagined", said Blake. I have to combat every day those really sincere people, but limited, who deny the superior logic of metaphor in favor of their perfect sums, divisions and subtractions. They cannot go a foot unless to merely catch up with some predetermined and set boundaries, nor can they realize that they do nothing but walk ably over an old track bedecked with all kinds of signposts and "championship records". Nobody minds their efforts, which frequently amount to a great deal,—but I object to their system of judgment being so regally applied to what I'm interested in doing. Such a cramping cannot be reconciled with the work which you have done, and which I feel myself a little beginning to do. The great energies about us cannot be transformed that way into a higher quality of life, and by perfecting our sensibilities, response and actions, we are always contributing more than we can realize (rationalize) at the time. We answer them a little vaguely, first, because our ends are forever unaccomplished, and because, secondly, our work is self-explanatory enough, if they could "see" it. I nearly go mad with the intense but always misty realization of what *can* be done if potentialities are fully freed, released. I know you to feel the same way about your camera,—despite all that you actually *have* done with it already. In that sense I hope to make it the one memorable thing to you in this letter that I think you should go on with your photographic synthesis of life this summer and fall, gathering together those dangerous interests outside of yourself into that purer projection of yourself. It is really not a projection in any but a loose sense, for I feel more and more that in the absolute sense the artist *identifies* himself with life. Because he has always had so much surrounding indifference and resistance such "action" takes on a more relative and limited term which has been abused and misunderstood by several generations,—this same "projecting". But in the true mystical sense as well as in the sense which Aristotle meant by the "imitation of nature", I feel that I'm right.

I shall go on thinking of you, the apples and the gable, and writing you whenever I can get a moment. So much has to be crammed into my narrow evenings and holidays, that I am becoming a poor correspondent with everyone, I fear. You will realize how much I am with you, I feel sure, by other signs. I am sending you a roughly typed sheet containing some lines from the *Bridge*. They symbolize its main intentions. However, as they are fragmentary and not in entirely finished form, please don't show them around. I only want you to get a better idea of what I'm saying than could be "said" in prose. Some of the lines will be clear enough to give a glimpse of some of my ideas whether or not the Whole can be grasped from such fragments or not. Please write me often, and in answering I'll do my best.

Affectionately—to both you and O'Keefe, Your Hart Crane

To Charlotte Rychtarik

Dear Charlotte: July 21, 1923

Your lovely letter came to me this morning. . . . I read it on the way to work. And I am full of happiness that you think of me as you do,—both you and Richard. Yes, it is my birthday and I must be a little sentimental,—especially as all my friends have recently left the city for places more cool and green and watery. It has been a frightful day, torrid and frying. And I have just come back from a lonely meal in Prince street,—the place where Richard ate with me, and where I have been many times since he left. Ah, yes, *there* is wine, but what is wine when you drink it alone! Yet, I am happy here in my room with the Victrola playing Ravel,—the Faery Garden piece which you and I heard so often together up in my room in Cleveland. When I think of that room, it is almost to give way to tears, because I shall never find my way back to it. It is not necessary, of course, that I should, but just the same it was the center and beginning of all that I am and ever will be, the center of such pain as would tear me to pieces to tell you about, and equally the center of great joys! *The Bridge* seems to me so beautiful, —and it was there that I first thought about it, and it was there that I wrote "Faustus and Helen", which Waldo Frank says is so good that I will be remembered by that, whether or not I write more or not. And all this is, of course, connected very intimately with my Mother, my beautiful mother whom I am so glad you love and speak about. Indeed it was fine of you to go over and see her as I asked you to do, Charlotte and Richard! And may I also say, in the same breath, that your letter was very painful? It really was,—because I have known all the things you said about her unhappiness for many, many months. *And* there is really nothing that can be done: that is the worst of it. I am sure if you think a minute about my Grandmother's age you will realize from that alone that my Mother could not possibly leave her to come here or anywhere else. And my Grandmother, at her age, cannot move. My mother has had her full share of suffering and I have had much, also. I have had enough, anyway, to realize that it is all very beautiful in the end if you will pierce through to the center of it and see it in relation to the real emotions and values of Life. Do not think I am entirely happy here,—or ever will be, for that matter, except for a few moments at a time when I am perhaps writing or receiving a return of love. The true idea of God is the only thing that can give happiness,—and that is the identification of yourself with *all of life*. It is a fierce and humble happiness, both at the same time, and I am hoping that my Mother will find that *feeling* (for it need not be a conscious thought) at some time or other. She must *accept everything* and as it comes (as we all must) before she can come to such happiness, glorious sorrow, or whatever you want to call it. You must never think that I am not doing all I can to make my Mother's life as bright as possible, even though I do not always succeed. I am doing work of a kind which I should not choose to do at all except that it makes me (or will make me) more money in the end than the simpler things which would satisfy my own single requirements—and just because I want to provide for my mother's future as much as I can. We shall be together more and more as time goes on, and this separation at present is only temporary. You don't know how grateful I am that you have given her your sympathy and love, and that has been *real* or she would not have confided in you the way she has.

It is fine that you had your luck turn so good on Friday, the 13th! The fact that you have found some new friends, too, is fine. One cannot live in these days and in such places as cities without at least a few friends that like the same things as you do and have minds and souls. I have made several fine friendships since I came here this time, and one that is a very great joy to me. Are you planning to go and see your Mother in Prague? I meant to have asked you before how she is, how she took the journey etc. She was so fine that day when we put her on the boat that I shall always remember her delicate smile.

I hope that I have not put you and Richard to too much trouble about those books. They will be fine here with me in my room. Mother sent me my trunk (that much debated question which you will remember!) this week, and it was full of all kinds of dear familiar things that you have seen and touched in my room. There is that ivory Chinese box, for instance, which is here before me as I write. It looks very charming on the black table next to the jade Buddha that Harry brought me from China.

I have not written much this last week,—too hot for one thing,—and then there are always people dropping in in the evening. But I am sending you a copy (to keep) of the last part of *The Bridge* which is all that I have done so far, that is, in a lump. You will remember enough of what I told you a long time ago about my general ideas and the plan of the entire poem to understand it fairly well anyway. It is sheer ecstasy here,—that is, all my friends who have seen it, say that. It was written verse by verse in the most tremendous emotional exaltations I have ever felt. I may change a few words in it here and there before the entire poem is finished, but there will be practically the same arrangement as what you see. If I only had more time away from office work I should have made much faster progress,—but I am perfectly sure that it will be finished within a year,—and as it is to be about four or five times as long as the enclosed fragment when it is complete,—I shall have been working about as fast on it as I have ever worked in the past. I am especially anxious to finish it, however, because then I shall have all my best things brought out in book form, and with a jacket or cover by Richard Rychtarik, I hope. Waldo Frank is anxious to introduce me to his publisher when the right time comes, and so there is no doubt but that the book will come out evenutally. In the meantime there is a long essay that I hope to write on the photography of Alfred Stieglitz. I ought to have about two weeks for that *away from everything*, when I could shut myself up somewhere and not have my mind taken away from it for a moment. In it I shall have to go very deep,—into, perhaps, some of the most delicate problems of art in the future. You see, I too, have my moments of despair,—for there is so little time for me to think about such things. I am succeeding in my position with the advertising agency quite well,—but all that means *more* work there, and even *less* time for what I want to do. I am forced to be ambitious in two directions, you see, and in many ways it is like being put up on a cross and divided. I hope to succeed in them both,—the reasons you will easily understand. This last week I got promoted to the copy department, and on Tuesday night I shall take the train for Chicago. Business of the company, of course, which will keep me out of New York for probably about ten days or two weeks. Being with the largest advertising agency in the world is giving me fine experience that will get me higher-paid positions in other places after a while. In many ways I have been very lucky to get placed so well at my age, so I complain about nothing except that I would like to have the days twice as long as they are—for all I want to do.

Richard will hear from the *Dial* about his work sometime soon, I think. I know that Dr. Watson has made his selection anyway. Do not worry if I am unable to get the rest of the pictures back to you for several months,—they are always taken good care of at the *Dial* office. It might even be a good thing to keep them on here until fall when some of the galleries begin to sell things again. I wish you would let me know what you think about such a plan.

Willy and I were going to write you a little note last Sunday when I was visiting him and his hosts, the Fords, out at Rye. But there was too much activity to do anything of that sort at all,—we spent many hours out in a sail boat with charming people singing songs and eating and swimming. I enjoy Willy here much more than I ever did in Cleveland, maybe because he has changed a little since his trip to Europe, but more likely because he is not bothered by some of the things which he used to find ugly in Cleveland. He came to town last Thursday and spent the night here with me in my cubic room (it is just the shape of a cube) (this doesn't mean that it is terribly small,—because the ceiling is immensely tall).

Charles wrote me a birthday letter which I appreciate very much, in fact I am very grateful to you all. You mustn't think I don't want your letters or as many as you can write! I only meant that I cannot always get around to answer them as soon as I would like.

Love to Richard, too, your Hart

To Alfred Stieglitz

45 Grove Street

Dear Stieglitz: August 11, 1923

The imagination dwells on frangible boughs! For ten days now I've been travelling through the middle west on *business* for the company. Investigating certain sales facts and figures among hardware and paint dealers on Barrelled Sunlight, a kind of white paint! My mind is like dough and *The Bridge* is far away. Your card was a warm signal to me on the morning of my joyful return. I never saw the Venus in her sphere before— looking on the world with the wind from Delphos in her hair! How do you do it? You have the distinction of being classic and realistic at once. That, of course, is what *real* classicism means. You don't know how much I think about my essay on you and your work! Please don't think me faithless. I fly in a rage when I think of the sacrifices I pay just to feed myself in the hope of time—a rightful heritage of all of us—and it takes time to say and think out the things I feel in your photographs. I'll try and write you more soon, but don't misunderstand any silences from me. *I am your brother always—*

Hart Crane

To Jean Toomer

Dear Jean: Sunday, August 19

Your little note was on the table when I came roistering in with Burke and the Cowley's after much to drink. The evening was dull, however, and I'd much better have talked it out with you!

There's nothing to tell except that I had a very doleful tired reaction to my western trip which I'm just pulling out of—into the merest static acceptance of things on a physical plane. For a while I want to keep immune from beckonings and all that draws you into doorways, subways, sympathies, rapports and the City's complicated devastations. Besides, the new copy-writing work at the office is a strenuous spending. A fine lot of dross to write to you about! But it will serve to accent somewhat, I hope, your chrysalis in the mountains.

I want words from you without reciprocal anticipations till I am solider. Just had breakfast with Gorham and Liza—with eggs of the usual sculptural perfection!

                                                        Hart

To Alfred Steiglitz

                                          45 Grove Street
                                          New York City
Dear Stieglitz: Sunday, August 25, 1923

I am hoping that you have seen Waldo, as you mentioned in your letter, by this time. The idea seemed so sensible to me, knowing as I have, the uneasy frictions that have bothered both of you and having regretted so much the evident mis-understandings all around. It is very important for us all—that is, all who are trying to establish an honest basis for what work we get a chance to do. It isn't, as you say, a matter of politics, —but something akin to our spiritual bread and butter. Not all our manna comes from the skies. And we suffer all-too-much from social malnutrition once we try to live *entirely* with the ghostly past. We must somehow touch the clearest veins of eternity flowing through the crowds around us—or risk being the kind of glorious cripples that have missed some vital part of their inheritance.

It's good to hear that you have been "at the camera" again and that you are recovering, with physical and nervous rest, that extremity of delicate equilibrium that goes into your best activities. I know what it is to be exiled for months at a time. They're the usual things with me, and lately it has been especially hard to be cut up between the necessities of a readjustment at the office (they've put me into a new department and I enjoy writing copy again to some extent) and the more natural propulsion toward such things as *The Bridge*. I've been in such despair about this latter for some time!—not seeing my way to introduce it in the way I want (the end and climax, what you have seen, is all that's done so far) and not getting the needful hours to ripen anything in myself. If I can once get certain obligations disposed of in my family, I shall certainly break loose and do only such simple labor for my room and board as will not come into my consciousness after "working hours". Streams of "copy" and ad layouts course through my head all night sometimes until I feel like a thread singed and twisted in the morning. This has been, very likely, as strenuous a year and as wasteful a one as I shall encounter for a long time, although you can never foretell such things as long as you have a family and connections. But I am looking forward to a more equable program when winter comes, when people's windows are shut, cats are quieter and the air more bracing.

Every once in a while I get a statement or so noted down in regard to my interpretation of you and your photographs. There are still many things in the lucid explanation of them that simply baffle me. To use a modern simile that occurred to me in that connection—it's like trying to locate "the wires of the Acropolis"; indeed, I may call my essay by that name before I get through. A little recent study of Picasso and his Harlequins has been illuminating on the inner realities and spiritual quantities that both of you possess, and perhaps by the time you get back to town I'll have some other comparisons ready for you to deny or substantiate. I certainly miss seeing you, now, and wish you might send me one or two of those prints that are otherwise committed to the waste basket sometime soon.

My love to you both, as ever Hart

To Jean Toomer

Dear Jean: September 28, 1923

Cane has come and I am grateful—and happy for your words. My mood is naive and somewhat awed today. The strange tempest has left off. It has as quietly settled as it suddenly rose. It has left one conscious thing (at least this and perhaps more) that evil accumulates, if not *in* us, at least in pockets and domains of the world without. And that the mark + gauge of our progress is quite obviously to be told in the successively more intense attacks of the dark force upon us—as we continue to defy it always more persistently. It takes flesh against our bodies, it assumes terrific marks and celebrations against our souls. The pointed finger appears through keyholes of our most sacred sanctuaries.

There were premonitions of a recent climax in the poem I sent you. The greater forces that we are encountering appear less and less recognizable in proportion to their more calamitous results. I have prayed to my perfect stone image, my Buddha with his frightful smile, the nick of fate upon his brow.

Isn't it fine that we can answer one another?! I mean the *three* of us.

Hart

To Jean Toomer

Dear Jean: Wednesday, October 2, 1923

The other side betrays my present whereabouts and "interests" (alas!) I've been stirred to a lot of imaginary conversations with you by your letters—one yesterday and another this morning. We must have that evening together! I'm going to see if I can get some wood and coal for a fire in my chimney.

I've been reading "Kabnis"—my first opportunity and feel I know your future better—but more when I see you. I hear from Lisa that the Neighborhood Playhouse crowd is waxing enthusiastic. More power to you! You don't know how I appreciate your note on "Possessions". It needs repairs however in more places than you pointed. At least I am inclined to think. Plan on staying with me when you come in if it suits you.

Your, Hart

To Grace Hart Crane

Grace, dear!   Friday, October 5, 1923

I had just got my pajamas on last night when there was a rap on the door. I opened and in walked Waldo Frank—behind him came a most pleasant-looking, twinkling, little man in a black derby—"Let me introduce you to Mr. Charles Chaplin", —said Waldo, and I was smiling into one of the most beautiful faces I ever expect to see. Well!—I was quickly urged out of my nightclothes and the three of us walked arm in arm over to where Waldo is staying at 77 Irving Place (near Gramercy). All the way we were trailed by enthusiastic youngsters. People seem to spot Charlie in the darkness. He is so very gracious that he never discourages anything but rude advances.

At five o'clock this morning Charlie was letting me out of his taxi before my humble abode. "It's been so nice", he said in that soft crisp voice of his, modulated with an accent that is something like Padraic Colum's in its correctness. Then he, blinking and sleepy, was swung around and was probably soon in his bed up at the Ritz.

I can't begin to tell you what an evening, night and *morning* it was. Just the three of us—and Charlie has known Waldo quite a while—They've been in Paris together and have a few mutual friends.

Among other things Charlie told us his plans (and the story of it) for his next great film. He has a five acre studio all his own now in Berkeley, and is here in New York at present to see that the first film he has produced in it gets over profitably. He doesn't act in it. But he wrote the story, directed and produced it entirely himself. It's running now for just a week or so more at the Lyric theatre to box prices. Then it will be released all over the country. *A Woman of Paris* it's called. I haven't seen it yet.

Our talk was very intimate—Charlie told us the complete Pola Negri story—which "romance" is now ended. And there were other things about his life, his hopes and spiritual desires which were very fine & interesting. He has been through so much, is very lonely (says Hollywood hasn't a dozen people he enjoys talking to or who understand his work) and yet is so radiant and healthy, wistful, gay and *young*. He is 35, but half his head is already grey. You cannot imagine a more perfect and natural gentleman. But I can't go on more now. Stories (marvelous ones he knows!) told with such subtle mimicry that you rolled on the floor. Such graceful wit, too—O that man has a mind.

We (just Charlie & I) are to have dinner together some night next week. He remembered my poem very well & is very interested in my work.

There's nothing else worth telling you about since my last letter. I am very happy in the intense clarity of spirit that a man like Chaplin gives one if he is honest enough to receive it. I have that spiritual honesty, Grace, and it's what makes me clear to the only people I care about.

Love, Hart

To Grace Hart Crane and Elizabeth Belden Hart

New York
45 Grove Street,

Dear Grace and Grandma: Oct. 12th, '23

This is a holiday: consequently I have had a late snooze and am left to read and write and do as I will for the rest of the time. It has been a very busy week. I have not seen Chaplin as I expected to, he has been under the weather up at the Ritz with too much champagne, parties and a bad cold. But Jean Toomer, Margaret Naumburg and Waldo Frank have been very much in evidence, and to the extent of a very fine home-cooked chicken dinner one evening at Margaret's which almost left me gasping—I ate so much. Toomer and I are great friends. I want to send you a copy soon of his book of short stories and a play which has just come out. It may interest you to read the inscription which he placed in the copy of this book which he recently gave me:—

> For Hart,
> instrument of the highest beauty, whose art,
> four-conscinal, rich in symbols and ecstasy,
> is great—
> whose touch, deep and warm, is a sheer illuminant
> with love
>   Jean   New York
>   24th Sept 23

I want you to meet Jean sometime. I can't begin to tell you my impressions of him now, but the biographical introduction to one of his reviews in the Dial last month is amusing in a certain sense:—"Jean Toomer, who is of negro extraction, is the grandson of P.B.S. Pinchback, the governor of Louisiana during the reconstruction. He was born in Washington, D.C. in 1894, and has travelled extensively throughout America. He studied at the University of Wisconsin, New York University and the College of the City of New York, and later taught in the University of Chicago." etc. Jean is only partly negro, looks more like an indian in color. In feature he is sharp and graceful.

Gorham and Liza were satisfactorily moved before G returned to the country last Monday. He was evidently better, even from his short stay before, but he intends, I think, to remain away for most of the winter. At least I hope so. We have all been very much implicated (entirely on the spiritual plane) with the present crisis in Frank's life, precipitated by the separation that has evolved between him and Margaret. It is a long story, very deep and interesting, which I shall speak more about when we get together. Waldo has never faced certain spiritual issues in his life—and now we all realize that he must either do so squarely and firmly, or else curtail his future development to a disastrous extent.

Since the weather cooled I have felt almost a new being. Having had the gas turned on in my radiator and tried it out several times, I am now confident that I shall be able to keep quite warm during the winter. Two friends of mine have offered me the use of their tubs and faucets whenever I want a hot bath, which I shall avail myself of, providing I cannot succeed in persuading the landlady to instal a hot water heater here. I do not think I shall have to buy any more clothes before spring what with the suit you are sending and what I have on hand to use. This certainly is fortunate, as my present salary at Thompson's just suffices for rent and food, really nothing more. I am waiting until the end of this month, the sixth month, to inquire about the possibilities of a raise. If I find that I am stalled off, I shall quietly investigate for a position elsewhere. I hear from all sides that Thompson's are famous for their low salaries anyway. A few people get vast amounts, and the rest are left to compensate each other with so called "cultured" environment. I have been working very hard this week on a stiff sort of proposition. So far they have given me only tough little nubbins to handle—jobs that didn't pay them anything and could best be turned over to a cheap man,—these little left-overs are, however, very often the most uninspiring and difficult things to handle.

I hope that your efforts for Glenn are going to have strong results. Please give him my heartiest salutations and good wishes when you meet him next. I think of you a great deal, and you must not be lonely. We are all going on in the regular course of things toward a higher consciousness of life and what it means. We have no reason or right to suppose that it should be predominantly happy—seen completely, from end to end, however, I think it is a great happiness. We must keep on overriding the details of pettiness and small emotions that dwarf it to keep on seeing it that way, and that can't be done without a real conscious effort and vision. We know each other too well to let physical separations mar very much. Christmas is not far away now, either, and then I shall see you for several days.

I meant to thank you for the five dollars before this, it enabled me to pay the advance deposit on my gas. You ask me if there is anything else I need in the way of clothing. Only a few soft collars, size 15 "Ideflex" brand, style "Montebrook". Don't bother much about them though,—I think I can manage that alright.

Remember that I am all right, and please don't worry any more. I have grown more in this last year than I can account for yet. I think we all have, and that's what matters. Love from

your

Hart

P.S.—If you ever want to write Gorham or Lisa—their new city address is *144 West 11th Street*. Give "Clip" a kiss for me.

To Grace Hart Crane

Dear Grace: Friday, Oct. 26th, '23

I am not going to the Island, but I expect to go up state to Woodstock for 6 weeks, leaving late next week. Have been invited to stay with Nagle and Brown in a house they have taken there for the winter. Please arrange to send me $15.00 per week while I am there. That will buy the necessary food, etc. When I get my rest and come back to town I expect to try some other kind of literary work, maybe with a publishing house, before accepting Thompson's offer again. They pay so damned little and expect so much—that I might do better another place.

At any rate I am going to have some time in the country and in the open air. Just now I am very exhausted, as I have said. Thank you for inviting me back to Cleveland, but you know there are too many people to talk to there and, after all, it's city life too. My present plan is much cheaper and better. The Island would have been best of all, but feeling that it was for sale and might move out from under my feet any moment I certainly should not enjoy it there now. I am very very sorry that you are selling it. Don't let yourself get taken in on any fake deal of exchange by this Cleveland man.

I'll write you more very shortly. Thank you for the contribution.

Love,

Hart

To Alfred Stieglitz

45 Grove Street
New York City
October 26, 1923

Dear Stieglitz:

I hardly know how to begin—such confusion reigns at present. It's the usual state, however, with the additional complication that my nerves are a little frazzled. In fact they got so on edge writing that damned advertising under the pseudo-refined atmosphere of the office I was working in that I had to resign the other day to save my mind. I have the prospect of coming back after a six week's vacation if I want to—but I don't want to, and as things stand at present, haven't got the money to carry me through the rest and contemplation that I need. Rather wound up, you see!

Your mention of the "sky" pictures really excited me. The greatest beauty comes out of repose, and I knew that as certain disturbances settled (were fought through) you would recapture the basis (on a higher plane than ever) for new penetrations and syntheses of vision. I had hoped to go down to a plantation that my grandmother and mother own in the West Indies this winter, in fact that was largely the basis of my leaving the job. My intention was to get the unbroken time there to write the essay on your work which I have never had the opportunity of doing here. I was also expecting to finish my *Bridge* poem (which, done, would complete the material for my first book of poems.) But these things must evidently wait. It is certain that they cannot be undertaken while my mind is divided between them and an office job. They are both of them too large conceptions to be accomplished under such tour de force conditions. Now, my mother writes me that the place may be sold at any time and that it is out of the question for me to go at all. *If* I can get somebody to lend me the money, however, I may possibly go right ahead, regardless. Both of my parents are interested in money only in connection with my actions, and I have never been persistent enough in the past to really clear that notion away.

Munson said that he had a fine letter from you, and he has probably answered it by this time telling you a number of things about his present position with regard to *Broom* and *Secession*. He is the noblest young man I know in this country. Experience seems only to sharpen a native integrity and an almost clairvoyant sense of spiritual values. He was obliged to leave the city for his health, and while I miss him a great deal, I hope that he will remain where he is for the rest of the winter. Waldo, as you know, leaves for Europe tomorrow. I am sorry that he couldn't get time to make you that visit. I have seen him going through a good deal, both in work and experience, and there is no use of trying to write out any details of these things. We shall talk about it some time. Margaret has also meant a great deal to me lately. Isn't this little handful of us fighting though?!

My love to Georgia too—Hart Crane

To Jean Toomer

Woodstock, New York
Dear Jean: Monday eve, November 4, 1923
A roisterous time! Cider, belly dances and cake walks over Sunday at O'Neills, and we didn't go to bed until daylight. Got here at Brown's and Nagle's place last night for dinner. Long walks today, wrestling matches and hide and seek on the lawn. My biceps are certainly swelling. The house is just right and the month promises very very much for me. I shan't be able to get down to any ratiocination until the Cowleys leave tomorrow, but I can see some sturdy days ahead, even though no pen shall touch the paper and the typewriter remains clickless. After all, it's been a good thing that I haven't had the time or the privacy to give myself to the recollection of the sad and wondrous night before I left. It keeps coming to me, though, in a kind of terrific rawness. And causes were outside of myself—and its gift a broken thing. It does cry for words, however,—and I'm wondering if I am equal to such an occasion, such beauty and anquish, all in one.
Saw Gorham for a moment in the village this morning, and expect to have a talk with him tomorrow. Matty J. is coming

to *this house* for a visit next week end! It doesn't especially disturb me if they don't stay too long. How is the Vic going, and Margy?

Love, hart

To Elizabeth Belden Hart

Sunday
Nov. 10th. '23
Woodstock, N.Y.

Dear Grandma:

Before I got your letter mailed your check came, but as I was at the postoffice at the time, there was no chance to open up the letter and include my thanks to you. I was sorry that the letter contained no words from either of you, but I suppose you were in a rush of some sort and maybe the election excitement had not yet subsided enough. I am going to assume at least that you are all well, or you would have said something.

It is a rainy day, but the last two days have been superb. We climbed up halfway on one of the mountains near here one afternoon. You could see for miles around, the same as the postcard that I sent you shows. I am getting myself hardened up—not wearing too much clothing and keeping meanwhile in motion a good deal. As I may stay here all winter I think it is a good way to avoid the possibility of later colds. At all odds it is certainly much better than stuffy offices, they are the worst things in the world for one. I remember last winter was quite miserable with all the colds I had.

I suppose Zell and Helen have been in the City and gone by this time. Sam has lost his job again, and writes me very touchingly. Eglin has taken a partner and pushed him out. Have you seen the Rychtarik's lately? Charlotte says she is studying music (piano) under Beryl Rubenstein. Richard LeGalliene, the poet, is living just half a mile away from us, and Gaston Lachaise and Mme. arrived last evening to spend the winter in a house they have taken for the winter here. We are going to have a great celebration on Thanksgiving. John Dos Passos (author of Three Soldiers) and some other folks are coming out from N.Y.

I'll write more very soon. Much love,

hart

To Jean Toomer

Woodstock, New York
Dear Jean: November 23

   Your letter voiced a mood that is still rather matching my
own. I am rather dissatisfied with the dormant state of my fac-
ulties, yet not enough so to make excuses even to myself. I
really am happy to hear the wind in the boughs, use the axe
and saw and even enjoy the bit of cooking which I share in
doing. There is not much time for other things except on rainy
days like the last, when I sat reading the *Golden Bough* and
alternating black cat "Jazz"—for tiger, "Chauncey Depew"
(on account of his dinner visits across the fields to neighboring
plantations) in my lap, now well protected with cordoroy. The
three of us got drunk on the wine filched last night from the
private cellar of the owner of this house. Great defense of
the MACHINE by Brown opposed by Crane and Nagle. Went
furious to bed. The night before it was Marinetti, John Brown,
KKK and Jesus Christ. Thanksgiving brings out Dos Passos
and a couple of women of good fame from the big city. Three
days of revelry are promised, and then I shall settle down to
something constructive as I'm due now to stay out here all
next month. Burke wants to rent my room and I'm tickled to
death to have some more calm and exercise and perfect my
mustache which makes me look very Breton, so B says. Every
day I have a walk and talk with Gorham into town for the
morning's mail and marketing. I am trying to get him out of
the fixed ideas relevant to the *Broom* rumpus, duel and person-
alities. I think the whole business has preyed upon his work
long enough and deserves to be dismissed in favor of more
worthy pursuits on his part—regardless of any actions on the
part of his opponents.

   The boat for Antwerp and Jerry still haunt me. Aside from
the three briefers I have done for the *Dial*, that poem has been
my only immeadiate concern. It is growing very slowly. I
doubt the possibility of ever printing it, but don't care. Signif-
icances gradually lift themselves from the trial lines. I send you
some of the poem as it stands at this hour, as you are fine
enough to be concerned. It was great to have your inquiry

about it. I think I shall call it "White Buildings" perhaps. Certainly it is one of the most consciously written things I have ever attempted, whether or not it has any sense, direction or interest to anyone but myself. Let me know if anything in it gets through at all to an outsider.

Brown and Nagle made the suggestion recently that they very much hoped you would feel like coming out here sometime in December for a few days. I've no idea how it strikes you, but you will get a real welcome from us all. I'll be back in town for better or worse around Jan. 1st. I don't think I can afford a trip before. How is Margey? I shall try to write her, but there have been entirely too many letters forced upon me here and I won't get around to it as soon as I should like. Give her my love.

As always, your Hart

This way where November takes the leaf
to sow only disfigurement in early snow
mist gained upon the night I delved, surely
as the city took us who can meet and go
(who might have parted, keen beyond any sea,
in words which no wings can engender now).

For this there is a beam across my head;
its weight not arched like heaven full, its edge
not bevelled, and its bulk that I accept,
triumphing not easily upon the brow . . .

And, margined so, the sun may rise aware
(I must have waited for so devised a day)
of the old woman whistling in her tubs,
and a labyrinth of laundry in the courted sky;
while inside, downward passing steps
anon not to white buildings I have seen,
leave me to whispering an answer here
to nothing but this beam that crops my hair.

(other verses even less developed—poem ends with following lines:)

Vaulted in the welter of the east be read,
"These are thy misused deeds."—
And the arms, torn white and mild away, be bled.

I think I ought to apologize for this page as it stands! h

To Elizabeth Belden Hart

Woodstock, New York
My dear Grandma: December 5, 1923

Your interest in my culinary triumphs is certainly very much appreciated. I've been waiting quite a while for the moment to tell you about the Thanksgiving dinner, etc. and have just about got adjusted again, the house in order and our simple program restored although the last guest left on Monday. Altogether, the party and every detail of the festivities was quite a success. Some things were very funny and some were a little aggravating. I think I did most of the cooking when it came right down to the last moment, as both my confreres were so occupied with their lady friends and rather daffy that they went around like dizzy roosters, and keeping the rest of the company entertained and out of the kitchen was some job, too.

The people we bought the turkey from had already cleaned it and plucked it, and had promised to make the stuffing. But at the last moment they went back on the stuffing, and so it was left to me entirely. You should have seen me going at it, sewing it up tight afterward and everything! Everyone said the stuffing was great, and I liked it myself. I rubbed the outside all over with salt and butter, and then the ten pound bird was put into a wonderful roasting machine that Lachaise brought out from New York which he got in the French bazaar. You put the bird on a long spit which had a crank and catches. One side of the cage was entirely open and that was turned toward the fire in the big studio. I never ate more luscious turkey than this process produced. You must have seen one of these roasting devices because similar ones have been used in New England for many many years. It's a large, fat oval shape and looks a little like a big tin pig on its legs. We kept turning the bird around inside until it was a rich brown and thoroughly done. The meal began with potato and onion soup made by Nagel. Then turkey with mashed potatoes, cranberry sauce, squash and gravey. Celery too. Then I made some fine lettuce salad with onions and peppers and french dressing. Dessert was composed of pumpkin pie and mince pie and the marvellous fruit cake. We had cider in abundance, Marsala wine and red wine as well as some fine cherry cordial. Nuts, raisins, etc. Quite a dinner, you see. And everyone went wild about the cake. We had all the walls hung with candles as well as the table. Sat down at five and didn't get up to dance until eight. I danced fat Mme Lachaise around until we both fell almost exhausted. Then there was a girl who could match me on my Russian dance and we did that together at a great rate. I forgot to mention that we had a Victrola, of course, which Lachaise bought in Kingston just the day before. Lots of jazz records, etc. Most of the guests had left by the following evening, but we have spent most of the time since in getting things straightened around again and catching up on our supply of wood.

While I had a wonderfully good time, I am hoping that we have no more company for the rest of this month. It's too much work and is distracting. I want things as quiet and restful as possible, and guests are always interfering with more personal pursuits. I was very much surprised, of course, to hear about Grace's job. Who is Josephine? and where is the establishment, what sort, etc.? I am glad that she has got into some kind of action other than housework, and I hope that it will not seem too strenuous for either of you. I keep thinking that an apartment would be so much better for you both. Rent out the house and let that pay your expenses in a smaller place. But maybe you can't get up the steam to move.

It is raining steadily today, and you can't even see the mountains through the overhanging mists. I like this country here more and more. In all kinds of weather it has unique beauties and I shall be sorry to leave it in January, which I must do, of course, as I must find some kind of work again. Your check was very welcome. I had begun to think that much embarrassment was due to come to me if I couldn't meet the modest demands of my board here, especially since both Brown and Nagel have just enough for themselves and no more, regardless of their generosity. Fifteen dollars a week is cheaper than I have ever been able to live before, but they pay the rent and fuel, etc. and would have to do so to the same extent whether I were here or not, so I am very lucky to share only in the cost of the groceries and meat.

I see you won't give me the chance to try out the dumplings! Perhaps it's just as well. I've been kidded a great deal about the apple sauce, or rather my 'temper' about it, as it has all been eaten up with avidity by all of us. Recipes or no recipes, I hope you will write me another such a good letter as the last one, Grandma, and soon! I'm not flattering you when I say you are superb. I hope that Grace will feel like writing me a longer letter than the last one soon. My love and deepest thanks to you both.

as ever, Hart

To Charlotte Rychtarik

Woodstock, New York
(2500 feet) verrückt!
December 10, '23

Dear Lotte:

I guess you and Richard have deserted me . . . . anyway I don't hear from you any more.

It may happen that I go to live on the top of a mountain near here very soon, I am not sure yet. But if I don't do that I shall have to go back to the City and take some tiresome job. On the top of the mountain I could be paid and have my expenses paid besides—just to take care of two horses, a cow and some chickens. The view is magnificent. And I should be alone —too much so, perhaps. Snow would come and for weeks I could not get down to see a single human being. Rather nice, though. I am thinking seriously of taking that job.

You should see me in my hunters coat, cordoroy pants and heavy shoes. This country is like the Tyrol, so Brown tells me, who was there last year. I have been chopping down trees and very strong. I have also grown a mustache—only it is very blonde and scarcely shows at all—very sharp and scratchy, however.

How is Charles? He doesn't write me any more, either. And I suppose you have had many letters from WE Lescaze, the thief and liar. He is a jolly bird, and not quite clever enough with his feathers to keep amusing one forever. He is being exhibited (one picture at least) at Wanamaker's Belmaison Galleries, so the paper says. That is the easiest place in NY to get into.

You should not forget me. I am free now—at least more so than ever before in my life, but that doesn't mean that I forget such people as you and Richard who have been so fine to me and whom I shall love always—even though I haven't any way of proving it but to just keep on saying so. I hear that my Mother has taken a Job of some kind and is working very hard. I am sorry to hear it, but I also know that she did not need to do it unless she felt like it. Everything is being sold as soon as possible. Only I refuse to sell myself any longer than I absolutely have to. I shall beg and steal when necessary to avoid it.

This letter is very intimate, and I have written it at the risk of a great deal of misunderstanding from you, I well know. Who knows,—perhaps you have some quaint ideas about me by this time. But I do hope that you will write me soon—if you feel like it—and tell me all about yourselves, how you are playing and how R is painting. I am sure you are gaining on Time! One must.

> your affectionate
> hart

To Grace Hart Crane

Woodstock, New York

Dear Grace: December 21, 1923

If it's as warm in Cleveland as it is around here—people must be hunting around to find Christmas, and Santa Claus must be still in Alaska waiting for more proper signs. I have just come back from town and all in a sweat with a few packages of provisions. The lilac bush beside the house has begun to sprout several times, and there is an epidemic of butterflies around Toronto, so the paper says. You don't like winter, so I suppose you are in comparative comfort so far. If you are using coal in the furnace it will make it easy to care for, which is good.

Grandma says that you are very much exhausted and too tired to go down to Zell's for the day. I'm sorry, because I think it would do you good in the end despite the extra effort involved. We are, all of us, in something of a strained state this Christmas but I don't think we need to be so much wrought up about it as you and Grandma apparently are. After all, Christmas is only one day in the year—and as a special day, I don't get half so excited about it (and haven't for some years) as I used to. It's too bad that we can't all be together, but that can't be helped. It wouldn't have made any difference so far as I could see, had I remained at Thompson's during all this time—so far as money side it goes. I was just keeping things going as it was, and had nothing left over for travelling expenses, and had I remained I might have incurred much more expense by this time by being flat on my back. I think you take my little rest and vacation a bit too strenuously. I'm going back to NY on the second or third of January (if I can get the carfare) and after that I won't ask for any more money. I don't know what I'm going to do, but I can probably wash dishes or work on the docks or something to keep skin and bone together. I shall keep my old room at 45 Grove Street (which is as cheap as any that can be found anywhere) as long as I can bamboozle the landlady. After that I'll have to depend on my good coat, or the kindness of friends. I've been able to store up a sufficient reserve of physical and nervous force while out here in the country to last me quite awhile, I think. I am not at all discouraged about anything, and I think that if you and Grandma will use your natural wits at a little better planning— you'll be able to get along fairly comfortably without working so hard. One can live happily on very little, I have found, if the mind and spirit have some definite objective in view. I expect I'll always have to drudge for my living, and I'm quite willing to always do it, but I am no more fooling myself that the mental bondage and spiritual bondage of the more remunerative sorts of work is worth the sacrifices inevitably involved. If I can't continue to create the sort of poetry that is my intensest and deepest component in life—then it all means very little to me, and then I might as well tie myself up to some smug ambition and "success" (the common idol that every Tom Dick and Harry is bowing to everywhere). But so far, as you know, I only grow more and more convinced that what I naturally have to give the world in my own terms—is worth giving, and I'll go through a number of ordeals yet to pursue a natural course. I'm telling you all this now, dear, because I don't want you to suffer any more than inevitable from misunderstandings—for once we see a thing clearly usually nine tenths of our confusion and apprehension is removed. Surely you and I have no quarrels, and I think you understand me well enough to know that I want to save you as much suffering from Life's obstacles as can be done without hypocrisy, silliness or sentimentality. You may have to take me on faith for some things, because I don't know whether it is possible for all people to understand certain ardours that I have, and perhaps there is no special reason why you, as my mother, should understand that side of me any better than most people. As I have said, I am perfectly willing to be misunderstood, but I don't want to put up any subterfuges before *your* understanding of me if I can help it. You didn't follow certain convictions that you had when you were my age because it wasn't easy enough; and I know what strong obstacles were put in your way. I, too, have had to fight a great deal just to *be myself* and *know myself* at all, and I think I have been doing and am doing a great deal in following out certain natural and innate directions in myself. By Jove—I don't know of much else that is worth the having in our lives. Look around you and see the numbers and numbers of so-called "successful" people, successful in the worldly sense of the word. I wonder how many of them are happy in the sense that you and I know what real happiness means! I'm glad we aren't so dumb as all that, even though we do have to suffer a great deal. Suffering is a real purification, and the worst thing I have always had to say against Christian Science is that it willfully avoided suffering, without a certain measure of which any true happiness cannot be fully realized.

If you will even partially see these facts as I see them it will make me very happy—and we can be much closer and more "together" that way than merely just living in the same house and seeing each other every day would ever bring about alone.

I have been thinking much about you and about dear Grandma —and I shall have you with me much on Christmas day. We'll be dancing a little, and are invited around to a couple of celebrations at other houses here, but there will be no such pretensious preparations as for Thanksgiving and no extra guests here. I really hope there will be a little snow both here and in Cleveland. It adds to things.

I am hoping that you will find time and will have the inclination to write me soon. It has been over a month now since your last. I want to thank Grandma for her check—and do, both of you,—have a little fun. I'm sure your friends must mean something to you, and they will not all forget you.

Love, Hart

To Charlotte Rychtarik

45 Grove St.,
New York City
Jan. 6, '24

Dear Charlotte:

Your lovely gift and long beautiful letter made me feel a little bit ashamed that I had written you such a hasty and doubting letter. Isn't it funny that just about the time one doubts humanity and begins to take some kind of active resentment against it, along comes fresh proof that there are, after all, many, many noble people that make life worth all kinds of trouble for the reward of having known them, kissed or shaken hands! I have been looking into your eyes—whether you knew it or not; you looked into mine in that letter—and I'm grateful for the confidence that you had in me, even though something made you doubt me a little. I really am just the same old person—just as moody and unreliable as ever I was in Cleveland when we used to exchange our troubles and get rid of them in some music or over a book or a picture.

What I said about "prostituting my mind", etc., I really mean't I *do* resent it—and because so many others as good and better than myself must also do the same in order to live and breathe doesn't help things at all. I shall keep right on talking that way—and probably not practice what I preach at all. I seemed very bitter in my letter because my mother seemed to think that a vacation was an extravagence—while I knew that it was the only thing for me to do in order not to go all to pieces. I feel now like a new man—better than I can ever remember feeling and realize that the country and hard work out in the keen sparkling air are the finest things in the world. Of course I should like to have stayed in the mountains even longer, but I know that I must now get to work again and earn some money. And I don't mind it a bit, either, feeling as I do. I have two appointments tomorrow and I don't think I shall have such a slow time finding work as before. It is a better season, "business is better" and I have had "experience in N.Y." which counts some.

I should have written you before this, but you know what the holidays are like, and I've also been very much on the move. There have been so many people here to see since I arrived and so many literary and artistic occasions that it really gets tiresome. Time just rushes by before one knows it.

My mother writes me that you and Richard are going to sail in May. I was hoping I should see you before that, but we'll have a great time whenever you come. This letter has been stupid after all—all about myself and "myself" isn't always interesting.

Please write me soon—and I hope you have time to see my mother once in awhile. She is so lonely!

Love and gratitude to you both.

Hart

To Gorham Munson

45 Grove Street

Dear Gorham: January 9, 1924

Back in the welter again. I've been so pressed with various desires and necessities that the thought of writing any one at all has seemed nearly impossible. I've lunched and dined with Burke and the Cowleys, seen the new Stieglitz clouds, Sunday-breakfasted with Jean and Lisa, argued an evening with Rosenfeld and Margy, chatted with O'Neill, Macgowan & R. Edmond Jones—Wescott, Matty, Light, and been to concerts with Jean—etc. etc. All this besides running around and looking for jobs. As all these contacts have brought so much in my mind to talk to you about, I began to and still do despair of including anything but the above catalogue in this letter. It will, after all, be only about a week longer before I see you and then we can have an extensive outburst. Meanwhile—I somehow feel about as solitary as I ever felt in my life. Perhaps it's all in the pressure of economic exigencies at present—but I also feel an outward chaos around me—many things happening and much that is good but somehow myself out of it, between two worlds. Of course none of this would be were I creating actively myself. It certainly helps things a lot that you are working on so well and it is very gratifying to see Burke and Cowley gravitating constantly more parallel to your initial theories and convictions. Cowley's gaucheries in admitting his mistakes and *tactics* are really funny. But I can't write you more details now.

Along comes a letter from my father this morning offering me a position with him as travelling salesman! This is unacceptable, of course, even though I now can't complete the rent on the room for the rest of this month and simply don't know what is going to happen. If worse comes to worse I can go back to Woodstock and stay with Fisher who urgently invited me to stay a month or so whenever I liked. Just now I haven't made up my mind about anything. I have no more illusions about advertising, yet that is the only thing I can talk about at all. Leffingwell (at Thompson's) is out of town, so I have not been able to attempt any reinstatement there. The lady at Machinery says she wants to use me there sometime and *may soon*, but the vacancy so far doesn't exist there. Hal Smith at Harcourt seems to be neither sufficiently interested in me nor my work to fulfill any of my hopes there. And so it goes. There's no point in going into more details.

Jean's new hygiene for himself is very interesting to me. He seems to be able to keep himself solid and undismayed. Certain organic changes are occurring in us all, I think, but I believe that his is more steady and direct than I have been permitted. My approach to words is still in substratum of some new development—the same as it was when we talked last together—and perhaps merely a chaotic lapse into confusion for all I dare say yet. I feel Stein and E.E.C. as active agents in it, whatever it is, and I've a short poem to show you soon which presents more interesting speculation to myself than it does to anyone else. Suffice to say that I am very dissatisfied with both these interesting people and would like to digest their qualities without being too consciously theoretical about it.

Stieglitz liked the drawings I brought back—and you'll like the one of Brown I think. I'd like to paint and draw half of the time, and write the rest. "Prince Llan" is published and I admire its strenuous prose. Its ideas are beyond criticism after a mere hasty first reading. Kenneth leaves for the South in another week, and I shall be sorry to miss him.

with love and haste! Hart

To Clarence Arthur Crane

45 Grove Street
New York City

My dear Father: January 12, 1924

Your letter has been on the table for longer than I had expected. I had wanted to answer it more promptly in view of your real consideration in offering me such a favorable opportunity in your business, but I've been so altogether occupied since I came back from Woodstock in looking around here for a new position, interviewing people and answering advertisements, that there has been only the evenings—when there was either someone in to call, or I was too tired to write you as I wanted.

By all this you will probably have guessed that I don't find it practical to accept your offer, kind as it is, and beyond all that I must also add in justice to us both that it would also not be honest of me to do so, either. I realize that in order to be understood in both the above reasons it is necessary that I at least attempt to explain myself in more detail than I may have gone into with you ever before, and as that is rather an unwieldy process within the limits of a letter I may only touch on a few points about myself and try to make them clear, leaving the rest to some later date when you may care to look me up in New York, provided I am here at your next visit. In what follows, father, I hope that you will take my word for it that there is no defense of my personal pride involved against any of the misunderstandings that we may have had in the past. I have come to desire to talk to you as a son ought to be able to talk to his father, that is, in a pure relationship, without prejudices or worldly issues interfering on either side. That was the basis of my first letter to you in three years—that I wrote a little over two months ago, and I hope it may be the basis of your interpretation of what I am writing you now. I, at least, am doing the most honest thing I know to do in whatever I have said to you and in whatever I may say to you since that time. That's a pledge from the very bottom of my heart.

In your letter you carefully advise me to turn a deaf ear to your offer if I find my advertising work so absorbing, pleasant and profitable that I might in later time regret a transfer into so widely divergent an enterprise as your business. You were perfectly right in presupposing that I had a considerable interest in this sort of work, for in less than three years I had got into the largest agency in the world and was to all outward appearances very much engrossed in carrying myself through to a highly paid and rather distinguished position.

But if there had been any chance to tell you before I should have stated to you I had no interest in advertising beyond the readiest means of earning my bread and butter, and that as such an occupation came nearest to my natural abilities as a writer I chose it as the quickest and easiest makeshift known to me. Perhaps, in view of this, it will be easier for you to see why I left my position at J Walter Thompson's at the last of October, unwise as such an action would be understood from the usual point of view. I went to the country because I had not had a vacation for several years, was rather worn with the strain of working at high speed as one does in such high geared agencies, and above all because I wanted the precious time to do some real thinking and writing, the most important things to me in my life. The director of the copy department asked me to see him when I came back to New York, but he has not returned yet from out of town and I don't know whether or not I shall return there. I told Grace that they had asked me to return definitely because I didn't want her to worry about me: she has enough worries as it is. But so much for that. . . .

I think, though, from the above, that you will now see why I would not regard it as honest to accept your proposition, offered as it was in such frankness and good will. I don't want to use you as a makeshift when my principle ambition and life lies completely outside of business. I always have given the people I worked for my wages worth of service, but it would be a very different sort of thing to come to one's father and simply feign an interest in fulfilling a confidence when one's mind and guts aren't driving in that direction at all. I hope you credit me with genuine sincerity as well as the appreciation of your best motives in this statement.

You will perhaps be righteously a little bewildered at all these statements about my enthusiasm about my writing and my devotion to that career in life. It is true that I have to date very little to show as actual accomplishment in this field, but it is true on the other hand that I have had very very little time left over after the day's work to give to it and I may have just as little time in the wide future still to give to it, too. Be all this as it may, I have come to recognize that I am satisfied and spiritually healthy only when I am fulfilling myself in that direction. It is my natural one, and you will possibly admit that if it had been artificial or acquired, or a mere youthful whim it would have been cast off some time ago in favor of more profitable occupations from the standpoint of monetary returns. For I have been through some pretty trying situations, and, indeed, I am in just such a one again at the moment, with less than two dollars in my pocket and not definitely located in any sort of a job.

However, I shall doubtless be able to turn my hand to something very humble and temporary as I have done before. I have many friends, some of whom will lend me small sums until I can repay them—and some sort of job always turns up sooner or later. What pleases me is that so many distinguished people have liked my poems (seen in magazines and mss.) and feel that I am making a real contribution to American literature. There is Eugene O'Neill, dramatist and author of *Anne Cristie, Emperor Jones, The Hairy Ape*, etc., Waldo Frank, probably the most distinguished contemporary novelist, and others like Alfred Stieglitz, Gaston Lachaise, the sculptor who did the famous Rockefeller tomb at Tarrytown and the stone frescoes in the Telephone Building, and Charlie Chaplin who is a very well read and cultured man in "real life". I wish you could meet some of my friends, who are not the kind of "Greenwich Villagers" that you may have been thinking they were. If I am able to keep on in my present development, strenuous as it is, you may live to see the name "Crane" stand for something where literature is talked about, not only in New York but in London and abroad.

You are a very busy man these days as I well appreciate from the details in your letter, and I have perhaps bored you with these explanations about myself, your sympathies engaged as they are—so much in other activities, and your mind filled with a thousand and one details and obligations which clamour to be fulfilled. Nevertheless, as I've said before, I couldn't see any other way than to frankly tell you about myself and my interests so as not to leave any accidental afterthought in your mind that I had any "personal" reasons for not working in the Crane Company. And in closing I would like to just ask you to think some time,—try to imagine working for the pure love of simply making something beautiful,—something that maybe can't be sold or used to help sell anything else, but that is simply a communication between man and man, a bond of understanding and human enlightment—which is what a real work of art is. If you do that, then maybe you will see why I am not so foolish after all to have followed what seems sometimes only a faint star. I only ask to leave behind me something that the future may find valuable, and it takes a bit of sacrifice sometimes in order to give the thing that you know is in yourself and worth giving. I shall make every sacrifice toward that end.

Affectionately, your son

To Grace Hart Crane

Grace, dear: Sunday, February 3, 1924

I had meant to have a special delivery for you and Grandma today, but the time I usually get for such writing was taken up this week, and yesterday afternoon I had a long talk with CA up at the Waldorf. He phoned me at my office yesterday morning and asked for that time. He had been here since the morning before, but had been so tied up with engagements, he said, that there had not been time even to phone me before. Frances was also along, but I didn't have to see her. They are returning home tonight.

We talked from 3 until five—and in the end it was very satisfactory. He began in the usual arbitrary way of inquisition into my attitude toward business life, etc. just as though there had been no exchange of letters and recent understandings on that subject, and did his best to frighten me into compromises. I parried these thrusts very politely, although it was very hard many times not to jump up and begin declaiming. However, I realized this time that my ordinary language about such topics is simply beyond his comprehension, so I quietly kept on doing my best to explain myself in terms that he would understand and not resent any more than possible. He finally ended by accepting me quite docilely as I am: in fact there was nothing else to do, especially as I did not so much as hint that there was anything I hoped he would do for me—or was ever planning that he would do for me.

Then he talked to me, as usual about his own affairs, and finally came around to asking my advise on a new product of his, its proper naming, and the best way to advertise it. He is going to send me data on the subject, and wants me to write some ads for him about it! You see, from this alone (and I have also other grounds to judge by) that he really respects me. He inquired in detail about you and Grandma and seems to have the right sort of interest in you. He also came around to aggree that I was quite exemplary of both sides of my family in not being made of any putty—knowing what I want to do, and sticking it out despite adversities. At parting he spoke of his anticipations of more extended contact with me on his next visit here, urged me to write him often, and thrust a greenback in my pocket. So that's that!

The work at the office goes smoothly enough to reassure me somewhat. My copy of the cheese book went over without any changes whatever, and that makes one write the next job a whole lot faster and imaginatively. Your own dear special has just come, and I'm awfully glad to know that things are alright and that my letters are worth something to you in spite of the haste they always have to be written in.

Tonight is the opening of a new play at the Provincetown Theater and I am invited to attend with Sue, who is the wife of James Light, the stage director. Through Light and O'Neill I know the whole crowd over there now, and it is very interesting to watch this most progressive theater in America in the details of its productions,—going behind scenes, watching rehearsals, etc. I have changed my opinions, or rather prejudices, about Clare Eames since meeting her there and watching her work in two recent productions. She isn't at all stiff or pompous,—and as an artist she is very flexible and exact. O'Neill, by the way, recently told a mutual friend of our's that he thinks me the most important writer of all in the group of younger men with whom I am generally classed.

Last night I was invited to witness some astonishing dances and psychic feats performed by a group of pupils belonging to the now famous mystic monastary founded by Gurdjieff near Versailles, (Paris,) that is giving some private demonstrations of their training methods in New York now. You have to receive a written invitation, and after that there is no charge. I can't possibly begin to describe the elaborate theories and plan of this institution, nor go into the details of this single demonstration, but it was very, very interesting—and things were done by amateurs which would stump the Russian ballet, I'm sure. Georgette LeBlanc, former wife of Maeterlinck, was seated right next to me (she brought them over here, or was instrumental in it, I think) with Margaret Anderson, whom I haven't seen since she got back from Paris in November. Georgette had on the gold wig which the enclosed picture will show you, and was certainly the most extraordinary looking person I've ever seen; beautiful, but in a rather hideous way.

If I can scrape up any of the recent newspaper notes on the dances of these people I'll send them on to you. These certainly are busy days!

Love, Hart

To Allen Tate

15 Van Nest Place
New York City
March 1, 1924

Dear Allen:

Somehow I imagine that you aren't finding it so bad to stand on the platform and dispense judgement and information after all! Whatever your attitude may now be, I must say that I am damned glad that you got the job,—first because its remunerations may bring you to me here in NY and less self-ishly, because I think that the activity will put you in better spirits, whatever erosions and disgusts the job may incidentally incur.

I'm dead tired. . . . You will note by the above that I am finally moved. It has taken more time and consternation than seems believeable,—all for just a few clothes, books, knick-nacks and pictures: but while I'm against my will now in a furnished room, I must admit that it seems good to get to a comfortable bed that hasn't ridges in the middle! and to have someone to clean things up for me (the old room I had was conducive to more dissipation and unease in some ways than any place I have ever been, and I seem to have had to get away before realizing it!). Forgive all this domestic bosh, please,—and consider my mind for just what it is at present,—a mellon sort of pulp, recuperating into better shape.

Your comments on my poems were so sharp, yet at the same time so pleasing to me, that I had to read them to Munson when he came in yesterday. "Possessions", it gives me much joy to know, hit you squarely as you say: I cannot help thinking that more of "Recitative" will get over better at some later date if you happen to re-read it. It *is* complex, exceedingly,—and I worked for weeks, off and on, of course,—trying to sim-plify the presentation of the ideas in it, the conception. Imag-ine the poet, say, on a platform speaking it. The audience is one half of Humanity, Man (in the sense of Blake) and the poet the other. ALSO, the poet sees himself in the audience as in a mirror. ALSO, the audience sees itself, in part, in the poet. Against this paradoxical DUALITY is posed the UNITY, or the conception of it (as you got it) in the last verse. In another sense, the poet is *talking to himself* all the way through the poem, and there are, as too often in my poems, other reflexes and symbolisms in the poem, also, which it would be silly to write here—at least for the present. It's encouraging that people say they get at least some kind of impact from my poems, even when they are honest in admitting considerable mystification. "Make my dark poem light, and light," however, is the text I chose from Donne some time ago as my direction. I have always been working hard for a more perfect lucidity, and it never pleases me to be taken as wilfully obscure or esoteric.

Your second version of "Light" was much improved, I think. But still I don't like it as well as that charming

To Jean Toomer

15 Van Nest Place
New York City
March 2

Dear Jean:

However much one must resent this mood we are both more-or-less contained in at present—one must still bow to it, however, without including a sense of fear. My excesses have added to my strength,—I am sure of it, but I feel the need of pausing now and then to accumulate these added but scattered perceptions,—to draw them inward toward a reserve that must be a unity if it shall ever conduce to a truly creative vision. I think I understand, then, the feelings that your brief note indicated. ONLY—the admission of "brokenness", or rather the constant conviction of it in yourself I feel to be unnecessary, not to say false, unless it is really desired. This division between mind and spirit is only a matter of will, desire, and I hope that some limited theories of science, "advanced" or not "advanced" will not succeeed in subduing your faith in exactly "the miraculous" which you doubt as a consistent basis for yeielding pure contacts from brokenness, I.E., your present state of uncertainty.

I am very tired . . . And you'll note by the above address that I occupy a familiar room. Its comforts so extra to the facilities at 45 Grove are having a good toning effect on me already. Good bed: good sleep! good plumbing: good hygiene. And there is, at last, sunlight through my windows! So I hope I shall not have to move again for a long while. Enough money came from both sides of the family in Cleveland to keep me, I think, until I can get new work, which, when I get it, I shall pursue with vigor but without illusions, as you know.

Burke is back for three months work at the *Dial*: also has some remunerative trans work to do. Said he wanted to look you up in Washington, but had only an hour in the station after all. Fitts and Wheelwright have practically aggreed to bring out his book. I have not been to any concerts. Tomorrow is the opening of Stieglitz's and O'Keefe's exhibition at the Anderson Galleries which Gorham and I'll probably attend.

Write me a word or so, now and then, just according to your mood. My above "advice" was not reflective to our correspondence and the general slackness of this note of mine is the best proof that I can give of aggreeing with you that there is little use in anything but a beck or a nod when the pulse is slightly debile.

Affectionately, Hart

To Grace Hart Crane

15 Van Nest Place,
New York City

Dear Grace: March 15th, '24

Of course I was glad to get your letter eventually, and be relieved of the possibility that something disastrous had happened to either you or Grandma to keep you from writing. And yesterday came your note about the suit, which I'll be awfully glad to get as soon as the rails can carry it here.

Just now I haven't a cent,—that's literally true, and must ask O'Neill for a loan this afternoon. My rent for the last week has not been paid, and I've given the landlady a box of Mary Gardens to appease her for the time being. None of my calls this last week have turned up anything particularly promising, and if Mr Leffingwell, of J Walter Thompson's, doesn't meet me for lunch on Monday as he has promised I think I'll go up an scalp him this time.

On my visit to CA's new office and store room on E 42nd St day before yesterday I was told that shortly after his visit to NY (when I saw him) he had had a "nervous breakdown". He wrote me in the one letter which I've had from him since then that he had just returned from out of town and had missed my letter when it first arrived—on that account. On further inquiries at the office, I found that he has been back in Cleveland for sometime, so I guess he has had plenty of time to read my two letters sent to him since then,—the last one written last Sunday, and appealing for the little loan. But no word comes back, either of help or denial, and I guess he is not so interested in me as to care one mite what happens. He may be trying to draw me back to Cleveland by these tactics, but he's a long way from the right method, I can only say!

I am in a strange state: feeling very well (everyone keeps saying, "how well you look!") and yet not knowing what is going to happen next. Yet I know that there is a limit to the uncertain trend of my existence as it is now, and I'll have to drive a truck, stevedore, or dig ditches if my profession can't afford me some relief pretty soon. Is it any wonder that I don't write you oftener than once a week when there is so little pleasant to tell?! At least, you, in Cleveland (however much you may dislike that place) are sure of a place to sleep next week,—which is much more than I am sure of!

About my poem:—there wasn't any other place to publish it but in "Secession". The main pity of that is, that I didn't get any money for it. Gorham had to pay for the entire issue himself. But if you look over the rest of the contents you will see that I am in very good company,—there is nothing in the issue which is not both dignified and creative. My work is in advance of the times, and I'll probably have to wait for a good while before getting my dues. At present—only writers, themselves, and a few advanced intelligences understand me. That has been true of many others in the past. But I am proud of my admirers.

Keep on writing me here—at least until you hear further from me. If I have to pile out I can still come around for mail for a few days. I'm sorry I cannot be more interesting in this letter, but what's the use, when the present state of things overbalances anything pleasant or entertaining I might have to tell.

My love to you both,
Hart

To Grace Hart Crane

15 Van Nest Place
Dear Grace: Sunday, March 23, 1924

I expect to be beheaded very neatly in your next letter for this failure to page you with the usual Sunday special delivery. However, the whirl during the last three days has been too much for me to write you anything but the merest note, and I've kept on postponing even that in favor of a lengthier pause. Before anything else I want to thank you for the fine long letter you wrote, its assistance and thoughtfulness and its unwavering confidence in me—the last named most of all! And the suit came, too,—and seems to look better than ever on me.

Your advice about self-reliance, etc. is, of course, quite right. But there are times when everyone I know has had to ask for a little help. This has been one of those times with me:— otherwise you would not have known by this time quite where even to write me. I went over and saw O'Neill, but finally didn't ask him for any loan whatever. Instead, almost right out of the sky the next day came a cash gift from a friend of mine who was managing editor of the *Dial* when my first poem was accepted there, and who simply had heard from others that I was in a predicament. Consequently, my rent is now paid for two weeks more, and I can keep on feeding a few more days. I've been invited out for dinner considerably, and have accepted more generally than I should if I had a job—for the obvious reason that free meals are a considerable help. The Habichts last Sunday evening, Claire and Hal on Friday night, and I generally eat with Gorham and Lisa one night a week, if not oftener. Then there are numerous other friends of mine about whom it is useless to mention much as they are too unfamiliar to you. I certainly am developing some interesting and perhaps valuable connections here as time goes on, and my natural manners seem to induce a certain amount of popularity and comment. How strange it seems to me sometimes to be gradually meeting and talking with all the names that I used to wonder over years ago,—and to find how, in most cases, I am valued as an individual—for the attributes most natural to myself! It does give me more confidence than I ever thought I should have.

"Well,—and what about the job?"—I can hear you asking, quite naturally. And I can only answer,—"Well, I don't know —yet". I have been up to see some people who advertised in the paper last Sunday, and they are considering me—as they sit in their offices up on top of the Flatiron Building. Mr. Leffingwell (curse him!) of Thompsons baulked me again. I shall not attempt another interview,—there, I mean. This is (for the next six weeks) the dull season for all advertising work, but I am pretty sure to land something within the next two weeks. Malcolm Cowley, the poet, who works at one of them says that there are about to be two vacancies—and I'm sure to get a bid at one of them within the next month. So things are. I don't see any use at present on planning to return to Cleveland (much as I should love to see you!) I have revived confidence in humanity lately, and things are going to come very beautifully for me—and not after so very long, I think. The great thing is to Live and Not Hate. (Christian Science, in part, I think; and a very important doctrine of belief. Perhaps the most important.)

I hope that CA will realize just a little bit of this truth before it is too late for him to think of anything at all,—even his business! But we are really so far apart, I'm afraid, that I have few ways of knowing whatever he does think about practically anything. I shall keep on doing my best to NOT DENY him anything of myself which he can see as worth realizing (which means *possessing*, also) meanwhile not depending on him either in thought or deed for anything whatever. He has not answered my letter yet. And despite what you say about his probable need for quiet and recuperation, he must be reading his mail all the time. The trouble is that he might much prefer me off the scene anyway,—and it's just possible that such a thought was behind his urging me when he was last here to go to the Isle of Pines (not a bad idea, I think, myself), but I realize your feelings on the subject. His problems are many, and I think he may realize in time that they are more than strictly those concerned with his business, however much and fast they multiply. What I love to think about is the way YOU have come through! And myself! It's a great game. We may realize that we are always losing, but it means a lot to realize that; also, all the while you are losing you are also gaining! And I think we both understand what that means.

Tell Grandma that I hope to hear directly from her whenever she can get around to write me. She is famous in NY already,—for her vitality and temperament! Gosh! I hope you both come down here this summer for a visit to Zell's place.

Write me soon, and forgive my tardiness!

devotedly, Hart

To Grace Hart Crane and Elizabeth Belden Hart

110 Columbia Heights
Dear Grace and Grandma: Brooklyn, NY

As I said in my wire, your gifts were an almost overwhelming surprise and certainly both a necessity and a delight. In each case the selection was perfectly to my taste, so I need not envy the haberdasher's windows so much for awhile as I have been lately.

It is, as usual, hard to believe that this is Easter. It has been raining and shining, and raining *while* shining ever since I woke up this morning. I had intended to attend mass at St. Patricks (the Fifth Avenue structure, very beautiful, which you will remember) but a drinking bout with some Danish friends of mine last night proved to much for an early rising. Emil Oppfer, an old man but very distinguished as an editor and anarchist, and whose two sons, Ivan and Emil, jr. I am very fond of, dines at a certain Italian restaurant on West Housten St every evening, and it was there that the party was held. In fact he is the same old fellow whose room I am to have in this same house when he moves out at some indefinite date, but soon. I have a small room in the front now, which is quite clean and comfortable. But when I get his present room on the back of this same floor, I shall have the finest view in all America. Just imagine looking out your window directly on the East River with nothing intervening between your view of the statue of Liberty, way down the harbour, and the marvelous beauty of Brooklyn Bridge close above you on your right! All of the great new skyscrapers of lower Manhattan are marshalled directly accross from you, and there is a constant stream of tugs, liners, sail boats, etc in procession before you on the river! It's really a magnificent place to live. This section of Brookyn is very old, but all the houses are in splendid condition and have not been invaded by foreigners . . . It's quieter than 115th Street, by a good deal and that's saying a lot for any locality near one's business in NY. In fact I can ride to Times Square, under the river and all and without changing cars on the subway in twenty minutes. This is the finest place to write in the world, and it will be well for me to be removed just as much as I am here from my friends over in Manhattan. I'll be able to do more reading and writing.

You'll be glad to know that everything is going along in excellent style up at my office. As I said, the work is very exacting, but I am catching up on some of the special requirements necessary which I lacked somewhat at first. You cannot easily imagine how difficult it has been moving here and there, for such a long time without any money. There will be a burden of debts to carry I don't know how long now, but good sleep and a place that you feel is your own help a lot in alleviating. I'm glad I shall not feel that I am extravagent about the rent here . . . What I pay here is about the lowest on record,—six dollars a week. The Back room will cost 2 more, but that will be very reasonable.

I'm awfully anxious to hear all about you both. Our correspondence on both sides have been curtailed a good deal of late, and I hope you realize that it has been quite unavoidable on my own part. In about ten days the Rychtariks will arrive, at least so I understand. Wouldn't you care to ask them out to the house some evening before they leave, or at least make a call on them? I have conjectures that they will probably not return to Cleveland at all *to live* when they get back from

Europe, but I may be wrong about that. At least Charlotte wrote me a very spirited letter in which she announced plans of storming the city here for work for Richard on their return from abroad. The dear lady has the usual expectations of recognition which are liable to cause her a great deal of pain before shes through, I imagine. It takes months and years of steady effort to get any sort of artistic recognition in New York,—at least for the kind of work that Richard does. But, of course, this is the place they should be, and I have always thought it unwise for them to spend so much money on this trip when it might well suffice to start them out on their board and keep here where they so much want to be. But do phone them, whatever happends. . . They think a great deal of you, and it would be too bad to have them leave town without some little fuss being made.

Be sure to return the letter from Waldo in your next to me. I think it contained some splendid praise and understanding. I keep thinking about a visit to you these days, but I guess it's a long way off yet. But sometime before next Oct. we'll have to get together. I'll get a few days vacation on pay if this job continues.

                         With much thanks and love,
                                              Hart

To Waldo Frank

                                    110 Columbia Heights
                                    Brooklyn, New York
Dear Waldo: April 21, 1924

For many days, now, I have gone about quite dumb with something for which "happiness" must be too mild a term. At any rate, my aptitude for communication, such as it ever is!, has been limited to one person alone, and perhaps for the first time in my life (and, I can only think that it is for the last, so far is my imagination from the conception of anything more profound and lovely than this love). I have wanted to write you more than once, but it will take many letters to let you know what I mean (for myself, at least) when I say that I have seen the Word made Flesh. I mean nothing less, and I know now that there is such a thing as indestructibility. In the deepest sense, where flesh became transformed through intensity of response to counter-response, where sex was beaten out, where a purity of joy was reached that included tears. It's true, Waldo, that so much more than my frustrations and multitude of humiliations has been answered in this reality and promise that I feel that whatever event the future holds is justified beforehand. And I have been able to give freedom and life which was acknowledged in the ecstacy of walking hand in hand across the most beautiful bridge of the world, the cables enclosing us and pulling us upward in such a dance as I have never walked and never can walk with another.

Note the above address, and you will see that I am living in the shadow of that bridge. It is so quiet here; in fact, it's like the moment of the communion with the "religious gunman" in my "F and H" where the edge of the bridge leaps over the edge of the street. It was in the evening darkness of its shadow that I started the last part of that poem. Imagine my surprise when Emil brought me to this street where, at the very end of it, I saw a scene that was more familiar than a hundred factual previsions could have rendered it! And there is all the glorious dance of the river directly beyond the back window of the room I am to have as soon as Emil's father moves out, which is to be soon. Emil will be back then from S. America where he had to ship for wages as a ship's writer. That window is where I would be most remembered of all: the ships, the harbor, and the skyline of Manhattan, midnight, morning or evening,— rain, snow or sun, it is everything from mountains to the walls of Jerusalem and Nineveh, and all related in actual contact with the changelessness of the many waters that surround it. I think the sea has thrown itself upon me and been answered, at least in part, and I believe I am a little changed—not essentially, but changed and transubstantiated as anyone is who has asked a question and been answered.

Now I can thank you for the wisdom of your last letter to me, and most of all for your confidence in me. (It is strange, but I can feel no place for paragraphs in this letter!) (Yet one goes on making paragraphs.) It came at the very moment of my present understanding, and it is as though it, in some clairvoyant way, included it. Only, I so much wish you were here these days for you are the only one I know who quite encircles my experience. I shall never, of course, be able to give any account of it to anyone in direct terms, but you will be here and not so far from now. Then we shall take a walk across the bridge to Brooklyn (as well as to Estador, for all that!). Just now I feel the flood tide again the way it seemed to me just before I left Cleveland last year, and I feel like slapping you on the back every half-hour.

Malcolm Cowley was very nice in telling me about an opening in the office of Sweet's Catalogues (architectural and engineering), and for the last two weeks I've been up there at five dollars a week the better salary than Thompson's gave me. The work involves no extraneous elements like "human interest" and such bosh, albeit a great deal of care and technical information: but so far I've been able to straddle it, and here's hoping.

If it hadn't been for the delicacy and generosity of people like Gorham, Sue Light, Stewart Mitchell, and at the last, Emil, I might have been back in Cleveland long ago. My family did, I suppose, what they could, but finally stopped at everything but my carfare back. I'm glad now that I refused that. My father is still silent after over two months since, when I asked him for a slight loan. The past would evidently like to destroy me, at least I can interpret things in no other light.

But you, Cummings and Gorham are good people to talk to, and I guess I get along without the past entire! And my eyes have been kissed with a speech that is beyond words entirely.

Allons! but I have written few poems during all this rumpus. I enclose what I have,—the "Lachrymae Christi" written two months ago, and a kind of sonnet written last week and, still unfinished. Write me soon, Waldo, if activities permit. You're doing a lot, I know!

with love, your friend, Hart

"Lachrymae Christi"

Recall to music and set down at last
What stain could hold my eyes
From joy so long in perjury . . .

What, but Thy silence shall I ask, that holds
Me, newly bright to bear no penitence
But song, as these, Thine everlasting fountains here
While every margin, wide
With fear, with scorn or terror,
Clasps no more now, nor rends.

Stream, Thou,—most effluent,
And knowing best what call the earthly rose
Obtains in Thee, Whose auspices
Are of most clear and vast attendance, white!

—Names falling from Thine eyes
And their undimming lattices of flame,
Whisper and spell out in palm and pain
Translation of Thy praise and Thy prevail,—
Compulsion of the Cross, at last
In liquid, perfect, stricken spheres,—the claim
And shining message, Christus, of Thy Grail.

"Sonnet"

What miles I gather up and unto you
are lost not one stroke ever in your sides:
nor in your breath that overcomes all tides:
nor in your fingers that reside forever here.

What if I turn toward you the gentle and
most terrible of all denials (shall I say
that you can give me) in intimation of the end
and all of praise—It is the light
that you have seen to reel
and whisper out to you upon the wine
and tables (yes always between us, two).

Now, in the encrusting edge of years,—
the definition of eternity—call
one work back now, that is your name,
that I may still be, as it is, one half to blame!

                                                        hart

To Grace Hart Crane and Elizabeth Belden Hart

110 Columbia Heights
Brooklyn, New York
May 11, 1924

Dear Grace and Grandma:

I am told that this section of Brooklyn around here (Brooklyn Heights) is very much like London. Certainly it is very quiet and charming, with its many old houses and all a little different, and with occasional trees jutting up an early green through the pavements. I have just come back from breakfast and saw some tulips dotting the edge of one of the several beautiful garden patches that edge the embankment that leads down to the river. It certainly is refreshing to live in such a neighborhood, and even though I should not succeed in acquiring a room that actually commands the harbor view I think I shall always want to live in this section anyway. Mr. Opffer, who has such a back room in this house, has invited me to use his room whenever he is out, and the other evening the view from his window was one never to be forgotten. Everytime one looks at the harbor and the NY skyline across the river it is quite different, and the range of atmospheric effects is endless. But at twilight on a foggy evening, such as it was at this time, it is beyond description. Gradually the lights in the enormously tall buildings begin to flicker through the mist. There was a great cloud enveloping the top of the Woolworth tower, while below, in the river, were streaming reflections of myriad lights, continually being crossed by the twinkling mast and deck lights of little tugs scudding along, freight rafts, and occasional liners starting outward. Look far to your left toward Staten Island and there is the statue of Liberty, with that remarkable lamp of hers that makes her seen for miles. And up at the right Brooklyn Bridge, the most superb piece of construction in the modern world, I'm sure, with strings of light crossing it like glowing worms as the Ls and surface cars pass each other going and coming. It is particularly fine to feel the greatest city in the world from enough distance, as I do here, to see its larger proportions. When you are actually in it you are often too distracted to realize its better and more imposing aspects. Yes, this location is the best one on all counts for me. For the first time in many weeks I am beginning to further elaborate my plans for my *Bridge* poem. Since the publication of my "Faustus and Helen" poem I have had considerable satisfaction in the respect accorded me, not yet in print, but verbally from my confreres in writing, etc. Gorham has made the astounding assertion that that poem was the greatest poem written in America since Walt Whitman! Malcolm Cowley has invited me to contribute about a dozen poems to an anthology that he is planning to bring out through a regular publisher, and I am inclined to assent, as the other contributors are quite able writers and it will be some time before my *Bridge* poem is completed and I bring out my efforts in individual book form.

This week has been quieter than the last, I'm more than glad to say. I had a terrible and ominous cold for several days but that has cleared up now, and as there have been no more people from the west to entertain nor others to see off on transatlantic liners, I feel considerably relieved. Helen and Dorothea had me out for dinner and the evening last Wednesday before Helen left, Thursday morning, and I only hope I successfully preserved the camouflage of my genuine boredom. A continuous round of puns and tittering really strains me more than some more difficult exercises. I enjoy Helen very much when we are alone together, but her friends allow one less control of the conversation, and in spite of all their good intentions one is glad to get away.

Before the day is over I hope to get a special from you, or at least some word tomorrow. You both have at least a little more time than I do for writing, and you should practice better what you preach than to go for ten days without sending me a word. I'm not complaining: nor should you, for all that, against me. But you must allow me to murmur back at you whenever I get the chance. Just because you are so ready to do it yourself. I do hope you are both alright, and shall begin to worry if I don't hear from you soon.

Work goes steadily on at the office. There is little to report excepting that I am living as economically as possible in order to pay back some rather overdue bills and obligations. It's a long drawn out matter that has just begun, but with an even regularity I can gradually relieve myself. Sometime in the next six weeks I am pretty sure to make you a Sat-Sunday visit, but I can't be more definite than that at present.

Much love, as always, your Hart

To Grace Hart Crane

Dear Grace: Tuesday
This little personal write-up of O'Neill I discovered in Sunday's TIMES. Inasmuch as it was written by a friend of mine about another friend of mine, and as it says a number of very interesting things about Gene, I'm sending it to you to read. Please hold on to it, and RETURN it to me soon, won't you!

Your last letter, arriving Sunday afternoon (after I had written you) was very encouraging and cheering to me. I'm just starting the day, so addios, for now. . . . . .

love,
Hart

P.S. Those two dogs, "Finn" & "Mat Burke", are out at Ridgefield. I was almost presented with "Matty" the last time I was out there. The picture of Gene is very fine in the original —taken on the roof of his home last summer in Provincetown.

"All God's Chillun" opens this Thursday night. I've been invited by Gene to attend. Forgot to tell you that I dined with Robeson, the negro actor, and his wife, at Sue's & Jimmie's last Sat. evening. Robeson is one of the most superb sort of people. Very black, a deep resonance to his voice and actor eyes. Phi Beta Kappa, half-back on Walter Camps all-star eleven, and a very fine mind and nature.

To Jean Toomer

110 Columbia Heights
Brooklyn, New York

Dear Jean!   May 28, 1924
I have not written—even in answer to your note of last—I don't know how many weeks ago. And I can't answer yet. Heaven and Hell has transpired in the meantime, but I hope

to know them both better before I get through, and before I say good-bye to you.

I think some of your (not concerns, but) *approaches* have been either worded badly, or too willful. I refer to your letters solely to me. But that should be no cause for resentment either on your side nor mine. Life is running over me and destroying me. That I confess, and you can boast about indifferences or immunities or victories as much as you wish. I have not gone this far for any kind of victories.

I understand you wrote me last at some old address. Therefore you must understand that nothing has reached me for some time: and while I am to blame anyway, I want you to know that, for your essential and pure self, I am as open and knowing as you once gave me credit for.

With love, Hart

To Jean Toomer

110 Columbia Heights
Brooklyn, New York

Dear Jean: Monday, June 16, 1924

Inasmuch as you have asked me for such a 'large order' I shan't think of trying to make a final definition of my own in reply during my present weakened condition. My last note to you was perhaps rather ill advised; I do not even remember my precise statements. It was written and mailed in a state of almost hysterical despair. What I am much more able to appreciate now is your admirable reply. I have had other spiritual reassurances, also, since then, and while I am suffering much from almost chronic acidosis and am subsisting on milk and water, I feel very much at peace with experience, so-called, which at present I feel inclined to believe, is the effort to describe God. Only the effort,—limitless and yet forever incomplete. But I want to elaborate my ideas a little longer before I admit that as complete. It is so much a matter of terminology, after all. I try to make my poems experiences, I rather don't try, when they are good *they are*—like "Possessions". And bright stones—in the end.

I shall probably never be able to be very personal about it, yet sometime I'll have more to say to you than now and here, about the maelstrom of the last three months,—what unbelievable promises it has not only fulfilled, but what complications, also, it has placed and replaced again and again between such beautiful realizations as it has, in the end, accomplished. And to *know* that such a love would forever be impossible again—that it would never be met with again, if only because one knew that one would never have the intensity to respond to a repitition of such even though it seemed worthy enough! I have not the initial exaltation (which you may see in the poem enclosed) but at least as much in some other way— which is new to me. I have never been given the opportunity for as much joy and agony before. The extreme edges of these emotions were sharpened on me in swift alternation until I am almost a shadow. But there is a conviction of love—that is the only way I can name it—which has somehow arrived in time, and which has (now so much has proved it) an equal basis in the both of us.

Allen Tate is enjoying himself very much, and is situated at 65—just below me. He seems to admire *Cane* very much. He had some other friends to see in Washington, so your absence didn't mean complete disappointment.

Love, from Hart

"Voyages"

Whose counted smile of hours and days, suppose
I know as spectrum the sea and greet
now vastly entering the reach and swarm of wings
unknown to me;—

              from palms the severe
chilled albatross's high immutability
advances still no stream of greater love
than, singing, this mortality in singleness
aflow through clay immortally to you . . .

All fragrance irrefragibly and claim
madly meeting logically in this hour
and region that is our's to wreathe again—

shall they not stem and close in our own steps
bright staves of flowers and quills today as I
must first be lost in fatal tides to tell?

In signature, then, of the incarnate word
the harbor shoulders to resign in mingling
mutual blood, transpiring—knowing and foreknown,
and widening noon within your breast forgathering
all bright insinuations that my years have caught
for islands where must lead inviolably
blue latitudes and levels of your eyes—

in this expectant, still exclaim, receive
the secret oar and petals of all love.

To Gorham Munson

                                        110 Columbia Heights
Dear Gorham: July 9, 1924
     It does seem regretable that I missed a few parting groans
and counsels with you before you took to the hills, but you
will resist the convenience of a phone, and I was in my usual
rush. And just a week ago today the Rychtariks sailed in for 4
days on their way back to Cleveland. I must say I'm a little
peeved at them—as they haven't even yet explained their ab-
sence from a performance of *Fashion* last Friday night when I
waited in vain in front of the theatre an hour and then walked
up to your place—to be equally cooled, again. I do want to
thank Lisa especially—however late—for the last and very pleas-
ant evening at your place. Allen enjoyed it, he told me, more
than any evening he had had in NY, and I admit to a gratifying
sense of excitement when I left that recalled some of the ear-
lier Munson-Burke-Toomer-etc. engagements that took place
before the grand dissolution, birth control, re-swaddling and
new-synthesizing, grandma-confusion movement (of which I
am probably the most salient example) began. Allen has a very
good mind and a kind of scepticism which I respect. I got a
very few chances to really talk with him, but I suspect that at
least we have established an idiom or code for future under-

standings which may make our correspondence at once a simpler and more comprehensive pursuit. The boy left NY in a frightfully feverish state, however, and I am a little worried about what's happening to him since. He was to have written over a week ago. I shall be pleased to know what he eventually comes to think about this bronco-busting city. I liked his sense of reserved opinion on some matters, and it may well be that a place like NY means less to him than to the usual young literary man.

I have just re-read your Eliot article in *1924*, and hope I may congratulate you again on some very accurate estimates and constructive motives. The little magazine is better than I thought it might be,—really quite sensible looking, and better in its initial contents than several issues of *The Trans-Atlantic Review* that I have seen. (Even Seaver's poetry surprises me!) It certainly is to be hoped that the *Secession-Broom* crowd can supply it to the point of crowding out the ever willing members of the milky way that flutter into every little magazine around the place.

I envy you the long walks and cool evenings. The office and all it means gets rapidly unbearable again with this anvil weather. I feel less querulous today, however, as E. is back with me again—to stay an indefinite brevity but under much more favorable circumstances than before. You will have at least a little more time to write than I, so be generous. And give my love to Lisa.

as always, Hart

To Elizabeth Belden Hart

110 Columbia Heights

Dear Grandma: July 10th, '24

In order to balance the scales of Time properly in deference to your date of birth I really should wait until August 11th to greet you now—for one can hardly have a birthday *every* month, and I certainly was early enough in greeting you once before—I refer to my June telegram. But it's nice to be exactly on time once in awhile,—and this time, if I may trust the airship that is supposed to carry this letter to you—I shall be. Of course I should like to be much more personal and have the airship bring myself along, with a posy in my buttonhole and a bouquet of roses for your own sweet self. I will make a wish, however, that you'll have enough more birthdays for that to be not only possible, but plausible. Then I shall drop down on you out of a perfectly clear sky, guiding my parachute so as to land right on the front porch. You will then serve me with fresh doughnuts and coffee and all will be merry!

I have been very much pleased to notice in recent letters from Grace that you have been feeling quite well, at least there has been no mention of anything to the contrary. I have said it many times, but I must keep on repeating that I think you remarkable in this and many other ways,—your animation, interest and courage have been so unflagging through many trials that we have gone through together,—and how many more, too, when one stops to think that my years are so small a share in your's! I'm awfully proud of you, as you know already. I'm very undemonstrative at times, but I think you know me well enough to believe in my constant affection and admiration for you. I only wish I could be with you more, but after all, you and I have had many more months and even years together than are usually granted the first and third generations. And our intimacy and comradeship have been unusual;—you've always been such a good sport.

There isn't very much news to write this week as yet. I'll try to get a letter to Grace by Sunday, however. Meanwhile I have been very glad to hear such rather pleasant news as her letter brought today—simply that my last letter pleased her, that it's not too hot (although it probably is NOW), that she may get off to Buffalo for a little trip with Zell, etc. I hope that you won't celebrate your birthday with too much strenuosity, upsetting tables, breaking chandeliers, or scuffing the floor with high kicking. Above all, don't drink too much, that Jamaica Rum, you know, always does go to one's head in hot weather!

Your devoted grandson,

Hart

To Grace Hart Crane and Elizabeth Belden Hart

110 Columbia Hts

Dearest Grace and Grandma: July 22nd, '24

I have been trying to write you for over three days. Now, I feel very neglectful indeed, especially after your two fine letters of last Sunday and the lovely gifts which arrived this morning. I hardly know how to explain myself nor to adequately thank you for so much love and attention. I know that I scarcely deserve it all, but certainly that makes it all the more pleasant. I am wearing the new dressing gown this minute. The handkerchiefs and case of Grandfather's are lovely to have and to use— as are also the socks and tie. The deep wine color of the silk handkerchief is one of the rarest shades I've ever seen, and I'm wondering if that wasn't also a possession of Grandfather's; one doesn't see such shades very often.

Altogether, my 25th birthday was quite happily passed. Emil Oppfer, whom I've mentioned to you before, and who is staying with me since he came back from his last trip to the West Indies, spread the news around and before I knew it a dinner had been arranged. Sue gave me a necktie and brought her husband, James Light, and Slater Brown, who arrived in town last Saturday for a week, was also along. There was much white and excellent wine and general hilarity. Emil even hired a taxi for transportation and I was re-christened "child of the earthquake".

Aside from all this there is very little to report. Work at the office becomes more and more hectic, and I'll be very glad when the extra strain of my hay fever relaxes. It isn't as bad as it always is in Cleveland, but enough to be very irritating to say the least. You will notice the two photographs enclosed and wonder where on earth they were taken. My expression is amusing enough, I think, even though it isn't a very good picture. To explain, Emil and I spent most of last Sunday afternoon cooling off on the roof of the house here, and looking out over the river. There is just one little piece of the panorama in the phto herewith—looking to the right and toward Brooklyn Bridge. The Wall Street section is directly opposite, and the whole bay to the left. I include a snap of Emil, also, who looks cooler than I do (in a sweater of his which I liked so much that I had to have myself taken in it). Emil, by the way, is a very lovely person, and I know you would like him very much. He will probably start working on The Leviathan (bound for England) next Saturday, but will stay with me always while he is in New York.

I hope that the trip to Buffalo with Zell was a real diversion. Being on a boat is wonderful—and I can't tell you how I am tempted to jump some boat for Europe or South America and get away from the stuffy confines of an office and office work for awhile. I think I might really save more money that way than this, and really consider taking a boat job with Emile for awhile before many months. I hope you approve.

My thanks again for all your love, and remember I love and think of you both very constantly, even if I seem to be slow in writing.

your sonny—"grand" and otherwise
Hart

To Grace Hart Crane and Elizabeth Belden Hart

Dear Grace and Grandma: September 14, 1924

I have just come back from a breakfast with Sam, and he has left to spend the rest of the day with the widow of Edgar Saltus (whom you must have heard him talk about enough to identify). I have been greeted so far mostly by his coat tails, so occupied has Sambo been with numerous friends of his here ever since arriving; Miss Sonia Green and her piping-voiced husband, Howard Lovecraft, (the man who visited Sam in Cleveland one summer when Galpin was also there) kept Sam traipsing around the slums and wharf streets until four this morning looking for Colonial specimens of architecture, and until Sam tells me he groaned with fatigue and begged for the subway! Well, Sam may have been improved before he left Cleveland, but skating around here has made him as hectic again as I ever remember him, and I think he is making the usual mistake of people visiting NY, attempting too much, getting prematurely exhausted, and then railing against the place and wanting to get back home. This last alternative is really what I am expecting him to do, although he has not yet finally decided. But he does think that NY is too swift for him—and perhaps it is, I don't know. Sam is so often in an unsettled state of mind, however, that it is hard to know in what direction to urge him. I have been able to offer him a temporary room on the same floor with me, at the back,—the same room, in fact, that I have been hoping to acquire for myself sometime. As Mr. Opffer, the father of Emil, who has been at the hospital for an operation, succumbed and died, the room is unoccupied until taken over sometime soon by Ivan, Emil's brother, who says he expects to take it for himself. So Sam has had at least several days lodging free, and a room that is most beautifully located. He is to see some hotel man tomorrow about an advertising job, and that may determine whether he remains here or returns to Cleveland. So far, his most coherent and welcome conversation has been about you, Grace, and several matters that you seemed to think were inadviseable to put on paper to me.

But why you have been so cautious, or sweetly shy, I'm at a loss to understand, because I certainly would never be timorous about writing you any news about myself, however intimate, and feeling quite sure enough that you would not be apt to quote it either far or near—just from the very facts of our relationship. However, I don't want you to think that I in the least minded hearing such delightful news quite orally from dear old Sam: good news is too welcome, only too welcome, however it comes. And now I want you—or rather want to reassure you about something that I have intended to write for some time, and in which you must believe my fullest and most intense sincerity is voiced.

When grandma wrote me awhile ago about Mr. Curtis and his devotion to you—describing as she did, such a human and very loveable person, I was exceedingly happy. But when— later in the course of the letter she mentioned that you felt that no alliance was worth anything that "broke" our relationship —that made me very worried and sad. I have spoken to you about this attitude of your's before, and you should not persist in assuming what I feel is a somewhat biased and un-natural attitude toward it. I also feel that you are unduly influenced by what Zell has to say on such subjects, and you should know that she is a very different type of personality than you and is in a very different relationship to life. The same differences—you should be aware of in whatever opinions you hear from other people on the same subject. (And remember that people—sometimes no matter how much they like you—are quite ready to sacrifice your personal happiness to prove or falsely prove their own merely personal theories, etc.) What I want to repeat to you again—and with emphasis—is that I, first, have an incessant desire for your happiness. Second, that I feel you are naturally most happy—or would be, given the proper opportunity—as a married woman. And thirdly, that I have perfect faith in your ability to select a man that loves you enough, and who has spirit and goodness enough to not only make you happy,—but to please *me* by his companionship. And you must remember, that *whoever you chose and no matter what the circumstances might be, no such element could possibly affect our mutual relationship* unless you positively willed it,—which doesn't seem likely by the undue circumspection you feel about the matter.

You must remember, dear, that nothing would make me happier than your marriage—regardless of such matters as money. And for God's sake don't marry—or least *seek* to marry a mere moneybag. It has always hurt me to hear you jest about such matters. A few material limitations are not so much to the heart that is fed and the mind that is kept glowing happily with a real companionship. That's what I want to caution you now, —and I must speak plainly before it is too late, because you have made as many mistakes in your life as the average, and I don't want you to persist in what is a very sentimental attitude, I fear, regarding my reactions to your natural inclinations. As the years go on I am quite apt to be away for long periods, for I admit that the freedom of my imagination is the most precious thing that life holds for me,—and the only reason I can see for living. That you should be lonely anywhere during those times is a pain to me everytime I contemplate the future; you have already had a full share of pain, and you must accept —learn to identify and accept—the sweet, now, from the bitter. And that you are able to do that if you follow your trained instincts—I have not the slightest doubt. I'm not urging you to do anything you don't want to; you, I hope, will see that clearly enough. I only want you to know that life seems to be offering you some of its ripeness now, and that if you will stop trying to reconcile a whole lot of opposing and often very superficial judgements—and recall some of the uninjured emotions of your youth which have revived, very purely in your heart, I know—you will better decide *your happiness* and *mine* than if you allow a clutter of complex fears and unrelated ideas to determine your judgement. I shall always love you just the same, whatever you do; and you know that. I can't help but say that I shall respect you even more as a woman, however, if you learn to see your relationship to life in a clear and coherent way; and you are doing that, I must say, with more grace and rectitude every day.

Do not, please, hesitate to write me your feelings after this. You should not fear—and you should trust to my understanding at least as much as to anyone I know.

My everlasting love,—your Hart

To Grace Hart Crane and Elizabeth Belden Hart

110 Columbia Hts
Tuesday—
Dear Grace and Grandma: Oct. 21st, '24

The last day of my vacation, and somehow the best! So cold and sharp it is, you might think it time for turkey. You know how keenly brilliant the atmosphere around these parts can be—frequently in any season. On such days one gets an even better edge to this glorious light here by the harbor. The water so very blue, the foam and steam from the tugs so dazzlingly white! I like the liners best that are painted white—with red and black funnels like those United Fruit boats across the river, standing at rest. And you should see the lovely plumes of steam that issue from the enormous heights of the skyscrapers across the way. I've been toasting my feet at an electric stove, a kind of radio heater that I have in my room, and glancing first at the bay, then with another kind of satisfaction at my shelves of books and writing table,—for a long time unable to think of anything but a kind of keen sensual bliss, that is in itself something like action—it contains so much excitement and pleasure.

After breakfast I called up Zell and Helen. They arrived yesterday but I was too occupied with other things to look them up that early. I see them at the Waldorf at four this afternoon. Which reminds me that I have already posted a steamer letter, or rather, poem, to Zell, which she won't glimpse, I hope, until she starts down the bay. She had written me, asking for a poem in this connection, and knowing how hard such "occasional" pieces are for me to write, I worried considerably. But it's not so bad for a piece of pure invention. I enclose it here for your amusement,—the only thing lacking is the photo of myself looking out my window here, of which I haven't a copy now to send you.

On going up to "headquarters" the other day for chocolates for my friends, I learned that CA had been here during September,—just how long I didn't ask. Which shows that I'm to expect the complete "go-by" from him in the future. He must be mortified about something—too much so to show his head. I'll send him a Christmas card once a year, and bless his soul! Which reminds me that I certainly do hope to join you at Christmas,—it will be high time, and we'll celebrate. I shall bring two quarts of something good from the metropolis and you'll BOTH have to break ALL THE RULES! I also want Mr. Curtis to join us during part of it. I'm sure to like him, and we'll tching-tching your health.

Give Margaret and Ralph my regards when you think of it.

Love, as always—

Hart

To Grace Hart Crane

Columbia Heights
Brooklyn, New York

Dear Grace—   Sunday evening, November 16, 1924

Another very active week. Luncheon with someone different every day,—and nearly always someone to take up the evening. But I have been so interested in several incompleted poems that I've sat up very late working on them, and so by the advent of Saturday felt pretty tuckered out. There's no stopping for rest, however, when one is in the "current" of creation, so to speak, and so I've spent all of today at one or two stubborn lines. My work is becoming known for its formal perfection and hard glowing polish, but most of those qualities, I'm afraid, are due to a great deal of labor and patience on my part. Besides working on parts of my *Bridge* I'm engaged in writing a series of six sea poems called "Voyages" (they are also love poems) and one of these you will soon see published in *1924*, a magazine published at Woodstock and which I think I told you about heretofore.

It darkened before five today and the wind's onslaught across the bay turns up white-caps in the river's mouth. The gulls are chilly looking creatures—constantly wheeling around in search of food here in the river as they do hundreds of miles out at sea in the wakes of liners. The radiator sizzles in the room here and it is warm enough for anyone's comfort, even your's. I feel as though I were well arranged for a winter of rich work, reading and excitement—there simply isn't half time enough (that's my main complaint) for all that is offered. And the weeks go by so fast! It will soon be sneezing season again before I know it.

O'Neill has a new play at the Greenwich Village Theatre—a tragedy called *Desire Under the Elms* which I'll see sometime this week. He and Agnes were in town for the premiere and I called on them at their rooms in the Lafayette one evening. They have gone back to their place at Ridgefield for a few days and then are going to Bermuda—perhaps to remain all winter. I'm reminded every now and then that I might have sent you interesting clippings and articles about O'Neill and his work in papers and magazines, and I intend to do better in the future and send some of them to you. I think you'ld be interested. Rheinhardt is staging his *Hairy Ape* in Berlin this winter, and dozens of performances of his other plays are being produced in Vienna, Paris, Copenhagen, Budapest, Munich etc. He seems to have Europe in applause more than America. That is true of Waldo Frank's work in France, also, where he has been much translated and more seriously considered, far more so, than here at home. The American public is still strangely unprepared for its men of higher talents, while Europe looks more and more to America for the renascence of a creative spirit.

Your letter came last night—was tucked under my door when I came in at one o'clock. Its tenderness and affection were welcome adjuncts to a good long sleep. I thought of you, too, just "turning in"—very likely—after the dance you mentioned, and I was very happy to think of your having had a lyric evening, dancing as you so enjoy doing. I'd like to see the Amsdens and the Patnos myself. They were a little unfair to me,—but good sports too, in a way and unusually merry bosses. I still like to think of those five o'clock booze parties we had in the office and how giddily I sometimes came home for dinner. You were very charming and sensible about it all, too, and I thank my stars that while you are naturally an inbred Puritan you also know and appreciate the harmless gambols of an exuberant nature like my own. It all goes to promise that we shall have many merry times together later sometime when we're a little closer geographically.

My—but how the wind is blowing. Rain, too, on the window now! There was a wonderful fog for about 18 hours last week. One couldn't even see the garden close behind the house—to say nothing of the piers. All night long there were distant tinklings, buoy bells and siren warnings from river craft. It was like wakening into a dreamland in the early dawn —one wondered where one was with only a milky light in the window and that vague music from a hidden world. Next morning while I dressed it was clear and glittering as usual. Like champagne, or a cold bath to look it. Such a world!

Love, as always, your Hart

To Grace Hart Crane

110 Columbia Hts
Sunday morning
Nov. 30th, '24

Dear Grace:

When I look back on the last 48 hours I must think myself lucky to be able to sit up to the table and write you at all. As it is, I feel both a little giddy with pleasure—and otherwise on the edge of a spell of grippe. But I seem to have an amazing amount of energy, and with regularity and quiet for a few days I think I'll pull through all right. My reading last night at the Rosenfeld party was a considerable success. The wonder is that I was able to attend.

On Friday night I am quite certain that I suffered at least a mild attack of the real ptomaine poisening from something I ate at dinner. I started to walk home after dinner, and before I got half way I began to swell up and burn like fire. Just the usual and bad-enough case of the hives, I thought at first. I finally managed to get to my bed, but was deathly sick besides. My pulse was pumping so that at the sink, as I was drinking some bicarbonate of soda, I lost my sight and hearing in a kind of rushing and smothering of the blood, and would have fainted had I tried to stand up any longer. Later on, when the case had apparently subsided and I was lying rigidly still in bed, it began all over again. It was perfectly maddening, and I never slept a wink all night. All this convinces me that my malady was something more than urticaria, and that I had eaten something positively poisenous. I was able to evacuate in both directions during the night, however, and somehow managed to go up to the office yesterday morning, retiring back to bed again as soon as work was over and not getting up until it was time to go to Rosenfeld's. In the meantime I had refrained from practically all food and taken a great deal of alkalithia and milk of magnesia, hot bath, etc. I was still very weak when I got to the party, but as whiskey and soda was served I quickly revived, and everyone thought I was a picture of health.

I'm very glad to have made the effort, after all, for I have reason now to feel more assured than ever in regard to my poetry. The crowd was representative as I had expected, delightfully informal, and proved very receptive. I had met at least half of them before,—Steiglitz, Georgia O'Keefe, Seligman, Jean Toomer, Paul Strand and his wife, Alfred Kreymborg, Marianne Moore, Van Wyck Brooks, Edmund Wilson and Mary Blair, Lewis Mumford, etc. etc. There was music by Copeland, a modern composer, and after that the readings by Miss Moore, myself, Kremborg and Jean Catel (who read a long poem in French by Paul Valery) occupied the rest of the time until one-thirty when the crowd broke up. I began by reading three of my shorter poems: "Chaplinesque", "Sunday Morning Apples" (the poem to Bill Sommer which seems to be talked about everywhere since it was printed last summer in "1924") and thirdly, a new poem which has not been printed, called "Paraphrase". As I was urged to read "Faustus and Helen" I finally did so. Kreymborg came to me afterward and said that it was magnificent and even the conservative Van Wyck Brooks clapped his hands, so Toomer told me. I certainly read more deliberately and distinctly than I ever thought I should be able to, and I find I have already been recognized with the applause of the most discriminating.

No more today in the way of writing. I shall look out the window or read until bedtime.

Hope I hear from you soon. Love to Grandma—

Hart.

To Gorham Munson

110 Columbia Heights
Brooklyn, New York
December 5, 1924

Dear Gorham:

I'm extremely sorry to have caused you such doubts and misunderstandings by what I said yesterday at lunch, and I'm further glad to say that I do not deserve all of them. In fact before your letter reached me I suddenly remembered my mention of the proposed attack on you and Waldo, and that I had given you a very incomplete account of it.

When this came up at the coffee house a week since yesterday I at once interrupted it by offering to withdraw from any participation in the issue whatever. Allen Tate was there at the time, and as a fairly neutral party I think you can rely on him to check my statement as a fact. At any rate I hope you will ask him about it when you next see him. I have so consistently defended you and Waldo in that particular company that I have so far derived little from the meetings but an unnecessarily aggravated state of nerves and feelings.

From your standpoint, I have long been aware, there is no excuse for my association with people whose activities are so questionable from several angles. And especially since I have been as strong in denunciations of them as anyone. (And let me add that I have taken no pains to conceal these opinions from anyone whatever.) Yet, at the same time, and whether fortunately or otherwise, I have not been so situated that I could possibly maintain the complete isolation which it has been your desired good fortune to maintain. While there is danger, and a good deal of it, I dare say, in my position, I have also felt that in yours, Gorham, lurked the possible blind-folding of certain recognitions, which, attached personalities being removed, you would have naturally found interesting and worthy. I can summon very little that is definite to support my feelings about this at the present time. Issues are not at all clear, and I am disgusted most of the time. You have set your-self to a rigorous program, part of which I subscribe to in ac-tion, a larger part of which I applaud you for as a critic, and another part of which I feel is unnecessarily unwieldy, limited and stolid. Perhaps all this assurance-plus is necessary in fighting as stringently as you have done and are doing, but so far I am not crystallized enough, as it were, to accept the whole lock-stock-and-barrel of it. To a certain extent, as Wyndham Lewis says, one must be broken up to live. Which I defend myself by interpreting—the artist must have a certain amount of "confu-sion" to bring into form. But that's not the whole story, either.

Regardless of these issues you will be assured, I hope, that I have so far found nothing in either your work or Waldo's which I would wish to attack. Your generosity, meanwhile, certainly deserves my thanks for appreciating the sometimes necessary distinctions between a personal friendship with a man and one's opinion of his work.

My rewards or discredit from participation in a magazine is-sued by your enemies will be bound to be, to a certain extent, somewhat embarrassing, yet, as you recognize, I still feel that I can owe myself that freedom on a clear responsibility. I am growing more and more sick of factions, gossip, jealousies, re-criminations, excoriations and the whole literary shee-bang right now. A little more solitude, real solitude, on the part of everyone, would be a good thing, I think.

Let us have lunch together soon. I won't take absolute "vows" before that, for this letter is a very crumb of my feelings.

Hart

To Gorham Munson

Dear Gorham: December 8, 1924
   Reflecting on our conversation at lunch today I have come
to feel bound to suggest that you take whatever decisions or
formalities are necessary to "excommunicate" me from your
literary circle. How much further you may wish to isolate me
depends entirely on your own personal feelings, but I am not
prepared to welcome threats from any quarters that I know
of—which are based on assumptions of my literary ambitions
in relation to one group, faction, "opportunity," or another.
                                            Yours, Hart

To Grace Hart Crane and Elizabeth Belden Hart

                                            Sunday morning
Dear Grace and Grandma: Jan. 4th, '25
   I might say that this is the first "day of rest" that I've had
since I came back,—but fortunately that doesn't mean that I am
all fagged out by any means. I've managed to get some regular
sleeping hours, have curtailed my liquor rations (since New
Year's eve) and am feeling as well as anyone could ever ask. Just
came back from a luscious breakfast (I make a practice of a reg-
ular meal on Sunday mornings because I sleep so late and also
walk a good distance to the restaurant) and have bought some
gay margolds and narcissi from the funny little florist woman
nearby who has a regular case on me, or rather has an amusing
way of flattering one. She's a sight, alright! Bumpy body,
pocked face, mussy hair and a voice that simply barks at you
it is so raucous. I can't be seen passing her place without her
glimpsing me, and signaling. When I enter she jumps at me
with such phrases as—"Well my handsome Good Looking
again!, How's my big boy?; Ain't he a dandy!", etc., etc, etc. I
generally get enough from her to make my room gay on a
quarter, and indeed, today, with my Christmas decorations still
up and the snow-light coming in from the roofs of the piers

below me—it is festive. Allen Tate, Sue and Brown are coming over for tea this afternoon, so I won't be the only one to look past the little flying swan still dangling in the window.

Tuesday night as I sat alone in my room I pictured you at the "Miracle". You must tell me how you liked it, and what you did on New Year's eve. Our party at Squachaloupi's (what a name!) was a delight. I was sent out to get some more Victrola needles about midnight, and before I got back the whistles began to blow. Even though it was in an uncrowded neighborhood—people began throwing their arms around each other, dancing and singing. Whereat I went into such an ecstasy as only that moment of all the year affords me. I hugged my companion and started singing Gregorian chants or something of my own version approaching them, and I hope in good Latin. O New York is the place to celebrate New Year's! There is such spirit in everyone, such cordiality! Your telegram came next morning before I was up (I didn't retire until 6) and I trust you got my answer on my way to breakfast. I am very happy these days and the more so because I trust you are.

Friday night I had a very pleasant dinner and evening with Waldo Frank. Dorothea was very lovely to ask me to dinner on New Year's afternoon, but I was wise (knowing how much I would want solitude and rest about that time) in excusing myself on another pretext, and I have invited her out to dinner some evening next week. On Satuday night I am taking Waldo to the Stravinsky concert (if he comes to Cleveland you must hear him conduct his own works. He is the greatest composer living today). And the rest of the week is already dotted with all sorts of occasions.

I enclose the trunk key, which I at last found in my little ivory box. Let me know when Nancy is coming next.

Love to you both, and remember me to Charles.

Hart

To Grace Hart Crane

Sweet's
noon-hour,
Dear Grace:—   Feb. 10th, '25

I suppose you've been reading about the great unprecedented fog here, which still more-or-less continues. Well, it's just been hell for me over at Columbia Heights. I haven't had 6 hours of solid sleep for three nights, what with the bedlam of bells, grunts, whistles, screams and groan of all the river and harbor bouys, which have kept up an incessant grinding program as noiseome as the midnight passing into new year. Just like the mouth of hell, not being able to see six feet from the window and yet hearing all that weird jargon constantly. It does no good to go to bed early under such circumstances, yet I'm forced to do so, just because I'm too tired to do anything else. I hope tonight will be somewhat better.

I didn't see Zell at all when she was hear, as you possibly know by this time. I phoned her hotel several times, and left messages for her to phone me at the office, but never got a reply. I was busy with another engagement Saturday afternoon and evening, and, as I understood she was to leave for the west that evening, I haven't made any further efforts. Gooz finally came, too, I understand. If Zell wants to get miffed at my "neglect" she'll have too—I couldn't do any better.

Friday night I went up to a party at Dorothea's—and I haven't been the same since. Imagine making anything fit to put in one's stomach out of two quarts of heavy cream, a dozen eggs and a bottle of Johnny Walker whisky! It was the richest and most disaggreeable egg gnog I have ever had, and it tasted just like ivory soup melted down in a wash tub. Saturday and Sunday I spent as quietly as possible—that is, as previous engagements would permit me—and I must say that I am far from desiring any excitement further this week or next.

I may be invited to a trip to Denmark, Norway and Sweden (perhaps including Paris) very soon—all expenses paid. But it is too uncertain yet to give you the details. I might be gone anywhere from 8 months to a year, and I certainly think I'd be a considerable fool not to take the opportunity. Emil Opffer will probably come into about 2 thousand dollars soon, and that is what he proposes to do with it. It is certainly magnificent of him to ask me to share this bounty with him, don't you think so?

I'm hoping to hear from you today or tomorrow. Please give my best to Charles, which reminds me that I do not share your trepidations concerning him which you expressed in your last letter. I don't think you ought to let such minor doubts annihilate the affection and devotion that he has proffered you so beautifully. I'm really planning on your marriage this spring, and I think you will be foolish to delay it until later.

Love, as always to you both—

Hart

To Charlotte and Richard Rychtarik

Dear Lotte and Ricardo: February 28, 1925

My grandmother sent me a picture of the artist before the Public Hall garden model, clipped from the paper—and as tonight is the night the beds were announced as being supposed to first bloom, I think of you as walking in a perfect Venusberg of flowers and shrubbery. Alas for me! I have only one white hyacinth in my window and a bad breath from last night and luncheon today. But, for once, I was able to retire to my room—away from friends and "enemies" and spend a quiet and economical Saturday evening. I owe enough answers to letters to keep me in a week, but I know well enough that tomorrow night will find me in a Spanish restaurant near here, recently discovered, which serves the finest ruby-colored and rose-scented wine in N.Y. besides delicious smoky tasting sardines and hidalgoesque chicken. Waldo Frank knows Spanish very well, and was able to convince the management, thereby, that we were not revenue officers. Since then life even in "my" retired neighborhood in Brooklyn has been gay. I know you think me terrible, and given over entirely to pleasure and sin and folly. Certainly I am concerned a great deal with all three of these—and even so, don't get *all* I want. What worries me is that I'm so restricted in other ways besides. Even, yea, on the holiest impulses. For didn't I promise to take Richard's drawings or rather photos around to the *Dial*—and haven't I, so far, completely failed to make a move? Really, I ought to sob in your laps for forgiveness. But to save your patience, I won't even mention excuses. I'll only mention that the matter has been frequently on my mind and that I'll try to do something about it very soon. I'll also try to get back to you somehow without damage the drawings (originals, etc.) which I've kept so long.

It's fine to know you have a new piano. Sam says that it's a beauty. If I ever get any money that is one of the first things I shall put it into. After so many years of negligence, however, I doubt if I shall be able to perform much on it! Which reminds me that I almost never get to hear any of the fine concerts here, after all. Money, lack of time and other things conspire to keep me away. Only once this winter have I stared at the baton,—and that was Stravinsky's. But he disappointed both Waldo and myself by not including the "Sacre du Printemps" on the program. I don't care for what I heard of his latest work. Indeed, the "Petrouchka" was the only fine thing on his program. I can probably bet on your having heard him in Cleveland.

My book is indefinitely stalled as the printer has run out of money, but I've been working hard to get finished with a f!!!?!!?!

18 hours later
Sunday, March 1, 1925

WELL! It isn't often that one gets an earthquake inside a letter, but this letter carries the evidence of one to you this time! Thank God I'm living still to finish the ending of that last sentence. I had, as you see, started the word "few" meaning to follow it with "poems"—when the room began swaying frightfully and I had the most sickening and helpless feeling I hope to ever have. By the time I got down the stairs people were coming out of other rooms all over the house, etc. I ended up with making a call and drinking wine, and so your letter has been waiting almost twenty-four hours for me to recover. The feeling was simply frightful. But you have probably read all the details in the papers by this time. I understand it was even noticed in Cleveland.

Love to you both, and write me soon, Hart

To Waldo Frank

Patterson, New York
Dear Waldo: Friday

I'm awfully sorry about the Jimenez translations: they are locked in my trunk at Columbia Heights in my letter file. But I'm going back to New York about a week from tomorrow and I'll be glad to copy them—and either send them on to you—or directly to the New Republic, as you may direct. That would be—at most—only a few days later than they would arrive had I sent them along with this letter. I don't know what you are accenting in your thesis on the poet, but I think short poem on the Virgin better than the one called "The Three". I think you sent me only these two.

Along with your letter today comes the news from my mother that transactions are about completed for the sale of our home in Cleveland. If this really eventuates I may be called upon to help them move—which will defer my plans for sea roving at least until after September. However, I may decide to evade the moving: I can't at present see my way to make any definite plans without risking some kind of unpleasant entanglement. I wish that "wile" and "guile" were easier instruments for my imagination to use! There is always some other immeadiate duty or requirement for me to perform than creation. I've had only about five hours at the writing table since I came out here, and now it's about time to look for a postage stamp —I mean the wherewithal for it—to post this letter! Of course I've had a good time, find I enjoy painting house, gardening, etc. BUT—.

At any rate your sanguine hopes for "White Buildings" warms me. It came back from Harcourt yesterday. They couldn't make anything out of most of the poems. My "obscurity" is a mystery to me, and I cant help thinking that publishers and their readers have never heard the mention of Sir Thomas Davies, Donne, Baudelaire, Rimbaud, Valery or even Emily Dickinson. Within a few days, probably, I'll get time to make you a copy of the mss. It has been loutish of me not to have delivered the poems to you long before this, but hurry and general confusion have been mainly responsible. In looking over the selection I hope you will (when the leisurely moment arrives) have the impulse to make what comments and criticisms occur to you. I am dissatisfied with at least half the poems, but I realize that this will possibly always be so with regard to poems written more than two years back. Reason seems to dictate, then, a certain amount of necessary indifference, that is, if I'm ever to print any collection of poems before the grave.

I shall do my praying for that year of unadulterated liberty for the creation of your next novel! When I am "settled again", or at least momentarily poised upon some perch—I want to read your MALVA if you will let me. Meanwhile we'll at least keep in touch with each other. Use my old address unless you write immeadiately on receipt of this.

as ever,
Hart

To Waldo Frank

1709 East 115th Street
Cleveland, Ohio
Dear Waldo: August 19

I have been trying to get time and clarity to write you for the last two weeks—ever since I sent you the mss. of *White Buildings*—but the nightmare hurly-burly and confusion here intercepted me consistently. Three more weeks of it and I shall be able to get back to Brown's place in the country and collect myself. Our old home will be rented by its new owner to a fraternity, my mother and grandmother will be leaving for Miami, and Cleveland will become for me, I hope, more a myth of remembrance than a reality, excepting that my "myth" of a father will still make chocolates here.

There has been one bright afternoon, however—last Sat.

when I went out to Brandywine valley (between here and Akron) and revisited Bill Sommer. The old baldpate was asleep on a sofa when I looked through the screen door and knocked. Arose a great bulk in white undershirt and loose white duck pants—the black eyes revolving in the pallid or rather, dusty-white miller face like a sardonic Pierrot's. The few hours I was there were spent with him out in the old school-house studio, surrounded by a flower garden and filled with plentiful new wonders of line and color. I wish you could have seen several of the oil childrens' portraits that he has been doing! And there is a line drawing of a head and hand that I am bringing back to New York that you will greatly care for. While we were both chewing, smoking and listening to the crickets I finally found out why Sommer has been so remiss about joining in with me in my several efforts to expose him to fame and "fortune". He hates to let his pictures leave him. Against that impasse, I guess, nobody's efforts will be of much avail. It's just as well, of course, if he has triumphed over certain kinds of hope. I admit that I haven't, at least not entirely. I still feel the need of some kind of audience.

By the way—do you know if O'Neill is at present a resident anywhere on Nantucket? He has promised to write some kind of notice for my book, and I should like to get in touch with him. He wrote me from Bermuda, but where he has settled since returning from there I don't yet know. If he has been near you I hope that you have got together.

I am enclosing an improved version of "Passage,"—the poem I wrote in the country this summer. It should replace the version that is in the mss. you have. To me it is still the most interesting and conjectural thing I have written—being merely the latest, I suppose. I'm particularly anxious to know what you think of its form. On sending it to the *Dial* I recently got this comment from Miss Moore:

"We could not but be moved, as you must know, by the rich imagination and the sensibility in your poem, Passage. Its multiform content accounts I suppose, for what seems to us a lack of simplicity and cumulative force. We are sorry to return it."

It seems almost as though Miss Moore might be rather speaking of her own poems with such terms. . . . Allen Tate is writing a short essay (he intends a longer one later) on my work to appear along with four of the "Voyages" in the next copy of the *Guardian*. You will probably see it. It does hearten me somewhat that you and a few others have been so actively interested in what I'm trying to do. Certainly I have never done anything to personally deserve it, but I think my personal and economic embarrassments and frustrations have curtailed a good many of my intentions.

Please do not feel constrained to write me during any of your active days . . . I know you are very busy this summer and I'm only afraid that my letters may have proved one more distraction from your writing.

As ever, Hart

To Charlotte and Richard Rychtarik

30 Jones St
New York

Dear Charlotte! dear Richard!   Sept. 15th, '25

Instead of being the guest of the Tates I have had the pleasure of an apartment all to myself, Jimmie Light's, in fact, and if you remember backwards enough you can picture my surroundings. Jimmie returns from London next week (I hear Sue is coming to town to meet him!) and he will have to rush into production work at the theatre madly. I hear that his production of *The Hairy Ape* met with great success in London, that he has been invited to return next year for another production etc. He says that conditions and interest in such matters are ideal there, which is a surprise to me as I had thought the British were notably indifferent to American plays—that is of the better sort. This reminds me that I am ready to send you one of the Light masks (from last year's production of *The Ancient Mariner*). Jimmie promised me one of them, and I can think of no one better to send it to than you. I'll get a box tomorrow, pack it and send it along. You can have some great fun playing with it in pantomime around the house. The effect is unearthly—the mask belonged to one of the angels, in fact, that are described as standing on the deck of the ship as it reaches the harbor in Coleridge's poem.

I plan to go up to the country next Friday. I shall need all the time meanwhile to try and locate some work to take up there with me—for I shall have barely enough to make the carfare. Shall call on your frind, etc. Yesterday along came the answer from my aunt. I had expected a refusal, but I'll be damned if I had calculated on such a lot of insulting assumptions and advice as she packed onto me. The letter is enclosed for your amusement. It is a perfect document of typical American conduct and should be preserved in a museum. Well, I'm through with her. In a way, too—it's a relief. There need be no more useless simpering, smiles and hypocritical assumptions between us. In other ways, too, the Cleveland trip did me good by opening my eyes more fully than ever. I'm glad of it on the whole. My aunt knows what I think of her by this time: I answered at once. But please save the enclosed letter from her and return it to me when you next write.

I am so afraid that the land up there will get away from me before I get there that I can hardly sleep nights. I find that O'Neill is not in town and the other person, the publisher, from whom I had planned to possibly borrow the money is away also. Would it strain your pocket-book at this time to lend me the amount, so that I can at once clinch the bargain? It was so good of you to make the offer in the first place that I feel am possibly taking advantage of your friendship. But if I could just settle the matter there before it is too late, I could later borrow the money from O'Neill of someone else and return you at once the money borrowed. I will need a little over two hundred dollars as otherwise I shall not have anything to pay the lawyer's fees with for looking up the deed, etc. Would $25.00 extra be too much? You must allow me to pay 6% interest on the loan—and to send you a regular note for the money. I would like the time stipulation about 5 years, but I would repay, it as soon as possible before that. I know you trust me, but I also want to assure you of protection in the matter.

If I can hear from you by next Friday or early the following week it will be a Godsend. The address will be as before: *Patterson, New York, care of Slater Brown*. I shall write you again as soon as I get there and look the situation over.

Everyone likes the picture you drew of me, Richard. I like the other one (side view) even better, and hope to have a photostat of it sometime. Saw Sam yesterday—restless as ever. He hopes to get a job at Brentano's. Emil wanted me to go down to a Danish ship today for dinner and spree on the real stuff but I was too afraid of it to go along. Those ship dinners are marvellous affairs from all I have heard!

Please excuse this chatter and haste. There is such a lot to do and think about that I can think of nothing so good to express the situation as your "red excitement!". Please remember me to Bahn.

With Love and Gratitude—
Hart

To Susan Jenkins and William Slater Brown

110 Columbia Heights
October 21, 1925

Dear Tories:

There have been numerous "celebrations" besides the already recounted one (by Bina) on the great transaction, and the Punch Palazzo has had due patronage. The engrossing female at most of these has been "Rideshalk-Godding", as I have come to call her, and thus far the earnest ghost of acidosis has been kept well hence. My real regret, however, is that I just missed getting the pick of jobs of the S. Am. line, last steamer—said occupation being deck yeoman at 20 minutes work a day, all freedom of ship, mess with officers or any first class passengers that seemed colloquial, white uniform, brass buttons, cap, meditation on the sun deck all day long, and seventy-five dollars a month clear sailing! The chief officer had already approved me, but before I could get over to the offices for final approbation they had already sent someone else over to the ship. We must have passed under the river. However, I noticed that my questionnaire (filled last June) had won an OK sign in the upper right corner, and I have been told to come around again on the 26th when the next boat arrives. I'm not waiting for that, however, as I need instant cash and there is not one chance in a hundred of a similar vacancy soon. Otherwise I have finished "The Wine Menagerie" and have sent it off, along with "Passage," to *The Criterion*. Since the last (yesterday) *Guardian* has come out *without* the "Voyages" I am thinking of trying to become a literary ex-patriot. It's just as tiresome as ever. This issue contains a lot of tommy-rot by Seaver and an "announcement" in the bargain that reads unforgivably: "Voyages, four remarkable poems by Allen Tate" will appear in the next issue!

Emil took me to see *Arms and the Man* last night, and I found it very amusing, if ancient. Have not seen Chaplin yet. Broadway is, to me, a depressing promenade, and unless someone urges me thither I don't seem to trickle up there. Have you heard about the death of Matty's father? (I don't know why I cram so many divergencies into one paragraph). Elbano is here at 110 packing up his ditty boxes, etc. to go to St. Louis today. I have had a room to sleep in at 65 Columbia Hts. as the Opffer Bros. have kept this joint well filled, but this is still my address, and I expect to re-instal myself very soon.

Am on my way to the *Dial* to have lunch with K. B. and shall try to bag a review or briefers from the Rt. Rev. Miss Mountjoy. A momentous morning: Frank is going to try to corner Liveright on my vol., also.

Mrs. Boving tells me you have been pressing apples, grapes and everything in sight. I wish I could be with you. The city certainly isn't pleasant for long. Meanwhile I hope for money and good luck before June.

Love,—Hart

To Waldo Frank

"At Melville's Tomb"

How many times the jewelled dice spoke
Beneath this ledge, beneath the wave;
Their numbers broken not by wave or rock,
Only by our unchiseled, beated dust.

Yet in the circuit calm of one vast coil,
Its lashings charmed, malice reconciled,—
Some frosted altar there was kept by eyes
Unanswering back across the tangent beams.

Compass, quadrant and sextant contrived
No farther tides . . . High in the azure steeps
Our monody shall not wake the mariner
Whose fabulous shadow only the sea keeps.

Dear Waldo: October 26
   Your advice and stimulation are still with me. Your solidity
and conviction seemed never more firm or luminous than
during our last talk. —I was glad to see you looking so well. I
wrote this out this morning, thinking it might go well in the
book. No other news yet.

                                                    Love, Hart

To Clarence Arther Crane

                                          110 Columbia Heights
                                          Brooklyn, N.Y.
Dear Father: Nov. 4th, '25
   I'm back in town looking for work, and without money, at
least until a couple of editors decide they want some of my
writing which they have. I'll have a job within two weeks, but
I hate meanwhile to borrow any more from friends, willing or
generous as they may be. Will you advance me some small sum
on the understanding that I repay it when I get work located?
   I know that you aren't interested in your son any more. You
said that last summer when I called on you at the factory and I
certainly didn't feel like inflicting myself on you again during
my visit. But in view of the fact that the world about us simply
doesn't seem to understand such an attitude toward an only
son, I, too, find it hard to reconcile my understanding to such
a unique situation. My book has been taken by the publishers,
Boni & Liveright, for spring publication, probably with a
Foreword by Eugene O'Neill, the playwright: and there will
be considerable public recognition for me when it comes out.
Probably it will be much easier for me to acquire the more lit-
erary kind of work for which I am best fitted after that. Mean-
while it seems a little too bad that my family can't muster up a

better appreciation of me than the forlorn picture of shiftless indigence and feeble will which you seem to think I represent.

I know three critics who regard my forthcoming book as the most important first volume of poetry to be issued in America since 1855, when Whitman's "Leaves of Grass" was issued. To have won a distinction of this sort without practtically any outside help, working every day at routine and (to me) unimaginative drudgery, has been no small task; and merely because I haven't naturally inclined to fall in love with the ideals of commercialism seems like a small item to attempt to discount it with. If I never wrote another line my reputation would last as long as that of any living banker, and I shouldn't think you would carc to bc put down in the eventual biography for posterity as the disgruntled, narrow minded commercialist who went about apologizing for his son's "failure".

Can't you rub some of the prejudice from your eyes, and see me a little clearer? It will honestly hurt me to receive help from you unless I can believe that a little of your father's pride and heart is in it.

Your son,
Harold

To Clarence Arthur Crane

Dear Father:

I was very glad to hear from you and it was generous of you to thus come to my aid. The only pity is that artificial theories and principles have to come so much between us in what is, after all, a natural relationship of confidence and affection.

You may not believe it, father, but in spite of what opinions you may hear that I have against you (and, not knowing what is told you, I still refuse to acknowledge them either way) I still resent the fate that has seemed to justify them and God Knows how much we all are secretly suffering from the alienations that have been somehow forced upon us. If we were all suddenly called to a kind of Universal Judgment I'm sure that we would see a lot of social defences and disguises fall from each other and we would begin from that instant onward to really know and love each other.

I feel rather strange these days. The old house sold in Cleveland; Grandmother ill in Florida; Mother somewhere in Cuba or the Isle of Pines; and I not hearing from either of them for the past month. Altogether, it's enough to make one feel a little foot-loose in the world. But I'll have a job soon, and will probably be reassured in the mail that everything's alright. At such times, though, I realize how few we are and what a pity it is that we don't mean a little more to each other.

Please let me hear from you when the spirit moves you.

Sincerely and gratefully, your son

To Charlotte and Richard Rychtarik

110 Columbia Heights
Brooklyn, New York
Dear Charlotte and Richard: December 1, 1925

I have kept putting off writing you because I wanted to have some kind of pleasant news to report, but it seems useless to defer any longer; I certainly have thought of you often enough . . .

The facts are hard, but true, I have not yet succeeded in finding myself a job, and even after trying every sort of position, like selling books in stores during the Christmas rush, ship jobs, etc., etc., and I have just been kept going by the charity of my friends. The nervous strain of it all has about floored me, and I feel as though the skin of my knees were quite worn off from bowing to so many people, being sniffed at (to see whether I had "personality" or not) etc. How I shall love it when, some day, I shall have a little hut built on my place in the country to live in—and get out of all this filthy mess!

Even the publication matter of my book of poems has not come through the way I had expected. O'Neill is writing the Foreword, after all, but he took so long to notify Liveright (the publisher) about it that I must now try to place it somewhere else. This may not be so hard, but it probably means that it will not come out until next autumn, and I had so hoped to have it printed before that. . . .

So you see how it's been! I don't mean to wail, but it is hard to keep up and going sometimes. To make matters worse, my mother and grandmother have both been sick in bed (grandmother seriously) at Miami. I have only heard about it through Mr Curtis whom they sent for to come down and bring grandmother back to Cleveland. Neither of them have written me for many weeks, and I have even myself stopped writing them. They could have at least answered my letters, I think, and what it is that they are angry about I really don't know. Their whole trip has ended just as badly as (you'll remember) I predicted. And what my mother wants to remain down in that silly and expensive place for any longer I can't guess. My grandmother is possibly already back at Wade Park Manor, and if you feel like cheering up an old lady you might telephone her or call. She will be more lonesome now than ever.

I have been very anxious to hear more about your plans. How have they come out, and why didn't Richard look me up when he was last in New York? The phone number here is *Main* 2649 and these days I am liable to be in at almost any time.

The reproduction of Richard's drawing of me is very deft and clear. Sometime I might use a dozen or so of them if it is not too much trouble to have them made. I have an appointment tomorrow with a possible job. I certainly hope to get it, and begin paying back what you were so kind in lending me. The *Dial* bought my "Wine Menagerie" poem—but insisted (Marianne Moore did it) on changing it around and cutting it up until you would not even recognize it. She even changed the title to "Again". What it all means now I can't make out, and I would never have consented to such an outrageous joke if I had not so desperately needed the twenty dollars.—Just one more reason for getting my book published as soon as possible!

Write soon. With love, Hart

To Clarence Arthur Crane

                                        110 Columbia Heights
                                        Brooklyn, New York
Dear Father: December 3, 1925

Your letter was appreciated in many respects and I don't want you to think that I wasn't glad to hear from you. But there were recriminations in it which assumed a basis for apologies and regrets on my part which I don't feel I at all suggested in my last letter and which I certainly cannot acknowledge now or later. In fact, you always seem to assume some dire kind of repentance whenever I write you or call on you, and so far as I know I have nothing in particular to repent. I simply said I was sorry that you could not see me in a clearer light, and it seems I shall have to go on lamenting that to some degree for the rest of my life. If I began to make recriminations on my behalf there wouldn't be any use writing at all, for though I have plenty to mention, I don't see what good it would be to either one of us to embark on a correspondence of that sort. My only complaint right now is that you seem determined to pursue such a course, and I can only say that if you persist I have no answers to offer. You and I could never restore our natural relationship of father and son by continually harping on all the unnatural and painful episodes that life has put between us via not only ourselves but other people during the last ten years, and if you are not willing to bury such hatchets and allow me, also, to do so, then I'll have to give up.

For the last six weeks I've been tramping the streets and being questioned, smelled and refused in various offices. Most places didn't have any work to offer. I've stepped even out of my line as advertising copy writer, down to jobs as low as twenty-five per week, but to no avail. My shoes are leaky and my pockets are empty: I have helped to empty several other pockets, also. In fact I'm a little discouraged. This afternoon I am stooping to do something that I know plenty of others have done whom I respect, but which I have somehow always edged away from. I am writing a certain internationally known banker who recently gave a friend of mine five thousand dollars to study painting in Paris, and I'm asking him to lend me enough money to spend the winter in the country where it is cheap to live and where I can produce some creative work without grinding my brains through six sausage machines a day beforehand. If he refuses me I shall either ask Eugene O'Neill who is now writing the Foreword to my book and won't refuse me for some help to that end, or I'll take to the sea for a while—for I'm certainly tired of the desolating mechanics of this office business, and it's only a matter of time, anyway, until I finish with it for good. I can live for ten dollars a week in the country and have decent sleep, sound health, and a clear mind. I have already bought ten acres near here in Connecticut and it's just a matter of time until I have a cabin on it and have a garden and chickens. You see I have a plan for my life, after all. You probably don't think it's very ambitious, but I do. As Dr Lytle said to me when I was last in Cleveland, "What does it all amount to if you aren't happy?" And I never yet have had a happy day cooped up in an office, having to calculate everything I said to please or flatter people that I seldom respected.

I wish you would write me something about yourself. Let's not argue any more.

As always,

To Otto H. Kahn

110 Columbia Heights
Brooklyn, New York
Dear Mr. Kahn: December 3, 1925

Yesterday I telephoned Mr. Sharpp, your secretary, to request an interview with you regarding some temporary assistance which I felt you might possibly care to render me under the pressure of my present circumstances. Mr. Sharpp advised that I write you first, explaining the exigencies of the situation and the application I wished to make. I shall try to be as definite and as brief as possible.

My first collected poems are about to be published (probably next spring) with a Foreword by Eugene O'Neill. Although my poems have appeared from time to time in various magazines such as the *Dial* and the *Little Review*, I am not yet well enough known to reap any substantial benefits from what I have written. I am twenty-six years of age, and for the last seven years I have been entirely dependent on my efforts as an advertising copywriter for my living. What real writing I have done has had to be accomplished after office hours and sometimes at the risk of losing my position. Last June, as a result of ill health and nervous exhaustion, I had to resign my position with Sweet's Catalogue, regardless of my dependence on my salary there, and live in the country until my health recovered.

For the past eight weeks I have been back in New York, endeavoring by every means to secure work again as a copywriter. As I have been unfortunate in not finding any openings I have recently attempted to get any other kind of work available, but as I find myself now completely without funds, my circumstances seem to be rather acute. One of my friends has suggested that you might be sufficiently interested in the creation of an indigenous American poetry to possibly assist me at this time. As I have never before asked for such assistance I run the risk of writing you quite presumptuously, and I certainly wish to beg your pardon if my letter seems so.

Besides the poems collected into my forthcoming volume I have partially written a long poem, the conception of which has been in my mind for some years. I have had to work at it very intermittently, between night and morning, and while shorter efforts can be more successfully completed under such crippling circumstances, a larger conception such as this poem, *The Bridge*, aiming as it does to enunciate a new cultural synthesis of values in terms of our America, requires a more steady application and less interruption than my circumstances have yet granted me to give to it.

If the suggestion seems worthy and feasible to you I should like to borrow the sum of a thousand dollars, at any rate of interest within six percent. With this amount I could live in retirement and cheaply in the country for at least a year and not only complete this poem, but also work on a drama which I have in mind. As security I can only offer an unconditional sum, amounting to five thousand dollars, which by the terms of my deceased grandparent's will, I inherit on the death of his widow. I do not know whether such bequests are open to outside inquiry, but the proper reference, in case you are interested, is Mr. Stockwell, Trust Department, Guardian Savings & Trust Co., Cleveland; estate of C. O. Hart.

As to the estimation my work deserves, I naturally do not feel free to do more than quote a few statements from critics who have seen my poems in print and read my mss. I include these on a separate sheet herewith. Let me say in concluding that I should appreciate an interview with you at your offices, Mr. Kahn, and that I honestly feel that my artistic integrity and present circumstances merit the attention of one like yourself, who is and has been so notably constructive in the contemporary and future art and letters of America.

Very truly yours, Hart Crane

Statements on my writings—
"It is time that your poetry should appear in a volume. You know what I think of it. I have done my best these years to spread my recognition of your genius not alone here but abroad. But it has been hard, without a volume of your work to go on. *White Buildings* will be an event in American poetry —a major event. Not the sort of event that journalists make paragraphs about, three times a week. But the sort of event that literary historians make chapters about—years later. You are a real poet.

"I promise you, that when your volume appears, I shall devote a long article to your work, in one of our leading literary magazines."

Waldo Frank

"The publication of *White Buildings* is one of the five or six events of the first order in the history of American poetry. It is doubtful if any other first volume since Whitman's, in 1855, has so definitely exceeded promise and reached distinction on its own account. Hart Crane's poetry, even in its beginnings, is one of the finest achievements of this age. So one must predict the reviewer's protest—'Incomprehensible!'"

Allen Tate
Reviewer for the *Nation, New Republic,* etc.

"Many thanks for sending me copies of your recent poems. I have taken them with me on my brief vacation and I have greatly enjoyed reading them. They have refreshed my conviction that you are writing the most highly energized and the most picturesquely emotionalized poetry in 'These United States.' 'Voyages' is the finest love suite composed by any living American."

Gorham B. Munson
Managing editor of *Psychology,* and critic;
contributor to *Dial,*
New Republic, Criterion, New Age, Europe, etc.

Other references—Eugene O'Neill, Greenwich Village Theatre, or Ridgefield, Conn.; James Light, Provincetown Theatre; Miss Eleanor Fitzgerald, Provincetown Theatre; Waldo Frank, 150 East 54th St., N.Y.C. Telephone: Plaza 2342; Marianne Moore; Jane Heap; Harrison Smith; Paul Rosenfeld.

To Grace Hart Crane

My dear Mother: December 9, 1925

For almost six weeks, now, I have not heard from you or Grandma. Though Mr. Curtis was thoughtful enough to notify me that you had been taken ill, the circumstances did not seem to describe a situation so severe that you could not have taken pen in hand and at least have written me once yourself during that time—especially, it seems to me, since you know by my several last letters that I was having a difficult time and was without funds entirely. I have put off writing you under these conditions; there was enough reason to so do simply on the basis of your own indifference, or possible disgust with me. And I admit that it was a shock for me to realize that you needed me so little. I have gone through a good many realizations of various sorts—during the last six months—and they are not without echos of certain things you said to me last summer, trying as I may have been.

I don't know where you may be at this time, but in case you may for any reason wish to write to me I am writing to say that

I shall be probably for the next year at the following address: c/o Mrs. Addie Turner / Patterson, New York / R.F.D.

I am unusually well provided for and shall leave for the country next Saturday. Yesterday afternoon I had the pleasure of being rewarded in some measure for some of the work I have been doing. You have probably heard of the banker, Mr. Otto H. Kahn, who has kept the Metropolitan Opera and various other artistic ventures endowed for years. After an interview with Mr. Kahn at his home at 1100 Fifth Ave. I was given the sum of two thousand dollars to expend on my living expenses during the next year, which time is to be opened in writing the most creative message I have to give, regardless of whether it is profitable in dollars or cents or not.

Mr. Kahn was keenly interested in what Waldo Frank and Eugene O'Neill had said about my work, and it makes me very happy indeed to have this recognition from a man who is not only extremely wealthy and renowned on that account, but who is also very astute and intelligent. I am very tired now—with all the strain and effort of the last two months, but I shall probably pick up as never before when I get into the quiet of the country and have the first real opportunity of my life to use my talents unhampered by fear and worry for the morrow.

If you are not too prejudicial about me by this time, you may also interested in this turn of affairs.

Let me hear from you sometime soon.

I certainly hope you and Grandmother are feeling better.

Love—Hart

To Charlotte and Richard Rychtarik

Dear Charlotte & Ricardo: New Year's Eve 1926

Here I am at this date and sixty-six miles from a drink. Isn't it tragic! And there will not be a whistle or a shout to tell me it is a new year. I shall probably be fast asleep, unless I get scared and stay up blinking over a book—for it must be a bad omen to be asleep at the switch of the new twelvemonth. But tomorrow night I shall make up for it. That is, if certain friends come out from New York with all their bottles on them.

Life out here so far has been ideal—even if it has been below zero much of the time. But I came prepared for all kinds of weather and dress every morning in boots, woolens, and furs. I shall have my picture taken and you shall see how very impolite I look.

Imagine paying only ten dollars a month for the rent of a whole house (8 rooms)! I share it with Allen Tate and his wife and have a suite all to myself on the second floor—1 room I do not use at all, a bedroom with a fine old "sleigh bed" and a study, spacious and light, in which the sun streams every morning. My pictures and nick-knacks look wonderfully jolly on the simple kalsomined walls and the books fairly glisten on the shelves. This room is kept well heated by two oil stoves. Downstairs we cook and heat with wood-burning stoves which means enough daily exercise to keep us glowing.

Otherwise all I have to do is wash dishes. Mrs. Tate cooks lunch and dinner and Allen gets breakfast! This routine plan is the only way for all of us to get each his work done—I mean our writing. Mrs. Tate is writing a novel (her second) and Allen is *supposed* to be writing reviews, etc. Nothing much *yet*, however, has been done by any of us. There have been food supplies, appliances and sundries of all sorts to order—and then came Christmas with flocks of people visiting Brown's place (about 1/2 mile away) and drinking and talking day and night. Allen also has dissipated terribly with a gun he bought (called The White Powder Wonder)! and has so far spent most of his time ranging over the hills shooting at sparrows. He did get a squirrel one day, however, and we had an exclamatory time over the stew it made. —There are all kinds of game around here, even deer, and it's a temptation to hunt, of course.

Well, the expected results have already been noticed on my family! Long and ardurous letters from uncles, aunts, etc. (not Zell but she's in Europe anyway), and a fat check from my father for Christmas. They all want me to come out and visit again—which I see no reason for doing at this time. I want to get into my work. My God, it's the first time anyone paid me to do it or even encouraged it in any substantial way! Of course —to them the $2,000 seems like some kind of shower bath without any connection with any conceivable responsibilities. You can have responsibilities toward your time clock, your cow or your maiden aunt, but you can't mean to say that poems or pictures demand anything but aimless dreaming! No. I'm not coming until spring—unless there is a serious need of me.

Mother, it seems, has been terribly ill in Miami, and did not even go to the Isle of Pines. As she was scheduled to leave for there on a certain day and, failing to, did not inform me I went on writing her there as I got no word of her from *anywhere* I finally gave up writing at all. Finally I got word through Mr. Curtis that he had been called to Miami to take care of them both—but I still didn't understand her not writing me in all that time, and thought she must be angry about something.

Everything was all mixed up. And I finally had a long letter from her rejoicing in my good luck and full of the harrowing details of how very ill she had been with all sorts of complications. Miami turned out to be more terrible than even I had predicted—and what this folly has cost those women in pain and in expense God only knows. Both in bed for weeks. Six doctors, nurses, compartments on trains, etc., etc., Grandma got back about 2 weeks before Grace was able to leave. The latter joined her finally and they are living at the Manor— where they should have been all the time, of course. I'm sure they would love to see you both, and believe me, there were no complications, as I had thought, between us.

I'm expecting you both to visit me here next summer. Plenty of room for you—and you'll be sure to relax. I bought some wonderful snow shoes with some of Otto's money and so I pray for heavy storms.

It is still hard to believe how much has really happened. And I'm longing to launch into the creative stream of things again. Wish I could see "Capt. Gulliver's" face. What a wonderful subject for your style, Richard! Do write me more about yourselves—that promised long letter "after Christmas".

Love, as ever—Hart

To Malcolm Cowley

Dear Malcolm: Sunday, January 3

The poem has been read with approval—is flatteringly apocalyptic and has the proper nautical slant. . . . Seriously, though, it seems to stand on its own feet as a poem and I appreciate a very great deal the tonality and direction of it in its more intimate aspects. You and Peggy have been more than good in remembering me—thanks for the photo, too.

Allen probably gave you enough of a picture of our daily operations and dissipations out here. In point of fact, I'm just beginning to get down to work—after a cyclone of mail ordering, food choring, etc., etc. We have to be provided, of course, against severe snow and a siege of weather—though there may be the mildest of days ahead.

Are you reviewing *Doc. Transit* anywhere? Schneider finally sent me out a copy. It intrigued me more than any such tour de force since Poe, though it has its obvious weaknesses. Some chapters, however, of great imagination. I didn't anticipate half so much from the earlier things I've read by Schneider.

I'm coming in town probably about two weeks from now, and should like to know what day or days about that period you'll be there also. You know what the Governor of North Carolina said to the Governor of S. Carolina—! I'm such a rum-scallion that I never even planned to stay put anywhere very long in the woods. Let me hear from you soon. Allen will probably write you about the outcome of his interview (along with Wilson) with the Adelphi Press. It looks as though we'd all be published next fall.

My love to you both—Hart

To Waldo Frank

Patterson, New York

Dear Waldo: January 18, 1926

I am not through working on it yet, but I thought you might care to see this last part of *The Bridge*, oddly enough emergent first. It is symphonic in including the convergence of all the strands separately detailed in antecedent sections of the poem—Columbus, conquests of water, land, etc. Pokahantus, subways, offices, etc. etc. I dare congratulate myself a little, I think, in having found some liberation for my condensed metaphorical habit in a form as symphonic (at least so attempted) as this.

The bridge in becoming a ship, a world, a woman, a tremendous harp (as it does finally) seems to really have a career. I have attempted to induce the same feelings of elation, etc—like being carried forward and upward simultaneously—both in imagery, rhythm and repetition, that one experiences in walking across my beloved Brooklyn Bridge. I'm now busy on the *Niña, Santa Maria, Pinta* episode—Cathay being an attitude of spirit, rather than material conquest throughout, of course.

I know I can depend on you to mention the flaws and shortcomings. This section seems a little transcendental in tendency at present,—but I think that the pediments of the other sections will show it not to have been.

Write me, but only when you have abundant time and feel so inclined. My Grandmother is on her deathbed and I may be called to Cleveland any moment.

Much love to you,—Hart

To Gaston Lachaise

Patterson, New York

Dear Lachaise: February 10, 1926

Constantly your seagull has floated in my mind—ever since I saw it, and it will mean much to me to have it. I can't thank you enough. I am enclosing an amount which I hope will to some extent defray the cost of materials, and you must let me know if more is needed.

I envy you your occupation out here in the extreme cold of the last two weeks—wiggling a pen or tapping a typewriter is hardly as conducive to good circulation or warmth while every breath one takes comes out like a steaming snort from a dragon! At present the snow is so deep that we are obliged to use snow shoes or skis to get anywhere. Fortunately we are well supplied with wood and oil and provisions.

When I get to New York—probably not for six weeks or

so—I hope to find you in. If the white bird is done before then you can express it out to Patterson, or I'll be glad to carry it back when I come in. Please give me best salutations and wishes to Mme. Lachaise and les Nagles.

Faithfully yours, Hart Crane

To Charles Harris

Patterson, New York
Dear Charles:　　　　　　　　　　　Febuary 20, 1926

I'm glad you are determined to go to Europe—and hope nothing has or will come to break the plans stated in your letter. You must let me know where to find you in New York if you are there any length of time before sailing—I *may* be able to come in about that time.

At present (and for the months past nearly) we have been snowbound. The snowshoes I bought before coming out here have been useful, despite the amiable jeers from the natives with which they were greeted. On the whole I'm a little bored with the ultimate privacy of a rural winter—supplies and mail so difficult of access and stiff fingers and chilblains. I could stand a few cocktails and taxis for a change. But this is the place for me to work—and I'll be here indefinitely and unregretfully.

It's been great to have time for some reading and I've been delving into everything from Spanish history to New Bedford whaling records, from D. H. Lawrence to Lord Bacon. Meanwhile the scaffoldings for the *Bridge* jacknife upward a little and a few stanzas seem to have been evolved. Being actually paid to write poems in advance like this, however, is a weighty problem and I'm a bit uncertain of acquitting myself as well as I hoped. So remember me in your prayers!

All luck to you Charles, and write again soon.

Hart

To Charlotte and Richard Rychtarik

Patterson, New York

Dear Charlotte et Ricardo: March 2

What is the red excitement that keeps you from writing me?! Br-r-r! It is still cold here, and for the last six weeks we have had no mail deliveries—that is, to our doorstep. Most of the time we have had to snow-shoe over to the next farm—about a mile away—as the snow was piled so deep on the road to our house that nothing could get through.

In spite of many inconveniences, however, I am glad of coming out here. Temperate living, good sleep and considerable outdoor exercise have had their usual effects. The cold has kept us hopping, though, and I'll be glad to greet the first warm days that come. Then there will be both more time and more comfort for reading and *The Bridge*. The finale of which is just about completed—but the antecedent sections will take me at least a year yet. At times the project seems hopeless, horribly so; and then suddenly something happens inside one, and the theme and the substance of the conception seem brilliantly real, more so than ever! At least, *at worst*, the poem will be a *nuge* failure! If you get what I mean. When I am a little better satisfied with certain details of the part already finished I'll send it on to you, although I really shouldn't—as isolated from the rest of the poem it would probably not be interesting.

Mother wrote me that you called on her. She was extremely pleased, and remarked how beautiful and youthfully radiant my Charlotte was! I am really longing to see you "all"—as the Southerners say—and aren't you coming east this summer? For a long time I expected to be called to Cleveland at any moment, but since Grandma is so much better I doubt if I shall come for awhile. Spring will be marvelous here—and we are going to have a large vegetable and flower garden. I'm *planning* to get up at dawn every day and cultivate it!

Please write me a copious letter soon. There must be a great deal of news.

Love—Hart

To Gorham Munson

Patterson, New York

Dear Gorham: March 5

The long siege of snow—the mail delivery has been discontinued for six weeks, and isn't resumed yet—despite occasional sportiveness with snow shoes and skis, has been a burden. Especially as I was swindled on a fifty-gal. drum of kerosene I bought for the stoves in my study, and have had to risk chapping hands every time I came near the typewriter to say nothing of tumbling through many a chilly night with chilblains from cold floors, damp, etc. It really would have been alright had I had pure kerosene, though. Nothing but the swindler is to blame.

None-the-less, I've read considerably—Aeschylus (especially the *Oresteia*) was a revelation of my ideal in the dynamics of metaphor—even through the rather prosy translations one gleans the essential density of image, impact of substance matter so verbally quickened and delivered with such soul-shivering economy that one realizes there is none in the English language to compare him with. —Then Prescott's *Ferdinand & Isabella*, journal of Columbus, a book on Magellan by Hildebrand (this was rather inexcusable), Melville's delightful *White Jacket* as well as a marvelously illustrated book on whaling and whaling ships, published by the Marine Research Society, Salem, Mass . . . In the midst of my readings of *Science & the Modern World,* Whitehead,—along comes *Virgin Spain.* I'm about half way through this at present and feel like telegraphing Waldo my immediate uncontrolled and unstinted enthusiasm! As prose it certainly is his climax of excellence—and as a document of the spirit one of the most lively testaments ever written. I had been dwelling with a good deal of surprise in a pleasant conviction that Lawrence's *Plumed Serpent* was a masterpiece of racial description. It certainly is vividly beautiful, its landscapes, theatrical vistas, etc.—but Waldo's work is a world of true reality—his ritual is not a mere invention. Only my interest in Maya and Toltec archeology led me to order Lawrence's book. It was poor in this—at least regarding the details I had hoped for, but I was rather astonished at the calibre of much of the prose.

As Waldo may have mentioned, the finale of the *Bridge* is written, the other five or six parts are in feverish embryo. They will require at least a year more for completion; however bad this work may be, it ought to be hugely and unforgivably, distinguishedly bad. In a way it's a test of materials as much as a test of one's imagination. Is the last statement sentimentally made by Eliot,

> "This is the way the world ends,
> This is the way the world ends,—
> Not with a bang but a whimper."

is this acceptable or not as the poetic determinism of our age?! I, of course, can say no, to myself, and believe it. But in the face of such a stern conviction of death on the part of the only group of people whose verbal sophistication is likely to take an interest in a style such as mine—what can I expect? However, I know my way by now, regardless. I shall at least continue to grip with the problem without relaxing into the easy acceptance (in the name of "elegance, nostalgia, wit, splenetic splendor") of death which I see most of my friends doing. O the admired beauty of a casuistical mentality! It is finally content with twelve hours sleep a day and archeology.

I am glad that you have switched over to the more profitable and leisurely programme which you describe. And that you've gone back to writing again with such vim. The social distractions of NY are so terrific that I hope to never live there again beyond six months at a period. I'm really just getting around to a working basis, the first real platform of my life—here. In many ways it proves to be a revelation of certain potentialities.

Do send me your comments on Crane. And may I be frank —without seeming to reflect on any personal relationships of the past—in stating my reactions? Not that I shall desire to exert any changes, but that there may possibly arise (between ourselves) certain questions of direction, aims, intentions, which I may feel are erroneously ascribed to me. At least my agreements or objections may interest you.

With my love to Lisa, as ever Hart

To Gorham Munson

                                      Patterson, New York
Dear Gorham: March 17, 1926

My rummy conversation last Monday offered, I fear, but a poor explanation of my several theoretical differences of opinion with you on the function of poetry, its particular province of activity, etc. Neither was I able to express to you my considerable appreciation of many accurate distinctions made in your essay which certainly prompt my gratitudes as well as applause. It would probably be uninteresting as well as a bit excessive for me to enumerate and dwell on these felicitations, however gratifying to myself I may feel them to be. Your essay is roughly divided in two, the second half including our present disagreement, and inasmuch as I have never attempted to fulfill the functions therein attributed to the poet, your theories on that subject can be discussed from a relatively impersonal angle so far as I am concerned. Furthermore, it is *one* aspect of a contemporary problem which has already enlisted the most detailed and intense speculation from a number of fields, science, philosophy, etc., as you, of course, know. I'm not saying that my few hasty notes which follow are conclusive evidence, but the logic of them (added to the organic convictions incident to the memorized experience of the creative "act", let us say) is not yet sufficiently disproved for me by such arguments, at least, as you have used in your essay.

Poetry, in so far as the metaphysics of any absolute knowledge extends, is simply the concrete *evidence* of the *experience* of a recognition (*knowledge* if you like). It can give you a *ratio* of fact and experience, and in this sense it is both perception and thing perceived, according as it approaches a significant articulation or not. This is its reality, its fact, *being.* When you attempt to ask more of poetry,—the fact of man's relationship to a hypothetical god, be it Osiris, Zeus or Indra, you will get as variant terms even from the abstract terminology of philosophy as you will from poetry; whereas poetry, without attempting to logically enunciate such a problem or its solution, may well give you the real connective experience, the very "sign manifest" on which rests the assumption of a godhead.

I'm perfectly aware of my wholesale lack of knowledge. But as Allen said, what exactly do you mean by "knowledge"? When you ask for exact factual data (a graphic map of eternity?), ethical morality or moral classifications, etc., from poetry—you not only limit its goal, you ask its subordination to science, philosophy. Is it not equally logical to expect Stravinsky to bring his fiddles into dissent with the gravitation theories of Sir Isaac Newton? They *are* in dissent with this scientist, as a matter of fact, and organically so; for the group mind that Stravinsky appeals to has already been freed from certain of the limitations of experience and consciousness that dominated both the time and the mind of Newton. Science (ergo all exact knowledge and its instruments of operation) is in perfect antithesis to poetry. (Painting, architecture, music, as well). It operates from an exactly opposite polarity, and it may equate with poetry, but when it does so its statement of such is in an entirely different terminology. I hope you get this difference between *inimical* and *antithetical*, intended here. It is not my interest to discredit science, it has been as inspired as poetry,—and if you could but recognize it, much more hypothetically motivated.

What you admire in Plato as "divine sanity" is the architecture of his logic. Plato doesn't live today because of the intrinsic "truth" of his statements: their only living truth today consists in the "fact" of their harmonious relationship to each other in the context of his organization of them. This grace partakes of poetry. But Plato was primarily a philosopher, and you must admit that grace is a secondary motive in philosophical statement, at least until the hypothetical basis of an initial "truth" has been accepted—not in the name of beauty, form or experience, but in the name of rationality. No wonder Plato considered the banishment of poets;—their reorganizations of chaos on bases perhaps divergent from his own threatened the logic of *his* system, itself founded on assumptions that demanded the very defense of poetic construction which he was fortunately able to provide.

The tragic quandary (or agon) of the modern world derives from the paradoxes that an inadequate system of rationality forces on the living consciousness. I am not opposing any new synthesis of reasonable laws which might provide a consistent philosophical and moral program for our epoch. Neither, on the other hand, am I attempting through poetry to delineate any such system. If this "knowledge", as you call it, were so sufficiently organized as to dominate the limitations of my personal experience (consciousness) then I would probably find myself automatically writing under its "classic" power of dictation, and under that circumstance might be incidentally as philosophically "contained" as you might wish me to be. That would mean "serenity" to you because the abstract basis of my work would have been familiarized to you before you read a word of the poetry. But my poetry, even then,—in so far as it was truly poetic,—would avoid the employment of abstract tags, formulations of experience in factual terms, etc.,—it would necessarily express its concepts in the more direct terms of physical-psychic experience. If not, it must by so much lose its impact and become simply categorical.

I think it must be due to some such misapprehensions of my poetic purpose in writing that leads you to several rather contradictory judgements which in one sentence are laudatory and in other contexts which you give them,—put me to blush for mental attitudes implied on my part. For instance, after having granted me all the praise you do earlier in your essay for "storming heaven" as it were, how can you later refer to that same faculty of verbal synchronization as to picture me as "waiting for another ecstasy"—and then "slumping"—rather as a baker would refer to a loaf in his oven. Granted your admiration for the "yeastiness" of some of my effusions, you should (in simple justice to your reader and your argument) here also afford the physical evidence (actual quotation or logical proof) of the "slump", the unleavened failure. There really are plenty of lines in this respect which could be used for illustration. What I'm objecting to is contained in my suspicion that you have allowed too many extra-literary impressions of me to enter your essay, sometimes for better, sometimes for worse. The same is true of your reference to the "psychological *gaming*" (Verlaine) which puts the slur of superficiality and vulgarity on the very aspects of my work which you have previously been at pains to praise.—And all because you arbitrarily propose a goal for me which I have no idea of nor interest in following. Either you find my work poetic or not, but if you propose for it such ends as poetry organically escapes, it seems to me, as Allen said, that you as a critic of literature are working into a confusion of categories. Certainly this charge of alternate "gutter sniping" and "angel kissing" is no longer anything more than a meretricious substitute for psychological sincerity in defining the range of an artist's subject matter and psychic explorations. Still less should it be brought forward unless there is enough physical evidence in the artist's work to warrant curiosity in this respect on the part of the reader.

Your difficulties are extra, I realize, in writing about me at all. They are bound to be thus extra because of the (so far as the reader goes) "impurities" of our previous literary arguments, intimacies of statement, semi-statements, etc. which are not always reflected in a man's work, after all. But your preoccupations on the one hand with a terminology which I have not attempted and your praise on the other hand of my actual (physical) representation of the incarnate *evidence* of the very knowledge, the very *wisdom* which you feel me to be only conjecturally sure of—makes me guilty of really wronging you, perhaps, but drives me to the platitude that "truth has no name". Her latest one, of course, is "relativity".

Apropos of all this the letter by Nichols in the *New Criterion* will interest you when you read it; there are interesting quotations from Goethe, Santayana, Russell, etc. And I am enclosing a hasty bundle of notes written at O'Neill's request for what angles they might suggest to him in writing a foreword for my book. (This, I hope, may be returned.)

Allen tells me that he has just mailed his note on me—for possible use in the new *Masses*. I told him to do this, not remembering definitely what you had told me about it before. It can do no harm anyway. I'm enclosing copies of the poems which Potamkin had intended using. It certainly was very kind of you to have suggested these matters to the *Masses* editor. Do let me hear from you soon.

Hart

P. S.—Needless to say, the notes for O'Neill contain repetitious matter for you, and certain accents were especially made against biases and critical deficiencies which I felt lead to unwarranted assumptions, misplaced praises, etc. on his part. But the definitions of the "logic of metaphor", "dynamics of inferential mention", etc. I think are quite exact.

To Otto H. Kahn

Patterson, New York

Dear Mr. Kahn: March 18, 1926

You were so kind as to express a desire to know from time to time how *The Bridge* was progressing, so I'm flashing in a signal from the foremast, as it were. Right now I'm supposed to be Don Cristobal Colon returning from "Cathay", first voyage. For mid-ocean is where the poem begins.

It concludes at midnight—at the center of Brooklyn Bridge. Strangely enough that final section of the poem has been the first to be completed,—yet there's a logic to it, after all; it is the mystic consummation toward which all the other sections of the poem converge. Their contents are implicit in its summary.

Naturally I am encountering many unexpected formal difficulties in satisfying my conception, especially as one's original idea has a way of enlarging steadily under the spur of daily concentration on minute details of execution. I don't wish to express my confidence too blatantly—but I am certain that, granted I'm able to find the suitable form for all details as I presently conceive them, *The Bridge* will be a dynamic and eloquent document.

As I said, I have thus far completed only the final section,—about one hundred lines. I am now going straight through from the beginning. There has been much incidental reading to do, and more study is necessary as I go on. As I cannot think of my work in terms of time I cannot gauge when it will be completed, probably by next December, however.

There are so many interlocking elements and symbols at work throughout *The Bridge* that it is next to impossible to describe it without resorting to the actual metaphors of the poem. Roughly, however, it is based on the conquest of space and knowledge.

The following notation is a very rough abbreviation of the subject matter of the several sections:

I   Columbus—Conquest of space, chaos

II   Pokahantus—The natural body of America-fertility, etc.

III   Whitman—The Spiritual body of America (A dialogue between Whitman and a dying solider in a Washington hos-

pital; the infraction of physical death, disunity, on the concept
of immortality)

IV   John Brown (Negro porter on Calgary Express making
up berths and singing to himself (a jazz form for this) of his
sweetheart and the death of John Brown, alternately)

V   Subway—The encroachment of machinery on humanity;
a kind of purgatory in relation to the open sky of last section

VI   The Bridge—A sweeping dithyramb in which the
Bridge becomes the symbol of consciousness spanning time
and space

The first and last sections are composed of blank verse with
occasional rhyme for accentuation. The verbal dynamics used
and the spacious periodicity of the rhythm result in an unusu-
ally symphonic form. What forms I shall use for the other sec-
tions will have to be determined when I come to grips with their
respective themes.

I would gladly send you the completed section for present
reading, but unless you especially wish to see it now I should
prefer your judgement on it later when a more synthetic
reading will be possible.

I hope that this extended amount of particulars,—evidence,
perhaps, of an excessive enthusiasm on my part, has not been
tedious reading. Your interest and confidence have proved to be
so great a spur to me that I must mention my gratitude again.

Very faithfully yours, Hart Crane

To Waldo Frank

Mid-channel
March 20, 1926

I

Be with me, Luis de St. Angel, now—
Witness before the tides can sweep away
The word I bring, O you who reined my suit
Into the Queen's great heart that doubtful day:
For I have seen what now no spicy breath
Of clown or courtier riddles or gainsays;
And you, Fray Juan Perez, whose counsel fear
And greed adjourned, I bring you back Cathay!

Dear Waldo:

Just a word to say I have finished my first reading of your *Spain*. It is a book I shall go back to many times. Its magnificence and integrity are so rare that they constitute an embarrassment to our times in some ways. "The Port of Columbus" is truly something of a prelude to my intentions for the bridge —which I seem to have got back to today after a hideous experience in New York and in spite of a very bad cold I seem to have caught from overheated city buildings.

I can't resist sending you the first verse at this early time, along with the revised version of the finale. Your discipline and your confidence are so dear to me that in moods like this today (adrift a music that is almost a burden) I have to be a little uncontained and remind you of my love. Will send the Kahn article next week when a fresh copy arrives . . .

> Here waves climb on the sliding back of day;
> Invisible valves of the sea, locks, tendons
> Crested and creeping, troughing corridors
> That fall back yawning to another plunge.
> And now the sun's red caravel sequesters light
> Once more behind us . . . It is morning there,—
> O where our other cities, mountains steep
> White spires in heaven, yet balanced in this keel!

Temporarily—Don Cristobal—

To Malcolm Cowley

Dear Malcolm: Sunday, March 28

The news of your plans for the summer is good to hear! We're all anticipating the first of May—though you *will* be a little distant. Five miles walking says Mrs. Turner, coming out of her aunt's part with the tea.

After a perfect spasm of sentiment and "inspection" I was released from the fond embrace of my relatives in Cleveland— only to fare into rather more than less spasmodic embraces in

N.Y.—a one night spree—on my way back. Since which I have been reading the philosophies of the East until I actually dream in terms of the Vedanta scriptures. Also am finding Marco Polo pleasant to incorporate in the subconscious.

I've often wondered how you got home that night. After you left I was roused from my stupor by an amazing scandal at the next table. Benét, Wylie and some others discussing Nathalia Crane—who, it seems, doesn't write at all. Her father does the trick—works off "suppressed desires" that way, etc. etc. I was very good after that and stormed over to the Albert, lectured the clerk for not admitting my friends, and went to bed, tout seul.

The next morning after the next I was discovering that my mother knows how to mix the best cocktails I ever drank.

Are you going ahead with the Boyd proposal? I think you should—a fine weapon against further attacks from that gent. again—and not, however, implying any concession whatever on your part.

I wish I had a lyric or so to circulate, like Allen. He suddenly sprouted last week and has been going ever since. A letter from Eliot indicates that the *New Criterion* may take some of his poems. The Adelphi matter had definitely fallen through.

Carolyn has gone to Washington and points south for a coupla weeks.

Wish you'd write. Best to Peggy.

Hart

To Grace Hart Crane

Patterson

Dearest Grace: Sunday

Your letter came yesterday. And I was *immensely* glad to hear from you. Altogether, the news seemed good, too, and I'm *so* glad you and Charles have made a definite decision! By *all* means make the little Church the scene. Then I can be there and we can all take a bus ride afterward. Of *course* you'll be acceptable—who ever heard of such distinctions being made in any Protestant church against widows and widowers, grass or otherwise! Then maybe you could make my humble domicile one of the stops on your celebrations.

I, too, think I made my visit at just the proper time. I'll never forget how really eloquently Grandma looked, how intelligent and fresh. And *you* looked so good to me, too! Remember, that suffering does, if borne without rancour, it does build something that only grows lovelier with time—and it is a kind of kingdom among those *initiated,* a kingdom that has the widest kind of communion. You and I can share our understanding of things more and more as time goes on. I loved you *so much* for many of the things you said when I was with you.

Yes, I hope you never will turn your back on me, as you say. And this is not to say that there may come occasions for it—but there may, after all, be times of temporary misunderstandings as there have been before. I can be awfully proud of *you*, however less occasion I may have to feel similarly about myself. I do some awfully silly things sometimes—most of which you don't know about, but which I sometimes (not always) regret. Don't let this stir your apprehensions any, however, I'm in no particular pickle at present.

We have had another snow—and I'm just disgusted. I had counted on modified weather on my return and instead it's been just one snow flurry after another. Sore throat is some better, but I'm still threatened with tonsilitis. No chance to start gardens yet.

I'm gonna gotta kinda sorta hit the hay now—so good Night. Here's a kiss for you X and one for Grandma X
>   Give Charles and Miss Wilson my best.
>   Hart

To Gorham Munson

>   Patterson, New York
Dear Gorham: April 5

It seems evident that I somewhat too egoistically argued what I intended as simply a defense of the position and province of poetry, as an art form, rather than any claims my work might or might not have to critical praise. This has been my attitude throughout our discussion, and though certain contentions are still unresolved, it doesn't in the least conflict with what you say in your last letter. Indeed, I should say that your essay rather overestimates my achievements in some particulars. Please don't think me ungrateful or disgruntled, anyway.

Rorty was so swift in returning Allen's NOTE that I have been wondering if he had actually taken some interest in the "Voyages" I sent you. I should have sent them direct to him had I known that he was subsequently to write me a request for something. Sheer inadvertency on my part not to have mentioned my intentions in sending them to you. Allen gave Untermeyer and Kreymborg such digs that it's not surprising that Rorty summarily returned the mss. I shall be surprised if he fancies my work.

The Cowleys move up here May first. I hope to have a few "animations" with Malcolm before I, the climate, the solitude, or whatever it is, drives him into the kind of shell that Brown and Tate seem to have retired into lately. My mood being preeminently N. Labrador these days—I should like a little good company immensely. A life of perfect virtue, redundant health, etc. doesn't seem in any way to encourage the Muse, after all. I almost feel like coming to town and seeking a job, at least that would make me part-time useful, meantime there wouldn't be the suspense of weeks going by without a written line. I'm afraid I've so systematically objectivized my theme and its details that the necessary "subjective lymph and sinew" is frozen. Meanwhile I drone about, reading, eating and sleeping. It's really quite agonizing. For in so many ways I know what I WANT to do. . . . The actual fleshing of a concept is so complex and difficult, however, as to be quite beyond the immediate avail of will or intellect. A fusion with other factors not so easily named is the condition of fulfilment. It is alright to call this "possession", if you will, only it should not be insisted that its operation denies the simultaneous functioning of a strong critical faculty. It is simply a stronger focus than can be arbitrarily willed into operation by the ordinarily-employed perceptions. Do you find anything in my rough notes that's interesting?

Love, Hart

To Otto H. Kahn

Patterson, New York
Dear Mr. Kahn: April 10, 1926
  Your kind answer of the 8th instant is most gratefully acknowledged. I shall not require additional funds for a month, at least, but if you wish to forward the amount mentioned in your letter about the 1st of May it will thereby assure the maintenance of a proper balance at my bank.
  I hope I may be pardoned for the mention and possible correction of a reference in your letter concerning the date of your initial interest in my behalf. Not that your extreme kindness deserves such trivialities of "button-holding"—but that my gratitude prompts me to preserve at least as favorable an impression of conduct in your eyes as facts permit. I dislike to seem extravagent of your benefits, therefor, and hope I may say without offense, that I should certainly feel myself to have been so, did I not recognize what appears in your letter to have been a mistaken recollection in point of time.
  It was early in December, I believe, instead of February, when our meeting occured. The difference in time is perhaps slight, but the duration of funds in the present case I consider as of some moral purport. In view of this I hope my motives will not be misunderstood.
  With deepest regard and best wishes, believe me,
                    Most faithfully yours, Hart Crane

To Grace Hart Crane

Patterson, New York
Dear Grace: Sunday, April 18
  It would be a relief to be able to talk with you an hour or so today. I'm in such an uncertain position in regard to a number of things that I feel as though it would be a fitting end to settle it with powder and bullet. The whole benefit of my patronage from Kahn, my year of leisure, my long fight with the winter, etc. out here is about to be sacrificed to the malicious

nature of a person I thought to be friendly—but who turns out to be quite otherwise. I refer to Mrs. Tate, and Allen. But primarily it has been Mrs. Tate who has influenced matters until they came to a head the other day, since which time I have had a note from each of them, respectively; including insults and malicious remarks to an extent which amazes me.

I am accused of having victimized their time and their quarters by intruding without regard to their wishes, etc. This is in part justified,—justified, I say because the contingency of such a matter was bound to exist between two families which had agreed on sharing a common water pump. I had to have access to it as much as they did, and had to pass through their kitchen occasionally on my way. When Mrs. Tate—this occured last week—instead of simply telling me that she wished I would avoid such passage in the future—when she began putting bolts on her doors, and all that—I could take the *hint* without having to be knocked down by a hammer, and so removed my shaving utensils, etc. which had been beside the pump, into Mrs. Turner's kitchen. Why this should make them mad, I don't know, and why it should make them mad because I immediately began avoiding their parts of the house *completely* (not being invited to do otherwise) I can't see, either.

Of course when I encountered them outside, and saw how sulky they behaved, etc. I began to lose all respect for such behavior—made up my mind to ignore them as much as decency permitted, although I realized that with such an atmosphere about the place it would be very difficult to procede with any creative work. Matters came to a climax day before yesterday, shortly after breakfast I had been talking to Mrs. Turner around on "our" side of the house about some plans for cleaning up some rubbish, etc. when suddenly a door opens from the Tate's kitchen and Allen shouts out, "If you've got a criticism of my work to make, I'd appreciate it if you would speak to me about it first!" Then the door savagely banged, and Mrs. Turner and I (who hadn't mentioned him or anything that concerned him) were left staring at each other in perfect amazement. I can't easily describe how angry I was. I felt myself losing all control—but I managed to address the Tates without breaking anything. Mrs. Turner came in with me and corroborated the facts of the matter, and it turned out that the

Tates hadn't heard actually a thing I was saying—their imaginations, they evidently felt, were perfectly justified in building up a perfect tower of Babel out of nothing.

Nothing was touched on at that fiery moment, but the immeadiate circumstances of what I had said and what I hadn't. Tate finally admitting that he was all wrong. My feelings remained little cooled, however. The rest of the time since then has been simply hideous. The next morning (I, not sleeping had heard the Tates getting out of bed during the night and pounding out something on the typewriter) I found a couple of the nastiest notes under my bedroom door that I ever hope to get from anyone. Mrs. Tate began by saying that they had arrived in the house first; that they had invited me to share quarters with them in the first place because I was penniless in New York at that time, and that as soon as they found out that I had been fortunate in acquiring funds they immediately had begun to doubt the adviseability of inviting me out, but *of course* hadn't felt privileged to say anything about such matters before this. I'm not quoting *insinuations* in any of this, I'm using practically their own words. Then she went on to say that they had alotted me one room only (this is an absolute lie; they assumed that I was to have a bedroom and my study besides) and that I had from the moment of arrival proceeded to spread myself and possessions all over the house, invading every corner; and so on,—finally ending up with the assertion that I had been busy ever since I arrived in trying to make them menial servants of my personal wants. The contents of Mr Tate's letter were about the same, a little more gracefully phrased, that's all.

As a matter of fact, I have never, so long as I've been here, requested a single favor from either of them. You know the story about the cooking arrangements already—how I changed over to Mrs. Turner because Mrs. Tate's ill temper made it impossible for me to perform my share of duties with her in the kitchen. She has never gotten over that—and all her talk about patronizing me from motives of "charity", etc. appears very likely to come from a regret that I didn't continue to buy most of the food, etc. Since then—even though I derived no benefit from the wood stove that the Tate's use in their kitchen—I've been careful to go out and help Allen cut and saw, etc. And made it a point to mention—that while I couldn't constantly keep after him with questions as to when he wanted to saw and when he didn't—if he'd let me know about such occasions I'd be glad to join him whenever possible.

It's all simply disgusting. I don't know how much money they owe me exactly—but I have told them that I was always glad to advance them funds whenever needed, and while they haven't been extravagent—they have nevertheless been momentarily relieved from sudden circumstances by frequent access to my funds. On top of all this I have practically given Allen the fare for two trips to New York (on one occasion I was so anxious for him to have the chance to hear a certain opera that I gave him ten dollars to get a good seat), I've had them in to dinner with Mrs. Turner and myself frequently, I gave Carolyn my old typewriter to work on her novel that she pretends to make all this fuss about. She didn't have one herself and would otherwise have had to depend on such moments as her husband wasn't using his to write at all, while I on the other hand, should certainly have been able to make a good discount on my new machine by turning in the old had I not purposely wished to be amiable about the matter. There have been lots of other amenities which I enjoyed extending. And you know me not to obviously hold such things over people's heads. *Doesn't* it all look as though *as Mr. Tate says*, I valued their friendship only for the purpose of exploiting their services to me!

Mrs. Turner has cried for two days and nights about the matter—she hates to have me leave so. She says there is another room in the upstairs which I can use and not be obliged to have anything to do with the Tate's part of the house, their rent or their arrangements. I must say I'm stumped. How can I, on one hand, persist in staying here after such an insulting statement from the Tates to the effect that I was originally their guest and that I was invited on the grounds of charity rather than from any other motives? This is one of the hardest matters I have ever had to decide. For I feel that I owe some sense of economy to Mr. Kahn, who didn't give me money to keep moving about merely out of the way of disagreeable people. My money is very low now. The first thousand is gone —it cost me more than I ever would have guessed to have just got settled here with all my books and materials at hand as they are. I wrote Kahn recently that I needed more money, and he very speedily and kindly replied with a check for five hundred. At the same time the Rychtariks wrote from Cleveland that they needed the money they had loaned me for my land—that they required it for the summer trip to Europe, etc. And so two hundred will have to be taken out of the Kahn money at once.

It really is tragic. The whole fruit of the first opportunity of my life to write an extended poem is apparently about to be blighted by the cankerous bile of a narrow, jealous mind! As I say I don't at this moment know which way to turn. If I remain here (spring is just coming on—and the best time for work, so long waited for, has come!) if I remain here under such unpleasant relations it is very doubtful whether or not I can overcome the hypnosis of evil and jealousy in the air enough to get back into my poem, really just started. But if I move away it means that so much of my slight funds will be wasted in just the cost of travel, etc. that in less than a month I'll be back looking for a job again—and in the middle of the summer, the most devilish and exhausting time to work in the city. I don't feel that I ought to let my indignation and pride effect me so far as the hasty and ill-founded remarks of the Tates are concerned, I would sacrifice all that to my work and remain here if I felt enough assurance of being *able* to work under such circumstances.

If you feel at all sympathetic to this situation of mine I wish you *this time* be generous to let me go to the Island and finish my poem there. At least I should not have to fear being put off the little land that is still ours in the world. I have ample money to get there and to live economically for some time. It may reasonably be expected that Mr Kahn will come forward with another five hundred which he promised within a certain time, meanwhile I can't ask him for more before six months without risking the charge of extravagence. I think that I can re-sell the land I bought to Miss Flynn from whom I purchased it. Summer in the tropics isn't of course the paradise of the winter months, but it is a thousand times better than a hall bedroom in New York without light or air, to say nothing of the fact that it might cost me a hundred or so of what I have left just spent in looking for work. You know how long it is sometimes.

If I can't somehow succeed in taking advantage of this one opportunity given me by Mr. Kahn, I don't know how I'll feel about life or any future efforts to live—and if you can't see how it is reasonable for me to request under the circumstances some privileges from my family I shall be amazed. You've already said that you didn't think I'd like Mrs. Simpson, etc. Well do you think *that* is half so important to me or to anyone else after all. I'm not able to reason why this issue should hang on the whimsical temper of an old woman. If I went to the Island I should do my best to preserve the most pleasant relations with Mrs. Simpson, and I haven't much doubt but what I should succeed. I ought to be able to live a few months in the house my grandfather built without being put off by a hired keeper of the place—especially when I am much better fitted naturally, by simply being a male, for keeping up the place than she is.

I'm asking you for this refuge. I've always been refused before. If you deny it now I'm not sure how much farther away I'll go to accomplish my purposes. Perhaps to the orient, even if I have just enough to get there and no more.

I shall go into New York early in the week, perhaps tomorrow. Perhaps several days later. I'll let you know where I settle and what plans are finally adopted. Meanwhile please write me here, as before; Mrs. Turner will be sure to send my mail to whatever address I have at the time.

I'm sorry to have such melancholy news, especially after such lovely letters as recently came from you and Grandma, but it can't be helped. It all may be very much for the best in the end. I do hope you'll be generous enough to give me your sanction on the Island matter—that's all I'm requesting. I can always get money enough to get back (from at least 5 people) and go into an office again. But that isn't the issue now. I'm writing a poem that is bound to be a magnificent thing *if* I can escape the wolves (and weazels!) long enough to build it. Won't you help?

With love—Hart

To Caroline Gordon and Allen Tate

Carolyn and Allen:

Your letters represent an array of such indiscriminate slanders directed to practically all my motives and intentions that I admit myself baffled in answering them. I can't answer the "challenge" you suggest, Allen. Several such references as my *desire to exploit my friends as menial servants* emanate from such an obscure source that if I hazarded the mention of what seem to me to be the only plausible emotional causes beneath such charges, I should run the risk of doing you a graver injustice and of offering you a deeper insult than you have offered me.

You will have to continue in your belief, then, that I engaged Mrs. Turner to cook for me because I wanted Carolyn Gordon to peel more potatoes, wash more dishes and begin serving me my breakfast in bed. Etc. The logic of your deductions in this regard is beyond mine. Perhaps Sue and Bill had some inkling of my designs on your services and wished to help. They suggested this plan, however, as offering relief to the Tate family, not especially to me.

When it comes to my decorum and conduct the matter is quite otherwise. Although you attribute all sorts of conquests and ambitions to me which I've never been aware of, perhaps such inferences are more deservedly drawn. For I acknowledge gross errors of taste and many, many lapses of decent consideration for your privacy and working time. I'm a comparative barbarian in many ways and certainly was not raised by the lack of education and social chaos that my family accorded my adolescence. If I have been so course-grained as not to have apprehended many of your implied correctives in such instances, it has not been due, believe me, to ill-will or mere stubborness. I have lived quite alone, without any real social relations with people for many years. My enthusiasms and hilarity seldom stop at considerate limits. I probably ought never to attempt to live with others whom I care for, in any domestic arrangement.

This same obtuseness also probably accounts for my complete obliviousness to the real motives actuating the invitation you extended me to join you here this winter. (Don't let the irony of my intonation suggest any insincerity in my words; I'm too deeply hurt to simulate any tricky indifference). It had never occured to me that the chief bond of attachment between Allen and myself was a pity on his part for certain material difficulties I have encountered frequently, and I'm stubborn enough and I hope, just enough, to persist in believing that such was the case—at least not until the first of December, 1925. However, I didn't realize it then, and haven't until very lately—which circumstances now make it a doubly embarrassing gratuity for me to acknowledge, since it is then obvious that I have presumed on a great many extraneous factors in our relationship for a long, long time.

You are wrong, Allen, in predicting my opposition to your poetry. It hasn't changed in any of the qualities that matter most to me. It doesn't, and doubtless will never be dominated by that particular supine narcissism which charms so many in the poetry of our friend Eliot. But this is no place for me to offer assurances which are not desired, nor defenses of my tastes, which are already too familar and monotonous.

I have rented the northeast bedroom, which Mrs. Turner assures me, much to my surprise, had not hitherto been formally included in the number of rooms allotted for rent. In view of this I am assuming that it will not be presumptious in me to store my things there for an indefinite period and under separate arrangements with Mrs. Turner.

The immediate future with its long expected outdoor freedom and relative ease will, I hope, quickly heal the rancor that my infringements and inadvertences have incurred. Certainly I desire that recent events and my image, howsoever it stands in your recollections, shall be erased as speedily as possible.

Sincerely,

To Allen Tate

You expect me to "welcome" failings that haven't yet appeared in your work merely because I detest a certain narcissism in the voluptuous melancholics of Eliot—which you admire, and I don't—. We should be able to agree to disagree about such matters without calling in dish pans, saws and slop jars. You claim I have involved these factors in my relation with you—I have torn up a letter, long and tiresome, detailing my own convictions that my motives have been more detached and less ridiculously subjective and selfish than you assume.

It's all wrong—all the way through—and unfortunate. Although I have no apologies to make—because I can't see my frequent vulgarities and assumptions as totalling the *real* causes you and Carolyn have mounted against me—I don't see any use in being either defensive or ironic. These are easy and obvious modes and I think it better to let the matter rest as you want to believe it.

I'm sorry for my failings wherever they have incured your inconvenience and displeasure, and ask you to forget them and me as soon as possible.

Hart Crane

To Otto H. Kahn

Dear Mr. Kahn: On Board S. S. *Orizaba*

I am on my way to a plantation owned by my family on the Isle of Pines, W.I. My decision to move there was sudden, and while I had intended to write you before leaving the country I was detained by the usual errands and preparations rather unavoidably.

The move has not been capricious by any means. I don't want to inflict a series of details which would be lengthy and tedious, but I have really felt it necessary to go to a place where I feel reasonably certain, this time, of no unpleasant disturbances to my work; and even though the summer months are not exactly the most propitious time to live in the tropics I trust that I can overcome such discomforts at least as well as the icy conflict I have carried on recently in the country.

For purposes of economy I attempted to share quarters with some friends of mine last winter. After much pain and disturbance to my work I find that such arrangements are never again advisable. This time I am going to a place where I have a greater prerogative of occupation. I shall probably remain until our *Bridge* is completed. I shall have few expenses, no rent, etc., and I hope it will be evident that I have not followed a merely personal impulse.

Faithfully yours, Hart Crane

To Susan Jenkins and William Slater Brown

c/o Mrs. T. W. Simpson
Box 1373
Nueva Gerona, Isle of Pines, West Indies
Dear Sue and Bill: May 7

It is still one day less than a week since we sailed, our second on the island. Frank got Ward Line accomodations, which cut a day off the sea; and we were rather sorry. Still, passing Pam Bitch, My ammy and other Coney islands at midnight wasn't especially thrilling; that part of the trip was too close shore. But Havana was more and better than I had imagined. Architecture rather like Chirico—some Spanish plateresque—and physical metaphysically suggestive. But mostly on the surface, there isn't other evidence.

F's Spanish brought us off all beaten paths. We didn't visit an American haunt except the steamship office. The rest was mostly bars, cafes and theatres—filled with blacks, reds, browns, greys and every permutation and combinations of Southern bloods that you can imagine. Corona-Coronas, of course, for 15¢, marvelous sherry, cognac, vermouth and "Tropical"(the beer that I was talking about). Am. boats seem to be easy, by the way; we had St. Julian and Sauterne all the way down at table. Then we went to the Alhambra, a kind of Cuban National Winter Garden Burlesque. Latin "broadness" was somewhat veiled from me as far as the dialogue went, but actions went farther than apparently even the East Side can stand.

Gratings and balconies and narrow streets with plenty of whores nodding. The day of our departure a great fleet of American destroyers landed. Streets immeadiately became torrents of uniforms—one sailor had exactly the chinese mustache effect that I aspire to. But no Jack Fitzin—his boat must have passed to Brooklyn—passed in the night. Taxis anywhere in town for only 20¢, but that's about the only cheap feature. Great black bushed buxom Jamaican senoritas roared laughter at us, old women hobbled up offering lottery tickets (I finally got one on a hunch). The whole town is hyper-sensual and mad—i.e. has no apparent direction, destiny or purpose; Cummings' paradise. I shall have to go up for a real spree sometime when cash is plentiful, meanwhile this isle is enough Eden.

Poor Mrs. Simpson hadn't expected us for at least three days more—and F, of course, the extra party, almost bowled her over at first sight. She had a violent coughing fit, at which I thought the fragile frame of her would break and during which a parrot screamed from a corner somewhere, "damned poor dinner!" She has recovered, and is really loveable and quite the contrary of all I had expected. I've had one pleasant shock after another. The house is much more spacious than I had remembered, the island much more beautiful . . . The approach from the sea is like the Azores, F. says. To me, the mountains, strange greens, native thatched huts, perfume, etc. brought me straight to Melville. The heat *is* different from northern summer heat and the parroty phrase does hold—"it's always cool in the shade." It was cool enough for F to put a coat on at sundown today, "breezes prevail". Oleanders and mimosas in full bloom now make the air almost too heavy with perfume, it's another world—and a little like Rimbaud. I'm surprised that I didn't carry away more definite impressions from my first visit 11 years ago.

We discovered a beach yesterday, very near our house. We bathed late in the day and the water was almost too warm. The rest of the time we've wandered over the grove, bought fish, played with a baby owl that suddenly appeared, drunk punch, picked coconuts (which are a meal by themselves). You ought to see that owlet (Pythagoras) make away with a chameleon. No bigger than a fat sparrow, it blincked and swallowed a lizard whole. I've nearly died laughing at the creature. We brought it to table and it turded in F's salad, it sits on your finger and squeaks like Peggy does when she gets tipsy. I'll probably be taking it to bed with me, like Buff, when I first get tipsy (NO I haven't been tipsy since I left NY).

I spose Bina has already told you the details of the parental wedding in NY. Those last three days in town were mad ones for me. Sibyl Fiske, Agnes' sister, gnawed at my hand for quite a while at the dinner with the Cowleys. I don't remember what it was all about, but I think we fell in love with each other. I finally brought the bridal pair to lunch with Lachaise and Mme. A good time was had by all. L insisted on my bringing the famous bird with me. All my fears about the trunks were wrong, they brought everything in fine shape, even china unbroken.

I feel like a gastric museum at present, a cross cut of Tahitian stomach coast—but not in especial distress—at least so far. Uric acid won't have a whispering chance in a few days what with all the strange fruits and vegetables I'm trying. Casavas, guavas, bread fruit, limes, cumquats, kashew apples, coconuts, wild oranges, bananas, God I can't remember any more of the damned names. O yes, mulberries and avocadas and papayas. And mangos! Maybe I don't get enough of it yet! Tamarinds . . . pomegranates . . . guabanas . . . O sacre Nom de. . . .

Please tell Mrs. Turner that I'll write her soon. I'm trying to get a few letters on the first boat. Tell her to put the above box number on my mail instead of "Casas Villa".

Love, hart

My mother finally said she envied me going to the island—and the only time we had an argument was after the second act of *The Great God Brown* —which left us in a bad state.

To Grace Hart Curtis

Nueva Gerona
Villa Casas

Dear Grace: Saturday, May 8th

Well, here we are! We got in Havana Tuesday (a day earlier than expected—it seems the Ward line is faster) and Wednesday night we were on the boat leaving Batabano. We enjoyed Havana immensely while we were there, but wouldn't have stayed longer for the world. Waldo's Spanish proficiency carried us everywhere—Cuban hotel (Isla de Cuba) and Cuban cafes and theatres. We kept entirely away from American haunts, and I discovered that Havana gives you a better impression from that angle. But it's too noisy everywhere, and we were glad to get away. A knowledge of Spanish surely does save one money here.

I am constantly being suprised at the novelties the island has to offer. I'm astonished that I carried away such vague impressions before—but being only 15 and being here so short a time accounts for it, I spose. First of all—the approach in the early morning was simply gorgeous, then all the varied plant life, the fruits etc. I discover I never really got acquainted with. This is only our third day here, but it has meant more vivid and exact impressions than would be easy for me to enumerate.

The weather has been wonderful—and except for the fact that May is the worst month in the year for mosquitoes everyting would be perfect. Breezes have kept up, and the only rain we've had was last night. The sky is somewhat different though; you'd know it was the rainy season. I've been again surprised at the spaciousness of the house—much larger than I had remembered. The bathroom, etc. is of course entirely new to me. I have your old room on the front west corner, and Waldo has the room next to it. Mrs. Simpson has been goodness itself, and while she was very much surprised at our early arrival, she has been pleased, I think, at the prospect of some company about the place. She has written you, she says, and you will probably gain from her letter the impressions she has formed of Waldo and me. I hope they are as favorable as we have of her.

Waldo is having the time of his life. I was so worried for fear I had perhaps gotten him into a perfect furnace—but his ease and comfort is evident—he even felt like putting on a coat for supper yesterday—it seemed so cool to him. He has only 20 more days to stay—even less, I guess—so Mrs. S won't be especially burdened, especially as we are making a point of performing numerous chores for her, etc. I haven't yet settled on the amount of board I am to pay, but we had an immeadiate understanding that such was to be the general arrangement. It is sure to be settled satisfactorily, and I thought it would be better to wait a few days before discussing such matters in complete detail. A little acquaintance with our tastes, requirements, etc. I thought would better determine in her mind what money was needed.

All my baggage arrived in perfect condition, I didn't have to pay duty on anything, even the Lachaise bird. Which reminds me that we had some good hours and happy ones together in NY. Charles was such a good sport and you looked so scrumptious! The flowers we took from the cabin to our table. We also had a moderate amount of good wines or cordials for a reasonable price (all French) served right on the table. Apparently the Am. boats aren't bound so tight as they were for awhile. And how good the cigars were in Havana! I find I don't feel like drinking much in hot climates, though; it's too heating.

Herrin is about the only person I've met yet whom you recommended me to. I was introduced very hastily to a number of others by Mrs. S. on Wednesday morning when we went to town, but I haven't wanted or had the need to go around much yet. Waldo and I walked over to the coast nearest the house the other day—and had a pleasant swim. The water is almost too warm, however, by afternoon. They really have discovered a little beach there, and people do bathe there often, it seems. I've been too tired to attempt such sudden or strenuous exercise in the heat.

Besides, I suspect that I ought to be rather careful for a week or so, after coming right out of a long severe winter. It taxes the body to make such sudden changes.

Waldo has been having the best time with a baby owl which flew on the porch the other morning—we all have, in fact. Mrs. S. is very sociable and jolly, doesn't mind my smoking a bit, she says. We really like her very much, her wit, her good sense and lack of all sentimentality. She and Waldo have just come back from town—with the mail. It will interest you to know that it contained a letter from the Dial (forwarded, of course) accepting a poem of mine which I sent them recently. There is another of mine in the current issue which I brought down with me.

My navy pants, etc. have proved to be just the right thing here. I bought some hemp-soled shoes at Waldo's recommendation at one of the Cuban shops. They are the kind the peasants of Spain have worn for centuries and they are the coolest thing on a hot road that you ever tried. Mrs. Simpson knows a native woman who will launder for me.

I reserve comments on conditions, etc. until later—naturally I haven't been able to make any especial observations as yet. Before this goes to the boat I may have a picture or so to send you—taken on the boat. Next boat I expect a letter from you. Give Grandma my deepest love and Charles my very very best.

Yours devotedly,
Hart

To Waldo Frank

Camerado: Saturday, May 22

In the middle of the terrible little performance we left you to attend and below the crash of floods on the roof—I was astonished to hear the whistle of your boat, whooping, I hope, a really final salute: I had supposed the Cristobal Colon long since departed. After so long a wait I hope you at least had a private and quiet rest in your stateroom, or rather, cabin.

Today frequent downpours and your card from Havana. Also a letter from O'Neill—more mysterious than ever. I'll quote exactly and all the words pertaining to the Liveright matter:

"There seems to be a misunderstanding about this Liveright matter somewhere. He isn't waiting for any foreword from me yet—at least not according to what he said when I saw him last before I wrote you the last time. He was waiting for more stuff from you apparently. And he spoke of having talked about you with Otto Kahn and so forth.

"However, I expect to be back in New York within a month and I will see him then and get this matter straightened out."

You will remember my descriptions of the situation up to this point with sufficient accuracy without further repititions; I can only say with regard to it all that Gene has either misinformed me in his previous letters or else is suffering from a lapse of memory. At any event, I hope that the conversation with Kahn alluded to, hasn't twitched Liveright into the decision to hold up my book until the *Bridge* shall be completed. If he doesn't really want the book of course nobody can force him to take it,—in which case I hope it won't be too much trouble for you to return the mss to the Boni Bros. There seems no end to the complications with L. The mysterious "yet" in Gene's statement (my underlining) is simply inexplicable.

Mrs. Simpson is having some duplicates made for you of the beach pictures and wishes to be remembered to you. Attaboy frequently calls out "Waldo!" Mrs. Durham (whose name I remember always just in time by thinking of the Bull) has come to stay at least for the week-end. And I have just written a little unconscious calligramme on the mango-tree which I enclose. I must apologise for opening a parcel of yours, patently a book from Spain, and squinting at it before remailing it. Otherwise only two letters have been forwarded.

I somehow have a suspicion that your sail was rainy; I hope not. Tell me how the migration reacted on your return to the polar regions and how you find Tom to be. You are much missed hereabouts.

Love, Hart

To Susan Jenkins Brown

Nueva Gerona, Isle of Pines, Cuba

Dear Sue: May 22

The post-Crane period in Patterson seems to have been full of excitements. Your letter, with its news about the incomparable Jack was corroborated in the same mail by no less than a letter from the noble tar himself. Poor Jack spent no little time and trouble, coming clear up from Norfolk. Mrs. Turner had been forwarding warnings of the impending disaster, first a letter from Norfolk on the date of landing, then a letter on the Patomac boat bound for Washington; I began to feel as though the wireless would be necessary to save my honor. His people live at Passaic and it was there, after his excursion north, that he finally got a card I had mailed from Havana explaining things. He's back on the job now, but quits June 6th. I commend your control under the penetrating gaze of Mrs. T——. Jack's letter contained a closing greeting from " 'me' John's sister, Mary" written in a very elegant hand, so I guess I'm well introduced when I come to Passaic. Anyway, he bane good company and I'm awfully sorry to have missed him.

Yesterday I got tight for the first time, on Bacardi. Cuban Independence day. Falling in with a flock of goats on my way home (I was trembling at what Mme Sampsohn would say) I stubbed my toe and skinned my knee. Arrived home in a somewhat obvious condition, there was nothing to be done but have it out with Mme . . . Waldo having left Tuesday night, we had it fair and square. It is now established that I can drink as much as I damned please. A couple of murdering desperadoes got loose from the penitentiary here recently—and I think she's glad to have my company. But she's been so damned pleasant and considerate that I haven't any reason to think she doesn't like me on less forceful grounds. I'm rather jealous of Mrs. T's old love, the weather, however.

Yes, Marianne took the little specialty I wrote for her, and even proof has been corrected and sent back. This time she didn't even suggest running the last line backward. "Again" is in the May issue; I spose you've seen the happy mixture. I enclose an accidental calligramme committed this morning accidentally on my way to the *Bridge*. I'm convinced that the Mango tree was the original Eden apple tree, being the first fruit tree to be mentioned in history with any accuracy of denomination. I've been having a great time reading *Atlantis in America*, the last book out on the subject, and full of exciting suggestions. Putting it back for 40 or 50 thousand years, it's easy to believe that a continent existed in mid-Atlantic waters and that the Antilles and West Indies are but salient peaks of its surface. Impossible forever to prove, however.

I'm glad that Malcolm has had such luck. It's likely he's made for life—once he enters the Lorimer field; and the articles ought to be interesting, certainly the material is. Because Poole's book, *The Harbour*, was said to have been written while looking from the windows of 110 Col. Hts., I had the idea that it might contain something—and have just finished reading it, a thin-chested little affair if there ever was one! I wonder if McFee's books are quite so ordinary.

Tell Bill to hurry up—and the Cowleys to write. My love to Bina and Romolo—

as always, Hart

To Waldo Frank

Nueva Gerona, Isle of Pines, Cuba
Dear Waldo: June 19, 1926

Late amends for your last three letters, the first of which I got just as I was taking the schooner for Cayman; the last two yesterday when I returned. The trip was strenuous, four days instead of the expected two—each way, on account of head winds and calms. And let me tell you that to be "as idle as a painted," etc under this tropical sun with thirty-five cackling, puking, farting negroes (women and children first) for a whole day or so (the water like a blinding glassy gridiron) is a novel experience. The first moral of the sea with the white man is clean decks; it's the last considered with the Indian black. Vile water to drink, etc. etc. there's no use recommending the facts further. And the much bruited Grand Cayman was some torment, I can survive to tell you. Flat and steaming under black clouds of mosquitoes, and not a square inch of screening on the island. I had to keep smudge fires burning incessantly in my room while I lunged back and forth, smiting myself all over like one in rigor mortis and smoke gouging salty penance from my eyes. The insects were enormous; Isle of Pines species can't compare in size or number. After nine days and nights of that I staggered onto the schooner—and here I am—with a sunburn positively Ethiopian.

I have pleasantly proved to myself, however, that under more sociably agreeable circumstances there is nothing to compare with a sail boat. The motion made me anything but sea-sick, with a good wind the rhythm is incomparable. More gorgeous skies than even you saw, acres of man-sized leaping porpoises (the "Huzza Porpoises" so aptly named in *Moby Dick*) that greet you in tandems (much like M & Mme Lachaise if you have ever seen them out walking together) and truly "arch and bend the horizons". One enormous shark, a White-Fin, lounged alongside for awhile. Had there been a place to sit or stand a few moments in the shade and fewer basins and chamber pots under the nose the trips would have been far from onerous.

In spite of all, I find myself rather toughened and well. The exasperations and torments of such a siege make one grateful for modest amenities. Mrs Simpson yesterday for the first time appeared to me as the Goddess of Liberty.

I am not writing to O'Neill about *White Buildings*—and do not expect to write him until I hear directly from him. He is supposed to be back in NY by this time, and in his last letter he said that he expected to see Liveright on his return and talk things over. He knows that I have prepared in mss all the poems which are to be included in the book and that all that can now hold it back is the lack of his foreword. It was hard for me to ask him to write such thing for my book, and it has been harder and more embarrassing for me to have kept trailing him with letters of urgence. . . . It's impossible for me to address him again on the subject. I'm sorry that whatever-it-was made him feel constrained to promise the favor initially. It will be just as well for me to forget publishers for awhile, I think, though I can't forget how steadfastly you have perservered in helping me—whatever the results have amounted to. And don't think too much about me; my judgements are too un-settled these days to make me feel that I deserve much atten-tion, much less the faith that you assure me of. The situation is really unique with me; it is absurd to say that one is battling indifference; but neither does one build out of an emptied vision. Mere word-painting and juggling, however fastidious, —a prospect of this doesn't excite one very much. At times it seems demonstrable that Spengler is quite right. At pres- I'm writing nothing—would that I were an efficient factory of some kind! It was unfortunate to have been helped by our friend, the banker,—with my nose to the grindstone of the office I could still fancy that freedom would yield me a more sustained vision; now I know that much has been lacking all along. This is less personal than it sounds. I think that the artist more and more licks his own vomit, mistaking it for the common diet. He amuses himself that way in a culture without faith and convictions—but he might as well be in elfin land with a hop pipe in his mouth. . . . No, the bridge isn't very flambouyant these days.

I'm glad that the "Mango" poem meant something to you, I'm cooking up a couple of other short poems to go with it ("Kidd's Cove," & "The Tampa Schooner") under the common title of "Grand Cayman." Maybe I can sell them to Marianne M. Word was just forwarded from Patterson that Edgell Rickword, who edits the *Calendar* (London) has taken three poems I sent him about eight weeks ago, "Melville's Tomb," "Passage" and "Praise for an Urn." The *Calendar* is a very decent quarterly, and I'm glad to get the "Melville" in print—not one magazine in America would take it. You ought to send them something of yours—(1 Featherstone Buildings, London, W.C.1.)

So far no zonite, but gratitude none the less. The only people who can get records to me securely are the Victor headquarters, I'll order direct from them. There's a duty of about 90% on all records! But I do wish you would have the *New Rep.* send me the Gide article. . . . As much of your work as is printed there and elsewhere. I read *Moby Dick* between gasps down in Cayman—my third time—and found it more superb than ever. How much that man makes you love him!

I'm so glad to know that Tom is better than reports warranted believing. But I wish you weren't so tired with overwork. Don't let that world of phantoms drive you too hard.

Love to you, as always—Hart

Let me know where to send Spengler.

To Waldo Frank

Dear Waldo: June 20

Recollection of certain statements made in yesterday's letter to you prompt me to a little better account of myself—not that I committed any insincerities (though the letter might seem to solicit sympathy or encouragement) but that I feel guilty of an injustice to you in some sort of way. You certainly do not deserve to have such fare set before you. . . .

So I apologize for my crudity, with the foreknowledge of your understanding that there are times when it is a torture to write anyone sincerely—as I must always write to you. My statements may appear in a less insane light after you have read what has principally spurred them—the Spengler thesis. This man is certainly fallable in plenty of ways but much of his

evidence is convincing—and is there any good evidence forth-
coming from the world in general that the artist isn't com-
pletely out of a job? Well, I may not care about such
considerations 2 hours from now, but at present and for the
last two months I have been confronted with a ghostliness that
is new.

The validity of a work of art is situated in contemporary re-
ality to the extent that the artist must honestly anticipate the
realization of his vision in "action" (as an actively operating
principle of communal works and faith), and I don't mean by
this that his procedure requires any bona fide evidences
directly and personally signalled, nor even any physical signs or
portents. The darkness is part of his business. It has always
been taken for granted, however, that his intuitions were salu-
tary and that his vision either sowed or epitomized "experi-
ence" (in the Blakian sense). Even the rapturous and explosive
destructivism of Rimbaud presupposes this, even his lonely
hauteur demands it for any estimate or appreciation. (The ro-
mantic attitude must at least have the background of an age of
faith, whether approved or disproved no matter.)

All this is inconsecutive and indeterminate because I am
trying to write shorthand about an endless subject—and more-
over am unresolved as to any ultimate conviction. I am not
fancying I am "enlightening" you about anything,—nor, if I
thought I were merely exposing personal sores, would I con-
tinue to be so monotonous. Emotionally I should like to write
the bridge; intellectually judged the whole theme and project
seems more and more absurd. A fear of personal impotence in
this matter wouldn't affect me half so much as the convictions
that arise from other sources. . . . I had what I thought were
authentic materials that would have been a pleasurable-agony
of wrestling, eventuating or not in perfection—at least being
worthy of the most supreme efforts I could muster.

These "materials" were valid to me to the extent that I pre-
sumed them to be (articulate or not) at least organic and active
factors in the experience and perceptions of our common race,
time and belief. The very idea of a bridge, of course, is a form
peculiarly dependent on such emotional convictions. It is an
act of faith besides being a communication. The symbols of re-
ality necessary to articulate the span—may not exist where you

expected them, however. By which I mean that however great their subjective significance to me is concerned—these forms, materials, dynamics are simply non-existent in the world, I may amuse and delight and flatter myself as much as I please—but I am only evading a recognition and playing Don Quixote in an immorally conscious way.

The form of my poem rises out of a past that so overwhelms the present with its worth and vision that I'm at a loss to explain my delusion that there exist any real links between that past and a future worthy of it. The "destiny" is long since completed, perhaps the little last section of my poem is a hangover echo of it—but it hangs suspended somewhere in ether like an Absalom by his hair. The bridge as a symbol today has no significance beyond an economical approach to shorter hours, quicker lunches, behaviorism and toothpicks. And inasmuch as the bridge is a symbol of all such poetry as I am interested in writing it is my present fancy that a year from now I'll be more contented working in an office than before. Rimbaud was the last great poet that our civilization will see—he let off all the great cannon crackers in Valhalla's parapets, the sun has set theatrically several times since while Laforgue, Eliot and others of that kidney have whimpered fastidiously. *Everybody* writes poetry now—and "poets" for the first time are about to receive official social and economic recognition in America. It's really all the fashion, but a dead bore to anticipate. If only America were half as worthy today to be spoken of as Whitman spoke of it fifty years ago there might be something for one to say—not that Whitman received or required any tangible proof of his intimations, but that time has shown how increasingly lonely and ineffectual his confidence stands.

There always remains the cult of "words", elegancies, elaborations, to exhibit with a certain amount of pride to an "inner circle" of literary initiates. But this is, to me, rivalled by numerous other forms of social accomplishment which might, if attained, provide as mild and seductive recognitions. You probably think me completely insane, talking as obvious hysterics as a drunken chorus-girl. Well, perhaps I need a little more skepticism to put me right on *The Bridge* again. . . . I am certainly in a totally undignified mind and undress—and I hope to appear more solidly determined soon.

Please don't think that the O'Neill foreword has precipitated anything, nor that I am burning manuscripts or plotting oriental travels. . . . Desolately I confess that I *may* be writing stanzas again tomorrow. That's the worst of it.

Mrs. S. asks to be remembered to you.

My love always—Hart

—All this does not mean that I have resigned myself to inactivity. . . . A *Bridge* will be written in some kind of style and form, at worst it will be something as good as advertising copy. After which I will have at least done my best to discharge my debt to Kahn's kindness.

To Wilbur Underwood

Dear Wilbur: Nueva Gerona, Isle of Pines, Cuba

Both your letters have been a kind of solace to me during a period of most acute distress. I can sympathize with your despair more than you probably would expect. I should have answered sooner had I not been driven nearly mad the last two weeks with two abscesses—one in each ear—which are just beginning to heal. Along with them I had such a fever, pains in my chest, night sweats etc. that I finally went to Havana last week and had it out with a doctor.

The situation is not serious, after all—except my state of mind. The boils or abscesses are one of the several unpleasant results of a short sailing trip I recently took to Grand Cayman, an island 150 miles south of here—we lay for several days on waters like gridiron—and the sun's to blame.

But the sudden change from a New England winter to a summer in the tropics has really been devastating. Add to that the fact the natives all aggree that this is the extremest heat hereabouts for many years and you can imagine my discomfort.

The details are too trivial and stupid to ask you to read— nevertheless the malice of one Mrs. Allan Tate prompted my sojourn here at so miserable a time,—simply for the economic reason of making my Kahn money (what there was left of it) last as long as possible and thus to prolong my opportunity for completing the poem I am supposed to be working on. I have not been able to write one line since I came here—the mind is completely befogged by the heat and besides there is a strange challenge and combat in the air—offered by "Nature" so monstrously alive in the tropics which drains the psychic energies. —And my poem was progressing so beautifully until Mrs Tate took it into her head to be so destructive! How silly all this sounds! Howsoever—it's a cruel jest of Fate—and I doubt if I shall continue to write another year. For I've lost all faith in my material—"human nature" or what you will—and any true expression must rest on some faith in something.

It has been so disgusting to note the sudden turns and antics of my "friends" since I had the one little bit of help I ever had toward my work in the money from Kahn. Every time I came into N.Y. from the country I'd hear new monstrosities of fables going about town as to how I was squandering money on pate de foie gras, etc. And worse whisperings. It's all been rather tiresome—and I'd rather lose such elite for the old society of vagabonds and sailors—who don't enjoy chit-chat.

Two of the latter, by the way, are keeping up a regular flow of letters and cards to me here. One, Fitzin, came clear up to Patterson to see me during May—but found me gone, of course.

I was very touched to hear that he had journeyed all the way from Norfolk—in memory of two evenings in Brooklyn last January. Immortally choice and funny and pathetic are some of my recollections in such connection. I treasure them—I always can—against many disillusionments made bitter by the fact that faith was given and expected—whereas, with the sailor no faith or such is properly *expected* and how jolly and cordial and warm the touseling *is* sometimes, after all. Let my lusts be my ruin, then, since all else is a fake and mockery.

If you feel like sending me any old papers or magazines down here, they'd help. I have nobody to talk to or even drink with—and live in a house with 2 old women.

Write again soon—Hart

To Waldo Frank

Nueva Gerona, Isle of Pines, Cuba

Dear Waldo: July 3, 1926

I must thank you immeadiately for your wireless. The news is most welcome—and your affectionate haste in notifying me is not without results in piercing the miasmas of these tropics.

Also comes a letter from Sue. It seems the news has reached Patterson via Jimmy Light. I copy Sue's account of the circumstances given her by Jimmy, as having been so active an agent in the matter you probably will be interested. "The way it came about is not without interest. About a month ago Liveright, Jimmy and others were at Otto Kahn's for a week-end. L had the mss with him at that time and on the boat coming back he said he had decided not to publish it—that he didn't care for the poems and so far as he could see, nobody understood them. Then, a little over a week ago, Jimmy and O'Neill were in L's office on business and your mss was on the table. Jimmy asked him if he had stuck to his decision and he said 'yes'. Then Jimmy and Gene both told him they thought he would eventually he 'proud' of having published your first volume, so that even if he himself did not care for the poems, as a publisher he was failing to take advantage of an opportunity. So finally L came around to his old position of saying that he would publish them if Gene would write a preface. (Previously L had said that he did not want to publish the poems at all—preface or no preface.) Gene protested some, saying that while he liked the poems he wasn't at all sure that he could tell why he liked them, that he was by no means a critic of poetry, and that L was preparing a fine opportunity for him (O'Neill) to make a fool of himself. But finally it was decided that the preface would be written, L phoned immeadiately to the printer and dictated the announcement. And I understand that the preface is already written and in L's hands."

Probably I'll hear something direct from Liveright within the next week; nothing so far has reached me. If the book is really scheduled for fall it will relieve me of numerous embarassments, especially with the family, who I think have already ceased to believe any statements from me about my work, publications, etc.

Last Sunday I was obliged to go to Havana to consult with a doctor. For the last two weeks I have been suffering intensely from two abscesses, one in each ear, added to which apparently alarming symptoms of fever, and lung trouble had seemed to develop. Of these latter the doctor says there is no need to worry, but the abscesses have not healed yet, and are distracting to say the least. I shall be glad sometime to get a good night's sleep. Doctor says they were caused by sun-exposure on my boat trip.

I have been reading *Quixote* and *Swann's Way*. My money is practically exhausted, but I think I can get a hundred by writing to Patterson and having my property there sold. The final 500 from Kahn can't be solicited until August or later—if at all, for I shan't ask for it unless I am writing again by that time. Mrs. Simpson has been so kind and altogether gracious that I couldn't ask for better care.

When I'm feeling better I hope to write you a decent letter the last two have been so haphazard, violent and vulgar. I hope these days of sea and sunshine and breezes are resting you and improving Tom. In Havana I bought a *New Yorker* and read your Van Loon snapshot—marvelling again at your flexibility and dash. Otherwise I was sipping the glorious limonades most of the time: couldn't get my mouth open wide enough to receive much other nourishment! Took long walks around the harbour and along the Malacon. A lovely city, albeit insipid; full of white and gold and azure buildings. Even plaster has something to say.

My love and gratitude always—Hart

To William Wright

Box 1373
Nueva Gerona
Dear Bill; Isle of Pines

After the last few weeks I can never again claim any indifference to an equatorial sun! My cruise to Grand Cayman was pleasant in some respects—but a little schooner "as idle as a painted—etc." (recall your Coleridge) is no place to spend a sunny day, especially in the tropics. I returned minus 3 coats of skin and the cartilage of my ears so cooked, broiled and sun-basted that for nearly a month I've been wondering whether my hearing would survive, to say nothing or the tortures of earache.

Completely recovered now, however, though I think my brains are rather "sweet-breadish" if you'll forgive the term. The sun so diddles one's brains that I've given up trying to think or even "emot"—so what writing I manage to do won't be very lively, I guess.

Nothing "happens" down here. There's everything fine in the world to drink—but nobody to drink with—so I haven't even sampled the many various labels that deck the bar—beyond some delicious Bacardi (15¢ a throw) some French Cognac and beer, the latter my staple beverage. Strange, too, how the removal of all *verboten* signs vitiates one's appetite.

By *your* letter I see you have been through some strenuousities, too! But I'm glad that you haven't encountered anything more fatal than the wedlock vows which you seem destined to make. Good luck to you, Willy and may you live to see all your grandchildren riding over the North Pole on week-ends. I have hovered on the brink several times—but finally decided that I was too ridiculously romantic for marriage—which shows me to be cautious and wise in the extreme! I was glad to hear that your parents are so well and happily located: you may remember that when I lost touch with you your father's health worried you a good deal.

I liked the poem from the Bookman—even, if as you say, you don't attempt more than a play of words. Convictions of any sort are hard to maintain these days—and maybe Spengler is right. Have you read his "Untergang des Adendlandes"—now translated (Knopf)? I envy people like Wheeler Lovell—who have intensive work to do without having to wrestle with either angels or devils to continue with it. I get awfully exhausted sometimes, trying to achieve some kind of consistent vision of things. But I don't seem to be able to relax—and knowing quite well all the time that most of my energy is wasted in a kind of inward combustion that is sheer nonsense. All else seems boresome, however,—so I must continue to kill myself in my own way.

The *Little Review* poems are so horribly mutilated by apparently a total neglect of proofreading—that I don't feel like sending them without some inky corrections. I would send the magazine entire except that new and insane Cuban postal ordinances make it next to impossible to send papers, books, etc. out. Let me end in the good old adolescent way by asking you what are you reading lately—and adjuring you to read by all means such "late" enthusiasms of mine as

Melville's "Moby Dick" and "Israel Potter"
Fielding's "Jonathan Wild" (Greenburg, Ed.)
Emily Dickinson's Poems
Cummings' "Enormous Room"—

Hope you are feeling less "hearty" and as cool as possible.

Yours,
Hart

To Marianne Moore

Box 1373
Nueva Gerona, Isle of Pines, Cuba
Dear Miss Moore: July 22

I enclose another poem for the *Dial,* if you wish to use it; "To Brooklyn Bridge." As I can't procure U.S. postage here I beg you to pardon the ommission of the return ticket.

With best wishes, believe me

Faithfully yours, Hart Crane

To Waldo Frank

Nueva Gerona, Isle of Pines, Cuba
Hail Brother!   July 24, 1926

I feel an absolute music in the air again, and some tremendous rondure floating somewhere—perhaps my little dedication is going to swing me back to San Cristobal again. . . . That little prelude, by the way, I think to be almost the best thing I've ever written, something steady and uncompromising about it. Do you notice how its construction parallels the peculiar technique of *space and detail division* used by El Greco in several canvasses—notably the *Christus am Olberg?* I've just been struck by that while casually returning to my little monograph as I often do.

> And obscure as that heaven of the Jews,
> Thy guerdon . . . Accolade thou dost bestow
> Of anonymity time cannot raise;
> Vibrant reprieve and pardon thou dost show.

Read above between the 6th & 7th stanzas of the last I sent— and you have the poem complete. It's done, and I won't bother you with any more scraps. . . .

The news of Allen Tate's generosity refreshed me a great deal; truly beautiful of him. You must know by now, how little I credited the Light gossip; I simply thought you'd be interested in hearing the sort of thing that goes around. I don't mean to say I sensed the ultimate facts as your enclosures establish them—but I have always known that your efforts were the sine qua non in this situation . . . your devotion and courage the sustaining factor.

I shall not write Kahn for awhile, or if I do it will be in a different mood than you need to fear of. I sent Spengler to you registered, two weeks ago. Don't know any exact date for the appearance of *White B's*, the contract specifies only in "the fall of 1926"; November, perhaps.

—Awfully glad to hear that you are taking things easier, and that rest is fertile with design and plan—

Love ever, Hart

To Allen Tate

Nueva Gerona, Isle of Pines, Cuba
Dear Allen: July 25, 1926
Will you preserve my appreciations somewhat in secret? I allude to some news received subsequent to my last writing

you. It was very refreshing (in the deeper sense of this abused word) to be told of the extremity of your interest (may I say generosity or *friendship* without too much transgressing appropriate boundaries?). It may be I can say more later; for the present I'm bound otherwise. I wouldn't be so—rather fitgety —were I not specifically charged to delicacy by someone else whose efforts in my behalf have been equally obstinate and sincere.

I've been writing the last few days—and turned out the enclosed "Dedication" for the *B* poem. It sounds suspiciously like clichee somewhere in the works; let me know if you notice any echoes.

With love, Hart

To Waldo Frank

Gerona
Dear Waldo: July 26, 1926

Dear repository of my faith, will you also serve as sanctum of some of my "works"? By which I mean that, though I shouldn't bother you now while you are busy with inner work of your own, I still must ask you to keep the enclosed somewhere. One never knows what may happen, fires burn the house here, etc and mss be burnt or otherwise lost—and in the case of this *Bridge* I feel enough honor-bound to desire preserved whatever evidence of my industry and effort is forthcoming.

I don't presume to ask you for comments. Read it if you like and fold it away somewhere. You have the last section ("Atlantis", as I have decided to call it) haven't you? I have discovered that it IS the real Atlantis, even of geology!

My plans are soaring again, the conception swells. Furthermore, this "Columbus" is REAL. In case you read it—(I *can't* be serious)—observe the water-swell rhythm that persists until the Palos reference. Then the more absolute and marked intimation of the great Te Deum of the court, later held,—here in the terms of C's own cosmography.

Mrs. S is the god's own gift. This were a perfect place for

work but for the prostrating heat. I think of next winter! Last night a wonderful breeze came up—and you can walk singing through the grove with a great moon simply bending down.

Love, Hart

To Malcolm and Peggy Cowley

Nueva Gerona, Isle of Pines, Cuba
Dear Malcolm and Peggy: July 29

I've been wanting to tell you how glad I've been to know about your good luck with the *Post* business, etc. but you probably know by this time what I've been going through with. . . . There's really no news except that I'm better and have begun to write—for a period until prostrated by the heat —like mad. "Columbus" has been cleared up—and a lot of other things started within ten days.

In the middle of the *Bridge* the old man of the sea (page Herr Freud) suddenly comes up. I enclose the section hoping you'll like it. Please mention or display it to no one but Allen and Les Browns for the time; it makes me nervous to have parts of an unfinished drama going about much before the curtain goes up.

It happens that all the clippers mentioned were real beings, had extensive histories in the Tea trade—and the last two mentioned were life-long rivals. Rather touching. . .

Write when you get time, Love—hart

To Grace Hart Curtis

Gerona
Dearest Grace: Friday   July 30th

Last boat brought your splendid letter from NY—welcome news, all of it. I'm so glad that you were invited, went and had the chance for a little rest and diversion. Thank you for the birthday gift, the best form in which you could have remembered me. Everything new sent down here now incurs terrific customs duty, so don't send me any luxuries—or necessities either until I ask for them. Waldo sent me some ointment for bug bites after he went north—and the duty came to over the original price in NY; I was so angry I threw it back into the post office and refused to have anything more to do with it. (by which please understand I *didn't* pay the duty)

You already have most of the news from Grandma's letter, and Mrs Simpson's letter also must have arrived explaining the cable matter. I wasn't worried about it because I was certain that you had received my letter almost immeadiately afterward —couldn't have *before* or else how could my *whereabouts* have been questioned in the cable. I am feeling quite well now—all but sleep, and whether that's due to the heat, chronic insomnia or my present ferment of creative work, I don't quite know. Certainly the hayhennies and crowing roosters (at all times of nights) and the breathlessness of the "air" don't encourage one to slumbers. In a number of ways, however, I'm better acclimated, and I don't need to memorize your advice to know enough to keep out of the sun and physical work! My spasm of hay fever seems to have gone—at about the same time it leaves in the north, that is, the spring session.

In all other ways this is the most ideal place and "situation" I've ever had for work. Mrs. S——lets me completely alone when I'm busy; lets me drum on the piano interminably if I want to—says she likes it—and has assumed a tremendous interest in my poem . . . She reads and sews a great deal and just talks enough to keep on splendid and equable terms with me. She's a perfect peach, in other words. The result is—that now that my health's better I'm simply immersed in work to my neck, eating, "sleeping", and breathing it. In the last ten days I've written over ten pages of the Bridge—highly concentrated stuff, as you know it is with me—and more than I ever crammed in that period of time before. I can foresee that everything will be brightly finished by next May when I come north, and I can make a magnificent bow to that magnificent structure, "The Brooklyn Bridge" when I steam (almost under it) into dock! For the poem will be magnificent.

Meanwhile my other book "White Buildings" will have been published. It comes out sometime this fall. I have my contract and the $100. advance royalties mentioned in Grandma's letter. O'Neill finally backed out on the foreword, as I thought he would. He's enthusiastic about my work, I've never doubted that, but he didn't have the necessary nerve to write what his honesty demanded—a thoroughly and accurate appraisal of my work. He can't write criticism, never has tried even, and I foresaw the panic that this proposal on the part of our mutual publisher would precipitate in his bosom . . . None other than Allen Tate! it seems is to write the foreword. I was informed by my publisher of all this—along with the acceptance. Has written it, in fact . . . And (mums the word on this!) I was very much touched to hear from Waldo, who knows all the inner workings on this, that Allen offered his foreword under O'Neill's signature when he heard that O'Neill had backed out. Of course O—— wouldn't think of anything like that—so the foreword goes back to its own name. I'm very glad things have turned out this way. My umbrage toward Allen is crushed by the fidelity of his action, and I'm glad to have so discriminating an estimate as he will write of me.

We'll try to find out as much as possible about the roofing details. You must write Mrs. Simpson—what do you mean by saying that she owes you and the bank in correspondence!— she hasn't had any answer to her last *five* letters, that note I brought down was all she'd heard from you this winter. Wake up! Remember to take your blue-prints of the house along with you when you talk to AE Brown, for the area to be covered, etc.

My best to Charles

Love
Hart

To Isabel and Gaston Lachaise

This quarry is in the mountains, near our place. There's plenty to work on anytime you come! Your bird (the gull) is divine, produces sea music, even winks at times!

Salutations, Hart Crane

To Waldo Frank

Nueva Gerona, Isle of Pine, Cuba

Dear Waldo: August 3

Enclosed is "Atlantis," there have been variances since your copy whether you have it now or not.—So will you kindly humor my present little neurosis, and take care of this. I feel as though I were dancing on dynamite these days—so absolute and elaborated has become the conception. All sections moving forward now at once! I didn't realize that a bridge is begun from the two ends at once. . . . Don't bother to read what I send you; ye Gods I hope to preserve at least the credit of not presuming on you to the point of total vulgarity. It's all right to be elegant—if you are rebellious like Rimbaud, however I have to admit grosser preoccupations so I'm sloppy.

Gorham sent me Allen's Preface, which I also enclose (you're quite sure to want to read this, if you haven't already). I think it clever, valiant, concise and beautiful. I'm more fortunate than I might have been had things gone as they were supposed to have gone. Gorham said he'd been up to see you. I'm trying to let down completely for awhile and "recuperate". "Powhatan's Daughter" must be that basic center and antecedent of all motion—"power in repose" . . .

Mrs S—has been following me in some of my recent reading,—with the result that she has named one of her roosters "Ferdinand, Count Fathom"! It's a good thing you aren't near to hear our piano going it these days!

Love—Hart

I've just sent Kahn the "Dedication" and "Ave Maria." Please return me A's preface. Don't know whether I'll use the enclosed "Notes" or not. A reaction to Eliot's *Wasteland* notes put them in my head. However, the angle chart from the *Scientific Am.* embodies a complete symbolism of both Bridge and Star, even including the motif of the "holy tooth". And I should like to use it on the cover. If the notes amuse you at the moment—as I wrote them—

Have you read how handy our *Orizaba* recently proved in the cyclone off Florida—when "Cutty Sark" was bobbing up?

To Waldo Frank

Nueva Gerona, Isle of Pines, Cuba
Dear Waldo: August 12

Your Menorah scolding is good and proper. . . . When all
America, not only the Jew, takes that to heart it will be well for
all of us. I know a number of prosperous jew families in Cleve-
land, among my best friends there, but they're mostly alike,
sadly similar to your catagorical disposals. . . . And, has the
Gide essay appeared yet? Remember your promise.

I want to meet Ornstein someday. But I never seem to read
or hear of any of these concert tours he is supposed to make
for bread, etc. Mrs. Simpson was enormously pleased at your
postcard; and I with your praise of the Dedication. You gener-
ally do pick the weakest link; that verse has bothered me, and
will undoubtedly be somewhat amended before the book. I've
sent it to the *Dial* and the *Criterion* (London), the little
money may help, IF they take it. Probably won't let anything
out of the bag on this side of the water, though, for sometime
yet. It keeps too many question marks in my head, albeit a
little change in the purse. I play the lottery, though, and like it.
I'm going to win a thousand before spring; you see. *"I knew
I'd see a WHALE!"*

I'm reading the *Prairie Years* now. More of "Powhatan's
Daughter" later. It ends up with the prodigal song from the
'49. There's to be a grand indian pow-wow before that. Two
of three songs have just popped out (enclosed) which come
after "Cutty Sark" and before the "Mango Tree." The last,
"Virginia" (virgin in process of "being built") may come along
any time. I skip from one section to another now like a sky-
gack or girder-jack. Even the subway and "Calgary Express"
are largely finished. Though novel experiments in form and
metre here will demand much ardor later on.

I'm happy, quite well, and living as never before. The accu-
mulation of impressions and concepts gathered the last several
years and constantly repressed by immeadiate circumstances
are having a chance to function, I believe. And nothing but this
large form would hold them without the violences that mar so

much of my previous, more casual work. *The Bridge* is already longer than the *Wasteland*,—and it's only about half done.

But enough of this shop talk. I'll exhaust your patience with it someday. You know I don't expect comments of any sort, except when they're easy and spontaneous.

Don't work too hard. You needed more rest than you got here.

Love, Hart

Much hoeing, "hedging" and mowing have made the place much more attractive than when you left. We have the Joneses here for dinner occasionally (Mrs. Jones continually talks about "mind stretching,") but I otherwise hardly see anyone. My reputation has spread enormously, however, according to Mrs. Simpson. Recently attempted some kind of portrait for Liveright to use possibly. I enclose two results.

"Virginia's" included after all.

To Marianne Moore

Nueva Gerona, Isle of Pines, Cuba
Dear Miss Moore: August 12, 1926

I was very pleased to receive your acceptance today of the poem, "To Brooklyn Bridge"for publication in *The Dial.*

As I have a suggestion to make in regard to the alteration of one line of this poem (or rather a substitution), I'm writing you at once. "Towers blot the drowning west in spooring steam," the third line of the sixth stanza, has bothered me. I am wondering if you would care to consider substituting the following for this line:

"All afternoon the cloud-flown derricks burn."

This seems superior to the other line as far as my personal intentions in the poem matter.

However, please regard this suggestion purely from your own standpoint and judgment. I certainly have no right to trespass with more than a suggestion, since you have been so kind as to accept the poem in its original form, and not necessarily otherwise. I shall, accordingly, not alter this line in the proof, when I receive it, unless I have previously received specific directions to do so.

Faithfully yours, Hart Crane

To Waldo Frank

Nueva Gerona, Isle of Pines, Cuba
Dear Waldo: August 19, 1926

Here, too, is that bird with a note that Rimbaud speaks of as "making you blush". We are in the midst of the equatorial storm season; every day, often at night, torrents engulf us, and the thunder rods jab and prospect in the caverns deep below that chain of mountains across. You can hear the very snakes rejoice,—the long, shaken-out convulsions of rock and roots.

It is very pleasant to lie awake—just half awake—and listen. I have the most speechless and glorious dreams meanwhile. Sometimes words come and go, presented like a rose that yields only its light, never its composite form. Then the cocks begin to crow. I hear Mrs. S— begin to stir. She is the very elf of music, little wrinkled burnous wisp that can do anything and remembers so much! She reads Dante and falls to sleep, her cough has become so admireably imited by the parrot that I often think her two places at once.

I have made up a kind of friendship with that idiot boy, who is always on the road when I come into town for mail. He has gone so far as to answer my salutations. I was unexpected witness one day of the most astonishing spectacle; not that I was surprised.—A group of screaming children were shrieking about in a circle. I looked toward the house and saw the boy standing mostly hid behind the wooden shutters behind the gratings; his huge limp phallus waved out at them from some opening; the only other part visible was his head, in a most gleeful grin, swaying above the lower division of the blinds.

When I saw him next he was talking to a blue little kite high in the afternoon. He is rendingly beautiful at times; I have encountered him in the road, talking again tout seul and examining pebbles and cinders and marble chips through the telescope of a twice-opened tomato can. He is very shy, hilarious,—and undoubtedly idiot. I have been surprised to notice how much the other children like him.

Mrs. Durham is leaving us. I'm glad because she has been so obviously unhappy. And when she told Mrs. S— the other day that she didn't like "playing third fiddle" I knew that nothing could be done about it. Besides she is a strain on Mrs. S— who even admits it.

I'm glad to know that the *Bridge* is fulfilling your utmost intuitions; for an intuition it undoubtedly was. You didn't need to tell me that you had "seen" something that memorable evening, although I was never so sure just what it was you saw, until now. But I have always carried that peculiar look that was in your eyes for a moment there in your room, it has often recurred in my thoughts. What I should have done without your love and most distinguished understanding is hard to say, but there is no earthly benefit for which I would exchange it. It is a harmony always with the absolute direction I always seek, often miss, but sometimes gain.

Your answer to G— on his essay was much more adept than any of my critical armament. It was complete. My greatest complaint against G— is (apparently) an incorrigible streak of vulgarity, arising no doubt from some distrust in experience. Sometimes it makes him obviously ridiculous in the eyes of all; sometimes it makes him personally dangerous when he doesn't intend such. Not especially par example, BUT: when I last dined with G— much happened to be said about my "extravagences"—how I spent K's money, etc. Snowshoes, African sculptures, etc. I happened to mention how useful the snowshoes had been during the storms at Patterson, etc. G— recently visited the Tates and went up to my room, accompanied by Mrs. Turner, who writes me, most unwittingly of the circumstances, that the main thing he quizzed her about was whether I used my snow shoes or not! Really, it is all so ridiculously small.

You may think I'm wasting paper on such a silly story. But in any kind of friendship I like to have my honesty sometimes granted on my oath of it, and this is only one of many such little evidences of a real lack of perspective and innate taste on G's part. It does leak into his work, the vision of his world.

He'd better memorize the last stanza of Baudelaire's famous "Epilogue" to the *Petits Pòemes en Prose*; as, indeed, I may sometime tell him to do. His definition of "knowledge" in that essay incorporates the savour of just such a mind as is preoccupied with such details as I've mentioned.

Yes, I read the whole of Spengler's book. It is stupendous,— and it was perhaps a very good experience for ripening some of the *Bridge*, after all. I can laugh now; but you know, alas, how little I could at the time. That book seems to have been just one more of many "things" and circumstances that seem to have uniformly conspired in a strangely symbolical way toward the present speed of my work. Isn't it true,—hasn't it been true in your experience, that beyond the acceptance of fate as a tragic action—immeadiately every circumstance and incident in one's life flocks toward a positive center of action, control and beauty? I need not ask this, since there is the metaphor of the "rotted seed of personal will", or some such phrase, in your *Spain*.

I have never been able to live *completely* in my work before. Now it is to learn a great deal. To handle the beautiful skeins of this myth of America—to realize suddenly, as I seem to, how much of the past is living under only slightly altered forms, even in machinery and such-like, is extremely exciting. So I'm having the time of my life, just now, anyway.

Love, as ever—Hart

To Waldo Frank

Nueva Gerona, Isle of Pines, Cuba
Dear Waldo: August 23

I feel rather apologetic about sending you so many photographs—but the last seemed to me more what I wanted you to think of me—than any others heretofore.

Work continues. "The Tunnel" now. I shall have it done very shortly. It's rather ghastly, almost surgery—and, oddly almost all from the notes and stitches I have written while swinging on the strap at late midnights going home.

Are you noticing how throughout the poem motives and

situations recur—under modifications of environment, etc? The organic substances of the poem are holding a great many surprises for me. . . . Greatest joys of creation.

Forgive me for telling that anecdote about G—, I don't want to seem stubborn or prejudiced, but you, on the other hand, are one who ought to know more or less *why* it is hard for me to maintain a steady sort of whole-hearted confidence and enthusiasm with such constantly recurring "obscurations," if you will. I'm not saying that these ultimately or "aesthetically" matter, but they enter the moral picture of the personality.

Let's hear from you soon. . . . Love, Hart

Did I tell you that M. Moore has taken the "Dedication?"— needless to say, without alterations.

To Kenneth Burke

Nueva Gerona, Isle of Pines, Cuba

Dear Kenneth: August 25

No; you don't need to worry about cones, nor octorones. They aren't (to me) attractive enough. Some of the fairer Cubanos, well! but I don't spik the languish quite well yet! I'm banking on some obscure senorita, giving her quite a load, these days; she keeps me sweating, and sometimes I feel like a burning bush.

But there is that bird here that Rimbaud refers to as making you blush. In fact birds don't sing here; they throttle, gag, cuspidor, hiss and swivel! And there are goats, whose eyes I always make a fuss over (ask Bill) and oxen, dumb, white and otherwise—which would delight you. There are mosquitoes, jiggers, ticks, hayhennies (no kidding) and orrydorries. These last two you will have to be introduced to sometime. So you see I have plenty of company.

You must notify me sometime when the *Dial* gets ready to get out a poetry number; I'll soon have enough to complete that number very roundly! *The Bridge* is coming along very well (The Brooklyn B poem is the dedication by the way) and Gorham has section I. Tell him I said to give it to you if you care to look it over. Later on, when I get section II finished I think I'll sumbit it to the *Dial* if it isn't too long,—probably about six or seven *Dial* pages. It's got real Indians in it!

The subway (next-to-last section) I'm working on now; and I shall certainly want your opinion on it, though it may be a mistake to ask anyone's judgment on any one section of the poem,—isolated, that is. Your statement on ideological organization of my work in general was very gratifying news, and no doggerel; for that particular organic incorporation of concepts has been a very conscientious pursuit of mine, even before I was conscious of it as an indispensable quality.

I've thought of writing you a number of times, and wondered where you were. Isn't there a new family arrival? or due? And what are you writing these days? The news from Patterson all sounds so wild, woolly and full of relatives, quaint visitors and gastronomics—that I'm beginning to congratulate myself on having found a quieter, *if* hotter corner in the world wherein to drink real beer, real Bacardi, real smoke and lay an egg or so.

Write again when you have time, best wishes, and to all the household.

yrs, Hart

To Clarence Arthur Crane

Habana,

Dear Father: Sept. 2 '26

I've been up here a few days to get away from the hay fever season on the Island. It's really as bad (for *me* at least) as anywhere north—in spite of all they say about its absence there. Well, it *has* been a relief—and I'm going back tomorrow quite refreshed.

I hope there'll be news from you waiting me. You haven't written for quite a while. Could you advance me fifty dollars or so—until I get my next installment from Mr. Kahn? It would help me out with the cost of this little vacation.

Havana is lovely despite many drawbacks. Excellent food if you go to the best Cuban places—and avoid American imitations. Of course you wouldn't like this summer heat—but I'm so used to it by now—anyway—that it doesn't bother me.

It's great fun walking the quaint old streets and alleys—you don't need any company. Last night I took a long cool drive along the Malacon—by the sea, you'll remember.

Write soon—with love,

your

Harold:

To Waldo Frank

Dear Waldo: September 3, 1926

I'm having my last bottle of "Diamante" before leaving for la Isla tonight. A petulant Abbé is gulping olives at the next table, and my waiter is all out of patience with him. But I cannot conceal my mirth—cheeks bulge and eyes strain at suppression. "Fuck la Cubans!" says the waiter who is Spanish. Well I never had such a fiesta of perfect food and nectar in my life. Furthermore, if you were St. Valentine—well, maybe you are! So here goes—even if you call my little story stale.

Perhaps you have also experienced the singular charm of long conversations with senoritas with only about 12 words in common understanding between you. I allude to Alfredo, a young Cuban sailor (most of them are terrible but Alfredo is Spanish parentage and maybe that explains it) whom I met one evening after the Alhambra in Park Central. Immaculate, ardent and delicately restrained—I have learned much about love which I did not know existed. What delicate revelations may bloom from the humble—it is hard to exaggerate.

So there have been three long and devoted evenings—long walks, drives on the Malacon, dos copas mas, and a change from my original American hotel to La Isla de Cuba, sine commotion, however.

I'm going back much relaxed. I got on a terrible tension—not a tennis court on the island! Just day after day in the heat and the house. Now I shall get a fresh view of what I have written and have still to write—and with an internal glow which is hard to describe. Silly of me to say so—but life can be gorgeously kindly at times. I'll hope to find word from you.

Love, brother, Hart

To Waldo Frank

Nueva Gerona, Isle of Pines, Cuba
Caro Hermano: September 5

Estoy en casa ayer de madrugada. No dormaba la noche a bordo mar. Mucha calor, y pensaba en el carinoso Alfredo y los calles blancas Habaneros, de consigniente dulces con Mi Bien. Encontreremos de nuevo en Deciembre . . . Busco en diccionario y gramatica, sudo, raspo polo de suerte que el tierno Cubano-Canario (parentela los Canarios) mi carta apprenderá.

Tell me if any of it is sensible. I am now, more than ever anxious to learn the most beautiful language in the world. And I suddenly conceive it as a necessary preparation for my next piece of work just apprehended in the form of a blank verse tragedy of Aztec mythology—for which I shall have to study the obscure calendars of dead kings. If I have the leisure for this study I shall certainly go to Spain sometime in the next five years. . . . In fact I must manage this anyhow.

Your letter, awaiting my return, conveyed much goodness, the sense of "wholiness"—of a complete return to yourself, from which I hope much; in fact, I'm *sure* of much therefrom. I am so glad that my progress has meant so much to you. More later; here comes a flock of people that Mrs S has invited for dinner, and I won't get opportunity to write again before night, when the boat leaves.

Love always,—Hart

To Otto H. Kahn

Nueva Gerona, Isle of Pines, Cuba
Dear Mr. Kahn: September 19, 1926

I am very much in need of additional funds to carry me through the remaining construction of *The Bridge*. Am I presumptious in asking you for the additional help of $500.00? This will certainly suffice, as I am three quarters through with the poem at the present date. Check, registered and sent to the above address can be deposited to my account here.

I should like to send you more of *The Bridge* herewith, but the 2nd and 3rd sections are apparently to be the last to be completed, so I must still (possibly) appear to be "stalling", i.e., if we stick to the "consecutive reading" preference. But I can warn you, albeit with no excess of modesty, that the poem is already an epic of America, incomplete as it is. And it is well worth the faith which you have so kindly volunteered,—a little of which, on the part of my father, who still stubbornly sulks, would also be welcome.

May I thank you for your kind answer to my Mother's recent letter to you? She mentioned it in her last letter to me. I don't mean to urge your attention toward intimacies of such nature, nor should I have advised her writing to you, necessarily; but your response to such humanities is distinguished, prompting even rather blatant gratitude, I fear.

With best wishes, faithfully yours—Hart Crane

To Kenneth Burke

Dear Kenneth: September 28

As you are so well known as an enthusiast when any new or "old" literary problems of form and content creep up, I can't resist inviting your attention to the Oct. no. of *Poetry*— wherein I have a discussion with Harriet Monroe on the "famous" Melville poem, in re the dynamics of metaphor.

I'm not modest in saying that I think I come off very well with the woozy old spinster,—but that isn't why I'm speaking to you about the matter. I refer, better, to your past preoccupations with such squabble—or, rather, questions,—and as nobody ever peeps at Miss M's one-time famous sheet any more, I'm flagging the event, as it were,—and making the usual fool of myself.

If you have a thought militant enough to demand registration, on one side or t'other,—why don't you mask it in perfectly decent terminology and frighten the dear old wench, or cheer her up. It would be more than fun. The problem under the gavel is vital in modern art (as well as ancient) and the linsey-woolseys of the great mid-west and corn belt ought to be given their money's worth.

Yours for Bacardi, clear and shining! Hart Crane

P.S.—Please don't take my suggestion as too personally motiviated or at all clamant. But I would like you to at least see the discussion—because we have had so many words (mine were always stupid enough to surpass the memory the day after) over the same drink in the *dolce far niente*. . . . I'm going to spur you toward the "feast" by flattery. I was most happily surprised at your review of Spengler in the recent *Dial*. It's hard to find a man, these days, or any, that doesn't swallow the whole hook and sinker in favor of his private predilections. . . . Your analysis of that book (and the psyche behind it) was amazing. One of the most magnificient and formidable books I ever read, but falsely led and falsely leading. You can see it when you get under the shell of certain parts of it. You have to live in or under a Greek sky like this, down here, to know why the ancients had a different idea of the space or "futurity" of *blue*—than did the monks and denizons of the northern abbey's, half the time fog-filled, of the *middle ages*.

To Yvor Winters

Nueva Gerona, Isle of Pines, Cuba
Dear Yvor Winters: October 5, 1926

It is just a 10–1 accident that I didn't write you first. What little of your work I have occasionally seen has stuck in my mind—as little else I see does. And I was recently so grateful to you for what was quoted to me as your opinion of "Faustus & Helen"(I refer to the current correspondence between Aunt Harriet and me, printed in *Poetry*) that I was restrained only by the fear of immodesty.

I think that the scene, so far as poetry goes, has never been quite so clouded as right now. In many ways, it would be much better if so many people weren't even mildly interested in "poetry". We have had the scullery permutations of Amy Lowell, and the batter bakes thick and heavy even on the charcoal embers! Sometime in the saturnalian past Elbert Hubbard found the ghost of Harriet Beecher Stowe, and on a slab of the sunburnt West they managed to conceive Carl Sandburg, a tiresome half-way person, even though a poet. (I am trying to wade through all the homespun crinoline of his recent and much lauded "Lincoln", but find I'd almost prefer some cold-hearted academic treatise without so much wet dreaming on Nancy Hanks, daisys, and prairie prostrations: "milk-sick" is a word that often occurs, and too symbolically, I fear.) One goes back to Poe, and to Whitman—and always my beloved Melville—with renewed appreciation of what America really is, or could be. And one may go back to Frost with the same cer tainty,—a good, clean artist, however lean. Cummings (at times) and Marianne Moore, too. As you say, Williams can shed his shirt,—but I think he is too much a quick-change artist. His specialty is both hairshirting and war-whooping: never more than constant experimentation. There are some things that are certain, after all; Kit Marlowe is one kind, and Menchen is another. I'm with the former.

Miss Moore's paces are stubborn, and once, in my case destructive. "Repose of Rivers" escaped her clutches successfully, as must everything else of mine published henceforth. But that frightful "Again" (what she must have said with lifted brows and a ? mark when she opened the envelope) was the wreck of a longer and entirely different poem "The Wine Menagerie" which I hope you will see in its original nudity when my book, *White Buildings*, comes out from Boni & Liveright sometime around December. I was *obliged* to submit to her changes, not only because I was penniless at the time, but because I owed money to others at the time equally penniless. When I saw that senseless thing in print I almost wept.

The "new Metaphysics" that Whitman proclaimed in *Democratic Vistas* is evident here and there in America today. I feel it in your work and I think I can sense it in some of my own work. (Probably Whitman wouldn't recognize it in either of us, but no matter.) That *sine qua non* evidently has to be fought for and defended. I'm doing my best about it here and now, fighting off miasmas, bugs, hay fever, bats and tropical sqeks and birds—toward *The Bridge* a very long poem for these days, extending from Columbus to Brooklyn Bridge and Atlantis. It is three-fourths done, and I may have to flee the torments (now settled in my nerves) to New Orleans soon to finish it. It will be a book by itself. And in it I shall incidentally try to answer all my friends who have for three years, now, sat down and complacently joined the monotonous choruses of *The Waste Land*. ("The Dedication" to it you may soon see in *The Dial*).

These preoccupations make me an inactive enthusiast toward the sensible proposals you make in your letter to me. I simply haven't time to copy out anything, nor extra energy. But I have more than time and energy to read anything of your's that you'll be kind and patient enough to send me. Won't you do so, saving such things as translations until later? Another admirer of your's, Allen Tate, RFD, Patterson, NYork, might be more energetic. I'm sure he would be glad to hear from you about the matter, anyway. I don't recall anything whatever about "Walsh", whom you refer to. I have never met Wrynn, but I am distinctly grateful to him for the story in the last *Dial*, especially the very beautiful close of it. Kay Boyle's stuff has always seemed a kind of diluted solution of some kind. She's still in France, n'est ce pas?

I don't mean to bluster on forever. But do write me again—with the proper enclosures! And thank you for your letter. Present address is good regardless of what changes ensue. Please offer my salutations to Janet Lewis.

Yours most faithfully, Hart Crane

To Clarence Arthur Crane

New York
Dear Father: Oct. 31st, '26

It is, of course, quite possible that you have not cared to answer any of my letters to you this summer, addressed from the Isle of Pines. Since my return to New York this week, however, I discover from various friends of mine that many of my letters have not reached their destination, and that much mail addressed to me on the island was never delivered. This is due, I understand, to the corrupt manners of the Havana postoffice. Letters are often opened in the hope of finding American currency, and not reforwarded . . .

So, in view of this, I feel prompted to at least express my regrets to you—in case you have been as mystified at *my* silence as I have been at yours. If you care to write me, I'll be here another week in all probability.

Sincerely, your son,
Harold

To Yvor Winters

Rural Delivery
Patterson, New York
Dear Winters: November 12

Although the hurricane experience (and engineering my way off the island aftward) were strenuous experiences, it is the previous heat and subsequent chaos of worries and details and travel which, I believe, account for my present vacant state of mind. At any rate, this may partially serve as an excuse for the present dullard answer to your very pleasant letter just arrived here via the Isle of Pines. I'll probably recover myself better later on; meanwhile I greatly appreciate your interest in a number of ways.

I am back where I started from last May, a farmhouse with an old woman to cook for me. It seems good to "experience" nights again—not filled with the overweening, obscene vitality of the tropics which never lets you (a northerner) rest. And though fate seems to throw me into sudden extremes, winters in polar regions and summers under the equator, I can at least hope to rest up a little, i.e. if I am not yanked to Cleveland on account of growing difficulties there, where my family is immersed in sickness, etc. The above address will always be good, however, as I maintain a room here permanently for a few personal belongings. Letters are quickly forwarded.

Your suggestion regarding the instructorship would certainly interest me very much were I at all equipped to respond. I'm not being merely modest when I say that my French is weak and my Spanish nil. I've never been through high-school, even. So you can see what a splurge I'd create! I always envy people like yourself—their entry into pages I shall never see. . . . And, after all, your isolation and work is much pleasanter than newspaper reporting and ad-writing, such as I've been raised on.

The Aunt Harriet harangue makes an interesting story. What gave her any initial impetus toward taste or selection was immeadiately withdrawn when Pound stopped sending her lectures and material. Now she is back on the ancient journalistic footing where he found her. Her "position" and excessive self-confidence, however, will never forsake her. She is the kind of person who would run up to Newton, and in behalf of all good easy-going "hopefuls" of the middle-west, would query, "But aren't you a little bit too mathematical, Sir Isaac?" There is good antidote for the kind of criticism she writes in Edwin Muir's last book, *Transition*. You may have already seen it; I like especially his treatment of Eliot and Joyce. He is the only one I've read who touches the real weaknesses both in Eliot's poetry and criticism.

My reference to Williams' work did me no more justice than him, it was too hasty to be representative. I have not read all the poems that you mention of his, but I've read about two-thirds of them. Some of them are truly unforgettable, especially the "Postlude." And I remember a suite published once in the *Little Review* called "To Mark Antony in Heaven". . . . Or was it a single poem? I have *Sour Grapes*, and had *Spring and All* . . . until the hurricane. I don't want to read *In the American Grain* until I get through with *Bridge* because I hesitate to complicate the organization of a work, which, from what I've heard of his chronicle, is on such similar subject matter. Certainly Williams is brilliant, and occasionally profound. Full of clean recognitions and discoveries. And I like Williams much personally.

I am eagerly awaiting your poems, the mss. your letter promised. If they get lost on the way back through Havana postoffice I shall be much disappointed. At any rate, the mss of your book had probably not been sent to that address before the storm. Your expressed esteem for certain of my poems makes me doubly anxious that *White Buildings*—in regard to such work as you haven't seen—will entertain and please you. It ought to be out in about two weeks.

Faithfully yours, Hart Crane

To Yvor Winters

Patterson, New York
Dear Yvor Winters: November 15, 1926
"—seeds that no sparrow will ever crack"—! I feel almost like shouting *Eureka!* Your letter of Oct. 20th has just reached me from the Island. And I must thank you for the most intimate sort of critical sympathy—not only with my work, but my aims—that I've about ever been given. I am convinced now that telepathy is constantly at work, for I have, I confess it now, been so impressed by a certain kinship in certain stray poems I have seen of yours at wide intervals—that I have thought at times, when pausing over certain lines of my own, —"well, Winters, I think, would like this line". But one scarcely dares expect (any more) such explicitness as yours in locating and justifying that code of reference, that metaphysical common denominator upon which our composite values seem to rest. We may differ in many a detail, but I'm amazed at our essential sympathy. (You see, it's most pleasant to find someone who (regardless of whether he wants to crack them or not) values the hard little kernels (really bombs) which most other people blame you for having "spoiled" the "clarity" of your work with,—especially when these kernels are (to me) the élan-vital of the poem!)

Your quotations are, several of them, old favorites of mine. And you are right about modern epics—except—until somebody actually overcomes the limitations. This will have to be done by a new form,—and, of course, new forms are never desireable until they are simply forced into being by new materials. Perhaps any modern equivalent of the old epic form should be called by some other name, for certainly, as I see it, the old definition cannot cover the kind of poem I am trying to write except on certain fundamental points. At least both are concerned with material which can be called mythical. . . . But what is "mythical" in or rather, of the twentieth century is not the Kaiser, the sinking of the *Titanic,* etc. Rather it is science, travel (in the name of *speed*)—psychoanalysis, etc. With, of course, the eternal verities of sea, mountain and river still at work.

The old narrative form, then—with its concomitant species of rhetoric, is obviously unequal to the task. It may well be that the link-by-link cumulative effect of the ancients cannot have an equivalent in any modern epic form. However, there are certain basically mythical factors in our Western world which literally cry for embodiment. Oddly, as I see it, they cannot be presented completely (any one of them) in isolated order, but in order to appear in their true, luminous reality must be presented in chronological and organic order, out of which you get a kind of bridge, the quest of which bridge is—nothing less ambitious than the annihilation of time and space, the prime myth of the modern world.

The labor in locating the interrelations between sources, facts and appearances in all this is, believe me, difficult. One may be doomed to the kind of half-success which is worse than failure. I could write reams in regard to certain startling discoveries made along the way, simply in trying to handle my subject in an organic way. One of them is the currency of Indian symbolism in whatever is most real in our little native culture, its persistence, despite our really slight contact with that race, into architecture, painting, etc.—cropping out in the most unexpected places.

> A cyclone threshes in the turbine crest,
> Swooping in eagle feathers down your back.

I may exaggerate, but why did I really *have* to employ mention of the turbine engine to really describe the warrior's headdress? Etc. Of course the head could have been elaborated in prose, but the psychic factor would have been lost via a delayed delivery. Our metaphysical preference for condensation, density—has a correspondence, an intense one, in the very elements of Indian design and ritual. I have, by the way, an Indian dance as Part 4 of "Powhatan's Daughter," the second section of the *Bridge* immediately following the "Ave Maria" which you have. I don't want to send it to you, however, until the other sections of this section are completed.

I'm glad you get the essential thing in "Cutty Sark"—written immediately after "Ave Maria," symbolically touching not only on the sea—and its presence under the center of the bridge (this comes about midway in the poem)—but the depth and hazards of the psyche, as well—a plumb line.

The green eyes, the drums, the Rose theme, precursor of the Atlantis theme which closes the poem on the pure Mythos of time and space. In a way, the calligramme, the regatta is the "sublimation" of the "raw article" as seen personified in the bar-cafe.

Forgive my rambling. It could go on unforgiveably and confusedly. I'm engrossed in a thousand problems of form and material all at once these days. One can go only so far with logic, then willfully dream and play—and pray for the fusion. —*When* one's work suddenly stands up, separate and moving of itself with its own sudden life, as it must; quite separate from one's own personality.

Your letter offering such kind help after the hurricane was forwarded also. You have my profoundest thanks for *all* of this. I trust you are not leaving for France until next spring; but in case it's considerably earlier be sure to let me know. I should like to have a few hours talk in NY before your departure.

Best wishes and sincerest affection,—Hart Crane

To Waldo Frank

Patterson, New York
Caro hermano: November, 21
   I am hoping that your country retreat is as pleasant to you as mine is to me. . . . It seems marvelous to sleep again, buried under the sound of an autumn wind—and to wake with the sense of faculties being on the mend. Now I can look back and enjoy "every moment" of the summer Carib days,—so gracious is the memory in preserving most carefully the record of our pleasures, *their* real savor, *only*.

When are you coming back to town? Will you for a moment consider coming out here for a week-end (or longer) sometime before you leave for Europe? It would be pleasant and quiet, and the country is still interesting if one doesn't demand too much tropical splendor. We could have the good deliberate talk that we couldn't get in NY, of course.

Haven't got my book yet, but expect it next week. Nor am I at work yet on the *Bridge* again . . . But I'm not worried. I know too well what I want to do now, even if it doesn't spill over for months and months. It must "spill", you know. The little thing above I did yesterday. Write me when you have time. Aunt Sally sends you her best (sometimes "love"!) in her every letter.

Good luck and my love, Hart

Williams'—*American Grain* is an achievement that I'd be proud of. A most important and *sincere* book. I'm very enthusiastic—I put off reading it, you know, until I felt my own way cleared beyond chance of confusions incident to reading a book so intimate to my theme. I was so interested to note that he puts Poe and his "character" in the same position as I had *symbolized* for him in the "Tunnel" section.

To *Yvor Winters*

Patterson, New York

Dear Winters: November 28, 1926

Don't scratch your head further about "taeping." It's not a fish, or any manner of coitus. *Taeping* and *Ariel*, one British and the other Yankee, were noted clipper rivals in the India tea trade races of '46 or thereabouts. . . . And accept my hearty thanks for your corrections on the Spanish and Latin. I must have been taught Main Street pig-latin to have so slighted the penultimate; however, I may possibly let this remain Elizabethanly porky, regardless. But the holy mother has already been restored to proper syllable.

I've been too harried and scrambled lately by a hundred little decisions and hesitancies incident to forms and material for the *Bridge* to give anything a fair reading, but I've immensely enjoyed the time spent with your poems. There isn't a bad poem in the ms, nor a weak one. Your "passion is resistant like a pane of glass", through which you filter strict pictures. Cold, sleep, stone, glass—these recurrent qualities, becoming touchstones of consciousness—are driven into the brain. They become the chain-links of your observations and evocations.

Your landscape is always solid, even when the fragility of the theme is a little tenuous, as it seems in several of the shorter, hokku-like forms.

You seem to have deliberately chosen very definite boundaries—and this certainly *helps* give your book a genuine unity. . . . The first stanza of "Song" (p 34) seems to me to present possibly as accurate a definition of your particular aims as could be mustered,—your self discipline implied in the "stiff wild hall of light". You emphasize the static element, the picture, the moment of realization,—a moveless kernel that glimmers like some mineral embedded in native rock. These:—

> My very breath
> Disowned
> In nights of study,
> And page by page
> I came on spring.
>
> — — —
>
> Dry penguins
> On the cliffs of light
>
> — — —
>
> Unlit windows, coffee hour by hour
> And chilling sleep—

are the kind of gleaming "facts" that hold my enthusiasm throughout your work. Such felicities, and one's exact reasons for so liking them, are hard to explain clearly. I always have to rush to metaphysics, and then I come back with tomes of complicated fragilities. I'll spare you that. . . .

My favorite is "The Rows of Cold Trees". Here, as in "Eternity", "The Passing Night", "The Moonlight" and "The Crystal Sun", also—you are on "the mythical and smoky soil"; your "wave-length" deepens, the structure of thought and emotion is amplified. Here the real weight of your stones and hills comes closer, with a threat. You are more discursive—and with no loss of intensity. "José's Country", with its last line, "a fern ascending", is beautiful. Likewise "The Precincts of February" and "Resurrection".

Truly, throughout the book, you come off with all you attempt,—or seem to attempt,—"solid in the spring and serious" (I love that phrase!); a rare example in "these days of hard trying", as Marianne Moore puts it; free from affectation, stained glass effects, or nervous antics. Is the book coming out next spring? If I have developed any editorial connections by that time I should like to review it. At present—up to the present—I have never been able to persuade any editor that I could lisp in anything but numbers. A true deduction, possibly, as you may judge by this letter.

Aunt Harriet has just taken "O Carib Isle", a rather violent lyric urging the hurricane on the Isle of Pines, which, of course, *came*. I hope to get *This Quarter* etc sometime, but I'm afraid they're lost. Do write again when you have time.

With best wishes, Hart Crane

To Mrs. T. W. Simpson

Patterson, New York

Dear Aunt Sally: Sunday, December 5, 1926

From hurricane to blizzards—all in six weeks! The fates sure do give me immoderate changes. It's "two below naught" outside, as they say in Hicksville; snowdrifts on the hills and windows, and my room isn't so warm but what tickling the typewriter keys is a stiff proposition. My nose got so cold last night it kept me awake, besides I could hear the congealing water click into ice in the pitcher on the washstand, ticking, ticking—every few moments. But my kerosene stoves are doing better than last winter—better oil, and I think with considerable economy I'll be able to finish the winter here, if I'm not called back to Cleveland.

Utter silence, by the way, from that quarter. It will make it a month since I heard from my mother, who evidently is displeased. It certainly is too bad that she doesn't write you; I guess she is in a pretty disorganized state of mind.

I should have known when they said that my book would be out "in two weeks" that it meant a month, but it's promised for certain late this week. I'll be glad when it's over—for though it, or rather the prospect of its appearance doesn't give me such a thrill after all, yet it does keep me a little distracted. I'm sure I shall be better able to work on the new stuff once this first book is really launched and off my mind. Work is going very slowly on the *Bridge*, but I'm not worried. Eventually it's going to be done, and in the style that my conception of it demands. Winters continues to write me most stimulating criticism; his wide scholarship, not only in English literature but in Latin, Greek, French and Spanish and Portuguese—gives his statements a gratifying weight. I have heard nothing whatever from Waldo since I reached Patterson (a month now), but he was going away to some country retreat himself for awhile. Is very busy writing a play of some kind.

Got a letter from Alfredo (you remember the Havanese sailor?) yesterday. The second since I got back. I have a great time translating his Spanish without a dictionary of any size. Once he got his niece to write me a letter in (broken) English. One of the statements ran, "*Maximo Gomez*, my ship—him sink in ciclon. All my clothes drowned." When I was going through Havana I asked another "Gomez" mariner if he knew anything about the fate of Al. in the storm. I gathered from his signs and contortions that Al. was badly laid up with a broken arm and a smashed shoulder. But later learn that he escaped at least as whole as the Adonis Crane refered to in your last letter. I'm still bent on learning Spanish as soon as my fortune or inheritance permits. With enough Spanish and enough reputation as a poet,—someday I might be appointed to sell tires or toothpaste in Rio de Janeiro!

I was amused to hear about the drunken outbreak of the very red, butter-faced hurricane friend of "ours"—who was looking for an isle of pines retreat for his mother—among the ruins. Certain of the actors in the melodramatic episode of wind, rain, ligntnin', plaster, shingles, curses, desperation and sailors—will never leave my mind. Especially our little one-step together the morning after, to the tune of "Valencia"! And pillows wobbling on our heads!

I'm glad you have got under a good roof again. You're such a good brick, you ought to get dried before some of the rest. I hope you got my letters, especially the one *containing* the check. The other was self-explanatory, of course, in case anything circumvented the registered letter. I mailed it a day later on purpose. One has to be sly with the Havana post office. I'm eating like a horse, losing my becoming tan, and getting fat, I fear. How I would like—at the present moment—to step into a grove of royal palms, doff these woolens—and have a good glass of Cerveza with you! The storm is increasing, howling loudly. It looks as though we were to be snowed in for the rest of the winter. Really! —And I may be a good time getting this letter to the PO if mail delivery is delayed, as usual under such circumstances.

Don't work too hard!

Lots of love, Hart

To Wilbur Underwood

Patterson, New York
Dear Wilbur!   December 16

I'm laid up with tonsilitis—but must somehow thank you for your pleasant N.Y. letter and wish you as amusing a New Year as possible. As for myself—I don't expect much.

Nothing but illness and mental disorder in my family—and I am expected by all the middle-class ethics and dogmas to rush myself to Cleveland and devote myself interminably to nursing, sympathizing with woes which I have no sympathy for because they are all unnecessary, and bolstering up the faith in others toward concepts which I long ago discarded as crass and cheap.

Whether I can do it or not is the question. It means tortures and immolations which are hard to conceive, impossible to describe. There seems to be no place left in the world for love or the innocence of a simple spontaneous act. Write me here.

As ever, Hart

To Samuel Loveman

Dear Sam: Patterson, New York

It's frightfully cold out here—and I've had tonsilitis for two weeks. Everyone but the old woman and the cats has gone into town for the rest of the winter.

How have you been? Do wish you would write once a year or so. Have you foresworn all correspondence? I have so little news that there is no excuse for this except it's Christmas time and I want to wish you the best for 1927.

Complications in Cleveland seem endless—and I may have to give up everything and go out and struggle some more in the chaos. As it is—I can't get my mind free enough of it to accomplish any work here. . . . Yes "God is love"—as Mary Baker Eddy says!

As ever—Hart

To Grace Hart Crane

Patterson, New York
Dear Grace: December 22, 1926

Your letter came yesterday and I am glad that you can once more write. Yes—it is a very melancholy Christmas for all of us. . . . I am certainly anything but joyful.

Insomnia seems now to have settled on me permanently—and when I do "sleep" my mind is plagued by an endless reel of pictures, startling and unhappy—like some endless cinematograph.

Am making as much effort as possible to free my imagination and work the little time that is now left me on my *Bridge* poem. So much is expected of me via that poem—that if I fail on it I shall become a laughing stock and my career closed.

I take it that you would not wish this to happen. Yet it may be too late, already, for me to complete the conception. My mind is about as clear as dirty dishwater—and such a state of things is scarcely conducive to successful creative endeavor. If it were like adding up columns of figures— or more usual labors—it would be different. . . . Well, I'm trying my best —both to feel the proper sentiments to your situation and keep on with my task. *The Bridge* is an important task—and nobody else can ever do it.

My *White Buildings* is out. A beautiful book. Laukhuff has been instructed to send you out a copy as soon as he receives his order.

I'm glad you have taken up CS again. You never should have dropped it. But it seems to me you will have to make a real effort this time—with no half-way measures. It isn't anything you can play with. It's either true—or totally false. And for heaven's sake—don't go to it merely as a *cure*. If it isn't a complete philosophy of life for you it isn't anything at all. It is sheer hypocrsy to take it up when you get scared and then forsake it as soon as you feel angry about something. Anger is a costly luxury to you—and resentment and constant self-pity. I have to fight these demons myself. I know they are demons—they never do me anything but harm. Why look at yourself as a martyr all the time! It simply drives people away from you. The only real martyrs the world ever worships are those devoted exclusively to the worship of God, poverty and suffering —you have, as yet, never been in exactly that position. Not that I want you to be a martyr. I see no reason for it—and am out of sympathy with anyone who thinks he is—for the *real* ones don't think about themselves that way—they are too happy in their faith ever to want to be otherwise.

If this sounds like a sermon it's the last I offer sincerely. I'm not well and still have the tonsilitis. Write me again as soon as you feel able.

Love, Hart

To Wilbur Underwood

                                    Patterson, New York
Dear Wilbur: January 3,

I love the poetry book you sent, especially the beautiful Denmark poem; and it was the only gift I received this holiday season. . . . Surely I didn't deserve it after the woeful little note I sent you!

I shall send you a copy of my *White Buildings* as soon as I get extra copies. It's out, finally, and not so badly printed.

Will you continue sending the *Times* (London) when you're through with them? I can afford to take no magazines (most of them I wouldn't take anyway) but it is amusing to get scraps from the outside world. Winter means almost complete isolation out here. And I'm rather curious to know what "London" thinks of my little verses; I sent the *Times* a copy for review. It will probably be among the briefer notices toward the back.

Do write me more about the brass-buttoned-tattoed vision that you carried with you from the metropolis to the capital! My faithful has forsaken me, at least I have no postal for many weeks.

> O, the navies old and oaken,
> O, the Temeraire no more!
>   as Melville says . . .

I ran across some London letters of Harry's the other day; it seems hard to realize that he's gone. Life was a frightful torture to him after all, though . . . and we all end up rather mad.

Love to you, Hart

To Yvor Winters

Patterson, New York

Dear Winters: January 3, 1927

Your enthusiasm prompted me to read *The Time of Man*. It's a superb piece of work and I *almost* share your statement that it's the greatest piece of narrative prose that has come out of America. It *is* in its particular *genre*. And you feel that it will stand all kinds of tests.

I also share your interest in boxing matches. But I've seen so few that I'm no critic. And when I come to put on the gloves myself I'm about as agile as a polar bear and wheeze like a gander. I have heard of Tiger Flowers but never followed his career. There's much in a name and he never should have been beaten.

The booklets from the Isle of Pines have finally reached me. And there are several things which regret are not included in the covers of your new book. "The Wizard" and "My Memory" are among them—and the title poem of the same booklet. Many of the poems seem to lack the "edge" that you have in your later work, however. This is very possibly due to a lack of confidence which I'm sure in my own case, is responsible for certain obscurities that I'm constantly accused of.

My *White Bldgs*, now out, shocks me in some ways. I think I have grown more objective since writing some of those poems —more sympathetic with the reader. "Make my dark heavy poem light—and light" is a line from Donne which has always haunted me. But on the other hand some of Donne's greatest complexities have most delighted me. This gentleman, by the way, somehow escaped mention in Tate's introduction but verily, I think he should have been. But I seem to have a queer mixture of tastes.

Allow me to thank you—or the Fates, if you prefer, for securing my book for review in *Poetry*. I want to read MacLeish's work as soon as possible. He is so far a complete stranger. He and Tate are now at work compiling an anthology of French and Anglo-American romantic poetry. Liveright is going to publish it, I think. I may be ill advised in mentioning this at present,—so please don't advertise the project in any incidental way.

You will excuse the dull and egocentric tenor of my correspondence lately, I hope. Certain worries and tonsilitis which seems to linger indefinitely make me a forbidding grouch. However, you must know how much I enjoy hearing from you—and that I hope you'll not give me up entirely. I enclose a little poem written lately to "our Emily".

Best to you and to your wife— Hart Crane

To Edgell Rickword

Patterson, New York
Rural Delivery
Dear Mr Rickword: January 7th, 1927
You have doubtless received the cabled 'yes' sent yesterday in answer to your very kind proposal . . . My publisher, Mr Horace Liveright, 61 West 48th St. N.Y.C. has sheets which he will send to Wishart & Co immeadiately on order, though I am not sure as to the quantity available. I wrote him yesterday,

however, and you may already have a letter from him regarding such details. On the other hand he may be waiting to hear from your publisher before writing. I am not exactly in conversational touch with him from my present rural isolation . . .

I hope that you have received the copy of White Buildings by this time, addressed to Mr Garman. If Wishart & Co after reading the book, desire to issue it in England will you kindly ask them to send me some form of contract or understanding . . . I am not anticipating any such sales from the book as to make royalties any particular item; however, the tenure of copyright must allow the author some claim on a share of the profit *should* the book in the long run prove remunerative. I know nothing about foreign copyright matters and leave the arrangements largely to your personal discretion. My contract with Liveright gives me 10% on the retail price of the first 1000 copies sold. This, I am told, is the average royalty allowance this side of the water. I should be very interested in seeing the Wishart announcements that you mention. Would it be desireable to issue the book in the Spring? I rather presume this from your letter. There is probably no specail need to mention it, but as a precaution—any cables sent to me should be addressed to Mr Allen Tate, 27 Bank St., New York, or to *Liveright, New York.* I'm too isolated here to be certain of getting such communications. I can't imagine a occasion for keeping the wires hot, however . . .

I enclose three poems: O Carib Isle, Cutty Sark and The Harbor Dawn. There is a general emphasis on the *marine* in all of them, and if you should care to use them all I suggest that the sequence in which I have named them above would chart an interesting curve of the underlying element.

I must risk a presumption on your interest in the poems in order to emphasize the necessity of printing Cutty Sark as closely as possible to the form as typed herewith, especially in regard to the third page, which is a "cartogram", if one may so designate a special use of the calligramme. The "ships" should meet and pass in line and type—as well as in wind and memory, if you get my rather unique formal intentions in this phantom regatta seen from Brooklyn Bridge.

Probably no one should be 'thanked' for taking an interest in poetry, but your kindness and interest in what little I've so far accomplished are much appreciated. It is re-assuring to me—especially from the fact that a couple of years ago I found so much in your Rimbaud volume which was sympathetic and critically stimulating.

Please pardon my failure to send the subscription; I shall have to wait until I get into Town where I can send a money order.

Sincerely yours,

To Allen Tate

Patterson, New York

Dear Allen: Friday

I'm tremendously obliged to you for all this British business . . . I really hope it will go through. I've written Rickword today immeadiately on receipt of your letter. I also wrote Liveright yesterday, where to write and who; he forgets things said in conversations very quickly sometimes. Let me know the cost of the cable and I'll send you a check at once.

The company that R is lined up with called Wishart & Co., address same as *Calendar,* which is continuing, by the way, as a quarterly. A new publisher just starting business in the Spring. You ought to send them something. Garman has gone to Russia for a considerable period, but Wishart is bringing out a book of his poems. As for the preface—your foreword is entirely good enough both here *and* there. Besides, it would destroy all the economic advantage in buying sheets from L if they had much extra printing to add over there. I therefore made no mention of the idea in my letter. Hope to God, though, that Schneider had sent the copy of *WB* to them that I put on my review list. As I understood from you all review copies were sent out some time ago. A detention of the book much longer is going to ruin all chance of sales from Waldo's article. Lord! is there anything else that can happen to that book? How long *will* it take them to put in those new title pages, I wonder. All of my friends have got tired of asking for the book in Cleveland and I expect that there will be a record of less than the famous Stevens-35 to my credit.

Your comments on Gorham's shrine and gland-totemism convince me that Orage talked as vaguely and arbitrarily in your presence as he did in mine on a similar occasion. Some great boob ought to be hired as a kind of heckler and suddenly burst out in one of those meetings held each year to attract converts,—"Come on now, do your stuff—there's millions waiting!" Or some such democratic phrase.

As I seem to be going through an extremely distrustful mood in regard to most of my own work lately, perhaps some of my present temper may unduly limit my perspective in regard to your Ode. I have a kind of perpetual dull cold in the head, however, which may better account for my reactions. But if you can bear to listen awhile to Aunt Harriet then here goes . . .

The obscurities bother me. Stanza I, OK; and I get along very well until I come to "ambitious" Novembers in II. Why this special epithet—this particular designation for the whole season in relation to the headstones, in fact? As it is stressed so much one chafes against the stubborn dullness that blocks one's apprehension of your precise intention. The last six lines are particularly fine and The *last*—!

There is no doubt that you make the theme of the poem a living continuity with the exception of the several places where, I admit, I find it difficult to follow you. The theme of chivalry—a tradition of excess (not literally excess, rather, active faith) which cannot be perpetuated in the fragmentary cosmos of today—"those desires which *should* be yours tomorrow" but which, you know, will not persist nor find way into action. . . . Your statement of this is beautiful, and the poem is a POEM with splendidly controlled rhythms and eloquence. But when you come to such lines as "From the orient of the sublime economy / Remember the setting sun" I suddenly feel the thread cut. *Sublime economy* misses its aim with me, I suddenly seem to see a little of Laforgue's mannerism too wittily on the scene. What *is* meant here?

I fancy that you could go much better directly from Bull Run to "You hear the shout", etc. The next verse is superb. The last 7 lines are the climax of the poem. The intensity of this "meditation" gives the lie, of course, to all previous factual statements regarding the impermancy of your grief . . . But you are, of course, speaking throughout less from a personal angle than a social viewpoint. Or are you? Both, of course. It was fatuous to have raised this point . . .

Then you go back to speculation in the next stanza. You go *too* far in the succeeding, I think. And it, again, is rather obscure—exactly what you mean. The capitalization of sentiment, I take it. A good dig at certain people, but I think the sarcasm is over-bitter, marring the beauty of the poem as a whole. The fierce resignation at the last is beautiful, that irony *will* sell, if you get what I mean.

Carolyn said you sent it to the *Nation*. I hope they have sense enough to reward you; on the other hand, though, how can they take such a chance with their average reader? Hang crepe on your door and wait . . . The sonnet makes me merry, though it's the lovely last four lines that I like best. They're almost too good for the rest. The rest is too complicated. I'd chop it apart and put the lovely windows in another room.

I enjoyed Carolyn's letter and hope you'll both write as often as possible. How is the anthology coming on?

Love, Hart

Further readings may reveal to me the folly of some of my objections. . . . Take issue with me meanwhile wherever you feel justified.

To Wilbur Underwood

Patterson, New York

Dear Wilbur: January 11

Unable, for various reasons, to carry my work any further—I spend the time reading and studying Spanish. Yes—I hope to live in some other country someday. Or if not to live—at least to make a long visit. Spain and Mexico, Peru, etc fascinate me. What little of the Spanish character I saw in Cuba I liked and the language is quite beautiful. Someplace where there is *some* liberty of action, where one can take one's time—and perhaps have something good to drink. All this is a dream—of course, —I'm already looking around for a job in N.Y. Money is low,

etc. But I have to have something to think about besides the
Times and H. G. Wells' prophecies.

Your letter was delightful. I've just rec'd a most scrumptious
N. Years card from Gibraltar—with verses! about waking up in
the morning-dew and all that. The author's name isn't
printed, but Jack's is written instead below the lines. Well, he'll
be back in May and I probably won't miss him as I did last year
—guess I told you about his coming out here after I'd left for
the Island. He always (also) writes—"Just a line to say I'm in
the best of health and wish you the same." Anything beyond
that must demand too great an effort ever to be attempted.

Thank you for the *Literary Supplements* which just came.
I'm sending the book to you—and hope you'll find some
poem or other in it that doesn't bore you. Don't try too hard
to like them—for Heaven's sake.

With love—Hart

To William Slater Brown

Turners corners

Mio caro Tortola Fandango-Con-Carne!   Thursday Jueves

How I envy you your new pequeno cubbhole in hermosa
ciudad Brooklyn! Mucha calor, I hope, for it is too cold por
harvest any alelies hereabouts. Basta! The cats and feo Senora
Turner, buena mujer pero consada. Ah, el bueno Havanese, he
has forgotten, having got no nifty new pantalons y camisa from
Sand St! Mais Don JF sends from Gibraltar a thrilling Maxfield
Parrish salvo por el anno nuevo, with verses! which makes up
for it.

Was it Romolos wood they dumped up in front of your
house? At any rate all is well at Tory Hill with the exception of
sundry raids made by that notorious Hart Crane. He will have
drink,—and one day went up and when I called again I found
a can of Mate mixture missing, the Shakes-p-heri-an beverage
that makes the llamas caper. Another time he took away a per-
fectly comfortable cot mattress, the Sybarite! And I under-
stand he lounges while the old woman starts the fire!

He reports having sent you two envelopes that looked like

dividends, both to your former Coney Island barricado, though I suspect that one of them may have failed to reach you. Let me know about this. "Brooms" says he, "WHOOPS, I can bedevil the deck as well as anyone"!

Saluts a la Missus tu bueno pequeno muchacho

To Yvor Winters

Patterson, New York

Dear Winters: January 19, 1927

Your letter of the 10th most welcomely breaks a rather long and sober rumination I've been indulging in lately on the defects of several of the *White Buildings.* . . . I'm elated that you think so highly of the book, and if subsequent readings leave you with even half the admiration expressed in your letter I shall be grateful to the Powers that give as well as take.

I have been unexpectedly lucky, I think, for one whose work is obviously so 'extreme'. Waldo Frank has written a quite vociferously friendly review which may already be out in the *New Republic.* Who else, besides yourself, is to review the book I don't yet know. But two *such* are certainly more than compensation for the drubbing the book is sure to get from most other hands. Then, too, Edgell Rickword, editor of *The Calendar*, London, is placing the book with a new publisher there, to whom he is acting as advisor. However, the terms of the arrangement have not been settled yet.

I am enclosing the Indian dance section of "Powhatan's Daughter", which is a kind of fiery core to this part of the *Bridge*, (II). I had hoped to send you the section complete, so you would get the gradual ascent from Manhatten harbor, etc. but I'm a little too impatient to ask you a question to delay longer—and I don't know when the three antecedant sections will be finally completed. It's a minor matter, but I'm anxious to know if there is an Indian philology or symbolism concerned in the name "Maquokeeta". I chose the name at random, merely from the hearsay of a NY taxi driver who was obviously of Indian extraction (and a splendid fire-drinker by the way) who said that his indian name was "Maquokeeta". I think he came from Missouri, or thereabouts. You know much more about Indian fable, symbolism, etc. than I do. Will you let me know if the name is 'sufficient' to the rôle it plays in the poem? Intuitions are surprising sometimes: I didn't know at the time of writing that the serpent and eagle were such valid Indian symbols of time and space, respectively, as to have stood thus in the ritual of the Aztecs.

We are snowed in here, though it can't be as bitterly cold here as it must be in northern Idaho. I find that my summer of suffocating heat and the consequently violent efforts made to adjust myself to it, have made me susceptible to all sorts of chilblains, tonsilitises and other rheumatics. I'm studying Spanish with the one dream of sometime living in Havana, Cardenas, Guadalajara, Toledo or Morocco!

Best wishes— Hart Crane

P. S.—If any better name occurs to you please suggest it to me. From a purely "physical" standpoint—(sound, quantity, cadence) I'm perfectly satisfied—but it may possess some jarring connotations for all I know.

To Grace Hart Curtis

Patterson, New York

Dear Grace: Sunday, January 23, 1927

Your good letter and the photographs arrived in the same mail—yesterday. I was awfully glad to hear from you; and your letter was a perfect volume of news. I had heard nothing of the death of Frances until Grandmother's letter reached me, last Friday, I think. CA did not trouble to answer the letter I wrote him in November, and though I shall probably not hear from him, even now, until God knows when—I wrote him a short note of condolence as soon as I heard.

I liked the pictures, especially the one with the hat, and the frame is beautiful. I shall take them with me into NY when I get the job (whatever it shall turn out to be) that I'm at present fishing for. I am trying to get a line on something before going in, as I have scarcely any money left, and I would like to avoid any charities from my friends on this occasion if possible.

Meanwhile I am doing what writing I can, and studying Spanish.

I'm very much amused at what you say about the interest in my book among relatives and friends out there in Cleveland. Wait until they see it, and try to read it! I may be wrong, but I think they will eventually express considerable consternation; for the poetry I write, as you have noticed already, is farther from their grasp than the farthest planets. But I don't care how mad they get—*after* they have bought the book! It is going to get some excellent and laudatory reviews. Waldo Frank's in the *New Republic* (a full page) out to be out any day. Matthew Josephson is reviewing it in the *NY Herald*, Yvor Winters in the *Dial*, Archibald MacLeisch in *Poetry, A Magazine of Verse* (Chicago), etc.

Yvor Winters, who is a professor of French and Spanish at the Moscow University, Idaho, writes me the following: "Your book arrived this evening, and I have read it through a couple of times. It will need many more readings, but so far I am simply dumfounded. Most of it is new to me, and what I had seen is clarified by its setting. I withdraw all minor objections I have ever made to your work—I have never read anything greater and have read very little as great." Etc. So you see what kind of a review he is apt to write.

Waldo Frank ends his article in the *New Republic* by saying: "At present Hart Crane is engaged in a long poem that provides him with a subject adequate to his method: the subject indeed which Mr Tate prophecies in his introduction. Yet already *White Buildings* gives us enough to justify the assertion, that not since Whitman has so original, so profound and— above all, so important a poetic promise come to the American scene."

In a way it's a pity that none of the Crane family are readers of anything more important than such magazines as the *Saturday Evening Post* and *Success*. Which reminds me, in contradistinction to all this, that Clara Risdon wrote me a jolly little Christmas card, mentioning the fact that she had been inquiring for *White Buildings*, having seen it advertised. I wonder what her address is; I should like to return the greeting somehow.

You are probably getting tired of all this egotism and lit'ry

news, but this is the last for the present. . . . A publisher in
London (Wishart & Co.) has written me proposing a London
edition of the book; and I think that arrangements will be
concluded within a few weeks. Mail is slow, of course. But I
am glad to have the book reissued there, as I may live abroad
sometime and a reputation in London might help me.

You asked me about my 'domestic arrangements' here . . .
Well, the Tates are in New York for the rest of the winter, and
so are the Browns. I have the house to myself, and Mrs.
Turner has forsaken her Aunt's 'part' for the time being, and
cooks, washes and mends for me—all for the round sum of
seven dollars a week! If I had the slightest sort of income I
could live on here forever at such a rate. One would simply
have to make an expedition to NY once in two months or so
for a few days, however, as there are some limitations to the
fascination of the 'scene'.

Grandmother's letter to me was a perfect marvel of lucidity
after all she's been through. I was amazed! I gathered from
it—as well as from your letter—that you are both seeing a
good deal of Bess and Byron lately. I suppose the unusual prox-
imity of your present location to theirs makes visiting easy. I've
always thought that Bess was pretty good company, and so is
Alice Crane. I'm glad that they have proved their friendship
and given you a somewhat graceful surprise at the same time.
I'm wondering what has become of the Rychtariks—true, I
had a Christmas card from them, but for some reason they
have written me only one letter in the last eight months. Do
you see them any—lately?

The delay in the divorce proceedings may mean that Charles
is reconsidering—and it might be just as well all around if he
did. I have the idea that you both care about each other much
more than you thought you did. Such thoughts are neither here
nor there, however, and I'm in no position to form judge-
ments or advise. I've never been able to figure out what the
quarrel was 'all about'—i.e., the issue involved. I think you
had probably better keep your mind off the subject as much as
possible, assuming the issue as closed. But you must get some-
thing to do as soon as you are physically able . . . I mean—
that without some kind of activity you'll remain in a morbid
condition—and your viewpoint will be more warped all the

time. People just have to have some activity to remain healthy-minded.

But you seem to be already much better; and I'm enormously glad. Don't think I don't care for you,—I can't help it, no matter how I feel about some things. I must write Grandmother a letter now. I hope you'll write me again soon.

Much love, Hart

P. S.—I enclose the Dedication to my long poem, *The Bridge*, —the *Dial* bought this part last summer, but so far it hasn't appeared.

To Yvor Winters

Patterson, New York
Dear Winters: January 27th, 1927
    Your account of Pablo's sad end—that is the dialect of it—reminds me of the speech of the Cayman niggers, whom I 'visited' last summer during their annual season of mosquitoes . . . I'll never forget that trip. The sixty-foot schooner had *only* 35 on it (myself the only white); the sun was practically 'equatorial' at that time and latitude; and we were becalmed—dead still—under that sun for two days (which made the whole trip 4 instead of 2) until I felt 'the very deep did rot'. But nothing stopped the enchanted tongues of those niggers . . . I was marooned on the island of Grand Cayman for ten days, mostly in my room, for there wasn't an inch of screening on the Island,—windows down and a smudge fire going all the time. My eyes disgorged more than one smoky tear over the pages of *Moby Dick*—which I think saved my mind.

This sounds exaggerated, but wait until you follow the pirate's tracks! My northern blood was simply ice cream and strawberry tarts to those various families of tiny vampires—and thin it as I would, by all sorts of dieting, I was always a popular pasture . . . Cayman, by the way, is the 'scene' of O Carib Isle, which ought to be out in Aunt Harriet's breviary and—aviary—soon.

I am certainly far from certain that you ought to feel that your surroundings, that is their lack-Easty-yeastiness, have deprived you of much. Of course there's no way of computing such matters for yourself, and how much less for another! But NY costs like hell in nerves and health. I should have been dead by this time if by a lucky hunch I hadn't written Otto Kahn a letter and secured the loan of enough money to get out awhile—over a year since, that was, and now it's about gone. I'm expecting to go back soon. And there's just as much 'metaphysics' in your landscape as mine; I know   not because I once made a flying trip to the coast and across the Canadian Rockies back—but because (and whether you like your bare hills and drunken miners or not) you've done some beautiful clean mining. That proves you enough to prove the soil too. That perfect thing, "The Moonlight," is just one of a dozen other substantiations in your work. In a queer kind of way all of your book is 'growing on me'.

I suppose the sheer and enormous waste of oneself—seeing oneself go under a little deeper every day in a place like NY proposes a challenge which sometimes seem best answered by a kind of word-grenade that puzzles in most cases as much as it pleases. Or neither. But after boundless literary chatter and philandering I've come to prefer some bare hill and more solitariness than I'm strong enough to gain in the city. For approach me at any hour but the 'morning after', and I'm all for the Mermaid again. I've worn out several kidneys and several bladders already on bootleg rum, but I seem always ready to risk another. Havana was almost a paradise to me—to have a little civilization mixed with one's food! I am going to write a Habanera in memory of it, someday. . . .

In most all your judgements on *white buildings* I agree with you. "The Voyages" (that is the series as a whole) I think are more articulate than you judge them, and "Grandmother's Love Letters"—while a very slight theme—seems to me to have sufficient organization to claim form.

Several I should never have included had I not felt necessary to fill out space. This terrible admission need not be followed, I hope, by a darker truth as to why I felt it necessary to publish! These include the "Fernery" (a fussy little Laforguian thing that I pottered on intermittantly over a longer period than anything I ever wrote,—*why* God only knows, except that Cleveland is a hellish place). Then, "In Shadow", a relic of my

Margaret-Anderson adolescence. "Chaplinesque" is fairly good as writing and as a description of the comedian of *The Kid*, but it's mood isn't matched to the bulk of my work, or related at all to the rest of the book. I care little for "North Labrador" and "Legend", and should have omitted both had Tate not urged the contrary. Etc. etc. But I must stop monopolizing your generous indulgence somewhere. I'm looking forward to a session with you at the aforesaid Mermaid when you come east. Rum has a strange power over me, it makes me feel quite innocent—or rather, guiltless.

Slater Brown writes me interesting news: that our 'Taeping' was originally 'T*ai*ping', and the name of some town or port in China. I wish I had a map to tell. He finds this in a history of the clipper *Cutty Sark* that he's reading. This is writ by Lubbock, too,—the same who wrote the *China Clippers* wherein *Taeping* and *Ariel* keep eternal company. If I still had this book (it went with the hurricane) I'd send it on to you. You would enjoy it immensely. Lubbock writes only for professional mariners, no concessions in vocabulary. And some of the anecdotes and logs quoted are marvellous. O all the gorgeous terminology of the sea . . . most of it gone forever now, with the sails that gave it wings. 'O the navies old and oaken/O the Temeraire no More!' sings Melville in one of the tragic little poems he wrote those last years when he was forgotten down on a customs wharf . . . It was coined all of hemp, oak, air and light. Logan Pearsall Smith pays an interesting tribute to the sea in his book on Idiom.

Brown says that Cutty Sark means a short shirt and is also the name for a kind of witch mentioned in "Tam O' Shanter":

> When ere to drink you are inclined
> Or cutty sarks run in your mind . . . etc

He further adds that *Cutty Sark* is still afloat in England where she is being reconditioned. Hooray!

Yours, ship-shape & Bristol fash'n, Hart Crane

To Waldo Frank

Patterson, New York

Querido hermano Waldo: January 28

Just a little note to say hello. It's sixteen below and the sun brightly shining. I'm living in practically one room—the kitchen—with the old lady these days—to keep warm. Writing a little again on the *Bridge* and studying Spanish.

Thank you so much for having the *Menorah* people send me out your review of Spengler. It's a magnificent rebuttal of the man's psychology. I don't need to know your philosophical references well enough to check up on them to feel that. I've sent the paper on to Tate who was somewhat bowled over by Spengler—as wasn't I?—thinking it will prick him a bit.

WBs is getting—or is going to get—wonderful reviews. Not to mention yours, there's a great explosion coming from Yvor Winters in the *Dial*; another from Mark Van Doren (of all the unexpected!) in the *Nation* this week. Seligmann has written a sincere and just estimate in the *Sun*; Josephson in the *Herald-Tribune*; MacLeish in *Poetry*, etc. I don't know any further, but there may be other surprises. I certainly feel myself very fortunate, considering the type of stuff in *WB*.

Also, Edgell Rickword, who is editor of the *Calendar*, London, has proposed the book to a new publisher starting up this spring—so there may be an English edition. But I'll be glad when all reviews and arrangements are over—so I can put the book definitely behind me. Present preoccupations tend to 'exteriorize' one entirely too much. Winters has a lovely book of poems coming out this spring, by the way,—and Ford Madox Ford has recommended Allen's poems highly to Duckworth, his London publishers. I hope they take it; Allen needs some encouragement very much.

Remember me in your mugs—though I guess you never get in far enough to become as sentimental as I do. Mrs. Simpson isn't very well, has overworked since the hurricane. Will you drop her a postcard from some hofbrau? It would tickle her to death. I've an amusing story to tell you sometime about one instance of the 'mysticism of money'—it refers to Kahn and the 'gift'. It seems I have to pay $60 odd the rest of my mortal term on life insurance to the Kahn estate, which, of course I was dumb bell enough not to understand when he proposed it. Not that I especially mind or that I'm at all embittered, but I think I have discovered a new way to avoid income taxes and become heroic—both at once, if you get what I mean.

Love to you—Hart

To Samuel Loveman

For the Memoires of a Man-Eater

There once was a cannibal nigger
Who ate up his enemy's frigger;
His dozens of wives
Had the time of their lives;
He grew bigger and Bigger and BIGGER.

Your valentine was the same as I sent to Emil—who is now more silent than ever. I'm passing this along—

To Susan Jenkins and William Slater Brown

Patterson, New York

Dear Bill and Sue: February 16

I left town last Sunday—so there was no time to see you again—and (already) scarce enough cash left to tip the conductor. The last two nights in town were mainly spent on the Hoboken waterfront, where you want to go (though it's for men only) if you want the good old beer, the old free-lunch counter and everything thrown in—for 15¢ a glass. Whiskey and gin are also much superior to the other side of the River and cheaper. Take the Christopher St ferry. Walk up *past* Front St. There are three in a row. Begin with McKelly's—or some such name.

The last night went flying back to Brooklyn with a wild Irish red-headed sailor of the Coast Guard, who introduced me to a lot of coffee dens and cousys on Sands Street, and then took me to some kind of opium den way off God knows where. Whereat I got angry and left him, or rather Mike Drayton did. Returning here to the home roost I found six cards from Jack the Incomparable with much more than the usual brief greetings, so Caramba!

Mrs Turner was laid up all day Monday from an excess of oatmeal eaten at breakfast in celebration of my return. Went up to Tory Hill yesterday and found everything just as I left it. Encountered Mrs Powitzki at the Jennings and think she is marvelous. Did you ever talk to her? I never heard such locutions. I should love to tickle her. Since which I've been reading the *Cock also Rises* (sent me by a Cleveland friend) and have developed a perfect case of acidosis. No wonder the book sold; there isn't a sentence without a highball or a martini in it to satisfy all the suppressed desires of the public. It's a brilliant and a terrible book. The fiesta and bullfight best. No warmth, no charm in it whatever, but of course Hemingway doesn't want such.

Love, Hart

To Allen Tate

Patterson, New York

Dear Allen: Thursday, February 24

I wish I could keep up with Winters. I already owe him several letters, besides comment on the ms of his *Fire Sequence*, which awaited me when I returned from town. All his work is so genuine that it takes close attention, meditation and blood and bone to answer . . . At present it's too much for me, so I've sent the manifesto on with a brief note to the effect that I agree with most of your marginalia, i.e., where I differ with him. Though I go further than you do in qualification of the Loeb-physics-etc. recipe . . . Pure hocus-pocus for the poet. Just one out of a five thousand other scientific similes, equally good to go by (regardless of their veracity)—and I venture to say that Winters' work suffers already from such arbitrary torturings—all for the sake of a neat little point of reference. What good will it do him to go on repeating in the background of every poem, that 'life is some slight disturbance of the balance', etc. etc.?! But we all must have some kind of incantation, I suppose. Though I'd rather adopt some of Blake's aphorisms. They're abstract enough. And a lot truer than the latest combination of scientific terms.

Glad you liked the Joyce lyrics. I make the following choice from my own work. If they seem to fit your requirements let me know, and I'll send you copies:

> "Passage"
> "The Springs of Guilty Song"("F & H," II)
> "Voyages"(V)
> "Powhatan's Daughter: The Dance"
> "To Emily Dickinson"
> "Repose of Rivers"

"The Dance" has been expanded to 104 lines, and is now the best thing I've done. I shall send it soon to you—regardless of the Anthology, as I want you to see and adjudge it. I've had to submit it to Marianne Moore recently, as my only present hope of a little cash. But she probably will object to the word 'breasts', or some other such detail. It's really ghastly. I wonder how much longer our market will be in the grip of two such hysterical virgins as the *Dial* and *Poetry*!

We have been without mail service all week. They may get the roads cleared out before Easter, I don't know. To have the sun again and a little warmth again! My present quandaries, that extend to every detail of my life, personal and artistic, have brought me near lunacy. I couldn't go on much longer on such a strain as the last year. Can you send me a few stamps? About a dozen—to last until Andy gets back on the rode.

Love, Hart

To Yvor Winters

Patterson, New York

Dear Winters: February 26, 1927

I can't say exactly why, but I have the suspicion that you will somehow be disappointed in my judgment for liking "Bison" the best of any poem in the *Sequence*. And I think that "November" and "Snow Ghost" both fall in the same superlative class. In each of these your theme and emotion develop without break—to the end. Of course I'm not giving much consideration to your Loeb-biochemic theories, and it may be that you succeed in certain other of the poems much better—in that regard. But I like such things as the marvelous suggestion of purity in "Snow-Ghost," like the dissection of a veritable nerve-fibre,

'invisible save on this plane of light'

and the sustained assault and vibration of "November." "Bison" is one of those things beyond analytic appreciation, like your "Moonlight."

At times you betray a kind of moral zeal—a preoccupation with the gauntness and bareness of things which sometimes gets in my way in trying to discover the particular properties of certain poems. It is so evident as to be distracting at times, and I cannot help feeling it to be a fault—at least it hinders the reader from accepting your poem on its pure aesthetic merits —and isolates or tends to isolate the poem from a spontaneous reception into the reader's sensibility. But since reading your Manifesto I'm better prepared to reckon your intentions, perhaps. Laying Life bare is all very well, but I think the Lady is best approached with a less obvious or deliberate signal than an upraised ax, if you get what I mean. It might be better in some cases to swim around with her a little while. For I feel a kind of vertical strain in some of your poems; and I am either not keen enough to follow you as far below the surface as you go, or else you don't penetrate the surface as readily always as you imagine you do.

Thus, out of "Coal" I get little more than expository statement of what is later evident as your main intention in the succeeding poems. That makes it the best poem for the start of the book. No. 2 is a good 'humanization' of the same theme— 'your thighs that seethe interminably'—a beautiful dynamic metaphor. No. 3 is a sharp, clean watercolor. Nos. 4, 5, & 6 puzzle me. As impressions they continue like 3—to relate man to the landscape, the idiom is forceful—but I feel myself missing many of the connotations or implications beyond that. I get more from 7, "A Miner," than from the sum of the other three, despite their brilliant counterpoint.

It seems to me that your general practice (and it is true likewise of nearly all imagists) has been too exclusive a concentration on the epithet—and the cost of the verb-dynamics of the poem as a whole. And consequently at the expense of the organic movement of the poem. Your poems never fall apart in the sense that one portion is out of key or focus with another, but they sometimes seem to lack the kind of progression which gives them the necessary conviction—the necessary completion or 'overtone' identifying them or their details with what I must call for lack of a better term—universal experience. I feel some of them to be too arbitrarily directed, if anything—too 'pure'—sometimes as isolated as a chemical experiment. The intellect is capable of emotional fire, but far from all its 'moods' seem to me emotionally adaptable to the creation of poetry. At least that's my feeling about your 'cold eye for the fact' though, paradoxically it would be hard for me to find two poems which better express the pure functioning of the intellect (and the beauty of such) than the very poem where that 'eye' is mentioned, and the aforepraised "Snow-Ghost." But that is because you got 'emotional' about your intellect and allowed your experience more imaginative range than you sometimes do when bent on objectifying something outside yourself.

No. 8 I like—as a keen drawing. No. 9 seems to me again too 'chemical,' also 10, excepting the 'globe of winter.' 11 is too obscure, to me; 12 seems strained. 14 moves—and is beautiful, and the next two are certainly fine. The painter-poem begins a little like one of Cummings'—"To Picasso"—but resemblances stop at once. "The Orange Tree" is the perfect type of imagist poem, even to the 'classic leaf' which it convincingly bears. "Los Angeles" and "Idaho" achieve a perfect contrast. "The Bitter Moon" and "December Sunset" get lost in abstractions that don't carry over—at least to me. The beautiful rhythm of "The Deep," despite several fine lines, leaves me 'cold,' indeed, as may be intended.

But this *Sequence* has a unity which your *Bare Hills* did not have—at least to the same solid degree. I envy you your method on one hand, and decry you for it on another. For I feel you are very consciously limiting yourself at times, and much more so than I should care to do. Not that I haven't a 'method'—but that our methods differ more than at first I thought they did. You want to strike directly inward, whereas I never consciously premeditate striking at all; I am interested mainly in a *construction*, autonomous,—the validity of whose abstract 'life' of course, is dependent on organic correspondences to Nature. In this sense *While Bldgs.* has two symbolic meanings, or connotations, its primary one being metaphysic-mechanical: it is only secondarily 'Woolworthian'.

For such as the above reasons you will possibly forgive me for feeling my method as inherently much more 'dynamic' than Williams'—though it would take a lot of space to qualify this. I do not think that your method—as I understand it—is any less dynamic than mine. (Your manifesto has started me on all this). I merely question the fertility of your key-symbol for it, the Loeb doctrine,—your (to me) superstitious conviction that Science strips Nature bare, and all that. Science may not decorate nature the way a minor poet does, but it nevertheless substitutes just one costume (set of terms) after another, one more split hair after another falls on Nature's bosom—the ultimate truth of any of which has been as well expressed by poetry—long since. Blake expressed the concept of Relativity long before science invented the term. Science is awfully stimulating—and should be used, but since it has become, as lately, an actual emotion, I think it is dangerous when uncontrolled. To me it must always remain an implement, not an oracle.

Living expansively enough in the current of the times—one becomes sufficiently infected, I suppose, to faithfully represent in one's reactions the characteristics of the period. If one is an artist the harmonious organization of such prejudices, aptitudes, etc.—sub speciae aeternitis—tends to determine the cultural history of the age. But I think one has to turn away from the age at times—as much as possible—in order to see it all intensely or synthetically. For as our vision of 'eternity' is itself a product of the age we live in—it can't very well be overlooked. At least I must conceive all or most of my poems under this process, regardless of whether or not they 'fit' the time. I *must* perforce, use the materials of the time, or the terms of my material will lack edge,—reality; one doesn't have to feel any great enthusiasm for one's age before utilizing the immediate materials it proffers. Personally—I think that these materials contain enough direction—enough dynamism in themselves—to eradicate the question or the primal importance of the question—as to just *where* they are taking us. Our intuitive selection of these materials on the basis of their appeal to us (their power) will ultimately determine our 'position' in time, historically speaking. We can't but be intuitive—our logic, the logic we choose to balance our 'intuitions' is intuitively selected. I must always write from the standpoint of Adam,—or rather, I must always fool myself that Adam 'felt the same way about it'. And you have granted me the feat at least of digesting machinery as successfully as nightingales!

There are other things that your manifesto prompts me to question, but I must break off this wild nonsense somewhere. . . . I've felt quite guilty for having put you (and others) to such lengthy pains anent the investigation of Maquokeeta. I feel perfectly reassured, however, for obviously the name isn't some notorious joke. Even if it has no existence as a name it's quite practical for my purposes, as it certainly *sounds* Indian enough to apply to a redskin. Thanks for forwarding the Cartwright notice.

I haven't yet had time to study the translations the way I want to. Your scholarship simply amazes me. I find several of the poems in a little anthology I have—*Las Cien Mejores Poesias*—, but I make slow progress in any language. But the pure sensuous appeal of Spanish is—almost—enough to induce me to struggle with it. They may be a messy lot, as you say—but their architecture, customs and general 'air' please me immensely—from the little I've seen. We all have some such personal and inexplicable impulses.

Please pardon this long harangue—and let me hear from you soon. Is the *Bare Hills* out yet?

All best to you and Janet Lewis,

Hart Crane

To Allen Tate

Patterson, New York

Dear Allen: March 10

I abducted a copy of your *Sewanee Review* essay from the envelope before sending it on; I hope you don't mind. As you had already promised me one I thought it would save you the trouble of mailing it back. Winters is sure to be interested, and I'm glad you're sending him one.

I'm too addled these days to have any ideas. And I may have a better perspective later—on Ransome. Just now, though, he doesn't impress me very much, at least this last book. But I haven't read nearly so much of him as you have. He, oddly, partakes somewhat of both Hardy and Wallace Stevens. Not that he imitates . . . but that in my 'reading' he seems to share certain aspects of both. And though I grant him a distinct personality I can't feel that either his technique or his attitude come half way up to the importance of either of them. He exploits his 'manners' a great deal. But his viewpoints don't seem to me very profound, nor does he possess any overwhelming graces. He never has succeeded—and probably never will—in writing anything that compares with your "Idiot" in respect to these qualities. He can satirize well at times, very well.

Hardy is a marvel in skill. If it weren't for my indifference to his never-absent 'message' I think I'd regard him as next to Shakespeare in sheer dexterity. I've been reading him rather thoroughly lately, instigated by Winters' frequent mention of him, I suppose.

Hope Torrence treats us well . . . I haven't heard anything yet. Nor from Marianne. What strange people these old virgins (male and female) are. Always in a flutter for fear bowels will be mentioned, forever carrying on a tradition that both Poe and Whitman spent half their lives railing against—and calling themselves 'liberals'. . . . I hear that Matty has a job writing a biography of ?—he won't tell, and that Malcolm is back. There's no news here.

best to you both—HART

To Allen Tate

Patterson, New York

Dear Allen: March 14, 1927

Miss Torrence won't even take tea, you know, because she finds it too 'stimulating'. I've been to her house, so I know. AND so, what can we expect! I got my verses back also. They seemed to be too spacious for the *New Republic*. . . . Your letter was of course a piece of folly, but justified. It won't do Miss T any good, but it's an admirable relief to me, and probably to you. I envy buckandwing dancers and the Al Jolsons of the world sometimes. They don't have to encounter all these milksops . . . and they do *please*. They're able to do some 'good' to somebody. And when they laugh people don't think they are crying. Out here one reads the paper—one sees evidence mounting all the time—that there is no place left for our kinds of minds or emotions. Unless we can pursue our futilities with some sort of constant pleasure there is little use in going on—and we must apprehend some element of truth in our mock ceremonies or even our follies aren't amusing. I'm looking around for some new sort of 'avocation', but having gone half-blind with conjunctivities (better known as 'pink-eye') I waiting for the cornea to clear before taking any leap.

Phallus-es have been known to slyly leap out of some of Mr Gilmore's poems published in the *Little Review*, so Miss Moore had better watch out. But she probably doesn't know one when she does encounter it! His poems, about as long as a cicada's whirr, might make an amusing booklet. His plays are even briefer, I'm told.

Thanks for the *NR* copies. Miss T had informed me of the matter, saying 'you must look out for it (sic), so that I felt I might be standing in the middle of Seventh Avenue with a huge truck bearing down suddenly. Having bothered you so much lately I thot I'd worry Bill for awhile, so I asked him to send me copies. I'll certainly have plentEE now! I note that the one quotable paragraph (from the publisher's standpoint) has been lopped off: the last, with the allusion to Whitman. The rest will be a sufficient warning to most readers not to read the book, for it's one long dissertation on the subject of OBSCURITY.

The genial tactics of the editorial proofreader have even helped Frank on a little by falsifying his ms—at least the copy I hold. For instance, 'the obscure poet he is likely *for long* to remain' has been changed to read '*ever* to remain'. This not only alters the time-limit before my possible admission to the panting bosom of the generous reader, but changes the emphasis of the context in such a way that the reader infers the reviewer's prophecy to be that I shall probably *never* write anything that is comprehensible! With the world flying into trillions of tabloids I probably shall not!

Your review of Laura was just according to my estimates. If I'm as obscure to others as she is to me—then I won't even rail any more at Miss Torrence.

Love, Hart

GOLDEN TEXT:
>Wondrous the gods, more wondrous are the men,
>More wondrous, wondrous still, the cock and hen!
>
>—Blake

To Yvor Winters

Patterson, New York
Dear Winters: March 19, 1927

It's reassuring to know that you care for the "Three Songs". Doubts, accidentally or justifiably, accumulate sometimes around certain pieces of work that never touch others. Sometimes they are based on the fear that the material or viewpoint featured is too personal to the writer, or again it may be the question of technique employed—questions of pure form. No amount of ragging would ever have convinced me, for instance, that "Ave Maria" wasn't primarily solid and valid, and I could say the same of the Indian dance, and certain other poems. I hope you don't mind my rather impertinent practice of 'trying out' so many things on you! In this respect I consider that our differences of 'experience' and our differences on theoretical matters are all to the good. I only regret that my ideas, as such, are so relatively incoherent—especially now, owing to a thousand quandaries in grappling with resistant materials—that I'm not able to offer more interesting or pertinent comment on the things you've been sending me.

It's impossible to imagine without undertaking a like problem oneself—what endless problems arise in carrying forward the conception of a theme like the *Bridge*. It takes more than ordinary mental logic, of course, to fuse all multitudinous aspects of such a theme—I carried the embryonic Idea of the poem about with me for six years before I ever wrote a line. Then there was a sudden impetus, the results of which you have seen almost entirely. I am beginning to think it may be six more years before the materials for the rest of the poem shall have reached a sufficiently mature organization to be ready for paper. Logic or no logic, I can never do anything that is worth while without the assent of my intuitions. The logical progression of the *Bridge* is well in my mind. But one has to even fight that! At least one has to be ready to doubt its validity thoroughly on the slightest whispering approach of what I might call 'temperature'—the condition for organic fusion of experience, logical or no. Melville didn't write good verse, but the following lines at least show him to have realized the nature of the problem:

> In placid hours well pleased we dream
> Of many a brave, unbodied dream;
> But form to lend, pulsed life create,
> What unlike things must meet and mate;
> A flame to meet, a mind to freeze;
> Sad patience, joyous energies;
> Humility, yet pride and scorn;
> Instinct and study; love and hate;
> Audacity, reverence. These must mate
> And fuse with Jacob's mystic heart,
> To wrestle with the angel—Art.

This is not quoted for your edification or information. It gives you or at least is so intended—nothing more than the primitive attitude I take toward both materials and aesthetic dogmas. There seems to me really no convincing modus operandi but what you might call alert blindness. Aesthetic speculations, etc. are of course endlessly interesting to me and stimulating. But not one that I have ever encountered has been quite equal to the necessary assimilation of experience—the artist's chief problem. I admit many biases. For instance, that I have a more or less religious attitude toward creation and expression. I respond more to revelation—or what seems revelation to me—than I do to what seems to me 'repititious'—however classic and noble. That is one reason why Williams probably means less to me than to you. I wish we could have a conversation on the subject of Williams—one is so at a disadvantage in writing out paragraphs which a monosyllable would settle in conversation.

There is no doubt of the charm of almost all of W's work. I except the "Paterson" and "Struggle of Wings" lately published in the *Dial*. I think them both highly disorganized. But in most of Williams' work I feel the kind of observations and emotions being 'made' which seem to me too casual, however delightfully phrased, to be especially interesting. I feel much the same about most of Whitman. But with Whitman there is a steady current—under or overtone—that scarcely ever forsakes him. And a rhythm that almost constantly bespeaks the ineffable 'word' that he has to speak. This 'tone', assertion, or whatever—emerges through all the paradoxes and contradictions in his work. It doesn't try to be logical. It is an 'operation' of some universal law which he apprehends but which cannot be expressed in any one attitude or formula. One either grasps it or one doesn't. When it comes out in a thing like the first 'paragraph' of "Out of the Cradle Endlessly Rocking" it is overwhelming. The man is both distant and near:

This is the far-off depth and height reflecting my own face;
This is the thoughtful merge of myself, and the outlet again:

Williams writes poems to the household gods—and you get a picture of a delightful man bent on appreciating the best that is given to him—sometimes, too often—dramatizing trifles in the classic manner of the old Chinese poets, and occasionally giving a metaphysical twist to his experience which is truly marvellous. To my mind he has written at least a dozen superb poems: "Postlude," "To Mark Antony in Heaven," "A Goodnight," "The Hunter,"—these are my favorites added to some things in *Spring & All* which I haven't had with me since the hurricane. I see nothing whatever Shakespearian about him however—unless you mean that he is in attitude not over-weeningly romantic. You mistake me if you think that I value non-representative art more than representative. That isn't at all what I meant by my little recipe. It must be both, of course —I mean a poem or a picture must have its own legs—no matter what it's carrying. But it must convey and even accen-tuate the reality of it's subject. That's the service of metaphor. And it must not only convey but locate and focus the *value* of the material in our complete consciousness. W's goes far this way in many poems—in others he seems to me to go off the track as badly as I often do, to judge by some of the strange in-terpretations I get of some of my poems. Personally I often delight in some of these excursions of W's—but I don't 'ap-prove' of them. They are too precious, insulate to all but—at least I fancy—a few 'choice spirits' and even then rather toy-like. I don't mean that I'm a democrat. But I don't believe in encouraging the fancy—as long as there is imagination. To me, "The Rose is Obsolete," represents this phase of W's.

I must stop rambling—if for no other reason than that the RFD is approaching. Have you really read much of Cum-mings' poetry? I suspect you haven't—else you would have more to say for him. Have you read his privately printed book called *&*—or the *IS₅* (Boni & Liveright) which contains some of the best in the former—? *Tulips & Chimney's* contains some of his worst sentimentalities. But the sensibility of the man is equal to Donne's—and if he had only cared to take a little more pains and organize—he'd be superb. I wish you'd let me know if you haven't read *&*. I'd like to make you a few copies of my favorites if you haven't.

I wish you would maintain a better opinion of your *Se-quence*. It deserves it. You haven't quite the range of Williams —at least I don't quite think you have—but you're much more essentialized and certainly as adept. At any rate—I don't believe in impeccability—hang it all, let yourself go more, re-gardless of poetics.

Best wishes—Hart Crane

To Allen Tate

Patterson, New York

Dear Allen: March 21, 1927

Mrs T and I made an extensive search for all items mentioned—but found only the following:

> dress shirt / black tie
> patent leather shoes (high)—no pumps in sight

These are enclosed with remnants of both garden and orchard in a package which we're mailing with this. I also included my black dress vest which you are welcome to use until I may sometime need it. I certainly can't use it out here—and we couldn't locate yours.

Bobbas and Browns drove up Saturday and left last evening. The Bobba casques are 150 gallons full of successful and highly combustible nectar. —I celebrated to the full—returning to my boudoir late Saturday night and knocking Señora Turner down besides hurling my Corona from the window in a high dudgeon because it wouldn't write to President Calles automatically in Spanish and express my "untold" admiration for his platform. Bill has taken it to the hospital for long and I fear expensive treatment.

It's turned cold again—rain and "ice forming on the trees" as Addie says. Browns leave Thursday for a wonderful tour of the West Indies on a fruit freighter. I've been dying to go with them. After 3 weeks of that they're coming directly up here. They're staying at 30 Jones St.

Marianne has taken "P's Daughter"—which comes to 4 *Dial* pages and helps my nerves considerably. Eyes are much better, due to a new pair of specs.

Best to you all—Hart

To Allen Tate

Patterson, New York
Dear Allen: Sunday, March 27
   Snow all piled up again. . . . I'm so damned sick of it! I'm
asking Bill to mail this in town tonight. He has told me about
the MacLeish fiasco. From what I hear, I think you accepted
with considerable patience. I'm afraid I should not have been
able to resist writing him that he had acted very unfairly, that
he had wasted considerable of my time without giving me any
return whatever, and that he was morally involved at least to
the extent of carrying through, regardless of his opinion of me
or my criticism.
   As to the *briefer*, I think that you give good reasons for as-
suming that Aiken wrote it. It might be more satisfying to
ascertain this more definitely—but I do not feel that beyond
that there is any particular justification for attacking him. He
has a perfect right to claim that many of the poems are spe-
cious and call them intellectual fakes etc. He may quite well
believe that he is right on this score. For years, remember, per-
fectly honest people have seen nothing but insanity in such
things as "The Tiger"—the only pity is the review wasn't
signed. But I don't see what can be done about it. You have
Aiken's sentimentality beautifully defined. Personally the man
is rather likeable, but I think he is full of poison. Let people
like Hemingway have every convert they want. When he writes
something vulnerable and signs it—we can backfire—and
publicly—and that's the only worthwhile way to spend—"we
have so little breath to lose." Thanks for the Davidson review.
I certainly appreciate its tone of honesty and sincerity. A copy
of *transition* #1 has reached me—and I'm enthusiastic about it.
By all means send Jolas some poems—and why not your article
on Marianne Moore? It doesn't spoil re-sale of ms over here,
you know. *transition* has some weak contribs, of course, but
the majority is respectable. Joyce, Gertrude Stein, Williams,
Winters, Laura, Larbaud, Gide, MacLeish, Soupault, etc. It's a
wedge that ought to be used. Malcolm also ought to send
things—and it seems to have a proof-reader!
   Aunt Harriet has taken "Cutty Sark"—of all things—and I

feel more cheerful. Have you sent her anything recently? Now seems to be the time.

I confided in Sue regarding "my biography". She says the Collinsons know the Roeblings well. She is having lunch with them Monday—so something *may* develope. She thinks the idea is rather promising.

Love to Carolyn, Hart

To Grace Hart Curtis and Elizabeth Belden Hart

Patterson—
Dear Grace & Grandma: March 28

I've been slow writing—but the Browns and others have been back and forth— I've had a lot of letters from all sorts of people to answer—and the last few days Mrs. Turner has been in bed on the verge of la grippe. She's up today, however, and I guess isn't going to succumb.

Thanks for the travel supplement. I'm wild to travel. A sailor friend of mine in the Navy writes me cards from the Mediterranean. I've been getting them now for nearly a year—and it keeps me stirred up and "rarin' to go" most of the time. I want to go to Spain—then Paris—and when things have cooled down there perhaps live in Mexico for a year or so.

My typewriter's on the bum—and I'm just lost. One gets so used to one that you're very dependent. I've been reading little and fretting much—but my eyes are better. Glad you liked Mrs. Simpson's letter. She was good as gold to me—and I have a very high opinion of her—shall always do what I can to liven up the rather bitter monotony of her position there on the Island. Very few people understand—and I suppose if we hadn't been thrown so very close together I shouldn't have discovered so much to love and admire.

By the way—if you really meant what you suggested about sending Mrs. Turner some old things I hope you wont forget about it. Some old house dress—even under wear—you've no idea how tattered and forlorn she looks. It's really kind of hard to look at her. But don't send anything the least bit fancy! You can't imagine how awful that would make her look—she's absolutely toothless and a kind of brownish-grey complexion.

Your last letter was so welcome—and I'm so glad to know you are facing things so bravely. I feel sure that with your recent attitude you'll fare a thousand times better.

There is so little happens here that I *have* to talk about my literary news whether or not it bores you. Last Sunday's N.Y. Times had a fair review of my book along with several others. They often bunch them that way. Then I just got a letter from Wilbur Underwood containing a very nice review from the London Times—it was short, but they don't give much space to any American editions anyway. The Nashville-Tennesseean is running a long review, etc. I may send some of these later—meanwhile don't loose the ones I have already sent. Keep the Frank one . . . Harriet Monroe has bought another section of The Bridge for Poetry, etc. I have lately been travelling on the Mississippi—in that part of The Bridge, I mean.

Spring has turned out to be slower than at first it promised. But I am grateful for what we have. It's at least a month ahead of last year—which was awful! I was leaving here—and that was around May 1st with snow still melting in some parts of the wood. Forgot to mention that Claire looked me up when I was in N.Y. over a month ago. As beautiful as ever—but not very happy. Plenty of money of her own—and was about to leave for a trip to Haiti to paint. Pat has become a Wall Street wizard, etc.

Will write more soon. Lots of love to you both—

Hart

To Allen Tate

Patterson, New York

Dear Allen: March 30

Thanks for *The Times* review. I am looking for *Poetry* review today—and, by the way, Carolyn forgot to enclose the Fletcher letter to the *New Rep*. I'm curious to know what it was about.

It's damned interesting to notice how evident it is that your Foreword set the key—at least to a large extent—for most of Gorman's comments on all six poets reviewed. I consider his comments on *W.B.* quite unexpectedly favorable. What they would have been without your preface is hard to imagine. . . .

I see we have come to the same conclusions about the Aiken debate—and shall leave him in his achin' void! I enclose a remarkable little surprise from the London *Times*. Altogether it's the most satisfying newspaper mention we have had. One wonders who wrote the notice. As for space—they seldom give more to any foreign *editions*. Please don't lose this, as I may want it for quotation—Liveright, I mean.

Altogether, I think this is the last time in our lives to be badly discouraged. The ice is breaking—and I'm beginning to detect many salutary signs. Apparently our ideas and idiom evoke some response—however slow. And what we do win in the way of intellectual territory is *solid*—it can't be knocked over by every wave that comes along—as could Masters, Bodenheim, Lindsay, etc. We wouldn't believe the developements of the next five years if they could be detailed now!

I'm *so* unhappy without a machine. Hope I get my new one soon. Let us know as much beforehand as possible if (and when) you intend coming. We're down to the last crust in the pantry—and no conveyance in sight to get any marketing done.

Love to you both—Hart

To Clarence Arthur Crane

Patterson,
Dear CA: Saturday

I found the old woman all dolled up in a new flaming orange dress she had made—and the cats all with their tails up!

It was good, better even than I expected, to get back, and I slept like a log, hitting the hay about 7:30 Wednesday evening. Next morning I got your note and a telegram from Grace, explaining that the trial had lasted all day Tuesday—was very 'trying'—and that the judge was suspending judgement for several days while he considered the evidence. No further word has since reached me, but I'm expecting something in today's mail.

Your feeling as regards the photomaton proposition was pretty much as I had expected, and I think you are dead right in what you say about dealing with the Isrealites when they have popular commodities for sale. Besides, your new store will be a considerable undertaking and will probably absorb plenty of energy.

I am still thinking about some of the pleasant hours we had together recently. Altogether it was the most satisfactory visit we have ever had together. And this despite the fact that, as I well realize, you were far from gleeful much of the time. If I was able to alleviate, even for only a short period, some of depression that you were struggling under I shall feel very happy —for it is a good thing to be of some use to one's father, especially when he's been so good to me as you have.

I hope you won't change your mind about the Canadian trip, for I think it will do you a world of good to get out of cities for awhile. Be sure to take plenty of woolens, though. We're back to the normal chilly April weather again, at least in these parts. Give my best to Bessie, Freddie, Joe and Sing— and write me soon.

with much love,
Harold

To Yvor Winters

Patterson, New York

Dear Winters: April 29, 1927

I got back here over a week ago, but have hardly yet settled down or managed to collect myself for any thought or occupation. However, I have all summer to plan on, that is, if there isn't too damned much weekending and visiting around the neighborhood. Much talk tires me terribly: and that is what Cleveland and my relatives, sick or well, always accomplish on my visits there!

Yesterday came two delightful Polelonemas. They are already perched on my walls. The female figure seems so far to be the more original, but what lovely feet they both have! Yes, they are truly "seeds no sparrow cracks"—and the kind of thing that time helps you to further appreciate. Your Hartley image was vastly amusing. I've met Hartley a couple of times, admire his painting (mainly for color)—and can readily recognize the amazing physiognomy of the original.

Enclosed are the last two sections of the *Bridge*, parts of which I am still somewhat anxious about, most notably the first page of the "Tunnel." Yet I may have to leave it largely as it is, for the rawness of the subject necessarily demands a certain sort of sensitizing introduction—which, if it savors a little of Eliot and his 'wistfulness', seems nevertheless indispensable toward the fixation or due registration of the subsequent developements of the theme. I flatter myself that I drop off the Eliot mood quite a ways before Chambers Street. And I venture to think that you will like the various throwbacks to Part I, and the Columbus theme.

As for the "Atlantis"—I imagine it to be too subjectively written for me to legitimately explain or condone. It was the first part of the poem to be written—and that in a kind of three-days fit, the memory alone of which is enough to justify it with me. I have later discovered that it contains a number of things like aeronautics, telegraphy, psychoanalysis, atomic theory, relativity, and what not! It aspires a little (perhaps far too much!) to the famous Pater-ian 'frozen music', i.e. it may rely too much on a familiarity with the unique architecture of Brooklyn Bridge, to me the most superb and original example of American architecture yet hinted at, albeit accidentally; and I may have to ask all willing readers to take a walk across same to get the marvellous feeling the webbed cables give (as one advances) of a simultaneous forward and upward motion. In any case "Atlantis" stands or falls as my synthesized vision of the poem as a Whole.

I should perhaps apologize for the apparently affected device of the quotation preceding each section: it is my hope that such a device may possibly alleviate the by-now chronic bewilderment of my *general* reader! Section One has the famous lines from Seneca's Medea (Ultima Thule, etc.); II, the lines quoted from some colonial chronicle about Pocahontas 'wheeling the boyes,' etc.; "Three Songs" takes a line from "Hero & Leander"; and so on. . . . I can hardly resist mentioning that all the place-names in "The Tunnel" actually do exist, and I honestly regard it as something of a miracle that they happened to fall into the same kind of symbolical functioning as the boat-names took in "Cutty Sark."

I have never been to Floral Park nor Gravesend Manor, but

you do actually take the 7th Avenue Interborough to get there, and you change for same at Chambers Street. A boozy truck-driver I used to talk with a good deal in a lowdown dive lived out there, used to talk about the girls 'shaping up,' and finally died at Floral Park, Flatbush. There are some new timbres and tonalities, I think, in the "Tunnel"—at least if I know what nearly maddened me for three years until I got a few of the acid tremors down on paper—if I have!

Don't strain your good will trying to like these sections: I shall be glad if you give me a few shots where the main failings are.

Faithfully yours, Hart Crane

To Wilbur Underwood

Hotel Albert
11th Street & University Place
New York City
Dear Wilbur: Wednesday, May 4, 1927

I think you must have offered the requested Tues. night prayer! At any rate the gods were never so good indeed. I think Apollo himself may have been sojourning in Gob blue—but that aloof rather chilly deity would hardly have qualified so well!

Am leaving for the woods this afternoon. A great time yes-terday afternoon on the U.S.S *Shawmut*, marvelous old Johnny Walker and Bacardi from the officers—such hospitality!

It's nice to be in love again. . . . I haven't your address with me, hence the Patterson postmark. Write soon. Hope you continue to improve.

Hart

To Wilbur Underwood

Patterson, New York
Dear Wilbur: May 12

Indeed it is no wonder you speak of your afflictions! Your letter has haunted me ever since I read it, yesterday. I pray that this is the last trial before a complete recovery. . . . Your experiences and others of my friends and relatives suffice to keep me humble before the sudden day when I, too, shall most surely 'lay my head on the table.' If I find anything which I think you would care to read I'll send it to you from NY. . . .

For I'm going in for the weekend to see Phoebus Apollo again. I quote the close of a letter just received: 'If you are in the city I should like very much to see you. I cannot come to you; for the last silver dollar is squandered and gone. Yet, omnia vincit amor. It is a little life and tomorrow—we may die. Dum vivimus, vivamus. May I see you? A morte, E.'

He is in the quartermasters div. and has brains as well as beauty and—! Dear Wilbur, you must get well and fall in love again!

H

To Yvor Winters

Patterson, New York

Dear Winters: May 29, 1927

You need a good drubbing for all your recent easy talk about 'the complete man', the poet and his ethical place in society, etc. I'm afraid I lack the time right now to attempt what I might call a relatively complete excuse for committing myself to the above sentiments—and I am also encumbered by a good deal of sympathy with your viewpoint in general. Wilson's article was just half-baked enough to make one warm around the collar. It is so damned easy for such as he, born into easy means, graduated from a fashionable university into a critical chair overlooking Washington Square, etc. to sit tight and hatch little squibs of advice to poets not to be so 'professional' as he claims they are, as though all the names he has just mentioned have been as suavely nourished as he—as though 4 out of 5 of them hadn't been damned well forced the major parts of their lives to grub at *any* kind of work they could manage by hook or crook and the fear of hell to secure! Yes, why not step into the State Dept and join the diplomatic corps for a change! indeed, or some other courtly occupation which would bring you into wide and active contact with world affairs! As a matter of fact I'm all too ready to concede that there are several other careers more engaging to follow than that of poetry. But the circumstances of one's birth, the conduct of one's parents, the current economic structure of society and a thousand other local factors have as much or more to say about successions to such occupations, the naive volitions of the poet to the contrary. I agree with you of course, that the poet should in as large a measure as possible adjust himself to society. But the question always will remain as to how far the conscience is justified in compromising with the age's demands.

The image of 'the complete man' is a good idealistic antidote for the horrid hysteria for specialization that inhabits the modern world. And I strongly second your wish for some definite ethical order. Munson, however, and a number of my other friends, not so long ago, being stricken with the same urge, and feeling that something must be done about it— rushed into the portals of the famous Gurdjieff Institute and have since put themselves through all sorts of Hindu antics, songs, dances, incantations, psychic sessions, etc. so that now, presumably the left lobes of their brains and their right lobes respectively function (M's favorite word) in perfect unison. I spent hours at the typewriter trying to explain to certain of these urgent people why I could not enthuse about their methods; it was all to no avail, as I was told that the 'complete man' had a different logic than mine, and further that there was no way of gaining or understanding this logic without first submitting yourself to the necessary training. I was finally left to roll in the gutter of my ancient predispositions, and suffered to receive a good deal of unnecessary pity for my obstinacy. Some of them, having found a good substitute for their former interest in writing by means of more complete formulas of expression have ceased writing now altogether, which is probably just as well. At any rate they have become hermetically sealed souls to my eyesight, and I am really not able to offer judgement.

I am not identifying your advice in any particular way with theirs, for you are certainly logical, so much so that I am inclined to doubt the success of your program even with yourself. Neither do you propose such paradoxical inducements as tea-dansants on Mt Everest! I am only begging the question, after all, and asking you not to judge me too summarily by the shorthand statements that one has to use as the makeshift for the necessary chapters required for more explicit and final explanations. I am suspect, I fear, for equivocating. But I cannot flatter myself into quite as definite recipes for efficiency as you seem to, one reason being, I suppose, that I'm not so ardent an aspirant toward the rather classical characteristics that you cite as desirable. This is not to say that I don't 'envy' the man who attains them, but rather that I have long since abandoned *that* field—and I doubt if I was born to achieve (with the particular vision) those richer syntheses of consciousness which we both agree in classing as supreme; at least the attitude of a Shakespeare or a Chaucer is not mine by organic rights, and why try to fool myself that I possess that type of vision when I obviously do not!

I have a certain code of ethics. I have not as yet attempted to reduce it to any exact formula, and if I did I should probably embark on an endless tome with monthly additions and digressions every year. It seems obvious that a certain decent carriage and action is a paramount concern in any poet, deacon or carpenter. And though I reserve myself the pleasant right to define these standards in a somewhat individual way, and to shout and complain when circumstances against me seem to warrant it, on the other hand I believe myself to be speaking honestly when I say that I have never been able to regret—for long—whatever has happened to me, more especially those decisions which at times have been permitted a free will. (Don't blame me entirely for bringing down all this simplicity on your head—your letter almost solicits it!) And I am as completely out of sympathy with the familiar whimpering caricature of the artist and his 'divine rights' as you seem to be. I am not a Stoic, though I think I could lean more in that direction if I came to (as I may sometime) appreciate more highly the imaginative profits of such a course.

You put me in altogether too good company, you compliment me much too highly for me to offer the least resistance to your judgements on the structure of my work. I think I am quite unworthy of such associates as Marlowe or Valery—except in some degree, perhaps, 'by kind'. If I can avoid the pearly gates long enough I may do better. Your fumigation of the Leonardo legend is a healthy enough reaction, but I don't think your reasons for doubting his intelligence and scope very potent. —I've never closely studied the man's attainments or biography, but your argument is certainly weakly enough sustained on the sole prop of his sex—or lack of such. One doesn't have to turn to homosexuals to find instances of missing sensibilities. Of course I'm sick of all this talk about balls and cunts in criticism. It's obvious that balls are needed, and that Leonardo had 'em—at least the records of the Florentine prisons, I'm told, say so. You don't seem to realize that the whole topic is something of a myth anyway, and is consequently modified in the characteristics of the image by each age in each civilization. Tom Jones, a character for whom I have the utmost affection, represented the model in 18th Century England, at least so far as the stated requirements of your letter would suggest, and for an Anglo-Saxon model he is still pretty good aside from calculus, the Darwinian theory, and a few other mental additions. Incidentally I think Tom Jones (Fielding himself, of course) represents a much more 'balanced' attitude toward society and life in general than our friend, Thomas Hardy. Hardy's profundity is real, but it is voiced in pretty much one monotonous key. I think him perhaps the greatest technician in English verse since Shakespeare. He's a great poet and a mighty man. But you must be fanatic to feel that he fulfils the necessary 'balanced ration' for modern consumption. Not one of his characters is for one moment allowed to express a single joyous passion without a forenote of Hardian doom entering the immeadiate description. Could Hardy create anything like Falstaff? I think that Yeats would be just as likely—more so.

That's what I'm getting at . . . I don't care to be credited with too wholesale ambitions, for as I said, I realize my limitations, and have already partially furled my flag. The structural weaknesses which you find in my work are probably quite real, for I could not ask for a more meticulous and sensitive reader. It is my hope, of course, not only to improve my statement but to extend scope and viewpoint as much as possible. But I cannot trust to so methodical and predetermined a method of developement, not by any means, as you recommend. Nor can I willingly permit you to preserve the assumption that I am seeking any 'shortcuts across the circle', nor willfully excluding any experience that seems to me significant. You seem to think that experience is some commodity—that can be sought! One can respond only to certain circumstances, just what the barriers are, and where the boundaries cross can never be completely known. And the surest way to frustrate the possibility of any free realization is, it seems to me, to willfully direct it. I can't help it if you think me aimless and irresponsible. But try and see if you get such logical answers from Nature as you seem to think you will! My 'alert blindness' was a stupid ambiguity to use in any definition—but it seems to me you go in for just about as much 'blind alertness' with some of your expectations.

If you knew how little of a metaphysician I am in the scholastic sense of the term you would scarcely attribute such a conscious method to my poems (with regard to that element) as you do. I am an utter ignoramus in that whole subject, have never read Kant, Descartes or other doctors. It's all an accident so far as my style goes. It happens that the first poem I ever wrote was too dense to be understood, and I now find that I can trust most critics to tell me that all my subsequent efforts have been equally futile. Having heard that one writes in a metaphysical vein the usual critic will immediately close his eyes or stare with utter complacency at the page—assuming that black is black no more and that the poet means anything but what he says. It's as plain as day that I'm talking about war and aeroplanes in the passage from "F & H" (corymbulous formations of mechanics, etc) quoted by Wilson in the *New Republic*, yet by isolating these lines from the context and combining them suddenly with lines from a totally different poem he has the chance (and uses it) to make me sound like a perfect ninny. If I'd said that they were Fokker planes then maybe the critic would have had to notice the vitality of the metaphor and its pertinence. All this ranting seems somehow necessary. . . . If I am metaphysical I'm content to continue so. Since I have been 'located' in this category by a number of people I may as well go on alluding to certain (what are also called) metaphysical passages in Donne, Blake, Vaughan, etc. as being of particular appeal to me on a basis of common characteristics with what I like to do in my own poems, however little scientific knowledge of the subject I may have.

I write damned little because I am interested in recording certain sensations, very rigidly chosen, with an eye for what according to my taste and sum of prejudices seems suitable to— or intense enough—for verse. If I were writing in prose, as I sometime shall probably do, I should probably include a much thicker slice of myself—and though it is the height of conceit for me to suggest it, I venture to say that you may have received a somewhat limited idea of my interests and responses by judging me from my poems alone. I suppose that in regard to this limitation of poetic focus one should consult the current position of poetry in relation to other intellectual and political characteristics of the time, including a host of psychological factors which may or may not promote the fullest flowering of a particular medium such as verse. I am not apologizing. Nor am I trying to penetrate beyond a certain point into such labyrinths of conjecture and analysis. It seems unprofitable. One should be somewhat satisfied if one's work comes to approximate a true record of such moments of 'illumination' as are occasionally possible. A sharpening of reality accessible to the poet, to no such degree possible through other mediums. That is one reason above all others—why I shall never expect (or indeed desire) *complete* sympathy from any writer of such originality as yourself. I may have neglected to say that I admire your general attitude, including your distrust of metaphysical or other patent methods. Watch out, though, that you don't strangulate yourself with some countermethod of your own!

Best wishes, Hart Crane

To Grace Hart Crane

Patterson, NY
Dearest: June 18th, 1927
I'm enclosing a fragment of the Bridge, part of the River section that I'm working on now, the end of it, in fact, where you suddenly find yourself adrift on the vast flow of the Mississippi. I think it one of the finest things I've written, and I think

you will enjoy the epic sweep of the thing—like a great river of time that takes everything and pours it into a great abyss. After this comes a great Indian dance which I wrote on the Island but which is too long for me to take time to copy now. The Dial has taken it. The Brooklyn Bridge dedication is out this month, in the June Dial.

I've been so pleased to hear about the divorce terms, though a little sorry that they could not have covered a longer period than two years. But I'm sure that Payer has done everything possible. I shall write Payer soon and thank him, without revealing any exact knowledge of the terms, or violating your tact.

I am glad that you have a location where you can have a view of trees and some natural scenery. Just now my hay-fever is unexpectedly bad for this locality, and I'd just as soon not have so much 'natural scenery'—nor tall grass either! I am immensely surprized that Ted Robinson should have noticed me. Yes, send the clipping on; and also the notices you have never returned which I left with you on my visit. Please remember them before they get lost! CA sent me the amusing Press clipping. It was a better ad for him than for me, and of that I was genuinely glad. I think his vanity is becoming a little tickled.

I wish you would give Bess, Byron and the rest of the Crane family my best when you see them. I don't get time to write these days, but I often think of them. The same might be said to Grandma. But all my letters to you—include her too, of course. Can't you make me a visit before the job begins?

Love ever,
Hart

To Clarence Arthur Crane

Patterson,

Dear Father: June 21, 1927

We have just had a long twenty-four hours of rainfall, and it being Sunday besides, I'm in one of those rather bluish hazes that such conditions usually induce. Besides I'm itching, tickling and sneezing incessantly with the fever, always worst in damp weather. When I get through my present enterprise I'm in for a life on the sea. I'd rather swab decks than keep on swabbing my face all the time!

I don't wonder that business is depressed. For over a month we haven't heard, read, eaten or been permitted to dream anything but airplanes and Lyndberg. After reading a good deal about it I've decided that the world is quite mad. I'm sure it will take months for people to get their eyes out of the sky and their necks uncrooked and back to their stomachs. Time and Space is the myth of the modern world, however, and it's interesting to see how any victory in that field is heralded by the mass of humanity. In a way my Bridge is a manifestation of the same general subject. Maybe I'm just a little jealous of Lindy!

Canary Cottage is a fine name for the Inn, much better than the Nest, which I wasn't particularly enthusiastic about, if you noticed. I'm glad that you've got a line on a good caretaker and hostess. There's no particular news here, either, but I'll write again soon anyway. The old woman is all up in the air with expectancy now that the chocolates are on the way!

With love always,
Harold

To Grace Hart Crane and Elizabeth Belden Hart

Patterson, N.Y.

Dear Grace and Grandma: July 4th, 1927

The date carries me back to the Fourth on the Island last summer, when I felt pretty lonely and dejected. I certainly feel a lot better these days, even though I haven't any beer to add to my sorrows (and joys!). It looks as though it were going to be a pretty dry Fourth up here with not only myself but all my friends. No firecrackers—no firewater, not even Crane's chocolates, although after my third mention of it, CA wrote a few days ago that he had sent some on.

I'm especially happy lately on account of having finished up one of the long sections of the Bridge which has been bothering me for a long time, the difficulties seemed unsurmountable. I enclose it for you to read. What I'm trying to do is tell the pioneer experience of our forefathers in terms of the present, and finally via the hobos get back to an entrance into the original world of the American Indian, symbolized by Poca-hontas. The hobos are really just "psychological ponies" to carry the reader along without mention of mares and prairie schooners, etc. I think I do it pretty smoothly, so that the reader is really led back to the primal physical body of America (Pocahontas) and finally to the central pulse and artery, the Mississippi. The description of that great river of time is one of the statliest things I've done, I think. Read it carefully, and tell me what you think of it. The introductory speedy vaude-ville stuff (what comes before the line beginning "The last bear . . ." is a kind of take-off on all the journalism, adver-tising, and loud-speaker stuff of the day.

I'm looking forward to a letter from you in the mail that takes this. Miss Gracie hasn't written her son for quite awhile, and I'm wondering what new things she is up to. As for me— I have so little news beyond my day-to-day writing (and I think about little else) that it's no wonder I write you scantily. I'm in a heated spell of brain fever again, and hope I can keep in it for awhile, for that's the way I was during that great month of work last summer down on the island. Which re-minds me that you must write Mrs Simpson soon. It's not fair to neglect her kindnesses. She wrote me recently—was awfully poor and tired—and as usual said she could get no answer whatever from you, despite several urgent proposals she had submitted to you.

It's awfully hot in Cleveland, I hear. But around here we still have a comforter on the bed every night. Let me know the new Payer developments, and write soon.

Love always,
Hart

To Mrs. T. W. Simpson

Patterson, New York

Dear Aunt Sally: July 4, 1927

Sunshine and a certain amount of heat seem to stimulate me to writing, that is, judging by the intensive work I did on the Island with you last summer, and by the returned activity I've been having lately. We haven't had any particularly hot weather, but it's been warm enough to sweat a little, and that seems to be good for me. As a little evidence of my activities I'm enclosing a new section of *The Bridge*, called "The River." It comes between "Van Winkle" which I sent you in the last letter and "The Indian Dance" which you are familiar with.

I'm trying in this part of the poem to chart the pioneer experience of our forefathers—and to tell the story backwards, as it were, on the 'backs' of hobos. These hobo's are simply 'psychological ponies' to carry the reader across the country and back to the Mississippi, which you will notice is described as a great River of Time. I also unlatch the door to the pure Indian world which opens out in the "Dance" section, so the reader is gradually led back in time to the pure savage world, while existing at the same time in the present. It has been a very complicated thing to do, and I think I have worked harder and longer on this section of the *Bridge* than any other.

You'll find your name in it. I kind of wanted you in this section of the book, and if you don't have any objections, you'll stay in the book. For you are my idea of the salt of all pioneers, and our little talks about New Orleans, etc. led me to think of you with the smile of Louisiana. I continue in a kind of 'heat' —and I may have another section or so finished up before August. I sure want to get it *all* done by December.

Well, here it is the Fourth again. I keep thinking of last year at this time. I guess my ears were about healed by that time, but I was still in a blue funk, and I remember how I went to town and after four or five Tropicals came home again and read. We aren't having much of any celebration up hear this year. The Browns are rather broke, and so am I—neither of us able to indulge in either firecrackers or firewater to any extent. Eleanor Fitzgerald is going to give a little levee down at her place, however, and maybe there will be some cider.

I got a card from NY the other day saying that my old jack tar friend, Jack Fitzin, was back from his long trip in European waters, so I just piked in and saw him! He was standing up on the forward deck when I saw him from the pier head, and after taking me all over the ship (a destroyer) we had a very pleasant evening, taking in a movie on hunting in a jungle, full of marvelous tiger close-ups and elephant stampedes.

Your last news sounds as though the Island had become

pretty depopulated. Are all the old saloons still there? You made my mouth simply water telling about your party and the 14 'dead soldiers.' I do hope you succeed in selling your place. Then you must come up here and make me a visit. I nearly went up when you spoke of Mrs (Bull) Durham still vainly trying to make up her mind about her baggage and the next boat! She's harmless, but buggy as a bat, I'm sure.

I get very little news from Cleveland. But from all I have heard mother and grandma are both fairly well. They have moved into a new apartment, but I guess I mentioned that change as well as the address in my last. I have stopped writing anything whatever to mother about the Island and the Island property, because I don't get any more return comment from her on that subject than you seem to get. She doesn't seem to be able to get her mind settled on any matters relating to that problem, I don't understand why, but I'm sure of this, and I hope you will believe me—she hasn't anything but gratitude to you for all you have done, and certainly entertains the most friendly sort of sentiments toward you constantly.

I can't make out yet whether Leffingwell is actually living at House house or not. Of course, I feel sure that grandmother would like to sell the place, even at a very moderate sum, but if they won't write, they won't, I s'pose. If I only had the title to the place!

I can't get over thinking how sweet it was of you to sell the four copies of *White Bldgs*. Did they arrive alright from the publisher? If they didn't I will see to it that they do! I somehow think of you as being out on the Golfo de Batabano today in a sailboat. Am I right? How I should like to be on the water! The sea's the only place for me, with my *nose*. I'm just getting a little over my spring attack of hayfever now. And the next session begins before September.

Sorry to hear that Mrs Jones isn't so well. Please give them both my best. By the way, if you have any extra pictures of the Hart house for me to look at you might stick one or two in your next letter. I'm sorry I didn't take more when I was there. Your idea about shipping the books, etc. when you leave the island is fine and suits me perfectly.

Love always, Aunt Sally, Hart

Wish I could read "The River" out loud to you as I used to do last summer! Too damned bad the hurricane came—I liked my little study room there so much, with the mango tree to look at through the back window. . . . I achieved some triumphs in that little room.

To Yvor Winters

Patterson, New York

Dear Winters: July 18, 1927

I can't tell you how your praise and approbation heartens me! Believe me, though, when I call myself most fortunate in having a reader who simply gets everything on the page! My expression is so limited today, due to a cyder spree with friends yesterday, that I'm not attempting much of a letter. I'll try to do better anon when I'm more 'assembled'. Meanwhile it is not my intention to allow you the least bit of rest!

Here is the corrected version of "The Air Plant," as well as two other pieces recently written and belonging to the Carib suite that I've been meditating. (It's rather good to get off *The Bridge* for awhile). Two remain to be written, but I think I'll group them together under the common title of "The Hurricane," beginning with

> "O Carib Isle!"
> "Quarry"
> "The Air Plant"
> "Royal Palm"
> "The Idiot" (still to be written)
> & "Eternity" (a description of the ruins)

with maybe one or two more items, as my tropical memories dictate.

I tried "The River" on *The Dial*, but it came back. Am trying *The Nation* now, where it will probably evoke just plain bewilderment. Glad to hear about your book. I want to write a review of it for *transition*, but I make such a mess of things whenever I try to formulate any sort of formal criticism! If I can't leave you as clean and direct as you are it'll go into the wastebasket.

all best, Hart Crane

To Wilbur Underwood

Patterson, New York
Dear Wilbur: August 17, 1927

Thanks again for the *Times*—which came today. It is so cool here these days that I'm wondering if even torrid Washington is milder than usual at this time of the year. For I think of you in that hot oven in the State Dept.

All my activities can be summed up in a few lines of verse—and then not very good. Nothing happens here but a cider party now and then with neighboring friends and a few games of croquet. It's no use to tell you how futile I feel most of the time—no matter what I do or conceive doing, even. Part of the disease of the modern consciousness, I suppose. There is no standard of values in the modern world—it's mostly slop, priggishness and sentimentality. One had much better be a wild man in Borneo and at least have a clear and unabashed love for the sight of blood.

Well, I'm looking around for a job in New York again—though when I'll find one remains to be guessed. I wouldn't stay here another winter alone in a heatless house with an old hag and her two cats even though I could afford to.

Have you read Doughty's *Arabia Deserta*? That and books of exploration and West Indian travel have been my summer reading.

Do write me how you are—despite my dull returns.

Love ever, Hart

To Otto H. Kahn

Patterson, New York
Dear Mr. Kahn: September 12, 1927

I am taking for granted your continued interest in the progress of *The Bridge*, in which I am still absorbed, and which has reached a stage where its general outline is clearly evident. The dedication (recently published in *The Dial*) and Part I (now in *The American Caravan*) you have already seen, but as you may not have them presently at hand I am including them in a ms. of the whole, to date, which I am sending you under separate cover.

At the risk of complicating your appreciation of Part II ("Powhatan's Daughter"), I nevertheless feel impelled to mention a few of my deliberate intentions in this part of the poem, and to give some description of my general method of construction. Powhatan's daughter, or Pocahontas, is the mythological nature-symbol chosen to represent the physical body of the continent, or the soil. She here takes on much the same rôle as the traditional Hertha of ancient Teutonic mythology. The five sub-sections of Part II are mainly concerned with a gradual exploration of this 'body' whose first possessor was the Indian. It seemed altogether ineffective, from the poetic standpoint, to approach this material from the purely chronological historic angle—beginning with, say the landing of *The Mayflower*, continuing with a resumé of the Revolution through the conquest of the West, etc. One can get that viewpoint in any history primer. What I am after is an assimilation of this experience, a more organic panorama, showing the continuous and living evidence of the past in the inmost vital substance of the present.

Consequently I jump from the monologue of Columbus in "Ave Maria"—right across the four intervening centuries— into the harbor of 20th-century Manhattan. And from that point in time and place I begin to work backward through the pioneer period, always in terms of the present—finally to the very core of the nature-world of the Indian. What I am really handling, you see, is the Myth of America. Thousands of strands have had to be searched out, sorted and interwoven. In a sense I have had to do a good deal of pioneering myself. It has taken a great deal of energy—which has not been so difficult to summon as the necessary patience to wait, simply wait much of the time—until my instincts assured me that I had assembled my materials in proper order for a final welding into their natural form. For each section of the entire poem has represented its own unique problem of form, not alone in relation to the materials embodied within its separate confines, but also in relation to the other parts, *in series*, of the major design of the entire poem. Each is a separate canvas, as it were, yet none yields its entire significance when seen apart from the others. One might take the Sistine Chapel as an analogy. It might be better to read the following notes *after* rather than before your reading of the ms. They are not necessary for an understanding of the poem, but I think they may prove interesting to you as a commentary on my architectural method.

1. "The Harbor Dawn":

Here the movement of the verse is in considerable contrast to that of the Ave Maria, with its sea-swell crescendo and the climacteric vision of Columbus. This legato, in which images blur as objects only half apprehended on the border of sleep and consciousness, makes an admirable transition between the intervening centuries.

The love-motif (in italics) carries along a symbolism of the life and ages of man (here the sowing of the seed) which is further developed in each of the subsequent sections of "Powhatan's Daughter," though it is never particularly stressed. In 2 ("Van Winkle") it is Childhood; in 3 it is Youth; in 4, Manhood; in 5 it is Age. This motif is interwoven and tends to be implicit in the imagery rather than anywhere stressed.

2. "Van Winkle":

The protagonist has left the room with its harbor sounds, and is walking to the subway. The rhythm is quickened; it is a transition between sleep and the immanent tasks of the day. Space is filled with the music of a hand organ and fresh sunlight, and one has the impression of the whole continent— from Atlantic to Pacific—freshly arisen and moving. The walk to the subway arouses reminiscences of childhood, also the 'childhood' of the continental conquest, viz., the conquistadores, Priscilla, Capt. John Smith, etc. These parallelisms unite in the figure of Rip Van Winkle who finally becomes identified with the protagonist, as you will notice, and who really boards the subway with the reader. He becomes the 'guardian angel' of the journey into the past.

3. "The River":

The subway is simply a figurative, psychological 'vehicle' for transporting the reader to the Middle West. He lands on the railroad tracks in the company of several tramps in the twilight. The extravagance of the first twenty-three lines of this section is an intentional burlesque on the cultural confusion of the present—a great conglomeration of noises analogous to the strident impression of a fast express rushing by. The rhythm is jazz.

Thenceforward the rhythm settles down to a steady pedestrian gait, like that of wanderers plodding along. My tramps are psychological vehicles, also. Their wanderings as you will notice, carry the reader into interior after interior, finally to the great River. They are the leftovers of the pioneers in at least this respect—that their wanderings carry the reader through an experience parallel to that of Boone and others. I think I have caught some of the essential spirit of the Great Valley here, and in the process have approached the primal world of the Indian, which emerges with a full orchestra in the succeeding dance.

4. "The Dance":

Here one is on the pure mythical and smoky soil at last! Not only do I describe the conflict between the two races in this dance—I also become identified with the Indian and his world before it is over, which is the only method possible of ever really possessing the Indian and his world as a cultural factor. I think I really succeed in getting under the skin of this glorious and dying animal, and in terms of expression, in symbols, which he himself would comprehend. Pocahontas (the continent) is the common basis of our meeting, she survives the extinction of the Indian, who finally, after being assumed into the elements of nature (as he understood them) persists only as a kind of 'eye' in the sky, or as a star that hangs between day and night—'the twilight's dim perpetual throne.'

5. "Indiana":

I regret that this section is not completed as yet. It will be the monologue of an Indiana farmer; time, about 1860. He has failed in the gold-rush and is returned to till the soil. His monologue is a farewell to his son, who is leaving for a life on the sea. It is a lyrical summary of the period of conquest, and his wife, the mother who died on the way back from the gold-rush, is alluded to in a way which implies her succession to the nature-symbolism of Pocahontas. I have this section well nigh done, but there is no use including in the present ms. without the final words.

The next section, "Cutty Sark", is a phantasy on the period of the whalers and clipper ships. It also starts in the present and 'progresses backwards'. The form of the poem may seem erratic, but it is meant to present the hallucinations incident to rum-drinking in a South Street dive, as well as the lurch of a boat in heavy seas, etc. So I allow myself something of the same freedom which E.E. Cummings often uses.

"Cutty Sark" is built on the plan of a *fugue*. Two 'voices'— that of the world of Time, and that of the world of eternity—are interwoven in the action. The Atlantis theme (that of Eternity) is the transmuted voice of the nickel-slot pianola, and this voice alternates with that of the derelict sailor and the description of the action. The airy regatta of phantom clipper ships seen from Brooklyn Bridge on the way home is quite effective, I think. It was a pleasure to use historical names for these lovely ghosts. Music still haunts their names long after the wind has left their sails.

"Cape Hatteras," which follows, is unfinished. It will be a kind of ode to Whitman. I am working as much as possible on it now. It presents very formidable problems, as indeed, all the sections have. I am really writing an epic of the modern consciousness, and indescribably complicated factors have to be resolved and blended . . . I don't wish to tire you with too extended an analysis of my work, and so shall leave the other completed sections to explain themselves. In the ms., where the remaining incomplete sections occur, I am including a rough synopsis of their respective themes, however. The range of *The Bridge* has been called colossal by more than one critic who has seen the ms. And though I have found the subject to be vaster than I had at first realized, I am still highly confident of its final articulation into a continuous and eloquent span. Already there are evident signs of recognition: the following magazines have taken various sections:

Dedication: "To Brooklyn Bridge"	*The Dial*
"Ave Maria"	*The American Caravan*
"The Harbor Dawn"	*transition* (Paris)
"Van Winkle"	"
"The River"	*The Virginia Quarterly*
"The Dance"	*The Dial*
"Cutty Sark"	*Poetry* (Chicago)
"Three Songs"	*The Calendar* (London)
"The Tunnel"	*The Criterion* (London)

(I have been especially gratified by the reception accorded me by *The Criterion*, whose director, Mr. T. S. Eliot, is representative of the most exacting literary standards of our times.)

For some time past I have been seeking employment in New York, but without success so far. It's the usual problem of mechanical prejudices that I've already grown grey in trying to deal with. But all the more difficult now, since the only references I can give for the last two years are my own typewriter and a collection of poems. I am, as you will probably recall, at least avowedly—a perfectly good advertising writer. I am wondering if you would possibly give me some recommendation to the publicity department of The Metropolitan Opera Company, where I am certain of making myself useful. I was in New York two days last week, trying to secure employment as a waiter on one of the American lines. I found that I needed something like a diploma from Annapolis before hoping for an interview. A few years ago I registered with the Munson Line with reference to my qualifications for a particular position which every ship includes—that of 'ship's writer', or 'deck yeoman'; but I always found that such jobs were dispensed to acquaintances of the captain or to office workers, and that my references were never taken from the file. I am not particular what I do, however, so long as there is reasonable chance of my doing it well, and any recommendation you might care to offer in any practical direction whatever will be most welcome. My present worried state of mind practically forbids any progress on *The Bridge*, the chances for which are considerably better under even greatly limited time conditions.

I am still assured of a definite inheritance, previously mentioned in my first letter to you; and if you care to consider advancing me, say 800 or 1,000 dollars, on the same basis of insurance security as your previous assistance I should be glad to come into New York and talk it over. There is no monetary standard of evaluation for works of art, I know, but I cannot help feeling that a great poem may well be worth at least the expenditure necessary for merely the scenery and costumes of many a flashy and ephemeral play, or the cost of an ordinary motor car . . . *The Aeneid* was not written in two years—nor in four, and in more than one sense I feel justified in comparing the historic and cultural scope of *The Bridge* to that great work. It is at least a symphony with an epic theme, and a work of considerable profundity and inspiration. Even with the torturing heat of my sojourn in Cuba I was able to work faster than before or since then, in America. The 'foreign-ness' of my surroundings stimulated me to the realization of natively American materials and viewpoints in myself not hitherto suspected, and in one month I was able to do more work than I had done in the three previous years. If I could work in Mexico or Spain this winter I could have *The Bridge* finished by next spring. But that is a speculation which depends entirely on your interest.

Please pardon the inordinate length of this letter. I shall, of course, hope to hear from you regarding your impressions of the poem as it now stands. Along with the ms. I am enclosing three critical articles which may interest you to see.

Believe me, with all good wishes,

Sincerely yours, Hart Crane

To Wilbur Underwood

Dear Wilbur:

You've possibly wondered at my "quietude." However, I've been anything but quiet in the other senses of the word. Everywhere and nowhere: out to Cleveland to see my mother and grandmother off for Los Angeles, then back to the country, then, finally, here. You may remember the house. You were here at tea time one afternoon about three years ago. I am glad to find quarters in the old houses—anything else in NY gives me the creeps.

Kahn recently gave me a little more, and I was already to embark for Martinique (where champagne is only a dollar a quart—and where truly golden Carib primitives abound) but family worries too complicated to explain made it seem useless to attempt—at least for the present—any sort of creative work, far or near. So—and I think I've been lucky—I've found a little job working in a bookshop on 57th St. I'll try to hold my little 'nest egg' together meanwhile, and maybe later kick the traces. For you know I'm none too much in love with civilization, especially the 18th amendment!

I am wondering how you are. Your thoughtfulness of me is more than I deserve. I refer to the papers which you send and which I always enjoy reading. Recently I wrote a letter (perhaps you recall your suggestion) to Jimmy Foster at the address you gave, suggesting that we meet. Perhaps he has moved. Anyway I have had no answer. Are you planning on a NY visit next month! Let me know. I hope to see more of you than before.

Affectionately, Hart

To Susan Jenkins and William Slater Brown

Columbia Heights
November 16, 1927
alias 2160 Mar Vista Avenue
Dear Bill & Susie: Altadena, Cal.

Traintime approaches, but I hope life does not continue to grow accordingly more hectic, as has been the rule so far! Several times I have all but lost my ticket, presented several days ago. Notably Tues. night in jail. . .

After a riotous competition with Cummings and Anne in which (I don't *know* but I'm sure) I won the cocktail contest I found myself in the Clark St. station along about 3 o'clock playing with somebody's lost airdale. The cop who rushed at me, asking me what I was doing is reported to have been answered by "why the hell do you want to know?!!!" in a loud tone of voice, wherat I was yanked into a taxi and was sped to the station (slyly and en route tossing all evidence such as billets doux, dangerous addresses. etc out the window) and the next I knew the door crashed shut and I found myself behind the bars. I imitated Chaliapin fairly well until dawn leaked in. or rather such limited evidences of same as six o'clock whistles and the postulated press of dirty feet to early coffee stands.

I was good and mad. Made an impassioned speech to a crowded court room, and was released at 10 o'clock without even a fine. Beer with Cummings in the afternoon which was almost better than evening before, as C's hyperbole is even more amusing than one's conduct, especially when he undertakes a description of what you don't remember. Anyhow, I never had so much fun jounced into 24 hours before, and if I had my way would take both C'gs and Anne along with me to heaven when I go.

The Breughel is a belated wedding memento which I hope will bring warmth to your lips and a smile to your hearts occasionally. Had dinner with Isidor and Helen last night—who asked to be remembered. I don't know your new address, so you must write me soon and let me know. Mine is included above.

Love, Hart

To Yvor Winters

2160 Mar Vista Avenue
Altadena, California
November 23, 1927

Dear Winters:

Ye Gods! what a pink vacuum this place around here is! I just arrived day before yesterday, and already I'm beginning to wish I had jumped off the train around Albuquerque. I sort of sensed it at the time—and almost did. The hybrid circumstances of my immeadiate environment make it all the worse: a millionaire neurotic (nice as he is) with valet, chauffeur, gardener, and all the rest. This house seems to be all bath rooms and bad furniture, about which my boss suffers about as much as I do, but apparently the president of the American Express, who rented it to him, isn't afflicted by anything. I have already limousined around enough to wince at the 'sculptural' advertising which you mentioned. If the bull that advertises some eating place were only a bit more gilded, not to say gelded, I'd approve of that one piece, however, as a symbol at least, of the whole shebang. Did some one say Spanish architecture?!!!!

I won't promise not to blow off more steam before seeing you—when you'll get aplenty—but this will do for now. I'll try to keep the home fires burning somewhere within me without exploding and thereby losing my job. They say that work is hard to find in California . . .

Yes, I went to see Elizabeth Madox Roberts. It was certainly worth while, and she was most cordial, though I never felt that society could torture any human being so much before without intending to. I thought of a sibyl writhing on a tripod. No one, with any amount of deliberation, could have so taken the part. But I doubt if I should have remained any longer than I did, regardless of a previous engagement that took me away within a half hour. We talked about you, California, her book. This latter I had hurriedly read a day or so before meeting her. There is no doubt about its permanence as a major accomplishment. And one feels the sense of form, a relentless pattern, from the 20th page or so right on to the terrific torture of the climax—and then the beautiful 'dying fall', the unforgettable pathos of the obscene inscriptions in the w.c. It's a marvellous book. But I don't think it necessarily diminishes the stature of *Ulysses*. It's range is more limited, and its intentions are different. Formally, yes, of course—it *is* more solid. Such debates are useless, however, with our present lack of any absolute critical logos.

I'm a bit muddled, and may remain so for awhile, especially as my situation demands a good deal of egg-stepping here. But I'll do my best to avoid boring you, and with the avid hope that you will support me to some extent by whatever rages, deliberations, constatations, etc. may seem worth while putting on paper for the nonce or otherwise. I ordered your book from Four Seas months ago; has it come out yet?

Faithfully, Hart Crane

To Yvor Winters

2160 Mar Vista Avenue
Altadena, California
December 8

Dear Winters:

I am anticipating your Christmas visit a great deal. Please do get in touch with me right away on your arrival: phone *Niagara 2684*. I have just located a court near here, where, if I am a great deal improved in my technique by that time, we may possibly have a game or so. Right now I'm lamentable.

This locale is certainly growing on me. No, I'm not turning

up my nose. For one thing I've been too much out of breath! Movie studios have so far occupied a good deal of the time, mainly owing to my boss's curiosity in that direction. And I've looked up a couple of minor constellations (Alice Calhoun and Robert Graves) whom I used to know in school in Cleveland. Your kind introductions have been unemployed so far—simply owing to the rush. The world is small . . . Ran into a very pleasant fellow who used to know Tate at Vanderbilt, etc. Meanwhile I'm becoming gradually accustomed to the formalities of a broker's household. AND begin to worry a little about having too good a time—that is for the approbation of the muses.

But I have at least read his copies of Richard's *Principles*— and Weston's *Ritual to Romance*. The former is damned good. I look forward to a detailed talk with you about it. The latter is especially interesting as revealing to me my unconscious use in the *Bridge* of a number of time-honored symbols. Wise (my boss) has a substantial enough stack of good things to read to keep me busy for some time.

I'm enclosing a review of *W.B.* which was a good while getting to me, but which opened a slight correspondence between author and critic, which, if I ever go to Spain for a visit, may be profitable. Marichalar writes the Madrid letter for the *Criterion*. Perhaps you're already familiar with his work,— prolog to the trans of Joyce's *Portrait*—, etc. I had Macauley send him a copy of the *Am. Caravan*, which, he says, interests him very much. I hope later to see what he writes about it in the *Revista de Occidente*. Please don't lose this clipping. I had to correct him about the Statue of Liberty. That was a gift from the great Republique Francaise, you know!

All best to you—Crane

To William Slater Brown

Breaker Club, Santa Monica, California

Dear Bill: Monday, December 19, 1927

Yes, one can hear the sea seven flights below—and I've been walking on the beach most of the day. The boss, finding that I didn't get along any too well with some of his Hollywood weekend guests, advised me taking a vacation and with means happily provided here I am until tomorrow night. Wall Street seems to carry a slight oppression and madness with it wherever it "extends." It has been good to come over here where places are rather deserted of crowds and hear the gulls cry overhead and watch the solemn pelicans eye you awhile and then hawl up their legs and sprawl into the air.

Viennese cooking with cavier and port every night for dinner is playing hell with my waistline—and I sleep as never before, excepting the cradle. One can't seem to wake up out here without the spur of scotch or gin. There has been plenty of that—in fact last Saturday night I danced the "Gotzottski" right on Main St., Los Angeles, while Chuck Short, an aviator from Riverside and a Kentuckian danced the Highland Fling or as good an imitation of it as he could manage. This after having invaded the Biltmore ballroom and dancing with fair ladies of the haute mondaine. Albeit—and having got our waiter drunk and having left in high dudgeon—I don't think I'll dare attend their supper club again.

After a good deal of "sailing" since arriving here—I am now convinced that "flying" is even better. Right now however—and until next week-end—I am "all fives" on the ground and life can run as high as it wants to over in our villa without my batting an eye. And it *is* running high, I can tell you; that's why I'm here just now . . . I never could stand much falsetto, you know.

God! you never know who you're meeting out here . . . First there was a snappy collegiate hanging around the studios, who turned out to know Allen—and then today on the beach a mile below here, at Venice, I found myself talking literature, Spengler, Kant, Descartes and Aquinas—to say nothing of Maurras and Massis—to a Bostonian of French descent who knows Stewart Mitchell, and especially his aunt, very well! He turned out to be one of the best scholars I've ever met—a great reactionary toward the same kind of classicism that Eliot and Lewis are fostering in England. I had him spotted as a Romanist in less than five minutes—but he wouldn't admit it until we parted. The dialectic we had was more rousing than the aforesaid tonic combustions of alcohol, I admit.

Winters and wife will be here visiting relatives during Christmas week—and I look forward to that as a real event. Really, it's terribly dull having so many servants around, so much food, so much tiptoeing and ceremony. But it takes some of these Hollywood fays to revolutionize all that. Whoops! and whoops again, dearie, and then more warbling, more whiskey and broken crockery and maybe broken necks, for all I know, when I get back and view the ruins! (and please be kind enough to burn this page). The present "star" was once "Ariel" in the *Tempest*—and though she still makes the welkin ring I fear her voice will never do again. She has adopted the pronoun "we" to signalize her slightest thought, whim or act—and her conceit was so wounded on spying my "Chaplinesque" during her drunken and exclamatory rampage through *Edificios Blancos*—that she nearly passed out and insisted on the spot that I make instant amends by composing a sonnet to her superb P.A. (Hollywood shorthand for "physical attraction") as displayed in her erstwhile success in *Peter Pan*. Hence here I am by the sea—and mightily pleased—until the storm subsides.

My Spanish quotation from Slater Brown reminds me that I now have Joyce's *Artista Adolescente*—a translation sent me by Marichalar who wrote a very interesting introduction. He was greatly interested in *Caravan* and is going to review it in *Rivista de Occidente*. I must get started at my Spanish again. Richards' *Principles of Literary Criticism* is a *great* book. One of the few—perhaps the only one in English excepting stray remarks by Coleridge—that gets to bedrock. Weston's book, *From Ritual to Romance* was quite fascinating—but Winters claims that scholars regard half her data and deductions a imaginative bunk. Did I speak to you about Elizabeth Maddox Roberts' new book—*My Heart and Flesh*—before? Anyway, I hope you'll read it. I think it a great performance.

Poor Addie! I got a most doleful letter from her not long ago—but she seemed to see *some* light in the improbable possibility of joining you in Bernardsville. I hope that plan will materialize. And how is Sue? Wish she would write when there isn't anything else better to do.

I'm glad you liked the Breugel book. Its humor really belonged to you, if you get what I mean, and you therefore were more capable of "owning" it than anyone I ever knew. If you were dead and gone I think it would have been a better commemoration than flowers—so take good care of it—and hand it on to your grandchildren—for you never can tell—you may have them, you know!

Love always, Hart

To E.E. Cummings

Dear C'gs—   December 21

Take my word for it—and get *A Survey of Modernist Poetry* (Heinmann, London) by Laura Riding and Robt. Graves. 3 bucks. . . . Holliday Bookshop. 49 East 49th St has it.

It has more gunpowder in it than any other book of contemporary criticism I've ever read—and as you (and Shakespeare) are the hero you certainly shouldn't keep the cotton in your ears any longer. . . .

Hart Crane

To Yvor Winters

2160 Mar Vista Avenue

Dear Winters: January 20, 1928

I can't help rejoicing that someone has come to the rescue of my "Grandmother", for above and beyond the bellowing and wallowing, there was the obviously patronizing reference to one of my relatives, which I may yet feel justified in answering, albeit it can only provoke mirth, no matter what *I* may say. The admirable *temper* of your letter, however, should prompt me to let well enough alone. After all, anyone who reads "My Grandmother's Love Letters" will notice that Kay Boyle hasn't. . . . But it's really the spectacle of anyone getting away with such snottiness that gets my goat. She apparently has no sense of pride or professional integrity.

I'm glad that Laura likes me and my work, but I hope she never gets herself (and incidentally me) so wound up again in a ball of yarn. Is she trying to evolve a critical style from Gertrude Stein? My God, what prose! Honestly, if I am forced to read much more of that sort of thing I'll go back and join hands with Morley and Canby. I've got as far as "Trinc" already. Damned if I don't like that "Ballad of a Strange Thing" more and more. It has an integrity of rhythm which isn't obvious at first. And I like a number of other things in the book without, however, thoroughly approving them. Putnam really has just as much to say as MacLeish, perhaps more, but isn't quite so devious in saying it. My favorites turn out to be just those of everybody else: "Memorial Rain," "Selene Afterwards," "Nocturne," "Signature for Tempo" (1), and "Immortal Helix." That Fragment in the *Caravan* was the best yet. Certainly MacLeish arouses one's speculations as much as anyone these days.

The epistemology of the Fernandez book is difficult for me to grasp. I started the initial chapter several days ago and soon found myself horribly muddled. I have an idea that he is awfully long winded and somewhat pretentious—but that is no better than a prejudice, so far. Meanwhile I shall lay the blame on myself and pray for the advent of a gleam of revelation when I pick up the book again, which will be soon. Did I shock you once while you were here by the admission that I had never read *Wuthering Heights*? Well, I have made up for lost time. Captain Ahab now has a partner in my gallery of demon-heroes, for I'll not soon forget Heathcliff! You probably read Proust "in the native," but if you should care to read the translation of *Sodom & Gomorrah* which is just out let me know and I'll send you my copy. The Stanford library will *not* have that, I feel sure, and as the edition is limited to subscribers you may not find it accessible. I've just about finished it.

I'm sorry I haven't been able to do more justice to the admirable lyrics that you have sent me lately. But as I have more than hinted by numerous actual demonstrations of critical ineptitude lately—I find myself less and less sure of a number of previous persuasions. Finding myself completely disoriented I can hardly pretend to the capacities of a firm judgement on anything but mere technical details. And even these are involved in—and justified or disqualified by—the intention or direction of the work as a whole. All this may well be less evolution than involution. But until I get back on the tracks again my word isn't worth much.

Getting back to *transition*—it was a pleasure to see the two

"Tonita Penas," and the "Fixer" (Hemingway) story was good burlesque. His *Men Without Women* is a book you ought to read. The short story called "The Killers" makes one doff one's hat.

Please remember me to Janet Lewis—and I can't help thanking you for your letter to *transition*!

Crane

To Yvor Winters

Altadena, California

Dear Winters: January 27, 1928

I hope you are in no great rush for the return of that Hopkins book. It is a revelation to me—of unrealized possibilities. I did not know that words could come so near a transfiguration to pure musical notation—at the same time retaining every minute literal signification! What a man—and what daring! It will be long before I shall be quiet about him. I shall make copies of some of the poems, since you say the book is out of print. As yet I haven't come to the theoretical preface—nor Bridges' notes—excepting a superficial glance. Actually—I can't wean my eyes from one poem to go on to the next—hardly—I'm so hypnotized. . . .

Having jumped from Proust into *this*—I haven't yet got to the Fernandez vol. Nor have I had time to do justice to Janet Lewis' poems—for which, please tell her, I am most thankful —and also for the line drawing—which looks a great deal like you.

I happen to have felt a good deal in one of those parturition times lately—with the clamant hope that I was about to yield "Cape Hatteras" or something equally ambitious at almost any moment . . . but have been so subject to interruptions that I guess the fit has passed off . . . leaving only an irritating collection of notes and phrases defying any semblance of synthesis. I'm going to stop all reading soon in a more-or-less desperate effort to digest and assemble what I've been consuming—or maybe to put it even out of mind. I'd like to get a little work done soon—or else take up copywriting, plastering or plumbing again. . . .

To go back beyond your last—to the mention of Tom Nashe—you named one of my greatest Elizabethan enthusiasms—though all I know of him is his *Unfortunate Traveller*.

With thanks again to you and Janet Lewis—Hart Crane

To Peggy and Malcolm Cowley

Dear Peggy & Mal: January 31, 1928

Writing is next to impossible—what with the purling of fountains, the drawling of mockingbirds, the roaring of surf, the blazing of movie stars, the barking of dogs, the midnight shakings of geraniums, the cruising of warships, etc., etc. not to mention the dictates of the Censor, whose absence will be welcome sometime, I hope, when we get together again at the Dutchman's or some rehabilitated Punch Palace where I'll at least be able to offer some new words to the (albeit) ancient tunes! My philosophic moments are few, but when they do occur it is almost always possible to turn on the radio and immeadiately expose my soul to the rasping persuasions of Aimee Macpherson, eternally ranting and evangelizing to packed houses at the great palm-flanked arena of Angelus Temple. She broadcasts the news that people are frequently carried out in pieces, arms broken, heads smashed in the stampede for salvation which she almost nightly stages, thereby emphasizing the need of arriving early (so as to save one's body as well) and thereupon lifts her voice into a perfectly convulsing chant, coaxing and cuddlingly coy about "Come, all ye—" (You can catch her in it on the Victor) the chorus of which would make a deacon's bishopric leap crimson and triumphant from the grave . . . I haven't seen her, but they say she has beautiful, long, red, wavy tresses . . .

The peculiar mixtures of piety and utter abandon in this welter of cults, ages, occupations, etc. out here make it a good deal like Bedlam. Retired schoolmarms from Iowa, Ohio, Kansas and all the corn-and-wheat belt along with millions of hobbling Mathuselahs, alfalfa-fringed and querulous, side by side with crowds of ambitious but none-too-successful strumpets of moviedom, quite good to look at, and then hordes of rather nondescript people who seem just bound from nowhere into nothing—one can't explain either the motives nor means of their existance. One can generally 'place' people to some extent; but out here it's mostly nix. One begins to feel a little unreal as a consequence of this—and so much more, like the perfect labyrinth of 'villas'—some pseudo-Spanish, some a la Maya (the colour of stale mayonnaise), others Egyptian with a simply irrisistable amphora perched on the terrace, and some vaguely Chink. Our house, a large *U* with patio and fountain, rambles all over the place, and is almost vertical to the observatory on Mt. Wilson. Plenty of roses, camillias, oleanders, acacias, etc. as well as a good wine-cellar. I've just been interrupted by the butler bringing in a makeshift for champagne, composed of carbonated apple-juice with a sling of gin; so all attempts at epistolary consecutivety are hereby and henceforth abandoned! San Pedro No, I'd better give up—I was just about to say something about the pool rooms down at San Pedro where the battle fleet rides close at anchor. Gradually I'm becoming acquainted with all the brands of bootleg that the Westcoast offers. I haven't been blinded by anything yet but beauty and sunshine, however; but I did have to get glasses to shield me from the violet rays, which are terribly strong out here. I'd better stop, I guess.

Love to you both, and peace to all our bladders! Hart

To Waldo Frank

2160 Mar Vista Avenue
Altadena, California
Dear Waldo: February 1, 1928

I thought the enclosed poems might interest you as souvenirs of our tropical sojourn together. The quarry and the road leading to it, the idiot boy, etc. and the Overhead which mocks the manner of the typical American settler's comments on the natives . . . There is another poem, "The Air Plant," properly belonging to this series, which ought to be out soon in *The Dial*. And there was another, "O Carib Isle!," published earlier in *transition*, which also belongs. In "The Hour" I attempted to secure the ground-rhythm of the hurricane.

You have been silent for so long that I cannot but doubt your interest in hearing from me. Yet I so often think of you that I have risked the intrusion regardless. Gorham may have already mentioned the conditions of my present residence out here. Before leaving NY I heard indirectly of your marriage, and hope you'll allow me to offer my felicitations. Do let's hear from you sometime.

with love, Hart

To Samuel Loveman

2160 Mar Vista Ave.,
Altadena, Cal.
Dear Sam: 5th Feb. 28
It's been so difficult to give any adequate sort of resume of the variety and humor of my life out here that I've started more than one letter to you, been interrupted, and then given up. Under any conditions I'll have to save the most amusing details until I see you, on account of the Censor. Meanwhile I hope you'll pardon my abbreviations, omissions, etc. . . .
First of all: my "boss" has never once failed to play the admirable host, and what is more, I continue to find him at all times most agreeable and entertaining. We are located in a large house, U-shaped, with a patio in the centre; palms, fountain, oleanders, camillias, etc.; almost at the foot of Mt. Lowe. Very comfortable indeed, almost too much so, considering the marvelous cooking of the Viennese cook, the wine cellar, etc. These are perhaps vulgar details, but they contrast so to my rubbery beef and boiled spuds of last winter that they seem notable; besides which I am becoming so rotund that you should be forewarned in case I do come back next Spring and shock you with my bulk.
I see my mother on the average of twice a week. She is located so far away that it takes a good two hours to reach her, so it nearly always means devoting practically a whole day to the occasion. My grandmother is better off than at any time for the last three years—the climate has done wonders. They have a small cottage and would be quite comfortable were

they more satisfied with the general temper of the woman they brought out here to live with them. I'm not capable of judging the situation very accurately, but there's been a good deal of fretting and umbrage, very discouraging indeed to me at times. Wise has practically asked me to accompany him to Europe in the Spring, but their situation may deny me that opportunity. Mother asked immeadiately about you. She would rejoice at any word from you whatever.

We have met some movie actors, attended some studio screenings, etc. And I have had a fair amount of swimming and tennis. (The beaches—Long Beach, Venice, Santa Monica—are really a delight, and I have spent whole days watching the gulls, sandpipers, pelicans in their manouvres). But I am especially enjoying the wealth of reading and music around the house. Wise is buying all the albums of symphonies, quintettes, concertoes and what-not on the Victor list. So I'm living on intimate terms for the first time with Brahms and Beethoven—the two most exciting of all to me.

"The Grandmothers", I agree with you, is damned fine, although I think it weakens towards the last; Westcott seems to lose his grip. Then I've immensely enjoyed the trans. of Proust's "Sodome et Gomorrhe", as well as Gide's "The Counterfeiters". I also am now introduced to Heathcliff (whom I have put beside Ahab) thanks to your mention of "Wuthering Hts." And by the way, I'm terribly excited about the poems of Gerard Manley Hopkins. Winters loaned me his copy recently (I had never read any of Hopkins before) and I have discovered that I am not as original in some of my stylisms as I had thought I was. Winters tells me that the book (Oxford edition, edited by Robert Bridges) is now out of print. I'm simply wild to secure a copy—and am wondering if you could locate me anything around New York. I'm willing to pay anything up to $10.00. Failing this, I think I shall go to work and type out the whole volume, for I've never been quite so enthusiastic about any modern before.

You ask me not to "congratulate" you yet on your new enterprise—so I'll try to be moderate in my words. Nevertheless I can't help feeling that you are to be saluted. And I think that you'll very likely prove successful. Anyway, God bless you, Sam! I've been homesick to see you more than once. There may be roses, surf and sunshine out here—but so far as I've yet been able to discover, there are very few *people* as yet!

Love always,

Hart

P.S.—Recently saw Chaplin in "The Circus". Hope you like it as much as I do! I met him one evening in a Hollywood cafe (which he is reputed to own) and had a few words with him. White hair, the old flashing smile—a strange luminosity about him as always.

To William Slater Brown

Dear Bill: February 22, 1928

I am above all, anxious to hear about Sue and the enfant sublime! My blessings—from the fairy God Mother in her native clime, here where the evenings are made lustful and odorous with the scent of lemon flowers and acacias on the sea-salt air!

A paean from Venusberg! Oy-oy-oy! I have just had my ninth snifter of Scotch. O shades of Bert Savoy! They say he had a glass eye as the result of some midnight with a mariner. But I have had no such dire results as yet. OH BOy! Try to imagine the streets constantly as they were during that famous aggregation last May in Manhattan! And more, for they are at home here, these western argosies, at roadstead far and near—and such a throng of pulchritude and friendliness as would make your "hair" stand on end. That's been the way of all flesh with me . . . And wine and music and such nights—WHOOPS*!!!!!!!*

Besides which I have met the Circe of them all—a movie actor who has them dancing naked, twenty at a time, around the banquet table. O Andre Gide! no Paris ever yielded such as this—away with all your counterfeiters! Just walk down Hollywood Boulevard someday—if you must have something *out* of uniform. Here are little fairies who can quote Rimbaud before they are 18—and here are women who must have the tiniest fay to tickle them the one and only way! You ought to see Betty Compson shake her tits—and cry *apples* for a bite!

What can I write about? Yes I am reading Wyndham Lewis'
Time and Western Man, Fernandez' insufferable *Messages* and
all the other stuff. But I would rather do as I did yesterday—
after a night of wine—wake up at dawn and dip into *The Tem-
pest*, that crown of all the Western World. What have I to say
after that event, I wonder. ???

> —The charm dissolves apace
> And as the morning steals upon the night,
> Melting the darkness, so their rising senses
> Begin to chase the ignorant fumes that mantle
> Their clearer reason. . . .

Maybe with me someday, as good Prospero says. Perhaps—as
Ceres says in the same play—

> Spring come to you at the farthest
> In the very end of harvest!
> Scarcity and want shall shun you;
> Ceres' blessing is upon you.

But you will tear this up—and keep me true. Bill. And if I come
back to you and to the dear hills of Connecticut again, as I
hope to, I shall have a cargo for your ears. My love to Sue and
to you.

as ever, HART

Enclosed is a souvenir of a night with Circe. A most affection-
ate red-haired mariner—who brought credentials.

To Yvor Winters

2160 Mar Vista Avenue
Dear Winters: February 23, 1928

Since I am become chronically remiss in responding to all
the epistolary courtesies of my friends for so long a time past as
to be (or to have been) long since disparaged—I make no more
excuses in detail, beyond the passing recognition of that im-
perfection, its millionth confirmation, as it were, with the
added addled protest that I am still, as always, your friend, and
that silence is not more mysterious, in this instance, than (at

least) cordial. Further, I have at present a little Spanish port in my noddle. And who knows (quien sabe) perhaps the wine is to blame for the conceit of writing you. But enough of bows and furbelows!

Your friend Fernandez—his epistomology and indirections are on the verge of forcing me to hurl his pretentious tome into the fire—which is what Wise tells me he did long since, before enduring half so much of his insufferable prose as I have already! I have to take long vacations and dissipations between glimpses of those great messages of his, so it is taking me a long time to come to any decision about him. Meanwhile I'm susceptible to a thousand and one temptations as momentary reliefs. I am especially consoled by Wyndham Lewis's latest, *Time and Western Man,* which at least has a vigorous style, whether or not you agree with all he says: a bull-headed man, astonishingly sensitive in many ways—who is a lot better than the usual Doug Fairbanks of controversies. I advise you to read the book, even though it costs—Well, let me know, and I'll send it to you. . . .

Yes, Williams would naturally prefer such a secondary item as "See L.A. First" to your better things. I've always had my finger on that soft spot in his—no, not brain—but character! He's almost as bad as some of the "revolutionary simpletons" that Lewis lays out, excepting that I'll always concede him a first-rate talent for language. If he'd only let himself alone! He's so afraid he'll find the Zeitgeist at his heels—not realizing that by means of that very attitude it's been *riding* him for some time since.

In "The Vigil" you are at your best, in action, but at something less than that in "registration" . . . I can't help telling you that in such a poem you do not carry me beyond the level of my own station in the laboratory of a like quandary. There is a certain lack of synthesis. I'm in the same fix in regard to my "Cape Hatteras"—a bundle of smoldering notes, no more. I don't know when the proper moment may arrive to grasp them and make them a whole . . . It's a damned hard time we live in. And I think you stand a much better chance of biding your time beyond it than I do—for a number of reasons.

Glad you liked the Blake. It really IS worth having. I am still discovering new marvels in Hopkins. Do, please, forgive me for withholding these books so long. I'll return them soon. My heartiest greetings to Janet Lewis. . . .

as ever, *Crane*

To Susan Jenkins and William Slater Brown

1803 North Highland
Hollywood, California
Dear Sue and Bill: March 27, 1928

As I don't seem to get anything more out of you by means of postcards, telegrams, and such-like shorthand signals I guess it's up to me to get busy on the typewriter and pay you your due torture—though I'll try and not inflict such piercing shrieks on you again, such as my last epistle! When I get to feeling like that again I'll begin on Pres. Calles first—and that will probably save you a great deal of amazement and conjecture.

This time the news is more diverse . . . Life is nothing if not exciting wherever Emil happens to land, if only for a few hours. It took him (or his presence) to arrange the most harrowing week-end yet, and I'm only praying that he's still alive, for when I left him in his berth in the "glory-hole" of the *California* last Sat. night he looked as though he were nearing the Pearly Gates. We were held up and beaten by a gang in San Pedro. . . . The story is complicated and lengthy—and Emil will probably give you the full version or as much as he can remember when he sees you.

I left Wise's ménage a week ago today. However, as E somehow failed to get my ship letter announcing same and the hour at which I would meet him—he flew right up to Altadena, leaving me to wait a *full 8 hours* by the gangway before I saw my dear "Goldylocks". By that time I had about finished a half pint of alcohol which I had brought for our mutual edification, and he had completely emptied a quart of Bacardi, also originally intended as a mutual benison.

Scene Two. Speakeasy joint with booths. Many bottles of dubious gin and whiskey—with much "skoling"—Emil flashing a fat payroll—and treating three or four still more dubious "merry andrews" who had invited themselves to our noisy nook. It being midnight, all ordered out.

Scene Three. A street, or rather, several streets. Our "guests" very insistent on taking a hotel room in which to finish the fire water. Emil & I both reeling but refractory. I finally noticed Emil being spirited away by three of them, while it was evident that I, who had been more emphatic in my wishes, was being guarded by two others. I broke away—and all five started slugging us. I put up quite a fight, but neither of us were in much condition. They all beat it as a car turned on a nearby corner. Both of us robbed of everything, and E. practically uncon-scious. After reporting at police headquarters I don't know how I would have got E back to his ship without the help of a sailor friend of mine whom I had run into earlier in the evening while waiting for E. We roused several of his shipmates—and I'm only hoping that his bumps and bruises haven't been any more fatal than mine. I finally had to finish the night in a ward of the Salvation Army Hotel, and it was five o'clock Sunday before I got enough money to get back to Hollywood. On his way back from Frisco I'm hoping to see E again—but not in Pedro! Probably nothing of this had better be mentioned to the Bovings . . . I don't mind my losses, but I feel terribly about Emil's luck. He always seems to get the hardest end of things.

As you can see, we didn't get much time for any gossip. But he did say that you had the most beautiful baby in the world! Wish I could see him! Besides which I get terribly homesick out here, but might as well not indulge myself in that emotion. My resignation from the Wise entourage was encouraged by a number of dissatisfactions, but as much as anything by the recognition of the fact that I must settle here for a while at least, and do whatever I can to help my mother during her at-tendance on grandmother. The two of them being completely alone out here, and none too well provided for, I couldn't get a good night's sleep in Conn. So I might as well relinquish my own wishes for awhile and try and earn some cash. Maybe sce-nario writing eventually. Meanwhile there are mechanical jobs such as title-writing, gag-writing, "continuity" writing, etc. I just had an interview with "Papa" Kahn this morning who is out here for a couple of weeks. He promises to help me connect with Lasky, Paramount, Wm. Fox, etc. At least I have "broken in" the movies in one way, for Pathe News-reel or some such torture swooped down on us while we were talking in the patio of The Ambassador, and for all I know we may be thrown upon the screen together all the way from Danbury to Hong-Kong and Mozambique! I'm wearing horn-rims now—so don't be shocked.

As for my late employer—the situation became too strained to be continued. If I had only had some definite duties I could have kept my self-respect, but the tip-toeing, solicitous, willy-nilly uncertainty of everything, besides his interminable psycho-analysis of every book, person, sausage and blossom got to giving me the heeby-geebies. And when he finally secured a quite cultured little piece of Pear's Soap (remember the slo-gan) to console him in all ways at once, then I began to feel al-together too extraneous for words. Such circumstances don't promote a very lively morale—and it's probably better for me to lose a little of the attendant avoirdupois in favor of a more exhilarating outlook. But we are still friends so far as I know.

Every week I scour the pages of the *New Rep.*, *Nation*, and *Herald-Tribune* for the names of our "rising generation." Have seen nothing by Malcolm for sometime. Does this cor-roborate the news I got from Mrs. T. some weeks ago that Malcolm has been laid up? Much by Robert Penn Warren, but little by his friend Tate, excepting a recent review of Winters which I thought excellent. Slater Brown, I long since ne-glected to mention, scored keenly in tussle with the milksop critic of Estlin C'gs in the Canby Crap Can. "The point was well taken," as my grandmother would say. And how is C'gs? for I think you told me he was pretty hard up. Mitchell seems to be bursting with new energy by the evidence in recent num-bers of *The Dial*. And last, but not least in this litry column, how goes it with your translations—and—how is "Amos"? No, your not the last, either! I must say that I haven't yet been able to decipher that defense of me by Laura, published in *Transition* along with Kay Boyle's explosive boil. I wrote her promptly, thanking her for her sentiments, but questioning her style. Her latest book announced by Jonathan Cape, is *Anarchy is Not Enough*—and so she seems to be maintaining her consistency. Judging by the time she has already taken before answering me, I judge that I'm off her correspondence list. I shouldn't have been so rude had I thought her tender-hearted. But I can't believe that anarchy is enough—or Gertrude Stein, either.

I imagine that you'll receive this at a rather busy period—re-settling in Patterson, swimming in the gully-torrents, planting the new garden and tripping over croquet wickets—but try to get me some words on paper somehow as soon as possible, for I'm devilish anxious to hear from you. My love to the bambino!

Yours ever, Hart

To Charlotte and Richard Rychtarik

1803 North Highland
Hollywood, California
Dear Charlotte & Richard: March 28, 1928

No doubt you think me late in keeping my word about the money. I am terribly sorry. I had difficulties with my late employer—if he can be called that, for I had no salary—and recently left his place. I am now with my mother and grandmother and am looking for work, as their circumstances make it necessary for me to remain out here and be of whatever help I can.

I shall try to borrow the money as soon as possible and send it on to you. Please do not think me callous or ungrateful. My mother joins in sending love.

As ever, Hart

To Waldo Frank

Dear Waldo: April 4 1928

The date on your generous and welcome letter is an accusation. It is true that I haven't lacked time to answer it, long since—but the desire to give you something more than a muddled confusion of cross purposes—and my confidence in your preference for reason and order—have detained me, though I am still by no means settled in my present environment nor do I seem any too happily disposed. But at least I have decided on a few details, for better or worse. . . .

My association with Mr. Wise, who brought me out here as private secretary, terminated about two weeks ago. Although it was unsatisfactory (my duties were extremely vague and I was neither servant nor guest) I might have stuck it out until May (when Wise returns to NY) had I felt justified in leaving my mother and grandmother alone out here in their present predicament. However, the experience of the last two years has taught me the futility of any retreat from what I, after all, must regard as my immeadiate responsibiltities. The further I might go from the actual 'scene' of operations the more obsessed I tend to become by the inert idea. So I am remaining here with the hope of securing some 'literary' connections with the movies which will net me enough to be of some substantial help. When all this is over—someday—I may be able to regain the indispensable detachment from immeadiate concerns that such a work as my *Bridge* demands. Needless to say, I find Hollywood far from tempting in any way—but my people had moved here before I arrived, and as my grandmother is unable to move more than a few steps from her bed she is hardly in the tourist class.

Your letter was as usual—bracing! You probably don't realize it, but it had been a year since I had heard anything from you excepting a postcard. I was beginning to fear that something spurious had been repeated to you as an emanation of mine, for NY is so full of fabrications of all kinds—so, to know better was a welcome relief, also! I can well appreciate the many preoccupations which beset and hindered you. The marvel to me is the glamor and precision of your new work; I refer to the installments of it in the *N.R.* Some of my copies were lost when I was moving—and my readings were frequently interrupted and only partially realized—but the luminous impulse and essential direction I think I have apprehended. It is something more than mere analysis. Like most of your work it postulates a 'Way'. I have tried reading Fernandez' *Messages* and Lewis' *Time and Western Man* without being able to wholly approve a single page of either, though Fernandez is more profound. But his style (or the translator's) is abominable as compared to L's direct though misdirected thrusts. But L just goes round in a desolate circle of elaborations—I can't see anything creative in his offering. Beginning with Spengler and Wells, this age seems to be typically encyclopaedic. This may assist the artist in time—by erecting some kind of logos, or system of contact between the insulated departments of highly specialized knowledge and enquiry which characterize the times—God knows, some kind of substantial synthesis of opinion is needed before I can feel confident in writing about anything but my shoestrings. . . . These Godless days! I wonder if you suffer as much as I do. At least you have the education and training to hold the scalpel.

If I can't send you a new poem of my own I can at least send you a better new-old one (for I don't think you have yet read him) by Gerard Manly Hopkins (Oxford) now out of print—a Victorian, posthumously printed, whose work has been a revelation to me.

"Pied Beauty"

Glory be to God for dappled things—
    For skies of couple-color as a brinded cow;
        For rose-moles all in stipple upon trout that swim;
Fresh-firecoal chestnut-falls; finches' wings;
    Landscape plotted and pieced—fold, fallow, and plough;
        And all trades, their gear and tackle and trim.

All things counter, original, spare, strange;
    Whatever is fickle, freckled (who knows how?)
        With swift, slow; sweet, sour; adazzle, dim;
    He fathers-forth whose beauty is past change:
                    Praise him.

When you see Gorham please tell him that I have intended writing him long since—and shall soon. I should love to hear from Gene, but know nothing whatever about his doings or whereabouts. And remember me to Stieglitz. I think I met Alma Veder once, long ago. At any rate I do hope she is now much improved in health and that your whole household is redolent-beaming.

                                        Love ever, Hart

To Clarence Arthur Crane

1803 North Highland,
Hollywood, Calif.
Dear Dad: April 14th, 1928

You may have a whole family of *petit bon-bons* in New York, as you say, but for the chow pups which you mentioned in Chagrin—I think Sing is to be congratulated. As for the good Dr. Jekyl and the bad Mr. Hyde, I'm getting used to them gradually, but hope you won't make any more quick changes than usual; meanwhile, may M. Cartier prosper! His mustachios have the true pistachio twist!

Which reminds me of a recent scandal in the life of our Uncle Cassius, the verification of which we are all awaiting with bated breath. It seems that on his way back east Mr. Williams, an old Ravenna croney of Unk. Cash's, stopped off at Albuquerque, N.M. and met a woman there who claimed to have got along very well with Cash. during one of his stopovers there. Williams writes Ralph that the lady was trundling around a most unusual infant of remarkable size and thickness. Uncle Cash. is loud in his protests and has written for further details. He won't answer charges, he says, until he hears the necessary and final specification—is the baby bald? as well as bearded!

Last Sunday we all (by whom I mean Ralph and family including Cassius) got up at 3 AM and went up to Easter Sunrise services at the Hollywood Bowl—a huge amphitheatre in the crotch of the hills nearby. Before the sun rose or services began I was so disturbed by the amount of matutinal liquids concentrated in my bladder that I had to wedge my way out of the mob (50,000 strong) and hit for the nearest bushes as fast as possible. The singing was very good, so I was told. No, Grandmother did not attend this function.

I didn't accompany my Wall St. invalid back east as I had expected to do. Grace is almost entirely confined to the house by the constant demands created by grandmother's helpless condition. And to have left the two of them out here alone under such conditions as prevail would have promised me anything but peace of mind on the opposite coast of the continent. I am accordingly on the lookout for some work with one of the moving picture companies. Not acting, but scenario writing, title writing, etc. which would prove more interesting as well as more profitable than any of my previous commercial connections.

I'm not as enthusuastic about *all* aspects of California as I may have seemed to be, but there are certainly far worse places. Employment is a real problem here. This southwestern center is already overcrowded, especially with numerous semi-invalids who have come out here from the east for their health AND very often with just enough independent income to encourage them to work for what are starvation wages to a man whose total income is dependent on his wages only. As one doesn't run into that sort of competition so much in the movies I'm all the more anxious to get located there as soon as possible.

On his recent visit here I had a very pleasant talk with Mr. Kahn. Already his recommendation has secured me one promising interview (Wm Fox Studios) but the present lull in production and the surplus of experienced help in practically all the departments creates a dubious situation for many who are regular old-timers. But my purpose in staying is to be of some real practical help, and I'm making a stab at something this time which offers real opportunities for big money provided I prove to have the proper knack. And I'm pretty damn sure that I have!

Grace is looking well and enjoyed both of your recent letters. She says to tell you that she now knows the buzz of bumble-bee from afar, and needs no further warnings! As for this little Bumble—that's yours truly—his eyes are kept busy these days in Hollywood. There's a regular stampede of trim ankles, silken calves, dimpled knees and laughing eyes. I'm wearing (not the "gold-rimmed testicles" mentioned by Mandy in her description of the churches new "rectum") but some new horn-rimmed dark spectacles with blinkers on the sides . . . And with that reassuring note I feel safe in closing this chapter.

Don't keep me waiting so long for your next letter, please! Best to Sing

and my love to you.
Harold

To Gorham Munson

1803 North Highland
Hollywood, California
April 17, 1928

Dear Gorham:

I certainly feel guilty—and the evidence of your cordiality in sending me your *Destinations* has not made me feel any more exemplary—for not having written you before. However, you *are* exacting in the level of response which you expect from your friends, and inasmuch as I have been involved in a general state of doldrums so far as any creative progress has been concerned for well nigh every moment since I left NY I haven't felt like burdening you with the mere minutiae of personal trifles in lieu of more "decisive developements" if I could help it. But here goes—anyway—if only to signal to you my pleasure in receiving your opus and to assure you that at any rate my affections are not defunct.

With the general exhortation of your book (as a whole) towards more definite spiritual knowledge and direction I find myself in close sympathy. The spiritual disintegration of our period becomes more painful to me every day, so much so that I now find myself baulked by doubt at the validity of every metaphor I coin. In every quarter (Lewis, Eliot, Fernandez, etc.) a thousand issues are raised for one that is settled and where this method is reversed—as with the neo-Thomists— one has nothing as substitute but an arbitrary dogmatism which seems to be too artificial to have any permanence or hold on the future. This "future" is, of course, the name for the entire disease, but I doubt if any remedy will be forthcoming from so nostalgic an attitude as the Thomists betray, and moreover a strictly European system of values, at that. Waldo's acute analyses now running in the *NR* strike me as wonderfully promising. He hasn't come to the constructive part of his program yet—but his ideas are promising; in a way they come to closer grips with American bogeys and vampires than any European is probably capable of seeing.

I think that *Destinations* is a transitional book with you. It contains a lot of splendid analysis, especially your discussions of technical procedures and the historical positions and relationships of various writers. Above and beyond (or enclosing) these considerations I think your demand for more order, clearer direction, etc. well justified, but on the other hand, too vaguely articulated to offer any definite system in contrast to the distraction, indifference to major issues, mere intuitiveness, etc. which you complain of in a number of writers whose work you otherwise admire. This was almost inevitable, I am forced to acknowledge, especially as I have already admitted my own quandaries in the face of such problems—but the challenge still rings for all of us. You have certainly done this much: if you have not definitely (or even begun to) articulate the concrete values of the ideal *100* per cent you have at least done some wiping on the slate and postulated *000*, or the position of the questionable ciphers. Skepticism may stop there and still claim gratitude and respect, but I am not exactly satisfied by that, and I doubt if you are. I still stake some claims on the pertinence of the intuitions; indeed some of Blake's poems and Emily Dickinson's seem more incontrovertible than ever since Relativity and a host of other ideologies, since evolved, have come into recognition.

As close and accurate scrutinies I like the Moore and Williams studies best. I don't know Dreiser well enough to judge your opinions. As for Hart Crane, I know him too well to disaggree on as many points as I once did, two years ago when I first read the essay. I am certainly grateful for such expert attention, and especially on the technical side I think you express my intentions with a very persuasive gusto that has recently revived in me some conviction of "reality" here and there in my scrap heap.

I probably won't see you for some time. My employer is soon to return east and though it would have been more attractive to have continued with him, I long since came to the conclusion that it would be inadviseable. My grandmother (now 89 yrs) is dependent on my mother for every move, and my mother's confinement with her makes it necessary for me to remain here with them for at least a while to come and to do what I can to help. Perhaps I can find something with one of the movie studios in the way of scenerio editing, title-writing, etc. I am striking out in that direction now. It promises more money than anything else out here—there's a terrible lack of employment—and that is the major need right now.

From what I have heard and read it has been a wonderful winter season in NY—unprecedented as far as music goes, at least. The aridity of social life out here is simply appalling. The nearest thing to reality is the greasepaint and vulgarity of the boulevard that runs through Hollywood. Broadway around Times Square at any time of the day is better. Expensive cars by the legion—and frizzed poodles and parading vampires. The golden west is a great pink vacuum filled with machinery and chewing gum and millions of "up-to-date" little stucco pseudo-Spanish villas. Thank God the sea is near, that's all I can be grateful for.

My love to Lisa, and genuine apologies for such a scrawny letter.

as ever, Hart

To William Slater Brown

Dear Bill: April 27

Your salute to the comments of the ny critics cracks at *him* displayed more life than I have seen around here since I arrived. Although I am still holding my sides, I'm a little sad; for I would like to have been there. Especially with Anne drinking gin and Emil sporting his shiners and shirt front and all the tumult and guzzling there must have been afterward! As for the critics—C'gs can be envied, in the same manner that even I can be envied, whereby I refer to the "clever" handling I recently got from Benet in the Canby crap can. At least we both have managed to evade the proverbial faint praise! Your clipping was the only one I've seen excepting a letter from Dos in the last Sunday Times, and a laudatory review in the Wall Street Journal which Wise had noticed. I hope you and others will make as much of a controversy about it as possible. That's one thing good about Frank—he never hesitates a moment and never tires.

Since the Fleet with its twentyfivethousand gobs has left for Hawai I have had a chance to face and recognize the full inconsequence of this Pollyanna greasepaint pinkpoodle paradise with its everlasting stereotyped sunlight and its millions of mechanical accessories and sylphlike robots of the age of celleloid. Efforts for a foothold in this sandstorm are still avid, but I have had little yet in encounter. "Crashing the gate" is a familiar expression out here, and it seems to be exclusively applied to the movie industry. To cap the climax I have to endure my mother's apparently quenchless desire that I become an actor! But if I can hold on until the middle of May I'm due for an interview with Jesse Lasky (HIMSELF) and maybe through that entree I can creep into some modest dustpan in the reading dept. of Paramount. Your friend Dietz, by the way, draws a cool $750.00 a week as their ad. mgr.

It's good to think of you as back near Patterson. I had a good letter from Malcolm. It all makes me homesick. Things like that croquet game in the rain, the afternoon at the cider mill, the skeleton surry ride and the tumble down the hill! I haven't a thing to send for the *transition* Am. issue. I can't imagine ever having anything to say out here except in vituperation of the scene itself. If I could "afford" to go to work on some ranch it might be otherwise.

Have just discovered the presence here of Mrs Alice Barney, the world-famous grande dame and mother of Nathalie Clifford Barney of Paris, friend of Valery, translator, ~~noted Lesbian~~, etc. As she is a great friend of Underwood of Washington I have been invited to her next weekly "evening". She ought to be a little different than the typical Hollywood hostess— perhaps mildly Proustian. God knows I need some sort of diversion besides bus rides and the rigor mortis of the local hooch. Forgive this spasm and write again soon.

yrs
hart

To Wilbur Underwood

1803 North Highland
Hollywood, California
April 27, 1928

Dear Wilbur:

I owe you fervent apologies, and offer them! But I have found it almost impossible to maintain any correspondence with anyone since coming out here last November. Invalid Wall St brokers have a way of disrupting one's customary mental habits—and the situation until a month ago, when I left my invalid's employ—was a little too complicated to promote much correspondence. Someday I can tell you more of the details. You were right in your guess, though you may have had several wrong slants on the situation as far as my duties extended. Rest assured, however, that when I become a concubine you shall be told all the dirt. In this case I was merely a sort of "safe and interesting" person to have around, and my calls were never made between the sheets. I had hoped to accomplish some creative writing with my free time, but the atmosphere of the household was too neurotic to encourage a single strophe, besides which I was constantly preoccupied with the concern of my mother and grandmother who had moved out here several months before I came—and on whose account I have remained here instead of returning to NY, as I had planned, with my invalid.

So the above address may be considered as permanent. I am trying to find some scenario or other literary-mechanical work with some movie company out here. My ad-writing experience ought to count some to the good in this direction, and though I hate the thought of the cheapness of such work (and would rather dig honest ditches) I must earn as much money as possible to be of help to the family, and there is no doubt left that movie connections offer the only large rewards out here. Other kinds of work are hard to get and badly paid.

But you can't imagine the cheap desolation of the populace out here—a spiritual vacuum, all grease-paint, pretense, expensive motors and chewing gum! If it weren't for the Fleet I should scarcely be able to endure it. Gobs always are amusing, as you know. And out here the selection is positively bewildering in beauty, not to mention friendliness. One of my "duties" over at the Pasadena menage was to dash out every week end and come back with some sort of story of my adventures—and adventures there have been, too numerous to describe! To begin with, the number of faggots cruizing around out here is legion. Half the movie stars are addicts, and Pershing Square in the center of Los Angeles is an even livelier place than Lafayette in Washington. The miles of beaches are the best feature of the place. I could live in the water and be quite contented.

But I really long for the east—for my few friends, and the simple habits of my recent life out on the farmstead in Conncticut. The stereotyped sunlight here, day after day, which everyone thinks is so inspiring is to me merely monotonous and depressing. Babbitts and Pollyannas make up the majority of America today. I wonder if I can give them enough of their fodder (in my movie plans, etc) to ever earn me anything but poverty! In a way you are luckier than you think. At least your work is largely mechanical, and it doesn't involve the prostitution of every natural impulse you have.

Your friend Mrs Barney is out here now, has bought a house and apparently intends to remain for some time. I have been so starved for company that I took the liberty of using your name and asking to see her. "Oh I am *so* fond of Wilbur!" she replied, and I'm invited to call during her next "evening". I don't know just why but I am expecting an atmosphere mildly Proustian, anomalous enough in Hollywood!

How have you been? I am anxious to hear, and hope you will forgive.

                                        as ever, hart

To Clarence Arthur Crane

                                        Patterson, New York
Dear Father: June 14th, 1928

It's going on to three weeks since I got back here in the country, and in spite of my sincere fondness for certain features of the Coast I can certainly say that I feel more in my element here in the East. Maybe it's my room—with my desk and my books—or old friends nearby—or the more stimulating mental atmosphere. But at any rate I don't miss the parade of movie actors nor a lot of other artificialities of Hollywood, though for a time I was rather amused by such matters.

I should have stayed on however, according to my announced intention, had I finally felt that there was any opportunity to be of help to Grace. But as the employment situation out there seemed only to grow worse with time and as I didn't above all want to become a burden to the household I decided to go while the going was good—and the remainder of my savings went toward carfare. Living isn't so cheap as it's cracked up to be out there, and though Grace was very generously inclined and urged me to stay I felt that it was taking too big a chance. So when you come down to New York next time perhaps we can get together for an evening.

As it was just as cheap I took a southern route back: across Texas to New Orleans and thence by boat to New York. I had a day in New Orleans and was treated like a senator by some writers on the *Times-Picayune* who had a considerable enthusiasm for my poetry. It's a beautiful old town, full of history and with the kind of mellowness which I prefer to all the boomed-up modernity of Los Angeles and environs. And the boat ride down the delta of the Mississippi (we were from 10 till 5 p.m. completing it) was one of the great days of my life. It was a place I had so often imagined and, as you know, written about in my River section of *The Bridge*. There is something tragically beautiful about the scene, the great, magnificent Father of Waters pouring itself at last into the oblivion of the Gulf!

Then five days on the boat. As I don't seem to get sea-sick any more I was grateful that the meals had been included in my ticket, for I only had $2. and an entirely disproportionate appetite. Although I'm not as keen about New York as I once was, it looked damned good to me. People aren't as indifferent and impersonal there as they are in the west despite all the slogans and catchwords to the contrary. I soon had the carfare to complete my journey out here—and here I've been ever since, thanks to my good credit with the old woman and the famous cat! There seems to be no possibility of finding any kind of work until after election, but at least I can live here at the most utter minimum of cost imaginable. I hope you can help me out a little as you did last summer. It's just a question of your interest in the matter, for I'm not claiming that you necessarily ought to. I hope to have some advance royalties on my new book within a couple of months.

I neglected to mention how much I enjoyed your last letter. You must be getting a lot of real satisfaction out of your country retreat, *this* summer, now that it is really a completed article and in all probability running pretty smoothly. Recently I came across the enclosed poem by Guest in a newspaper. I don't know whether or not it tells of *all* the trials of a confectioner or not, but at any rate it certainly suggested that Eddie had recently been sampling some of *Crane's Best.* Which reminds me that I'm sort of candy hungry these days, as well as the old woman. And I can't help recalling the delicious assortment we received from you last summer.

Please give my best to all the folks including Joe—and do let me hear from you real soon.

With love, as ever—
Harold

To Yvor Winters

Patterson, New York
June 27, 1928

Dear Winters:

I left the Coast on the 15th of last month. I had thought that I had given the hasty signal of at least a postcard dropped off the station platform at Houston or San Antonio, but evidently not, judging by your good letter received this morning via Hollywood. I left in a hurry, but not without due deliberation. You already know my grudges against the L.A. population, but perhaps you don't know my full distaste for family turmoils. At any rate . . . here I am again in the old house with the old woman and her cats, and sneezing as strenuously as ever at the date of roses . . . and damned good and glad to rejoin a few human associates who live around here and to smell a little horse manure again.

The boat ride down the Mississippi to the Gulf was, of

course, something of a heart-throb to me. One day only is enough to make one sentimental about New Orleans. I never before felt as in the presence of the "old" America—not baldly "confronted" with it, as at places like Salem, Mass.—but surrounded and rather permeated by it. But I suppose pewter is the more representative, and the old tarnished gold of Orleans belongs rather to the traditions of Martinique than to the spirit of the Minute Men. I'd like to spend a winter there sometime, anyway. And the Mississippi delta is all that I ever dreamed it to be. Then I had four more days on the water before a sight of land. It's just as cheap as the northern routes, and to me a lot less tiresome, though longer.

Nathan Asch and his wife as well as the Cowleys and Josephsons are close neighbors of mine this summer. There is also a cashiered army officer turned bootlegger over on Birch Hill, who makes very good apple-jack. But in spite of all this whirl, not to mention the usual croquet tournaments up at Slater Brown's place, I intend to get something done before going to N.Y. later for a job. I've met Williams before, but I'm hoping to know him better when he comes out here soon as a guest of the Asches. They are also hoping to get Morley Callaghan down from Canada for a brief spell . . . but I am beginning to sound like a maitre d'hotel.

To get back in the files a little—I am glad that my dear olde Kit still gives you so much kick. I am always amazed at the glorious cornucopia that Tamburlaine shakes page after page. I enjoy the antiquated spelling even in this case, of the Oxford edition, wherein the buskins of Hero are described as a "woonder to behold". Truly, the very prologue to *Tamburlaine* and the very first words set the key for the divinest human feasting:

> From iygging vaines of riming mother wits,
> And such conceits as clownage keepes in pay . . .

What a "flourish without" to signal the whole Age of Elizabeth! and a promise that was truly kept! I have been haunted by those two lines so many times, and always wonder in what consists their strange combination of tangibility and illusiveness. You get it also in Keats' "Eve of St. Agnes", but not in quite so joyous, so robust a form. The very kindly jaggedness of the Marlowe lines endears them more, at least at times, than the suave perfections that somehow reached a little over the line, into death, with Keats.

The tremendous lines from Blake that you wanted are on page *763*. They always strike me as about the most *final* words ever written. At your mention of Traherne I have been looking over some specimens in an anthology I have, and can't imagine why once, years ago, I failed to appreciate his astonishing validity. Vaughan, whom he certainly bears a likeness to, really does bore me excepting a handful of complete poems and scattered lines in others. It lies rather with a kind of Presbyterianism that infects Vaughan, I surmise; whereas Traherne's piety is more universalized, more positive. You even begin to suspect him of apocalyptic casuistry here and there, so crystalline and capable is his bended head, when lo! by adding even more wit to the occasion he convinces you of his complete absence of vanity. Almost a Brahmin in some ways.

I'll follow your advice and read more of Herbert. Cowley has a copy down the road. But please don't bother about the proffered copy of Traherne—not that I wouldn't love to have it, but I'm so near N.Y. now, that such books are once more accessible. You may be interested in watching for some forthcoming articles in the *Outlook*: Cowley on Poe; Tate on Emily; Burke on Emerson (I think), etc. I haven't been able to get advance carbons from any of them, but these three generally have something worthy of interest. Cowley has a rather slow, laborious mind that simply cannot turn out a shoddy sentence. I would rather talk to him about the sheer mechanics of poetry than anyone I know—that is since Tate has become too pontifical for any discussions whatever. Which reminds me of the protests you mention receiving for your *Fugitive* review. I suspect you irritated a great deal by spelling his first name All*an* instead of All*en*. He raised such a row with Liveright about that misdemeanor on the title page of *White Bldgs*. that the whole edition was torn up, new title pages inserted and rebound. As to the locutions of Marianne—she seems to have had at least a good time with her briefer on your book. I never shall be able to make out the meaning of "apperceptions . . . whose cumulative elequence recedes in geometric inverse ratio to imperativeness". For God's sake, somebody play the "Kitten on the Keys", PLEASE! All this exudes a "flabby algebraic odor"—which in one of Cumming's poems is descriptive of a good-sized c—t.

I didn't mean to end matters so oderiferuously; I'm sure I can congratulate you on your pups, anyway, if not on your Turgid Mention.

All best, *Crane*

To Clarence Arthur Crane

501 East 55th Street,
New York City
c/o Malcolm Cowley
Dear Father: August 14th, 1928

Your letter, forwarded from Patterson, reached me yesterday. I have been offered the use of the flat of a friend of mine who is spending the summer in the country, and I'm fortunate enough to have it for several weeks. I've been cooking my own meals and doing my best without the help of a flatiron to keep myself looking spruce, but my shoes are giving out as well as the several small loans that friends have given me—and so far I haven't been able to make any connections with ad. work. I guess I'll have to give that up.

I agree with you completely in what you say about learning a trade; in fact I have wanted to learn some regular trade like typesetting, linotyping, etc. for a long time back. However, connections that pay anything whatever while learning these trades are hard to find out about. And, of course, I need something more than air to live on in the meantime. I'm going to do my best during the next few days to find a job as a plumber's or mechanic's helper. The work is physically heavier than I have been used to for a long time, but I fancy I can make the adjustment in due time. The way things are now I'll consider myself lucky to get anything.

Last week was terrific here in New York, but we got relief Sunday. Now the heat is in full blast again, and I suppose you are also getting some of it out in Cleveland. I'll be at the above address for awhile, at least, and hope I shall hear from you again soon. Did you hear that Joe Smith of Canton recently died? Bess is simply prostrate with greif, so I hear.

Yours, with love,
Harold

To Yvor Winters

77 Willow Street
Brooklyn, New York
Dear Winters: September 9, 1928

I'm back again where I can see the harbor from my window, and Brooklyn Bridge. Also I've found a job (copywriting) as well as a remedy for hay fever that really seems to work. In regard to the last, if you have any other sneezing critters among your friends who need relief remember to tell them of the following two remedies which team beautifully—*Rinex* (internally) and *Estivin* (for eyes). More violent cases should apply to Miss Jessicum North, Mother Superior of Thunder Mug University, Illinois, for summary advice and parsing treatment. . . .

Have been reading Laura Riding's *Contemporaries & Snobs* (Jonathan Cape) and recommend parts of the first 100 pages as some really remarkable analysis, fumblingly expressed, but damned suggestive. *And* have you heard Bach's Toccata & Fugue in D Minor on the Orthophonic yet? The Philadelphia Symphony gives it wonderful volume. The pattern and purity of it are beyond praise. The sublimest rhetoric I have ever heard!

My mind is mostly a flat blank these days, that is—what is left of it after it has been crammed and unloaded several times every day, the material being CALOROIL HEATERS, FOS-FOR-US MINERAL MIXTURE (for hogs, cattle, poultry) and FLOWERS OF LOVE WEDDING RINGS, etc. etc. The high tension rush of an agency office is only to be compared with a newspaper office. Inserts, folders, circulars, posters, full pages and half pages, a two-column twenty-liner here, there this, there that! But I'm not sorry to be working and, in fact, was damned lucky to get anything as good right now.

When I get a little back on my feet financially I'll feel a little more like a man. Meanwhile you seem to have the gracious facility of making me believe that I am possibly at least a poet.

All best, hastily Hart Crane

To Charlotte and Richard Rychtarik

77 Willow Street
Brooklyn, New York
Dear Charlotte and Richard: September 16, 1928

It has hurt me to think that you thought me indifferent about returning the remainder of the money that you so kindly loaned me. I confess my guilt: it *could* have been done before. But nevertheless at *no* time since you wrote me asking for it. Owing to the recent death of my Grandmother Hart (in Hollywood) I shall, however, be able to discharge the obligation fairly soon, as I come into a slight inheritance which will take care of several debts. I have been struggling without any money for weeks, but have finally secured a decent job with an advertising agency here.

This is perhaps a futile letter to write, since our friendship seems to have been already sacrificed. But I owe it to myself perhaps as much as to you to give you rightful evidence of my continued intention of honest behavior, no matter what you may have thought of me. You don't know how often I have thought of you and regretted the circumstances of your recent loss of interest in me. You don't know the extent to which I feel gratefully indebted to you both for many things outside the realm of money or anything that money could ever buy. But there is no use in trying to make apologies. As long as I believe in myself I shall insist in my good intentions and with the ultimate faith of putting them into practice. I can never, of course, ask others as much as that.

If you will be friendly enough to answer *this* letter sometime in the next three months I shall be glad to know that at least I may be sure of your present address. Otherwise, I'll have to ask someone in Cleveland to look you up in the directory or telephone book to ascertain your present whereabouts at the time I'm able to write a check out.

With best wishes always, Sincerely, Hart

To William Carlos Williams

77 Willow Street
Brooklyn, New York
September 16

Dear Williams:

At times I'm prompted to wonder why in paradise we don't once in a while get together. Especially since I'm told that you frequently get over to Manhattan. I'm a stranger in N.J. But from what Nathan Asch says, it's a good place—and you live on a magistral hill in a venerable mansion, not to speak of governmental rations. No; that's not what I mean . . .

But do look me up sometime. I know how busy you are—and perhaps the liveliest man in America. Phone me at *Vanderbilt 2970* between dawn and dark, please, sometime when it's convenient. There are so many things to talk about—with you.

Sincerely, Hart Crane

To Wilbur Underwood

77 Willow Street
Brooklyn, New York
October 5

Dear Wilbur:

How are you these days? I'm just getting on my feet again after a hell of a time finding work, etc. For awhile it seemed good to get back in the city—but now it's getting on my nerves again.

Haven't you been owing me a letter for a long time—or is it the reverse? Anyway—don't think too badly of me. I'm doing no writing—America seems to be so comfortably dead—you see it in millions of faces—that there's nothing left to struggle for except "respectability".

Occasionally some sailor gives me a jolt—but I guess I'm getting old. My grandmother recently died—out west—which releases some money previously left me in my grandfather's estate. When I get it—later, toward spring, I may go to Europe for awhile. I've never been, you know. Hope to see you here in the meantime.

I noticed a favorable mention of your book (Elkin Matthews) in the new *Criterion* today. Write me soon.

Affectionately—Hart

To Yvor Winters

110 Columbia Heights
Brooklyn, New York
October 23, 1928

Dear Winters:

I won't enumerate all the excuses I've had for my negligence of you. They wouldn't seem valid to you without inexcusable details on my part, and perhaps even then you'd need a slice of Babylonian routine yourself, directly experienced, before you'd be able to summon the necessary charity.

I've started two or three letters, been interrupted or obliged to complete some office work at home, etc. etc. But I have wanted to say something about the three sonnets you sent, along before this, and even now they aren't with me. So I can only give you my preferences: the Emily one first, the one ending—"I'm dead, I'm dead" next. But the other one, though ambitious and solid emotionally, somehow falls short of a sufficiently rich intonation. Allen Tate is more successful sometimes at expressing something of the same feeling of cerebral thunder in a vacuum, "invisible lyric seeds the mind", etc. But I think this group is superior, less strained than the sonnets in the *Caravan*.

Your review of Tate in the *N.R.* strikes me as nothing less than noble. Of course I resent being posed in a kind of All American Lyric Sprint with anyone, as the competetive idea seems foreign to my idea of creation. But that is probably too personal a reaction to have any pertinence to the major critical issues of the review. I also think that while Tate has a very complex mind and possibly a wider grasp of ideas than I do—

he nevertheless has not come to any closer grips with his world than to simply state the dilemma in a highly inferential manner, which we're all obliged to do most of the time. Tate's greatest rage against me at times has been on account of my avowed (and defended) effort to transcend these Eliotish sighs and tribulations, and to reach some kind of positive synthesis.

Tate faces the issues more squarely than the later Eliot. I like your appreciation of his really unflinching valor. But when you speak of my "illusions" you convince me that you surely are mistaken in a number of my intentions. I am not content with being an absolute Stoic. I mean, stoicism isn't my goal, even though I'm convinced as much as you and Tate are of the essentially tragic background of existence. There's something entirely too passive about stopping there (I don't care if even so great a poet as Hardy did!) and counting out, like the beating of a clock, the "preconceived" details of disappointment. For that is the stoic's pride—that all will pass but his endurance. It seems to me that Aeschylus, assuming the same materials, does a lot more with them. At least he *makes* something out them, call it all illusion or not.

After many inquiries and some intrigue, even, I'm back in the old house where I have a view of the harbor again. Rooming houses depress me terribly, and this is about the only one that sets me reading and writing a little, though I actually haven't had time, with the rush at the office, to read more than the usual reviews on the can or in the subway. I suspect I'll soon be off your list if I don't do better.

Yours, *Crane*

To Charlotte Rychtarik

110 Columbia Heights
Brooklyn, New York
October 23, 1928

Dear Charlotte:

Sam is in Cleveland this week, and maybe you have already seen him. Anyway, he said that he was going to phone you. If you do see him he can tell you more about my life the last year than I could get on paper in three weeks—and some things, especially my recent relations with my mother, I couldn't write about anyway. They are too complicated, too depressing, too inconclusive.

Your letter made me feel a lot better. It lifted a load from my spirit that I had felt for many months. I really need to *see* you, *talk* with you to explain what a hell the last two years have been. Perhaps you'd then see how it has been almost impossible for me to write anyone. For who wants to hear nothing but troubles? I've waited, putting off writing again and again, hoping to have something interesting to offer—for that is what such friends as you and Richard deserve.

I can realize how deeply you have felt the loss of your mother. You seem to have been having your share of tribulations . . . O, I know. . . . How I wish I could have seen you on your way through New York when you came back from Europe! Now it may be some time before we get together again. There is much to say, but little to tell—if you get what I mean. I haven't had a creative thought for so long that I feel quite lost and *spurlos versenkt*. My present job lasts another week, and then I must tramp around again to find another. Moving around, grabbing onto this and that, stupid landladies—never enough sense of security to relax and have a fresh thought—that's about all the years bring besides new and worse manifestations of family hysteria. It's a great big bore! I feel like saying what the Englishman did: "Too many buttons to button and unbutton. I'm through!"

Well, I don't deserve another letter from you, but I'd appreciate getting it, just the same, whenever you feel like writing.

Love, Hart

To Malcolm Cowley

110

the 20th of the 28th

Dear Malcolm: at the A.M. 7-thirtieth

After the passionate pulchritude of the usual recent maritime houreths—before embarking for the 20th story of the Henry L Doherty Co's 60 on Wall Street story—I salute your mss which arrived yesterday morning—as well as the really cordial apologies accompanying them for the really unhappy hours inaugurated last week by the hysteria of Sue (personally, sub rosa, between ourselves on the terrible Q.T.—I think that Sue has gone mad—having gone around to live with Jimmy Light and Patty as I hear). Poor Bill! God damn the female temperament! I've had thirty years of it—lacking six months—and know something myself.

It's me for the navy or Mallorca damned quick. Meanwhile sorting securities of cancelled legions ten years back—for filing—pax vobiscum—with Wall Street at 30 per—and chewing gum for lunch—while my supposed mother solicits every available streetwalker of the Coast to write me tearful threats—O yes, I saw Art Hays about it all. Nothing can be done, but to—

But hear I am—full of Renault Wine Tonics—after an evening with the Danish millionaire on Riverside—and better, thank God, a night with a bluejacket from the *Arkansas*—raving like a'mad. And it's time to go to work. So long. . . . I'll be careful of the mss. And your book'll be out within 7 months . . . About time! God bless you and give my love to Peggy! And as W. J. Turner says: "O hear the swan song's traffic's cry!"

Love ever, Hart

To Malcolm Cowley

Dear Malcolm: Tuesday night

Forgive me for that—whatever it was I wrote and sent this morning. Please destroy it, if you haven't already. The truth is, I've been nearly cookoo with the kind of letters my mother has been getting folks on the west coast to writing. She is now stooping to anything.

I've telephoned to the bank today. And declared her irresponsible. The bank seems to agree with me, having just had a 5 page letter from her which declares her refusal to sign until I agree to join her on the Coast and share the funds with her.

I have demanded immeadiate payment and think I'm going to get it without her signature. That means that I must rush to a gangplank as soon as I can buy a ticket. Hell of a situation! I'm apparently to be a new kind of literary exile!

Excuse all this, but I had to explain a little of my confusion.

Hart

To Malcolm Cowley

110 Columbia Heights
Brooklyn, New York
December 1, 1928

Dear Malcolm:

It has been a pleasure for me to spend part of the last two days in typing the mss of your book. Certainly I have been on more intimate terms with the poems than ever, and my enthusiasm has been heightened thereby rather than in any way diminished.

I now have two copies, one to turn over to the "secret" arbiter here and one to take with me to England. Whatever may or may not happen over there I'll at least be sure of having you along with me—which is much. By the way, if the mss. is returned to you, refused, be sure to send it at once to Coward-McCann, who, I understand, are calling for new poets and planning some kind of series of them. Hanna spoke to me about this yesterday.

Although I hope to get off next Saturday (probably on the *Tuscania*) I'm not at all certain. The bank behaves too strangely—now ignores my letters not to mention telegram. The meddlesome old nanny that is handling the matter there will soon hear from me through a lawyer if things don't take a new turn by Monday. That's the only way to handle it, I guess. I'm to see Art Hays Monday and talk it over. At any rate, I think it would be foolish to bring my troubles over to London with me and have them poison my first impressions of the place.

To get back to the poems: I omitted practically nothing but the "Decorations." The arrangement you made is ideal. As to the places for the following, I think you'll agree that they are ideal:

"Tumbling Mustard" just before "Memphis Johnny"

"Still Life" just before "Seaport" (it doesn't fit in the "Grand Manner" section particularly)

"Two Winter Sonnets" just after "St. Bartholomew" (they come in eloquently there)

Really the book as we now have it has astonishing structural sequence. Most of the more doubtfully important poems come in the central section. There is the fine indigenous soil sense to begin with in the *Juniata*, and the eloquent and more abstract matter mounting to a kind of climax toward the end. Hope you don't mind my enthusiasm!

See the *Show Boat* when you come to town. Wise took me last Tuesday night; the beautiful new Ziegfeld Theatre has them all beat—and the settings, song, costumes and glistening lithe girlies! Like greased lightning— the suave mechanical perfection of the thing.

You may not hear from me again if I leave next Saturday, but Mrs. Turner will be informed when I leave anyway. I'll see that your mss. (the original) is remailed to you registered, early next week. Lorna and I went on the best bat ever last night— Sam's old place—finally two cops came in and joined the party at three o-clock—asked Lorna to marry me and live with me in Spain—but she's got to wait for her divorce from the Danish gaucho now on the pampas.

My love to you both, as ever, your, Hart

To Charmion von Wiegand and Hermann Habicht

Rumrunia
off the coast of Ireland
near Christmas 1928

Dear Charmion and Herman:

My performance given at the Anderson party last summer was but a slight forecast to the splendors of my behavior night before last—when at a bal masque, dressed in a red coat of a sergeant-major, sailor hat, shark swagger stick etc.—I essayed a dervish whirl. But I seem to have made no enemies, and rum has become the favorite drink throughout the cabin.

If anything, I've had almost too good a time! I have been the only native American in the whole tourist cabin. The rest being Britishers, Canadians, Australians visiting relatives abroad, etc—and all of them the pleasantest crowd I ever met. Think I'm going to like London entirely too well for an early take-off to Spain. One old squire took me for a Cambridge man—and I admit that after a day or two in conflab with some of these natives one does tend to lose one's "middle-western accent."

You must excuse my exuberance momentarily at least. I can't stop being tremendously pleased at the wonderful ale, the pleasant manners of practically everybody (and one gets such graceful and attentive service everywhere), the balmy spring air, and the prospect of meeting more of such people soon on foreign shores. I feel really rested now, despite a hectic round of pleasures.

It was so nice of you to come to the little beer party. When I think of the mad rush of that last day I'm moved to wonder how I ever kept on my feet. But I enjoyed the evening after all. Hope you met some people you liked. I'm always a little vain about my friends.

The box of sweet meats has been a pleasure all round my table in the saloon. And as I haven't been seasick a moment I've been able to eat a full share, in fact an incredible amount every day. I'm enclosing a little reminder of past favors on your part.

Do let me hear from you soon. And please give my best to Max and Ilyena!

Your affectionate comrade, Hart

To Waldo Frank

Dear Waldo: December 28, 1928

Landed here with incipient flu but have managed to stave it off with good Jamaica rum and quinine. The city is soberly impressive—full of courtesy and deep character. I feel now as though I'd like to settle here—and even might—and I'm apt to be off to Paris next week. Shall not stay there very long, either, as I want to get settled and at work.

Am expecting to meet Edgell Rickword soon but not many others. Laura Riding and Robert Graves (friend of Col.

Lawrence and the one who introduced Cummings here) have been delightfully hospitable. I had a most luscious plum pudding with them Christmas on their barge on the Thames at Hammersmith in front of Wm. Morris' old headquarters.

No snow here at all—and the grass as green as summer in the parks. I've already seen a great deal—tramping about by myself, drinking Australian wine with old charwomen in Bedford Street—talking with ex-soldiers, and then the National Gallery with the marvelous "Agony in the Garden" of El Greco. The beautiful black and white streaked stone facades of the buildings make me quite sentimental. London is negative (as Laura says) but one gets a chance to breathe and deliberate. And there is something genuine about nearly every Englishman one meets. I feel almost too much at home.

Your pipe grows mellower every day. It's a little like Paul Robeson's voice—and I've been enjoying him, by the way. He and Essie have taken a sumptuous home of an ex-ambassador to Turkey for the rest of his engagement. But he's anxious to get to Paris to earn some astonishing laurels offered him there.

Do write soon. c/o Guaranty Trust / 3, Rue des Italiens.

Love to you and Alma and Tom. As ever, Hart

To Joseph Stella

c/o Guaranty Trust
3, rue des Italiens
Paris, France

Dear Mr. Stella: January 24, 1928

Sometime before leaving America Charmion Habicht showed me a copy of your privately issued monograph called *New York*, containing your essay on Brooklyn Bridge and the marvelous paintings you made not only of the Bridge but other New York subjects. This has been the admiration of everyone to whom I have shown it. And now I am writing you to ask if you will give permission to an editor friend of mine to reproduce the three pictures—"The Bridge", "The Port", and the one called "The Skyscrapers". He would also like to reprint your essay.

I am referring to Mr. Eugene Jolas who is an editor of *transition*—a magazine which you have probably heard of. He would like to use this material in the next number if you will be so kind as to give us permission. *Transition* is able to pay little or nothing now for contributions, but, since our friend Varese has told me that your essay has never been printed in any journal, we feel that so splendid and sincere a document should have wider circulation than private printing has allowed.

I have also a private favor of my own to ask you. I should like permission to use your painting of the Bridge as a frontispiece to a long poem I have been busy on for the last three years—called *The Bridge*. It is a remarkable coincidence that I should, years later, have discovered that another person, by whom I mean you, should have had the same sentiments regarding Brooklyn Bridge which inspired the main theme and pattern of my poem. I hope I am not plaguing you too much by requesting your permission in these matters. I may not be in Paris by the time you answer, but the above address is "good" anyway—for forwarding mail wherever I may later settle down.

Sincerely yours, Hart Crane

To Lorna Dietz

Dinners, soirees, poets
(PARIS)
mad millionaires, painters,
(PARIS)
translators, lobsters,
music, invitations, prom-
enades, gendarmes, sherry,
aspirin, oysters, pictures,
cathedrals, Sapphic heir-
esses, editors, "Kiki", books,
limousines, absinthe, fog,
red pompons, matelots. . . .
And How!

To Gertrude Stein

Hotel Jacob
44, rue Jacob
Paris, France
Dear Miss Stein: January 31, 1929

May I introduce myself as a friend of your friend, Laura Riding?

And on that presumption may I ask to see you some hour early next week—whenever it may suit your convenience to have me call?

I am going away for the weekend, but shall probably be back by Monday evening. I hope I may hear from you.

Sincerely, Hart Crane

To Malcolm Cowley

Guaranty Trust Co.
3, rue des Italiens
Paris, France
Dear Malcolm—   February 4, 1929

Time here flies faster than I can count. And now along comes the good news from you about the book of poems. Of course I'm all the happier that you got better terms from Hal—it's all to the good. But I do hope that you have seen Munson by this time and at least thanked him for his interest. For the very fact that you were able to make such an announcement to Hal may well have influenced his interest to a great extent. Such matters are rather officious for me to mention, I fear, but I do feel that Munson deserves some real credit.

I'm sorry to hear that Peggy has been so afflicted. I came the nearest ever to flu in London and really have been tagging around with a bit of it ever since.

I'm dizzy, also, with meeting people. "Teas" are all cocktails here—and then that's just the start of the evening. And as lions come these days, I'm known already, I fear, as the best "roarer" in Paris.

Have just returned from a weekend at Ermenonville (near Chantilly) on the estate of the Duc du Rochefoucauld where an amazing millionaire by the name of Harry Crosby has fixed up an old mill (with stables and a stockade all about) and such a crowd as attended *is* remarkable. I'm invited to return at any time for any period to finish the *Bridge*, but I've an idea that I shall soon wear off my novelty. Anyway, Crosby who inherited the famous Walter Berry (London) library has such things as first editions of Hakklyt (I can't spell today) and is going to bring out a private edition of the *Bridge* with such details as a reproduction of Stella's picture in actual color as frontispiece. He's also doing Lawrence, Cummings, and Kay Boyle. It takes a book to describe the Crosbys—but it has (I mean the connection) already led me to new atrocities—such as getting drunk yesterday and making violent love to nobility.

As le comte was just about to marry, I couldn't do better, though all agree (including Kay Boyle and Lawrence Vail) that I did my best. These last named, by the way, are consuming each other in hymen's flame these days.

I'm supposed to be off for a short trip to Villefranche, Toulon and Marseilles this week—but keep on writing me here. I'm not going to Mallorca—want to learn French and stay here.

> Best love to Peggy, and write soon & often. Hart

To Waldo Frank

Yes, how can one help loving Europe!—And after such barbarous crudities—en famille—as I have tasted! Here I am in an old mill tower with an old peasant couple bringing me wood for the glorious hearth, and food and delicious wine—all by myself for a whole week of solitude and study! I walk in the beautiful snow-clad park of the chateau and dream of getting back to myself—and you! Which means healing, strength and love (another name for faith) you understand?

> Hart

To Samuel Loveman

Water Boy! What the hell's the matter with you—and you won't even write a word! Here, I'm in marble halls and palace walls with my bad reputation on walking terms with the Comte du Rochefocauld all through his magnificent estate, swans, sheep, pheasants and all—and deep on the "Road to Xanadu" and kindred matters. Love to Mony and Rose—and to you.

Hart

Here—so far as I'm concerned, Proust, Jean Jacques and Whitman join!

To Wilbur Underwood

Do you remember this? The greatest work of art here, I think. I'm going too fast, too happy and too tired, but riding a good horse. Shall stay here until summer then probably the Riviera. Do write me c/o Guaranty Trust / 3, rue des Italiens

Love—Hart

To Charlotte and Richard Rychtarik

c/o Guaranty Trust
3, rue des Italiens
Paris, France

Dear Charlotte & Richard: February 26, 1929

First of all—before you read another word of this—you must swear to me not to repeat to anyone that you have heard from me, not even that you know where I am. I hate to begin my letter so seriously, but in time you will know more about *why* I don't want my family to find my whereabouts right now. I am very serious about this request, and I'm sure that you have enough interest in my work to abstain from any action which would cripple me.

It was fine to hear from you—two good long letters—and to know that all is going along so well in every way. I'm especially glad that you, Richard, have received such good notice and representation in the theatre literature which you mentioned. And from the other matters mentioned, I judge that Cleveland has been far from a cemetery—part of the credit for which is due to you both, *I know*. The Christmas card was a beauty, but then, so are all that you have ever made!

I scarcely know how to begin to tell you all that's been happening to me during the last year. But here's a brief summary, omitting thousands of details, all of which, however, are really important. . . . During my sojourn with the millionaire in California last winter my mother made life so miserable for me with incessant hysterical fits and interminable nagging that I had to steal off east again, like a thief in the night, in order to save my sanity or health from a complete breakdown. I went back to Patterson and tried to pull myself together, without money or prospects of any kind. Then in September, after I had secured a good job with an advertising agency, my Grandmother died, leaving me the inheritance which my grandfather bequeathed me over fifteen years ago.

Of course there had been a coolness between my mother and me ever since I left California. The net result of this was that (being co-executor of the estate with the Guardian Trust Co) she held back her signature to the papers for weeks, pretending to be too ill to sign her name. And finally she threatened to do all sorts of things if I did not come at once to California and spend it with her—among which she said she would write to my father and try to get him to intercede with the bank against paying me! This could have no effect whatever, but you may gather a little bit from what I have said about just how considerate and honorable she was! I can't begin to tell you about all the underground and harrowing tactics she employed. Got people who were practically strangers to write me threatening and scolding letters, so that I never came home from work without wonder—and trembling about what next I should find awaiting me. She had, through abuse, destroyed all the affection I had for her before I left the west; but now she made me actually hate her. I finally had to consult a lawyer, who directed his guns on the bank. This finally brought results. In the meantime I had given up all my plans about buying a little country place in Connecticut, for her ultimate home as much as mine. There was literally no other sensible plan but to take my money and get out of communication as soon as possible.

After having received written promise from the bank (as well as an advance) that the money would be in my hands by a certain day, I went ahead and engaged steamer passage to London. But the bank did not even keep its word, and I did not actually get the money until a few hours before the boat sailed. You can imagine my state of mind. I got on the boat more dead than alive. And I have not since had the least desire to know what is going on in California, and doubt if I ever *shall* care. Since my mother has made it impossible for me to live in my own country I feel perfectly justified in my indifference. I have had no particular quarrel with my father, and shall write him sometime after the *Bridge* is done and I don't fear mental complications. Meanwhile I'm so sure that she has carried out her threat and written him certain things that I'd rather keep out of it all. Twenty-five years of such exhausting quibbling is enough, and I feel I owe myself a good long vacation from it all. Neither one of them really cares a rap for me anyway. I have much more to tell you sometime, but this is enough for now. . . .

I fought off the flu in London by drinking hot rum and walking, walking, walking. It's a wonderful but sad, heavy city. I didn't meet many people there, but saw Paul Robeson several times (who is the star in the London production of *The Show Boat*) and had a jolly Christmas with some friends who live on a barge on the Thames. Went to the famous dangerous and tough Limehouse section expecting some exciting adventures, but found that most of the young toughs drank only lemonade—and after I had had several swigs of Scotch they all seemed to be afraid of me! O life is funny! I'd like to go back to England sometime in the summer of the year. The damp, raw cold was like a knife in my throat—and the hotels like cellars. I left there on the 7th of January, and life has been like a carnival ever since—here in Paris!

I've never been in such a social whirl—all sorts of amusing people, scandalous scenes, cafe encounters, etc. Writers, painters, heiresses, counts and countesses, Hispano-Suizas, exhibitions, concerts, fights, and—well, you know Paris, probably better than I do. I had originally intended to stop here only two or three weeks on the way to a permanent location at Mallorca, one of the Balearic Islands (Spain). But I've fallen so much in love with the French and French ways that I've deceided to stay here until summer anyway, and try to learn the language before leaving.

All sorts of things have happened. Through Eugene Jolas, editor of *transition*, I met Harry Crosby who is heir to all the Morgan-Harjes millions and who is the owner of a marvelous de luxe publishing establishment here. He is so enthusiastic about the *Bridge* that he is going to bring it out here before it is published in America, as soon as I can finish it. He has renovated an old mill (16th century) out on the ground of the chateau of the Comte du Rochfocauld at Ermenonville where I have spent several wild weekends. Polo with golf sticks on donkeys! Old stagecoaches! Skating on the beautiful grounds of the chateau! Oysters, absinthe, even opium, which I've tried, but don't enjoy. I had the pleasure, last week, of spending five days out there working all by myself, with just the gardener and his wife bringing me food and wine beside a jolly hearthfire. And the beautiful forests all around—like the setting for *Pelleas et Melisande*! I'm going out again soon. Meanwhile I dream of how fine they've promised to publish the *Bridge*—on sheets as large as a piano score, so none of the lines will be broken—and they have already sent to the Brooklyn Art Museum to have the Stella picture of the *Bridge* copied in color for reproduction as a frontispiece!

Philippe Soupault and his wife are about the nicest French people I have met. Then there is Edgare Varese, Gertrude Stein, Glenway Wescott, Eugene MacCown, Kay Boyle, Man Ray, Robert Desnos and dozens of others who are not famous as artists, but who make things amusing and lively. I'm quite mad about Paris. One can take long walks without ever being depressed, for you can't walk a single block without encountering something gracious to the eye. When are you coming? I hope before too late in the summer, as I may be down on the Riviera then, or in Spain, especially as one or two people whom I have met have asked me to sail around with them, from port to port, on little boats they own. It would be great to be with you here in Paris! And I long to see you.

Write me soon, and I promise to do better about answering than before. And lots of love!

as ever, Hart

To Harry Crosby

Dear Harry: Sunday

I hear that you've been in bed with la grippe, but hope that she has slipped under other covers by this time—at least left you unravaged and lively as usual! The two antiquities you sent me are priceless, especially with their high-voltage inscriptions. It was almost too much for my slumbers to have undone the package and found so much, despite the hour, 7 AM, when I came back from wandering yesterday. I lay blinking quite awhile, with the sun climbing into the windows! —And I got a very unique pleasure from picturing your search for the talisman shark-tooth. Just so no one has swallowed it!

Yes, I'm longing for le Moulin, and anytime like next Thursday suits me perfectly. Meanwhile I'll try to add a few more paragraphs to the flying machine, scream awhile, dream awhile, etc. Your praise is very stimulating. My confidence revives! Love to Caresse!

Hart

To Otto H. Kahn

c/o Guaranty Trust
3 rue des Italiens
Paris, France

Dear Mr. Kahn: March 5, 1929

I think of you so often that I can't help wondering if it is not again somewhat near the time for one of your visits to the Continent. At any rate, I do hope to see you when you are next in Paris; and I shall be here until summer, probably, to greet you, should you chance to come.

Meanwhile, I hope you will grant me a particular favor. There is to be a special de luxe edition of *The Bridge* printed here, by Harry & Caresse Crosby (Editions Narcisse). The poem, per se, is not dedicated to anyone, but to The Brooklyn Bridge, as you know. But I should like the privilege of dedicating this special edition to you, if you will allow me, in token of my appreciation of all you have done to further the creation of the poem. The edition will be very beautiful, I can assure you; and regardless of your decision I shall take great pleasure in presenting you with a copy.

I hope to hear from you soon, and to know that you are in your usual good health and spirits.

Faithfully yours, Hart Crane

To Caresse Crosby

Hotel Bougnol-Quintana
Collioure, Pyrenees-Orientales
April 25, 1929

Dear Caresse:

I'm beginning to feel my feet a little nearer the ground already. Hot suns and rural surroundings and the sea can almost be counted on to relieve that suspended feeling that cities generally induce. . . . So maybe I can get some work done, after all. At least I don't feel as doubtful now as I did a week ago.

Your suggestion about immeadiate publication for the *Bridge* is very generous, indeed inspiring. I'm so glad to know that it strikes you as being already so organic as to satisfy the requirements that its general form demands. The fact of your having stated this may help me to relax my concern about the rest of it enough to possibly stimulate me to quicker results with the remaining projected parts. We'll see. At least I'm becoming weary of the burden and am ready for almost any compromise.

Suppose, then, that I agree to turn the thing over to you by the first of September, regardless of my success in the meantime? By that time we'll possibly all be in Paris (I *may* be much before) and can see the thing through the press together. If you like I'll give you my word about the matter, especially as I know you run your press on business principles and like to know your schedule sometime in advance. As you say, there can always be a second edition incorporating additions. For all I know, the *Bridge* may turn into something like the form of *Leaves of Grass*, with a number of editions, each incorporating further additions.

I'd love to see you on the beach here with your red herring suit. You're about the only thing lacking. I begin to look like a red herring myself—with my recently incurred coat of tan. The place is full of painters. Every nook, corner, alley, turret, parapet and sailboat simply screams to be painted. It's alright for me. But if I were a painter I'd be damned scared of the place. It certainly has spoiled all stage sets for me. They'll never be able to equal the genre of this place.

Do let me hear more from you and Harry. You don't know how I appreciate all your warmth and kindliness. What are your plans? Going later to Cannes with Pete and Gretchen? Understand they're having a bullfight here later on.

Affectionately, as ever Hart

To William Slater Brown

Collioure
Pyrenees-Orientales, France

Bill: 25 Avril 1929

Why the hell don't you write to me? You used to. And here I am, sitting by the shore of the most shockingly beautiful fishing village—with towers, baronial, on the peaks of the Pyrenees all about, wishing more than anything else that you were on the other side of the table.

This begins to look as good as the West Indies. Maybe—if I could talk Catalan it would be better. I began to feel as you predicted about Paris. Wish you were with me! I don't know whether you want to hear from me or not—since you have never written—but here's my love anyway, Bill—

Your, Hart

To Gertrude Stein

There has been too much wind to notice odors. I like it so far, and expect to stay awhile. Feel quite indigenous since spending last night out on a sardine schooner. The dialect isn't so easily assimilated.

Best wishes—Hart Crane

To Isidor Schneider

Collioure, Pyr.-Orientales, France
Dear Isidor: May 1, 1929
   I'm wondering if you and Helen aren't already out in the Pennsylvania countryside. I've been late in answering—hoping, in point of fact, that I'd have more "progress" to report than the usual preoccupations of a typical American booze-hound in Paris. But alas, I must bow my immodest head in resignation, while you must credit me with more attachment and affection than has seemed evident, to judge by my responses. And I *had* really counted on seeing you over here. . . . Too damned bad you didn't get it! I mean the Guggenheim prize. However, as regards creative writing—I can't say that I'm finding Europe extremely stimulating. I left home in a bad state of nerves and spirit and haven't exactly recovered yet, so perhaps my reactions are not as fresh as they might be. Perhaps a few weeks of the quiet of places like this ancient fishing port may change my mind—but at any rate I haven't so far completed so much as one additional section to the *Bridge*. It's coming out this fall in Paris, regardless. Limited edition of 200 copies, Black Sun Press (Harry & Caresse Crosby)—which won't complicate my contract with Liveright in any way. If it eventuates that I have the wit or inspiration to add to it later—such additions can be incorporated in some later edition. I've alternated between embarrassment and indifference for so long that when the Crosbys urged me to let them have it, declaring that it reads well enough as it already is, I gave in. Malcolm advised as much before I left America, so I feel there may

be some justification. The poems, arranged as you may remember, do have, I think, a certain progression. And maybe the gaps are more evident to me than to others . . . indeed, they must be.

Here's wishing you good luck—inspiration, celerity and response—on your novel. I'm sorry I was in such a state when I dined with you last. I should have liked to have had a calm discussion of it with you, your aims, ideas, etc. As it is, I know nothing whatever about it. In your next letter, please do tell me more about it. I suppose you dread to go back to the grind of the office, but I'm sure that Liveright has needed you back —and has realized it. Your temporary successor, whoever he may be, is lacking in all sorts of ways. I recently have been informed that the 1st edition of *White Bldgs.* is sold out. There won't be another for awhile, I guess. There were only 500 printed, just half the number that I until recently had supposed. But that's the usual number, I'm told.

I do hope you prevail on L. to bring out Hopkins' verse. But I doubt it. I think he's a bit thick-skinned to sympathize. Recently a friend of Laura Riding and Graves, Geoffrey Phibbs, whom I've never met, sent me a copy right out of a clear sky. I was dumfoundered—for it certainly is rare when such wealthy bibliophiles as Harry Crosby are unable through all their London agents to locate a copy. So when I come back, we'll have at least one copy "in the family" as it were! whatever Liveright decides.

London, I can still believe, might be delightful under proper circumstances. I had incipient flu before I landed, then the raw cold of the particular season, the bad hotel accommodations, the indigestible food and Laura's hysterical temper at the time —all combined to send me off with no particular regrets. It's certainly the most expensive place I can imagine—more than even New York unless you're really settled down. I loved its solid, ponderous masonry—and the gaunt black-and-white streakings and shadings. It's a city for the etcher. I must tell you about my excursion to Limehouse sometime—where, expecting to be blackjacked etc., I drank so many Scotch-and-sodas during a game of darts in one of the pubs, that I frightened people, actually scared some of the toughs about— all of whom struck me as being very pleasant people. I'd like to go there again and stay longer sometime—but not during the winter!

As for Paris, I'll have to wait until I see you to touch the subject. Philippe Soupault and his wife were about the most hospitable French people I met, and Gertrude Stein about the most impressive personality of all. That marvellous room of her's, the Picassos, Juan Gris and others (including some very interesting youngsters) on the walls! Then there were Ford Madox Ford, Wescott, Bernadine Szold (just back from the Orient), Richard Aldington, Walter Lowenfels (who has an interesting book of verse coming out in England (Heinemann), Emma Goldman, Klaus Mann, Eugene MacCown, Jolas (whom I like very much), Edgar Varèse, René Crevel, Kay Boyle (who has decided she likes me), and a hundred others just as interesting, or more so, who aren't particularly known. The Tates are living in Ford's apartment while he is away, and declare they never want to leave Paris. I like it all too well, myself, but would have to live there a long while before I could settle down to accomplish any work, I fear. And lately—all cities get on my nerves after a few weeks. I'd never want to settle down for good over here like many do, however,—town *or* country. For even here by the blue inland sea, with ancient citadels and fortifications crowning the heights of a lovely white-walled village—I can't help thinking of my room out there in Patterson. Silly, I know . . . but what can one do about it?

My plans are vague. May stay here two months more or only two weeks. Spain is very near, but also, I hear, very expensive. I'm crossing over to a nearby town to see a bull fight in a couple of days. But I may not explore it much further at the time, regardless of my intense interest. There are other small ports between here and Marseille which are very intriguing. I can't regret not seeing everything this trip—or even never. You see I like France pretty well! Guaranty Trust, Paris, is still my address. Write soon—please.

My love to you both, Hart

To Harry Crosby

c/o American Express
13, La Canabière
Marseille, France
Dear Harry:—   May 16, 1929

That's a fine picture—and if you want to turn it over to
Jolas I don't mind at all. My God! what I'm to do about
money *now*—since reading your instructions—is more than I
know. Methinks it means that I leave early for the States again
—as I don't think I have any bankbook even in my baggage
still in Paris. I have a coupla thousand in that account in New
York—perhaps I'll have to show my passport to them to iden-
tify my claim! Banking doesn't seem to be my strong point
. . . As it is, I have about enough for 2 more months on this
side of the water. I'll write the Paris office and inquire what
can be done about it.

Marseille's a delightful place—to *me*—and I want to stay a
week or so longer. Thank God, there's nothing much to gape
at—museums or otherwise—and the people seem (I mean the
citizens and residents) less French than anywhere else I've been.
I can think of my work here—get my feet more on the ground
—and dress and do as I please. Living at that one-and-only
boarding house at Collioure—with an international colony of
painters—got on my nerves. To see them so busy every day
with every nook and corner of the "picturesque" gave me the
"willies". Here there isn't one building that one wants to look
at twice. It's dirty, vulgar, noisy, dusty—but I claims whole-
some. Had a great time last Saturday visiting the whore houses
with an English sailor—whose great expression of assent and
agreement was "heave Ho!" And a row with one of the
officers later in the evening—a true Scotsman—who said he
would give the 16 (why *16* I don't know) remaining years of his
life to see America "humbled in the dust". He was a fine
looking old codger—with upturned whiskers and eyebrows—
looked like a Triton or Neptune but had too much beer in him
to float . . . There's a Danish cruiser here now—as far as I
can see the officers have better manners.

Did you send me some cigars? and where? I'm damned

sorry I missed 'em. I'm glad I got that bottle of "Cutty Sark" anyway. If it isn't tonsilitis it's hay fever! I'm having my usual spring touch of that down here—though I can't see any *fields* around here. No, Europe isn't my cure, after all! Even though someone sent me some damned-fool clipping from the *Tribune*, reporting me as "convalescing" at Collioure, "a tiny village far in the Pyrenees"! Christ Almighty! save me from such mention!

I've had enough Pernod to keep on forever—but it's time to stop boring you. Write me soon, Harry—and tell me, by the way, what date during the next 3 months is most convenient for the printing of the *Bridge*. . . .

I'm trying to write a gloss—but it's not easy to be consistent about it, as the poem is developed not on narrative lines nor dramatic—in the sense of any consistent theme, like the "Ancient Mariner". Shall we try to help the poor public or not? That's the question!

Hope all is well at Le Moulin these days. My love to Caresse and her rosebeds there!

Best ever to you, Harry! Yours, Hart

To Malcolm Cowley

23 May

Have been looking for your proofs. Hope you have sent me the promised set. I'm becoming very fond of Provence. Wish I could stay here forever. Spring has *finally* arrived. Very late here this year. I'm supposed to meet Roy Campbell here today but it seems he's just gone into Marseille! I'm going back tonight.

Hart

To Allen Tate

c/o American Express
Marseille, France
Dear Allen: June 11, 1929

You *have* had a time of it! But you deserve real congratulations on the amount of work which you've done despite so many obstacles. I wish I had something to show for the last two months—more than a coat of tan. I've really just "bummed around".

I didn't stay more than three weeks at Collioure. Since then I've been in and about Marseille, a city which has a great deal of interest to me, although there's nothing whatever here to interest the usual type of tourist. Have just come back from two weeks visiting Roy Campbell and family out at Martigues, a sort of Venice and Gloucester combined, being built on three islands made by canals joining the Etang de Berre with the sea.

I have come to love Provence, the wonderful Cezannesque light (you see him everywhere here) and the latinity of the people. Arabs, negros, Greeks, and Italian and Spanish mixtures. The Campbells rent a house and have a maid for almost nothing, but swimming isn't good there and there are other features which might not appeal to you as much as the country east of here where you are planning to go. Marsden Hartley whom I encountered here knows the whole coast, both sides of the Rhone, and prefers it here. I'm coming back to Paris within a couple of weeks but may take a swift excursion over to Nice and environs beforehand, just to see what I've missed by hanging around here so long. Then maybe my advice will be worth more than at present.

I'm planning on returning to N.Y. before very long. How soon depends largely on what I hear from the Crosbys on my return to Paris regarding their edition of the *Bridge*. I'm anticipating a good visit with you and Carolyn before many days. Thanks a lot for the money order, exactly correct in amount, and quite providential at the moment as the bank has been slow in forwarding me funds.

Yours ever, Hart

To Waldo Frank

June 17, 1929

Can't get around to that long and grateful letter to you that you so much deserve. Why?—don't ask me yet! But it isn't because I don't often long to see you. I have been in an undecided state since before we last met. I pray for relief.

Love, Hart

Have been here 5 weeks and love it. *All* Provence is "holy land" to me.

To Harry and Caresse Crosby

c/o Guaranty Trust
4, Place de la Concorde
Dear Harry and Caresse: July 1

A thick fog still envelopes my "memory" of the latter hours at your side last Saturday! I think Cutty Sark won that bout without the slightest doubt! I called next morning to find you had *both* gone—so Paris is going to be more lonesome than I thought.

I'm wondering if you have said anything to Mme Henri about my visiting the Moulin for a while, as you suggested. Perhaps since your change of plans it wouldn't be convenient. Please be thoroughly frank about it. But I'm in such a devil of a fix with all my money tied up in that savings account in New York that I'm naturally anxious to make plans regarding the next few weeks as soon as possible. I'm through playing around in any case—and the rest of my time here will be devoted entirely to preparing the mss. of *The Bridge* for your hands.

I don't want to borrow any more money from you than will be necessary for a second class or tourist cabin passage back to N.Y. More won't be necessary. But as by staying for a few weeks at the Moulin I might be able to get more work done and also possibly see you again your suggestion had a great appeal to me.

Yesterday, by the way, I met Edgar Varese, who told me that

Stella is still in Naples, and further—that there had already been a *colored* reproduction of the Bridge printed in some magazine, he didn't know which. Accordingly I've already written Stella for details—also to send us a copy of the colored picture if he has it with him. It may be that the color plates could be purchased from the magazine publisher. I'll write more as soon as I hear.

Hope you're enjoying that wonderful sun! Love and a thousand thanks!

As ever, Hart

To Malcolm Cowley

c/o Guaranty Trust
4, Place de la Concorde
Paris, France
Dear Malcolm: July 3, 1929

Since reading the proofs I'm certain that the book is even better than before. And the notes! —When you first mentioned them to me I admit having trembled slightly at the idea. But since seeing them I haven't a doubt. The maturity of your viewpoint is evident in every word. Humour and sincerity blend into some of the cleverest and adroit writing I know of, leaving the book a much more solidified unit than it was before. I haven't had the original mss with me for comparison, but wherever I have noted changes they seem to be for the better. Nor do I regret any of the additions. I like the added bulk of the book. Really, Malcolm—if you will excuse me for the egoism—I'm just a little proud at the outcome of my agitations last summer. *Blue Juniata* will have a considerable sale for a long period to come, for the bulk of it has a classical quality—both as regards material and treatment—that won't suffer rejection by anyone who cares or who will later care for American letters.

I would particularize more copiously except that I'm expecting to see you within relatively so short a time. . . . I'll be back in NY by the first of September at the latest, and I may be back a month before. Perhaps it's just as well that a good part of my money is tied up in a savings account in New York and inaccessible to me here. As it is, I haven't any great regrets about coming back at this time. When I come to France again I'll sail direct for Marseille—and it's certainly my intention to come again! I'm looking forward to talking it all over with you—so get a little cider ready for the occasion!

The Crosbys are bringing out the *Bridge* in December or January—that is, it'll be finished and on sale by that time. Yes, you can have a copy—but don't tell anyone about it. I don't get very many gratis—and I might like to sell a half dozen of them myself. Why not? Certainly that wouldn't be any more ignoble than the McSorley book-raid which you played such a friendly part in. I certainly *am* grateful!

I wish *Vanity Fair* could have something better than they likely got from the Isle of Pines period. But they'll probably have too good taste to use any of those anyhow—and anyway, I can't imagine a much greater absurdity than putting me, at this early date, in any of their public albums!

S'much for now, and as Jack Fitzin used to say—"it won't be long now" . . .

As ever, Hart

To Harry Crosby

Dear Harry: July 23, 1929

The *Cutty Sark* lasted 3 days, which is doing well for me—not to mention my steward and a nice boy from Wall Street both of whom have a sip now and then. The empty bottle is going to survive the customs tomorrow as a respectable souvenir of you and Paris even if I have to bring my little hatchet into play and "givim Hell"—as you say . . .

Last night I made it a point—along with three college boys—to get politely put out of the 1st class bar. After that I felt considerably better. The rest of the trip—which has been smooth as castor oil and sunny—will be celebrated with Bourbon and Soda. I haven't had any Bourbon since my sweaty days in Cuba and it almost makes me see palm trees on the horizon.

I've been reading John Donne's "Devotions" and Mase-field's "Sard Harker" and working on the new sections of *The Bridge*. You'll be getting something from me very soon. How long it will last I don't know, but the nearer we get to America the more "creative" I seem to feel. And we are sailing right into one of those fine heat waves in Manhatten if the wireless is to be believed.

Here are some stars, by the way. With rays and without 'em. I think that "A" is the best—if made smaller—for the end of book. And I'm not at all sure now that I want one *at all* on the title page. If so—it ought to be very small. But I leave it to your taste entirely. Please do put one at the end, however. "B" looks well—but I'm afraid reminds one too much of the date of Santa Klaus . . .

I've been enjoying a leisurely reading of *Transit of Venus*. My especial favorites are:

> "Beyond"
> "Were it not Better"
> "Eventuates"
> and "Fire-Eaters"

There is a Rimbaudian vigor to "Beyond" and I'll never forget your "deaf adder" poem.

I'll see the Brooklyn Museum about the Stella reproduction and write at once.

Meanwhile my gratitude, dear Harry, to you and to Caresse —well, for some of the happiest times of memory! I'm glad I have those snapshots you gave me, whenever I'll want two pleasant faces to look at.

Yrs—Hart

Love to Caresse!

To Caresse Crosby

Patterson, New York

Dear Caresse: August 8, 1929

Herewith are the gloss notes that I showed you, now cor-rected and ready to include with the composition of the first two sections of the *Bridge*. You will see where each block of them falls by the *key lines* typed at the left. I have kept them narrow as that seems to be the custom—and we don't want to crowd our margins. (See MacLeish's *Hamlet* and the version of the *Ancient Mariner* as printed in the *Oxford Anthology*.) I can't help thinking them a great help in binding together the general theme of Powhatan's daughter. As for the Columbus note, it simply silhouettes the scenery before the colors arrive to inflame it. . . .

I'm working on the other remaining sections indicated in the index of the ms. as you have it, and hope to get a couple of them off to you within ten days. I haven't had a chance to see Mr. Fox, director of the Brooklyn Museum yet as he has been away on his vacation, but have an appointment made with his secretary for early next week. I'm hoping to see Harry Marks as soon as he returns in order to ask his advice about having a copy made of the picture, the amount to pay, etc. Meanwhile, from what Harry said, I judge that you are going ahead with setting certain sections. Don't rush along too fast, though— please! If we get it out by the last of November it will be soon enough. Meanwhile I'm not negociating with Liveright or anyone else. I don't think there will be any difficulty whatever in disposing of the 250 which you are printing. I don't know how many people have already bespoken copies, and I'll send you a list of names later on which will be pretty sure-fire.

New York seems better than ever to me. The beaches are wonderful—and packed with pulchritude. Where are you these days? I somehow can't picture you as still in Paris.

Love ever, and more soon— Hart

P. S. Please ask Harry if he can think of any job for that nice Danish boy I introduced him to the morning I sailed. He's without work or funds—and starving. He's an expert trainer and keeper of horses (Danish Royal Artillery) and speaks English fairly well. *K.P. Christensen,* 7, rue Jean-Lantier, Paris. Honest, industrious, and will do anything that's honorable.

To Malcolm Cowley

130 Columbia Heights
Dear Malcolm: August 22, 1929

You're a lucky boy! I've been rereading some beautiful reviews of *Juniata*—especially Allen's in the *New Republic*—and then Kenneth's in the *H.-Tribune*, the *Nation*, and even Seaver in the *Eve. Post* for last Saturday. I'm very glad about it all.

When you or Peggy come in look me up in my new apartment as numbered above. There's no phone yet. But plenty of mariners! *And whisky, too*—

Love, Hart

To Harry and Caresse Crosby

130 Columbia Heights
Brooklyn, New York
Dear Harry and Caresse: August 30, 1929

I had my first visit with Harry Marks today and am glad to hear that he has nothing as yet to report about any work of yours on the *Bridge*. For, as you know, I am anxious to add more—the "Cape Hatteras" sections, at least—before you bring it out. This is now being worked out rapidly, and the aeronautical sections which you so much admired have been improved and augmented considerably. However, the line-lengths are longer than in any other section—so long, in fact, that to preserve them unbroken across the page I think we ought to change our plan regarding page size and use, instead of the previously-agreed on Perse book for a model, your *Mad Queen* volume—even better looking in other respects, too, I think. I hope I can ask you for this change without appearing too presumptuous!

How did you like the "gloss" I sent you recently? I'm passionately anxious to hear from you as soon as possible.

About the Stella reproductions . . . I've been over twice to the Brooklyn Museum, talked with the director and curator, and secured permission to have the picture featured any way we like. But when I came to question engraving companies on the cost of the necessary five plates for color reproduction I was surprised at the cost. At least $200. would be involved, it seems. Now I'm assuming that to be too steep for any of us, and, instead, am going to send a good photographer over to the museum to get a good, clear picture. Then I'll send that on to you. The plate for this can be made in Paris cheaper and possibly better than here. It may look better, even, without color—if we get a good photo and a sharp, clear half-tone.

I'm settled at last in a comfortable furnished apartment— not far from the navy yard. There have been great house-warmings, especially since I can buy corn whisky from my janitor for only $6. per gallon! No more querulous, farty old landladies for me for awhile. Write me from now on directly at the above address instead of Patterson. Liveright is issuing a second edition of *While Buildings*—*Vanity Fair* bestows laurels in the Sept. issue—Eliot urges me to contribute as well as old Mamby Canby of the *Sat. Review*, the old enemy camp. So I'm feeling optimistic to a large extent.

Yrs ever, Hart

To Caresse Crosby

130 Columbia Heights
Brooklyn, New York
Dear Caresse: September 6, 1929

Just received the first specimen proofs a little late, unfortunately, as my old landlady out at Patterson had thought they were "printed matter" and had failed to forward them as soon as certain other mail. But you'll be writing me direct to the above address in the future anyway.

Please go ahead and set up what sections you already have in the large sized type. I like it much better than the smaller sized Caslon. Only—don't you think that page (I'm using it as a model) would look better balanced, and certainly not crowded, with about four more lines of verse on it? I think the extreme depth of the bottom margin looks awkward rather than luxurious.

I have more to send—and it's very important. I am working like mad since I've found this apartment where I can keep my own hours, etc. I'm too rushed to type you out a final copy of this finale to the "Cape Hatteras" section yet—but you can get some idea of what I'm accomplishing by the muddled copy I'm including herewith. You'll have the final version—including what you read in Paris—within a few days, aeronautics and all. It looks pretty good to me, and at least according to my ideas of the *Bridge* this edition wouldn't be complete or even representative without it.

Then the "Quaker Hill" section—and "Indiana," the final subsection to "Powhatan's Daughter" (which won't require any gloss, I think) will come in quick succession. I know what to plan on fairly well when I get into one of these fevers of work. So please be patient. The book must have these sections and I can promise to have them in your hands by the second week in October! Then clear steaming ahead! I'm very happy about the paper, format and all which you have selected. I'll try to get you the fresh photo of Stella's picture within a few days.

I hope you and Harry are still planning on a visit here next winter. Then maybe I can make up for the kiss I missed when sailing! Do you really like that little necklace that much?!! My gifts seldom have so fortunate a reception!

Love, hastily, Hart

P. S.—Peter Christiansen writes me how cordial Harry has been and how helpful. Thank you both a lot!

To Caresse Crosby

Patterson, New York

Dear Caresse: September 17, 1929

I sent you, registered, the "Cape Hatteras" 1st version. But re-typing it for a magazine, I couldn't help glimpsing some necessary improvements. So please use this *second* version, as enclosed. I vow that you'll be troubled by no further emendations—excepting perhaps a comma or so on the proofs.

Since I'm writing I can't help saying that I'm pleased with

the way I've been able to marshal the notes and agonies of the last two years' effort into a rather arresting synthesis . . .

Gosh, how I'd like a bottle of Cutty Sark to-night to soothe my excited nerves! The countryside is the dryest here in years—and nothing to hope for next year, as frost and this later drowth have ruined the apple crop! I had to flee the heat in the city for a week's work up here in my old farmhouse room. It's lovely, too. Another week of it—by which time I expect to have finished the two remaining sections,—and I'll be back in city quarters (130 Columbia Hts). . . .

Love ever, Hart

To Otto H. Kahn

Dear Mr. Kahn—   5:20 Wednesday
    Lord Lymington and I were sorry to miss you. It was *not* a business call. I look forward to delivering the edition of the *Bridge* (and I shall hope to deliver dedication to you) this winter—provided your lackeys are not quite so imposing and insulting—

Yours affectionately, Hart Crane

To Lorna Dietz

Patterson, New York

Dearest Lorna: Wednesday
    I've been *weltschmerzing* a little bit all by myself here since last Saturday afternoon, when I suddenly picked up and left town. I've never seen such color as this year's autumnal shades, but the storm that began this morning after three wonderful days of sunshine probably won't leave so much on the boughs to be gazed at. . . . Nevertheless I'm staying on at least until next Monday—and maybe somewhat longer. I feel quite rested already, but I know that I need a little "reserve" after the way I've been acting. I'm *hoping* also, to complete the last two sections, God 'elp me! And then to come back to town and see you again in your sweet, new, cheerful, rosy little nest!

You've probably seen Emil, who left Monday for a few days with his mother.

Lots of love, Dear! from your Hart

To Harry and Caresse Crosby

130 Columbia Heights
Brooklyn, New York
October 29, 1929

Dear Harry Caresse:

Your last cable fairly met me at the door on my return from ten days out at Patterson. I was able to finish the enclosed ("Indiana")—but the "Quaker Hill" section is not yet ready to send. In view of the fact that you will soon be here (and I certainly hope to see you! God bless you!) and that my decision will apparently not hold you up materially on any of your other projects (since you will be away from Paris anyway) I have decided to adopt the latter choice mentioned in your cable—and let publication be postponed until the February date, as you know already from the cable I'm sending today.

I really do want to see at least the bulk of the poem in proofs. Also your visit here will provide a splendid opportunity for us to go over all final details with no chance of misunderstandings. I am sorry to have been so slow—but the muse, as you know, won't hurry, least of all when the brow becomes infected with the urgency for haste! Certainly you seem to have agreed that the "Hatteras" section proved worth waiting for, no matter what you may think of the succeeding sections. The symbolism of Indiana (metamorphosis of Pocahontus—the indian) into the pioneer woman, and hence her absorption into our "contemporary veins" is, I hope, sufficiently indicated without too great sacrifice of poetic values: line-by-line interest, I mean. It does round out the cycle, at least historically and psychologically—one leaves the continent surrounded by water (pure space) as one found it in the first place ("Harbor Dawn"), and "Cutty Sark" quite logically follows as "space" again.

What a treat it will be to see you again! Is Constance coming by any chance? Please allot me in advance as much time with you as possible. I am going out to Cleveland to visit my father (with whom a reconciliation seems to have been effected) during the next two weeks, but certainly shall hope to be back here before your arrival. Haven't been well lately, but hope to improve as soon as I can get the 5-year load of the *Bridge* off my shoulders. You can't imagine how insufferably ponderous it has seemed, yes, more than once!

Love always, Hart

To Caresse Crosby

To my loved Caresse—   December 3, 1929

"while through white cities passed on to assume
that world which comes to each of us alone"—

from forever her Hart

To Caresse Crosby

DECEMBER 12 1929

DEAR CARESSE YOU KNOW I WISH TO BE OF HELP CARESSE YOU ARE CARESSE YOU ARE MY FAVORITE FRIEND POLLY CARESSE I SAY CARESSE YOU ARE NOT ONLY ALL BUT YOU UNDERSTAND ALL

HART CRANE

To Allen Tate

130 Columbia Heights
Brooklyn, New York

Dear Allen: December 14, 1929

Despite the recent tragedy of Harry's death here Carresse Crosby is going to complete their superb edition of *The Bridge*. She is on the same boat that brings this to you.

You once suggested your willingness to collaborate in the final proofreading and I am hoping that you still feel the same as then. Caresse is very anxious to have your help, and will welcome any effort on your part to get in touch with her as soon as possible. You can reach her at home, 19 rue de Lille.

I've been all broken up about Harry. I had just had a party or so for them—and all our friends immeadiately fell in love with them both. I was with Caresse and Harry's mother the evening of so-called suicide, and had to break the news to them. I haven't been worth much since, so this letter is hasty and brief.

The advance interest in the appearance of the *Bridge* is amazing. Random House and others have been after Caresse to handle it. All this has made Liveright almost a fanatic on the subject. But he's got to wait a couple of months, according to my contract with Harry and Caresse, before bringing out the trade edition. He's furious, but—it can't be helped.

I hope you are all well, and look forward to your return . . . is it in February?

Love to Carolyn and Nancy,

yours ever, Hart

To Otto H. Kahn

Dear Otto Kahn:

A Merry Christmas to you! *The Bridge* is done—and I shall bring it to you soon!

Yours faithfully, Hart Crane

To Caresse Crosby

130 Columbia Heights
Brooklyn, New York
December 26, 1929

Dearest Caresse:

I am hastily enclosing the final version of "Quaker Hill," which ends my writings on the *Bridge*. You can now go ahead and finish it all. I've been slow, Heaven knows, but I know that you forgive me. I haven't added as many verses to what you took with you as I had expected. I had several more, roughly, in notes, but think that my present condensation is preferable. "Quaker Hill" is not, after all, one of the major sections of the poem; it is rather by way of an "accent mark" that it is valuable at all.

By the way, will you see that the middle photograph (the one of the barges and tug) goes between the "Cutty Sark" Section and the "Hatteras" Section. That is the "center" of the book, both physically and symbolically. Evans is very anxious, as am I, that no ruling or printing appear on the pages devoted to the reproductions—which is probably your intention anyway.

I have an idea for a change in one line of the dedication to B. Bridge. If you don't like it, don't change it. But I feel that it is more logical, even if no more suggestive. Instead of:

"—And elevators heave us to our day"

I suggest:

"—Till elevators drop us from our day"

I'll leave the choice to you.

I think of you a great deal. This letter doesn't represent *me* really, at all. But I must get it off for the *Mauretania* or else risk the delays of one of the slower steamers, and I fear that you are already impatient. I shall write you more very soon, meanwhile I hope that you have recovered somewhat from the exhaustion that must have followed on your brave and marvelous endurance at the time of your departure.

I have signed my contract with Liveright, which definitely states that he shall not offer his edition for sale (or review) before the first of April. He must, however, secure his copyright on the condition of offering 2 copies (only) and the usual registration *before* another edition is offered for sale in this country. All the details of this are included specifically in my contract, and I have guarded my understanding with you with complete fidelity. Please believe me . . .

And with love always, Hart

P. S.—please send a review copy to Yvor Winters—

To Caresse Crosby

190 Columbia Heights
Brooklyn, New York

Dearest Caresse: January 2, 1930

Your good letter today—and it was so reassuring to hear the first news of you! I saw your dear mother last week (thank you again for that photograph) and she said that she had so far had only a couple of cables, but that you seemed to be all right. With so many good friends around you again I know that you'll continue to be invulnerable as ever. I wish I could have been out at the Moulin with you on Christmas—it might not have been quite as gay as usual—but just as sweet, I'm sure.

I spent the day very quietly with Bob and incidental gin. Bob sailed away for manoevres today (off Cuba) and the U.S.S. *Milwaukee* won't bring him back here again until June. I am already missing him a lot.

In my last letter I forgot to mention that Paul Rosenfeld liked "Sleeping Together" a great deal, and was just stepping to the telephone to ask Harry if they could have it for the *Caravan* when his eyes fell on the news of Harry's death in the morning paper. Whether or not he has got in touch with you about it, I don't know. But I rather imagine that you would want the *Caravan* to have it. I'm hoping to see him soon, and have more definite word. I urged Smith to send Liveright's copy but haven't been up to their office since to judge reactions. If they don't want it I think some other publisher will.

Evans has been out of town with his family for nearly a week, mainly because he ran out of funds. He'll be awfully glad to get your letter when he comes back which will probably be within a few days. I liked that portfolio he sent you via Gretchen. I think that Evans is the most living, vital photographer of any whose work I know. More and more I rejoice that we decided on his pictures rather than Stella's.

I have moved down the street from the old place and you can be safe in writing me direct to #190 here for a good while. The place is smaller and considerably cheaper, but quite comfortable enough. I'm hot on the trail of a job now and am settling down to the prospect of quieter evenings!

I hope Allen Tate got in touch with you before he left. I didn't know he was sailing so soon. I don't suppose he could have been much help to you in such a general rush.

Please give my love to all—including Harry's mother, Crouchers, Evelyn—and the anonymous midget of a French sailor, if you ever see him again!

Love to you forever and ever—Hart

To Yvor Winters

190 Columbia Heights
Brooklyn, New York
Dear Winters: January 14, 1930

In this same mail I'm sending a complete copy of the *Bridge*—as it is being set up for the Black Sun Edition in Paris now. This edition will be ready about a month from now, the Liveright edition on April 1st.

"A fine time to be writing me!"—you may rightfully observe. But I am hoping that you haven't totally misunderstood my lengthy silence. To begin with, I haven't been in a mood for any sort of correspondence with anyone for a considerable time; and secondly, though you may not consider the statement as complimentary to your powers as I do,—I have not wanted, for the time being, to engage myself in any further controversies, metrical, theoretical, ethical or what not, which letters (especially from you) frequently occasion. That kind of stimulus is apt to be dangerous at the time when one is desperately trying to complete any preconceived conception like my *Bridge* project. But here the thing is, now—very much larger than I had originally planned it, and at long last, something of a satisfaction, at least to me.

I have asked Mrs. Crosby to send you a copy of the Paris edition for review—not that you actually need review it, but that I want you to have a copy of what is physically one of the most beautiful libros I know of. You ought especially to appreciate the three photographs therein, taken by Walker Evans, a young fellow here in Brooklyn who is doing amazing things.

There is much on which to congratulate you,—especially the superb essay in the *Caravan*. I have seen a couple of issues of the *Gyroscope* which were certainly not to be sneezed at. You may put me down as one of your subscribers—with as many of the earlier issues as are available. Also I hope I may hear from you sometime soon, however little I may deserve to.

Best wishes, as always, Hart Crane

To Yvor Winters

190 Columbia Heights
January 27

Dear Winters:

I'm glad to hear that you feel like commenting on the *Bridge*. Tate has made arrangements to review it for the *Hound & Horn*, Cowley for the *New Republic*, and Schneider for the *Chicago Eve. Post*. I don't know who has taken it for the *Herald-Tribune*, but out of the list for the Paris edition only two choices remain: *Poetry* and the *Nation*.

I recently sent the "Indiana" section to H.M. . . . Zabel replied that she was in the east and he was unable to accept it without her consent, however much he wanted to. His attitude was so complimentary and friendly that I judge there may have been some change of mind around their office. At any rate it offers a parallel to their recent invitation to you as described in your letter. I'm glad you're writing for them again. There aren't any too many openings for any of us. I'm eager to read your exposé of Jeffers. I've always felt that Jeffers was sincere,—but that doesn't quite suffice,—and somewhat "gifted" —to use a horrible word. But everything he has ever written, of any length, at least, excepting *The Tower Beyond Tragedy*, has given me a vague nausea. He really is a highstepping hysteric, I'm afraid.

You couldn't be expected to like Crosby's work. I find only a little pure ore here and there. I liked him personally, however, and was very disturbed at his death. . . . But since it is quite probable that he desired it as one more "experiment", I've reserved most of my sympathy for his wife.

Thank you for the promised *Gyroscopes*, though I'm sorry that there won't be any more. It won considerable and respectful notices, but I imagine took too much of your time.

Isn't there some chance of your coming east this spring?

Yours, Hart Crane

To Otto H. Kahn

190 Columbia Heights
Brooklyn, New York

Dear Mr. Kahn: February 28, 1930

It would give me great pleasure to see you sometime during next week, in order that I may personally deliver a copy of the Paris edition of *The Bridge*.

This first edition, as you know, is dedicated to you. There also has been printed a special copy for you personally. It was announced as having already arrived yesterday, in advance of the other copies, on the *Aquitania*, and I am hoping that I shall succeed in getting it through the customs before next Tuesday.

I was sorry not to have had the pleasure of speaking to you recently on the occasion of the dinner to Waldo Frank at the Hotel Roosevelt. You left, however, before the ceremonies permitted me the pleasure.

Faithfully yours, Hart Crane

To Isidor and Helen Schneider

190 Columbia Heights
Brooklyn, New York

Dear Helen & Isidor: March 16, 1930

I hoorayed when I heard, though you'd never think so by the time it's taken me to get my voice up to the megaphone!

Emily *is* a nice name. It makes me think of poetry, and a certain yacht at Cannes with lyrical white sails that went by the same name. So let me mix memory and metaphors and wish *your* Emily particularly smooth sailing.

I do want to see you *all* soon!

With love as ever, Hart

To Otto H. Kahn

190 Columbia Heights
Brooklyn, New York
Dear Mr. Kahn: April 6, 1930

I am hoping that I may have the privilege of a talk with you sometime this week. You may perhaps recall my mention recently, when I called to deliver *The Bridge*, that I was very much in need of work and had found nothing after persistent efforts.

This condition still continues, and I am the more discouraged now, since I realize that the general business depression renders any fortunate "break" quite improbable right now. I am earnestly looking, however, and shall continue to search for any kind of work that I can find to support myself. Meanwhile I have obligations to the landlord, and even distressing forebodings about the next meal.

Will you be so generous as to consider some temporary assistance for me during the present emergency? I should be glad to accept any kind of work that you might suggest or put me in touch with. Failing this, I am hoping that you might advance me sufficient funds to alleviate my present distress—until the reviews of *The Bridge* have had time to appear. Since so many of these will be highly favorable (I happen to know the sentiments of at least six of the prominent reviewers) I feel sure that the resulting réclame will ensure me editorial work, or some position with an advertising firm such as I have previously held.

The Liveright edition of *The Bridge* is now on sale. It represents, I think, a very fine job in format and printing. I hope it will please you. Believe me, with best wishes,

Sincerely and gratefully yours, Hart Crane

To Herbert Weinstock

Patterson, New York
Dear Herbert Weinstock: April 22, 1930

You have my sincerest gratitude for your enthusiastic review of the *Bridge*. Van Vuren had already sent me a copy, and I was just on the point of writing you my thanks when along came your good letter.

I hope I am deserving of such lofty companions as you group me with. I am almost tempted to believe your claims on the strength of your amazing insight into my objectives in writing, my particular symbolism, the intentional condensation and "density" of structure that I occasionally achieve, and the essential religious motive throughout my work. This last-mentioned feature commits me to self-consciousness on a score that makes me belie myself a little. For I have never consciously approached any subject in a religious mood; it is only afterward that I, or someone else generally, have noticed a prevalent piety. God save me from a Messianic predisposition!

It is pertinent to suggest, I think, that with more time and familarity with the *Bridge* you will come to envisage it more as one poem with a clearer and more integrated unity and developement than was at first evident. At least if my own experience in reading and re-reading Eliot's *Wasteland* has any relation to the circumstances this *may* be found to be the case. It took me nearly five years, with innumerable readings to convince myself of the essential unity of that poem. And the *Bridge* is at least as complicated in its structure and inferences as the *Wasteland*—perhaps more so.

I shall remember to write you my exact whereabouts in time to reach you before you leave for the East and Europe, and we shall meet somewhere in New York. At present the unemployment situation has me balked for any definite location beyond the next day or so.

With sincerest gratitude, Hart Crane
The above address is *always* good for letters.

To Yvor Winters

Patterson, New York

Dear Winters: June 4, 1930

Your disparagement of *The Bridge* and friendly counsel in
the current number of *Poetry* surprised me considerably; not
so much on account of the wide discrepancies between your
public and private opinions (I refer to your letters during the
last three years), as to see to what astonishing lengths of
misrepresentation your prejudices toward a biological (or is it
autobiographical?) approach to poetry can carry you.

You have the right, of course, to revise your estimates of any
work or personality as often as you see fit, but I am less certain
that your validity as a critic is strengthened by permitting your
own special notions about the author's personality to blur the
text before you on the printed page. In that regard I cannot
help thinking that our personal acquaintance proved to be a
handicap to a keener estimate, although, for all I know, it may
have accumulated as much or more bias in my "favor" in some
respects, as against it in others.

At any rate, you seem to have appropriated a good many of
my ethical and privately expressed aesthetic convictions, and
applied them pretty much to the advantage of your initial per-
suasions against certain features and directions repugnant to
you in *The Bridge*. How implicitly these convictions (or weak-
nesses) are actually represented as cases in point in the specific
sections and lines which you cite, does not seem to have
mattered much. You had a case to make out, and exaggeration,
misappropriation—or just confusion, all helped to make it
more convincing.

After some of your comments I am even left to doubt that
you actually read the lines referred to. Anyone, for example,
who can read "Indiana" and then refer to the son addressed
there as "adopted" certainly ought to read lines 6 & 7 again.
This isn't any profound memorandum on "individual human
relationships", nor an attempt to justify the "helpless" or
"mawkish", but it has some bearing on the symbolic place and
function of that section (mainly transitional) in the larger de-
sign of the poem as a whole.

I don't wish to quarrel with all of your judgments; I feel that some of them are illuminating. Nor should our philosophical differences be resurrected again except that you ascribe, again and again, quite different objectives on my part than anything said in the text could reasonably warrant. You then, on the same basis, pronounce the performance botched, and end up with a prognosis that is more pretentious and weightier than need be. Thus you can count "nine" as many times in succession as you like. But that doesn't prove that there was anyone in the ring. People can't be said to "fail" in matters they never thought of undertaking, though such re-iterations as yours may prove impressive enough to strangers.

Your primary presumption that *The Bridge* was proffered as an epic has no substantial foundation. You know quite well that I doubt that our present stage of cultural developement is so ordered yet as to provide the means or method for such an organic manifestation as that. Since your analysis found no evidence of epic form, no attempt even to simulate the traditional qualifications or pedantic trappings,—then I wonder what basis you had for attributing such an aim to the work,— unless, perhaps, to submit me to an indignity which might be embarrassing on the grounds that I could be stripped of unjustified pretensions.

The fact that *The Bridge* contains folk lore and other material suitable to the epic form need not therefore prove its failure as a long lyric poem, with interrelated sections. Rome was written about long before the age of Augustus, and I dare say that Virgil was assisted by several well travelled roads to guide him, though it is my posthumous suggestion that when we do have an "epic" it need not necessarily incorporate a personalized "hero".

Since you have seen conclusive proof of my respect for Whitman, I note that the bulk of "The River" seems to have become "turgid", "confused", and "unmastered" to an unforeseen degree. There had been, as you later discovered, bad influences at work. It is regrettable that an ignorance of the "source" of "The River" (now that you find Whitman in the upper reaches) should have betrayed you into such a premature gusto of acceptance as your letters record. But, as you say, so be it.

I'm more at a loss to explain the aims you postulate (mapping out heaven, or what not) as the inspirational basis of my anti-climax in "The Dance". Here, as often elsewhere, you confuse the intentionally relative with some interpolated "absolute" of your own, as though I had set out to offer some law of the Medes or Persais, or some immutable precept of Nirvana in every other line, mounting gradually to some unapproachable zenith presided over by some Krishna of moral infallibility. My intentions were less ambitious; therefore my failure may be less magniloquent, less dolorous. But there are the lines, anyway; and they attempt nothing more elevated than an identification of myself (or reader) for the moment with the Indian savage while he is in process of absorption into the elements of the pure nature-world about him. The climax of this is the "purple passage" you quoted. The remainder is a gradual decrescendo to a final repose and statement.

You still point with complacency, I see, to the infamous medicine-man passage, as you did once before in the Tate-Crane steeplechase. I've tried before to tell you how innocent that passage is, but you will probably cite it again, somewhere else, I am sure, as an example of "moral surrender", "reversion of the species", or heaven knows what. I'm not expressing nostalgia there, as you have already twice insisted. It is as laughable for you to distort the meaning of this passage into some kind of behavioristic betrayal as to accuse Shakespeare of homicidal inclinations because he created Macbeth. All I am saying amounts in substance to this: "Mimic the scene of yesterday; I want to see how it looked." Here again your notions of what is feeble in my character offered false premises.

My acknowledgment of Whitman as an influence and living force: "Not greatest, thou,—not first, nor last,—but near", as I qualify it,—apparently this discolored the entire poem in your estimation. Thereafter you can see little but red, and throw all logic to the winds. You can even commit the following example of pure non sequitur: "All three (Whitman, Jeffers and Crane) are occasionally betrayed by their talents into producing a passage better than their usual run, *but this only goes to prove the fallacy of their initial assumptions.*" This proves actually nothing whatsoever, unless it be your assumption that a horse cannot run without breaking out of harness. You might as well say that maples turn red in late autumn, but that only goes to prove the uselessness of rain.

I admire your pedanticism up to a certain point; but as your vision develops, narrows, or focuses (whichever term you find most flattering to accept) I'm wondering if it isn't, like Munson's, transcending the province of poetry altogether, in favor of a pseudo-philosophical or behavioristic field of speculation. I note that I am not the only tumbler who comes in for a reshuffling in your hierarchy of merit. You give every evidence of knowing exactly where you are bound for. But with my "moment-to-moment" inspirational limp (now that the public has been reliably informed of this limitation by both Munson and yourself (see his *Destinations*)) I'm sure I cannot be expected to follow. It took over five years of sustained something-or-other to compose *The Bridge*—with more actual and painful "differentiation of experience" into the bargain than I'll wager you will ever take upon yourself. The results have not been as satisfactory as I had hoped for; but I believe that such "wreckage" as I find remaining, presents evidence of considerably more significance than do the cog-walk gestures of a beetle in a sand pit.

Yours,

To Isidor Schneider

. Patterson, New York

Dear Isidor: June 8, 1930

I had wanted to get to see you and Helen before leaving town, but moving various belongings hither and thither and the crazy confusion of my affairs at the time were too much for me. I specially wanted to see Emily. From all reports all three of you are withstanding all onslaughts merrily enough, though I cannot but realize that these are not easy times for you in a number of respects. That makes me all the more grateful for the evident care which you took in your review of the *Bridge*. Certainly I don't see what more I could ask for—than your generous credit to and recognition of practically all the aspirations implicit in the poem. I hope the actual poem is deserving of it all. If you have read Winters' attack in the June issue of

Poetry you cannot have been more astonished than I was to note the many reversals of opinion he has undergone since reading my acknowledgment to Whitman in the later "Cape Hatteras" section.

Had it not been for our previous extended correspondence I should not, of course, have written him about it. But as things stood I could hardly let silence infer an acceptance on my part of all the willful distortions of meaning, misappropriations of opinion, pedantry and pretentious classification—besides illogic—which his review presents par excellence. I must read what prejudices he defends, I understand, against writing about subways, in the anti-humanist symposium. Poets should defer alluding to the sea, also, I presume, until Mr. Winters has got an invitation for a cruise!

I haven't any work whatever in mind. I guess I can trust my father's promise of a small allowance to carry me along out here until fall, when the gates of employment may prove better oiled than they have for some time past. If you hear of anything, Isidor, please let me know. I'm aching to get busy at almost anything. Maybe I'll be in town for a couple of days in about 2 weeks. If so, I'll do my best to see you. Many thanks again for your splendid review!

Love to Helen. As ever, Hart

To Allen Tate

R.F.D. 1
Gaylordsville, Connecticut

Dear Allen: July 13, 1930

Your last good letter and the admirable review of *The Bridge* in the *Hound & Horn* deserved an earlier response, but time has somehow just been drifting by without my being very conscious of it. For one thing, I have been intending to get hold of a copy of the *Hound & Horn* and give your review a better reading, before replying, than I could achieve at the tables in Brentano's when I was in town about two weeks ago. I still haven't a copy and consequently may wrong you in making any comments whatever. But as I don't want to delay longer I hope you'll pardon any discrepancies.

The fact that you posit the *Bridge* at the end of a tradition of romanticism may prove to have been an accurate prophecy, but I don't yet feel that such a statement can be taken as a foregone conclusion. A great deal of romanticism may persist—of the sort to deserve serious consideration, I mean.

But granting your accuracy—I shall be humbly grateful if the *Bridge* can fulfill the metaphorical inferences of its title. . . . You will admit our age (at least our predicament) to be one of transition. If the *Bridge*, embodying as many anomolies as you find in it, yet contains as much authentic poetry here and there as even Winters grants,—then perhaps it can serve as at least the function of a link connecting certain chains of the past to certain chains and tendencies of the future. In other words, a diagram or "process" in the sense that Genevieve Taggard refers to all my work in estimating Kunitz's achievement in the enclosed review. This gives it no more interest than as a point of chronological reference, but "nothing ventured, nothing gained"—and I can't help thinking that my mistakes may warn others who may later be tempted to an interest in similar subject matter.

Personally I think that Taggard is a little too peremptory in dispensing with Kunitz's "predecessors". We're all unconscious evolutionists, I suppose, but she apparently belongs to the more rabid ranks. I can't help wishing I had read more of Kunitz before seeing her review. He is evidently an excellent poet. I should like to have approached him, not as one bowing before Confucius, nor as one buying a new nostrum for lame joints. Taggard, like Winters, isn't looking for poetry any more. Like Munson, they are both in pursuit of some cure-all. Poetry as poetry (and I don't mean merely decorative verse) isn't worth a second reading any more. Therefore—away with Kubla Khan, out with Marlowe, and to hell with Keats! It's a pity, I think. So many true things have a way of coming out all the better without the strain to sum up the universe in one impressive little pellet. I admit that I don't answer the requirements. My vision of poetry *is* too personal to "answer the call". And if I ever write any more verse it will probably be at least as personal as the idiom of *White Buildings* whether anyone cares to look at it or not.

This personal note is doubtless responsible for what you

term as sentimentality in my attitude toward Whitman. It's true that my rhapsodic address to him in the *Bridge* exceeds any exact evaluation of the man. I realized that in the midst of the composition. But since you and I hold such divergent prejudices regarding the value of the materials and events that W. responded to, and especially as you, like so many others, never seem to have read his *Democratic Vistas* and other of his statements sharply decrying the materialism, industrialism, etc of which you name him the guilty and hysterical spokesman, there isn't much use in my tabulating the qualified, yet persistent reasons I have for my admiration of him, and my allegiance to the positive universal tendencies implicit in nearly all his best work. You've heard me roar at too many of his lines to doubt that I can spot his worst, I'm sure.

It amuses me to see how Taggard takes up some of Winters' claims against me (I expected this and look for more) in his article in the Anti-Humanist volume, especially as that borrowing doesn't seem to have obviated his own eclipse according to her estimate of the new constellation. I have the feeling that Miss Taggard is not only conducting her own education in public (as someone once said of George Moore) but also the education of her subjects. . . . At least she seems now to have attained that acumen which is a confusion to all.

I'm leaving this weekend for a visit to Cummings in New Hampshire. After a final row with Addle M. Turner (who is about to sell her place anyway) I have moved my things down the road to Fitzi's. Occasionally I am appalled at my apparently chronic inability to relinquish some hold or connection that has long since ceased to yield me anything but annoyance—until some violence of fate forces my release. That's one of many ways I seem to keep of wasting time.

There were three great Fourth parties. (1) at Schuyler's place, Amawalk, (2) at Peter Blume's, who has rented the abandoned chapel above Fitzi's, and (3) at Brown's. I'm just recovering. Bill goes in to work on the *New Republic* this week. That's about all the news. I look forward to seeing you again in the fall, when—God willing—I may find a job open somewhere. Meanwhile please let me hear from you. I picture you installed now, and very comfortable.

Best to all—Hart

To John A. Roebling

Gaylordsville, Connecticut
Dear Mr. Roebling: August 18, 1930

I am mailing to you under separate cover a copy of a long poem of mine, *The Bridge*, which I hope I have not been too presumptuous in inscribing to you in hommage to your family as builders of the Brooklyn Bridge, to which the poem is dedicated.

My devotion to the Brooklyn Bridge as the matchless symbol of America and its destiny prompted this dedication—as I dare say the particular view of the bridge's span from my window on Columbia Heights, where I lived for several years, inspired the general conception and form of the entire poem.

Months after its completion I learned on what I take to be good authority, that this address had once been the possession of Washington Roebling, which news certainly did not tend to decrease my sentiments towards the Builder of the bridge.

I hope that, as his son, you will find some element or occasional statement worthy of expression in a theme, which, in its way, is as ambitious and complicated as was the original engineering project which your father so nobly undertook and completed.

Very sincerely yours, Hart Crane

To the John Simon Guggenheim
Memorial Foundation

Plans for Study

My application for a fellowship is prompted by a desire for European study and creative leisure for the composition of poetry. I am interested in characteristics of European culture, classical and romantic, with especial reference to contrasting elements implicit in the emergent features of a distinctive American poetic consciousness.

My one previous visit to Europe, though brief, proved creatively stimulating in this regard, as certain aspects of my long poem, *The Bridge*, may suggest. Modern and medieval French literature and philosophy interest me particularly. I should like the opportunity for a methodical pursuit of these studies in conjunction with my creative projects.

My next volume of poetry will probably be issued by Horace Liveright, Inc. who has already issued my two previous books, *White Buildings* and *The Bridge*.

Hart Crane

To Allen Tate

Gaylordsville, Connecticut

Dear Allen: September 7, 1930

Have you ever had boils? I got my first specimen during my visit to the Cummingses six weeks ago, brought it home along with several up-and-coming progeny, and "the loyal and royal succession of the Plantaganets" (as E. E. referred to them) has not left me yet. Since the throne room is in my right arm pit, not to mention the chamber and royal nursery, I've scarcely been able to manipulate my right arm to the meek extent of writing a letter much of the time. I think that I have now established at least my better intentions!

The pictures of your homestead were much appreciated and widely circulated hereabouts. It's my opinion that you now have about all one could ask for in the way of rural comfort not to mention dignity. Certainly it surpasses anything owned and directed by any of our mutuals in this valley. I should enjoy the visit you suggested (many thanks!) but, boils or no boils, I've got to get located in some office as soon now as possible—or at least be on the scene of interrogation, prison, palace, and supplication. I hear that the Cowleys are shortly to investigate your premises on the way to Mexico; and I know that the Browns are highly anticipatory. Bill, by the way, is now definitely bound to the *N.R.* for three years, likes the work and salary and seems highly pleased, as am I.

I was glad to get your *Three Poems*. The distinguished diction throughout reminds me of the little advance I have ever made in essential flexibility and the finer intonations. These qualities seem most evident to me in the "Message from Abroad", which, though it is largely inferential to me in its substance, is in a way, all the more welcome as a poem to be re-read for a multiple suggestiveness that may very well take on clearer perspective with time. "The Cross" keeps me guessing a little too strenuously. I can't help thinking it perhaps too condensed, and, as Bill suggested, a not entirely fused melange of ecclesiastical and highly-personalized imagery. In which case you sin no more than Eliot in the recent "Ash-Wednesday". "The Ode to the Confederate Dead" is as excellent as ever, I don't think essentially improved except as regards rhythm: the wind-and-leaf interpolations adding a certain subjective continuity.

My summer seems like a blank to me right now. Perhaps my study of Dante—the *Commedia* which I had never touched before—will have been seen to have given it some significance, but that isn't much to boast of. Let me hear from you soon. I don't expect quite the full extent of Job's afflictions, and so can probably keep on reading, at least.

Best to all, Hart

To Otto H. Kahn

Gaylordsville, Connecticut

Dear Mr. Kahn: September 9, 1930

In my application for a Guggenheim Fellowship for Creative Writing (1931) I recently took the liberty of listing your name among other personal references. Needless to say, I hope that any consequent inquiries on the part of the Foundation will not prove annoying to you.

As you doubtless know, the next Fellowships are not awarded until March, 1931. I have a reasonable amount of confidence in the outcome, on the basis of the enthusiastic reception accorded *The Bridge*, aside from other reasons. But I still have no prospects of employment during this fall and winter. Sufficiency of zeal is beside the point, as you must know, realizing the unemployment situation as well as anyone. My recent experience proves it to be as hopeless this fall as it was last spring when I wrote you of my unavailing efforts.

I have been too harried by these exigencies to write more than a handful of poems during the last six months. If you still have the interest in my work which you once had—and I am not presuming *The Bridge* to have been a disappointment to you—I hope you won't consider me importunate in referring to my present predicament. The waste of energy consumed in worry could be avoided it I could have a modicum of security at this time, insuring at least the simple immunity from having to borrow from friends who, in most cases, are as hard-pressed as myself. I could then concentrate on my creative work and accomplish another book of poems without such needless delay.

Here in the country I can subsist decently on twenty-five dollars a week. If you would care to consider helping me to this extent, at least until I can succeed in locating a position in the city, it would, as I have suggested, result in a real economy of creative force. But regardless of your decision, Mr. Kahn, you are assured, as I hope you already realize, of my continual gratitude for all your previous benevolence in my behalf.

With all good wishes, believe me

Ever faithfully yours, Hart Crane

To Solomon Grunberg

45 Grove Street,
N.Y.C.

Dear Mony: Sept. 30th '30

Your letter reached me during a visit with Cummings on his place up in New Hampshire. I was mighty glad to hear from you again, although my extreme delay in answering would seem to emphasize that fact but slightly. You were not a little to blame for this, yourself,—for you told me so little about yourself, Mony, that—lacking any particular urge to describe my own bucolic, monotonous round of days—I hardly knew on what to hang a worthy reply. Now that I am back in town

again, looking for the needles in haystacks and jobs in limbo,
—now that the most monotonous and familiar situation of *all*
engrosses, nay inundates me, I'm taking "time off" to answer
in the hope that you'll write me more news and also be sure to
look me up on your next visit to these parts.

I'm most grateful for your continued interest in "The
Bridge". After so grandiose talk as I indulged myself in during
its interrupted progress it's a wonder if most of my friends
aren't appalled at its ultimate shortcomings. Some of them are.
It's gone into a second printing, however, which means a sale
exceeding the first thousand. If last spring hadn't ushered in
such a calamitous slump in all books I imagine I might have
been more fortunate; at any rate I can't complain about most
of the reviews.

My summer was a kind of steady doldrums, enlivened only
by a sudden insight into the values and beauty of Dante's
"Commedia". Not that I've learned Italian, but that I found a
decent translation (Temple Classics Edition) thanks to Eliot's
inspiring essay on Dante. My recent struggles with a poem of
large proportions and intricate framework, I think, gave me a
maturer appreciation of the "Commedia" than I could have
mustered ten years ago. Sometimes one feels that one's neglect
or "indifference" to a great masterpiece is almost justified,
pending the proper developement of one's own powers of per-
ception proportionate to the opportunity postponed. (I didn't
realize that alliteration was so "on the job" this morning!) Of
course I now realize how much more than ever I have to work
to accomplish anything whatever.

Some conversations with you again would be very welcome
interludes in my present job-obsession. Aren't you planning
on New York before long? That would be welcome news.

As ever,
Hart Crane

To Wilbur Underwood

Dear Wilbur: November 20
All my hectic efforts at concentation during your last few
days in New York have brought me nothing better than a cool

turning down from the editor of *Fortune*. Perhaps I should call it "Misfortune". At any rate I did, and still do regret not having had more time with you. In the state of mind I was in (you had already had a sample of it) I'm sure I should not have been worth talking with anyway, but at least I should have enjoyed your observations, and you could not have mistaken me for indifferent.

I can well imagine what a pleasant time you are having with Finley (or is it Fin*d*ley?). I wish you would ask him to write me, and tell him that I hope he'll look me up if he comes up this way soon. My friend Bob arrived last Saturday, his ship to remain here until January. I've been too rushed to see him but once, but the air has taken on a pleasant warmth. If I weren't so harried by problems! Could you advance me ten dollars for a few weeks? I still have the interview with Teagle (President of Standard Oil) to submit to *Fortune*. Maybe I'll get that "put over" and paid for.

Constant anxiety is wearing me out. It has already corroded my mind to the point where I can write neither poetry *nor* the most obvious hack work. Nor sleep nights—really insomnia is ghastly. And then these "times"! A steady job, though a bore, is certainly worth a lot.

I'm sorry to sound so funereal. But then we can't all be resourceful Finley Cases. My notebook containing your address got lost, so remember to write me the Connecticut Ave number.

Affectionately, Hart

To William H. Wright

St. George Hotel
Brooklyn, New York
November 21, 1930

Dear Bill:

Your good letter is really more than I deserve, which doesn't, however, diminish my relish in each and every detail of it. From June until September I was living out near Pawling, N.Y., less precariously, it is true, than during three previous months of job hunting in town, but still so continuously harried by anxieties regarding the immeadiate future as to be in anything but a writing mood. I did receive your announcement of your visit, and replied by letter addressed to the Hotel Governor Clinton that I expected to be driven into town by some friends in time to meet you. That trip didn't eventuate; and as I was dead broke at the time, I had to wire you that I couldn't make it. I felt badly about it, especially as I wanted to meet Margaret. You evidently didn't stop at the Governor Clinton, else you couldn't have missed my communications.

The details of your summer program and the description of your winter quarters reflect an enviable settled state of affairs. New York is full of the unemployed, more every day, and the tension evident in thousands of faces isn't cheerful to contemplate. It is a little strange to see the city so "grim about the mouth," as Melville might say. Yours truly has been having his grim moments, too; in fact, I'm pretty well convinced that unmitigated anxiety has a highly corrosive effect on the resilience of the imagination. I am trying to write a couple of articles for *Fortune*—that de luxe business-industrial monthly published by *Time*, Inc.—and I am appalled at the degree of paralysis that worry can impose on the functioning of one's natural faculties. One assignment is a "profile" of Walter Teagle, president of Standard Oil (N.J.). I managed to keep the oil king talking far beyond the time allotted, but when I come to write it up in typical *Fortune* style the jams gather by the hundred.

I am so pleased that you continue to enjoy the *Bridge*. I admit having felt considerably jolted at the charge of sentimentality continually levelled at the "Indiana" fragment, particularly when such charges came from people who aknowledged a violent admiration for Hardy's poetry. For many of his lyrics have seemed to me at least as "sentimental" as this "mawkish" performance of my own. But I approve of a certain amount of sentiment anyway. Right now it is more fashionable to speak otherwise, but the subject (or emotion) of "race" has always had as much of sentiment behind it—as it has had of prejudice, also. Since "race" is the principal motivation of "Indiana," I can't help thinking that, observed in proper perspective, and judged in relation to the argument or theme of the "Pocahontas" section as a whole, the pioneer woman's maternalism isn't excessive.

Did I mention my pleasure in reading a very skillful poem of yours about various types of fur. It came out in *Poetry*, I think. Certainly Baudelaire would have been charmed by its adept blending of beautiful names with a world of tactile associations. The geographical evocations implicit in the list of animals mentioned were delightful. I see a great many reasons for you to continue writing, especially since it brings you none of the pangs that accompany a more professional concern with the muses. I haven't written a line for over nine months, and nine months is not so promising a period in the seven arts as it may be in the physical sciences.

I'll try not to be so remiss in writing again. Would I be deemed insensitive in requesting a temporary loan to help carry me over till a check from *Fortune* can be expected. Please be very frank. Money is "hard" everywhere these days, and if you can't spare 25 or 50 dollars, or if you have any scruples against such transactions, I shall remain as affectionate and as spontaneous a partner to our friendship as ever. In fact I would prefer to shoulder double my present quandary before exposing you to any stringencies.

I have applied for a Guggenheim Scholarship (which would give me a year's study and creative freedom abroad) and hope to God that I'll gain approval. Announcements are made early in March. Meanwhile I'm praying that I can write well enough on industrial subjects to keep on with *Fortune*. My room here is surprisingly cheap—a weekly rate that barely exceeds rooming house costs—and with these articles I've had to be located where messages could be taken in my absence. The requirement of advance payment is none too comforting, however.

Will you be coming here for a few days before long? This time I shall surely see you, and Margaret, too, I hope. Please remember me not too darkly and give my warmest greeting to your Father and Mother.

Affectionately, Hart

To William H. Wright

Hotel St. George
Brooklyn, New York
Dear Bill: November 29, 1930

Your imagination is evidently as magnanimous as your hand is. . . . By ascribing my almost chronic indigence to so Nietzschean a program as the attitude of "living life dangerously" infers, you make me blink a little. For my exposures to rawness and to risk have been far too inadvertent, I fear, to deserve any such honorable connotations;—and my disorderly adventures and peregrinations I regard with anything but complacency. However, it isn't everyone who can lend help with such graceful tolerance of evident shortcomings; and your euphemisms make me doubly grateful.

The Teagle article is now awaiting approval. I hope to know more about my immeadiate fate early next week. If that doesn't eventuate in a check and another assignment, then my best bet lies in the direction of book selling in one of the many Doubleday-Doran shops in the metropolitan area. I know someone who may succeed in insinuating me there. In normal times, of course, I should have been located with an advertising agency months since. No, teaching isn't a solution for me, Bill. I haven't any academic education whatsoever. You may have forgotten that I left East High without even a diploma—in my junior year. Mirabile dictu! . . . Noblesse oblige! . . . . Pax vobiscum! . . . . Nunc dimittis est . . . so who am I, therefore, to rule a class!

I'm hoping that I won't need to cash your second check, a contingency which I'll do my best to avoid. You'll hear from me again very soon. Meanwhile I can't tell you how much I appreciate your kindness.

Affectionately, Hart

To Samuel Loveman

Dear Sam: December 29, 1930

To make partial amends for my neglect of you, I am, as you see, giving you the full, blazing benefit of the official stationary! Of course, had I been consulted, I should never have permitted so harmless a slogan as "The place to *bring* your guest". The fourth word would still have begun with "b", but there would have been more action implied in the order of the other letters substituted, or I'm no befriender of monks and monkery.

However, that might belie the nights hereabout. As I have just written to Bill Adams, *la vie sportif* continues its reckless pace hereabouts without any too great abundance of absinthe, gobs, apple-vendors or breadlines. It's too bad that all this drouth and quietude should have produced, so far at least, nothing better than a maidenly complexion and a bulging waist line. Gone is that glittering eye of Sands St. midnights, erstwhile so compelling; and the ancient mariner is facing the new year with all the approved trepidations of the middle west business man, approved panic model of 1931. So much for resignation. It brings me at least a little more sleep than I was getting in New York.

For about ten days I was busy at my father's store on Euclid, near Higbee's. Driving in from the Falls here, wrapping Xmas parcelpost bundles, and driving back at night, I lived in a veritable whirl of excitement. Now that the Xmas "rush" is a memory only, I am casting about for some connection or other with what remains of the direct mail advertising business here. So far it doesn't look promising. But unless I manage to turn a few honest pennies I mayn't get back to your skyline for many months. Of course I knew that when I came out here, but I had borrowed all I felt justified in borrowing and the situation in NY looked, and still looks, hopeless. As you had no doubt observed, it had gotten considerably under my skin.

I have yet to see Bill Sommer, yet to see Gordon, yet to try to see Don B. The Rychtariks asked about you. I hope you got the candy I sent. Please write me all the news from Harlem to the St. George. Best to Pat.

Affectionately, Hart

To Solomon Grunberg

Box 604
Chagrin Falls, Ohio
Dear Mony: January 10

Sam evidently hasn't seen you recently, as his letter of the other day makes no allusion to a visit with you. I've been out here with my father since the 12th of December and shall probably not return to Babylon for some time—unless there seems to be better opportunity for work than the present offers.

I got terribly run down with the worry of it all—and since my father had expected me out here for the holidays anyway I felt I owed him the courtesy of complying, especially since he had been so generous with me for some time past. Since the Teagle (Standard Oil) article proved to be a flop there wasn't much use in persisting longer—in the face of the bread lines.

This humiliation, severe for awhile, doesn't seem to have ruined me, however, and in view of certain recoveries and gains in poise, I don't seriously regret my move. My father, of course, expects me to remain in this locality permanently. I of course keep all contrary plans very much to myself, including the secret of a bank balance sufficient at least to my carfare east again, whenever my return seems advisable. But enough of such explanatory details!

I'm anxious to hear from you—and what your plans are, etc. This is dull enough around here to encourage a good deal of reading—which I am enjoying. Spinoza (Einstein's grandpop) furnishes plenty of discipline. Cleveland has one of the best libraries in the country, admirably conducted and with shelves practically wide open.

No writing is being done yet—or even in prospect. Can't fool myself that way, as you know. An old thing of mine from my West Indian days in a forthcoming issue of *The New Republic* which you may like, however.

Best luck, dear Mony, and let me hear from you soon.

Affectionately, Hart

To William H. Wright

Chagrin Falls, Ohio

Dear Bill: January 14, 1931

Your reiterated invitations are much appreciated, whether my actions would seem to prove my sentiments or not. My movements are however, more restricted these days than I have ever known them to be. The economic causes are too well known to you to need further substantiation, in addition to which I should be restrained here anyway, at least for the next three weeks; as my father and his wife have just departed for Havana, and there are, happily, some ways I can make myself useful here in their absence. It may well be that I shall not see you until March or April, during your projected tour of these parts. But if an opportunity is granted me before then to visit you, believe me I shall do so. Fate has not been very heavy handed with me, but I find that it can be persistent!

One day in Laukhuff's I came upon a copy of *The Book of the Rhymer's Club*, the first time I had seen one. Your two poems weren't as exciting to me as others I have read, being in somewhat a different vein, of course. Herman Fetzer I remember meeting years ago in Akron (he worked on a paper there, I think) during my days with my father's store there. But we just shook hands, and I'm surprised that he remembers me. It might be fun to go into the Press office someday and talk awhile. He boasts of being a first cousin to Rabelais, I hear. Certainly he looked the part.

You may, or may not be interested in the enclosed card. It has just met my eye in one of the local drugstores. Archeological discoveries in Ohio are just rare enough to excite me, especially as this one bears such an intimate relation to one of my metaphors in the *Bridge*:

"Time like a serpent down her shoulder, dark,
And space, an eaglet's wing, laid on her hair."

The native blacksmith who did this rock carving, I've just been told, was accounted most peculiar. His midnight whereabouts used to be quite a mystery—until someone tracked his lantern down to this rock on which he spent his midnight oil. I must visit the place and also find out more about him, H. Church, by name. For we both seem to have identical conceptions of Pocahontas. (Look directly under my marginal X and you will note the eagle partially outlined.)

Besides other carvings he executed his own gravestone, a lion couchant beside a lamb in company with a man standing. Most striking of all is the story of his funeral sermon, composed and committed by himself to a phonograph record, which was duly played at his obsequies. Well, Sherwood Anderson didn't quite catch all the incipient Blakes in this middle west! I don't know when anything has more refreshed me than this casual discovery.

I'm enclosing a check for ten dollars as a partial payment on the loan, not that I intend to bother you with continued dribblings in the same style, but simply in lieu, for the time being, of the total. It's possible that you can find use for it these days and I don't want to be any more laggard than I'm forced to be.

Why not send me some of your poems to read? Please write me soon, anyway.

Yrs affectionately, Hart

To Lorna Dietz

Dear Lorna: February 10, 1931

Since I wrote you I've had a molar removed and have listened to Chevalier on the radio. . . . Such is about all the news. No wonder I haven't written! One more excitement should be recorded, however, even though it is as recent as this morning: Bill Adams on the phone wanting to know why I hadn't written, etc. I must admit that all this interest sets me up considerably. After this I must hit the keys oftener if only to spare the budgets of my friends.

As nothing more has been said about photography, I guess I'm to be spared the useless apprenticeship to the village baby tickler; instead I've been hammering, waxing, rubbing, painting and repairing—odd jobs—around the place, and work which is rather amusing. Once a week I generally go into

Cleveland and spend some hours with my old friends, the Rychtariks (a Prague painter and his wife whom you must have heard me mention) who really "belong"—and are about the only people in this district that I enjoy seeing. I can be more or less myself with them, and that's a great relief after the unmitigated rigor of the parental regime. (Poetry or anything like that is an offense to mention here, as something belonging in the category with "youthful errors", "wild oats" et cetera, and the "reform" that has been inaugurated has brought me back to just that pleasantly vegetable state of mind that can read Coolidge's daily advice without a tremor of protest.) My father, you can visualize his type, is "enjoying" the depression, or at least his incessant howls about it. Despite the losses personally involved, I think he will actually be disappointed if matters improve in less than five years. From his standpoint at any rate, anything that disproved his doleful prediction would prove a calamity. His great reiteration being that everyone has been spending too much money. He is willing to admit, however, that it hasn't been spent on candy! (Which is among the luxuries, too, if I am not mistaken.) All of which makes very stimulating conversation, of course, especially when you are obliged to agree on each and every occasion and reiteration, ad infinitum. . . .

The possibility of a Guggenheim keeps me restive. That failing, I may hike back east in March anyhow. Too prolonged a stay here at my present age isn't sensible, whatever the alternatives may be right now, and however generously my father might feel.

You've been awfully generous in writing. Sounds as though your winter were being rather pleasant after all. How about Emil and Fitzi? Is he on the sea? Is Fitzi still involved in mortgages—and jobless? Partying seems to continue unabated as well as discussions of Communism. But Eda Lou Walton writes me that nobody is writing anything. Certainly I'm not either. Some reading, however. No wonder Fitzi liked *The Story of San Michele* so much; it's almost as full of dog sentiment as she is. But in some ways a marvelous book. A friend of mine on *Fortune*, Russell Davenport, has written a good book, *Through Traffic*, on a combined business and love theme. I'll send it to you to keep for me and read. I've just gotten around to read *Jurgen*! Always resented the pow-wow about it, but rather like it. Dos Passos' *42nd Parallel* is good—as far as it goes. But Dos has yet to create a full portrait. What did you think of Mumford's series of leaders in the *Tribune*, just concluded? I find myself agreeing pretty thoroughly with him.

I'm looking forward to Chaplin's *City Lights* wishing however, that you were to be seated beside me. I don't get the full delight of such spectacles without good company. Weren't Dressier and Beery splendid in *Min & Bill*! I'm going to see them again here at the village theatre this evening. My father will probably be too devoted to his Jeremaids to budge, but I'd like to get him to come along.

Let's hear from you soon again, dear Lorna!

Love, Hart

To Samuel Loveman

Chagrin Falls, Ohio

Dear Sam: February 16, 1931

No, I haven't quite decided to remain in chagrin. I'm planning, at least right now, to return to my darling Babylon within three or four weeks, but am hoping that there will be enough from the Guggenheim millions to launch me on the waters toward the south of France. Anyway and regardless, I shall have to move to save my soul. Physically I am altogether too completely recovered to risk it here another moment.

Our friend Bill Sommer has evidently heard a little scandal— for he refuses to see me. Too bad he isn't a little more stalwart, considering the boozing he once indulged in himself. But how I do enjoy the Rychtariks! They're the only people I see besides my aunt and few other relatives. I'm in town only about once a week anyway—the rest of the time I help out here, making repairs, whitewashing, painting, framing prints for my father, etc. The apprenticeship to the village photographer (it would have been mostly pinking babies' bottoms a la 1885) did not eventuate, parental cogitations having discovered more sensible employments for my time.

When I listen to Roxy's Sunday morning concerts I think of you—and imagine us both looking out that window on the harbor. Sundays are nightmares here to me—so many diners around, the endless conflabs enent the "masterpieces" that my father has around the walls, no privacy or chance to either relax, concentrate or really be serviceable. No one is to blame; I don't mean that at all. I've really been treated very squarely considering the family prejudices and limited imagination.

I'm glad to here that Pat's performance was a success. Please give him my thanks for the programme. I've been reading *Jurgen* and enjoying it! Don't wonder that it was a target for the censors however. Bob writes me regularly from Guantanamo and Panama, where they are maneuvering now. Quits the service in March. I may be around to see him again before he goes back to his Alabamy. He's true blue, navy blue included!

Write me again soon. Affectionately, Hart

To Waldo Frank

Box 604
Chagrin Falls, Ohio
February 19

Dear Waldo:

Your invitation to lunch has just reached me here in the middle west. I left the St. George Dec. 12th and have been out here at my father's place ever since. Derelict? Yes, but in view of the general depression there didn't seem to be anything else to do. I can at least be of some use around there, carpentering, painting, repairing etc. I suppose you know of my hopes to get back to Europe for awhile, since I took the liberty of giving you for reference to the Guggenheim foundation.

These are bewildering times for everyone, I suppose. I can't muster much of anything to say to anyone. I seem to have lost the faculty to even feel tension. A bad sign, I'm sure. When they all get it decided, Capitalism or Communism, then I'll probably be able to resume a few intensities; meanwhile there seems to be no sap in anything. I'd love to fight for—almost anything, but there seems to be no longer any real resistance. Maybe I'm only a disappointed romantic, after all. Or perhaps I've made too many affable compromises. I hope to discover the fault, whatever it is, before long.

Since you seem to have retired completely from any journalistic appearances I'm completely ignorant of your current opinions or reactions. Do write me soon and tell me what you're engaged in. And such of your plans as you care to divulge. I'd like to have heard your recent lecture mentioning the *Bridge*, as I gather. Present day America seems a long way off from the destiny I fancied when I wrote that poem. In some ways Spengler must have been right.

On the water wagon two months now . . . If abstinence is clarifying to the vision, as they claim, then give me back the blindness of my will. It needs a fresh baptism.

Love, Hart

To Henry Allen Moe

Chagrin Falls, Ohio

Dear Mr. Moe: March 16, 1931

My appointment as a Fellow of the John Simon Guggenheim Memorial Foundation is appreciated greatly, not only as a welcome opportunity to continue my creative endeavors, but also as a distinguished honor conferred upon me as a poet. In accepting this Fellowship for 1931–32 I feel a stimulating sense of pride and gratitude. Needless to say, this evidence of trust in my abilities and character, alone and quite apart from my instinctive response to such good fortune, would prompt me to my utmost efforts to justify such confidence as the liberal terms and generous conditions of the Fellowship imply. I fully subscribe to all these conditions as detailed in your announcement, —not, however, without realizing that I am assuming some serious responsibilities.

As I am at present among the vast horde of the unemployed —and with nothing of consequence to detain me, I should like to situate myself definitely as soon as possible in a favorable environment for constructive work and study. It will therefor be most gratifying to hear from you regarding the propriety and feasibility of taking up my projected foreign residence at an early date. To be specific, I should like to sail for France by the middle part of April, provided such proposal meets the unreserved approval of the Trustees of the Foundation. A statement from a local physician regarding my state of health will be sent to you very shortly.

In closing I hope I may reiterate my sincere gratitude to those comprising the Committee of Selection and to the Trustees of the Foundation, as well as to you personally, Mr. Moe, for such emininent associative privileges as you, conjointly, have deemed me worthy of. I shall take the liberty of telephoning regarding my temporary address when I get to New York at the close of this week.

With best wishes, believe me, faithfully yours, Hart Crane

To Charlotte and Richard Rychtarik

Dear Lotte & Ricardo: March 30
I am sailing to *Mexico* (damn the gendarmes!) next Saturday. The change was made without any trouble and I am too happy at change to a *really* (for *me*) creative locality to be anything but pregnant.

Have been having too wonderful a time to breathe—and it still goes on. Will write you more when I know my permanent address. First a week in Mexico City with my old and wonderful friend, Katherine Anne Porter (whom you will notice *also* was awarded)—and then on to some country location.

Meanwhile hope you will write me a boat letter—S.S. *Orizaba*, Ward Line, Pier 4 East River, NYC, sailing noon April 4th.

Your "Marius" shawl from Marseille is on the way to you. Best to Ward Lewis.

Love always, Hart

To Katherine Anne Porter

Dear Kathryn Anne:
Sailing for Vera Cruz on April 4th. What happens when Guggenheimer meet Guggenheimer? I'm to be with you for a year.

Love, Hart

To Caresse Crosby

Dear Caresse: April 5, 1931

I'm losing no time getting to work on the Guggenheim Fellowship just rec'd, and am on my way to a year's work in Mexico. As you know, I had expected to go to Martigues or Aix-en-Provence originally, but considering the Aztec theme of the work I have in mind, a drama featuring Montezuma and Cortez, it seemed much more logical to turn to Mexico. Besides, that is something I have been dreaming about for years.

I hear that you have bought a clipper ship (*Cutty Sark* #2?) and you can imagine how much I applaud your imagination in choosing a maritime existence. I had a fine time enjoying your poems in the *Caravan* all over again just before leaving NY— up at Russell Davenport's—and seeing the Walkers again. You must keep on, Caresse, and send me carbons as often as possible. After all, I'm not so bad at group titles, am I? It was I who thought of "Saggitarius".

I read in the *New Yorker* that the Alice book was a great success, and sold like hot cakes. Marks is still moaning, I presume, about his losses on *The Bridge*. He snubbed me so thoroughly the last time I called on him, last autumn, that I decided to leave him definitely without future interruptions.

Danes are proverbially good sailors; and so thinking that you may need as reliable help as possible on your nautical adventures, I'm hastening to recommend my old friend, K. Peter Christensen (my sweet tall boy friend whom you met more than once in Paris) to your mercy and consideration.

I had unfortunaly agreed to meet him in Paris before my plans for Mexico occurred. He's starving in Nice. No place for younger Danes in Denmark—and apparently no place else in these days of unemployment. It's really pitiful considering his sterling qualities and desire to work. He'd make a very dutiful and smiling helper on your boat, and I hope I'm not offensive in making my suggestion so urgent. I really feel, however, that should you need so ready a servant—*or any of your friends*—I won't regret my emphasis. His present address is Hotel Richmond, Nice. I'm including a picture of this loyal hearted and thoroughly unfrivolous creature.

There are millions of things I'd like to say and discuss with you, but I'll have to postpone them until I get settled near Mexico City. I'm going to take a small villa, settle down with a servant and get into one of the greatest themes that I ever heard of. Have wonderful letters of introduction to all the officials, poets and painters from Waldo Frank, Hal Smith and others. Am feeling as at the beginning of *The Bridge*,—only fresher and even stronger.

Write me, Caresse, and give my love to Peter and Gretchen, and Marcelle!

LOVE ALWAYS Hart

To Charlotte Rychtarik

Veracruz—April 10

On to Mexico City tomorrow. Have a very, very pleasant voyage. Love to you both!

Hart

To Samuel Loveman

Dear Sambo: April 12, 1931

Got here last night (I always seem to arrive in cities on Sat. nights) and have just had a Sunday dinner a la Mexicano. I begin to feel at home here already, despite my complete ignorance of the language. But kindly people and generous faces have a way of compensating for one's lack of palabra. The peons are the marvel of the place, just as Lawrence said. So lovable, and although picturesque, not in any way consciously so. What faces, and the suffering in them—but so little evidence of bitterness.

We had one evening in Havana, and one night in Vera Cruz on the way, the latter not to be repeated if I can help it. I had better than usual luck by meeting on the second day out the great Dr. Hans Zinsser, of Harvard, who is probably the world's greatest bacteriologist. And what a man besides! He arrived along with me last night with letters from the state and war departments and a half dozen rats in the hold loaded with the deadly typhus. He is to conduct some local experiments and then return to Harvard in two weeks, leaving his assistant, Dr. Maximilliano Castenedo here for 3 more months to complete the experiment. Castenedo being a native Mexican and very much a gentleman has and will continue to do all kinds of favors for me—and one thing is assured: I shall not lack proper attendance here if I ever get sick. "Max" as I call him, knows everyone from the president down.

Zinsser, a product of Heidelberg, the Sorbonne, Pasteur Institute and other places besides American Universities knows and has more interesting ideas about literature than almost anyone I have ever met. What conversations we had!—He's about 51, bandy legged from riding fast horses, looks about 40 at most, writes damn good poetry (which he claims he'd rather do than excel as he does in the scientific world) and in carelessness and largesse is a thoroughbred if I ever saw one. . . . But I could write ten books about him and his incredible adventures in the war and in various parts of the world. Next year he's going to Abassynia to fight hook worm and other complaints. Well—and what is the best of it—I guess I've made a friend who will be a perennial stimulus to the best that I can do.

The ride up from Vercruz was marvelous, not alone the scenery, but the country people all along the way who swarmed around the train selling fruits, cakes, tortillas, serapies, canes, flowers, pulque, beer and what have you! One rides up, up along incredible ledges over valleys filled with tropical vegetation, waterfalls, etc. for about 5 hours. Then in front of Orizaba everything suddenly begins to change. This is the great plateau that in some ways seems even more splendid. Very austere—and with the mountains rising in the distance on each side, here and there the feudal walls of some old rancho—and the burros and brown natives jogging along dry roads. How I wish you were here to witness it. But you will come sometime. I know.

Tomorrow I shall go around to the bank to see if any mail has arrived for me as yet. I hardly expect your books this soon. I shall be here in town at least a month as I must get my Spanish somewhat at least before venturing to settle down in any of the smaller native places.

I hope you understood how sorry I was not to have seen you again before leaving. God, but I'm glad all the rush is over now—let's hope for a long time to come. Write soon. Best to Pat.

Love, as always, Hart

To Otto H. Kahn

c/o Dr. Eyler N. Simpson, Apartado 538
Mexico City, D.F. Mexico,
Dear Mr. Kahn: April 24, 1931

I have intended several times before this tardy hour—to thank you for the recommendation you accorded me, as one of my intimate references, in regard to the Guggenheim Fellowship in present tenure.—At least, since I have been so fortunate as to receive the honor, I assume that you were favorable to the circumstances, and so, without further thought, I presume to thank you. Is that aggreeable to you? I hope so!

My application included such details as a year in France. Without being too specific, however, you may guess that my preference for France was rather half-hearted—especially in view of the treatment that I had received there a year or so earlier. To be plain, I had not realized that Mexico was a possibility, without special qualifications (under the conditions of the Fellowship) such as archeölogy, zoölogy, medicine, etc. But a few days before engaging passage for Marseille (and Provence, the Cezanne country which I love there best of all) kind friends, more familiar with the conditions of my fellowship, informed me that not only Shanghai, Singapore or Mozambique were possible residences under the freedom of the Fellowship, —but Mexico, also!

I lost no time in deciding. And I am not—nor shall be regretful! Perhaps you may remember my conception of a drama (a true tragedy) based on the circumstances of the Conquest here—I refer to the gorgeous Cortes-Moctezuma action. I conceived that idea during the composition of the *Bridge*. You, later, made a kind inquiry about that project. . . . But I was too depleted by my efforts on *The Bridge* to even discuss it then with any gusto. And the same condition (through long months of unemployment!) has persisted—until *finalamente*, with the Fellowship, has come the flame again! My choice of Mexico was unquestionable.

Well, here I am, happier than ever before in my life. And my brain literally teeming with work and projects. Not only the Moctezuma matter, but (surprizingly) short stories even. . . . Prose, criticism—and the promise of more than I have dreamed since my appreciation of the Roebling magnificence. It is only, now, a matter of getting it down. . . . And Mexico, and the Mexicanos are the most superb people I have ever encountered. (They must not be destroyed). Simply as a tribute to our friendship, and in gratitude to you as a man whom I profoundly respect, I hope you will receive this slight appreciation and *recuerdo* (you, who gave me the accolade for the *Bridge*!) of my constancy.

I have been honored here, thanks to my Fellowship and to certain letters from Waldo Frank to such people as Don Genaro Estrada, Minister of Foreign Relations, and to Monseñor Moises Saenz, Minister of Education—besides distinguished doctors (I came down here with Dr. Hans Zinsser, of Harvard), editors, poets, painters, etc. I must admit that already I feel very much "at home". I hope to deserve these attentions —which, apparently, in Mexico, are lavishly extended.

Enclosed is one of several interviews which, I hope, will not seem too frivolous—especially as your name appears therein. And may I hear from you from time to time? Old friends,—at least mine—are good friends. What more has the Almanach de Gotha to offer? My dear Monseñor, you are already an old friend, if I may say so.

Faithfully yours, Hart Crane

P. S. Don't you dare come to Mexico again without looking me up! I enclose my permanent address. A suburb of the City.

To Katherine Anne Porter and Eugene Pressly

DEAR KATHERINE ANNE & GENE—
HAVE GONE TO THE MANCERA UNTIL THE FIRST. EXCUSE MY
WAKEFULNESS PLEASE.

HART

P.S. NO. HAVEN'T BEEN BUSY WITH "LOVERS". JUST YEOWLS AND FLEES. LYSOL ISN'T NECESSARY IN THE BATHTUB. HAVEN'T GOT "ANYTHING" YET. IF YOU KNEW ANYTHING WHATEVER ABOUT IT, YOU'D KNOW THAT AT LEAST (AND THE LAST THING SYPHILLUS DOES) IT DOESN'T <u>ITCH</u>. OTHER MATTERS DO, SOMETIMES.

To Katherine Anne Porter and Eugene Pressly

Dear Katherine Anne and Gene:

This is as near as I dare come to you today. Shame and chagrin overwhelm me. I hope you can sometime forgive.

Yours—Hart

To Katherine Anne Porter

Darling Katherine Anne:

I'm too jittery to write a straight sentence but am coming out of my recent messiness with at least as much consistency as total abstinence can offer.

Your two notes were so kind and gave me so much more cheer than I deserve that I'm overcome all over again. God bless you!!! I've got myself in a fix with a hell of a bill at the Mancera—but I'll get out of it somehow. My father is sending me some money—meanwhile Hazel Cazes is going to advance some.

This house is a love—and I'm glad to know that it won't be ruined for me now by any absence on your part—and Gene's. The recent cyclone is my last—at least for a year.

Love and a thousand thanks. Hart

When I get D.T.s again I'll just take it out on police . . . They'll have at least a cell for me—or a straightjacket.

To Charlotte and Richard Rychtarik

Guest here recently at wonderful villa of Minister of Education. A great *fiesta* in progress. All *10* cathedrals ablaze with candles, songs. My bed heaped with confetti. Dancing, wine, *Courvoisier*! Heavenly! And the view through the mountains!

Love—
Hart

To Malcolm Cowley

Michoacan 15
Mixcoac, D.F., Mexico
June 2, 1931

Dear Malcolm:

Look up Bill Spratling, whom I saw off a week ago for NY. He's staying at 603 Park Ave. for a coupla weeks; then intends (or *intended*) to cruise back to his Taxco. Meanwhile I'm trying to take care of all his precious collection of timeless, or rather dateless, idols.

An even more "advance notice" concerns the early arrival (permanent) of Malu Cabrera, the nicest and most interesting woman in Mexico, who is coming up within three weeks or so to marry a guy named "Bloch," I think it's his name, who's a reader for Knopf. She hates his crowd, the Van Vechten set, from previous encounters. Let Spratling tell you about her. She is very much somebody—especially in Mexico. Have her around to one of those "ordeal" luncheons at the *New Rep.* because she'll always know so damned much more about Mexico than anyone else (including little Carleton Beals) who has ever stepped into the doors of your institution, that it'll pay to have her handy for a lot of timely references.

Malu will probably end up in NY by serving conventional enough "teas"—but here in Mexico, being the daughter of a great international corporation lawyer and a real Mexican patriot—(what a combination!)—she's considered more advanced and "independent" in her actions than any señoritas who ever left home and "earned her way" in convent and as school teacher. She's a beautiful and agile and strong, direct creature. And you'll miss a lot if you don't take her up—I.E. as far as her husband, who, I'm told, is pretty bad,—will let her'nyouboth. Failing due attentions, on your part, to Spratling,—I'll drive her to you with a letter. . . . As I am to the Davenports, Paul Rosenfeld, and some others.

Don't expect much more from me about Mexico for awhile. Maybe it's the altitude (which *is* a tremendous strain at times) maybe my favorite drink, Tequila; maybe my balls and beautiful people; or maybe just the flowers that I'm growing or fostering in my garden . . . but it's all too good, so far, to be true. I've been too preoccupied, so far, with furnishing, from every little nail, griddle, bowl and pillow, to look around much outside the fascinating city markets and streets and bars. No chance to stretch pennies—just to spend them. Ran out long ago on my Guggenheim installment. But a house just can't be lived in without a few essentials. And the main "standard American" essentials in Mexico cost like hell.

Lorna will have to relay to you the more complete details of my house, should such matters interest you. I found, by advice, that single mozos weren't apt to be much good. Pulque sprees three times a day, and the evenings never certain. Besides I needed a woman to cook. Consequently I have a delightful hide and seek combination—of both functions (page Mormon be sneezed BUnson) besides a new installation of electric lights with just enough "glim"—not to say Klim—to be pleasant.

Moisés has been swell to me. His innate Aztec refinement; his quiet daring; his generosity (one should avoid an *et cetera* in such exceptional cases!) has made me love him very much. He was very instrumental in my accidental possession of a real decoration: an ancient silver pony bridle (bells and all!) from the period of the Conquest, about my neck in a photo taken by Katherine Anne—you shall soon see, like it,—believe it, or not!.

I have a quilty, besides a guilty conscience! Haven't even written to Waldo, whose letters gave me a wonderful send-off with certain writers here. But Latin American manners, I have discovered, are rather baffling. Great dinners are planned, but never come off! If Katherine Anne couldn't explain it all away with references to certain previous experiences of her own, I'd feel quite crushed. As it is, I don't mind in the least. Because . . . . Mexico has incredibly fine native painters. (You should see the new Diegos in the Palace!) But all her pretenders to poesy have just read about orchids in Baudelaire, apparently. I have my most pleasant literary moments with an Irish revolutionary, red haired friend of Liam O'Flaherty, shot (and not missed) seventeen times in one conflict and another; the most quietly sincere and appreciative person, in many ways, whom I've ever met. It's a big regret that he's Dublin bound again after three years from home, in a few weeks. Ernest O'Malley by name. And we drink a lot together—look at frescos—and aggree!

You and Muriel have got to come visit me here before long. I can't dare to think how soon I'll be driven to fight for my little place here—and keep it. But I think I will. And it has an entire guest suite. Not that it's pretentious—anything BUT. BUT—it's the first real home I've ever had. And the devotion of my servants, for $8. total fees per month, and the flowers, and the fleas—well, Malcolm, I don't wanna ever leava!

Good night! Love to Muriel! and write me soon!

As ever, Hart

What's happened to Bill? He never answers my letters!!!

To Clarence Arthur Crane

Michoacan 15
Mixcoac, D.F., Mexico

Dear C.A.: June 5, 1931

I really owe you answer for two letters. The postcard was about all I could get time for the other day, and regardless of time, there happens to be very little more to report even now —without going far beyond a letter, in fact, clear into a couple of books, in order to describe some of the places, villages, rug factories, museums, etc. that I've been busy visiting. In any case, such descriptions will have to be postponed. It takes a while even to digest it all,—let alone relay it!

Regarding money—I shall economize and make out probably very well from now on—without any outside help. You know how grateful I am to you for seeing me installed here, and ultimately with the accepted indispensables. I'm feeling very well, am getting well into the language study and my work. And—in a certain way—the less news there is for awhile, the better it really is.

I don't see much of American papers here, so anything about the stock market would surprise me. But I am sorry to hear that the weather has been so inclement as to keep people away from the Cottage. April and May are always great lotteries, however. But you'll be sure to find more luck in June—and thereafter. You can't lose . . . Don't you remember the "Bright" prediction?

How is Sherlock Holmes these days? From over the wall I occasionally hear American programs from Los Angeles and other stations in California. But by and large, I enjoy my portable Orthophonic and a few symphony records much more. There are some wonderful native Mexican dances, Saints' Day songs, etc. that you would enjoy very much. And situated as I am—I can play them as late at night as I like. That's all to the good of my inspiration, as you may remember me saying.

More anon. Meanwhile send the next letter airmail, like the last. It took only two days en route.

                    Much love to you, and to all, Hart

PS—The enclosed photo was taken on a special occasion, the bard being gifted with a very old and rare solid silver pony bridle, from the period of the Conquest. The shirt and pants are part of my previous wardrobe—a French sailor's outfit—from days "over there." I don't look very sick however, do I?

To Waldo Frank

                              Michoacan 15
                              Mixcoac, D.F., Mexico
Dear Waldo: June 13, 1931

It seems to require much more determination to write a letter, so far, than to fuss around in my flower garden that skirts three sides of the house I have taken here in Mixcoac for a year. My long suppressed passion for a few plants and a "philosopher's walk" however, is far from being the sole reason for my neglectfulness of you. The novelty and turmoil incident to the first few weeks; then locating a house, then furnishing it with the indispensables, from broom to teakettle, from mop to mattress; then "breaking in" a native couple to cook and sweep—all with my limited native vocabulary! Well, it's been a good deal to have undertaken, freshly lifted, as I am, to this high altitude.

Despite this delay in getting down to work, I haven't any regrets. You may remember that I spoke of establishing a headquarters as soon as possible on my arrival? I've had to squirm for money temporarily, but corresponding later savings and the creative advantage of having a place of my own—really for the first time in my life—ought to justify my action.

As for Mexico—I'm not frothing over quite so much as I did for awhile, but I'm still so fascinated and impressed by the people that I want to stay much longer than one year, if I can manage to. You were right; it's a sick country; and God knows if it ever has been, or will be otherwise. I doubt if I will ever be able to fathom the Indian really. It may be a dangerous quest, also. I'm pretty sure it is, in fact. But humanity is so unmechanized here still, so immeadiate and really dignified (I'm speaking of the Indians, peons, country people—not the average meztiso) that it is giving me an entirely fresh perspective. And whether immeadiately creative or not, more profound than Europe gave me. . . . This is truly "another world." There isn't much use for the present in describing my reactions beyond saying that I find them all expressed in my emphatic aggreement with nearly everything said by Anita Brenner in her *Idols Behind Altars* which I've just finished reading. It would take me, I imagine, a long residence here to be able to contradict any of her statements, besides which I am so sympathetic to her attitudes, reactions and general thesis as not to care to court divergencies of opinion.

A few days after my arrival I took a taxi and delivered the letters of introduction that you so generously provided. I immeadiately heard from Leon Felipe, and a few days later had an audience with Estrada. The former I saw a couple of times later—and was introduced to a flock of writers, doctors, etc. one afternoon at the Café Colon. Camino seemed very cordial, but suddenly "dropped" me. Latin-Americans, I've been told (and now I *know*) have a way of inviting you out on some specific day, and then "letting you down" most beautifully—without notice or subsequent apology or explanation. I've got so that I take it quite for granted, and if any other more tempting occasion offers itself in the meantime, I, too, humor my whim.

Estrada gave me two de luxe volumes of his poetry in response to the copy of the *Bridge* (Paris edition) I brought up to him. I can't read Spanish well enough yet to even attempt his books, nor any other "Mexican" poetry; but off-hand I've more spontaneous respect for him than for Camino, who, as soon as he heard I was about to call on Estrada, began to ridicule both the man and his work in high glee. What makes me rather indifferent to all of them is the fact that not one of them is really interested one iota in expressing anything indigenous; rather they are busy aping (as though it could be done in Spanish!) Paul Valery, Eliot—or more intensely, the Parnassians of 35 years ago. And they are all "bored"—or at least pleased to point the reference. Estrada spoke very warmly of you, and after what some of the others said, I should consider him a real friend of yours. In contrast to their general directions and preoccupations, however, I still (to date, at any rate) harbor the illusion that there is a soil, a mythology, a people and a spirit here that are capable of unique and magnificent utterance.

Moisés Sáenz, who has had me out to his place at Taxco, and who has treated me as hospitably and generously as anyone I ever remember, has the same conviction. And he says that Casanova, whom I have merely met, has a more natural attitude than the typical Mexican *litterateur*. I hope to see more of Casanova later; he's been ill most of the time since I got here. I've not yet had a reply from Montéllano. Camino asked to do some translations from *White Bldgs* for "Contemporaneos." I gave him the book—and offered assistance. But since he found me out of the stiff black round-shouldered "elegance"—in fact in my usual household white sailor pants and shirt—he hasn't been heard from—by mail or otherwise. One must appear in veritable Wall street gear to impress the Mexican hidalgo!

He said that he was translating your new Latin Am. book, as I remember. Will you tell me something about its publication date, etc.—since I can't get any reply from Camino? And now, how about your new work, your novel? And your for this summer, etc? I hope you are having a smooth road toward some really individual expression. Hope you'll approve of my reference to you in the enclosed interview, from *Excelsior. El Universal* was also very kindly. Their feature writer, Rafael Valle, is a very decent and intelligent and constant friend of mine.

My love to Alma. Write soon, Waldo. And maybe I'll have something really interesting to say later on.

Love, as ever, Hart

Katherine Anne Porter and I are neighbors in Mixcoac. You really ought to get hold of her book *Flowering Judas.* The title story, and another called "Maria Conception" are very profound comments on Mexico.

To Ernest O'Malley

Dear OMalley:

Hope apologies for last night are acceptable . . . Please!

Can you come back with Miguel for "dinner" tonight? Or wouldn't you rather?

Katherine Anne is leaving me her extra bed for your use here. So come prepared to stay over night—at least—if the idea suits you.

Affectionately,
Hart

P.S. I'm keeping Miguel and María a week longer—provisionally—

To Morton Dauwen Zabel

Michoacan 15
Mixcoac, D.F., Mexico
Dear Mr. Zabel: June 20, 1931

The post (for books, etc. 2nd class) is apt to be very slow to Mexico,—at any rate unreliable. If this be not too great an impediment to either my reception or return of review books from *Poetry*—then let me ask for the two books suggested by you for review in your very kind letter of June 11th.

Further, I realize that my facilities for adequate reviewing of books are somewhat restricted here, there being no library handy for consultation on recent or even near-recent works on American poetry, etc. But if you are willing to take the risk— then so am I. And if you find the resultant estimates too biassed or unfounded, you certainly need be under no compulsion to print them.

Didn't Roy Helton compile an anthology, or rather a study interspersed with very good quotations, on negro folk songs, spirituals, etc.? I suppose the jacket of his book will contain whatever references to his earlier works are notable. But if not, please give me some word about the above.

Allow me to thank you and Miss Monroe for the copy of *Poetry* recently received. I hope, and very earnestly, that I shall soon have something worthy to submit to you. Since leaving the pattern of *The Bridge* the "new freedom" (call it rather a new restriction) has left me at least momentarily, rather speechless. I'm too attached to the consciousness of my own land to write "tourist sketches" elsewhere. Mexico is well enough. But I'd rather be in my favorite corner of Connecticut. The first requirement of a scholarship, however, is to leave the U.S.A. It doesn't matter much whither. It wouldn't so much matter if the entire outside world didn't positively hate us Americans so much. To create in such an atmosphere isn't so easy however!

Best wishes to you and to Miss Monroe.

Sincerely, Hart Crane

To Katherine Anne Porter

Dear Katherine Anne:

My apologies are becoming so mechanical as (through repitition) to savour of the most negligible insincerity. So I have to leave most of this to your judgement of the potency and the malfeasance of an overdose of tequila.

Let Theodora know—if I have any chance of talking with you and explaining. Otherwise I'll know that you don't want to be molested even to that point of endurance.

I spent the night in jail—as Theodora has probably told you. That was, in its way, sufficient punishment. Besides having made a fool of myself in Town. . . . However I was arrested for nothing more than challenging the taxi driver for an excessive rate. But if it hadn't been for waiting for you—hour on hour, and trying to keep food warm, cream sweet, and my damnable disposition—don't suppose I'd have yelled out at you so horribly en route to doom!

I don't ask you to forgive. Because that's probably past hope. But since Peggy C. will be here in a few days—I'd rather, for her sake as well as mine, that she didn't step into a truly Greenwich Village scene.

Very sincerely and contritely, Hart

To Lorna Dietz

Michoacan 15

Dearest Lorna: Mixcoac, D.F., Mexico

The arrival of the reviews you sent at least assured that you aren't angry with me. They certainly are *most* welcome—and if it isn't asking too much I hope you'll think of me again in that regard. What I most crave is a good long letter from you. Do you realize that I haven't heard from you for two months? And after that long, long shriek of excitement that I sent you— including a map of my house! I'm beginning to wonder now if you really received it. My father recently missed getting a letter I sent him . . .

Have you abandoned your vacation plans in Mexico? I spent a full paragraph urging you to come. Guess everyone is sore at me or whatever, I don't know. People don't like enthusiastic reports from me—and so from now on they won't need to read them any more. Not a word from Bill, Sue, Malcolm since I left. Peggy Cowley and Don Young as well as Bob Stewart (down home in Alabamy) haven't exactly snubbed me, however.

I read accounts of terrific heat up north. It's so chilly here during most of the day and *all* night as to be almost uncomfortable. I'm studying Spanish and the Conquest—and that keeps me busy enough. Have still a lot of sightseeing and traveling to do, but *that* later—when I'll know more about what I'm looking at. Had to "fire" my servants as the cook could only manage native dishes—*some* of which agree with me, but only *some*! I'm really better off without them since I can get a huge meal sent in every noon for less than 25 cents—and breakfast and supper are very light affairs to manage myself. A man comes and cleans every day for the same price. So Peter Blume need not write again so damned sarcastically about my basking and lounging in an orgy of luxury.

Peggy Cowley is due in a few days and I'll probably get an earfull about most everybody—but that will hardly do in your case! Do write. I need your moral support against all the things that Katherine Anne Porter has apparently been writing north.

Love always, Hart

To Henry Allen Moe

Dear Mr. Moe: July 8, 1931

Due to my Father's sudden death two days ago I cannot yet answer your recent notice beyond expressing my sincere regret that you felt so wholesale a condemnation was necessary. On my return to Mexico (if I go through New York) it may be possible to have a talk with you—when some rather gross misunderstandings can be explained.

Sincerely yours, Hart Crane

To William Slater Brown

Box 604
Chagrin Falls, Ohio
Dear Bill: July 15

I appreciate your letter a very great deal. Your surmise is very true: while the results of my visit with my father last winter make me feel the loss more keenly, there is some consolation, at the same time, in having realized his qualities and affection for me more fully than ever before. I'm glad, too, that at the time of his death—as well as for some months before—he had been in a singularly happy mood. And it might have been very painful had there been any protracted illness, invalidism, etc. Especially with his predisposition toward constant activity. As it was, I don't think he had more than a passing flash of recognition of what had occured.

I'm here for a month or so, at least. Mrs. Crane wants me to be of what help I can during the settlement of the estate, pending continuance of certain branches of the business and possible suspension of others. As she and I have always been great friends it's only natural that I should comply. Her grief has been genuinely severe; she's been really heroic in facing the burden of so many new responsibilities.

I'll write you more soon. Meanwhile do let me hear more details of your recent life. Thanks again for your thoughtful letter, Bill.

As ever, Hart

PS—Could you have my subscription address for the *New Republic* changed to Chagrin Falls again?

To Lorna Dietz

Box 604
Chagrin Falls, Ohio
Dearest Lorna: July 15, 1931

To begin with the same subject which you did in your last—and to continue with what has been almost an obscession with me for the last month—I want to say a few words about Katherine Anne Porter. Not that I can possibly give even the outline of the whole queer situation, but since she has done so much announcing, just a hint at the circumstances.

Katherine Anne's disposition, as I knew her initially in NY was considerably different than I found it to be with a sourish gentleman of Scotch descent, in Mexico. He can't abide most of her old associates in Mexico (nor they him) any more than I found he could abide me. Maybe you've known like circumstances with other couples. Anyway, they're very misleading, eventually in any case. Katherine Anne was quite lovely to me on more than one occasion, and since I have always liked her a lot, it was hard to relinquish her company.

The continuance, however,—and this is the only way I can put it—resulted in some very strained situations and outbreaks on my part—generally at times when I had had too much to drink. Since I have no very clear recollection of everything said during those times I presume I must have been pretty awful. Everything had been going very smoothly for some time, however; Katherine Anne frequently dropping into my place for afternoon chats, beer, etc. when the apparently decisive moment occurred.

I had asked them both to have dinner with me on a certain day at my house. It was well understood, etc. I made extensive preparations—and was left to keep things warm the entire afternoon, nipping at a bottle of tequila meanwhile, and going through the usual fretful crescendo of sentiments that such conduct incurs. Toward evening, having fed most of the natives in the vicinity and being rather upset, I went to town, where more drinks were downed. But in an argument with the taxi driver at my gate later in the evening I challenged him to arbitration at the local police station. Result: a night in jail; for feeling is so high against Americans in Mexico since the recent *Oklahoma* affair, that any pretext is sufficient to embarrass one.

K.A.'s place is just around the corner from the house I took, so on the way to the station I passed her gate. She and Mr. Pressley (the Adonis I have been speaking of) happened to be within speaking distance. I remember having announced my predicament and of having said, in anger at her response to the dinner engagement, "Katherine Anne, I have my opinion of you." I was furious, of course, and I still have no reason for doubting that Pressley simply devised that insult deliberately. I haven't seen Katherine Anne since, nor has she ever offered the slightest explanation of her absence. She told a mutual friend that I said something particularly outrageous to her that evening at the gate; but what it may have been beyond what I have just mentioned I don't know. I wrote her a very humble apology a few days later, but there was no response.

It's all very sad and disaggreable. But one imputation I won't stand for. That is the obvious and usual one: that my presence in the neighborhood was responsible for a break or discontinuance of Katherine Anne's creative work. K-A had been in Mexico a full year before I ever arrived without having written one paragraph of the book she had in mind to write when she went there. If her friends don't already know her habit of procrastinating such matters at least I do. If she wants to encumber herself with turkeys, geese, chickens and a regular stock farm for the fun of it then well and good; but I know that she spent many more hours in nursing and talking to them every day than she ever spent in my company. Neither did the slight amount of extra tippling incident to my arrival impair her health. She came down with an attack of gout, from which she quickly recovered; but I'm surely not responsible for the effects of strong Mexican gravies made by her own servant nor for the fact that, by her own admission, she and Pressley had been indulging in the most expensive foreign wines and liqueurs for many a month before my arrival. Katherine Anne hasn't a trace of T.B. left; that was all over long ago; and I think there is a great tendency among her friends to sentimentalize and exaggerate her delicate health. She isn't happy, that's true, and is constantly in a nervous flutter, talks more to herself than others lately, and is a puzzle to all her old friends—but those manifestations originated long before my arrival. I'm tired of being made into a bogey or ogre rampant in Mexico and tearing the flesh of delicate ladies. I'm also tired of a certain rather southern type of female vanity. And that's about all I ever want to say about Katherine Anne again personally.

My father was buried last Saturday. Mrs. Crane, despite the fact that the delay was really a great strain on her endurance, insisted on awaiting my arrival, which wasn't until late Friday, as I couldn't get airplane reservations beyond Albuquerque. She was so grief-stricken that I've been worried about her. I'm more impressed by her sincerity and dignity than I can tell you, however, and her feelings toward me make me feel that I have a real home whenever I want to claim it here with her. She had a room and bath all ready for me—and it's to be regarded as permanently mine.

I'm glad that I've already been able to be of some help to her in matters of the estate, etc. It will be some time before all inventories are taken of various departments of my father's business, and I'll certainly be here beyond the time of your trip west, in August. You must plan on stopping over at least a day. You really ought to see this country place, for I think it's worth more than a passing glance. And above and beyond such considerations, I have a great yen to look you over, as you might guess. Certainly you can "make it", and I'm sure that a day's break in that long trip would be refreshing. Let me know.

My father's will left very modest provisions for me, but they are as good as an annual Guggenheim, anyway, and that is all I really require. Quite properly, Mrs. Crane was left with the direction of most of his property and concerns—along with two other executors. The chocolate business will probably be discontinued, as it should have been anyway, as soon as one or two expensive leases can be disposed of. I may or may not take a hand in the picture business—but probably not. Nothing can be definitely decided until we know more about the total status of the estate.

As I just wrote Bill—who surprised me by writing a very thoughtful note—I'm increasingly glad that I had those three months with my father last winter. The enormous advance in mutual understanding and affection that was achieved left me a better and truer picture of my father than I had ever had before. It's good to remember, too, that he was unusually contented and optimistic during the last few months, about his business and all other concerns. And when he went he had no more than a passing flash of recognition of the event before complete unconsciousness supervened.

Various parts of this letter may have bored you, but since you're such a good and old friend, I like to impose on you.

Write soon, Lorna, and try to plan on a stopover here on your way west.

Affectionately, *Hart*

To Ernest O'Malley

Box 604,
Chagrin Falls, Ohio
Dear Ernest: July 19th
    I'm wondering if, besides forwarding to me what mail has come to me in Mixcoac, you'd mind going someday to the Anglo South American Bank, on Capuchinas, and forwarding whatever letters have been sent to me there. They won't be apt to question your identity if you just write out "cartas para Hart Crane" on a slip of paper and hand same to one of the attendants with the request to have the letters brought to you.
    I'm sorry I can't send you the extra postage needed, but it won't be much anyway, as there are probably relatively few pieces.
    I just had a brief note from Peggy Cowley who is apparently staying with the hypochrondriacs of Tiziano. You've met her ere this, I presume. She hinted that she'd like to stay awhile in my place after KA leaves and I've written her that I'd be glad if she would move in anytime. I have no way of knowing whether or not you or Lalla have been there a moment or not since my departure. But there's plenty of room for all three of you if you like. Incase you aren't making any use of the place, I've asked Peggy to come to you for the key.
    Please hurry up and write me soon. It's been two weeks since I left, and not a peep from you yet! You can't be in distant villages *all* the time. Maybe you'll still be there when I get back—a month or more yet anyway—which would be nice, for *me* at any rate.
    Lots of luck and best wishes,

Affectionately,
Hart

To Louis Untermeyer

Box 604
Chagrin Falls, Ohio
Dear Louis Untermeyer: July 24, 1931

I appreciate the honor of being included in your new anthology, *The Book of Living Verse*—and it is especially nice of you to request my opinion on the best poem to be used. In this regard I can't help thinking that "To Brooklyn Bridge" (Liveright version, *not* Black Sun Press) best answers what I conceive to be the requirements. Barring that, "Voyages II or VI" would be *my* second choice. You are free, of course, to make whatever selection you like. The fee will be the same as for your other anthology: $5.00 for each page or page runover.

Does anyone know what has happened particularly to Wallace Stevens of late? I miss fresh harmonies from him almost more than I can say. There never was anyone quite like him, nor will there be! I don't think any critic has ever done him full justice, either, and it's a temptation to attempt it sometime oneself. Even I may sometime try. I hope he's going into your anthology, as well as Cowley's (Malcolm) "Urn".

I'm in anything but a lyrical mood these days, but then that's the way Ohio always affects me, as your wife would seem to anticipate.

Faithfully yours, Hart Crane

To Samuel Loveman

15 Michoacan
Mixcoac, D.F., Mexico
Dear Sam: September 11, 1931

The trip down was pretty damned hot, but it's really cold here and will seem to be so until the end of the rainy season which is about finished. I found my house in fine shape. The servants had guarded everything beautifully and the garden surprised me with its miraculous growth—sunflowers 14 feet high—profusion of roses, nasturtiums, violets, dahlias, lilies, cosmos, mignonette, etc.

I have had the pleasure to meet a young archeologist from Wisconsin, who is studying in the University here and who thinks he has discovered a buried Aztec pyramid right in the vicinity of my house. Yesterday we took a pick and shovel and worked our heads off digging into the side of a small hill, itself on a vast elevation overlooking the entire valley of Anahuac. Except for a few flocks of goats and sheep the entire neighborhood has been abandoned since the Conquest. A marvelous stillness and grassy perfume pervade the district; one sees the two great volcanoes in the distance and a part of the horizon glazed by Lake Texcoco, seemingly below which floats, as in a dream, the City of Mexico. It was an arduous and rich afternoon. I have a lame back today, but also some very interesting chips and pieces of the true Aztec pottery picked up here and there on the surface and from our little excavation. The experience is haunting, melancholy too. But such "first hand" contact beats the more artificial contacts that museums proffer. We also ran across one of those incredibly sharp fragments of obsidian, part of a knife blade used either to carve stone and other materials or human flesh. It is still a mystery as to how they cut obsidian—but this shard was perfectly edged and graded as though it had been as conformable as wood.

Tomorrow morning we are leaving for a four days visit to Tepoztlan, the town Chase writes about. We shall have to sleep on the floors of schoolhouses or abandoned convents. I'm glad to have the chance to go with Rourke (the archeologist) as he speaks Spanish perfectly and also knows a great deal about customs, folklore, etc. He is light, slender, Irish of course, and makes me think a little of Pat. If all goes well it may not be our last trip together.

I'm enclosing some pictures of my place. My kodak works very well. Write me all about yourself, and the "doings" of our mutual friends. Sorry you couldn't get to the boat, but I can well understand the reasons.

Love, Hart

To William H. Wright

15 Michoacan
Mixcoac, D.F., Mexico
September 21, 1931

Dear Bill:

How are things going? I hear the heat continues up north. But you must have had a pleasant trip through the Adirondacks any way. Vera Cruz was a hissing cauldron when I got there; in fact the last two days on the boat were Turkish baths. But once here on the plateau—I went back to my nightly blankets and recovered quickly. The aforesaid port has had a pretty little hurricane since my debarkation. I knew it couldn't help but happen.

I felt awfully diffident about leaving the US, but I'm beginning to be entirely glad that I came back here after all. In the first place there was no settling down this time to be accomplished. I found my house in good order, the servants joyful to see me, and my garden a perfect miracle of growth and colorful profusion. I could begin "living" right away without a moment in a hotel, a blanket or kitchen implement to buy—having spent about three months in such preoccupations on my previous visit. The rainy season is lasting unusually long, but it keeps all the verdure so miraculously green that the countryside will hold its colors all the longer into the long 8 months of drowth to come.

During the mere two weeks since my return I've already had the most interesting adventure that I think I ever remember. I came back with the resolution to get out more into the smaller cities and pueblas, to get as thoroughly acquainted with the native indian population as possible. So when I met a young archeologist from Wisconsin who asked me to go along with him on a five days trip to Tepoztlan I didn't linger. Though two books and a dozen articles have been written about Tepoztlan (see Stuart Chase's *Mexico* and Carleton Beals' *Mexican Maize*) it has never been invaded by tourists. And isn't likely to be, either, for some time. As there is nothing remotely resembling a hotel or lodging house in the place I went prepared to sleep on the floor of the Monastery. One can sleep soundly almost anywhere and be thankful for the limited diet of beans and tortillas if one has spent the whole day walking, scrambling over dizzy crags or hunting fragments of old Aztec idols, of which the surrounding cornfields of Tepoztlan are full.

The town is practically surrounded by cliffs as high as 800 feet, basalt ledges with a perilous sheer drop sometimes of 300 feet, covered with a dense tropical foliage and veritable hanging gardens—with cascades and waterfalls galore. The descent begins about 3 miles from El Pargue where the train leaves one—about 4 hours from Mixcoac.

(Distances in linear miles are so deceptive here, since mountainous country necessitates such inclines and devious windings. One can watch the engine from the rear most of the way.)

But I'm not going to give an exhaustive description of the town as you can read that, and better formulated too in Chase's book, which everyone seems to be reading now anyway. The most exciting feature of our trip and visit was the rare luck of arriving on the eve of the yearly festival (fiesta) of Tepoxtéco, the ancient Aztec god of pulque, whose temple, partially ruined by the Spaniards and recent revolutions, still hangs on one of the perilous cliffs confronting the town.

Only a small fraction of the populace (they are all pure unadulterated Aztec) took part or even attended this ceremony; but we found those that did, largely elderly, the finest and kindliest of all the lovely people of the place. Aside from those who had climbed up to spend the night in watch at the temple there were only about twenty-five. These, divided into several groups around lanterns (of all places!) on the roof of the Cathedral and Monastery which dominates the town, made a wonderful sight with their dark faces, white "pyjama" suits and enormous white hats. A drummer and a flute player standing facing the dark temple on the heights, alternated their barbaric service at ten minute intervals with loud ringing of all the church bells by the sextons of the church. Two voices, still in conflict here in Mexico, the idol's and the Cross. Yet there really did not seem to be a real conflict that amazing night. Nearly all of these "elders" I have been describing go to mass!

And so kindly and interested in explaining the old myths of their gods to us! Fortunately my archeologist friend speaks perfect Spanish—besides knowing some Aztec and some local mythology. Meanwhile, if you can possibly imagine such a night, the lightning flickered over the eastern horizon while a crescent moon fell into the west. And between the two a trillion stars glittered overhead! It was truly the Land of Oz, with the high valley walls in the Wizard's circle. Rockets were sent whizzing up—to be answered by other rockets far up and over from the lofty temple. After nine, when the playing stopped, we asked the "elders" to a stall in the town market and served them each with a glass of tequila. We were invited to join them again at 3 A.M. atop the church again, for the conclusion of the watch.

I am sorry to say I didn't wake until five. But it was still pitch dark. And to hear those weird notes of drum and fife in the dark valley, refreshed as we were with sleep, it was even more compelling. We rushed from the baker's house (where we had found a bamboo bed and exquisite hospitality) over the rough stone streets into the church yard, stumbling up the dark corridors and narrow stairs of the monastery just as a faint light emerged over the eastern break in the cliffs. There was the same bundle of elders welcoming us and serving us delicious coffee, all the hotter for a generous infusion of pulque, straight pulque alcohol in each cup.

But the most enthralling of all was the addition of another drum—this being the ancient Aztec drum, pre-Conquest and guarded year after year from the destruction of the priests and conquerors, that how many hundreds of times had been beaten to propitiate the god, Tepoxtéco, the patron and protector of these people. A large wooden cylinder, exquisitely carved and showing a figure with animal head, upright, and walking through thick woods,—it lay horizontally on the floor of the roof, resounding to two heavily padded drum sticks before the folded knees of one of the indians. The people at the temple had played it up there the night before, and now someone had brought it down to be played to the rising sun in the valley.

Suddenly, as it was getting lighter and lighter and excitement was growing more and more intense, one of the indians who had been playing it put the drum sticks into my hands and nodded toward the amazing instrument. It seemed too good to be true, really, that I, who had expected to be thrown off the roof when I entered the evening before, should now be invited to actually participate. And actually I did! I not only beat the exact rhythm with all due accents, which they had been keeping up for hours; I even worked in an elaboration, based on the lighter tattoo of the more modern drum of the evening before. This, with such ponderous sticks, was exhausting to the muscles of the forearm; but I had the pleasure of pleasing them so that they almost embraced me. They did, in fact, several of them—put their arms around my shoulders and walk back and forth the whole length of the roof, when at the astronomical hour of six the whole place seemed to go mad in the refulgence of full day. It is something to hear bells rung, but it is inestimably better to see the sextons wield the hammers, swinging on them with the full weight of their entire bodies like frantic acrobats—while a whole bevy of rockets shower into such a vocal sunrise!

Well, after that there was the whole series of tableaus and performances incident to the Mexican Independence Day celebration (Sept 15–16–17) in which everybody took part. But of that another time. You can see how I am enthusiastic about Tepoztlan. I went bathing in mountain streams with a young indian, gorged on beans and tortillas, found idols in the surrounding cornfields and finally, the morning I was leaving, met the Vicar at stool in the Cathedral. On the climb back to the station we visited the ancient temple. It still has fragments of remarkable relief and is staunchly and beautifully constructed. I may go back to Tepoztlan for two weeks in October. I never left a town feeling so mellow and in such pleasant relations with everybody in the place.

Heavens, what a long letter! But there isn't much more to say right now. Except that I hope I won't be called back to "civilization" any too soon!

My love to Margaret and warmest greetings to your parents.

Affectionately, Hart

To Peggy Baird Cowley

                                              15 Michoacan
                                              Mixcoac, D.F.
Dearest Peggy: Monday noon

Sorry not to find you in. But come out before two if you can, and have lunch with me. If not then later in the day—as soon as convenient.

Just got back from Taxco last night. Have some fascinating children's paintings to show you—as well as puff or so left over from our private—and scandalous—fiesta last Saturday night.

                                              Love, Hart

To Malcolm Cowley

                                              15 Michoacan
                                              Mixcoac, D.F., Mexico
Dear Malcolm: October 5, 1931

Despite its aero stamp, I'm just today in receipt of your letter. Mail service seems to get a little worse and more doubtful here all the time.

Yes, Peggy must have been pretty close to danger for awhile judging by what she said about her symptoms. She stayed in bed for a week or so, but went to Puebla over last weekend and looked very well this morning when I called. I think she's got to keep pretty quiet, however, if relapses aren't to be expected. Bill Spratling wired me to bring her along with me to Taxco tomorrow for a few days, and I think she's planning on joining me since I've had no word to the contrary this afternoon. She was going to ask her doctor about it . . .

About cashing checks: I haven't made any connections myself yet, having depended on Eyler Simpson (of the Foundation) to cash mine up to the first of this month when my Guggenheim letter of credit became valid again. So I can't be of much help in that way. In Peggy's present quandary I suggest sending her (wiring her) American Ex. money orders. It costs more than postage but it isn't so high as direct through

Western Union, and it's worth the little extra to both of you to have more peace of mind. I think I paid only $.75 to send $150. to France recently, and they were certainly prompt and efficient. Wells Fargo may have the same service . . . They seem to have more business in Mexico.

As Bill has probably told you, the Katherine Anne upset accounted for my more than diffidence about seeing most of our mutual friends when I passed through NY. Sometime I may say more about it, but I'm sick of the subject just now; and since Mexico is proving to be so much more pleasant and absorbing to me during this second sojourn, I don't want to stir up any more unneighborly dust here in Mixcoac this evening than matches a pleasant mood.

But I do hope to have an answer from you sometime—a little longer than this last and more in proportion to the long letter I wrote you from here months and months ago, and which hasn't even yet been acknowledged. It's getting dark and I want to get this off before the post office closes, so more later. I'm glad to be of any help I can to Peggy, love her as always, and enjoy her company (and we see quite a lot of each other) immensely. Old friends are a God-send anywhere! Especially when they're as good sports as Peggy is . . . She's pretty fragile, but I think she's happy here, possibly more so than anywhere else right now.

I miss getting the *N.R.*—which is still probably being sent to Chagrin Falls. Could you have it switched back to Mixcoac?

All best to you and Muriel, besides Bill and Sue.—*AND LORNA!*

Hastily, Hart

I enclose a picture of the garden side of my house. Pretty good for $30 per month.

To Charlotte and Richard Rychtarik

When are you coming down? Mexico means more and more to me. I'll write soon. Meanwhile here is a sail carved out of stone.

Love,
Hart

To Solomon Grunberg

15 Michoacan
Mixcoac, D.F., Mexico
Dear Mony: Oct. 20, 1931

I hope I secure some pardon with this note! It seems that I often spend a lot of time writing to people who really care so little about hearing from me that I get no answers—among whom seems to be Sam, who always seems to get into some kind of huff every time I leave the dear old USA. When I get back to Fifth Ave. or Columbia Heights—try as I will—I can never seem to elicit anything more by way of explanation from him than a few cherubic smiles and immeadiate references to the attractions of the St. George subway station!

Well, much as I like that district, I think I'm happier here. With a bottle of "Old Nick" Jamaica rum, here I sit in my spacious salon, twenty feet high, which is only part of my eight-room, old-fashioned Mexican house—and rip off expletives and reviews for *Poetry*, scratching my head like mad to be impressive. I have the whole house, garden and what not, including devoted servants (who would cook for me if I relished their style of Mexican diet) for the price of $38. per month! Houses here are like fortresses, each with a gate, grill, walls etc. around it, and everything under a romantic spell of lock and key.

I wish I could tell you something about my travels into the country places hereabouts, finding ancient Aztec idols in the cornfields, swimming in mountain streams with handsome indians (whose courtesy, especially in the outlying towns and districts is phenomenal), beating the ancient drum of Tepozté-catl at Tepoztlan during the recent festival (on top of the church and to the tune of a pagan fife—and in view of the ancient Aztec temple perched on the lofty cliffs) etc. etc. But that would take a book. So would my sex life down here! I've been in jail twice, but that was only regarding arguments with taxi drivers when I was tight. Nobody but the Guggenheims seemed to mind, which reminds me that I had a right good dream the other night, seeing in headlines that the chief of them all had been murdered by some one named Abernethy!

You must have heard about my father's death. I'm so glad that I had a chance to know him before he died—it left me a lot more self respect than I had before, and it made him rather happy too, or so I hear. His will left me as good as an annual Guggenheim for some time, and that was considerably better than would have occurred a few years before. I'll be just extravagent enough to use it all up, month by month; but here in Mexico one sees so many gorgeous and inimitable handicrafts that the purse is always open. Besides, as you know, I always drink a lot. I nearly had a nervous prostration with "needle beer" in company with Bob Thompson one night in Hoboken before I left again for Mexico last month. But you can get anything safe or deadly that you like down here. Nothing quite so deadly as NY offers, however. Not even the native tequila, which approximates in power and concentration, vodka.

You should see these native indian people—not the people "in power"—of mixed Spanish and indian blood. They're dumb as hell in a thousand ways, but wiser, I think, than all our mad, rushing crowd up north. I'm cultivating (as you may observe) the virtues of UN-thought for awhile! The beautiful brown, "it's toasted"—flesh, dark eyes, big white hats, white pyjama suits, sandals, dirt, indigestion, faith, doubt, elation, resignation—but always something fundamental, a contact with the soil and earth and the blue of the mountains hereabouts! I don't know much Spanish, but I get along fairly well with them. Mexico is more foreign than anything remaining in the farthest districts of Europe. I'm glad I didn't go back to France, even though this country is a perfect Calvary in a thousand ways . . .

Every other night or so my servants bring in their friends— and we have a swell time dancing native dances, singing native songs to their guitar music, and clinking glasses of beer and tequila—a deadly but companionable mixture! Flowers! my dear Mony! I have all I can do to prevent my rooms from resembling mortuary chapels. . . . My servant is continually stacking sugar cane and corn stalks, besides hanging myrtle wreathes against the walls. From the garden come stacks of daisies, nasturtiums, roses, calla lilies, violets, heliotrope, cannas, enormous marigolds, cosmos, sun flowers, phlox, iris, geraniums, and a score of other tropical and typically Mexican flowers whose names I do not know. This sounds phoney, but it's true.

The climate here is the same, practically, the year round. Very, very cool at night and early in the morning—with sometimes considerable heat on the sunny side of the street at noon. The altitude accounts for it (I'm something like 8,000 feet above you here on this big plateau) but you can get any temperature you want at any time of the year by going a little more up, or down. The altitude is—especially at first—a strain on the nerves. One is always a little wild, but I doubt if I'm any wilder than usual, after all. I think I'll get used to it, and *maybe* stay here a long, long while. That is, if I find I get to writing poetry again. Certainly there is every other inducement here for me to remain. You'd love it, Mony; and if you feel that you can afford the trip, please remember that I'd love to have you come here and stay with me for awhile. I've this vast house, half of which isn't used at all. You could browse around and do just as you please, living on about $50. per month.

When I left New York I was pretty much discouraged with everything up north. I think our civilization is on the lurch, to say the least, which isn't, however, a very original thought these days. It will survive, but with considerable pain and a number of economic modifications. Of course this makes it the hardest time in world (known world history) to write a line of sincere lyricism. Wish I weren't so lyric, but I'm told I am and even Mr. Eastman would probably assent to that. Since both he and Mencken have taken recent cracks at me, I feel more than ever in the public eye. At such times it is fortunate to have a place like this, where I never even read the papers, and have developed a great incuriosity regarding most world doings. There's nothing else to do but stuff one's head continually with all that mess while in the states; but my garden (the first time I've ever had the chance to see things grow—and how they GROW here!) keeps me happier, at least right now.

I'm glad, in a way, to hear you announce your intention of going to France. I hope you don't go, however, before I see you again, because I don't feel at present as though I should ever have an excuse to go to France again. But maybe I'll get over my distaste for their horrible avarice and unkind manners over there. I can't blame you for taking a leap from Baltimore and the hat factory. . . .

I'm not going on any further in this tirade. . . . I know you think the "Old Nick" has got the better of me, but that wouldn't be the first time, would it? Certainly I've made up in *length* whatever I missed in *time*, and you can't complain at my neglect for awhile. But it's been fun writing to you this morning! . . . . I include a couple of pictures, one of my house, and one of me—gone a little native for the nonce. David Siqueiros, a Mexican painter, whom I regard as superior in depth of conception to both Rivera and Orozco, has painted a magnificent portrait of me, that I'm sure you'll like. But as it hasn't been photographed yet, I can't yet send you a reproduction. You might reciprocate, by the way, and give me a lasting glimpse of yourself! Please do! And remember how much I care for you, Mony, and write again soon!

Affectionately, Hart

To William Slater Brown

Dear Bill: October 22

Please tell Malcolm that his article on the Munson-Josephson "debate" has delayed my dinner by two hours of sore sides! "Old Nick" (Jamaica) Rum *may* have contributed a little to such pleasant distress, but I still owe a debt . . . I wish I had the two previous articles of the series at hand; can't you get Betty to sort them out and send them to me?

From cock-crow to sunset, here in Mixcoac, my life is extremely jolly. And then beyond . . . How I wish you and Sue were here sometimes! Guitars and *corridas* galore. Even *I* am learning how to sing! One thing I can't seem to get around to do—and that's the reviews I contracted to do for *Poetry*. Have you seen Putnam's new book of poems, *The Five Seasons?* I've got to 'do' that, and it's almost too big a job.

"Old Nick" and Nicotine keep me too occupied.

From the Hart

PS—Allen's note on Milton was one of the best things in modern criticism I expect to anticipate!

To Peggy Baird Cowley

Peggy Dear:

Why don't you come out and see my Siqueiros portrait before I have to take it away to the photographer! Come anyway; lots of flowers and a loyal welcome . . . Come, OH COME+

Hart

To Peggy Baird Cowley

Dear Peggy: Thursday

Don't fool yourself, as you seemed to do at the gate, this morning at 4 o'clock, that you have been abused in my house. I only hope that you got home all right, you having insisted, at the final cost of my temper, that you both adventure forth (and in Mexico!) at that ungodly hour of the morning, hurling, by the way, the most unfriendly sentiments back at me, who had only tried to be of service.

You can make all you want of this. It wasn't quite fair to me in the first place. But you didn't know on this occasion even quite as much as *I* understood.

I can't name "persecution complexes" and all that in this case, as you claim *I'm* entitled to. It was just a healthy case of drunken unreasonableness, apparently, on your part. And I have *no reason* this time to beg forgiveness.

Come out and see me soon. I'm generous as you are with friendship. If you wanted to go farther, as you claimed, last night—how could you expect me to, with Maria sick on the bed, and the floor covered with vomit! No apologies accepted or expected!

As ever, Hart

To Solomon Grunberg

Haven't heard since that long letter I wrote you. And wonder if you got it. Mail is sometimes opened here and not forwarded. I never know. If I'm tampered with any more I intend to object, to the Secretary of State who is a poet and knows me. Please write soon.

Affectionately, Hart

To Peggy Baird Cowley

Dear Peggy: November 13
   I don't think you need bother to consider me a friend any more.

Sincerely, Hart Crane

To Peggy Baird Cowley

Dear Peggy: Thursday
   I don't know why I felt impelled to write you that gracious note of yesterday, except perhaps on account of the heeby-jeebies—and the fact that when I called with Daniel in the morning I was refused admittance.
   Of course, if you really feel that strongly about it, for whatever causes I don't know, then we'll have to remain apart. Please let me contradict that note yesterday, anyway. And believe me, at least so far as I know, as always,

Your Hart

To Samuel Loveman

15 Michoacan
Mixcoac, D.F., Mexico
Dear Sam: November 17

Well, at long last it was fine to hear from you, and such a warm-hearted and characteristic letter, too! Your correspondence goes by fits and starts and long lapses, and I've noticed that the lapses have generally occurred when I was farthest away, just why I don't know. Perhaps distance doesn't make your heart grow fonder; certainly it doesn't agitate your pen. Letters certainly do fall short of the intimate and voluminous conversations that we two indulge in habitually, but don't forget that your letters mean a lot to me, and so pray do write oftener.

I haven't been any too well lately. First a week's spell of the grippe—then lately a kind of half relapse, bad cold, back ache, etc. All this in spite of heavenly weather, but not, I'm afraid, despite a strenuous program of dancing, tequila and amor. I'm on the water wagon for awhile . . . Meanwhile my house is in considerable tumult. David Siqueiros (who is certainly the greatest painter in Mexico) arrived Sunday night from his house in Taxco, with his wife and doctors—so deathly ill from malaria that he had to be carried into the house. No really expert medical attention being available in so small a town as Taxco—and after 8 days of mounting fever—there was nothing to do but rush to Mexico City. He contracted it during a long trip through the *tierra caliente*, or "hot country" which is the wild jungleland of Mexico near Acapulco along the Pacific coast. It is a marvelous trip, but very strenuous and dangerous, through native villages where a tax collector has never dared venture, and where the people wear the same Aztec costume that Cortez found them in, there being several towns entirely of negros (escaped slaves) who wear nothing but the slender loin cloths of Africa and who shoot with bow and arrows. It seems incredible, but Mexico is more vast than you can ever realize by looking at a map and more various in its population than any country on earth. Layer on layer of various races and cultures scattered in the million gorges and valleys which make the scenery so plastic and superb. Siqueiros is going to pull through all right, but I shall probably have him here with me for a couple of months. Malaria takes a long time. I'm glad to be of help in such a crisis, however, and since I had three rooms which I never used the house really isn't crowded.

I bought two fine paintings of S. which I hope someday you will see. I guess I wrote you that he painted a portrait of me (about 4 by 2½ ft) which is causing much favorable comment. Besides which I have a splendid watercolor of an Indian boy's head. You have never seen anything better by Gauguin, which, however, doesn't describe the originality and authenticity of these works. Then I have about a dozen small watercolors, mostly landscapes, painted by Mexican children none of whom are older than eight—these for about 20¢ apiece!

Of course the Siqueiros works cost me *considerably*, so much, in fact, that I've been worried about making ends meet until my next quarterly from the Guggenheim falls due, Jan. 1st. For what was my great shock after buying them to be notified that none of the income that I had been assured of from the estate would be paid, and would continue unpaid indefinitely! This meant that the paintings had to be paid for out of the Guggenheim allowance—and in consequence I'm stranded excepting for a few dollars remaining in my personal N.Y. account—until January 1st. And it will be hard to cash personal checks hereabouts. And if business doesn't pick up before next May it probably means that I can't continue to stay in Mexico for awhile longer, as I had hoped to do.

Those masks that you bought last fall are undoubtedly Mexican. Even the neo-Greek mask that puzzled me so. I am sure about them all being Mexican because I've seen dozens in private collections and museums here that have the same variety of stylizations. There is a great tradition of masks here, and while those of yours may not be extremely old they are decidedly not new nor sold around in the shops here, and are really valuable. You have to go out to some of the most remote settlements to get that sort, and they're seldom to be bought because of their religious significance.

I haven't been able to resist buying some other things like sarapes, giant hats, embroideries, laquer trays and Guadalajara pottery. You've never seen such beautiful arts and crafts as the indian element here has perpetuated. Wm. Spratling's collection at Taxco is one of the best, and when his book comes out, called *Little Mexico* (Cape & Smith) for heaven's sake read it. It's illustrations are many and will give you more detail than I could squeeze into twenty letters.

This letter is becoming ungodly long—and I haven't been able to tell one fragment of all there is to tell. I'm not upset about the Eastman and Menchen notices. There *was* a quite serviceable editorial in the *New Republic* on the former a couple of weeks back. And if it provides something for Burke and Cowley to write about—then so much the better. They're bound to be fairly loyal to my *style*, even if not to my "personality". It is even more consoling that a few people like yourself maintain a constancy to both. And so let's hear from you again, *real soon*.

Affectionately, Hart

To Eda Lou Walton

15 Michoacan
Mixcoac, D.F., Mexico
Dear Eda Lou: November 27, 1931

I'm very glad to hear that you are applying for a Guggenheim. You certainly deserve it and would make splendid use of it. Mr. Moe, the Secretary, has sent me a copy of your proposed program (this being part of the usual routine regarding references) and I shall be greatly disappointed if you do not have a chance to carry it out. Naturally my response to Moe will be very warm in your favor. However slight your hopes may be there is evidence that at least you are being considered seriously.

These are dull times for poetry, even as Mr. Menchen says, and I must admit that with all my present salutary circumstances my impulses in that direction are surprisingly low. A beautiful environment and economic security are far from compensating for a world of chaotic values and frightful spiritual depression. And I can't derive any satisfaction in the spinning out of mere personal moods and attitudes.

Meanwhile I am, however,—or at least I feel I am—penetrating to a new kind of world in the psychology of the Indians hereabouts, though it hasn't taken on any real outline as yet. Everyone says that it takes a long time to make an adjustment here. The infinite variety of climate, vegetation, and the distraction of a new language as well as thousands of fascinating sights and speculations, all combine to uproot one and hold one in a strange suspension. At least I feel that I am living fully and absorbing a great deal, whatever else. And that, I suppose, is a considerably better state to be in than the dubious tenure some office job would provide, if such indeed were even accessible! I like Mexico and the Mexicans (Indians) so much that I'd like to remain here permanently. I'm even thinking of attempting some work like teaching (English Lit.) in one of the many private colleges if I can locate such work before my Guggenheim fellowship expires.

I'm sorry that your book is receiving such scant attention. About all I get here is the *New Rep.* and consequently miss a great deal of what is being said. Please let me hear from you again before long. I'm not exactly teeming with ideas, nor am I a very prompt correspondent, but I do like to hear from people immensely.

All best wishes, Hart Crane

To Wilbur Underwood

15 Michoacan
Mixcoac, D.F., Mexico

Dear Wilbur: November 30

The nature of the Mexican Indian, as Lawrence said, isn't exactly "sunny", but he is more stirred by the moon, if you get what I mean, than any type I've ever known. The fluttering gait and the powder puff are unheard of here, but that doesn't matter in the least. Ambidexterity is all in the fullest masculine tradition. I assure you from many trials and observations. The pure Indian type is decidedly the most beautiful animal imaginable, including the Polynesian—to which he often bears a close resemblance. And the various depths of rich coffee brown, always so clear and silken smooth, are anything but negroid. Add to that—voices whose particular pitch will make the welkin ring—and you have a rather tempting setting for an odd evening. Even Lawrence, with all his "blood-fear" of them, couldn't resist some lavish descriptions of their fine proportions.

I was glad to hear from you again. And the amusing clippings! New York must have been depressing with all the derelicts haunting the streets and alleys. The parks were packed when I was there in August. Did I write you that my father suddenly died in July? I had been here since April, but came north again for two months to see about the estate, etc. It's a satisfaction to me to remember what a fresh and affectionate relationship grew up between us last winter during those months that necessity forced me into his hospitality. And he was doubly pleased and reassured when I got the Guggenheim scholarship.

I have a lease on a house here (eight rooms, flower garden) until next May. The exchange is so low that it only amounts to $30. per month; and servants come for only $8. per month more. I've been around to Tepoztlan, Toluca, etc. but no extensive trips as yet. The scenery is gorgeous and I'm in love with the simple country people whose heads still resemble the fragments of ancestral idols that one picks up in wandering through the corn fields. I have a project of a poetic drama on Cortes and Montezuma, but the more I see the more I realize how intricate the subject is—and how much longer it is going to take me than I had anticipated. If the estate can be made to yield me any income, however, I may remain here long after the term of my scholarship.

Write me at length soon. Whom did you see in New York, etc. I find myself more and more out of touch with that metropolitan world.

Affectionately, Hart

To Bessie Meacham Crane

15 Michoacan
Mixcoac, D.F., Mexico
December 12, 1931

Dear Bess:

There is a distinct smell of powder in the air this evening. But that isn't all! Rockets are whizzing up sporadically for miles around, and the sound of church bells far and near, has been incessant since dawn. All of which is to say that this is an important day in the Mexican calendar—nothing less, in fact, than the annual Feast of the Virgin of Guadalupe, the particular Patroness of all Mexicans. This year's celebration is all the more extravagant, as she is reputed to have "appeared" here (before a humble peon named Juan Diego) just four hundred years ago today.

For weeks the influx of Indians and pilgrims of all types from all the provinces and tribes of Mexico has been in progress. It is probably no exaggeration to say that there are two hundred thousand extra souls, pious and near-pious, who have flocked here to continue the fiesta until New Years. But today—all of them, including the majority of Mexico City's population of one million—went to the little town of Guadalupe Hidalgo, practically a suburb now, of Mexico City, where a great cathedral has been erected near the spot where the Virgin is reputed to have made her first appearance.

I engaged a cab the night before, and got up at four this morning to get an early start, arriving, before the Cathedral just at dawn. Even then one couldn't elbow one's way into the church without waiting in line for an hour. I gave that up, having come more to see some of the Native Indian dances that take place here and there throughout the town—some, in fact, right in front of the cathedral. The whole business is simply indescribable without ten reams of paper; but suffice to say that the dances were wonderful. Certain people are picked from each district or tribe for their marked ability—and there is quite a rivalry between districts in the excellence of their performance. There are from 24 to 45 in a group, generally in circular formation, with banners, guitars which they play as they sway and turn, and elaborate pantaloons, skirts, feather crests, etc. Death and the Devil weave in and out among them—and their masked figures, like wild boars and old man-of-the-mountain.

I pushed and prodded from one group to another, until by 9:30 I was ready to come home; and did. I had taken Daniel along, and was glad of it, since I just missed causing a riot by attempting to photograph some of the dancers in action, which is, it seems, forbidden. The dancing is all very serious and very set and formal; it generally derives from very ancient tribal rites. It isn't any sort of Mardi-Gras mood at all that the Indians express, despite the flamboyant colors of their costumes.

Well, when I consider that the Indians, all of those, at least, that I saw—had been dancing the same measure for practically all the night before—continued all day after I left and WILL continue on the same schedule for practically two weeks more—and ALL for the sake of a ritual and *not a cent of money*—I must say I admire their devotion to custom and tradition. The figure of the Virgin of Guadalupe miraculously unites the teachings of the early Catholic missionaries with many survivals of the old Indian myths and pagan cults. She is a typical Mexican product, a strange blend of Christian and pagan strains. What a country and people! The most illogical and baffling on earth; but how appealing! I enclose the authoritative portrait of this Virgin, who, I think, is quite beautiful. She is really the Goddess of the Mexican masses, and you will find her picture or image everywhere, even when you can't see it— as for instance, inside the hat bands of wide sombreros. It is rare to escape the sight of her—on a postcard or stencil above the windshield facing half the taxi drivers of Mexico. For protection and good luck! I think I shall have to "wear" her around with me for awhile—likewise for "Protection and good luck" against the wiles and extortions of some of those same drivers!

I haven't heard from you in a long while—no answer yet to my last. But I'm not complaining. I know the season, the other trials—and how filled your time is. Thank you very much, by the way, for having arranged the money payment for me through the Chase Bank. It saved me many pesos on the "exchange". I won't need to bother you again this month—nor next. Matters go more smoothly with me as I get myself more acclimated to Mexico, its habits and the peculiar strain of the high altitude here. I'm feeling very well, and am even accused of getting fat.

As Christmas draws near I think much of the Season's loss in all it can give to you and me this year. Christmas always probes the deepest memories, and the fondest; and I know what you will be thinking about this Christmas, and how apt it will be to make the hearth seem cold. I know your fortitude also, Bess, —and your natural, spontaneous response to all that is good and enduring. And I'm sure, therefore, that surrounded as you are by the loyalty and love of those whose names need no particular mention, you'll still find many reasons for gratitude and even a bit of seasonal merriment.

And so—good night. And Merry Christmas to you, to Ethel, to Anne, to Dorothy—and to all about the Cottage who care to remember me at all. Let me hear from you when you have time. If you haven't time—I can understand.

With love, Harold

To Peggy Baird Cowley

15 Michoacan
Mixcoac, D.F.

Dearest Peggy: January 6

I hope you got the $75. I sent yesterday afternoon. I went first to the Mancera where I ate like a horse; then rushed to the bank in time to get all I wanted. Daniel I found as drunk as usual when I got home, but he did manage to get me a hot bath before eight, after which I really began to enjoy my weariness. Slept fairly well—waking to find old Mizzentop flaunting the colors still in valiant dreams of you.

Milton was home, besides the family box of goodies and about a million letters. I'll just never catch up, I'm sure. M., as I expected, is as settled as ever. . . . I can foresee a number of needs, or rather uses for him in the next fortnight.

Lesley is coming to lunch with me at the Mancera this noon. All things considered, I am hoping that he rather than anyone else, will want to take over the house. For one thing it would mean that I could trust *all* my belongings to the premises—and be free-er than ever to move about as I took a notion to. I wouldn't lose any more money in the end than storage costs and transportation otherwise necessitated.

I'm in such a hectic rush this morning that I can't do more than remind you that you already know the depth of my love for you. The ride back yesterday was psychologically so strange and new a meditation to me that it seemed almost like sheer delirium. When I get more of the pressure of events eased and a moment for a little personal thinking I'll write you a more decent expression of my gratitude. I'm dying now to be off to Acapulco with you in two weeks time, and almost every moment must be bent to that end.

I'll see Mary today or tomorrow about your clothes. Has Malcolm replied yet? Let me know when to write him if he hasn't. DAMN that Putnam review! Of all times, now, to sharpen the critical blade! But that's what I get for procrastinating. Mexico doesn't look any more tempting and reassuring than I expected. It's cold, bloody cold, of course, too.

I'm expecting a letter from you tomorrow, and often afterwards, dear Twidget! Apply yourself well; don't forget the toilet paper, the water wagon, your typewriter, nor your Hart.

Hugs, kisses, and a long upward sigh! Hart

To Peggy Baird Cowley

Dear Twidget: Thursday

No letter from you in the first mail today, but perhaps later, I'm hoping! Lesley and I had a delightful afternoon together yesterday, eating heartily and discussing your charms and merits. He said he had promised you three copies of that photo of you, which you have doubtless received—so I didn't get one. But I intend to get one before long—from you or otherwise.

I learned that Malcolm had replied to your wire by sending L. $75.00—part of which L. had sent you already. I told you that L. took a paternal interest in you, and perhaps he is quite right in reserving some of the rest of it for scheduled remittances. Anyway, if you think otherwise you'd better write him about it. I also learned that there is little chance of L. taking my house over as Marion hasn't even started yet and may not reach Mexico before the end of the month. And since he (naturally) wouldn't want to commit himself without first consulting her wishes, I don't see much hope. Milton is going to help me as much as he can, but I may not be free to go to Acapulco before the end of the month. We'll try to find some way out.

I'm already tired—rushing through correspondence this morning. Neglected to mention yesterday that a long letter was waiting for me from old Aunt Sally Simpson, who hasn't kicked the bucket after all. Is very much alive and demanded a complete history of my doings during the last year. You can't expect me to have much breath left for you after just finishing that this morning!

Off to town again for lunch today. Not drinking, I feel I have a right to better meals. Maybe there'll be a snapshot or so to include with this. I missed your darling hands last night. Old Mizzentop doesn't like air pockets either! Nor standing so long without an occasional tumble . . . Remember me to Gretchen and Charles and Bill and Maria-Luisa.

Love ever, from your Hart

To Morton Dauwen Zabel

Dear Zabel: January 8, 1932

You may or may not have read the attack on the so-called "Unintelligibles" penned by Max Eastman in *Harper's*, of last Oct. or Nov. issue. But it *was* a nasty swipe at Joyce as well as me, and showed just how helpless a poet can be made in the face of the kind of testimony that Eastman offered.

I happened to show the article to Anita Brenner (author of *Idols Behind Altars*, the best book on the Mexican Revolutionary Art Movement, and a fellow Guggenheimer here this year) —and the enclosed dissertation is the result. She sent it to *Harper's* for publication, but they quite consistently refused it, writing in the same mail that if she had any books to place they'd like to see them.

I don't know what you'll think of it; but I think she raises some very pertinent points and issues. It's probably too lengthy for *Poetry* to use, even should you care to; but it may amuse you to read it over. People who are as damned unscrupulous and *canaille* as Eastman (and who make their living out of such attitudes) ought to be caught up, here and there, at least once in awhile.

This supplements my letter of this morning, though I haven't another air-mail stamp to speed it quite as fast—and there is probably no cause to. Should you care to use it, do so. Otherwise please return to me care Simpson.

Hastily, Hart Crane

To Malcolm Cowley

15 Michoacan
Mixcoac, D.F., Mexico
Dear Malcolm: January 9, 1932

I've just returned Maddow's poems to him with a brief note of appreciation, tempered by some objections to his chaotic structural tendencies, etc. It's hard to say much against a person who has so obviously experienced one's own temper and angle of vision. Furthermore, I suspect that he is no more obscure to me (at his *worst*) than I have been to hundreds of others. But what the hell! I don't pretend to excuse myself for a lot of things. He has power and original vision, though,—if he's got the conscience and brains to channel them. . . .

Peggy and I had the pleasantest Christmas and New Years together that I remember for ages. Peggy's usual mixed crowd appeared for the former date, but I stayed long enough to enjoy a week alone with her. Taxco is so extremely beautiful—and the townsfolk still so affable—that whatever one has to say about the Yankee occupation (and that ultimately seals its doom) it's still one of the pleasantest places to be. Peggy has probably written you about encounters with Brett, Bynner,

King, et al. Lewd limericks were shouted from the rooftops—your collection being more than ever in demand. A mad crowd, though. I had enough Duff—Brett's new name, or nickname, —preferring as I do, the nautical variety.

I enjoyed your attack on Munson very much,—that is, the initial broadside that appeared in the *NR*. But having read answers and replies since then in *Contempo*, I've lived to regret those later readings—from both sides of the battle line. Of course it was a great mistake for Munson to have replied at all. No dignity could be saved that way—and in the end it put you, too, into a rather apologetic position. Your advantage rests—not chiefly, but partially—in the fact that you initiated the fracas—and in a journal of vastly greater circulation than that little receptacle on Chapel Hill. Now people are beginning to accuse you of being a successful politician. But I hardly agree with that; I think that greater conquests are necessary for that title, even though Mr. Boyd lay flaccid under the same swipe.

I'm damned tired of Mexico City, and want to sublet my house for the remaining three months and get off into Indian towns and territories for awhile. If I'm lucky I may get off within three weeks. Hence, better address me, next letter c/o Eyler Simpson, Apartado 538, Mexico, DF. You owe me more than one full letter, old boy; and this may be my last for quite a while. Best to Bill and Sue and Muriel and Betty.

As ever, Hart

To Wilbur Underwood

c/o Dr. Eyler Simpson
Apartado 538
Mexico

Dear Wilbur:

Please use the above address in writing me again, as I'm trying to sublet my house here in Mixcoac and get off to some of the country towns for a spell.

Your Christmas gift was a great surprise—and an inspiration. Lawrence never wrote a greater story, nor one which provoked less divided feelings. It was a great revelation to me, and I shall read *The Man Who Died* more than once again. In all honesty —it has more to tell me—at least in my present state of mind—than any book in the Bible. It was originally published by the same people in Paris who brought out my *Bridge*— under the title of, *The Escaped Cock*; but I never happened to have read it before. I remember that they had a terrible time with the customs, getting it into this country—and largely on account of that title! Imagine!

Have you been noticing a recent burlesque-ad magazine, named *Hooey*? It's so frightfully vulgar from cover to cover that "O. Swish"—the temperamental pseudonym of the "editor" might be Chic Sales himself in disguise. Their ads for "B. Hinds" Cream and "More Bananas" however, are epochal.

I get tired of Mexico and Mexicans at times. Today is one of those times. But that's to be expected wherever one is; and wherever I am, I get homesick for Columbia Hts. once in awhile. I've broken ranks . . . I don't suppose you will ever forgive me . . . the ex-wife of an old friend of mine who's just got a divorce here in Mexico.

Affectionately, as ever, Hart

To Peggy Baird Cowley

15 Michoacan
Mixcoac, D.F.

Dearest: Wednesday

In case I don't get off tomorrow morning for Taxco—and hence anticipate this letter by kisses and much contentment— I want you at least to know that it won't be long before we are together again, for I shall be with you certainly before Sunday.

Your letter of this morning makes me ache for you. Why is it you love me so? I don't deserve it. I'm just a careening idiot with a talent for humor at times, and for insult and desecration at others. But I can, and must say that your love is very precious to me. For one thing it gives me an assurance that I thought long buried. You can give me many things besides—if time proves me fit to receive them: the independence of my mind and soul again, and perhaps a real wholeness to my body.

Do you remember my saying that I would *not* fall in love with you, or with anyone again? But I find that though I like to perpetuate that statement, I have really over-ruled it in a thousand thoughts and emotions.

(The period on the last sentence was accompanied by a convulsion under the table from Palome. Rather horrible, in fact. I roused Milton, we called a policeman; but though the dog has resumed all the appearances of his normality—we've relegated him to the shed-room in back of the kitchen. Rabies are common here, so Milton says, and I shouldn't wonder if we'll have to shoot the "dove".)

Since there seems to be such a slight chance of renting the house, and since I really can't welsh on Eyler Simpson (who is equally responsible, since he signed the lease with me) by just walking out—I've decided to pay the $70. odd dollars by just keeping it—wherever else I spend my time during the next three months. The family will just have to fork up a loan or something for me, and I feel sure they will. I'm going to try to avoid spoiling my remaining time in Mexico; and much more worry about the house and my few items of possession would succeed in doing so. Don't you think I'm right?

Besides Milton will be in on weekends, and will watch over the servant's care of things, and forward my mail wherever I am. I want you to go to Acapulco with me—and after that I'm going to spend some time up in Michoacan, Morelia, Lake Chapala, etc. I may end up in Jalapa (which is very near Vera Cruz) but by that time I rather expect you'll be with me. I feel serene and happy in your love today, mad dogs and convulsions notwithstanding!

Your, Hart

To Charlotte and Richard Rychtarik

Mixcoac,
Dear Charlotte and Richard—   Feb. 8 '32

Thanks so much for your last letter. Thought I would never hear from you. I'm too deep in work to answer now—but shall soon. Meanwhile—here is a photograph of my portrait by Siqueiros. It is making a sensation in the gorgeous exhibition of his recent work which is now on view here in Mexico City. The greatest one-man show I ever saw. He is coming to N.Y. soon and may bring it along with him. But because nearly everything is already sold—it would probably not pay him.

Am dying to see your new decorations.

Love,
Hart

To Solomon Grunberg

15 Michoacan
Mixcoac, D.F., Mexico
Dear Mony: February 8, 1932

As usual, I'm ignoring all the questions of your last letter. . . . Don't know how long I'm going to remain here, etc. Hate it and love it alternately, but am not, as you surmise, in a constant Bacchic state. Not by any means. However, I happen to be in something approximating it at this present moment, since I've got to work on the first impressive poem I've started on in the last two years. I feel the old confidence again; and you may know what that means to one of my stripe!

The servants are all asleep—and I'm in that pleasant state of beginning all over again. Especially as I'm in love again—and as never as quite before. Love is always much more important than locality; and this is the newest adventure I ever had. I won't say much more than that I seem to have broken ranks with my much advertised "brotherhood"—and a woman whom I have known for years—suddenly seems to "to have claimed her own." I can't say that I'm sorry. It has given me new perspectives, and after many tears and groans—something of a reason for living.

So much for "Mexico." I'm not able to write tourist sketches any more. They take too long—and are only the more incomplete. I've lots to tell you about all that some other day. And they needn't be the less stirring for a little delay. Meantime let me say that you are one of the few heroes I know. I love your steadfastness and uncompromising attitude, Mony. Have we the patience to endure? I say YES!

Under separate cover I'm sending you a photo of the

portrait that David Alfaro Siqueiros painted of me recently. He's having a one-man show now in the Sala Española here, and I've never seen such a show before. The picture I'm sending you is a sensation—and, I think, deserves to be. Not only is it a marvelous likeness of me—it's besides, a tremendously powerful piece of work, that Picasso would—and well might envy. The head is about 2 1/2 times life-size, so you can imagine the dimensions. I was so glad to have your picture—against the NY skyline.

Write me again, dear Mony,—SOON. We aren't so far away from each other!

Love, Hart

"The Broken Tower"

The bell cord that gathers God at dawn
Dispatches me—as though I fell down the knell
Of the new day . . . I could wander the cathedral lawn
Clear to the crucifix, and back again from hell.

Haven't you seen—or ever heard those stark
Black shadows in the tower, that drive
The clarion turn of God?—to fall and then embark
On echoes of an ancient, universal hive?

The bells, I say, the bells have broken their tower!
And sing, I know not where . . . Their tongues engrave
My terror mid the unharnessed skies they shower;
I am their scattered—and their sexton slave.

And so it was, I entered the broken world—
To hold the visionary company of love, its voice
An instant in a hurricane (I know not whither hurled)
But never—no, to make a final choice! . . . .

(More to follow—this is the new beginning) Hart

To Peggy Baird Cowley

15 Michoacan
Mixcoac, D.F.
Dearest: Wednesday, February 10

So glad to hear from you this morning! I have been up late for the past two nights, writing countless letters—and with a little tequila (a very little!) walking back and forth the length of the room to the tune of the records that we enjoyed so together. I haven't really seen anyone since you left, even Milton hasn't shown up for 48 hours again. The version of the be ginning of "The Broken Tower" that I sent you early this morning is probably to be changed a good deal yet. But you seemed to hanker for it—and so I let 'er fly.

I would be doing a lot these days, since I feel so much like working, if the tension were less, around here. Sr. Daniel Her nandez is morose and very threatening indeed, despite the fact that I haven't even reprimanded him for his recent drunkenness. Lisa is scared to death of him, & warns me that there may be all kinds of trouble in store if I fire him, since he knows about half the Police of Mixcoac, knows I have no firearms on the place, etc. Well, neither can I bring myself to endure his insolence and complete disregard of services much more. Sr. Lepine my landlord is going to try to corner and talk to him this afternoon, but Daniel won't be around at the time, as Lepine, who called this morning when D. was out, told his wife the hour when he'd return this afternoon.

Oh Hell! I say. I'm getting so tired of the whole problem. Lisa thinks she won't dare remain after Daniel leaves on account of his probably exposing her political affiliations. If you can't find someone from Taxco I shall probably be left here a perfect prisoner—without even a telephone, and afraid to leave the place a minute. Well, don't see how I'm going to get any work done *this* afternoon, nor probably tomorrow. Damned outrageous, I think. Daniel will probably come lurching in about 8 tonight and begin to flirt a knife and pistol about. Such a quiet life in this pretty retreat!

It's too bad you have to move so peremptorily—on the exact 15th. But those scorpions worry me—especially their generous numbers. That house will always attract them—being so on the side of a hill. I miss you a lot, dear. Somehow we have such a lot to talk about together. I am getting more and more serious and dignified day by day—getting maybe back into myself —as well as into you.

Love and kisses ever, from your harried Hart

To Peggy Baird Cowley

15 Michoacan
Mixcoac, D.F.
Dearest: Thursday, Feb 11

I was so tremulous and distracted with the domestic situation as described yesterday to you, that last night I went on a mild tear with Lisa here in the salon. I finally came to the decision of packing up and leaving for the states within a week; there just didn't seem to be any other way of proceeding. I certainly felt fed up! Lepine didn't come round until this morning, and if he hadn't offered me a new servant whom he swears is reliable, I think I should be sending you the telegram I typed out last night, announcing my departure.

Lepine is sending me an old man he has known for 14 years, the most honest soul, he declares, he has ever met. Lisa will stay, she says, and cook. The combination will be perfect, and will result in very little more expense than I have been under right along. Lepine says that Daniel has been wanting to work for "the general" for some time. I think they will leave within a few days—and without umbrage. Certainly they have no reason to resent my simple objection to constant drunkeness. Daniel came home stewed again last night, after working all day at "the general's". But I was too gay with Lisa and tequila and dancing—and my secret resolution to pull out, to mind very much. I have a notion that this re-arrangement will be satisfactory. Certainly I'm damned lucky to have Lisa here—so intelligent, generous, neat and efficient in a thousand ways. She doesn't ask for anything but her board and keep, but I shall try to induce her into some sort of salary.

These photographs I think, are perfectly splendid. I especially love those of you with the goat! And you *ought* to like the one of me. Remember, I was looking at you—and the expression seems to bespeak a lot of love and happiness. And what a scrumptious and monumental pose that is of Lisa's! Siqueiros really ought to see it.

Of course I'm anxious about your plans after leaving Natalia's. You know you're welcome—more than that, my dear, to make this your future headquarters. I miss you *mucho, mucho, mucho*! But I don't think that either of us ought to urge the other into anything but the most spontaneous and mutually liberal arrangements. I am bound to you more than I ever dreamed of being, and in the most pleasant and deep way. I think I have wandered back to some of my early idealism, and in the proper sort of way—without any arbitrary forcing or conscious reckoning. You're a great little "rouser," my dear!

I'm off for town now, where I shall mail this so you'll get it tomorrow.

Love ever, Hart

To Wilbur Underwood

15 Michoacan
Mixcoac, D.F., Mexico
Dear Wilbur: February 14, 1932

I disagree with you quite thoroughly about the Lawrence book. To me it yielded a great deal, almost an illumination. I wrote you more about it in an earlier letter, written before your's of early in January arrived. But, alas, I got drunk and don't remember whether that got mailed or not; so I'm writing you again to assure you of my gratitude.

Mexico still delights and puzzles me by turns; I've been spending much time in Taxco—a beautiful mountain-side town about 5 hours from here. A woman I have known and liked for years is renting a villa there, and I have the sad news to relate that for the first time in my life I have broken ranks with the "brotherhood" and extended my sexual dominions to some extent at least. I don't know how long this affair will last (I have engaged in no promises of any sort) but I think it has done me considerable good. The old beauty still claims me, however, and my eyes roam as much as ever. I doubt if I'll ever change very fundamentally. The gorgeous Jorge ended up running off with a suit of clothes—so I don't see him anymore. Nearly all Mexicans are petty thieves. But then I've met some Americans who were too.

I'm glad that your NY vacation brought you relief and some real diversion. I'm trying to get some real work done; but it's awfully hard to get down to anything in Mexico. Write me soon.

Affectionately, Hart

To Peggy Baird Cowley

15 Michoacan
Mixcoac, D.F.
Dearest: Tuesday, February 16
I was in the mood for swearing last night that I wouldn't write you for at least a week. My blast at the Kings, I felt, needed some very definite and concrete "substantiation"—such as a long, glum silence; which I hoped might worry you. But, really, I find daily communication with you quite irresistable. Especially when your reciprocation is so regular and—need I say?—charming. And then, besides, the entire household has been in such a perfectly delightful mood all day,—I can't really be sad or important.

True to my word last night, I got very lit. Daniel had come home that way anyhow, and I took the opportunity to talk to him about sobriety—meanwhile pouring him glass after glass of the Tenampa I'd bought for the Kings. The more he drank the more he talked of "his" or "our" Pegguie—accent on the penulte;—but you will be able to pronounce that without the acquaintance of Quintillian anyway, I'm sure. You're very popular around here, and I'm sure that if you care to come and stay with me awhile you will be regarded as the pet of the place—since Elise and Conrada both dote on you—as well as myself. Milton just isn't around for days and days any more.

Daniel is *not* drunk tonight; rather he appeared at 6 PM with a large bush of *buena de noche*, from the *jardine del general*, as well as a large bouquet of heliotrope. Judge what the sala smells like with a large bunch of tube roses also, which I purchased yesterday in honor of the Kings! Sometimes I think this house is the nicest place in the world. It certainly could be—in a not ambitious way. My tempermental reversals of opinion regarding Mexico are a joke. I now regard myself as a confirmed idiot who can't make up his mind about anything whatever any more.

I can't yet figger how Tommy could say we looked like "two waifs" sitting on a strange doorstep. Yes, that letter was distinctly below his usual level. Got a fine long letter from Peggy Robeson yesterday, which hints at the same relations with Don that you mentioned. Well, well, and *como no*! She also said that Malcolm (in long underwear) and Waldo left together in the same truck for the scene of action. Perhaps common suffering will weld a friendship there, after all. By the way, I don't believe a thing of your wagon wagon, water wagon story. Especially with Luz around, who Liza says is a great little tanker. I have my own ideas about the sobriety of those nights of yours in such company, and how "lonely" they are. Just as long as you don't let your right hand know what your left hand doeth, as they say. I'll keep the same code, at least with my index finger.

Ahoy and ahoy and AHOY! I'm off for the night! Here comes Elise, after cooking me a scrumptious meal. Wish you were here, darling!

Love, Hart

Lisa sends you "many kisses", she says.

To Bessie Meacham Crane

15 Michoacan
Mixcoac, D.F., Mexico

Dear Bess: February 17, 1932

This room is simply piping with the aroma of tube-roses and heliotrope, from two large bouquets that my servant brought this afternoon from the garden of a Mexican general who lives nearby. My white dog, "Paloma," whose appearance you admired so much in the photograph I sent, lies on the floor beside me, searching for fleas. He insists on lying at the foot of my bed at night; but the pleasure isn't all his. I have to go through about as much scratching as he does. But I wouldn't lose him for the world. There's nothing quite like the devotion and obedience of a dog. This one gets, or seems to get smarter and more accomplished every day. I think I wrote you about my servant problem. They seem to get dumber and dumber every day; but they're very fond of me (it's all like a big family, really) and when I can get the head of the family sober enough to really understand my lame Spanish, I can accomplish wonders—at least for the succeeding 24 hours.

I get so aggravated at times that I swear I'll pack up and leave for the States on the first available boat. Then the next clear and glorious morning comes around, with fresh flowers in the garden, good coffee on the stove—and the renewed vision that sleep brings . . . Then I change my mind all over again. For I know that as soon as I go back I'll regret it—and long and long for Mexico again. Not that I plan on staying here forever; but for the time being the business situation in the States is zero. There's nothing I can really do there. And although I've found that living here is far from being as cheap as it's cracked up to be, it *is* less, on the whole, and when one learns—and how long it takes!—to wade around and learn one's depth and altitude—one can make a good deal of a lame proposition. At least Mexico affords me time and space. I'm not so giddy as I once was about *all* its features; but a very pleasant residue remains. And I'm just getting to know it well enough to get down to work on my poetry and other creative work.

Bess, you certainly have given a demonstration of real heroism in handling the factory rent problem as you have. I sense a certain amount of weariness in your letter; and I can well understand the causes and the justifications. The sheer day-to-day strain of management, complicated as it is, I know to be a burden—a real cross to bear. You're one of the finest people I've ever met or ever expect to meet. I've always been so glad that Father found someone at last who really took the pains to understand him; because he was certainly a difficult person to comprehend. He had many faults, too. I only regret that I was so late in realizing his many virtues.

And believe it or not, that realization is one of the things I owe most of all, to you. I've said this before. But I like to repeat it again. Not that you'll necessarily care to remember or forget, but because it's the truth; and I like to bubble over with my gratitude and convictions at times, even though they're tiresome and repetitional.

Yes, it's true that I've fallen in love. I've known Peggy for years, as the wife of one of the editors of the *New Republic*. They came to swords points about a year ago. I was privy to the whole matter, but never dreamed of falling in love with Peggy—or any other woman. We won't probably ever marry. There are reasons against this which I needn't go into—at least until I can have your private ear. But meanwhile her devotion and companionship mean very much to me, Bess. I bear all that terrible virus of criticism that all the Cranes are born with. I think it's a great curse. But what the hell! When you have it, you can't get rid of it. I also carry a real appreciation of Peggy's virtues and companionship, which I have never completely realized before.

I must go to bed soon. It's getting very late, and the liquor is running out. (But don't doubt my complete sincerity merely on that confession.) Bess, as you may already know, there have been many years when I haven't cared about living much at all. I may care now, at times, and I suspect that *unconsciously* I'm very much on the side of Life. A great deal always depends on my associations, my associates, as to whether or not I think it worth while to continue. I'm not starting an oration; but if you care for me that much I wish you would consider my monetary affairs in the way of which I have spoken. If the Estate cannot pay me the dividends that Father desired, I can only ask you to help me for the present moment by *lending* me, if it comes to that, an income of some sort. You know as well as I, that within the four-year limit, when I come into the ultimate terms of the Estate, that I'll be able to discharge my obligations.

I have the need of a certain amount of assurance. That is, if I'm able to earn anything besides. You may or may not know the uncertainty and torture under which I have struggled for

many years. In my kind of work—the most difficult and susceptible in the world—such a constant hazard is far from being
a creative incentive. I need the assurance of an income—if I'm
ever to save myself and my creative powers. I've even almost
ceased to care about *them*. If you can manage to assure me of
$125 a month here, while I'm in Mexico, I'm sure that I can
repay the amount in actual value received. I'm leaving the
matter entirely in your hands.

Please give my love to Ethel, Anne, and Dorothy. I needn't
even mention my fondness for you. I hope Aunt Bess Madden,
and all the other Maddens are in the pink of health and contentment by this time.

Devotedly, Harold

P. S. I was so glad to have all those good pictures of you,
Ethel, Dorothy and the Cottage. Snow seems stranger and
stranger, although one can look up here towards the peaks of
volcanoes and see it every day.

I'm sending you a picture very recent of myself holding a
baby billy-goat, who has to be fed from a bottle. Goats have
wonderful eyes and other features. They never take a position
which isn't positively beautiful. But as soon as this one gets old
enough to munch all the flowers in my garden we're going to
skin and eat him. Isn't that horrible! But they say that young
goats are very luscious. And he's growing such delightfully
fragile horns!

To Malcolm Cowley and Muriel Maurer

15 Michoacan
Mixcoac, D.F., Mexico
Dear Malcolm and Muriel: Febrero 18, 1932

I hope it is no profanation of this sacred paper to offer you
my genuine and ultimate thanks for the pillow case; a vehicle
which ought to carry me, if not back to old Virginny, at least
to certain splendid heights of Old,—and Columbian at that!

Here in this pre-Columbian World, one often wonders how
much longer the fat will fry or the indians resist a wholesale
and picturesque slaughter. It is all this typewriter can do to

resist a rape of the tutelary Virgin. I never wrote on such rosy paper before but while it lasts it's yourn.

And by the good and generous goodbye, how is Waldo, since all the trucks broke down and bird-shot was welcomed by all? Or was it buckshot? I'm still ignorant about guns despite my sojourn in this gun toting peninsula. But, as you see I write ornamental letters. And How!

Bill Spratling is dizzy about finally seeing his book in print. Paca Toor and Anita Brenner continue their old feuds. Glad I'm not trying to get my teeth into Mexico—and pull *another* way. My best—and thanks—to you both. I'm here in Mixcoac for sometime yet, I conjecture, reckon—and fear. But I'll be sorry to leave, after all.

Affectionately, Hart

To Samuel Loveman

15 Michoacan
Mixcoac, D.F., Mexico

Dear Sambo: March 10, 1932

I can't remember whether or not I've ever answered your letter of January 5th; but I do know that I've sent you a photograph of my portrait by Siqueiros. I hope it reached you alright and that you liked it. It's one of the hardest pictures I ever saw to photograph, mainly because it is in such dark pigments. The original would move you very much, I am sure.

Rather amazing things have happened to me since Xmas. Peggy Cowley, whom you certainly remember as Malcolm's wife, and who is getting a divorce here in Mexico, is mainly responsible. You may have heard that we are now living together, and I must admit that I find conjugal life, however unoffical, a great consolation to a loneliness that had about eaten me up. Maybe I am fulfilling some of your theories and predictions. At any rate, if you hear (when you tune in on Mexico City some night) the sound of creaking bed springs—don't fancy it to be just "static".

Just about 20 more days before my scholarship is officially terminated. But I have my doubts about coming back before six months, and maybe not that soon. I can't hope to find any interesting work in the States for some time, meanwhile the estate has guaranteed me at least a portion of the yearly allowance left me by my father, which will go farther here than in the north. Besides I'm just getting to work on a few things —and Peggy and I enjoy Mexico more than ever, being together.

How I wish you could step into our house here some afternoon! Week by week I've collected more and more beautiful Mexican serapes, leather work, pottery, embroideries, laquers, etc. Fresh bunches of lilies, tube roses, violets, nasturtiums, etc. every day from the garden. The white iris is just coming out, too. When my lease on this house expires—6 weeks from now—we're going to do more traveling. There are at least twenty wonderful towns and places I haven't yet visited. Last week we went to Puebla. I only visited 2 of its 365 churches and chapels (one for every day of the year) and what gold and decorations I saw defies description. We came back laden down with gorgeous pottery and sarapes, etc. from the superb market there.

There's *so* much more to tell, Sam; but I somehow might as well stop early as late, anywhere short of a book. Do read *Little Mexico* (just out) by my friend Bill Spratling. It's different and more charming than any of the others. You will adore the illustrations too.

Much love, Hart

To Solomon Grunberg

15 Michoacan
Mixcoac, D.F., Mexico
March 20, 1932

Dear Mony:

What a fine, understanding and spirited letter that was from you! Proving not only your friendship again but the clean and heroic attitude you hold toward life also . . . Not that I have ever doubted either one, but reassertions of that kind are always highly gratifying. And I am very glad to know that your sister has agreed to set you up in business again as your own boss. I know you wont miss the straw braid and glue pot right away.

And then your second letter which came this morning! Of course I'll be glad to autograph the book for Hanna. I remember that long ago, when you had the store with Sam, something was said about that, and it's too bad that I have kept you waiting so long. The ivory knife will be a treasure to me always. It may be some time before I receive either of these items—as the mails are very slow here in delivering parcels. By the way if I find out that I can get a Mexican lacquer box or a hand woven fabric through to you you may expect a parcel from me soon. You have no conception of the beautiful handicrafts, pottery, etc. made here.

Peggy and I are still very happy together here. She is still married to Malcolm Cowley, editor of the *New Republic*, but her divorce will probably be tendered within a few weeks. We've known each other for nearly 12 years, intimately—but never dreamed, of course, of our present happy relationship. How permanent that will be is far from settled; but we have learned to enjoy the present moment without too much romanticising—which I think is wisdom.

Wish you could see—and smell—all the delicious flowers that surround our house: calla lilies, freesia, roses, calendulas, white iris, violets, cannas, a dozen colors of geraniums, pansies, feverfew, candy tuft, morning glories, etc. The days are getting warmer and all the deciduous trees are back again in fresh leaf. My fellowship is about terminated, but I expect to stay on here for several months longer if the income from my father's estate seems to warrant. Am even thinking of making my permanent home here. Mexico gets into your veins. Beautiful people, manners, scenery, speech and climate.

The poem ("Broken Tower") has undergone considerable change and extension since the version I sent you. I'm so glad that you liked it. I'm not sending any more of it to you, however, until it's quite finished.

There is a small group of quite interesting compatriots here which gathers occasionally at one or the other of our houses—most of whom are Guggenheim fellows like myself. Carleton Beals and wife, Anita Brenner, Marsden Hartley the painter who has just arrived and who is wildly enthusiastic, Lesley

Simpson (University of California) and wife, Pierre & Caroline Durieux, head of General Motors here, Wm. Spratling whose book *Little Mexico* (just out) you ought to read, etc. Plenty of good company, in fact, for one like myself who doesn't care for a great many people.

A way, way back you asked me a question about what I thought of *Moby Dick*. It has passages, I admit, of seeming innuendo that seem to block the action. But on third or fourth reading I've found that some of those very passages are much to be valued in themselves—minor and subsidiary forms that augment the final climacteric quite a bit. No work as tremendous and tragic as *Moby Dick* can be expected to build up its ultimate tension and impact without manipulating our time sense to a great extent. Even the suspense of the usual mystery story utilizes that device. In *Moby Dick* the whale is a metaphysical image of the Universe, and every detail of his habits and anatomy has its importance in swelling his proportions to the cosmic rôle he plays. You may find other objections to the book in mind, but I've assumed the above to be among them, at least, as I among others that I know, found the same fault at first.

Peggy and I may not keep this house more than a month longer, as the lease runs out in May. But I expect to hear from you anyway in the meantime. Many, many fond regards, dear Mony, and lots of luck!

Yours ever, Hart

To Malcolm Cowley

"The Broken Tower"

The bell-rope that gathers God at dawn
Dispatches me as though I dropped down the knell
Of a spent day—to wander the cathedral lawn
From pit to crucifix, feet chill on steps from hell.

Have you not heard, have you not seen that corps
Of shadows in the tower, whose shoulders sway
Antiphonal carillons launched before
The stars are caught and hived in the sun's ray?

The bells, I say, the bells break down their tower;
And swing I know not where. Their tongues engrave
Membrane through marrow, my long-scattered score
Of broken intervals . . . And I, their sexton slave!

Oval encyclicals in canyons heaping
The impasse high with choir. Banked voices slain!
Pagodas, campaniles with reveilles outleaping—
O terraced echoes prostrate on the plain! . . .

And so it was I entered the broken world
To trace the visionary company of love, its voice
An instant in the wind (I know not whither hurled)
But not for long to hold each desperate choice.

My word I poured. But was it cognate, scored
Of that tribunal monarch of the air
Whose thigh embronzes earth, strikes crystal Word
In wounds pledged once to hope,—cleft to despair?

The steep encroachments of my blood left me
No answer (could blood hold such a lofty tower
As flings the question true?)—or is it she
Whose sweet mortality stirs latent power?—

And through whose pulse I hear, counting the strokes
My veins recall and add, revived and sure
The angelus of wars my chest evokes:
What I hold healed, original now, and pure . . .

And builds, within, a tower that is not stone
(Not stone can jacket heaven)—but slip
Of pebbles,—visible wings of silence sown
In azure circles, widening as they dip

The matrix of the heart, lift down the eye
That shrines the quiet lake and swells a tower . . .
The commodious, tall decorum of that sky
Unseals her earth, and lifts love in it shower.

Dear Malcolm: Easter 1932
    Peggy and I think and talk a great deal about you. That means in a very fond way, or it wouldn't be mentioned. I'm wondering whether or not you'll like the above poem—about the 1st I've written in two years . . . I'm getting too damned self-critical to write at all any more. More than ever, however, do I implore your honest appraisal of this verse, prose or nonsense—whatever it may seem. Please let me know.
    And because I congratulate you most vehemently on your recent account of the Kentucky expedition—please don't tell me anything you don't honestly mean. This has already been submitted to *Poetry*—so don't worry about that angle.
    I miss seeing you a great deal. Peggy is writing you some sort of account of the Easter celebrations here. We're very happy together—and send you lots of love!

Affectionately, Hart

To Samuel Loveman

Easter 1932

What a jolly long letter from, Sam! I can't get the time to answer immediately, but here's a poem—about the first in 2 years —tell me if you like or not. Happiness continues, with also all of the gay incidentals of a Mexican Easter—exploding Judases, rockets, flowers, pappas (excuse me, that's the spelling for Mexican potatoes!), mammas, delicious and infinitesimal children wearing masks and firemen's helmets, flowers galore and a sky that carries you ever upward! More anon, and soon!

Love always, Hart

To Solomon Grunberg

15 Michoacan
Mixcoac, D.F., Mexico
April 12, 1932

Dear Mony:

So glad to hear that the lacquer box reached you—and I hope there wasn't any duty on it. Things often get through (small articles) I'm told—if not sent by registered mail. The cutter is awaiting me at the main post office. At least I take the notice just rec'd to indicate *that* as the article, as I'm not expecting anything else of late. I'll probably get it tomorrow when I go in town. Also, I've autographed the book for Hanna and shall mail that to you today.

I'm in a dull mood today, trying to get back into harness after a couple of feverish weeks spent in running thither and yon every day or so to borrow enough money to keep us going until my check from the estate finally arrived. Somehow I can't get people to understand that any break in schedule regarding remittances in a foreign country like Mexico is quite catastrophic, especially when, like myself, you're asking for a mere minimum for all expenses, and when the first of each month finds you with less than a shoe string to meet all obligations. Finally after borrowing money for wires, writing a dozen letters, etc. the check arrived; but I hope for a little more consistent treatment in the future. After all, it isn't like asking for a favor; the money was left me in the will, and the least the executors can do is to send it to me on the schedule agreed on.

Through the soninlaw of the President I'm acquiring a permanent passport; something damned hard to get here these days. Peggy and I shall probably stay here at least until next fall, and maybe longer. We like our isolation from mutual friends there in the north and our domestic life here with a house, servants, garden, pets etc. proves more satisfying every day. If I can avoid drinking too much I'm expecting to get nearer solid earth than I have for several years. Sheer loneliness had nearly eaten me up. Peggy has sufficient sportsmanship, mentality, taste and sensuality to meet me on practically every level. And I think I'm learning considerable that would hardly be possible from any other person.

I had a fine ample letter from Sam not long ago which I must answer soon. He complained of "doldrums", but the tone of his letter betrayed him. At least he could summon up enough jolly good spirits to reassure me of his old cantankerous self. But most all the letters we get from the north are pretty damned blue and dubious in tone. Well, no wonder, of course. I sometimes wonder if I shouldn't go back and wail around the grave of capitalism myself, adopting sackcloth and ashes too, instead of the beautiful bright woolen sarape worn around here on cold evenings. All my friends are turning at least a violent pink lately, and I'm almost convinced myself. In fact—by all the laws of logic I *am* convinced. But it goes so against my native grain—seeing nothing but red on the horizon.

Just finished reading Dos Passos' *1919*. I could scarcely stop five minutes to eat or sleep. A great book in its way. Do, for Lord's sake, read it; and give me your reactions.

Speaking of music, did you ever hear any *real* Mexican songs and dances? Some of the best of them are now on disks which can be ordered, if not in stock, at least from the factory through your dealer:

"Las Mañanitas" (Brunswick #40397) might have been composed by Bach. It's a ceremonial song played to one or another Mexican in honor of his birthday. Very solemn and eloquent.

"La Marihuana" (Victor 46107-A) a wild jargon about the native drug of the same name (generally smoked in cigarettes) and its effects.

"Capulin" (Victor 30323-A) a wild and throbbing native cancion that will set you prancing.

The Mexican singer uses a part of his throat or larynx never used elsewhere that I know of, except in the Orient or Arabia. It has great range, is generally shrill but capable of heart-wringing vibrations. Has the old Hawaiian gargling backed off the map. It is nothing to have four or five singers (masons, plumbers or pickslingers during the day) drop in here for an evening's singing. And to my mind they're generally preferable to all the trained and professional strummers and whoopers-up I've ever heard. Tequila is passed around; or beer; or coffee. And the corridas (endless ballads) and seranatas go on for hours and hours. There are endless corridas about "poor Pancho

Villa", Zapata and other dead revolutionaries. And then, if we're drunk enough, someone dances a *jarabe*, a dance that is all vibrant gristle, emphasis and exhausting grace.

Write me again soon, Mony. Much love to you. Better not send me a hat here. Too unlikely to reach me.

Hart

To Lorna Dietz

15 Michoacan
Mixcoac, D.F., Mexico
April 12, 1932

Dearest Lorna:

Peggy is out picking violets and incidentally tramping down my forget-me-nots quite barbarously; but she's made such a good cook out of the wife of my servant Daniel, that I never complain any more. We both have enormous appetites and wet our whistles with about 2 gals of beer per day. Lord, how we miss you at times! There are about 25 different grades and types of beer in Mexico—many of them from Milwaukee and St. Louis recipes. So whatever your favorite brew was—it here awaits you when you come down here to visit us.

And it looks, by the way, as though we'd both be here at least until next fall. The son-in-law of the President has promised to get me a permanent passport *muy pronto*, and with that I could probably stay forever. Six-month renewals of the usual tourist card are very expensive—but it's almost impossible to wangle a permanent out of them these days. They still aren't as impossible as our own tourist and emmigration laws, however.

Got a card from Don about two weeks ago, mailed from Porto Rico. Bound for some port of Columbia, SA and said he's given up drink; expecting to see us "next Summer", etc. but whether that was based on the assumption of our northward flight or a visit to us here—we can't imagine. It can't help but please him, I'm sure, to have a job again for awhile. La Robson hasn't answered a long letter I wrote her months ago, but I think it was you who wrote me that they were hitting it off together quite well there for awhile. I finally wrote Don a letter straightening out the misunderstanding between ourselves;

but wish I'd had a little more definite news in reply than the card contained.

Yes, the wholesale conversion of most of our friends around NY has made me feel quite guilty at times. Instead of donning the prevalent sack-cloth and ashes I've been sitting around cold evenings in the most comfortable and flamboyant serapes I could lay my hands on. I'm convinced of the logic of it all—perhaps also the inevitability, but it runs so against my precious individualistic "grain" (if I have any left) that I can't really feel very sterterous about it. Peggy and I have endless arguments which generally end by one of us tearing pages out of the Oxford Dictionary or slamming a door so hard that a pane of glass falls crashing on the floor. Maybe before long I'll make up my mind, reform, and become of some use to Humanity.

I'm wondering what you thought—or will think—of Dos Passos' *1919*. . . . I've just finished it, Claire Spenser and Mrs. Wm. Seabrook just having called on their way to Cuernavaca and left it, and have hardly bothered to eat or sleep during the reading. Certainly it's the best book Dos has ever written—the same technique as the *42nd Parallel*, but developed and perfected finally into an almost perfect instrument.

I get letters occasionally from Bob Thompson, Sam Loveman, Aunt Sally Simpson of the Isle of Pines (who hadn't kicked the bucket after all), Bob Stewart, my ex-gob now working the railroads in Alabama if he wasn't hurt or killed in the recent cyclones, and a few others whom you don't know. Never a word from Bill Brown however. I hear ominous rumors about Sue's threatening divorce, Bill's unhappy straits, etc. And it seems too bad they can't make up their minds and settle matters once and for all after so many years of tragic indirection.

My fellowship ended the last of March. I'm now just plain Hart Crane again, with the hope of living here awhile on what the estate can send me on the amount left me in my father's will. It isn't much, but can be made to go farther here than in the states; and since I can't find any work there for months to come I don't know why I shouldn't stay a while longer. It takes a great while to know anything very definite about Mexico. I do know, however, how emphatically I love it—population, customs, climate, landscape and all. So does Peggy, though I know she's had a hard time relinquishing the planting of her Patterson garden this spring—and all that.

This dullish letter reflects a full stomach and the siesta hour—with the weight of considerable beer besides. But it does bring you our love . . . Write soon, Lorna, and lots of love.

As ever, Hart

To Morton Dauwen Zabel

15 Michoacan
Mixcoac, D.F., Mexico
Dear Morton Zabel: April 20, 1932

I've suddenly been called north on account of business. Sailing immeadiately and probably won't return to Mexico. Will you kindly have my subscription address to my permanent residence: *Box 604, Chagrin Falls Ohio* . . .

About a month ago I sent you a poem, for possible use in *Poetry*, but have not as yet heard from you about it. The letter may have gone astray for all I know, as service isn't any too reliable here.

I hope I may hear from you soon after my arrival in Ohio. With all best wishes to you and Miss Monroe.

Very hastily, Hart Crane

To Solomon Grunberg

15 Michoacan
Mixcoac, D.F., Mexico
Dear Mony: April 20, 1932

Just a hasty note in the fever of packing and final arrangements. . . . My plans for staying in Mexico have been completely reversed by a suit against the estate which may cut me off from any income for years. Since I'm having to depend even now entirely on loans from my stepmother's salary the only thing possible to do is return to Chagrin Falls and try to work some of it out in service to the organization, several branches of which are approaching bankruptcy. Not a very happy prospect . . .

Am sailing for NY on the *Orizaba* from Vera Cruz on the 24th. Shall probably land in NY without a penny. Could you send me a small loan of some kind c/o Hotel Lafayette, University Place & 11th St.? It would be wonderful if you could happen to be in NY sometime during the three or four days I hope to be there before going into my middle western exile. This crash has prevented my collecting the cutter as yet, but I hope to get it before leaving if I have anything like the pesos to pay the duty charges. If not it may come back to you. I've had an awful time all round lately . . . will tell you later.

Write me Chagrin Falls, Ohio, Box 604—if not before during my stay in N.Y.

Much love,—hastily Hart

To Bessie Meacham Crane

15 Michoacan
Mixcoac, D.F., Mexico
April 22, 1932

Dear Bess:

Pardon me for wiring Byron about money, but so many difficulties came to a head at once here, and with myself weak from a fever and dysentery I had to use every way of impressing on you the urgency of my immeadiate needs. And I imagine that you well may have been too preoccupied to realize the situation here anyway—even in part.

Altogether I've had a terrible time lately. I can't begin to write the details now in the finalities of packing. I leave for Vera Cruz tomorrow night and sail Sunday morning on the *Orizaba* for New York. I was planning to return to Ohio even before the shocking news came about the Wilson matter. But with that having happened I wouldn't have thought of staying here another minute anyway. I may be able to be of some help to you this summer. Anyway I want to make the effort, especially since you must be quite crippled (at least at the Cottage) without Dorothy's help.

You can't imagine how difficult the Mexicans make it for any foreigners to remain here—comfortably. I love the country and the people (Indians) but certainly have had my fill of passport difficulties, servant problems and other complications for awhile. I have been not only ill—but frightened out of my wits because I happened, in all innocence, to put my passport-renewal problem in the hands of a lawyer crook. It's all right; I have clearance papers; but it involved me in a lot of expense, consultations with innumerable people and just endless worry. Then at the last moment my servant got roaring drunk and left, and came back and shook the gate to its foundations, yelling threats against my life, terrorizing us for days, until we had to call on the American Embassy for special police service. Etc. and so on . . . Do you wonder I've been anxious to get off as soon as possible. Thank God the lease on my house is already expired—and there can be no further complications that I know.

I have hated to draw on you so heavily for money lately, but after all, I had no way of knowing how matters would turn out with the estate; and the expense of coming home now certainly seems justified in view of the possibility of economizing later on. There are many things highly important for us to discuss together, and besides that I am looking forward to seeing you and the rest of our friends and relatives again. I am bringing back a lot of very interesting things, some very beautiful, that you'll enjoy seeing, I'm sure.

A case of books had to be sent collect (Wells Fargo) direct to the factory. Please be on the watch for it. The other things are all in a large hamper which will go with me on the boat and will be expressed to the factory later on from New York. I'll be in New York a couple of days as I simply must see some of my old friends after so long a time. I'll telephone you on the first night of my arrival around ten o'clock when the rates are reduced.

Please give my love to poor little Dorothy. I haven't had a moment to write to anyone lately or I should have written her long ago. Had to spend all day yesterday running around trying to get the telegraphed money cashed. Wasn't your fault, nor mine. Peggy nearly went crazy with her's sent from her former husband, too. The telegraph office paid us off in six hundred and some odd "Tostons" (about like getting it all in dimes) and neither the Ward Line office nor the official Banco de Mexico would accept them . . . It's seems there's a law against paying out any such currency beyond a certain small amount. But how should we know—and besides what does a government agency like the telegraph here mean by paying you in currency which the government itself, through its own official bank, turns around and refuses! We finally had to arrange a special interview with the president of the bank himself. I was already to complain to the embassy. So you see how slow things move here and what incessant obstacles one has to fight for the simplest sort of transactions. It certainly has about made a nervous wreck of me. But I'll rest up on the boat.

Lovingly, Harold

To Lesley B. Simpson

Very pleasant journey. Shall write when I get in the upper latitudes. Peggy sends *her* love, too.

Hart

To Mrs. T. W. Simpson

Off here for a few hours on my way north. Will write you soon. Am going back to Cleveland to help in the business crisis. Permanent address—Box 604, Chagrin Falls, Ohio.

Chronology

1899   Harold Hart Crane is born July 21 in Garrettsville, Ohio,
        to Grace Edna Hart and Clarence Arthur Crane. (Father,
        known as "C.A.," b. 1875, is the son of Arthur Edward
        Crane, an Ohio banker and owner of a maple syrup fac-
        tory, and Ella Beardsley. Mother, b. 1878, is the daughter
        of Clinton Orestes Hart, a successful Ohio businessman,
        and Elizabeth Belden, a schoolteacher. They married in
        1898 after a short acquaintance and stormy courtship.)

1901–07 In 1901 family moves to Warren, Ohio, where father es-
        tablishes successful syrup business of his own. A preco-
        cious and sensitive child, Harold is subject to bouts of
        nervous illness. Parents' marriage is troubled and marked
        by frequent quarrels; father is often away on business, and
        Harold becomes mother's ally in parents' battles.

1908   Father's business is bought by the Corn Products Re-
        fining Company, which hires him as a manager. Parents
        separate; father moves to Chicago, mother takes rest cure
        in a sanatorium, and Harold is sent to live with his ma-
        ternal grandparents at 1709 115th Street in Cleveland,
        where he grows especially close to his grandmother.

1910–12 Mother comes to live with Harold and the Harts in 1909.
        Temporarily reconciled, father joins family in Cleveland
        and the three move into a house together. Mother be-
        comes a devotee of Christian Science; father and Harold
        follow her example, although father's interest soon wanes.
        Father founds Crane Chocolate Company, which becomes
        a prosperous business. Harold shows an affinity for the
        arts, including music, painting, and poetry; tells aunt, "I'm
        going to be a poet."

1913   Maternal grandfather dies and leaves inheritance to
        Harold, which is held in trust. Family moves in with
        grandmother Elizabeth Hart.

1914   Harold enrolls at Cleveland's East High School and is an
        indifferent student. Father invents the Life Saver candy
        and sells product for $2900 to Edward J. Noble, who

eventually makes it the centerpiece of a multi-million-dollar business. Parents' marriage is severely strained.

1915   In January, family travels to the Isle of Pines, Cuba, where the Hart family owns property. Parents fight and father departs in anger. Harold attempts suicide by slashing his wrists; in another incident, he falls unconscious, most likely due to an overdose of mother's sleeping powder, and is treated by a local doctor. Parents attempt to reconcile when father returns to take the family back to Cleveland. Harold confides determination to be a poet to his friend William Wright. With father's support, spends late spring and summer in East Aurora, New York, at Roycroft, an artists' colony founded and run by writer Elbert Hubbard, who had praised father's business in essay "A Little Journey to Crane's Chocolate Company." Meets Harriet Moody, widow of poet William Vaughn Moody and an important figure in Chicago's cultural scene.

1916   Writes poetry influenced by late 19th-century aestheticism. Sends "Nocturne" to Harriet Moody in March. Spends summer with family friends Vivien and Hazel Brown at Chautauqua, New York, then accompanies mother on tour of the West, visiting Wyoming, San Francisco, and Alberta, Canada. Frequents new bookstore of Richard Laukhuff, which quickly becomes essential to Cleveland's artistic scene. Is published for the first time in September when "C 33," based on reading about Oscar Wilde's trial and imprisonment, is accepted by *Bruno's Weekly*; "October-November" is published in the November-December issue of *The Pagan*. When he submits poems to *Others*, associate editor William Carlos Williams replies that they are "damn good stuff." In November, father moves out and mother initiates divorce proceedings. Crane drops out of high school in his junior year and works briefly at a print shop. With plans to enroll eventually at Columbia University, leaves for New York shortly after Christmas and stays with Carl Schmitt, painter and family friend.

1917   After a brief stay in a boardinghouse on East 15th Street not far from Schmitt's studio, moves to a room on West 10th Street. Meets Irish poet Padraic Colum and wife, Mary. Makes frequent visits to editorial offices of *The Pagan*. Meets Margaret Anderson and Jane Heap, editors of *The Little Review*. Mother arrives in New York in

March, with Crane told to keep her visit secret from father; but when he borrows $168 from the Crane Company's New York offices to cover her expenses father demands (to no avail) that he return to Cleveland. "The Hive" is published in *The Pagan*; mother writes, "In signing your name to your contributions & later to your books do you intend to ignore your mother's side of the house entirely. . . . How would 'Hart Crane' be." Parents' divorce is finalized on April 14. With talk of a permanent move to New York, mother arrives with grandmother Elizabeth in May and rents an apartment at 44 Gramercy Park. Crane moves in with them, sleeping on the couch. Studies French with a tutor. Befriends Claire Spencer (later Smith, after marrying editor Harrison "Hal" Smith). Mother interprets father's letters as signs of possible reconciliation and returns to Cleveland with Crane at the end of July. Attempted family rapprochement goes badly, and mother attempts suicide by swallowing bichloride of mercury. Crane returns to New York by August 1. Signs August 8 letter to his father "Hart Crane." Moves from Gramercy Park apartment to boardinghouse on East 11th Street. Attempts to write short stories and movie scenarios. Asks father to increase allowance and is rebuked. ("Poetry is alright; your chosen vocation is alright, but when you are living in New York and spending $2 a week for tutoring, out of an allowance of $25, it is not alright; it isn't as things should be.") Mother visits New York in November and suffers nervous collapse; summons father who, suffering from laryngitis, refuses to come. "In Shadow" is published in *The Little Review* in December. Crane travels with mother to Cleveland, where they are feted as guests of honor at father's New Year's Eve party.

1918   Moves to 78 Washington Place. His allowance under threat of suspension by father unless he gets a job, begins working at Brentano's bookstore. Receives letter disparaging his poetry from Ezra Pound, who had read "In Shadow" and advised editor Margaret Anderson not to publish him. Reads poetry of Rimbaud. In March, is named associate editor of *The Pagan*; in its next issue, publishes two poems, the essay "The Case Against Nietzsche," and a review of one-act plays by Millay, Kreymborg, and O'Neill signed "A. Pagan Knight." Returns to Cleveland in May after father announces engagement to

Crane Company employee Frances Kelley. Works for about six weeks in an ammunition factory, tightening bolts on machine parts. Attempts to sign up for military service but is discouraged from doing so at the enlistment office, where he learns he would probably be assigned an industrial apprenticeship. Father marries Frances Kelley on August 14. Crane works for three weeks at a Lake Erie shipyard. Sends unsolicited proposal for "Six Lyrics" chapbook to Cleveland publisher Charles Bubb. In November, submits "Armistice Sonnet" (now lost) to the Cleveland *Plain Dealer* and is hired by the newspaper as a reporter, a job he quits after a few weeks.

1919   Reviews poetry collections of Lola Ridge and Maxwell Bodenheim in *The Pagan*. His relations with mother strained, he receives an unexpected offer of support from father and returns to New York, eventually sharing an apartment with Alexander Baltzly, recently a lieutenant in the army. Through Baltzly, meets and befriends Charmion von Wiegand. Meets Gorham Munson, who had read and admired Crane's "October-November." Publishes "To Portapovitch," dedicated to Ballets Russes dancer Stanislaw Portapovitch, in *The Modern School* in March. Is hired to work on commission selling advertisements for *The Little Review*; sells just two, to father and Portapovitch. Nearly broke when Baltzly moves to Boston, sublets from Hal Smith an apartment above the offices of *The Little Review* on West 16th Street; avant-garde poet Elsa von Freytag-Loringhoven ("The Baroness") lives in a basement apartment in the building. Meets Matthew Josephson. Agrees to be the Smiths' chauffeur and gardener at their summer residence in Brookhaven, Long Island, but the arrangement soon deteriorates and Crane returns early to New York, where he begins working for the art publishing firm of Reinthal & Newman. Publishes "North Labrador," "Legende," and "Interior" in the single issue of *The Modernist*. After enthusiastic review of Sherwood Anderson's *Winesburg, Ohio*, receives note of appreciation from Anderson, which initiates their correspondence. Begins working on "My Grandmother's Love Letters." Leaves job at Reinthal and Newman and is convinced by father to return to Ohio, where he is promised work with the Crane Company. Moves to Akron and mans a Crane Company counter in a drugstore; he is featured in a local newspaper article, "Millionaire's Son Is Clerk in an Akron Drug Store," which infuriates father. Meets Harry Candee and photographer Hervey Minns. Reads widely, including T. S. Eliot, the Elizabethan and metaphysical poets, and Waldo Frank's *Our America*. Is involved in a love affair that has him "broken in pieces most of the time," as he confides to Munson.

1920   Returns to Cleveland in early January when father summons him to work at Crane Company factory there; makes weekend visits to Akron. Is paid $10 for "My Grandmother's Love Letters" by *The Dial*. Factory accident inspires "Episode of Hands." Affair with Akron man ends in April. Crane writes "Garden Abstract" and "Porphyro in Akron." Visits New York for two weeks. Is sent by father to Washington, D.C., in an unsuccessful attempt to open up new sales territory; during seven-week stay meets Wilbur Underwood, State Department official and poet, with whom he will maintain lifelong correspondence that includes his frankest surviving letters about his homosexuality (Crane's mother destroyed many letters after his death). Reads Dostoevsky. Shortly before Christmas, becomes involved in passionate affair with a man called "Pierrot" in letters to Underwood. Moves out of mother's house and into the Del Prado residence hotel.

1921   Meets and befriends Samuel Loveman. Is transferred out of Crane Company factory to its warehouse and then to storeroom in its restaurant on Euclid Avenue. Writes "Black Tambourine." Moves back in with mother. Quarrels with father on April 19 and quits job; contact between them is severed for more than two years. Begins making weekend visits to painter William Sommer's studio overlooking Brandywine Falls outside of Cleveland. Befriends the painter (later architect) William Lescaze and stage designer Richard Rychtarik. Begins and soon abandons a play about John Brown; publishes essay on Sherwood Anderson, the poems "A Persuasion" and "Pastorale," and translations of Jules Laforgue's "Locutions des Pierrot." Sends Munson an early draft of the first section of "Voyages." Works sporadically for advertising agencies throughout the year; takes classes in advertising in September. In the fall, sees Chaplin's *The Kid*, deems the actor a "dramatic genius," and writes "Chaplinesque," published in *Gargoyle* in December. Takes Christmas-season job at a bookstore. Serves as pallbearer when Ernest Nelson, a Norwegian-American lithographer, is killed in a car accident.

1922   Starts work at the advertising firm Corday and Gross on January 3. Writes "Praise for an Urn," in memory of Ernest Nelson. Blackmailed by a former lover, is compelled to pay $10 a month to keep their affair secret. In April, Crane's friends Josephson and Munson found the review *Secession* in France, drawing Crane into their circle despite his reservations about Josephson's enthusiasm for Apollinaire's modernism: "Apollinaire lived in Paris," he remarks. "I live in Cleveland, Ohio." After reading Allen Tate's poem "Euthanasia," initiates correspondence with Tate, whose support for T. S. Eliot's disaffected, "pessimistic" modernism contrasts with Crane's "positive" answer to Eliot in a poem he begins to write, "For the Marriage of Faustus and Helen." In July, hosts Munson, who has smuggled him a copy of James Joyce's banned *Ulysses* from Europe; eagerly reads novel and writes to Underwood, "I feel like shouting EUREKA!" Reads Ouspensky's *Tertium Organum*. Friendship with Sherwood Anderson cools after Anderson and Munson argue at his house about William Sommer's works and the judgments of critic Paul Rosenfeld. Crane writes "Sunday Morning Apples." Leaves Corday and Gross for another advertising job at the NASP agency. Writes "The Great Western Plains." Continues work on "For the Marriage of Faustus and Helen." Reads Eliot's *The Waste Land* and calls it "good, of course, but so damned dead." In *The New Republic*, Louis Untermeyer includes Crane as one of "The New Patricians" (along with writers such as E. E. Cummings, Malcolm Cowley, John Dos Passos, and Edmund Wilson). In November, Crane begins correspondence with novelist and critic Waldo Frank. When mother forbids wine in the house, lives briefly in hotel until mother rescinds the rule. Sees Isadora Duncan dance on December 12.

1923   Completes "For the Marriage of Faustus and Helen" and sends it to Untermeyer, calling it "a more creative and stimulating thing than the settled formula of Mr. Eliot, superior technician that he is!" Reviews anthology *Eight More Harvard Poets*. Writes "Stark Major." Begins planning *The Bridge*, detailing his conception of the poem as "a mystical synthesis of 'America'" in his correspondence and showing fragments to Frank, Underwood, and other friends. His drawing, a caricature of Paul Rosenfeld made after Rosenfeld had dismissed William Sommer's work, is published in *The Little Review*. Receives praise for his poetry from Allen Tate and Waldo Frank, with whom his friendship deepens. Is laid off by NASP and decides to move to New York; to hide his unemployment from father, his boss, Stanley Patno, agrees to ruse in which Crane appears to be traveling to New York on business. Arrives March 25 and stays with Munson and his wife. Meets Waldo Frank, who provides letter of introduction to the J. Walter Thompson Agency, which offers him a job in May. In April, meets photographer Alfred Stieglitz, whose work he admires; begins writing essay on Stieglitz that he never completes. Befriends William Slater Brown. After staying with Slater Brown and at the Hotel Albert on East 10th Street, moves to second-floor apartment at 45 Grove Street. Meets Jean Toomer. Works on "Atlantis" section of *The Bridge*. In August, convinced that Lescaze has stolen his copy of *Ulysses*, ends their friendship. Meets Malcolm Cowley and his wife, Peggy. In August, writes mother that he "came near a collapse near the middle of the week." After rejection by several magazines, "For the Marriage of Faustus and Helen" is accepted by *Secession*, but, edited by poet John Wheelwright in Florence, section II is omitted and Crane is unhappy with edits and errors in the published version. In October, receives surprise visit from Charlie Chaplin, who admires "Chaplinesque." Meets Danish-born sailor Emil Opffer. Restores contact with father with brief (now lost) letter. Leaving the Thompson agency, goes to Woodstock, New York, where he lives with Slater Brown and painter Edward Nagle. Meets sculptor Gaston Lachaise, Nagle's stepfather. Writes early version of "Recitative." Reads manuscript poems of Samuel Greenberg, immigrant poet who died of consumption at age 24 in 1917, and chooses lines from Greenberg's poems to rewrite and shape into "Emblems of Conduct."

1924   Returns to New York City on January 2. Rejects father's offer to work as a traveling salesman for the Crane Company. Begins working for advertising agency Pratt and

Lindsay but is laid off after two weeks. Has amiable meeting with father, in New York on business. Attends lectures by Gurdjieff and his disciple A. R. Orage and is unimpressed; he grows distant from Munson and Toomer when they become followers of Gurdjieff. Begins work on "Lachrymae Christi." Is forced to vacate his Grove Street apartment and stays with Eugene O'Neill in Ridgefield, Connecticut, in a furnished room at 15 Van Nest Place, and at Susan Jenkins' apartment; makes unsuccessful bid for loan from father. Gets copywriting job at Sweet's Catalog Service, having been told of an opening by Malcolm Cowley, who also works there as a copywriter. Relationship with Emil Opffer intensifies into a passionate affair. Moves to 110 Columbia Heights in Brooklyn in house where Opffer's father lives, eventually moving into a room looking out over New York Harbor and the Brooklyn Bridge. Writes "Voyages" and "Legend." Meets Paul Robeson. Befriends Lorna Dietz. Meets Allen Tate in person for the first time. In September, to his dismay, mother puts Cleveland house up for sale. At reception for French critic Jean Catel given by Paul Rosenfeld, Crane reads "Chaplinesque," "Sunday Morning Apples," "Paraphrase," and "For the Marriage of Faustus and Helen." As friendship with Cowley deepens, relationship with Munson (who had quarreled with Cowley) is strained and Crane asks to be "excommunicated" from Munson's circle because he refuses to sever ties with Cowley. Visits Cleveland for Christmas and finds grandmother ailing and mother, now working in a shop, in reduced financial straits. Meets insurance adjuster Charles Curtis, his mother's suitor.

1925   Through Samuel Loveman, meets H. P. Lovecraft. Begins revising and arranging poems of debut collection *White Buildings*. After his request for a raise is turned down, quits job at Sweet's; rejects job offer from father. Accepts invitation to help with renovation of Susan Jenkins and Slater Brown's recently bought farmhouse (known as "Robber Rocks") near Patterson, New York. Works on "Passage." Hal Smith rejects *White Buildings* on behalf of Harcourt, Brace in July. Crane makes vow to stay sober for a year. Returns briefly to Cleveland to help his mother and grandmother move after the family house is sold.

Visits Robber Rocks before returning to New York City in October. Completes "The Wine Menagerie." Becomes friends with Laura Riding. Having long toyed with the idea of working on a ship, applies for job on a South American steamer. When Eugene O'Neill agrees to write preface for *White Buildings*, Horace Liveright expresses strong interest in having his firm, Boni & Liveright, publish it; Crane sends O'Neill "General Aims and Theories," notes about his poetics. Works on "At Melville's Tomb." With a $200 loan from Richard and Charlotte Rychtarik, buys ten acres of sloping, heavily wooded land in Sherman, Connecticut, on the New York border, and plans to build a house there (but never does). In November, Marianne Moore accepts Crane's "The Wine Menagerie" for *The Dial*, but cuts and revises it drastically, much to his chagrin, publishing it as "Again" in May 1926. Crane writes to banker and arts patron Otto H. Kahn for a loan; meets with Kahn in December and secures half of a pledged $2,000 gift to work on *The Bridge*. Withdraws "At Melville's Tomb" from *The Dial* after Moore demands the last stanza be cut. Moves in with Allen Tate and his wife (the novelist Caroline Gordon) in farmhouse owned by Addie Turner not far from Robber Rocks in Patterson, New York, with plans to complete *The Bridge* there. Rereads Whitman. Cowley dedicates poem "The Flower in the Sea" to Crane.

1926   Crane works on "Repose of Rivers" and the "Atlantis" section of *The Bridge*. On five-day visit to New York City, has fling with sailor Jack Fitzin. Reads widely, researching background for *The Bridge*. Works on "Ave Maria" section. Travels to Cleveland when mother asks for help with her upcoming wedding to Charles Curtis; en route, stops in New York City and sees Munson, whose essay on Crane, "Young Titan in the Sacred Wood," had recently been sent to him. Sends Kahn detailed outline of *The Bridge* in March; receives more money from Kahn. Relations with Tates fray, due to domestic squabbles as well as literary differences (having once called Crane the greatest living poet, Tate now bestows the honor on T. S. Eliot in *The New Republic*); quarrel on April 16 prompts Crane to move out. Asks mother if he can stay in family house on Isle of Pines, which she reluctantly agrees to, canceling

Cleveland wedding plans and traveling to New York with Charles Curtis so Crane can see them get married. Accompanied by Waldo Frank, sails for Cuba on the *Orizaba* on May 1. Settles in at family house with the caretaker, "Aunt Sally" Simpson; Frank leaves on May 18. O'Neill writes that he does not intend to submit introduction to *White Buildings*. Crane takes brief trip to Grand Cayman Island and, though finding the voyages there and back unpleasant (enduring severe sunburn, bites from swarms of mosquitoes, and unfounded fears of aural abscesses), the experience gives rise to poems "The Air Plant" and "O Carib Isle!" Sells Connecticut property back to its former owner, Bina Flynn. "Passage," "Praise for an Urn," and "At Melville's Tomb" are accepted for publication by Edgell Rickword, editor of London-based *Calendar*. Crane reads and is strongly influenced by Spengler's *Decline of the West*; reads Cervantes and Proust. Receives news that Horace Liveright nearly changed his mind about publishing *White Buildings* but was persuaded to go forward with it by Kahn, James Light, and O'Neill, under condition that O'Neill write foreword; receives confirmation of fall publication and a $100 advance from Liveright. O'Neill concedes that he will not write *White Buildings* foreword; Tate steps in and writes it instead. Begins intense period of sustained work on *The Bridge*, in which he drafts as much as half the poem; completes proem "To Brooklyn Bridge," which he sends to Waldo Frank and *The Dial*. Crane reads Thomas Nashe and first volume of Carl Sandburg's Lincoln biography. Takes break from writing *The Bridge* and visits Havana, where he has affair with Cuban sailor named Alfredo. Resolves to learn Spanish and envisions writing blank-verse tragedy about the Aztecs after *The Bridge* is completed. Receives news from mother that she and Charles Curtis have separated. Poet and critic Yvor Winters initiates correspondence. Crane's letter to *Poetry* editor Harriet Monroe defending "At Melville's Tomb" against her charge of obscurity appears in *Poetry*. In late October, a hurricane hits the Isle of Pines, causing severe damage and making the house uninhabitable (he describes the aftermath in poem "Eternity"). Crane returns to New York City, where he meets Kahn and receives final installment of the money promised him. Discouraged, goes back to Patterson, where he lives with Addie Turner (the Tates being in New York

City). Charles Curtis informs him of imminent divorce with mother. Reads and admires Williams' *In the American Grain*. In December *White Buildings*, dedicated to Waldo Frank, is published by Boni & Liveright ("a beautiful book," he writes his mother).

1927   From this time onward, Crane's alcoholism worsens. Father's second wife dies of cancer on January 3. Crane receives admiring letter from American expatriate in Paris, Eugene Jolas, who is about to start the magazine *transition*, in which a review of *White Buildings* and several poems, including "O Carib Isle!", are published. Discovers that his arrangement with Kahn requires that he pay the banker a $60 yearly premium on a life-insurance policy established on his behalf. Addie Turner allows Crane to live at the Patterson house on credit. *The Dial* and *Poetry* accept, respectively, "The Dance" and "Cutty Sark," sections of *The Bridge*. *The New Republic* publishes Waldo Frank's favorable review of *White Buildings* but edits out his more enthusiastic pronouncements; also publishes Edmund Wilson's essay "The Muses Out of Work," survey of contemporary American poetry in which he writes: "Mr. Crane has a most remarkable style, a style that is strikingly original—almost something like a great style, if there could be such a thing as a great style which was, not merely not applied to a great subject, but not, so far as one can see, applied to any subject at all." Crane hopes to write biography of Brooklyn Bridge architect John Roebling, which he thinks would have commercial appeal and attract attention to *The Bridge*. Accepts father's invitation to visit Cleveland, then travels back to New York City with father (going there on business), who offers Crane an allowance. Works on *The Bridge* in Patterson. Spends month in New York City, where he falls in love with a sailor named Evered (called "Phoebus Apollo" in letters to Underwood), who joins him for several weeks when he returns to Patterson. Sends Kahn detailed explanation of *The Bridge* along with a request for more assistance. Begins gathering shorter poems for a volume with eventual working title *Key West: An Island Sheaf*, which he never completes. Goes to Cleveland at the end of September to see his mother and grandmother off as they move to Hollywood, California. With money promised from Kahn, intends to work on *The Bridge* in

Martinique for two months; when mother hears of plans she demands he stay in the U.S., citing her fragile nerves and his grandmother's poor health. Crane works for a short time in a bookstore. Is hired as a secretary and intellectual companion by Herbert Wise, a wealthy 34-year-old stockbroker recovering from a nervous collapse who has planned a six-month rest cure in Southern California. "The Tunnel" is published in *The Criterion* in November. Shortly before leaving for Los Angeles in November, Crane is arrested after a "riotous" night drinking with E. E. Cummings and his wife, Anne. On November 21, arrives in California as part of Wise's entourage, which is installed at Spanish-style villa at 2160 Mar Vista Avenue in Altadena. During his stay at Wise's villa he visits mother and grandmother, two hours away in Hollywood, twice a week. At first beguiled ("everywhere such beautiful faces, bodies!"), quickly becomes disenchanted with the "great pink vacuum" of Southern California and his unusual position in Wise's household; writes no poetry during his California stay. Meets Yvor Winters at Winters' parents' house in Pasadena.

1928   After Kay Boyle publishes negative assessment of Crane's poetry in *transition*, Yvor Winters writes a letter in his defense. On Winters' recommendation, Crane reads poems of Gerard Manley Hopkins. ("What a man—and what daring!"; writes to Loveman, "I have discovered that I am not as original in some of my stylisms as I had thought I was.") Meets Bennett Cerf, Wise's nephew. Reads Proust, Gide, and Wyndham Lewis. Corresponds with Spanish critic Antonio Marichalar, who reviewed *White Buildings.* In March, Crane quits position with Wise and moves in with mother and ailing grandmother. Probably declares his homosexuality to mother. Sees Emil Opffer when his ship docks at San Pedro; after having drinks at a speakeasy with five strangers, Crane and Opffer are attacked and seriously injured. Kahn promises to offer a recommendation on his behalf to Paramount Pictures executive Jesse Lasky. Relationship deteriorates with mother and she asks him to leave, though when he starts packing she goes to hospital, complaining of kidney ailment. Secretly and in the middle of the night, Crane leaves California for New York in May, never to see mother or grandmother again. Returns to New York, (passing by ship through the mouth of the

Mississippi in the Gulf of Mexico.) Goes to Patterson, where novelist Nathan Asch and his wife are fellow tenants at Addie Turner's house. Regularly sees Malcolm and Peggy Cowley, who have bought property nearby in Connecticut. Father refuses request for loan to buy cottage in the area, citing financial problems. Crane acts increasingly wild and his drunken tantrums result in Turner asking him to leave; he stays briefly with Provincetown Players business manager Eleanor Fitzgerald in Connecticut before going to New York City, where he is invited to stay in the Cowleys' East 55th Street apartment until he finds work. Receives money from father to return to Ohio but spends it on immediate expenses; works temporary jobs at Samuel Loveman's bookstore and Griffin, Johnson & Mann, an advertising agency. Moves to 77 Willow Street, Brooklyn. Receives news on September 6 that grandmother has died. Is due to inherit $5,000 from grandmother's will but as co-trustee mother, insisting that he move to California so they can live off the inheritance, obstructs execution of will and makes exaggerated claims of illness in cables and letters. Moves back to 110 Columbia Heights. Befriends photographer Walker Evans, who helps him get a job at Henry R. Doherty and Co., which he quits after a month. Helps with editing of manuscript of Cowley's *Blue Juniata*. Considers legal action against mother, who remains intractable regarding grandmother's will; convinces the trust administering the estate to advance him money. Befriends Solomon Grunberg. Sails for London in early December. Sees *Calendar* editor Edgell Rickword and spends Christmas on Robert Graves and Laura Riding's houseboat.

1929   Travels to Paris in January and meets artists and writers (including Gertrude Stein and André Gide) in a "life like a carnival." Befriends Harry Crosby, wealthy poet and founder, with his wife Caresse, of the Black Sun Press, which specializes in limited editions of modernist writers including D. H. Lawrence and James Joyce. In February, makes weekend visit to Le Moulin du Soleil, Crosby's estate at Ermenonville near Chantilly, known for its lavish, hedonistic parties; Crosby offers to print private edition of still uncompleted *Bridge*. Crane accepts invitation to work on *The Bridge* at Le Moulin du Soleil, and for the next several weeks divides his time between Paris and

Ermenonville. Travels to south of France in April. The Crosbys plan to publish *The Bridge* later in the year in its current form, although Crane intends to keep writing and revising the poem. Crane spends a few weeks in Marseille, "a delightful place—to *me*," before visiting South African poet Roy Campbell at Martigues, a village on the Rhône. Soon wears out welcome and, asked to leave, returns to Paris via Marseille at the end of June. Broke, he stays with the painter Eugene MacCown. Is involved with the Danish sailor Peter Christiansen. On July 3, starts a fight after he is unable to pay bar bill at Café Select; after striking waiters and a policeman, is arrested and spends six days in jail. His ticket paid for by a loan from Crosby, returns to the United States. Sends marginal glosses for *The Bridge* from Patterson to the Crosbys in August, and works on "Cape Hatteras" section of the poem. Rents apartment at 130 Columbia Heights in Brooklyn and divides time between Patterson and the city. Meets Federico Garcia Lorca. Works on "Indiana" and "Quaker Hill" sections of *The Bridge* as Black Sun deadline looms. Phones father after a year of suspended contact. Publication of Black Sun *Bridge* is deferred so he can finish "Quaker Hill" and read most of the poem in proof. Visits father at recently established business, Crane's Canary Cottage, in Chagrin Falls, Ohio, and meets Bessie Meacham. Throws party in Brooklyn to mark completion of *The Bridge* on December 7, where he introduces the Crosbys, now in America, to his New York friends. A few days later, Harry Crosby and his mistress, Josephine Bigelow, in what authorities rule a double suicide, are found dead in a hotel room. Crane revises "Quaker Hill" and arranges to have Walker Evans' photographs of the Brooklyn Bridge included in the book (originally a reproduction of Joseph Stella's painting of the bridge was to be included, but reproduction costs were too high). Signs contract with Boni & Liveright for American trade edition of *The Bridge*. Spends Christmas with Bob Stewart, sailor with whom he is involved. Sends final *Bridge* revisions to Black Sun Press on December 26.

1930   In January, father marries Bessie Meacham. Crane moves to basement apartment at 130 Columbia Heights in Brooklyn. Writes "The Cloud Juggler" in memory of Crosby for *transition* but is unsatisfied with the effort. Is involved with Carl Carlsen, sailor with literary aspirations.

Black Sun Press publishes *The Bridge* in limited edition in Paris; American trade edition is brought out by Boni & Liveright in April. Reviews are mixed, but the negative ones hurt Crane; these are published in select literary magazines and in two cases are written by friends: Yvor Winters (*Poetry*) and Allen Tate (*Hound & Horn*). In June, Crane writes to Winters defending the poem, which ends their correspondence. Goes to Patterson and alienates everyone with his behavior, and is again thrown out of Addie Turner's house. Stays with Eleanor Fitzgerald and, accompanied by Lorna Dietz, visits E. E. Cummings in New Hampshire. Reads Dante. Applies for fellowship from Guggenheim Foundation in August. Moves back to New York City, staying at Fitzgerald's apartment and in cheap hotel rooms. In October, *The Bridge* is awarded *Poetry*'s Helen Haire Levinson Prize. *Fortune* assigns him articles about the nearly completed George Washington Bridge and Standard Oil president J. Walter Teagle, but the first is rejected and a rough draft of the second goes missing in the mail. In December, funds depleted, Crane goes to Ohio, and during his stay he visits the Rychtariks, William Sommer, and Crane family members in Garretsville. Works in the family store in Cleveland and at the Chagrin Falls business.

1931   Though three-month stay in Ohio is tranquil and his relationship with his father is as close as it has ever been, Crane grows restless. Is overjoyed to be awarded $2000 Guggenheim fellowship in March. Although he had proposed traveling to France, adopts Cowley's suggestion to go to Mexico, reviving vague plans to write verse play about the Aztecs. Gets thrown out of a *New Republic* party for fighting. Shortly before leaving New York, meets bacteriologist Hans Zinsser from Harvard Medical School, who is also traveling to Mexico on the *Orizaba*. Arrives in Mexico City in April, and stays with writer Katherine Anne Porter, another Guggenheim recipient. A series of drunken episodes alienates him from Porter; he moves to the suburb of Mixcoac and grows distant from his literary friends, with the exception of Malcolm Cowley, now an editor at *The New Republic*. Corresponds with old friends from Ohio, William Wright and Samuel Loveman, as well as Solomon Grunberg, a psychoanalyst in New York. Befriends Irish revolutionary and poet Ernest O'Malley. In

June, receives request from Morton Dauwen Zabel, editor of *Poetry*, for poems and is offered book reviews to write. Writes "Purgatorio" fragment. Mental state deteriorates. After Porter fails to attend a meal he had planned for her, Crane goes on drunken spree, acts outrageously at a reception at the American embassy, shouts obscenities at Porter outside her house, and spends night in jail. A complaint is lodged with the Mexican government, and the Guggenheim Foundation sends letter threatening to end fellowship. Father dies of heart failure and Crane returns to Ohio in early July for the funeral and to help settle the estate; discovers father's businesses are in trouble. Goes to New York for a few days before his return to Mexico but avoids most of his friends. Back in Mexico, meets archaeologist Milton Roarke and accompanies him to Tepotzlan, four hours from Mexico City; witnesses festival in honor of the Aztec god Tepoztecatl. Works on "The Circumstance." Befriends artist David Siqueiros, under house arrest for his communist ties, who paints Crane's portrait. Discusses his unwritten Aztec drama with historian Lesley Baird Simpson, who becomes a friend. Resumes friendship with Peggy Cowley, in Mexico in the midst of a divorce, and through her meets journalist Carleton Beals and historian Anita Brenner. His poetry is attacked in print by H. L. Mencken and Max Eastman in October. Agrees to host Siqueiros in November when the malaria-stricken painter has to be moved for medical treatment. Goes to Taxco and stays with Peggy Cowley shortly before Christmas and they become lovers (Crane continues to have sexual relations with men during their affair). Begins work on "The Broken Tower."

1932   Spends night in jail in Taxco on January 28. Returns to Mixcoac and a chaotic household; goes with Peggy to Puebla for a few days. Sends completed "The Broken Tower" to Malcolm Cowley, Samuel Loveman, and *Poetry* (which never receives it). When Guggenheim fellowship expires on March 31, Crane is low on funds because inheritance money from father's estate does not arrive; learns from Bessie Crane that although he will receive a small monthly allowance "nothing can be paid to you in the way of your bequest" because father had guaranteed a lease on a factory building that occupants cannot pay. He mutilates his portrait by Siqueiros. Talks of suicide and makes at least one will (destroyed or lost); swallows iodine and receives medical care. Feels compelled to leave Mexico and departs with Peggy from Veracruz on the *Orizaba*. Goes ashore for several hours in Havana. Rages drunkenly through ship after Peggy's arm is accidentally burned. Is badly beaten in the early hours of the morning of April 27. Around noon that day, in front of several witnesses, plunges to death by jumping off the deck of the *Orizaba*.

Biographical Notes

Sherwood Anderson (1876–1941), novelist and short-story writer. Born in Camden, Ohio, Anderson grew up in the nearby town of Clyde and moved to Chicago in 1895. His first novel, *Windy McPherson's Son*, was published in 1916. His collection of stories and sketches about small-town life, *Winesburg, Ohio* (1919), received an enthusiastic review from Crane in *The Pagan*; Anderson's appreciative note in return initiated their correspondence. Crane's second essay on Anderson's fiction was published in *The Double Dealer* in 1921. They did not meet until Anderson came to Cleveland in 1922, but by then Crane had developed reservations about his work. Anderson's other books include two poetry collections, *Mid-American Chants* (1918) and *New Testament* (1927); several novels, including *Poor White* (1920) and *Dark Laughter* (1925); and nonfiction such as *No Swank* (1934) and *Puzzled America* (1935).

Susan Jenkins Brown (1896–1982) befriended Crane in 1923, not long before she married William Slater Brown. Her first husband was Provincetown Players director James Light. She worked as an editor for the pulp magazine *Telling Tales*. Her *Robber Rocks: Letters and Memories of Hart Crane, 1923–1932* was published in 1968.

William Slater Brown (1896–1997), writer and editor. Born in Massachusetts to the family that founded the town of Webster, Slater Brown served in a Red Cross ambulance corps unit during World War I. After writing letters deemed seditious, he was incarcerated with his friend E. E. Cummings in a detention center in Normandy, an experience depicted in Cummings' *The Enormous Room* (in which he appears as "B."). He was briefly secretary for *Dial* owner James Scofield Thayer and worked at *Broom*, *New Masses*, and *The New Republic*. In 1923 he met Crane, who was immediately drawn to him (he recalled, "his long crushes on me he consistently treated with reticence and a high degree of delicacy"). He married Susan Jenkins, and they used his small inheritance to purchase a farmhouse in Dutchess County, New York, known as Robber Rocks and Tory Hill, which Crane helped renovate. Robber Rocks was not far from the house in Patterson that was Crane's home at various times from 1925 to 1930. Slater Brown wrote one novel, *The Burning Wheel* (1942), as well as nonfiction such as *World of the Wind* (1961), *World of the*

Desert (1961), and *The Heyday of Spiritualism* (1970). His marriage to Susan Jenkins ended in the early 1930s.

George B. Bryan, a childhood friend of Crane. In the summer of 1916, he was Crane's companion during a stay in Chautauqua, New York, under the supervision of family friends Hazel and Vivian Brown. Crane hosted Bryan in New York in April 1918.

Charles C. Bubb (1876–1936), Cleveland clergyman and publisher of the Clerk's Press. In 1918 Crane sent Bubb an unsolicited proposal for a chapbook called "Six Lyrics."

Kenneth Burke (1897–1993), critic, theorist, and poet. Born in Philadelphia, Burke went to high school in Pittsburgh with Malcolm Cowley and Susan Jenkins. He briefly attended Ohio State and Columbia universities before leaving school to become a writer and settling in Greenwich Village in the late 1910s. He worked for *Broom*, *Secession*, and *The Dial* in the 1920s. He met Crane in 1923. Burke's works of literary criticism and theory include *Counter-Statement* (1931), *Permanence and Change* (1935), *A Grammar of Motives* (1945), *A Rhetoric of Motives* (1950), and *Language as Symbolic Action* (1966). His fiction was collected in *The Complete White Oxen* (1968), his poetry in *Collected Poems 1915–1967* (1968).

Harry Candee (1887–1925). Son of the travel writer and art historian Helen Churchill Candee, Harold C. Candee met Crane in 1919 in Akron, where he worked as secretary to the businessman and philanthropist Edwin Coupland Shaw. In the 1920s he traveled with his mother to Southeast Asia and then settled in England, where, while serving as president of the Working Boys' Home in Birmingham, he contracted pneumonia and died on July 9, 1925. Grace Crane destroyed all of Crane's correspondence with Candee.

Malcolm Cowley (1898–1989), editor, poet, critic, and memoirist. Born in western Pennsylvania as the only son of a homeopathic doctor, he attended high school in Pittsburgh with Kenneth Burke and Susan Jenkins. He was awarded a scholarship to Harvard and, with an overseas interlude driving munitions trucks for the French army during World War I, graduated in 1920. He married Peggy Baird in 1919. Crane praised his early poems in a review of the anthology *Eight More Harvard Poets*; Cowley returned the compliment with a letter that named Crane "one of the two or three people who can write a twentieth century blank verse, about other subjects than love death and nightingales." They met in 1923, shortly after Cowley returned from two years in France, where he had been studying on an American Field Service scholarship. As a copywriter for Sweet's Catalog Service, he helped Crane get a job with the firm in 1924. He was Gorham Munson's literary adversary, and his friendship with Crane strained Crane's relationship with Munson. Cowley dedicated his poem "The Flower in the Sea" to Crane in 1925. The two men saw each other in the city as well as the country: the Cowleys' property in Sherman, Connecticut, was close to Slater Brown's Robber Rocks and Crane's residence in Patterson, New York. Cowley served as the literary editor of *The New Republic*, in which he gave *The Bridge* a generally favorable review while citing "obvious" flaws that he did not elaborate on; he wrote the magazine's editorial about Crane's suicide, "Death of a Poet." His first marriage had long since deteriorated when his divorce from Peggy was made final in 1932, the year he married Muriel Maurer. Cowley later served as literary advisor to Viking Press and edited anthologies of Faulkner, Hemingway, and Hawthorne. His memoirs include *Exile's Return* (1934) and *The Dream of the Golden Mountains* (1980).

Peggy Baird Cowley (1887–1970). Born Marjorie Frances Baird in Babylon, New York, she studied at the Art Students League in New York and was an active feminist. She married Malcolm Cowley in 1919. Her affair with Crane began while she was in Mexico in the midst of divorcing Cowley; she was traveling with Crane on the *Orizaba* when he committed suicide.

Clarence Arthur Crane (1875–1931), Hart Crane's father, candy manufacturer and businessman known as "C.A." He grew up in Garrettsville, Ohio, and attended Allegheny College in Pennsylvania but did not complete his studies. His brief courtship of Grace Hart in the spring of 1898 led to their marriage that year on June 1. After working in his father's maple syrup factory in Garrettsville, he went to the nearby town of Warren and established his own syrup company, which became a successful business. The Corn Products Refining Company bought his company in 1908 and hired him as a manager. He and Grace separated in 1908 and he went to Chicago, leaving his son in the care of the boy's maternal grandparents. The family reunited in Cleveland in 1910, though he was often away on business and domestic strife continued. He founded the Crane Chocolate Company, which grew into a flourishing concern; he developed innovative marketing strategies involving artists such as Maxfield Parrish and soprano Mary Garden. After inventing the Life Saver candy, he sold it to Edward J. Noble. He and Grace separated again in 1916 and were divorced the following year. His relationship with his son was often troubled (at one point they had no contact for more than two years) but not without periods of warm feelings toward each other, particularly after 1927. He was married to Frances Kelley from 1918 until her death in 1927; he married Bessie Meacham in 1930. During his final trip to Ohio in late 1930 and early 1931, Hart Crane spent much of his visit at one of his father's later business ventures, Crane's Canary Cottage in Chagrin Falls, Ohio.

Grace Hart Crane (1878–1947), Hart Crane's mother. Born in Warren, Ohio, she moved as a girl to the Chicago suburb of Oak Park. She married C.A. Crane in June 1898, and her only son was born the following year. Her marriage to C.A. Crane was characterized by bitter feelings and melodramatic displays on both sides, leading to divorce in 1917. After a failed attempt at reconciliation, she attempted suicide. Nine years after her divorce from C.A., she married Charles Curtis, an insurance adjuster, but the marriage soon ended. She moved to Hollywood, California, in 1927. After the death of her mother, she and Crane argued over the terms of Elizabeth Belden Hart's estate, and he refused to communicate with her again. After his death she destroyed a significant part of his letters, including all correspondence with Harry Candee and Emil Opffer. In the 1930s she moved to New York and worked as a hotel chambermaid and a maid's supervisor. She died in poverty from cirrhosis of the liver in a hospital in Teaneck, New Jersey. Her funeral was attended by Crane's friend Samuel Loveman, who, with Crane scholar Brom Weber, scattered her ashes from the Brooklyn Bridge.

Bessie Meacham Crane (1893–1977), C.A. Crane's third wife. She managed Crane's Canary Cottage in Chagrin Falls, Ohio.

Caresse Crosby (1892–1970), publisher and poet. Born Mary Phelps Jacob, she married the banker Richard Peabody, with whom she had two children. She divorced Peabody in December 1921 and married Harry Crosby in June 1922. (Known familiarly as Polly, she changed her name to Caresse after her marriage to Crosby.) The couple settled in France and established Editions Narcisse, later renamed the Black Sun Press, which published books by D. H. Lawrence, Kay Boyle, Ezra Pound, Marcel Proust, and James Joyce, as well as the first edition of *The Bridge*. Her books include the poetry collections *Graven Images* (1926) and *Painted Shores* (1927) and the memoir *The Passionate Years* (1953, enlarged 1955).

Harry Crosby (1889–1929), publisher and poet. Born in Boston, he was descended on both sides from wealthy families. He drove an ambulance in World War I, served at Verdun, and was awarded the Croix de Guerre in 1919. After graduating from Harvard in 1921, he married Polly Peabody (who soon changed her name to Caresse Crosby). With her two children from her previous marriage, the couple moved to Paris, where Harry worked for the bank Morgan, Harjes et Cie (J.P. Morgan Jr. was his mother's brother-in-law). He soon quit to devote himself to literature and an opulent, hedonistic lifestyle that included a private religion based on sun-worship. He published *Sonnets for Caresse* in 1925 and *Chariot of the Sun* in 1928; he kept a diary that was published posthumously as *Shadows of the Sun*. With Caresse, he founded Editions Narcisse, later renamed the Black Sun Press. The couple divided their time between Paris and Le Moulin du Soleil, a country house in Ermonenville, near Chantilly. They met Crane in February 1929 and, after inviting him to work on *The Bridge* at Le Moulin du Soleil, offered to print a deluxe edition of the poem, which was published in 1930. On a visit to America in December 1929, three days after Crane gave a party in the Crosbys' honor, Harry shot his mistress, Josephine Bigelow, in a room at the Hotel des Artistes in New York and, at least two hours later, shot himself; the deaths were ruled a double suicide.

E. E. Cummings (1894–1962), poet. Born in Cambridge, Massachusetts, Cummings began writing poetry at an early age. He graduated from Harvard in 1915 and served in the Red Cross ambulance corps during World War I; he was suspected of espionage and, with his friend William Slater Brown, was incarcerated in a French detention camp for three months, an experience that was the basis for *The Enormous Room*, published in 1922. He met Crane in 1923. Crane's "riotous" evening of drinking in November 1927 with Cummings and his wife, Anne, ended with Crane spending the night in a New York City jail. Cummings' many collections of poetry include *Tulips & Chimneys* (1923), *&* (1925), *XLI Poems* (1925), *Is 5* (1926), *ViVa* (1931), *No Thanks* (1935), and *XAIPE* (1950); he was awarded the Bollingen Prize in 1958.

Lorna Dietz, Wisconsin-born friend of Susan Jenkins who met Crane in 1924. He asked her to marry him several times, proposals she did not take seriously. They took a trip together to visit E. E. Cummings in New Hampshire in 1930.

Walker Evans (1903–1975), photographer. Evans became a friend of Crane's in 1928, having returned to the U.S. from France with the intention of becoming a writer. He soon began pursuing photography more seriously and eventually abandoned his literary aspirations. He lived near Crane in Brooklyn Heights and helped Crane get a job as a clerk at the Wall Street brokerage house of Henry R. Doherty and Co., where Evans worked the night shift filing sales receipts. He took several photographs of Crane, including some of the best-known portraits. His photographs of the Brooklyn Bridge were included in the Black Sun Press edition of *The Bridge* as well as the American trade edition published by Boni & Liveright. His photographs of the American South accompanyed James Agee's text in *Let Us Now Praise Famous Men* (1941).

Waldo Frank (1889–1967), novelist and cultural critic. Frank was one of the first critics to promote Sherwood Anderson, Jean Toomer, and Crane. He graduated from Yale in 1911, and was married to the progressive educator Margaret Naumburg until 1924. He was associate editor of *The Seven Arts* from 1916 to 1917, a member of the editorial board of *New Masses* from 1926 to 1930, and an editor of *The New Republic* from 1925 to 1940. *Our America* (1919) and *The Re-Discovery of America* (1929) are his major works of cultural and literary criticism in the period of his friendship with Crane. Other works of cultural criticism include *Salvos* (1924), *Virgin Spain* (1925), *America Hispana* (1931), *Dawn in Russia* (1932), *In the American Jungle* (1937), and *The Prophetic Island: A Portrait of Cuba*. His novels include *Dark Mother* (1920), *Rahab* (1922), *City Block* (1922), and *Holiday* (1923).

Solomon Grunberg, "Mony," a friend of Samuel Loveman who met Crane in 1928. He was a psychoanalyst in New York City.

Caroline Gordon (1895–1981), novelist and short-story writer. Born in Trenton, Kentucky, she was educated at Bethany College and married Allen Tate in 1924. She worked as a secretary to novelist Ford Madox Ford. Although she wrote throughout the 1920s, including while she and Tate were living with Crane in Patterson, New York, Gordon did not publish her fiction until 1929. Her books include *Penhally* (1931); *Aleck Maury, Sportsman* (1934); the Civil War novel *None Shall Look Back* (1937); and *The Malefactors* (1956), whose main characters are based on Tate, herself, and Crane. After a brief divorce she and Tate remarried, but they divorced again in 1959. She died in San Cristobal de las Casas, Mexico.

Charles Harris, Crane's friend in Cleveland. An engineer who wrote poetry, he was part of the forward-looking cultural circle that frequented Richard Laukhuff's bookstore and embraced the musical modernism of Cleveland Institute of Music director Ernest Bloch.

Elizabeth Belden Hart, Crane's maternal grandmother, a teacher. Born Elizabeth Belden, she grew up in Akron and was educated at Western Reserve Seminary, where she met her future husband, Clinton Orestes Hart. The couple were married in 1865. The Harts' son Harry died of scarlet fever in 1876; their son Frank, born in 1869, died from a morphine overdose in 1893; their daughter Grace was born in 1878. She grew close to her grandson when he lived with her during his parents' separation in 1908. After her husband died in January 1913, Crane and his parents moved in with her in the house at 1709 East 115th Street in Cleveland. She lived with Grace Crane for the rest of her life, including her last years in Hollywood, California, where she died in 1928.

Matthew Josephson (1899–1978), "Matty," editor and biographer. He met Crane in 1919, while Crane was living above the offices of *The Little Review*. In 1921 he went to France, where with Gorham Munson he co-founded *Secession* in 1922. He was also an editor of *Broom*. Crane embraced the Elizabethan and metaphysical poets that Josephson encouraged him to read in 1920, but he took issue with his friend's later enthusiasm for Dada and Apollinaire. Tensions between Josephson and Munson led to an acrimonious split in 1923; because Crane took Munson's side, his friendship with Josephson ended. Josephson's numerous books include the biographies *Zola and His Time* (1928), *Jean Jacques Rousseau* (1931), and *Edison* (1959); *The Robber Barons* (1934), a study critical of American capitalism; and the memoir *Life Among the Surrealists* (1962).

Otto H. Kahn (1867–1934), German-born banker and cultural philanthropist. As a young man he went to work in the London office of Deutsche Bank and became a British citizen; he went to New York in 1893 to work for Speyer & Company and within a few years was working for Kuhn, Loeb & Company. He became an American citizen in 1917. His cultural interests were primarily directed toward art and music: he owned an impressive collection of Old Masters and was the majority shareholder in New York's Metropolitan Opera Company at the time of his death in 1934. He gave Crane $2,000 to work on *The Bridge* in 1925–1926, followed by small cash gifts. Crane dedicated the Black Sun Press edition of *The Bridge* to him.

Gaston Lachaise (1882–1935), Paris-born sculptor who met Crane in 1925 while Crane was sharing a house in Woodstock, New York, with his stepson Edward Nagle, a painter. Crane dedicated "Interludium" to Lachaise, who showed his appreciation by giving Crane a cast of his *Sea Gull* sculpture. His work was featured in *The Dial* in the 1920s.

Samuel Loveman (1887–1976), book dealer, editor, publisher, and poet. A Cleveland native, Loveman knew Ambrose Bierce in his youth and edited a small edition of Bierce's letters in 1922. Crane met him in 1921 at Richard Laukhuff's bookstore in Cleveland and they quickly became friends; Crane worked briefly at Loveman's New York bookstore in 1927. He co-founded The Bodley Press, which published Brom Weber's *Hart Crane: A Biographical and Critical Study* in 1948. His poetry is collected in *The Hermaphrodite and Other Poems* (1936). He served as editor of the magazines *The Saturnian* and *Trend*. After Grace Crane's death, Loveman acted as Crane's literary executor.

Henry Allen Moe (1894–1975), principal administrator of the John Simon Guggenheim Foundation for nearly four decades after its founding in 1925. Moe's book *The Power of Freedom in Human Affairs* was published in 1977.

Marianne Moore (1887–1972), poet and editor of *The Dial* from 1925 to 1929. Notorious for revising poems accepted by the magazine, she rewrote Crane's "The Wine Menagerie" as "Again," much to Crane's dismay, and published her version of the poem in 1926. When she asked him to cut the last stanza of "At Melville's Tomb" he withdrew the poem. He referred to her as "the Right Reverend Miss Mountjoy." Moore's collections include *Poems* (1921), published in Britain without her knowledge; her debut American volume *Observations* (1924); *Selected Poems* (1935); *Collected Poems* (1951), which was awarded the Bollingen and Pulitzer prizes; and *The Complete Poems of Marianne Moore* (1967). She lived in Brooklyn with her mother, Mary Warner Moore.

Harriet Monroe (1860–1936), called "Aunt Harriet" by Crane, founder and longtime editor of Chicago-based *Poetry* magazine, which published the early poetry of Ezra Pound, H. D., T. S. Eliot, Marianne Moore, and Wallace Stevens. Her criticism of the supposed obscurity of Crane's "At Melville's Tomb" occasioned a long letter from Crane defending his work. She was the author of several collections of poetry and the autobiography *A Poet's Life: Seventy Years in a Changing World*, published posthumously in 1938.

Gorham Munson (1896–1969), literary critic and editor. Through Joseph Kling, editor of *The Pagan*, Crane met Munson in New York in 1919. In 1922, Munson co-founded (with Matthew Josephson) the magazine *Secession* in France. Like Jean Toomer, he became interested in the teachings of the Russian-born mystic G. I. Gurdjieff in 1924. Crane's friendship with Munson was strained when Crane became close with Munson's literary enemy Malcolm Cowley, and never really recovered. Munson's books include *Waldo Frank: A Study* (1923); *Robert Frost: A Study in Sensibility and Good Sense* (1927); *Destinations: A Canvass of American Literature Since 1900* (1928), a volume of essays that includes a chapter on Crane; *Style and Form in American Prose* (1929); and *The Dilemma of the Liberated* (1930). He wrote about Crane in *The Awakening Twenties: A Memoir-History of a Literary Period*, published posthumously in 1986.

Ernest O'Malley (1898–1957), Irish revolutionary and poet who befriended Crane in Mexico in 1931.

Emil Opffer (1896–c.1980s), born in Denmark, immigrated to the U.S. with his parents and brothers in 1905. The family had associations with the arts and the sea. Opffer's father published a Danish-language newspaper in Brooklyn, *Nordlyset*. His brother Elbano was a marine engineer; his brother Ivan was a musician and artist who worked with the Provincetown Players in Greenwich Village. Crane was introduced to the family through Susan Jenkins Brown, who was part of the Provincetown Players circle. Opffer's father and brothers lived at 110 Columbia Heights in Brooklyn in 1923 when Crane and Opffer met, and Crane rented an apartment in the building in 1924. Opffer's mother, after remarrying, lived near the Browns in Patterson, New York, and Opffer and Crane sometimes saw each other there. Opffer worked in the merchant marine from the 1920s until the 1940s. In later life he married and returned to Denmark. None of his correspondence with Crane survives.

Katherine Anne Porter (1890–1980), novelist and short-story writer. She was born Callie Russell Porter in Indian Creek, Texas. In the 1920s she made several trips to Mexico, became interested in Mexican revolutionary politics, and wrote the long essay "Outline of Mexican Popular Arts and Crafts" (1922). She was in Mexico on a Guggenheim fellowship when Crane traveled there in 1931 on a Guggenheim fellowship of his own. He had known Porter casually in New York and asked to stay with her when he first arrived in Mexico City; the relationship soon soured. Porter's novels and short stories include *Flowering Judas and Other Stories* (1930); *Pale Horse, Pale*

Rider (1939); and *Ship of Fools* (1962). Her *Collected Stories* (1965) won the Pulitzer Prize.

John A. Roebling, engineer and philanthropist, son of Brooklyn Bridge builder Washington Roebling and grandson of the bridge's architect, John Augustus Roebling.

Charlotte Rychtarik, Czech musician and painter who immigrated with her husband Richard and settled in Cleveland, where they became friends with Crane in 1921.

Richard Rychtarik (1894–1972), Czech stage and costume designer. He studied architecture in Prague and came to the U.S., settling with his wife Charlotte in Cleveland, where he worked for the Cleveland Playhouse creating sets and costumes. In the late 1930s, he moved with Charlotte to New York and worked for City Center Opera, the Metropolitan Opera, and, from 1949 to 1964, CBS television.

Isidor Schneider (1896–1977), novelist, poet, and editor. Born in what is now Ukraine, he immigrated to the U.S. as a child and as a young man worked in advertising and as an editor. His novel *Doctor Transit* was published in 1926, followed by poetry collections *The Temptation of Anthony* (1928) and *Comrade: Mister* (1934). A regular contributor to *New Masses*, Schneider was also a translator of Gorky and an anthologist.

Lesley B. Simpson, historian and translator, author of *The Encomienda in New Spain* (1929) and *Many Mexicos* (1941). Like Crane and Katherine Anne Porter, he was in Mexico on a Guggenheim fellowship in 1931–32.

Mrs. T. W. Simpson. Known affectionately as "Aunt Sally," she was the caretaker of the Hart family's property on the Isle of Pines, Cuba. She and Crane survived a hurricane together in October 1926.

William Sommer (1867–1949), painter and lithographer. Born in Detroit, Sommer moved to Cleveland in 1907. He was mostly a self-taught artist, though he received some training in Munich. Crane was shown his work by Samuel Loveman in March 1921 and, impressed, asked to meet him; soon he was making frequent weekend visits to Sommer's studio overlooking Brandywine Falls outside Cleveland. His poem "Sunday Morning Apples" praises Sommer. He was eager to publicize the artist's work, sending reproductions to little magazines and asking Gorham Munson to arrange a gallery show in New

York; when the critic Paul Rosenfeld dismissed Sommer's work Crane drew a caricature that was published in *The Little Review*. He also brokered the sale of one of Sommer's watercolors to William Carlos Williams. Later Sommer worked for the Works Progress Administration and painted murals for the Cleveland Public Library.

Gertrude Stein (1874–1946), American writer who, with her companion Alice B. Toklas, held a salon in their Parisian home at 27 rue du Fleurus that attracted the vanguard of experimental modernism. On his trip to France in 1929, Crane was provided an introduction to Stein by Laura Riding. Stein's works include *Three Lives* (1909), *Tender Buttons* (1914), *The Making of Americans* (1925), the libretto for Virgil Thomson's opera *Four Saints in Three Acts* (1927), *How to Write* (1932), *The Autobiography of Alice B. Toklas* (1933), and *Wars I Have Seen* (1945).

Joseph Stella (1877–1946), artist. Born in Italy, Stella briefly studied medicine in New York City, then attended the New York School of Art. His oil painting, *Brooklyn.Bridge*, was shown at a one-man exhibition at the Bourgeois Galleries in New York City in 1920. In that year, Stella joined the Societé Anonyme (whose directors included Man Ray and Marcel Duchamp) and participated in its exhibitions throughout the 1920s.

Alfred Stieglitz (1864–1946), photographer. Born in Hoboken, New Jersey, Stieglitz moved as a child to New York City and attended the College of the City of New York before spending nearly a decade studying in Germany and traveling in Europe. Returning to New York, he established himself as a photographer and campaigned for recognition of photography as an art form; he founded the groundbreaking quarterly journal *Camera Work* and (with Edward Steichen) the gallery known as "291" (1905–1917), and later the Intimate Gallery (1925–1929) and An American Place (1929–1946). He and Georgia O'Keeffe married in 1924. Crane met him in 1923 and they corresponded as he worked on an essay on Stieglitz's photography that he never finished.

Allen Tate (1899–1979), poet and critic. Born in Winchester, Kentucky, Tate attended Vanderbilt University and became (with John Crowe Ransom, Robert Penn Warren, and others) one of the poets affiliated with *The Fugitive* magazine. Crane admired Tate's poem "Euthanasia" and initiated their correspondence in 1922; they met in 1924. After working as a high school teacher in West Virginia, Tate went to New York in 1924 and worked briefly at the pulp magazine *Telling Tales* with Susan Jenkins. He married novelist Caroline Gordon and they moved to a rented farmhouse in Patterson, New York, supporting themselves with a meager income from his book reviews. Crane moved in with them late in 1925 but after a few months the arrangement collapsed, largely due to domestic squabbling. Nevertheless, Tate volunteered to write a foreword to *White Buildings* when Eugene O'Neill, who had agreed to do it, backed out. Tate published *Mr. Pope and Other Poems* in 1928, and spent more than a year in France (1927–1928) on a Guggenheim fellowship. He gave *The Bridge* a mixed review in *Hound & Horn*, criticizing "Indiana" in particular as a "nightmare of sentimentality and false writing" while praising other aspects of the poem. He co-edited and contributed to the Southern Agrarian manifesto *I'll Take My Stand* (1930); his books of poetry include *The Mediterranean and Other Poems* (1936); *The Winter Sea* (1944) and *Collected Poems 1919–1976* (1977). He served as the first Consultant in Poetry at the Library of Congress (1943–1944), and was awarded the Bollingen Prize in 1956. He wrote the novel *The Fathers* (1937) as well as biographies of Jefferson Davis and Stonewall Jackson.

Jean Toomer (1894–1967), writer. Educated at New York University and other colleges, Toomer taught in a rural black school in Georgia in the early 1920s, an experience that informed his first book, *Cane* (1923), a collection of poems, stories, sketches, and drama. Waldo Frank admired Toomer and wrote the foreword to *Cane*, in which he implied that Toomer had transcended his African-American identity; this angered Toomer, who saw himself as a member of the "American" race, neither black nor white. His affair with Frank's wife, Margaret Naumburg, ended the friendship and the marriage. Toomer met Crane in New York in 1923, the year before he became a follower of the Russian-born mystic G. I. Gurdjieff. (Toomer later devoted himself to other spiritual teachings.) After *Cane* he continued to write but limited publication to occasional pieces and privately printed tracts such as *Essentials: Definitions and Aphorisms* (1931).

Wilbur Underwood (1876–1935), State Department official and poet. Introduced through his Cleveland friend Harry Candee, Crane met Underwood in 1920 when he spent several weeks in Washington, D.C., on assignment for the Crane Company. Underwood's collections of poetry, including *A Book of Masks* (1907) and *Damien of Molokai* (1909), were all published in England.

Louis Untermeyer (1885–1970), anthologist, critic, and poet. He placed Crane in a group he called "The New Patricians" (including E. E. Cummings, John Dos Passos, and Edmund Wilson) in an article published in *The New Republic* in 1922, He was one of Crane's references on his Guggenheim fellowship application, submitted in 1930.

Eda Lou Walton (1894–1961), poet, critic, anthologist, and professor at New York University, who taught *The Bridge* in her contemporary poetry course. She lived with the novelist Henry Roth in the 1920s and 1930s.

Herbert Weinstock (1905–1971), editor, music critic, and biographer of composers. He reviewed *The Bridge* favorably in the Milwaukee *Journal* in 1930. For most of his career he worked as an editor at Knopf.

Charmion von Wiegand (1898?–1983), artist and journalist. Born in Chicago, she grew up in San Francisco and was educated at Barnard. She met Crane in 1919 through his roommate Alexander Baltzly, who had been a classmate of her first husband, Hermann Habicht. She spent part of the late 1920s and early 1930s as a Hearst correspondent in the Soviet Union. Novelist and *New Masses* co-founder Joseph Freeman was her second husband.

William Carlos Williams (1883–1963), poet and doctor. As associate editor of *Others* he encouraged Crane in 1916 by declaring his youthful poems "damn good stuff." The two poets were never especially close, although Crane said that he "like[d] Williams much personally" and remarked to Williams in a 1928 letter, "At times I wonder why in paradise we don't once in a while get together. . . . There are so many things to talk about—with you." Although he had mixed feelings about Williams' poetry, Crane admired his study *In the American Grain* (1925), though at first he avoided reading it because, as he worked on *The Bridge*, he feared that its concerns would overlap too much with his own. Williams was the author of numerous books, including novels and story collections as well as poetry. His long poem *Paterson*, published in five books between 1946 and 1958, received the National Book Awards' first Gold Medal for Poetry; he shared the 1953 Bollingen Prize with Archibald MacLeish.

Yvor Winters (1900–1968), poet, critic, and professor. Born and raised in Chicago, Winters attended the University of Chicago (1917–1918) but after being diagnosed with tuberculosis he moved for health reasons to Santa Fe, New Mexico. He published two poetry collections, *The Immobile Wind* (1921) and *The Magpie's Shadow* (1922), while teaching high school in coal-mining communities in New Mexico (1921–1923). He married poet and novelist Janet Lewis in 1926. He taught at the University of Idaho in Moscow from 1925 to 1927, then moved to California to begin doctoral work at Stanford University. Winters began corresponding with Crane in 1926; Crane provided extensive feedback about Winters' *The Bare Hills* and "Fire Sequence." They met at Winters' parents house in Pasadena in December 1927 while Crane was living in Southern California. Winters' unfavorable review of *The Bridge* prompted Crane to write a letter in defense of the poem, and their friendship ended. Winters published the poetry collections *The Proof* (1930), *The Journey* (1931), and *Before Disaster* (1934). He was named assistant professor (1937) and full professor (1949) at Stanford and remained in the English department there until his retirement in 1966. His later books include the poetry collections *Poems* (1940) and *The Giant Weapon* (1943) as well as the critical studies *Primitivism and Decadence* (1937, with a chapter devoted to Crane), *Maule's Curse* (1938), *The Anatomy of Nonsense* (1943; expanded as *In Defense of Reason*, 1947, with further comment on Crane and *The Bridge*), *Edwin Arlington Robinson* (1946), and *The Function of Criticism* (1957). He won the 1961 Bollingen Prize for the revised edition of *Collected Poems* (originally published in 1952).

William Wright (1900–1953), Cleveland friend of Crane's from East High School. Wright was educated at Ohio State, Columbia, and Yale, and published his poetry and fiction in *The Pagan*, *Poetry*, and *Story*. He was the owner and manager of a department store in Warren, Pennsylvania. He married and had a daughter. He committed suicide in April 1953.

Morton Dauwen Zabel (1902–1964), associate editor of *Poetry* magazine from 1928 to 1936, when he became editor-in-chief. He assigned Crane book reviews for *Poetry* in the early 1930s.

Carl Zigrosser (1891–1975), Indianapolis-born curator, critic, and writer. As editor of the magazine *The Modern School* he accepted Crane's "To Portapovitch" for publication in 1919. He later served as longtime Curator of Prints and Drawings as well as vice-director at the Philadelphia Museum of Art.

Note on the Texts

This volume contains Hart Crane's poetry collections *White Buildings* (1926) and *The Bridge* (1930); poems from the projected volume "Key West," which he never completed; 24 poems published in magazines between 1916 and 1932; and 50 poems and fragments not published during his lifetime. It also includes 14 essays and prose notes by Crane, along with a selection of 412 letters he wrote between 1910 and 1932.

The texts of the poems, except for "Mirror of Narcissus" and "Lenses," are taken from Marc Simon, ed., *The Poems of Hart Crane* (New York: Liveright, 1986). In a note to this edition, Simon writes that he aimed "to produce a text of the published and unpublished poems of Hart Crane that is as close as possible to his latest intention in his most authoritative form of each poem. Consequently, his latest copy meant for the printer, or the subsequent form of the text closest to that copy, has been chosen as Crane's intended text. . . . When the printer's copy has not survived—often the case with Crane's poems—the first printing, which is the next closest text to the printer's copy, is used for the text in this edition." For *White Buildings*, the first impression of the 1926 Boni & Liveright edition provides the basis for Simon's text; for *The Bridge*, the text is based on the proofs, with corrections in Crane's hand, of the 1930 Boni & Liveright edition.

"Key West" is a volume Crane began planning after writing several poems while living on the Isle of Pines, Cuba, from May to October 1926. A manila folder Crane marked *"KEY WEST"* contains 19 poems on 32 unmarked sheets and a table of contents listing 13 poems. "Key West," "—And Bees of Paradise," "To Emily Dickinson," "Moment Fugue," "By Nilus Once I Knew . . . ," and "To Shakespeare" are in the folder but not listed in the contents. Simon's edition classifies these six poems under the heading *"KEY WEST* Folder Subsection." The present edition, while noting the distinction, treats these poems simply as other titles in Crane's projected volume, presenting them in the order in which they appear in the folder. Except for "Bacardi Takes the Eagle's Wing" (taken from Crane's final version, which was published in *Contempo*, July 5, 1932), the texts of the "Key West" poems in Simon's edition are based on the typescripts in the *"KEY WEST"* folder.

The Simon edition arranges the remainder of Crane's poetry under four headings ("Poems Uncollected but Published by Crane,"

"Poems Unpublished by Crane," "Incomplete Works," and "Fragments"). Rather than reproduce Simon's four-part classification, this edition groups this portion of Crane's work in two categories: "Poems Published in Magazines" and "Unpublished Poems and Fragments," each arranged by approximate order of composition.

The "Poems Published in Magazines" section contains 24 poems, published in the following periodicals during Crane's lifetime (or, in the case of "The Broken Tower," just after his death): "C 33": *Bruno's Weekly*, September 23, 1916; "October-November": *The Pagan*, November–December 1916; "Carmen de Boheme": *Bruno's Bohemia*, March 18, 1918; "The Hive": *The Pagan*, March 1917; "Fear": *The Pagan*, April–May 1917; "Annunciations": April–May 1917; "Echoes": *The Pagan*, October–November 1917; "The Bathers": *The Pagan*, December 1917; "Modern Craft": *The Pagan*, January 1918; "Exile": *The Pagan*, April–May 1918, as "Carrier Letter"; "Postscript": *The Pagan*, April–May 1918; "Forgetfulness": *The Pagan*, August–September 1918; "To Portapovitch": *The Modern School*, March 1919; "Legende": *The Modernist*, November 1919; "Interior": *The Modernist*, November 1919; "Porphyro in Akron": *The Double Dealer*, August–September 1921; "A Persuasion": *The Measure*, October 1921; "Three Locutions des Pierrots": *The Double Dealer*, May 1922; "The Great Western Plains": *Gargoyle*, August 1927; "America's Plutonic Ecstasies": *S4N*, May–August 1923; "Interludium": *1924*, July 1924; "March": *larus: The Celestial Visitor*, March 1927; "The Broken Tower": *The New Republic*, June 8, 1932.

The Simon edition's texts of the remaining poems and fragments are each based on the last surviving version written by Crane. Two poems, "Mirror of Narcissus" and "Lenses," are not included in Simon's edition; the texts printed here are from Brom Weber, ed., *Hart Crane: A Biographical and Critical Study* (New York: The Bodley Press, 1948).

With two exceptions, the essays in the present volume are taken from Brom Weber, ed., *The Complete Poems and Selected Letters and Prose of Hart Crane* (New York: Liveright, 1966). The source for "Note on the Paintings of David Siqueiros," written for an exhibition of Siqueiros' paintings in Mexico City, is a typescript at the Rare Book and Manuscript Library, Columbia University. "A pure approach to any art . . . ," not published during Crane's lifetime, is taken from Brom Weber, *Hart Crane: A Biographical and Critical Study* (New York: The Bodley Press, 1948). The remaining articles and reviews were first published in the following periodicals and books: "The Case Against Nietzsche": *The Pagan*, April–May 1918; "Joyce and Ethics": *The Little Review*, July 1918; "Review of *The Ghetto and Other Poems*": *The Pagan*, January 1919; "Review of *Minna and Myself*": *The Pagan*,

February 1919; "Review of *Winesburg, Ohio*" : *The Pagan*, September 1919; "A Note on Minns": *The Little Review*, September–December 1920; "Sherwood Anderson": *The Double Dealer*, July 1921; "Review of *Eight More Harvard Poets*": *S4N*, March–April 1923; "A Letter to Harriet Monroe": *Poetry*, October 1926; "Modern Poetry": Oliver M. Sayler, ed., *Revolt in the Arts* (New York: Brentano's, 1930); "From Haunts of Proserpine": *Poetry*, April 1932. "General Aims and Theories" was not published during Crane's lifetime.

Of the 412 letters included in the present volume, most are taken from either Thomas S. W. Lewis, ed., *Letters of Hart Crane and His Family* (New York: Columbia University Press, 1974) [abbreviated *LHCHF* below], or Langdon Hammer and Brom Weber, eds., *O My Land, My Friends: The Selected Letters of Hart Crane* (New York: Four Walls Eight Windows, 1997) [abbreviated *OMLMF* below]. For letters from these editions, the name of the library or collection where the letter is currently located appears in parentheses in the list of sources below. The rest of the letters are transcribed from manuscript or typescript sources. Special thanks and grateful acknowledgment are extended to Professor Vivian Pemberton for permission to print several letters (marked with an asterisk in the list below) from the collection of Crane manuscripts at Kent State University, for her transcriptions of these letters, and her help with explanatory notes.

To Clarence Arthur Crane, June 2, 1910: Typescript, Rare Book and Manuscript Library, Columbia University.

To Grace Hart Crane, November 5, 1910: Typescript, Rare Book and Manuscript Library, Columbia University.

To Elizabeth Belden Hart, January 26, 1916: Manuscript, Rare Book and Manuscript Library, Columbia University.

To Clarence Arthur Crane, December 31, 1916: *OMLMF* (Rare Book and Manuscript Library, Columbia University).

To Clarence Arthur Crane, January 5, 1917: *OMLMF* (Rare Book and Manuscript Library, Columbia University).

To Grace Hart Crane, February 22, 1917: *OMLMF* (Rare Book and Manuscript Library, Columbia University).

To Clarence Arthur Crane, April 1, 1917: *OMLMF* (Case Western Reserve Historical Society, Cleveland).

To Clarence Arthur Crane, April 7, 1917: Typescript, Kent State University Library.*

To Clarence Arthur Crane, May 5, 1917: *LHCHF* (collection of Bessie Meacham Crane).

To Clarence Arthur Crane, May 19, 1917: Typescript, Kent State University Library.*

To Clarence Arthur Crane, August 8, 1917: *OMLMF* (Rare Book and Manuscript Library, Columbia University).

To Clarence Arthur Crane, September 18, 1917: *LHCHF* (collection of Bessie Meacham Crane).

To Grace Hart Crane, September 28, 1917: *LHCHF* (Rare Book and Manuscript Library, Columbia University).

To Grace Hart Crane, October 1, 1917: *LHCHF* (Rare Book and Manuscript Library, Columbia University).

To Clarence Arthur Crane, October 8, 1917: Typescript, Kent State University Library.*

To Clarence Arthur Crane, October 14, 1917. Typescript, Kent State University Library.*

To George B. Bryan, April 23, 1918: *OMLMF* (Ohio State University Library).

To William Wright, August 12, 1918: Manuscript, Beinecke Library, Yale University.

To Rev. Charles C. Bubb, November 13, 1918: *OMLMF* (Rare Book and Manuscript Library, Columbia University).

To George B. Bryan, December 28, 1918: *OMLMF* (Ohio State University Library).

To Carl Zigrosser, December 30, 1918: *OMLMF* (Van Pelt Library, University of Pennsylvania).

To George B. Bryan, January 8, 1919: *OMLMF* (Ohio State University Library).

To Carl Zigrosser, February 12, 1919: *OMLMF* (Van Pelt Library, University of Pennsylvania).

To Carl Zigrosser, late February 1919: *OMLMF* (Van Pelt Library, University of Pennsylvania).

To Grace Hart Crane, February 26, 1919: *LHCHF* (Rare Book and Manuscript Library, Columbia University).

To George B. Bryan, March 2, 1919: *OMLMF* (Ohio State University Library).

To George B. Bryan, March 17, 1919: *OMLMF* (Ohio State University Library).

To Grace Hart Crane, April 2, 1919: *LHCHF* (Rare Book and Manuscript Library, Columbia University).

To William Wright, May 2, 1919: *OMLMF* (Beinecke Library, Yale University).

To William Wright, June 17, 1919: *OMLMF* (Beinecke Library, Yale University).

To Grace Hart Crane, July 30, 1919: *LHCHF* (Rare Book and Manuscript Library, Columbia University).

To Gorham Munson, November 13, 1919: *OMLMF* (Ohio State University Library).

To Gorham Munson, November 22, 1919: *OMLMF* (Ohio State University Library).

To Gorham Munson, November 28?, 1919: *OMLMF* (Ohio State University Library).

To Gorham Munson, December 13, 1919: *OMLMF* (Ohio State University Library).

To Gorham Munson, December 27, 1919: *OMLMF* (Ohio State University Library).

To Gorham Munson, January 9, 1920: *OMLMF* (Ohio State University Library).

To Gorham Munson, mid-February 1920: *OMLMF* (Ohio State University Library).

To Gorham Munson, March 6, 1920: *OMLMF* (Ohio State University Library).

To Matthew Josephson, March 15, 1920: *OMLMF* (Beinecke Library, Yale University).

To Gorham Munson, April 14, 1920: *OMLMF* (Ohio State University Library).

To Gorham Munson, April 26, 1920: *OMLMF* (Ohio State University Library).

To Gorham Munson, September 24, 1920: *OMLMF* (Ohio State University Library).

To Gorham Munson, October 20, 1920: *OMLMF* (Ohio State University Library).

To Gorham Munson, November 23, 1920: *OMLMF* (Ohio State University Library).

To Sherwood Anderson, December 8, 1920: *OMLMF* (Newberry Library, Chicago).

To Wilbur Underwood, December 22?, 1920: *OMLMF* (Beinecke Library, Yale University).

To Wilbur Underwood, January 2, 1921: *OMLMF* (Beinecke Library, Yale University).

To Matthew Josephson, January 14, 1921: *OMLMF* (Beinecke Library, Yale University).

To Gorham Munson, January 28, 1921: *OMLMF* (Ohio State University Library).

To Wilbur Underwood, January 31, 1921: *OMLMF* (Beinecke Library, Yale University).

To Gorham Munson, February 11, 1921: Manuscript, Ohio State University Library.

To Gorham Munson, April 10, 1921: *OMLMF* (Ohio State University Library).

To Gorham Munson, April 20, 1921: *OMLMF* (Ohio State University Library).

To Wilbur Underwood, May 14, 1921: *OMLMF* (Beinecke Library, Yale University).

To Gorham Munson, early July, 1921: *OMLMF* (Ohio State University Library).

To Gorham Munson, October 1, 1921: *OMLMF* (Ohio State University Library).

To Gorham Munson, October 6, 1921: *OMLMF* (Ohio State University Library).

To William Wright, October 17, 1921: *OMLMF* (Beinecke Library, Yale University).

To Gorham Munson, November 26, 1921: *OMLMF* (Ohio State University Library).

To Gorham Munson, December 10 1921: *OMLMF* (Ohio State University Library).

To Gorham Munson, December 25, 1921: *OMLMF* (Ohio State University Library).

To Sherwood Anderson, January 10, 1922: *OMLMF* (Newberry Library, Chicago).

To Gorham Munson, January 23, 1922: *OMLMF* (Ohio State University Library).

To William Wright, February 11, 1922: *OMLMF* (Beinecke Library, Yale University).

To William Wright, March 2, 1922: Manuscript, Beinecke Library, Yale University.

To Gorham Munson, April 19, 1922: Manuscript, Ohio State University Library.

To Gorham Munson, May 16, 1922: *OMLMF* (Ohio State University Library).

To Gorham Munson, May 16, 1922: *OMLMF* (Ohio State University Library).

To Allen Tate, May 16, 1922: *OMLMF* (Princeton University Library).

To Gorham Munson, May 25, 1922: *OMLMF* (Ohio State University Library).

To Gorham Munson, June 4, 1922: *OMLMF* (Ohio State University Library).

To Allen Tate, June 12, 1922: *OMLMF* (Princeton University Library).

To Wilbur Underwood, June 15, 1922: *OMLMF* (Beinecke Library, Yale University).

To Gorham Munson, June 18, 1922: *OMLMF* (Ohio State University Library).

To Wilbur Underwood, July 4, 1922: *OMLMF* (Beinecke Library, Yale University).

To Allen Tate, July 19, 1922: *OMLMF* (Princeton University Library).

To Wilbur Underwood, July 27, 1922: *OMLMF* (Beinecke Library, Yale University).

To Gorham Munson, late August 1922: *OMLMF* (Ohio State University Library).

To Gorham Munson, late August 1922: *OMLMF* (Ohio State University Library).

To Wilbur Underwood, September 2, 1922: *OMLMF* (Beinecke Library, Yale University).

To William Carlos Williams, September 14 or 15, 1922: *OMLMF* (Poetry / Rare Book Collection, State University of New York, Buffalo).

To William Carlos Williams, September 1922: *OMLMF* (Poetry / Rare Book Collection, State University of New York, Buffalo).

To Wilbur Underwood, September 19, 1922: *OMLMF* (Beinecke Library, Yale University).

To Gorham Munson, September 29, 1922: *OMLMF* (Ohio State University Library).

To Wilbur Underwood, October 30, 1922: *OMLMF* (Beinecke Library, Yale University).

To Gorham Munson, November 20, 1922: *OMLMF* (Ohio State University Library).

To Gorham Munson, November 30, 1922: *OMLMF* (Ohio State University Library).

To Waldo Frank, November 30, 1922: *OMLMF* (Van Pelt Library, University of Pennsylvania).

To William Wright, December 4, 1922: *OMLMF* (Beinecke Library, Yale University).

To Wilbur Underwood, December 10, 1922: *OMLMF* (Beinecke Library, Yale University).

To Gorham Munson, December 12, 1922: *OMLMF* (Ohio State University Library).

To Gorham Munson, January 5, 1923: *OMLMF* (Ohio State University Library).

To Gorham Munson, January 14, 1923: *OMLMF* (Ohio State University Library).

To Louis Untermeyer, January 19, 1923: *OMLMF* (University of Delaware Library).

To Charmion von Wiegand, January 20, 1923: *OMLMF* (Beinecke Library, Yale University).

To Gorham Munson, February 6, 1923: *OMLMF* (Ohio State University Library).

To Allen Tate, February 6, 1923: *OMLMF* (Princeton University Library).

To Waldo Frank, February 7, 1923: *OMLMF* (Van Pelt Library, University of Pennsylvania).

To Gorham Munson, February 9, 1923: *OMLMF* (Ohio State University Library).

To Allen Tate, February 12, 1923: *OMLMF* (Princeton University Library).

To Allen Tate, February 15, 1923: *OMLMF* (Princeton University Library).

To Gorham Munson, February 18, 1923: *OMLMF* (Ohio State University Library).

To Wilbur Underwood, February 20, 1923: *OMLMF* (Beinecke Library, Yale University).

To Gorham Munson, February 27, 1923: *OMLMF* (Ohio State University Library).

To Waldo Frank, February 27, 1923: *OMLMF* (Van Pelt Library, University of Pennsylvania).

To Gorham Munson, March 2, 1923: *OMLMF* (Ohio State University Library).

To Charlotte and Richard Rychtarik, March 1923: *OMLMF* (Beinecke Library, Yale University).

To Waldo Frank, April 1, 1923: *OMLMF* (Van Pelt Library, University of Pennsylvania).

To Alfred Stieglitz, April 15, 1923: *OMLMF* (Beinecke Library, Yale University).

To William Sommer, May 9, 1923: *OMLMF* (Case Western Reserve Historical Society, Cleveland).

To Wilbur Underwood, May 9, 1923: *OMLMF* (Beinecke Library, Yale University).

To Grace Hart Crane and Elizabeth Belden Hart, May 25, 1923: *LHCHF* (Texas)

To Grace Hart Crane, June 10, 1923: *OMLMF* (Rare Book and Manuscript Library, Columbia University).

To Alfred Stieglitz, July 4, 1923: *OMLMF* (Beinecke Library, Yale University).

To Charlotte Rychtarik, July 21, 1923: *OMLMF* (Beinecke Library, Yale University).

To Alfred Stieglitz, August 11, 1923: *OMLMF* (Beinecke Library, Yale University).

To Jean Toomer, August 19, 1923: *OMLMF* (Beinecke Library, Yale University).

To Alfred Stieglitz, August 25, 1923: *OMLMF* (Beinecke Library, Yale University).

To Jean Toomer, September 28, 1923: *OMLMF* (Beinecke Library, Yale University).

To Jean Toomer, October 2, 1923: *OMLMF* (Beinecke Library, Yale University).

To Grace Hart Crane, October 5, 1923: *OMLMF* (Rare Book and Manuscript Library, Columbia University).

To Grace Hart Crane and Elizabeth Belden Hart, October 12, 1923: *LHCHF* (Rare Book and Manuscript Library, Columbia University).

To Grace Hart Crane, October 26, 1923: *LHCHF* (Rare Book and Manuscript Library, Columbia University).

To Alfred Stieglitz, October 26, 1923: *OMLMF* (Beinecke Library, Yale University).

To Jean Toomer, November 4, 1923: *OMLMF* (Beinecke Library, Yale University).

To Grace Hart Crane, November 10, 1923: *LHCHF* (Rare Book and Manuscript Library, Columbia University).

To Jean Toomer, November 23, 1923: *OMLMF* (Beinecke Library, Yale University).

To Elizabeth Belden Hart, December 5, 1923: *OMLMF* (Rare Book and Manuscript Library, Columbia University).

To Charlotte Rychtarik, December 10, 1923: Typescript, Beinecke Library, Yale University.

To Grace Hart Crane, December 21, 1923: *OMLMF* (Rare Book and Manuscript Library, Columbia University).

To Charlotte Rychtarik, January 6, 1924: Manuscript, Beinecke Library, Yale University.

To Gorham Munson, January 9, 1924: *OMLMF* (Ohio State University Library).

To Clarence Arthur Crane, January 12, 1924: *OMLMF*

To Grace Hart Crane, February 3, 1924: *OMLMF* (Rare Book and Manuscript Library, Columbia University).

To Allen Tate, March 1, 1924: *OMLMF* (Princeton University Library).

To Jean Toomer, March 2, 1924: *OMLMF* (Beinecke Library, Yale University).

To Grace Hart Crane, March 15, 1924: *LHCHF* (Rare Book and Manuscript Library, Columbia University).

To Grace Hart Crane, March 23, 1924: *OMLMF* (Rare Book and Manuscript Library, Columbia University).

To Grace Hart Crane and Elizabeth Belden Hart, April 20, 1924: *LHCHF* (Rare Book and Manuscript Library, Columbia University).

To Waldo Frank, April 21, 1924: *OMLMF* (Van Pelt Library, University of Pennsylvania).

To Grace Hart Crane and Elizabeth Belden Hart, May 11, 1924: *OMLMF* (Rare Book and Manuscript Library, Columbia University).

To Grace Hart Crane, May 13, 1924: *LHCHF* (Rare Book and Manuscript Library, Columbia University).

To Jean Toomer, May 28, 1924: *OMLMF* (Beinecke Library, Yale University).

To Jean Toomer, June 16, 1924: *OMLMF* (Beinecke Library, Yale University).

To Gorham Munson, July 9, 1924: *OMLMF* (Ohio State University Library).

To Elizabeth Belden Hart, July 10, 1924: *LHCHF* (Rare Book and Manuscript Library, Columbia University).

To Grace Hart Crane and Elizabeth Belden Hart, July 22, 1924: *LHCHF* (Rare Book and Manuscript Library, Columbia University).

To Grace Hart Crane and Elizabeth Belden Hart, September 14, 1924: *OMLMF* (Rare Book and Manuscript Library, Columbia University).

To Grace Hart Crane and Elizabeth Belden Hart, October 21, 1924: *LHCHF* (Rare Book and Manuscript Library, Columbia University).

To Grace Hart Crane, November 16, 1924: *OMLMF* (Rare Book and Manuscript Library, Columbia University).

To Grace Hart Crane, November 30, 1924: *LHCHF* (Rare Book and Manuscript Library, Columbia University).

To Gorham Munson, December 5, 1924: *OMLMF* (Ohio State University Library).

To Gorham Munson, December 8, 1924: *OMLMF* (Ohio State University Library).

To Grace Hart Crane and Elizabeth Belden Hart, January 4, 1925: *LHCHF* (Rare Book and Manuscript Library, Columbia University).

To Grace Hart Crane, February 10, 1925: *LHCHF* (Rare Book and Manuscript Library, Columbia University).

To Charlotte and Richard Rychtarik, February 28, 1925: *OMLMF* (Beinecke Library, Yale University).

To Waldo Frank, c. July 10, 1925: Typescript, Van Pelt Library, University of Pennsylvania.

To Waldo Frank, August 19, 1925: *OMLMF* (Van Pelt Library, University of Pennsylvania).

To Charlotte and Richard Rychtarik, September 15, 1925: Typescript, Beinecke Library, Yale University.

To Susan Jenkins and William Slater Brown, October 21, 1925: *OMLMF* (Rare Book and Manuscript Library, Columbia University).

To Waldo Frank, October 26, 1925: *OMLMF* (Van Pelt Library, University of Pennsylvania).

To Clarence Arthur Crane, November 4, 1925: Typescript, Kent State University Library.*

To Clarence Arthur Crane, mid-November 1925: *OMLMF* (Rare Book and
Manuscript Library, Columbia University).

To Charlotte and Richard Rychtarik, December 1, 1925: *OMLMF* (Rare Book
and Manuscript Library, Columbia University).

To Clarence Arthur Crane, December 3, 1925: *OMLMF* (Rare Book and
Manuscript Library, Columbia University).

To Otto H. Kahn, December 3, 1925: *OMLMF* (Princeton University
Library).

To Grace Hart Crane, December 9, 1925: *OMLMF* (Rare Book and
Manuscript Library, Columbia University).

To Charlotte and Richard Rychtarik, December 31, 1925: *OMLMF* (Beinecke
Library, Yale University).

To Malcolm Cowley, January 3, 1926: *OMLMF* (Princeton University
Library).

To Waldo Frank, January 18, 1926: *OMLMF* (Van Pelt Library, University of
Pennsylvania).

To Gaston Lachaise, February 10, 1926: *OMLMF* (Rare Book and Manuscript
Library, Columbia University).

To Charles Harris, February 20, 1926: *OMLMF* (Kent State University
Libraries, Ohio).

To Charlotte and Richard Rychtarik, March 2, 1926: *OMLMF* (Beinecke
Library, Yale University).

To Gorham Munson, March 5, 1926: *OMLMF* (Ohio State University
Library).

To Gorham Munson, March 17, 1926: *OMLMF* (Ohio State University
Library).

To Otto H. Kahn, March 18, 1926: *OMLMF* (Princeton University Library).

To Waldo Frank, March 20, 1926: *OMLMF* (Van Pelt Library, University of
Pennsylvania).

To Malcolm Cowley, March 28, 1926: *OMLMF* (Princeton University
Library).

To Grace Hart Crane, March 28, 1926: *LHCHF* (Rare Book and Manuscript
Library, Columbia University).

To Gorham Munson, April 5, 1926: *OMLMF* (Ohio State University Library).

To Otto H. Kahn, April 10, 1926: *OMLMF* (Princeton University Library).

To Grace Hart Crane, April 18, 1926: *OMLMF* (Rare Book and Manuscript
Library, Columbia University).

To Caroline Gordon and Alen Tate, n.d.: *OMLMF* (Beinecke Library, Yale
University).

To Allen Tate, n.d.: *OMLMF* (Rare Book and Manuscript Library, Columbia
University).

To Otto H. Kahn, May 4 or 5, 1926: *OMLMF* (Princeton University Library).

To Susan Jenkins and William Slater Brown, May 7, 1926: *OMLMF* (Rare
Book and Manuscript Library, Columbia University).

To Grace Hart (Crane) Curtis, May 8, 1926: *LHCHF* (Rare Book and
Manuscript Library, Columbia University).

To Waldo Frank, May 22, 1926: *OMLMF* (Van Pelt Library, University of
Pennsylvania).

To Susan Jenkins Brown, May 22, 1926: *OMLMF* (Rare Book and Manuscript Library, Columbia University).

To Waldo Frank, June 19, 1926: *OMLMF* (Van Pelt Library, University of Pennsylvania).

To Waldo Frank, June 20, 1926: *OMLMF* (Van Pelt Library, University of Pennsylvania).

To Wilbur Underwood, July 1?, 1926: *OMLMF* (Beinecke Library, Yale University).

To Waldo Frank, July 3, 1926: *OMLMF* (Van Pelt Library, University of Pennsylvania).

To William Wright, July 16, 1926: Manuscript, Beinecke Library, Yale University.

To Marianne Moore, July 22, 1926: *OMLMF* (Beinecke Library, Yale University).

To Waldo Frank, July 24, 1926: *OMLMF* (Van Pelt Library, University of Pennsylvania).

To Allen Tate, July 25, 1926: *OMLMF* (Princeton University Library).

To Waldo Frank, July 26, 1926: *OMLMF* (Van Pelt Library, University of Pennsylvania).

To Malcolm and Peggy Cowley, July 29, 1926: *OMLMF* (Princeton University Library).

To Grace Hart (Crane) Curtis, July 30, 1926: *LHCHF* (Rare Book and Manuscript Library, Columbia University).

To Isabel and Gaston Lachaise, early August, 1926: *OMLMF* (Rare Book and Manuscript Library, Columbia University).

To Waldo Frank, August 3, 1926: *OMLMF* (Van Pelt Library, University of Pennsylvania).

To Waldo Frank, August 12, 1926: *OMLMF* (Van Pelt Library, University of Pennsylvania).

To Marianne Moore, August 12, 1926: *OMLMF* (Beinecke Library, Yale University).

To Waldo Frank, August 19, 1926: *OMLMF* (Van Pelt Library, University of Pennsylvania).

To Waldo Frank, August 23, 1926: *OMLMF* (Van Pelt Library, University of Pennsylvania).

To Kenneth Burke, August 25, 1926: *OMLMF* (Pennsylvania State University Library).

To Clarence Arthur Crane, September 2, 1926: *LHCHF* (Rare Book and Manuscript Library, Columbia University).

To Waldo Frank, September 3, 1926: *OMLMF* (Van Pelt Library, University of Pennsylvania).

To Waldo Frank, September 5, 1926: *OMLMF* (Van Pelt Library, University of Pennsylvania).

To Otto H. Kahn, September 19, 1926: *OMLMF* (Princeton University Library).

To Kenneth Burke, September 28, 1926: *OMLMF* (Pennsylvania State University Library).

To Yvor Winters, October 5, 1926: *OMLMF* (Bancroft Library, University of California, Berkeley).

To Clarence Arthur Crane, October 31, 1926: *LHCHF* (collection of Bessie Meacham Crane).

To Yvor Winters, November 12, 1926: *OMLMF* (Bancroft Library, University of California, Berkeley).

To Yvor Winters, November 15, 1926: *OMLMF* (Bancroft Library, University of California, Berkeley).

To Waldo Frank, November 21, 1926: *OMLMF* (Van Pelt Library, University of Pennsylvania).

To Yvor Winters, November 28, 1926: *OMLMF* (Bancroft Library, University of California, Berkeley).

To Mrs. T. W. Simpson, December 5, 1926: *OMLMF* (Rare Book and Manuscript Library, Columbia University).

To Wilbur Underwood, December 16, 1926: *OMLMF* (Beinecke Library, Yale University).

To Samuel Loveman, December 20?, 1926: *OMLMF* (Rare Book and Manuscript Library, Columbia University).

To Grace Hart Crane, December 22, 1926: *OMLMF* (Rare Book and Manuscript Library, Columbia University).

To Wilbur Underwood, January 3, 1927: *OMLMF* (Beinecke Library, Yale University).

To Yvor Winters, January 3, 1927: *OMLMF* (Bancroft Library, University of California, Berkeley).

To Edgell Rickword, January 7, 1927: Typescript, Rare Book and Manuscript Library, Columbia University.

To Allen Tate, January 7?, 1927: *OMLMF* (Princeton University Library).

To Wilbur Underwood, January 11, 1927: *OMLMF* (Beinecke Library, Yale University).

To William Slater Brown, mid-January, 1927: *OMLMF* (Hay Library, Brown University).

To Yvor Winters, January 19, 1927: *OMLMF* (Bancroft Library, University of California, Berkeley).

To Grace Hart (Crane) Curtis, January 23, 1927: *OMLMF* (Rare Book and Manuscript Library, Columbia University).

To Yvor Winters, January 27, 1927: *OMLMF* (Bancroft Library, University of California, Berkeley).

To Waldo Frank, January 28, 1927: *OMLMF* (Van Pelt Library, University of Pennsylvania).

To Samuel Loveman, n.d.; February 1927?: *OMLMF* (Beinecke Library, Yale University).

To Susan Jenkins and William Slater Brown, February 16, 1927: *OMLMF* (Rare Book and Manuscript Library, Columbia University).

To Allen Tate, February 24, 1927: *OMLMF* (Princeton University Library).

To Yvor Winters, February 26, 1927: *OMLMF* (Bancroft Library, University of California, Berkeley).

To Allen Tate, March 10, 1927: *OMLMF* (Princeton University Library).

To Allen Tate, March 14, 1927: *OMLMF* (Princeton University Library).

To Yvor Winters, March 19, 1927: *OMLMF* (Bancroft Library, University of California, Berkeley).

To Allen Tate, March 21, 1927: *OMLMF* (Princeton University Library).

To Allen Tate, March 27, 1927: *OMLMF* (Princeton University Library).

To Grace Hart Curtis and Elizabeth Belden Hart, March 28, 1927: *LHCHF* (Rare Book and Manuscript Library, Columbia University).

To Allen Tate, March 30, 1927: *OMLMF* (Princeton University Library).

To Clarence Arthur Crane, April 23, 1927: Typescript, Kent State University Library.*

To Yvor Winters, April 29, 1927: *OMLMF* (Bancroft Library, University of California, Berkeley).

To Wilbur Underwood, May 4, 1927: *OMLMF* (Beinecke Library, Yale University).

To Wilbur Underwood, May 12, 1927: *OMLMF* (Beinecke Library, Yale University).

To Yvor Winters, May 29, 1927: *OMLMF* (Bancroft Library, University of California, Berkeley).

To Grace Hart Crane, June 18, 1927: *LHCHF* (Rare Book and Manuscript Library, Columbia University).

To Clarence Arthur Crane, June 21, 1927: *LHCHF* (collection of Bessie Meacham Crane).

To Grace Hart Crane and Elizabeth Belden Hart, July 4, 1927: *LHCHF* (Rare Book and Manuscript Library, Columbia University).

To Mrs. T.W. Simpson, July 4, 1927: *OMLMF* (Rare Book and Manuscript Library, Columbia University).

To Yvor Winters, July 18, 1927: *OMLMF* (Bancroft Library, University of California, Berkeley).

To Wilbur Underwood, August 17, 1927: *OMLMF* (Beinecke Library, Yale University).

To Otto H. Kahn, September 12, 1927: *OMLMF* (Princeton University Library).

To Wilbur Underwood, late October 1927: *OMLMF* (Beinecke Library, Yale University).

To Susan Jenkins and William Slater Brown, November 16, 1927: *OMLMF* (Rare Book and Manuscript Library, Columbia University).

To Yvor Winters, November 23, 1927: *OMLMF* (Bancroft Library, University of California, Berkeley).

To Yvor Winters, December 8, 1927: *OMLMF* (Bancroft Library, University of California, Berkeley).

To William Slater Brown, December 19, 1927: *OMLMF* (Rare Book and Manuscript Library, Columbia University).

To E. E. Cummings, December 21, 1927: *OMLMF* (Harry Ransom Humanities Research Center, University of Texas, Austin).

To Yvor Winters, January 20, 1928: *OMLMF* (Bancroft Library, University of California, Berkeley).

To Yvor Winters, January 27, 1928: *OMLMF* (Bancroft Library, University of California, Berkeley).

To Peggy and Malcolm Cowley, January 31, 1928: *OMLMF* (Princeton University Library).

To Waldo Frank, February 1, 1928: *OMLMF* (Van Pelt Library, University of Pennsylvania).

To Samuel Loveman, February 5, 1928: Typescript, Rare Book and Manuscript Library, Columbia University.

To William Slater Brown, February 22, 1928: *OMLMF* (Hay Library, Brown University).

To Yvor Winters, February 23, 1928: *OMLMF* (Bancroft Library, University of California, Berkeley).

To Susan Jenkins and William Slater Brown, March 27, 1928: *OMLMF* (Rare Book and Manuscript Library, Columbia University).

To Charlotte and Richard Rychtarik, March 28, 1928: *OMLMF* (Beinecke Library, Yale University).

To Waldo Frank, April 4?, 1928: *OMLMF* (Van Pelt Library, University of Pennsylvania).

To Clarence Arthur Crane, April 14, 1928: Typescript, Kent State University Library.*

To Gorham Munson, April 17, 1928: *OMLMF* (Ohio State University Library).

To William Slater Brown, April 27, 1928: Typescript, Rare Book and Manuscript Library, Columbia University.

To Wilbur Underwood, April 27, 1928: *OMLMF* (Beinecke Library, Yale University).

To Clarence Arthur Crane, June 14, 1928: *LHCHF* (collection of Bessie Meacham Crane).

To Yvor Winters, June 27, 1928: *OMLMF* (Bancroft Library, University of California, Berkeley).

To Clarence Arthur Crane, August 2, 1928: *LHCHF* (collection of Bessie Meacham Crane).

To Yvor Winters, September 9, 1928: *OMLMF* (Bancroft Library, University of California, Berkeley).

To Charlotte and Richard Rychtarik, September 16, 1928: *OMLMF* (Beinecke Library, Yale University).

To William Carlos Williams, September 16, 1928: *OMLMF* (Poetry / Rare Book Collection, State University of New York, Buffalo).

To Wilbur Underwood, October 5, 1928: *OMLMF* (Beinecke Library, Yale University).

To Yvor Winters, October 23, 1928: *OMLMF* (Bancroft Library, University of California, Berkeley).

To Charlotte Rychtarik, October 23, 1928: *OMLMF* (Beinecke Library, Yale University).

To Malcolm Cowley, November 20, 1928: *OMLMF* (Princeton University Library).

To Malcolm Cowley, November 20, 1928: *OMLMF* (Newberry Library, Chicago).

To Malcolm Cowley, December 1, 1928: *OMLMF* (Princeton University Library).

To Charmion von Wiegand and Hermann Habicht, near Christmas 1928: *OMLMF* (Beinecke Library, Yale University).

To Waldo Frank, December 28, 1928: *OMLMF* (Van Pelt Library, University of Pennsylvania).

To Joseph Stella, January 24, 1929: *OMLMF* (Beinecke Library, Yale University).

To Lorna Dietz, January 26, 1929: *OMLMF* (Rare Book and Manuscript Library, Columbia University).

To Gertrude Stein, January 31, 1929: *OMLMF* (Beinecke Library, Yale University).

To Malcolm Cowley, February 4, 1929: *OMLMF* (Newberry Library, Chicago).

To Waldo Frank, February 17, 1929: *OMLMF* (Van Pelt Library, University of Pennsylvania).

To Samuel Loveman, February 19, 1928: *OMLMF* (Rare Book and Manuscript Library, Columbia University).

To Wilbur Underwood, February 1929: *OMLMF* (Beinecke Library, Yale University).

To Charlotte and Richard Rychtarik, February 26, 1929: *OMLMF* (Beinecke Library, Yale University).

To Harry Crosby, March 3?, 1929: *OMLMF* (Morris Library, Southern Illinois University, Carbondale).

To Otto H. Kahn, March 5, 1929: *OMLMF* (Princeton University Library).

To Caresse Crosby, April 25, 1929: *OMLMF* (Morris Library, Southern Illinois University, Carbondale).

To William Slater Brown, April 25, 1929: *OMLMF* (Beinecke Library, Yale University).

To Gertrude Stein, April 29, 1928: *OMLMF* (Beinecke Library, Yale University).

To Isidor Schneider, May 1, 1929: *OMLMF* (Rare Book and Manuscript Library, Columbia University).

To Harry Crosby, May 16, 1929: *OMLMF* (Morris Library, Southern Illinois University, Carbondale).

To Malcolm Cowley, May 23, 1929: *OMLMF* (Library of Congress).

To Allen Tate, June 11, 1929: *OMLMF* (Princeton University Library).

To Waldo Frank, June 17, 1929: *OMLMF* (Van Pelt Library, University of Pennsylvania).

To Harry and Caresse Crosby, July 1, 1929: *OMLMF* (Morris Library, Southern Illinois University, Carbondale).

To Malcolm Cowley, July 3, 1929: *OMLMF* (Princeton University Library).

To Harry Crosby, July 23, 1929: *OMLMF* (Morris Library, Southern Illinois University, Carbondale).

To Caresse Crosby, August 8, 1929: *OMLMF* (Morris Library, Southern Illinois University, Carbondale).

To Malcolm Cowley, August 22, 1929: *OMLMF* (Princeton University Library).

To Harry and Caresse Crosby, August 30, 1929: *OMLMF* (Morris Library, Southern Illinois University, Carbondale).

To Caresse Crosby, September 6, 1929: *OMLMF* (Morris Library, Southern Illinois University, Carbondale).

To Caresse Crosby, September 17, 1929: *OMLMF* (Morris Library, Southern Illinois University, Carbondale).

To Otto H. Kahn, September 25, 1929: *OMLMF* (Princeton University Library).

To Lorna Dietz, October 25, 1929: *OMLMF* (Rare Book and Manuscript Library, Columbia University).

To Harry and Caresse Crosby, October 29, 1929: *OMLMF* (Morris Library, Southern Illinois University, Carbondale).

To Caresse Crosby, December 3, 1929: *OMLMF* (Morris Library, Southern Illinois University, Carbondale).

To Caresse Crosby, December 12, 1929: *OMLMF* (Morris Library, Southern Illinois University, Carbondale).

To Allen Tate, December 14, 1929: *OMLMF* (Princeton University Library).

To Otto H. Kahn, December 1929: *OMLMF* (Princeton University Library).

To Caresse Crosby, December 26, 1929: *OMLMF* (Morris Library, Southern Illinois University, Carbondale).

To Caresse Crosby, January 2, 1930: *OMLMF* (Morris Library, Southern Illinois University, Carbondale).

To Yvor Winters, January 14, 1930: *OMLMF* (Bancroft Library, University of California, Berkeley).

To Yvor Winters, January 27, 1930: *OMLMF* (Bancroft Library, University of California, Berkeley).

To Otto H. Kahn, February 28, 1930: *OMLMF* (Princeton University Library).

To Isidor and Helen Schneider, March 16, 1930: *OMLMF* (Rare Book and Manuscript Library, Columbia University).

To Otto H. Kahn, April 6, 1930: *OMLMF* (Princeton University Library).

To Herbert Weinstock, April 22, 1930: *OMLMF* (Beinecke Library, Yale University).

To Yvor Winters, June 4, 1930: *OMLMF* (Kent State University Libraries, Ohio).

To Isidor Schneider, June 8, 1930: *OMLMF* (Rare Book and Manuscript Library, Columbia University).

To Allen Tate, July 13, 1930: *OMLMF* (Princeton University Library).

To John A. Roebling, August 18, 1930: *OMLMF* (Kent State University Libraries, Ohio).

To John Simon Guggenheim Memorial Foundation, August 29, 1930: *OMLMF* (John Simon Guggenheim Memorial Foundation).

To Allen Tate, September 7, 1930: *OMLMF* (Princeton University Library).

To Otto H. Kahn, September 9, 1930: *OMLMF* (Princeton University Library).

To Solomon Grunberg, September 30, 1930: Typescript, Rare Book and Manuscript Library, Columbia University.

To Wilbur Underwood, November 20, 1930: *OMLMF* (Beinecke Library, Yale University).

To William Wright, November 21, 1930: *OMLMF* (Beinecke Library, Yale University).

To William Wright, November 29, 1930: *OMLMF* (Beinecke Library, Yale University).

To Samuel Loveman, December 29, 1930: *OMLMF* (Rare Book and Manuscript Library, Columbia University).

To Solomon Grunberg, January 10, 1931: *OMLMF* (Rare Book and Manuscript Library, Columbia University).

To William Wright, January 14, 1931: *OMLMF* (Beinecke Library, Yale University).

To Lorna Dietz, February 10, 1931: *OMLMF* (Rare Book and Manuscript Library, Columbia University).

To Samuel Loveman, February 16, 1931: *OMLMF* (Rare Book and Manuscript Library, Columbia University).

To Waldo Frank, February 19, 1931: *OMLMF* (Van Pelt Library, University of Pennsylvania).

To Henry Allen Moe, March 16, 1931: *OMLMF* (John Simon Guggenheim Memorial Foundation).

To Charlotte and Richard Rychtarik, March 30, 1931: *OMLMF* (Beinecke Library, Yale University).

To Katherine Anne Porter, March 30?, 1931: *OMLMF* (University of Maryland Library, College Park).

To Caresse Crosby, April 5, 1931: *OMLMF* (Morris Library, Southern Illinois University, Carbondale).

To Charlotte Rychtarik, April 10, 1931: Manuscript, Fales Special Collections, New York University.

To Samuel Loveman, April 12, 1931: *OMLMF* (Rare Book and Manuscript Library, Columbia University).

To Otto H. Kahn, April 24, 1931: *OMLMF* (Princeton University Library).

To Katherine Anne Porter and Eugene Pressly, April 28, 1931: *OMLMF* (University of Maryland Library, College Park).

To Katherine Anne Porter and Eugene Pressly, April 30, 1931: *OMLMF* (University of Maryland Library, College Park).

To Katherine Anne Porter, May 1, 1931: *OMLMF* (University of Maryland Library, College Park).

To Charlotte and Richard Rychtarik, May 14, 1931: Manuscript, Fales Special Collections, New York University.

To Malcolm Cowley, June 2, 1931: *OMLMF* (Princeton University Library).

To Clarence Arthur Crane, June 5, 1931: *OMLMF* (Rare Book and Manuscript Library, Columbia University).

To Waldo Frank, June 13, 1931: *OMLMF* (Van Pelt Library, University of Pennsylvania).

To Ernest O'Malley, June 1931: Manuscript, collection of Cormac O'Malley.

To Morton Dauwen Zabel, June 20, 1931: *OMLMF* (University of Chicago Library).

To Katherine Anne Porter, June 22, 1931: *OMLMF* (University of Maryland Library, College Park).

To Lorna Dietz, June 22, 1931: *OMLMF* (Rare Book and Manuscript Library, Columbia University).

To Henry Allen Moe, July 8, 1931: *OMLMF* (John Simon Guggenheim Memorial Foundation).

To William Slater Brown, July 15, 1931: *OMLMF* (Rare Book and Manuscript Library, Columbia University).

To Lorna Dietz, July 15, 1931: *OMLMF* (Rare Book and Manuscript Library, Columbia University).

To Ernest O'Malley, July 19, 1931: Manuscript, collection of Cormac O'Malley.

To Louis Untermeyer, July 24, 1931: *OMLMF* (Lilly Library, Indiana University).

To Samuel Loveman, September 11, 1931: *OMLMF* (Rare Book and Manuscript Library, Columbia University).

To William Wright, September 21, 1931: *OMLMF* (Beinecke Library, Yale University).

To Peggy Baird Cowley, late September 1931: *OMLMF* (Beinecke Library, Yale University).

To Malcolm Cowley, October 5, 1931: *OMLMF* (Rare Book and Manuscript Library, Columbia University).

To Charlotte and Richard Rychtarik, October 6, 1931: Manuscript, Fales Special Collections, New York University.

To Solomon Grunberg, October 20, 1931: *OMLMF* (Rare Book and Manuscript Library, Columbia University).

To William Slater Brown, October 22, 1931: *OMLMF* (Rare Book and Manuscript Library, Columbia University).

To Peggy Baird Cowley, November 4?, 1931: *OMLMF* (Beinecke Library, Yale University).

To Peggy Baird Cowley, November 1931?: *OMLMF* (Beinecke Library, Yale University).

To Solomon Grunberg, November 10, 1931: *OMLMF* (Rare Book and Manuscript Library, Columbia University).

To Peggy Baird Cowley, November 13, 1931: *OMLMF* (Beinecke Library, Yale University).

To Peggy Baird Cowley, November 14, 1931: *OMLMF* (Beinecke Library, Yale University).

To Samuel Loveman, November 17, 1931: *OMLMF* (Rare Book and Manuscript Library, Columbia University).

To Eda Lou Walton, November 27, 1931: *OMLMF* (Beinecke Library, Yale University).

To Wilbur Underwood, November 30, 1931: *OMLMF* (Beinecke Library, Yale University).

To Bessie Meacham Crane, December 12, 1931: *OMLMF* (Rare Book and Manuscript Library, Columbia University).

To Peggy Baird Cowley, January 6, 1932: *OMLMF* (Beinecke Library, Yale University).

To Peggy Baird Cowley, January 7?, 1932: *OMLMF* (Beinecke Library, Yale University).

To Morton Dauwen Zabel, January 8, 1932: *OMLMF* (University of Chicago Library).

To Malcolm Cowley, January 9, 1932: *OMLMF* (Princeton University Libraries).

To Wilbur Underwood, January 15?, 1932: *OMLMF* (Beinecke Library, Yale University).

To Peggy Baird Cowley, January?, 1932: *OMLMF* (Beinecke Library, Yale University).

To Charlotte and Richard Rychtarik, February 8, 1932: Manuscript, Fales Special Collections, New York University.

To Solomon Grunberg, February 8, 1932: *OMLMF* (Rare Book and Manuscript Library, Columbia University).

To Peggy Baird Cowley, February 10, 1932: *OMLMF* (Beinecke Library, Yale University).

To Peggy Baird Cowley, February 11, 1932: *OMLMF* (Beinecke Library, Yale University).

To Wilbur Underwood, February 14, 1932: *OMLMF* (Beinecke Library, Yale University).

To Peggy Baird Cowley, February 16, 1932: *OMLMF* (Beinecke Library, Yale University).

To Bessie Meacham Crane, February 17, 1932: *OMLMF* (Rare Book and Manuscript Library, Columbia University, and Kent State University Library).

To Malcolm Cowley and Muriel Maurer, February 18, 1932: *OMLMF* (Princeton University Library).

To Samuel Loveman, March 10, 1932: *OMLMF* (Rare Book and Manuscript Library, Columbia University).

To Solomon Grunberg, March 20, 1932: *OMLMF* (Rare Book and Manuscript Library, Columbia University).

To Malcolm Cowley, March 27, 1932: *OMLMF* (Princeton University Library).

To Samuel Loveman, March 27, 1932: *OMLMF* (Rare Book and Manuscript Library, Columbia University).

To Solomon Grunberg, April 12, 1932: *OMLMF* (Rare Book and Manuscript Library, Columbia University).

To Lorna Dietz, April 12, 1932: *OMLMF* (Rare Book and Manuscript Library. Columbia University Library).

To Morton Dauwen Zabel, April 20, 1932: *OMLMF* (University of Chicago Library).

To Solomon Grunberg, April 20, 1932: *OMLMF* (Rare Book and Manuscript Library, Columbia University).

To Bessie Meacham Crane, April 22, 1932: *OMLMF* (Rare Book and Manuscript Library, Columbia University).

To Lesley B. Simpson, April 26, 1932: *OMLMF* (Beinecke Library, Yale University).

To Mrs. T. W. Simpson, April 26, 1932: *OMLMF* (Rare Book and Manuscript Library, Columbia University).

This volume presents the texts of the original printings chosen for inclusion here, but it does not attempt to reproduce nontextual features of their typographic design. The texts are presented without change, except for the correction of typographical errors. Spelling, punctuation, and capitalization are often expressive features and are not altered, even when inconsistent or irregular. The following is a list of typographical errors corrected, cited by page and line number: 147.19, pig-headed,'; 173.17–18, considerable; 173.20, Siquerios'; 174.9, illusive; 174.17, workman; 174.17, chrildren; 174.18, enanations; 175.33, Alleghanies; 190.17, your; 205.24, palce; 246.18, no no; 335.12, neven; 373.18, every; 381.34, heldM.; 382.13, foreignersM . . . ; 382.30, hereM . . . ; 396.36, the railing; 400.15, chcolates; 414.26, asuprise; 433.7, snow-show; 499.9, hell; 503.28, It; 564.31, tkaing; 583.35, reassuraning; 595 33, fulls; 678.13, Any; 705.14, thcose.

Copyrights and Permissions

The writings of Hart Crane in this volume have been printed with permission of various copyright holders. The relevant permissions information is listed below:

The Complete Poems of Hart Crane and *The Complete Poems and Selected Letters and Prose of Hart Crane* copyright © 1933, 1958, 1966 by Liveright Publishing Corporation. Copyright © 1952 by Brom Weber. Used by permission of Liveright Publishing Corporation.

"Foreword" by Allen Tate, from *White Buildings* by Hart Crane. Copyright © 1926 by Boni & Liveright, Inc. Copyright renewed © 1954 by Liveright Publishing Corporation. Used by permission of Liveright Publishing Corporation.

O My Land, My Friends copyright © 1997 by The Estate of Hart Crane, © 1997 by Langdon Hammer and Brom Weber. Used by permission of Four Walls Eight Windows.

The Letters of Hart Crane and His Family copyright © 1974 Columbia University Press. Letters of Hart Crane copyright © 1974 Columbia University. Letters of Grace Hart Crane and Elizabeth Belden Hart copyright © 1974 by Helen Hart Hurlbert. Letters of Clarence Arthur Crane copyright © 1974 by Bessie M. Hise. Used by permission of Thomas S. W. Lewis.

Letters of Hart Crane copyright © 1952 by Brom Weber. Used by permission of The Estate of Samuel Loveman.

Hart Crane © 1948 by Brom Weber. Used by permission of The Estate of Samuel Loveman.

Letters to Bessie Meacham Crane and Clarence Arthur Crane courtesy of the Kent State University Library Special Collections. Used by permission of Vivian Pemberton.

Letters to Charlotte and Richard Rychtarik courtesy of The Richard W. Rychtarik/Hart Crane Papers, MSS 103, Fales Library & Special Collections, New York University. Used by permission.

Notes

In the notes below, the reference numbers denote page and line of this volume (the line count includes headings). No note is made for material included in standard desk-reference books. Biblical quotations are keyed to the King James Version. Quotations from Shakespeare are keyed to G. Blakemore Evans, ed., *The Riverside Shakespeare* (Boston: Houghton Mifflin, 1974). For further biographical background than is contained in the Chronology and Biographical Notes, see Susan Jenkins Brown, *Robber Rocks: Letters and Memories of Hart Crane 1923–1932* (Middletown, CT: Wesleyan University Press, 1968); Malcolm Cowley, *A Second Flowering* (New York: Viking, 1973) and *The Dream of the Golden Mountains* (New York: Viking, 1980); Clive Fisher, *Hart Crane: A Life* (New Haven, CT: Yale University Press, 2002); Philip Horton, *Hart Crane: The Life of an American Poet* (New York: Norton, 1937); Gorham Munson, *The Awakening Twenties* (Baton Rouge: Louisiana State University Press, 1985); John Unterecker, *Voyager: A Life of Hart Crane* (New York: Farrar, Straus & Giroux, 1969); Brom Weber, *Hart Crane: A Biographical and Critical Study* (New York: The Bodley Press, 1948).

1.1   WHITE BUILDINGS]   Allen Tate wrote a foreword for the 1926 Boni & Liveright edition of *White Buildings*:

FOREWORD

The poetry of Hart Crane is ambitious. It is the only poetry I am acquainted with which is at once contemporary and in the grand manner. It is an American poetry. Crane's themes are abstractly, metaphysically conceived, but they are definitely confined to an experience of the American scene. In such poems as The Wine Menagerie, For the Marriage of Faustus and Helen, Recitative, he is the poet of the complex urban civilization of his age: precision, abstraction, power. There is no *pastiche*; when he employs symbols from traditional literature, the intention is personally symbolic; it is never falsely pretentious with the common baggage of poetical speech, the properties coveted by the vulgar as inherently poetic.

Hart Crane's first experiments in verse are not, of course, collected in this volume, which contains with one or two exceptions only those poems exhibiting the qualities likely to be permanent in his work. Of these exceptions there is the perfectly written piece of Imagism, Garden Abstract. This poem evinces several properties of the "new poetry" of a decade ago, the merits and the limitations of the Imagists. To the Imagists Crane doubtless went to school in poetry. He learned their structural economy; he followed their rejection of the worn-out poetic phrase; he must have studied the experiments in rhythm of Pound, Aldington, Fletcher. From Pound and Eliot he got his first conception of what it is, in the complete sense, to be contemporary.

But Crane suddenly and profoundly broke with the methods of Imagism, with its decorative and fragmentary world. To the conceptual mind a world set up not by inclusive assertion but by exclusive attention to the objects of sense lacks imaginative coördination; a method which refuses to exceed the dry presentation of *petites sensations* confines the creative vision to suggestions, to implicit indications, but it cannot arrive at the direct affirmation, of a complete world. A series of Imagistic poems is a series of worlds. The poems of Hart Crane are facets of a single vision; they refer to a central imagination, a single evaluating power, which is at once the motive of the poetry and the form of its realization.

The poet who tries to release the imagination as an integer of perception attempts the solution of the leading contemporary problem of his art. It would be impertinent to enumerate here the underlying causes of the dissociation of the modern consciousness: the poet no longer apprehends his world as a Whole. The dissociation appears decisively for the first time in Baudelaire. It is the separation of vision and subject; since Baudelaire's time poets have in some sense been deficient in the one or the other. For the revolt of Rimbaud, in this distinction, was a repudiation of the commonly available themes of poetry, followed by a steady attenuation of vision in the absence of thematic control. Exactly to the extent to which the ready-made theme controls the vision, the vision is restricted by tradition and may, to that extent, be defined by tradition. In The Waste Land, which revives the essence of the problem, Mr. Eliot displays vision and subject once more in traditional schemes; the vision for some reason is dissipated, and the subject dead. For while Mr. Eliot might have written a more ambitiously unified poem, the unity would have been false; tradition as unity is not contemporary. The important contemporary poet has the rapidly diminishing privilege of reorganizing the subjects of the past. He must construct and assimilate his own subjects. Dante had only to assimilate his.

If the energy of Crane's vision never quite reaches a sustained maximum, it is because he has not found a suitable theme. To realize even partially, at the present time, the maximum of poetic energy demonstrates an important intention. Crane's poems are a fresh vision of the world, so intensely personalized in a new creative language that only the strictest and most unprepossessed effort of attention can take it in. Until vision and subject completely fuse, the poems will be difficult. The comprehensiveness and lucidity of any poetry, the capacity for

poetry being assumed as proved, are in direct proportion to the avail-
ability of a comprehensive and perfectly articulated given theme.

Crane wields a sonorous rhetoric that takes the reader to Marlowe
and the Elizabethans. His blank verse, the most sustained medium he
controls, is pre-Websterian; it is measured, richly textured, rhetorical.
But his spiritual allegiances are outside the English tradition. Melville
and Whitman are his avowed masters. In his sea poems, Voyages, in
Emblems of Conduct, in allusions to the sea throughout his work,
there is something of Melville's intense, transcendental brooding on
the mystery of the "high interiors of the sea." I do not know whether
he has mastered Poe's criticism, yet some of his conviction that the
poet should be intensely local must stem from Poe. Most of it, how-
ever, he undoubtedly gets from Whitman. Whitman's range was pos-
sible in an America of prophecy; Crane's America is materially the
same, but it approaches a balance of forces; it is a realization; and the
poet, confronted with a complex present experience, gains in intensity
what he loses in range. The great proportions of the myth have col-
lapsed in its reality. Crane's poetry is a concentration of certain phases
of the Whitman substance, the fragments of the myth.

The great difficulty which his poetry presents the reader is the style.
It is possible that his style may check the immediate currency of the
most distinguished American poetry of the age, for there has been
very little preparation in America for a difficult poetry; the Imagistic
impressionism of the last ten years has not supplied it. Although Crane
is probably not a critical and systematic reader of foreign literatures,
his French is better than Whitman's; he may have learned something
from Laforgue and, particularly, Rimbaud; or something of these
poets from Miss Sitwell, Mr. Wallace Stevens, or Mr. T. S. Eliot.

He shares with Rimbaud the device of oblique presentation of
theme. The theme never appears in explicit statement. It is formulated
through a series of complex metaphors which defy a paraphrasing of
the sense into an equivalent prose. The reader is plunged into a
strangely unfamiliar *milieu* of sensation, and the principle of its orga-
nization is not immediately grasped. The *logical* meaning can never be
derived (see Passage, Lachrymae Christi); but the *poetical* meaning is
a direct intuition, realized prior to an explicit knowledge of the subject-
matter of the poem. The poem does not *convey*; it *presents*; it is not
topical, but expressive.

There is the opinion abroad that Crane's poetry is, in some indefi-
nite sense, "new." It is likely to be appropriated by one of the several
esoteric cults of the American soul. It tends toward the formation of a
state of mind, the critical equivalent of which would be in effect an
exposure of the confusion and irrelevance of the current journalism of
poetry, and of how far behind the creative impulse the critical intelli-
gence, at the moment, lags. It is to be hoped, therefore, that this state
of mind, where it may be registered at all, will not at its outset be

shunted into a false context of obscure religious values, that a barrier will not be erected between it and the rational order of criticism. For, unless the present critic is deceived as to the structure of his tradition, the well-meaning criticism since Poe has supported a vicious confusion: it has transferred the states of mind of poetry from their proper contexts to the alien contexts of moral and social aspiration. The moral emphasis is valid; but its focus on the consequences of the state of mind, instead of on its properties as art, has throttled a tradition in poetry. The moral values of literature should derive from literature, not from the personal values of the critic; their public circulation in criticism, if they are not ultimately to be rendered inimical to literature, should be controlled by the literary intention. There have been poetries of "genius" in America, but each of these as poetry has been scattered, and converted into an *impasse* to further extensions of the same order of imagination.

A living art is new; it is old. The formula which I have contrived in elucidation of Crane's difficulty for the reader (a thankless task, since the difficulty inheres equally in him) is a formula for most romantic poetry. Shelley could not have been influenced by Rimbaud, but he wrote this "difficult" verse:

> *Pinnacled dim in the intense inane.*

The present faults of Crane's poetry (it has its faults: it is not the purpose of this Foreword to disguise them) cannot be isolated in a line-by-line recognition of his difficulty. If the poems are sometimes obscure, the obscurity is structural and deeper. His faults, as I have indicated, lie in the occasional failure of meeting between vision and subject. The vision often strains and overreaches the theme. This fault, common among ambitious poets since Baudelaire, is not unique with them. It appears whenever the existing poetic order no longer supports the imagination. It appeared in the eighteenth century with the poetry of William Blake.

ALLEN TATE.

1.2–3   *Ce* . . . RIMBAUD]   It can only be the end of the world, advancing. From "Enfance," IV, in *Illuminations* (1874).

4.14   *Emblems of Conduct*]   Crane rewrote lines from "Conduct" and other poems by Samuel Greenberg (1893–1917) to create "Emblems of Conduct."

4.24–25   Bowls . . . gates.]   Cf. lines 9–11 of Greenberg's "Immortality": "For bowls and cups found historians / Sacred adorations, the numismatist hath shown, / But only to be memories of spiritual gate."

6.2   *William Sommer*]   See biographical note.

6.24   *Ernest Nelson*]   Crane's friend, a Norwegian-born painter and lithographer, was killed in a car accident in 1921. (See Crane's description of Nelson's life and career on pages 262 and 284.)

14.8   *Lachrymae Christi*]   Christ's tears; also the name of a sweet red Neapolitan wine.

16.28   *The Wine Menagerie*]   Crane submitted this poem to *The Dial* and it was accepted by editor Marianne Moore, who rewrote it and published it under the title "Again":

> What in this heap in which the serpent pries,
> Reflects the sapphire transepts round the eyes—
> The angled octagon upon a skin,
> Facsimile of time unskeined,
> From which some whispered carillon assures
> Speed to the arrow into feathered skies?
>
> New thresholds, new anatomies,
> New freedoms now distil
> This competence, to travel in a tear,
> Sparkling alone within another's will.
>
> My blood dreams a receptive smile
> Wherein new purities are snared. There chimes
> Before some flame a restless shell
> Tolled once perhaps by every tongue in hell.
> Anguished the wit cries out of me, "The world
> Has followed you. Though in the end you know
> And count some dim inheritance of sand,
> How much yet meets the treason of the snow."

18.8   Holofernes']   In the Apocryphal Book of Judith, the Assyrian general Holofernes was sent by King Nabuchodonosor to "avenge himself on all the earth" (Judith 1:2). Like "Baptist John" (at 18.10), Holofernes was beheaded—when the Jewish woman Judith, to save her city, murdered him in his tent after a drunken banquet (Judith 13:1–10).

18.12   Petrushka's]   Eponymous puppet-hero of the 1911 ballet, choreographed by Diaghilev to music by Stravinsky, based on a Russian folk tale about a puppet come to life.

19.2–4   suspend us . . . like Absalom]   Absalom, son of David, rebelled against his father and was killed in battle when his hair was caught in a tree under which he was riding his mule, leaving him suspended in the air and easy prey for his assailants (2 Samuel 18:9).

19.13   *Faustus and Helen*]   In Christopher Marlowe's *The Tragical History of Doctor Faustus* (1589–92), Faustus, unsatisfied with mortal beauty, summons Helen from the underworld.

19.14–21   *"And so . . . Rome."*] Ben Jonson, *The Alchemist*, IV.v.25–32.

23.18   Anchises'] Anchises was borne away by his son Aeneas as Troy burned, then accompanied him on his wanderings before dying in Sicily.

25.11   Samite] "A rich silk fabric worn in the Middle Ages, sometimes interwoven with gold" (OED).

35.3–7   *Venient annis . . . ultima Thule.*] From Seneca's *Medea*: "A time will come in distant years when Ocean will loosen the bonds of things and the whole earth's surface will be open to view, and Tethys will discover new worlds; Thule will no longer be the outermost limit of the world."

35.9   Luis de San Angel] Collector of church revenues who advocated for Columbus' voyage in Queen Isabella's court.

35.15   Juan Perez] Rabidán friar who helped persuade Columbus to ask Ferdinand and Isabella to support his voyage, although they had rejected his previous proposals.

35.29   Chan] Title given to various dignitaries in the Near East and Central Asia, often spelled "Khan."

36.27   Palos] Spanish port from which Columbus sailed on August 3, 1492.

37.8   Teneriffe's] Largest of the Canary Islands.

37.10   Te Deum laudamus] O Lord we praise Thee.

38.3–7   *"—Pocahuntus . . . over."*] From William Strachey, *History of Travaile into Virginia Britannica* (1615).

41.9   Tintex—Japalac] Tintex was a brand of dye; Japalac, a varnish.

44.13   Dan Midland] Legendary hobo who died after falling from a train.

46.31   Maquokeeta] See Crane's letter to Yvor Winters, January 19, 1927: "I chose the name at random, merely from the hearsay of a NY taxi driver who was obviously of Indian extraction (and a splendid fire-drinker by the way) who said that his indian name was 'Maquokeeta'. I think he came from Missouri, or thereabouts."

49.22   fifty-nine] The Colorado gold rush of 1859.

51.2   *Cutty Sark*] A clipper ship and a brand of Scotch whisky.

51.3–4   *O . . . no more!*] Final lines of Herman Melville's poem "The Temeraire."

52.2   Popocatepetl] Volcano southeast of Mexico City.

53.16 *Thermopylae . . . Cloud*] Names of clipper ships, as are *Rainbow*, *Leander* (53.23), *Nimbus* (53.25), *Taeping* (53.27), and *Ariel* (53.28). Crane wrote to Yvor Winters on November 28, 1926: "*Taeping* and *Ariel*, one British and the other Yankee, were noted clipper rivals in the India tea trade races of '46 or thereabouts."

53.24 last trip a tragedy] The *Leander* sank off the coast of Australia in November 1853.

54.3–4 *The seas . . . done*] From Whitman's "A Passage to India" in *Leaves of Grass*, in the "Autumn Rivulets" section.

55.16 "—Recorders age hence"] Title of a Whitman poem from *Leaves of Grass*, in the "Calamus" section.

55.19 Paumanok] Algonquin name for Long Island meaning "fish-shaped," often used by Whitman.

59.17 *Panis Angelicus*] Bread of angels.

61.3 *The one . . . hight.*] From Christopher Marlowe's *Hero and Leander* (1598).

62.6 *National Winter Garden*] New York City burlesque house.

64.2 *Quaker Hill*] Resort near Pawling, New York, not far from where Crane lived in Patterson at various times between 1925 and 1930.

64.3–5 *I see . . . earth.*] From Duncan's *My Life* (1927).

64.7–8 *The gentian . . . red.*] Opening lines of a poem written by Dickinson in 1858.

67.3–4 *To Find . . . Wrath.*] From Blake's notebook poem "Morning" (c. 1800–06).

72.3–4 *Music . . . system.*] From *Symposium* (187a–c), spoken by Eryximachus.

75.3–5 *The starry . . . day.*] "Introduction," *Songs of Experience* (1794), last three lines.

77.1 *O Carib Isle!*] The present volume prints the text of "O Carib Isle!" from Marc Simon, ed., *The Poems of Hart Crane* (New York: Liveright, 1986), which is based on what is presumed to be the last of five worksheets with Crane's ink emendations. The poem, which Crane began writing in June or July 1926, was published in three distinct versions: in *transition* (April 1927), *Poetry* (October 1927), and in Eugene Jolas's French translation in *Anthologie de la nouvelle poésie américaine* (1928), edited by Jolas. For a textual history of the poem, see Edward Brunner, *Splendid Failure: Hart Crane and the Making of* The Bridge (Urbana: University of Illinois Press, 1985). This is the version published in *Poetry*.

O Carib Isle!

The tarantula rattling at the lily's foot,
Across the feet of the dead, laid in white sand
Near the coral beach; the small and ruddy crabs
Stilting out of sight, that reverse your name—

And above, the lyric palsy of eucalypti, seeping
A silver swash of something unvisited. . . . Suppose
I count these clean enamel frames of death,
Brutal necklaces of shells around each grave
Laid out so carefully. This pity can be told . . .

And in the white sand I can find a name, albeit
In another tongue. Tree-name, flower-name deliberate,
Gainsay the unknown death. . . . The wind,
Sweeping the scrub palms, also is almost kind.

But who is Captain of this dubloon isle
Without a turnstile? Nought but catchword crabs
Plaguing the hot groins of the underbrush? Who
The commissioner of mildew throughout the senses?
His Carib mathematics dull the bright new lenses.

Under the poinciana, of a noon or afternoon
Let fiery blossoms clot the light, render my ghost,
Sieved upward, black and white along the air—
Until it joins the blue's comedian host.

Let not the pilgrim see himself again
Bound like the dozen turtles on the wharf
Each twilight—still undead, and brine caked in their eyes,
—Huge, overturned: such thunder in their strain!
And clenched beaks coughing for the surge again!

Slagged of the hurricane—I, cast within its flow,
Congeal by afternoons here, satin and vacant. . . .
You have given me the shall, Satan—the ember,
Carbolic, of the sun exploded in the sea.

78.6–7   *And if . . . dominions*—] In the opening scene of Shake-
speare's *King Lear*, Kent criticizes the rashness of Lear, who angrily banishes
him at I.i.176–79: "If, on the tenth day following, / Thy banish'd trunk be
found in our dominions, / Thy moment is thy death. Away!"

79.2   *Harry Crosby*]   See biographical note.

83.17   Atahualpa]   Last emperor of the Inca, the "imperator victus" ("an
emperor conquered" in Latin) of the poem's title. Atahualpa (c. 1502–1533)
was ambushed, captured, and executed by the Spanish expedition led by
Francisco Pizarro.

87.14   Ormus] Or Hormuz, island in the Strait of Hormuz, the site of an important Arab emporium for the Chinese and Indian trade in the thirteenth century.

87.14   Ophir] Region mentioned in the Old Testament as famous for its gold and other expensive commodities. Also a pun on the name of Emil Opffer (see biographical note).

91.1   C 33] The cell in Reading Gaol in which Oscar Wilde was imprisoned.

97.8   Portapovitch] Stanislaw Portapovitch, member of Diaghilev's Ballets Russes who had settled in New York and become friends with Crane.

98.21   Porphyro] Lover of Madeline in Keats' poem "The Eve of St. Agnes," lines from which are quoted at 100.4–6.

99.20   Harry] Harry Candee (see biographical note); see p. 221 for another account of the occasion.

100.7   "Connais . . . pays] "Do you know the country?" in French: the opening words of a popular aria, "Connais-tu le pays où fleurit l'oranger," from the first act of the 1866 opera Mignon by Ambroise Thomas, with words by Michel Carré and Jules Barbier.

104.21   Lachaise] See biographical note.

120.5–6   es . . . DONNERHALL] A cry roars like the SOUND OF THUNDER: the first line of "Die Wacht am Rhein" ("Watch on the Rhine"), patriotic German song (1840) by Max Schneckenburger.

121.29–122.1   Laocoön . . . Lessing] Laocoön is a work on aesthetics (1766) by the German philosopher, playwright, and poet Gotthold Ephraim Lessing (1729–1781).

122.2–4   Guthries . . . Williams] American poets Ramon Guthrie (1896–1973) and William Carlos Williams (1883–1963).

123.1   Zell] Crane's godmother, Zell Hart Deming (1868–1936), a journalist and editor who traveled to Europe in 1924.

127.2–3   Holofernes . . . bosom] See note 18.8.

129.18–19   "How . . . shall—"] The opening of The Bridge.

129.24   Hammerfest] Norwegian town, one of the northernmost settlements in the world.

135.6   E. O.] Emil Opffer (see biographical note).

141.10   Havana Rose] The text printed here, from Marc Simon, ed., The Poems of Hart Crane, is based on the only extant holograph of the poem. Simon writes that Crane "clearly accommodated the line-breaks of his poem in prose to the space available on the two sheets," but nonetheless the poem is printed as lineated verse in his edition. As with "Supplication to the Muses on a Trying Day" (p. 129), the present volume prints the poem as prose, according to Crane's apparent intention.

142.30   was not]   The version in Marc Simon, ed., *The Poems of Hart Crane*, based on the poem's only surviving manuscript, puts the word "not" on a line of its own, because it appears that way in the manuscript. The word's placement there, however, appears determined by the space limitation of the sheet rather than Crane's intention.

143.2   *Xochipilli*]   Nahuatl for "Flower Prince," the name of the Aztec god of flowers. Crane appears to refer to a statue of Xochipilli found at Popocatépetl thought to depict the god in a trance brought on by hallucinogenic flowers.

SELECTED PROSE

147.21   *Menschliches, Allzumenschliches*]   Nietzsche's *Human, All Too Human* (1878).

158.25   Woodberrian]   Referring to the critic and poet George Edward Woodberry (1855–1930), whose books of poetry included *Ideal Passion* (1917) and *The Roamer* (1920).

162.37–38   We are led . . . the eye.]   Cf. William Blake, "Auguries of Innocence," lines 125–26.

165.1   *A Letter to Harriet Monroe*]   In response to Crane's "At Melville's Tomb," submitted to *Poetry*, Harriet Monroe, the magazine's editor, wrote to Crane:

> Take me for a hard-boiled unimaginative unpoetic reader, and tell me how *dice* can *bequeath an embassy* (or anything else); and how a calyx (*of death's bounty* or anything else) can give back a *scattered chapter, livid hieroglyph*; and how, if it does, such a *portent* can be *wound in corridors* (of shells or anything else).
>
> And so on. I find your image of *frosted eyes lifting altars* difficult to visualize. Nor do compass, quadrant and sextant *contrive* tides, they merely record them, I believe.
>
> All this may seem impertinent, but it is not so intended. Your ideas and rhythms interest me, and I am wondering by what process of reasoning you would justify this poem's succession of champion mixed metaphors, of which you must be conscious. The packed line should pack its phrases in orderly relation, it seems to me, in a manner tending to clear confusion instead of making it worse confounded.
>
> But pardon me—you didn't ask for criticism. Of course, I should not venture upon these remarks if I were not much interested.

Monroe's letter, with Crane's response and "At Melville's Tomb," were published in the October 1926 issue of *Poetry*.

167.5–6   "a *sigh* . . . King."]   From Blake's "Jerusalem."

167.8   "Every street . . . *drum*!"]   From "Rhapsody on a Windy Night" (1917).

167.32–33   "patient . . . table,"]   From the opening of "The Love Song of J. Alfred Prufrock" (1917).

167.35   dome of many-colored glass.]   From stanza 52 of Shelley's "Adonais"; also the title of Amy Lowell's 1914 collection of poems.

174.29   *From Haunts of Proserpine*]   A review of the verse novel *Green River* (1931) by James Whaler, about the Sicilian-born naturalist Constantine Rafinesque (1783–1840).

SELECTED LETTERS

181.21   Eva Tangua]   Vaudeville star Eva Tanguay (1878–1947), who became popular through her rendition of the song "I Don't Care" in the Broadway musical *The Chaperones* (1904). The "Hipp." is the Hippodrome in Cleveland.

181.27   Elmendorfs]   Most likely the popular lecturer Dwight Lathrop Elmendorf (1859–1929). Young Harold went to the lecture with his father's parents.

182.16   the island]   The Isle of Pines, Cuba, where the Hart family owned a house. The "Wilcoxs" (182.18) refers to the caretakers of the property at the time.

183.7   Carl]   Carl Schmitt, painter and family friend.

183.29–30   Mildred and Erwin]   Erwin Shoot, a Crane Company employee and his wife.

184.23   Hazel]   Hazel Hasham, an employee at the Crane Company office in New York City.

185.9–10   published . . . next month]   "The Hive" was published in *The Pagan*; after submitting poems to *Others*, Crane had received an encouraging reply from associate editor William Carlos Williams.

187.34   three more poems]   "Echoes," "The Bathers," and "Modern Craft."

190.3   The picture]   By Carl Schmitt, which C.A. Crane had bought.

190.11–12   shock . . . house]   Grace's attempted suicide (see Chronology, 1917).

190.12   Potapovitch]   Stanislaw Portapovitch (see note 97.8).

192.17   that bastard, T——.]   A Crane Company employee. According to

Crane's biographer John Unterecker, Grace believed the man "had poisoned C.A.'s mind against her."

192.29   Anna and Stan]   Stanislaw Portapovitch and his wife, Anna.

193.9–10   "The strongest . . . alone."]   From Ibsen's *An Enemy of the People* (1882), spoken by Dr. Stockmann at the end of the play.

199.9–11   you have published . . . Aldington]   Richard Aldington's *Reverie: A Little Book of Poems for H.D.* had been published in a limited edition by Bubb's Clerk's Press in Cleveland in 1917.

199.26   Laukhuff]   Cleveland bookseller Richard Laukhoff.

200.21   illustration . . . Stevens poem]   Rockwell Kent's illustration for Stevens' "Apostrophe to Vincentine" (see Crane's next letter to Zigrosser, p. 201).

202.1   Bourne]   American writer and cultural critic Randolph Bourne (1886–1918), who had died less than two months before Crane wrote this letter.

202.2   Floyd Dell]   Writer and editor (1887–1969), who worked on leftist publications such as *The Masses* and *The Liberator*.

202.28   Mr. Pound's . . . things]   Ezra Pound was *The Little Review*'s London editor at the time.

202.34–35   Walt . . . brands]   Walt Mason (1862–1939), poet published regularly in the *Emporia Gazette* in Kansas; Edgar Guest (1881–1959), folksy poet whose poems in the *Detroit Free Press* were widely syndicated; Robert Service (1874–1958), Canadian poet best known for his popular verse about the Yukon.

203.22–23   strike . . . shipyards]   Now the site of the Philadelphia International Airport, Hog Island was home to a huge shipbuilding complex that opened in 1918. The threatened strike would have involved 25,000 workers.

206.14   the date]   Grace's birthday, April 1.

208.4   Kreymborg]   Poet and playwright Alfred Kreymborg (1883–1966).

208.6   O'Neil]   Eugene O'Neill.

208.14   Hazel]   Hazel Hasham (see note 184.23).

208.38   Charley Bubb]   See biographical note.

210.40   a poem of mine]   "To Portapovitch," which had been published in *The Modern School* in March.

211.8–9   Hal Smith and wife (Claire)]   The daughter of one of Grace Crane's friends from Ohio, the novelist Claire Spencer had befriended Crane not long before marrying editor, publisher, and writer Harrison "Hal" Smith

(1888–1971), who, as well as starting several publishing ventures, worked as an editor for Harcourt, Brace.

215.8   Baroness] Elsa von Freytag-Loringhoven (1874–1927), notorious for her outrageous clothing, behavior, and poetry. When Crane roomed above the *Little Review* offices on West 16th Street, the Baroness was living in the building's basement apartment.

215.11   Grandame poem] "My Grandmother's Love Letters."

216.2   *Pavannes & Divisions*] Collection (1918) of essays, translations, and poems by Ezra Pound, later expanded as *Pavannes & Divigations*.

216.3   *L.R.*] *Little Review*.

216.14   Fawcett] *Modernist* editor James Waldo Fawcett; the magazine lasted one issue.

216.40–217.1   the poems . . . *Poetry*] Fourteen poems by Stevens were published in the October issue of *Poetry*, including versions of "Anecdote of the Jar" and "Fabliau of Florida."

217.17   Grandma] "My Grandmother's Love Letters."

217.25–26   *The Young* . . . Barrie)] *The Young Visiters*, novella by nine-year-old Daisy Ashford (1881–1972). J. M. Barrie wrote a preface to the book when it was published in 1919, and some have speculated that he was the book's author.

217.29   Joe Kling] Editor of *The Pagan*.

217.35   Mencken . . . with him] H. L. Mencken's *Heliogabalus: A Buffoonery in Three Acts*, written with George Jean Nathan, was published by Knopf in 1920.

218.2   enclosed booklet] Twain's *1601*, privately printed in 1880, was supposedly written by one of Queen Elizabeth's servants.

219.3   Waldo Frank's book] *Our America* (1919).

219.18–19   "our Caesar"] Zwaska, office boy of *The Little Review*.

220.26   Van Wyke Brooks] American literary critic and cultural historian Van Wyck Brooks (1886–1963).

220.29   Hackett's] Francis Hackett (1883–1962), critic and editor of *The New Republic*.

221.14–17   write up . . . headlines] Crane had been the subject of a feature article in the Akron *Sunday Times*, "Millionaire's Son is Clerk in Akron Drug Store."

221.25   Eugene Field] A joke. Field was a humorist and newspaper columnist (1850–1894), perhaps best known for children's poems such as "Wynken, Blinken, and Nod."

221.26   Burleson] Postmaster-General Albert S. Burleson (1863–1937) was involved in the government suppression of materials deemed subversive during World War I and its aftermath. For his role in the censorship of *The Little Review*'s serialization of Joyce's *Ulysses*, see note 236.16–18.

221.29   Edgar Saltus] Novelist, biographer, and translator (1855–1921) known for his *fin de siècle* decadence; his many novels include *The Pomps of Satan* (1904) and *The Perfume of Eros* (1905). Munson was working on a biography of Saltus at the time.

222.28–29   marvelous photographer] Hervey W. Minns (see Crane's essay "A Note on Minns," p. 153).

222.32   Coburn . . . London] Alvin Langdon Coburn (1882–1966), Boston-born British photographer known for his portraits and the nonobjective photographs he called "vortographs"; Emil Otto Hoppe (1878–1972), German-born photographer who established a studio in London in 1907.

223.8   Baroness] See note 215.8.

223.29   Comstock] Anthony Comstock (1844–1915), founder of the Society for Suppression of Vice.

226.7   "Sweeney"] Character in T. S. Eliot poems such as "Sweeney Among the Nightingales" (1920).

226.5   *Ploughshare*] *The Plowshare*, magazine edited by Hervey White (1866–1944), novelist, poet, and founder of the Maverick Art Colony in the Catskills.

227.21   Powys] Welsh novelist and poet John Cowper Powys (1872–1963).

228.32   Burke] Kenneth Burke (see biographical note).

228.37   my opus] "My Grandmother's Love Letters."

229.1   My poem] "Garden Abstract."

229.25   I've recently . . . something] "Episode of Hands."

230.6   lines of his] From "To a Friend Concerning Several Ladies," slightly misquoted.

230.15   Vildrac] French poet Charles Vildrac, pen name of Charles Messager (1882–1971).

230.26   Akron friend] Harry Candee (see biographical note).

231.5   your position] Munson was teaching at a boarding school for boys.

232.25   people here] In Washington, D.C. Crane's father had sent him there to try to open new markets for the Crane Chocolate Company in the region.

232.29   poet friend of his]   Wilbur Underwood (see biographical note).

233.1   Porphyro]   "Porphyro in Akron."

233.16–17   VICE-President, Franklin Roosevelt]   Franklin Delano Roosevelt, vice-presidential candidate in 1920, had been the head of an investigation of homosexual acts among naval personnel.

233.19–20   Lord Douglas]   Lord Alfred Douglas, Oscar Wilde's lover.

233.20   Amusing Household!]   Crane's translation of Rimbaud's "Drôle de ménage!," the final line of "The Foolish Virgin," first section of *A Season in Hell* (1873).

233.21   *The Rainbow*]   Novel (1915) by D. H. Lawrence.

233.24   Pollard article]   Essay on the novelist and critic Percival Pollard (1869–1911).

234.6–8   the latter . . . Underwood]   In *Their Day in Court* (1909), Pollard praised Underwood's volume of poems *A Book of Masks* (1907): "His verse had the proper solemn note of carnival leaping recklessly toward a bitter morrow."

234.26   Saltus]   See note 221.29.

234.27   Hampden]   American actor, born Walter Hampden Dougherty (1879–1955), known for roles in Ibsen's and Shakespeare's plays and as Cyrano de Bergerac.

236.14–15   *L.R.* . . . my poem]   "Garden Abstract" was first published in *The Little Review*, October–December 1920.

236.16–18   J. Joyce trial . . . Quinn and Burleson]   Beginning in May 1918, *The Little Review* had serialized Joyce's *Ulysses*. The publication of an excerpt from the novel's "Nausicaa" section in the magazine's July–August 1920 issue was met with an official complaint of obscenity from the New York Society for the Suppression of Vice. The postal service, headed by Postmaster-General Albert S. Burleson, halted mailing of the issue until the matter was decided in court. Lawyer and arts patron John Quinn (1870–1924) represented *The Little Review* in the case. An initial hearing was held on October 21, 1920. A panel of three judges later pronounced *Ulysses* obscene, fining *The Little Review* and prohibiting it from continuing the serialization.

236.26   jh]   Jane Heap, co-editor of *The Little Review* with Margaret Anderson; she signed her editorials in the magazine "jh."

237.3   David Pinski]   Yiddish-language playwright and novelist (1872–1959), who spent much of his career in New York City.

237.25   Pax vobiscum!!!]   Peace be with you.

239.9   Frank Harris]   Irish-born American novelist (1856–1931), biographer, and editor of the American edition of *Pearson's Magazine*.

240.7   Minns]   See Crane's brief essay, "A Note on Minns."

240.23   Akron suite]   "Porpyhro in Akron."

241.3   Mackensie]   Sir Compton Mackenzie (1883–1972), Scottish novelist.

241.10   Baroness]   See note 215.8.

242.10   Scarron . . . Anderson]   Paul Scarron, French poet, playwright
and fiction writer (1610–1660), known for his burlesque treatment of exalted
themes; Abbé de Brantome (c. 1540–1614), French memoirist whose *Dames
galantes* relates scandalous tales of the French court; Anatole France
(1844–1924), French novelist; American novelist James Branch Cabell
(1879–1958), author of *Jurgen* (1919), which was nearly suppressed on charges
of obscenity; Sherwood Anderson (see biographical note).

242.17–18   "The   everlasting . . . laughter."]   Conclusion   of   "The
Bridge of Estador."

243.7–8   "Under the Hill"]   Unfinished work of erotic fiction by English
artist and writer Aubrey Beardsley (1872–1898).

243.14   "baboon's"]   Underwood's friend "Madame Cooke," a male
transvestite.

243.18   Palmer vigilance]   Alexander Mitchell Palmer (1872–1936), while
serving as Attorney General (1919–1921), led a zealous battle against commu-
nism and related forms of radicalism.

243.24–25   gobs . . . forever]   Parody of the final lines of Tennyson's
"The Brook": "But men may come and men may go / But I go on forever."

244.20   "Contact"]   Little magazine edited by William Carlos Williams
and Robert McAlmon, which ran from 1920 to 1923 (a "new series" began in
1932 and ran for three issues).

245.36   *Sommers'*]   See biographical note.

246.1   Brzeska]   French sculptor and graphic artist Henri Gaudier-
Brzeska (1891–1915), killed in World War I.

246.1   Boardman   Robinson]   Artist,   illustrator,   and   cartoonist
(1876–1952), whose work was published in *The New York Times*, *The Masses*,
and *The Liberator*.

246.23   art]   Articles.

248.6   Mme. Cooke's]   See note 243.14.

248.9–10   "vine leaves . . . Hedda]   Vine leaves are a motif in Ibsen's
Hedda Gabler (1890). At the end of Act Two, Hedda imagines her former
lover Ejlert Lövborg "with vine leaves in his hair. Flushed and confident." In
Act Three, she tells a suicidal Lövborg that she doesn't "believe in those vine

leaves anymore" but hopes he would end his life "beautifully," and gives him a pistol.

248.39   2 poems]   "Black Tambourine" and "A Persuasion."

249.4   drawing]   By Sommer.

249.8   what they have there]   Crane had sent reproductions of Sommer's works to *The Little Review.*

249.17   De Zayas]   A member of Alfred Stieglitz's circle, the Mexican-born art dealer, critic, and caricaturist Marius De Zayas (1880–1961) founded the Modern Gallery (1915–1918) and the De Zayas Gallery (1919–1921).

250.25   Garden]   Born in Aberdeen, Scotland, the soprano Mary Garden (1874–1956) was an opera star who spent much of her career in Chicago. She entered into an endorsement deal with Crane Chocolate Company for their "Mary Garden chocolates" line.

251.9   poem]   "Pastorale."

251.21   Marginalia on Poe and Baudelaire]   Essay from the first volume of *Promenades Littéraires* (1904) by French critic and poet Remy de Gourmont (1858–1915).

251.23   "Bottom of the sea is cruel"]   A draft of the first section of "Voyages."

252.5   Morand]   French writer Paul Morand (1888–1976).

252.11   Zona Gale]   Regionalist writer (1874–1938) from Wisconsin; a stage version of her novel *Miss Lulu Bett* (1920) won the Pulitzer Prize for Drama in 1921.

252.35   "infinitely . . . thing"]   From "Preludes" (1917).

253.13   Willy Lescaze]   See biographical note.

253.19   Salmon]   Novelist and art critic André Salmon (1881–1969).

253.30   Liza]   Gorham's wife, Elizabeth Delza Munson.

254.23   Sara . . . Wilkinson]   American lyric poets Sara Teasdale (1884–1933) and Marguerite Wilkinson (1883–1928).

254.23–24   Lady Speyer]   American poet Leonora Speyer (1872–1956), perhaps called "Lady" because she was the daughter of a German count.

257.17   "Sacred Grove"]   Eliot's essay collection *The Sacred Wood.*

257.20   J]   Matthew Josephson.

259.4   *Ulysses* situation]   See note 236.16–18.

259.11   imminent suppression . . . Jurgen]   See note 242.10.

259.13–14   *Physique d'Amour* . . . Pound]   Pound's translation was published under the title *A Natural History of Love.*

259.30   Edgar . . . Service,]   See note 202.34–35.

260.11   author of *Tarr*]   Wyndham Lewis.

262.6   Paul Rosenfeld]   Critic and editor (1890–1946), a member of the cultural circle surrounding Alfred Stieglitz and his "291" gallery. His books include *Musical Portraits* (1920) and *Port of New York* (1926).

262.13   mutual friend]   Ernest Nelson (see note 6.24).

264.31–32   from John Donne]   From "The Second Anniversary."

266.10   the office]   The advertising firm Corday and Gross.

266.17   "ivory tower"]   Crane's room in his grandmother's house.

266.26   your magazine]   *Secession.*

272.30   your letter]   A word between "your" and "letter" is obliterated in the letter.

272.38   my portrait]   Lescaze's portrait of Crane.

273.27–28   poem by Allen Tate]   "Euthanasia."

275.35   Slater Brown]   See biographical note.

278.11   matchless passage]   *The Duchess of Malfi*, III.ii.58–62.

279.22   quite as]   The rest of this letter is lost.

280.1   simian favorite]   "Madame Cooke," Underwood's male transvestite friend.

280.15   my poem]   "Praise for an Urn."

280.22   *Memoirs of a Midget*]   Walter de la Mare's novel (1921) narrated by "Miss M.," a 20-year-old woman who is at most two feet tall and at times seems even smaller.

281.19   work on Greek Vases]   *Griechische Vasenmalerei* (*Greek Vase-painting*, 1912), by the German art historian and archaeologist Ernst Buschor (1886–1961).

284.34   papers]   Issues of the London *Times* Sunday supplements.

287.26   Colum's]   Irish poet Padraic Colum (1881–1972), one of the first people Crane met when he came to New York in 1916.

288.18–20   Anderson! . . . "trial"]   Sherwood Anderson had agreed to show Sommer's work to Paul Rosenfeld.

289.17   *Enormous Room*]   Autobiographical narrative (1922) by E. E. Cummings.

289.18   *Rahab*]   Novel (1922) by Waldo Frank.

291.15–16   Moss . . . *Plains*]   With Florence Gilliam, Arthur Moss (1889–1969) founded the little magazine *Gargoyle* in Paris in 1921. Crane's poem "The Great Western Plains" was published in its August 1922 issue.

291.21   Seldes]   Critic Gilbert Seldes (1893–1970) was editor of *The Dial* from 1922 to 1923.

293.15–16   any transcriptions]   On August 13, Crane had typed and sent to Underwood 16 pages from the "Nighttown" episode of James Joyce's *Ulysses*.

293.36–294.1   your Matisse poem]   "A Matisse," published in the second issue of *Contact* in 1921.

295.6   *Wave*]   Magazine based in Chicago.

295.9   that Ben Hecht novel]   *Gargoyles* (1922).

295.15   this Turkish situation]   In September 1922, during the Turkish War of Independence, the forces of Mustafa Kemal (later Kemal Atatürk) entered a neutral zone established by the 1920 Treaty of Sèvres, threatening a wider war.

295.16   Cuthbert Wright's]   Critic and poet (1899–1948).

296.32   Loeb]   Harold Loeb (1891–1974), editor of *Broom*.

298.6   Frank study]   Munson's *Waldo Frank: A Study*.

298.7–8   delightful name]   I.e., for the *Double Dealer*.

298.16   interest . . . *Court*.]   See note 234.6–8.

298.32   Macy]   Munson had reviewed *The Critical Game* (1922) by John Macy (1877–1932).

299.7   Fischer]   William Murrell Fisher, director of the Woodstock Art Gallery.

300.38   *Ryctarik*]   See biographical note.

304.17–18   "every   day . . . millions]   Emile Coué's   *Self-Mastery Through Conscious Autosuggestion*, published in the United States in 1922, urged its readers to repeat to themselves: "Day by day, in every way, I am getting better and better."

304.27   *Book of Masks*]   Underwood's 1907 collection of poems, published in London.

305.40   1709]   Address of the Hart family house on East 115th Street.

306.8   "prison, . . . reverberation"]   Cf. T. S. Eliot's *The Waste Land*, line 326.

306.14   *S4N*]   Magazine edited by Norman Fitts.

306.15   Paul R.]   Rosenfeld (see note 262.6).

309.12   (enclosed)]   A draft of Part III of "For the Marriage of Faustus and Helen."

311.18–19   *Griechische Vasenmalerei*]   See note 281.19.

311.21   Hermann]   Her husband, Hermann Habicht.

312.31   Farrar]   *Bookman* editor John Farrar (1896–1974).

313.10   Alec]   Alexander Baltzy (see p. 205.27–29).

314.17   enclosed review]   A review of the anthology *Eight More Harvard Poets*.

315.10–11   inadvertancy . . . *Broom*]   The second part of "For the Marriage of Faustus and Helen" was published in *Broom* under the title "The Springs of Guilty Song."

315.28   amusing parody]   "America's Plutonic Ecstasies."

315.35   promised portrait]   Crane had sent a photograph of Lescaze's portrait of him to Tate, who promised to send a picture of himself in return. The two poets did not meet until 1924.

317.25–26   two . . . Tate's]   "Tercets of the Triad" and "Pins and Needles," two satirical poems published in a pamphlet by Tate and Ridley Wills entitled *The Golden Mean and Other Poems* (1923).

319.38   *Fugitive*]   Literary magazine that published Tate and like-minded poets, who became known as the Fugitives.

320.18   "Belle Isle"]   A draft of the sixth section of "Voyages."

322.19   Wheeler and Wescott]   Publisher Monroe Wheeler (1899–1988) and his lover Glenway Wescott (1901–1987), novelist and poet.

322.22–23   Turbyfill in Chicago?]   Mark Turbyfill's collection of poems *The Living Frieze* (1921) was published by Monroe Wheeler in Evanston, Illinois.

323.4   my review]   Crane's review of *Eight More Harvard Poets*.

323.5   Wheelwright's]   John Brooks Wheelwright, American poet (1897–1940).

323.23–24   "bowels" poem]   "America's Plutonic Ecstasies."

325.28   Your book]   *Waldo Frank: A Study.*

327.6   Harrison Smith]   See note 211.8–9.

328.12–13   "Striated . . . heir to"]   From "For the Marriage of Faustus and Helen"; see 22.10.

330.14   letter of introduction]   At the J. Walter Thompson Agency.

334.11   Mart and Sam]   Sommer's wife and Samuel Loveman.

336.10   writer from the South]   Jean Toomer (see biographical note).

338.14   Miss Spencer]   See note 211.8–9.

338.39   Willy]   William Lescaze, painter and later architect.

339.2   Charlotte]   Rychtarik, temporarily in New York.

339.7   Binet's]   Swiss composer Jean Binet (1893–1960), who taught
eurhythmics and theory at the Cleveland Institute of Music.

339.12   Mrs. Walton]   Frances Walton, Crane's former landlady.

339.13   Mme Lebeque]   Eugénie Lebègue, Crane's former tutor.

339.17   The Smiths]   See note 211.8–9.

339.18   Habicht's]   Charmion von Wiegand and her husband, Hermann
Habicht.

339.25   J. Taylor, Esq.]   One of Grace's suitors, who bought her a car.

341.11   "What . . . imagined,"]   One of the "Proverbs of Hell" in Blake's
The Marriage of Heaven and Hell (1790–1793).

342.33   the Faery Garden piece]   Fifth movement of Ravel's suite *Ma
Mère l'Oye* (*Mother Goose*, 1910).

345.30   Dr. Watson]   Co-owner of *The Dial* J. Sibley Watson, to whom
Crane showed Rychtarik's pictures.

346.9   Charles]   Charles Harris (see biographical note).

349.18–19   poem I sent you]   "Possessions."

349.24   *three* of us]   Perhaps meaning himself, Toomer, and Frank, since
he enclosed a sketch he had made of Frank.

349.28   The other side]   This letter is written on the back of a page of
advertising copy for a new product, Naugahyde, from the editorial depart-
ment at J. Walter Thompson.

350.1   "Kabnis"]   The last section of *Cane* and the name of a character
based on Toomer.

351.7   Pola Negri . . . ended]   Chaplin had been engaged to Polish-
born actress Pola Negri (1894–1987).

351.36   Margaret Naumburg]   Waldo Frank's wife.

354.15   Nagle]   American painter Edward Nagle (1893–1963), stepson of
the sculptor Gaston Lachaise.

356.36   *this house*]   Rather than Munson's.

357.1   Margy?]   Margaret Naumburg.

357.13–14   election excitement]   Municipal elections on November 6 in Ohio had been marked by the success of many candidates belonging to the Ku Klux Klan, followed by large demonstrations.

357.31   Rubenstein]   Beryl Rubenstein (1898–1952) was head of the piano faculty and later dean of the Cleveland Institute of Music.

357.31–32   Richard LeGallienne]   English poet and essayist (1886–1947), father of the actress Eva LeGallienne, who moved into Crane's Gramercy Park apartment when he moved out in 1917.

357.33   Gaston Lachaise]   See biographical note.

358.10   *Golden Bough*]   Comparative study of myth (1890) by James George Frazer (1854–1941), a key influence on T. S. Eliot's *The Waste Land*.

358.11   "Chauncey Depew"]   Named after a character in Toomer's *Cane*.

358.33   that poem]   The fragment on pp. 359–60.

361.25   Grace's job . . . Josephine]   Grace had been hired to sell bric-à-brac in the Josephine Shop on Euclid Avenue.

362.18   verrückt]   Crazy.

363.2–3   Lescaze, the thief and liar.]   Convinced that Lescaze had stolen his prized copy of *Ulysses* from his bedroom in Cleveland, Crane ended their friendship.

364.4   Zell's]   See note 123.1.

367.36   Macgowan]   Producer and drama critic Kenneth Macgowan (1888–1963).

367.36–37   R. Edmond Jones]   Stage designer Robert Edmond Jones (1887–1954), who worked with the Provincetown Players and wrote *Continental Stagecraft* (1922) with Kenneth Macgowan.

367.37   Light]   James Light (1894–1964), English director and early member of the Provincetown Players.

368.23   Fisher]   William Murrell Fisher, director of the Woodstock Art Gallery.

368.28–29   Machinery]   A trade journal, which offered Crane a job in May 1923. He turned the position down because on the same day he was hired by the J. Walter Thompson advertising agency.

368.30   Hal Smith]   See note 211.8–9.

369.9   "Prince Llan"]   Kenneth Burke's "Prince Llan: An Ethical Masque in Seven Parts" was published in *Broom* in January 1924.

371.40–372.1　　　stone frescoes . . . Building] Lachaise had designed a frieze for the Barclay-Vesey building at 140 West St., designed by architects McKenzie, Voorhees and Gmelin.

373.3　　　Frances] C.A. Crane's second wife.

373.35　　　My copy] Crane had been hired as a copywriter by the advertising firm Pratt and Lindsay; he was dismissed on February 11.

374.1–2　　　opening . . . Theater] Provincetown Players' revival of Anna Cora Mowatt's 1845 comedy *Fashion, or Life in New York*, starring Clare Eames (374.8).

375.8　　　the job] A temporary teaching job at a high school in Lumberport, West Virginia, which began in late February 1924.

376.7　　　"Make . . . light,"] From Donne's "The Progress of the Soul," line 55.

376.13　　　that charming] The rest of this letter is lost.

377.34–35　　　box of Mary Gardens] See note 250.25.

378.28　　　my poem] "For the Marriage of Faustus and Helen."

379.25　　　friend of mine] Kenneth Burke.

379.33　　　Claire and Hal] The Smiths (see note 211.8–9).

385.6　　　Estador] See Crane's poem "The Bridge of Estador."

385.19　　　Stewart Mitchell] Poet, editor, and historian (1892–1957).

386.18　　　"Sonnet"] A draft of a poem probably related to "Voyages."

388.17　　　Helen] Helen Hart, Crane's cousin.

389.6　　　little personal write-up] A *New York Times* article entitled "O'Neill Defends His Play."

389.26–27　　　half-back . . . eleven,] While a student at Rutgers, Paul Robeson was twice named an All-American football player by the sportswriter Walter Camp.

392.22　　　performance of *Fashion*] See note 374.1–2.

393.15　　　Seaver's] Poet, editor, and publisher Edwin Seaver.

396.21　　　Sam] Samuel Loveman (see biographical note).

396.27　　　Lovecraft] Horror and fantasy writer H. P. Lovecraft (1890–1937).

397.32　　　Mr. Curtis] Charles Curtis, whom Grace married in 1926.

400.7　　　poem, to Zell] See p. 123.

401.34   Rheinhardt]   Austrian-born theater director Max Reinhardt (1873–1943), head of the Deutsches Theater in Berlin at the time.

403.33   Seligman]   French-born American art dealer and critic Germain Seligman (1893–1978), who had recently taken over as head of his father's firm, Jacques Seligman & Co.

403.36   Mary Blair]   Actress (1895–1947). She was Edmund Wilson's wife at the time.

404.24   proposed attack]   Malcolm Cowley had asked Crane to participate in the satirical magazine *Aesthete*. The magazine was intended to be hostile to Munson and especially H. L. Mencken's *The American Mercury*, which had published an attack on the circle of Cowley, Josephson, and Burke entitled "Aesthete: Model 1924," by the Irish journalist Ernest Boyd.

410.27–30   _fl!!?!!?! . . . earthquake]   While Crane was writing this letter, New York City was shaken by tremors caused by an earthquake with an epicenter near Île aux Lièvres, Quebec.

412.2   Sir Thomas Davies]   I.e. Sir John Davies (1569–1626), English poet.

412.17   your MALVA]   A play Frank was working on.

413.40–414.2   essay . . . *Guardian*]   Neither Tate's essay nor Crane's poem was published there.

416.16   Bina]   Sabina Flynn, friend of Susan Jenkins Brown and youngest sister of American Communist Party leader Elizabeth Gurley Brown.

416.18   "Rideshalk-Godding"]   American poet Laura Riding (1901–1991), whose first husband was the historian Louis Gottschalk.

417.13   Elbano]   Emil Opffer's brother, a marine engineer.

417.17   K. B.]   Kenneth Burke.

417.18–19   Mountjoy]   Marianne Moore.

417.21   Mrs. Boving]   Opffer's mother.

419.17   receive help]   C.A. sent a check for fifty dollars with a caustic letter complaining of his son's disrespectful attitude toward him and his work.

423.11   ten acres]   With a $200 loan from the Rychtariks, Crane had bought ten acres of heavily wooded land on Bina Flynn's property in Sherman, Connecticut.

429.36   The poem]   Cowley's "The Flower in the Sea," dedicated to Crane.

430.11   *Doc. Transit*]   Isidor Schneider's novel *Doctor Transit*.

430.23   Wilson]   Edmund Wilson.

430.30   last part of *The Bridge*,]   A draft of "Atlantis."

431.23   your seagull]   Lachaise gave a small sculpture of a seagull to
Crane, who had dedicated "Interludium" to him. The sculptor was the step-
father of painter Edward Nagle, with whom Crane and William Slater Brown
had shared a house in Woodstock, New York, in 1923.

434.21   book . . . Hildebrand]   Arthur Sturges Hildebrand's *Magellan:
A General Account of the Life and Times and Remarkable Adventures* (1924).

434.26   *Virgin Spain*]   Waldo Frank's book *Virgin Spain: Scenes from the
Spiritual Drama of a Great People* (1926).

435.10–12   "This . . . whimper."]   Final lines of "The Hollow Men."

435.31   comments on Crane]   Munson's essay on Crane's poetry entitled
"Young Titan in the Sacred Wood," collected in Munson's *Destinations: A
Canvass of American Literature Since* 1900 (1928).

439.24   bundle of notes]   "General Aims and Theories."

441.36   Fray Juan Perez]   See note 35.15.

443.7–8   Benét . . . Crane]   With a foreword by poet and editor
William Rose Benét (1886–1950), *The Janitor's Boy*, a book by child poet
Nathalia Crane, was published in 1924 and soon sold out several printings.
Elinor Wylie (1885–1928), American poet and Benét's wife at the time.

443.15   Boyd proposal]   The magazine *Aesthete*; see note 404.24.

443.23   Carolyn]   Tate's wife, the novelist Caroline Gordon (see bio-
graphical note).

443.33   little Church]   "The Little Church Around the Corner" is the
popular name for the Episcopal Church of the Transfiguration on East 29th
Street in Manhattan. Grace and Charles Curtis were married at City Hall in
New York City.

445.6   Rorty]   Editor of *New Masses*.

445.37   rough notes]   See note 439.24.

446.1   *Otto H. Kahn*]   On April 7, Crane wrote an elaborately polite
letter requesting further support from Kahn ("My funds are by no means
exhausted, but they are slight enough to claim anxiety as to whether I am
warranted in placing much further dependence on them or not"). Kahn
replied, "I am prepared to add $500 to the advance which I made to you last
February." His error—he had given Crane money not in February but in
December—elicited this letter.

447.5   note . . . them]   From the letter Gordon had written Crane:
"You knocked on our kitchen door day before yesterday for the first time this
winter. I do not think you realize, ever have realized in spite of various con-

versations on this subject, that some privacy and seclusion is necessary for Allen to carry on his work. Nobody has ever entered your room unannounced. A great many happenings which I am sure have been as disagreeable to you as to us have been the result of that sort of thing. Worse still the atmosphere of the household has been made unpleasant in a thousand ways. You complained of this as 'constricting your imagination.' What has it done to ours? Any social life which we all might have enjoyed together has been prevented by the feeling that we have to protect ourselves from you."

Tate's letter to Crane was longer than his wife's and attempted to articulate their differences more thoroughly: "Briefly, the difference lies in the point I indicated the night we were discussing the 'negativity' of Eliot, when I said you could not possibly see things divorced from the satisfactions of your own ego; ergo, negativity is simply the term you apply to any force not directly sympathetic to your own personal aims; and these aims include, incidentally, your poetry as well as your merely moral situations. . . .

"You have often referred to a 'demonic' possession, something like Marlowe's; that's quite all right; but you shouldn't act upon it in ordinary life, for you can't expect others to take it seriously. But naturally to a person so motived, disagreement is equal to indictment; and that predicament makes social communications impossible. I repeat that my feeling of fundamental difference in our respective attitudes is not a condemnation of yours. But I think it is significant that I find no difficulty in getting along with other persons whose attitudes, so far as mere ideas go, are just as basically different from mine as yours is. Our difficulty doesn't lie in a mere difference of ideas; it lies in the very structure of your mind. I think I am quite justified in attributing the difficulty to you; you are, as I have just implied, the exception in my entire experience."

451.8   Mrs. Simpson]   "Aunt Sally" Simpson, caretaker for the Hart family property on the Isle of Pines.

453.32   *Allen Tate*]   This fragmentary, unsent letter, found in a book Crane left in Cuba, may be a draft of the previous letter.

455.35   Jack Fitzin]   A sailor friend and lover of Crane's.

456.36   Peggy]   Peggy Cowley.

456.37   Buff]   Eleanor Fitzgerald's dog.

456.39   Bina]   Bina Flynn (see note 416.16).

457.1   Agnes']   Agnes O'Neill's.

457.6   famous bird]   Lachaise's sculpture "The Seagull" (see note 431.23).

457.24   *The Great God Brown*]   Play (1926) by Eugene O'Neill.

461.8   unconscious calligramme]   "The Mango Tree."

461.22   Jack]   Fitzin (see note 455.35).

462.28   Malcolm has had such luck]   Cowley had received a commission from *The Saturday Evening Post*.

462.29   Lorimer]   G. Horace Lorimer, *The Saturday Evening Post*'s editor.

462.35   McFee's books]   *Letters from an Ocean Tramp* (1908) and the novel *Casuals of the Sea* (1916) were among the popular books of sea writer William McFee (1881–1960).

462.37   Romolo]   The husband of Bina Flynn.

463.8–9   "as . . . painted,"]   Coleridge, "The Rime of the Ancient Mariner," line 117.

467.13   Absalom by his hair]   See note 19.2–4.

470.5   notifying me]   I.e., that Boni & Liveright had decided to issue a contract for *White Buildings*.

470.7   Sue]   Brown.

472.33–34   "Untergang . . . translated]   Spengler's *The Decline of the West*.

474.14   Tate's generosity]   After Eugene O'Neill failed to deliver a promised preface for *White Buildings*, Tate volunteered to write the essay.

479.25   "Ferdinand, Count Fathom"]   The hero of *The Adventures of Ferdinand Count Fathom* (1753), by the Scottish novelist Tobias Smollett (1721–1771).

479.36   handy . . . proved]   The *Orizaba* was one of several ships sent to assist an Italian freighter crippled by a hurricane in late July. It was hampered in the rescue effort because of continuing severe weather.

480.4   Menorah scolding]   Frank's essay "Toward an Analysis of the Problem of the Jew" was published in *The Menorah Journal*.

480.10   Ornstein]   Experimental composer Leo Ornstein (1892–2002).

480.23   the *Prairie Years*]   The first book of Carl Sandburg's three-volume biography of Abraham Lincoln, subtitled "The Prairie Years," had just been published.

482.8   Rimbaud . . . blush"]   See "Enfance," III, in *Illuminations* (1874).

485.27   Bill]   William Slater Brown.

487.7   *To Waldo Frank*]   This letter was written on the back of a menu from "La Diana, Gran Café, Reposteria (abierto toda la noche)."

487.22   Alhambra]   A burlesque house.

489.21   discussion with Harriet Monroe]   See "A Letter to Harriet Monroe," p. 165.

490.33   Elbert Hubbard] American writer (1856–1915), best known for his inspirational tract *A Message to Garcia* (1899). (See also Chronology, 1915.)

490.34–35   slab of the sunburnt West] Title of Sandburg's 1922 poetry collection.

491.4   Nancy Hanks] Abraham Lincoln's mother, who died in 1818 of so-called milk-sickness.

492.13   "Walsh"] Poet Ernest Walsh (1895–1926), editor of the magazine *This Quarter*.

492.14   Wrynn] Short-story writer and poet Anthony Wrynn.

493.9   hurricane experience] Crane left the Isle of Pines after a hurricane in late October. See the poem "Eternity" for an account of the hurricane's aftermath.

494.24   complicate] The word may be "contemplate" (the word is ambiguous).

495.4   "—seeds . . . crack"] Cf. Winters' poem "To the Painter Polelonema" (collected in *The Proof*, 1930), describing the essential elements in a work of art as a kind of indestructible kernel: "No sparrow / cracks these seeds // that no wind blows."

496.23–24   A cyclone . . . back.] From "The Dance."

498.5   little thing above] The poem "To Emily Dickinson," typed at the top of this letter.

498.20   *Taeping* and *Ariel*] Ships cited at the end of "Cutty Sark" in *The Bridge*.

498.32   the ms] The manuscript contained poems Winters was considering publishing in *The Bare Hills* (1927).

498.32–33   "passion . . . glass"] The lines quoted here are slightly different from the published version of the "Nocturne" section of Winters' "The Bare Hills": "their passion is / persistent like a pane of glass."

499.12–16   My very . . . spring.] From "Dark Spring."

499.18–19   Dry . . . light] See the first stanza of Winters' "The Grosbeaks": "The beauty of / these hard / small birds is / clean as scattered seed— / dry penguins / of the cliffs of light!"

499.21–22   Unlit . . . sleep—] See the ending of "The Streets": "I met God in the streetcar, but I could not / pray to him, and we were both / embarrassed; and to get away I chose / the first finality —black streets like / unlit windows, coffee hour by hour, / and chilling sleep."

499.38–39   "solid . . . serious"] See the description of a little goat in

"April": "Not a tremor— / solid in the / spring and serious / he walks away."

500.1   hard trying" . . . put it] Crane cites a phrase from the title of Moore's poem "In This Age of Hard Trying, Nonchalance Is Good And," collected in *Observations* (1924).

500.6   lisp . . . numbers] Cf. Alexander Pope's account of himself in "Epistle to Dr. Arbuthnot": "As yet a child, not yet a fool to fame, / I lisped in numbers, for the numbers came." "Numbers" refers to metrical verses.

504.1   C S] Christian Science.

505.11   as Melville says] In "The Temeraire," lines used as the epigraph to "Cutty Sark."

505.12–13   Harry's . . . gone.] Harry Candee had died in England in July 1925 (see biographical note).

505.20   *The Time of Man*] Novel (1926) by the Kentucky-born novelist, poet, and children's writer Elizabeth Madox Roberts (1881–1941).

505.28   Tiger Flowers] Boxer Tiger Flowers (1895–1927) had recently lost his world middleweight championship to Mickey Walker, in a split decision widely regarded as unfair.

506.7   line from Donne] "The Progress of the Soul," line 55.

508.3   your Rimbaud volume] Rickword's *Rimbaud: The Boy and the Poet* (1924).

508.28   Schneider] Isidor Schneider.

508.31–32   Waldo's article] Waldo Frank had written an admiring review of *White Buildings* for *The New Republic*.

508.33–34   new title pages] Tate's name had been misspelled "Allan" on *White Buildings*' original title page.

509.2   Orage] Gurdjieffian disciple Alfred Richard Orage (1873–1934), whom Crane and Munson heard lecture in 1926. Unlike Crane, Munson embraced Gurdjieff's ideas.

509.11   Ode] "Ode to the Confederate Dead."

510.14   sonnet] "The Subway."

511.6   Jack's] Jack Fitzin's.

511.28   Romolos] Romulo Bobba's, Bina Flynn's husband.

512.33   "Maquokeeta"] See note 46.31.

513.26   death of Frances] C.A. Crane's second wife, Frances, died of cancer on January 3.

514.12–14   Matthew . . . etc.] Neither Josephson nor MacLeish reviewed *White Buildings*; Winters' review was published in *Poetry*.

514.35   Clara Risdon] Crane's cousin.

515.20   Bess and Byron] The Maddens, C.A.'s sister and brother-in-law.

516.21   'the very deep did rot'] Coleridge, "Rime of the Ancient Mariner," part II.

518.13–14   history . . . reading] *The Log of the Cutty Sark* (1924), by Alfred Basil Lubbock (1876–1944).

518.27   book on Idiom] *English Idioms* (1923), by Logan Pearsall Smith (1865–1946).

518.29   "Tam O' Shanter"] Robert Burns's poem.

520.14   Emil] Emil Opffer.

521.2   Mike Drayton] One of Crane's pseudonyms while cruising, a sly homage to Elizabethan poet Michael Drayton (1563–1631).

521.4   Jack the Incomparable] Jack Fitzin.

521.9   the Jennings] Home of Charles Jennings, Crane's neighbor in Patterson, a farmer and a bootlegger.

521.24   his *Fire Sequence*] Provisional manuscript of a series of interrelated poems by Winters. He had included notes (what Crane called a "manifesto") with the manuscript.

521.31   Loeb-physics-etc.] Winters was influenced by the ideas of Jacques Loeb (1859–1924), a German-born biochemist with a mechanistic theory of causation discussed in books such as *The Mechanistic Conception of Life* (1912).

522.8   copies] For an anthology Tate and MacLeish were planning, which was never published.

522.29   Andy] The local mailman.

523.36   No. 3 . . . 6] Because Winters renumbered the poems in the sequence, it is impossible to know which poems Crane refers to.

524.17–18   'cold eye for the fact'] A phrase from Winters' poem "The Rows of Cold Trees," published in *The Bare Hills*.

526.34   Janet Lewis] Winters' wife, a poet and later a novelist (1899–1998).

527.10   Ransome] Poet John Crowe Ransom (1888–1974), who, like Tate, was a central figure in the Fugitive group. "This last book" is *Two Gentleman in Bonds* (1927).

527.29   Torrence] Ridgely Torrence, poet and editor of the *Saturday Review of Literature* (referred to as "Miss Torrence" in the following letter).

528.24   Gilmore's] Louis Gilmore.

528.29   NR] *New Republic.*

528.33   Bill] William Slater Brown.

528.35   one quotable paragraph] Crane quotes the paragraph excised by *The New Republic*'s editors in a letter to his mother, p. 514.25–31.

529.13   Laura] Laura Riding.

529.18–19   Wondrous . . . hen!] Opening couplet of Blake's "Imitation of Pope: A Compliment to the Ladies."

530.23   following lines] Melville's poem "Art."

533.13   Bobbas and Browns] Romolo Bobba, his wife Bina Flynn, and Susan and William Slater Brown.

533.18   President Calles] Plutarco Elías Calles (1877–1945), president of Mexico at the time.

534.6   MacLeish fiasco] The collapse of the anthology project Tate planned with MacLeish.

534.14   Aiken] American poet Conrad Aiken (1889–1973).

534.28   Davidson] American poet Donald Davidson (1893–1968), a member of the Fugitives.

534.31   Jolas] Expatriate writer Eugene Jolas (1894–1952) co-founded and edited *transition* in Paris.

535.3   "my biography"] Crane wanted to write a biography of John A. Roebling, architect of the Brooklyn Bridge, as a means to make money and attract attention to *The Bridge.*

536.20   Claire] Smith (see note 211.8–9). "Pat" (520.24) is her brother, Pat Spencer.

537.16   machine] I.e., a typewriter.

537.24   old woman] Addie Turner, owner of the farmhouse in Patterson where Crane lived off and on from 1925 to 1930.

537.29   trial] Grace's divorce suit against Charles Curtis.

538.29   Polelonemas] Works by Hopi artist Otis Polelonema (1902–1981), subject of a poem by Winters quoted here by Crane (see note 495.4).

539.19   Pater-ian . . . music'] Walter Pater wrote, "All art constantly aspires towards the condition of music" in "The School of Giorgione," collected in *The Renaissance* (1907).

541.24–25   Wilson's article]   "The Muses Out of Work," Edmund Wilson's survey of contemporary American poetry first published in *The New Republic* on May 11, 1927, and collected in *The Shores of Light* (1952).

560.19   Anne]   Cummings's wife.

560.29   Chaliapin]   Russian opera star, the bass tenor Feodor Chaliapin (1873–1938).

561.5   The Breughel]   A book of reproductions of the Flemish painter's work that Crane had given the Browns.

561.7   Isidor and Helen]   Schneider (see biographical note).

561.36   Elizabeth Madox Roberts]   See note 505.20.

562.7   her book]   Roberts' novel *My Heart and My Flesh* (1927).

563.20–23   enclosing . . . Marichalar]   Spanish critic Antonio Marichalar (1893–1973) wrote a favorable essay about Crane, "La Estética de Retroceso y la Poesía de Hart Crane," in the journal *Revista de Occidente* in February 1927.

563.29   correct him . . . Liberty]   In his essay Marichalar regards the Statue of Liberty as representing a distinctly American aesthetic.

563.14   "Gotzottski"]   Russian dance that Crane learned from Stanislaw Portapovitch.

564.33   Maurras and Massis]   Charles Maurras (1868–1952), French poet and political reactionary; Henri Massis (1886–1970), conservative Catholic literary critic who accused André Gide of corrupting public morals with his books.

564.34   Stewart Mitchell]   See note 385.19.

565.33   Addie]   Turner (see note 537.24).

565.35   Bernardsville]   New Jersey, where the Browns had moved in anticipation of the birth of their son, Gwilym.

566.20   "Grandmother"]   After Kay Boyle attacked Crane's "My Grandmother's Love Letters" in *transition*, Yvor Winters wrote the magazine a letter in Crane's defense.

566.30   Laura likes me]   Laura Riding reviewed *White Buildings* favorably in *transition*.

567.1   Morley and Canby]   Christopher Morley and Henry Seidel Canby, editors at the *Saturday Review of Literature*.

567.1   "Trinc"]   Debut poetry collection (1927) by H. Phelps Putnam (1894–1948).

567.13   Fernandez book] *Messages* (1927), a collection of literary essays on Balzac, Stendhal, Conrad, Freud, Pater, T. S. Eliot, and others, by the literary critic Ramon Fernandez (1894–1944).

568.1   "Tonita Penas"] Reproductions of works by Pueblo painter Maria Antonía Peña, also called Quah Ah (1893–1949).

568.19   Bridges' notes] Hopkins' poems were first published posthumously in 1918, in a book edited by Robert Bridges.

573.18   Bert Savoy] Stage name of female impersonator Everett Mackenzie (1888–1923), part of the vaudeville team of Savoy & Brennan.

573.35–36   Betty Compson] Movie actress (1897–1974) who starred mostly in silent films.

576.13   Pres. Calles] The president of Mexico. A discussion about Calles with the Slater Browns had led to Crane throwing his typewriter out the window (see p. 533).

577.22   the Bovings] Johanne and Henrik Boving, Opffer's mother and stepfather, were close friends of the Browns.

578.1   Lasky] Paramount Pictures executive Jesse Lasky (1880–1958).

578.14–15   the slogan] "He Won't Be Happy 'Til He Gets It."

578.28   Estlin C'gs] E. E. Cummings.

578.28   Canby Crap Can] *Saturday Review of Literature.*

578.30   Mitchell] Stewart Mitchell.

579.29   The date] February 9.

581.34   Alma Veder] Waldo Frank's second wife.

582.13   Uncle Cassius] Crane's great-uncle, the brother of C.A. Crane's father.

582.18   Ralph] Cassius' son.

583.38   Sing] C.A. Crane's dog.

584.6   *Destinations*] See note 435.31.

591.10   Guest] See note 202.34–35.

592.13   Nathan Asch] American novelist Nathan Asch (1902–1964), son of the Yiddish writer Sholem Asch.

592.21   Morley Callaghan] Canadian novelist and short-story writer (1903–1990), who had worked with Hemingway at the Toronto *Star*.

594.4   pups] Winters and his wife bred Airedales.

596.11   kindly loaned me]   See note 423.11.

598.28   "invisible . . . mind"]   From Tate's "Ode to the Confederate Dead."

600.18   *spurlos versenkt*]   Sunk without a trace.

600.24–25   the Englishman . . . through!"]   The suicidal Englishman is cited in Cocteau's *Le grand écart* (1923).

600.36   mss]   The working draft of Cowley's collection *Blue Juniata.*

601.11–13   supposed mother . . . Art Hays]   Crane's mother obstructed the execution of his grandmother's will, insisting that he move to California so they both could live off the inheritance. Crane considered legal action against her; Art Hays was a lawyer.

601.21–22   W. J. Turner says]   In "London After Noon."

603.19   Lorna]   Dietz (see biographical note).

604.26   Max and Ilyena]   Max Eastman and his second wife, Eliena.

606.6   Varese]   Composer Edgar Varèse (1883–1965).

607.21   from Hal]   Hal Smith (see note 211.8–9). *Blue Juniata* was published by Jonathan Cape & Harrison Smith in 1929.

609.7   Mony and Rose]   Solomon Grunberg (see biographical note) and his wife, Rose.

609.9–10   Here . . . join!]   This is written on the front of the postcard, which shows a photograph of Le Moulin du Soleil, Crosby's estate at Ermenonville, near Chantilly.

609.12   remember this?]   The interior of the gothic cathedral of Saint-Chapelle in Paris, which is shown on the front of the postcard.

611.29   some friends]   Crane spent Christmas 1928 on the houseboat of Robert Graves and Laura Riding.

614.5–6   dedicating . . . you]   Kahn replied on March 1: "As a general rule, I am not partial to dedications, but you and *The Bridge* do not come within the four corners of general rules. Therefore I accept with pleasure and appreciation the honor which you offer me, and I am looking forward to receiving a copy of that volume."

614.24   Your suggestion]   Caresse Crosby had written Crane on April 23 that *The Bridge* "seemed already to be one poem. Why do you think it must be added to? It is eternal and it is alive and it is beautiful—why don't you let us print it as it is?"

615.18   Pete and Gretchen]   Peter and Gretchen Powel, whose book of photographs, *New York 1929*, was published in a limited edition by the Black Sun Press in 1930.

616.2   to notice odors] Stein had warned Crane about open sewers in Collioure, from where he sent this postcard.

620.25   here] Martigues, France.

620.26   Roy Campbell] South African poet (1901–1957).

622.8–9   Have been . . . me.] This sentence was written on the front of the postcard, showing a view of Marseille from the sea.

623.1–5   Stella . . . colored picture] Crane had initially wanted a reproduction of Joseph Stella's painting of the Brooklyn Bridge to be included in the Black Sun Press edition of *The Bridge*.

625.8   stars,] Potential ornaments for the Black Sun Press edition of *The Bridge*.

627.6   Kenneth's] Kenneth Burke's.

627.30   "gloss"] Marginal gloss for "Powhatan's Daughter."

630.12   *Kahn*] This handwritten note was left at Kahn's door with his servant. Lord Lymington, Gerard Vernon Wallop, was a poet and bon vivant whom Crane met through Harry Crosby.

631.1   Emil] Opffer.

631.4   *Crosby*] This handwritten note (with a star beside the signature) probably accompanied a part or the whole of *The Bridge* in typescript.

632.11–12   "while . . . alone"—] Lines from "For the Marriage of Faustus and Helen."

632.16   OF HELP] Harry Crosby and his mistress Josephine Bigelow were found dead of gunshot wounds in a hotel room on December 10, apparently a double suicide.

632.17–18   POLLY CARESSE] Caresse Crosby was nicknamed Polly.

634.7   middle photograph] By Walker Evans.

635.13   Bob] Bob Stewart, a sailor who was Crane's friend and lover.

635.18   "Sleeping Together"] A sequence of prose poems by Harry Crosby.

635.31   Gretchen] Powel (see note 615.18).

637.3   *Gyroscope*] Short-lived magazine co-founded and edited by Winters

637.17   H.M.] Harriet Monroe.

637.17   Zabel]   Morton Dauwen Zabel (see biographical note).

639.35   gratefully yours,]   Kahn's next letter contained a check for $100.

640.4   enthusiastic review]   In the Milwaukee *Journal*, April 12.

643.18   medicine-man passage]   In "The Dance."

644.18–21   I believe . . . sand pit.]   Cf. lines 137.22–25 in the poem beginning "I rob my breast to reach those altitudes."

647.21   as someone once said]   Oscar Wilde.

653.1   turning down]   The article assigned by *Fortune* on the nearly completed George Washington Bridge was rejected by the magazine. No copy survives.

653.15   interview with Teagle]   Another *Fortune* article, on Standard Oil president J. Walter Teagle, was lost in the mail while still a rough draft; Crane abandoned the piece.

654.14–15   "grim about the mouth,"]   From the opening paragraph of Chapter 1, "Loomings," of *Moby-Dick*.

654.27–28   charge of sentimentality]   Allen Tate, reviewing *The Bridge* in *Hound & Horn*, called "Indiana" "a nightmare of sentimentality and false writing."

657.4   official stationary!]   The letter is written on the stationary for Crane's Canary Cottage, the business recently established by Crane's father in Chagrin Falls, Ohio.

657.22   on Euclid,]   In Cleveland.

658.14   Teagle . . . flop]   See note 653.15.

659.31   in the *Bridge*]   From "The River."

659.34   rock carving]   The carving shows an eagle and a serpent intertwined.

661.31   Emil and Fitzi?]   Emil Opffer and Eleanor Fitzgerald.

661.33   Eda Lou Walton]   See biographical note.

661.35–37   The Story . . . dog sentiment]   *The Story of San Michele* is the 1929 memoir of Swedish physician Axel Munthe, who adopted stray dogs as part of a menagerie he kept on the island of Capri.

662.1   pow-wow about it]   *Jurgen* was nearly suppressed on grounds of obscenity.

666.18   Alice book]   In 1930, the Black Sun Press published an edition of *Alice's Adventures in Wonderland*.

669.20 treatment . . . there] Crane had spent six days in prison after starting a fight outside the Café Select and striking a policeman.

670.27–28 Almanach de Gotha] Directory of European nobility.

671.21 Hazel Cazes] Formerly Crane Company employee Hazel Hasham, she had married and was an assistant to Eyler Simpson, official for the Guggenheim foundation in Mexico City.

672.12 Bill Spratling] Artist William Spratling (1900–1967), who expatriated to Mexico in 1929. Most of his work was done as a silversmith. Spratling introduced Crane to painter David Siqueiros.

672.26 Carleton Beals] Foreign correspondent and author of several books on Latin America, including *Brimstone and Chili* (1927) and *The Coming Struggle for Latin America* (1938).

673.28 Moisés] Moisés Sáenz, Mexican Minister of Education.

674.4 the new Diegos] Works by Diego Rivera.

674.7 Liam O'Flaherty] Irish novelist and short story writer (1896–1984).

674.14 Muriel] Muriel Maurer, who married Cowley in 1932.

679.17 Roy Helton] Zabel had asked Crane to review Helton's book *Lonesome Water*.

680.10–17 I spent . . . doom!] After Porter failed to attend a meal he had planned for her, Crane went on a drunken spree that culminated in his shouting obscenities at her outside her house. Crane spent that night in jail for his behavior. To this letter, Porter replied: "I have lived in Greenwich Village also, as you know, but I was never involved there in such a meaningless stupid situation as this. . . . You must either learn to stand on your own feet as a responsible adult, or expect to be treated as a fool. Your emotional hysteria is not impressive, except possibly to those little hangers-on of literature who feel your tantrums are a mark of genius. To me they do not add the least value to your poetry, and take away my last shadow of a wish to ever see you again."

681.31 recent notice] Moe had written to Crane on June 29: "There's no use in getting mad at this letter; protests have been made in several governmental channels and I cannot ignore them, which I have no desire to do anyway. So I put my cards on the table and tell you that you are making yourself liable to deportation; and, if that happens, your support from the Foundation must cease. I am far from saying that that is the only incident that would terminate the Fellowship either.

"So that's that, and that's flat. The Fourth of July is coming; and that will make a grand occasion for you to go on a *final* bust or quit making a nuisance and a fool of yourself and the Foundation. Take your choice and go to it."

683.33–34   recent *Oklahoma* affair]   On June 8, 1931, two Mexican college students studying in the United States (including a cousin of Mexican president Ortiz Rubio) were shot by sheriff's deputies in Ardmore, Oklahoma, causing widespread outrage in Mexico.

688.26   Chase writes about.]   In *Mexico: A Study of Two Americas* (1931), by Stuart Chase.

694.34–35   sail . . . stone.]   The image on the front of the postcard.

697.27   he . . . cracks]   H. L. Mencken and Max Eastman had attacked Crane's poetry in *The American Mercury* and *Harper's*, respectively, in October 1931.

698.25   Betty]   Elizabeth Huling, Brown's co-worker at *The New Republic*.

708.35   Lesley]   Lesley Byrd Simpson (see biographical note).

709.17   Putnam review!]   Crane had been asked to review H. Phelps Putnam's *The Five Seasons* for *Poetry*.

710.3   Marion]   Lesley Simpson's wife.

711.7   *canaille*]   Rabble.

711.19   Maddow's poems]   Youthful poems of Ben Maddow (1909–1992), later a novelist and screenwriter.

711.35   Brett]   Lady Duff Twysden, the model for Brett Ashley in Hemingway's *The Sun Also Rises* (1926); she married American artist Clinton King (see 712.1), her second husband, in 1928.

711.35   Bynner]   American poet Witter Bynner (1881–1968).

719.6–7   Natalia's]   Natalie Scott, who rented Peggy Cowley a house in Taxco.

720.17   Kings,]   See note 711.35.

721.16   scene of action]   Cowley and Frank were among a group of writers delivering food and support to striking miners in Kentucky.

724.30   this sacred paper]   This letter is typewritten on rose-colored paper with an image of the Virgin Mary in the center. Crane typed around the image.

725.9   Paca Toor]   Frances "Paca" Toor (1890–1956), author of several books about Mexico.

727.4   for Hanna]   The Grunbergs' daughter.

730.14   Kentucky expedition]   See note 721.16.

735.16–17   poem . . . it.]   "The Broken Tower" never arrived at *Poetry*.

736.21   Byron]   Madden, Bessie's brother, who was involved in settling
C.A. Crane's estate.

736.31   Wilson matter]   Several employees of Crane's Canary Cottage had
been injured, one fatally, in a car accident.

738.20   here]   In Havana, where the *Orizaba* had docked briefly. The
postcard shows a picture of Morro Castle in Havana as seen from the sea.

Index of Poem Titles and First Lines

Index

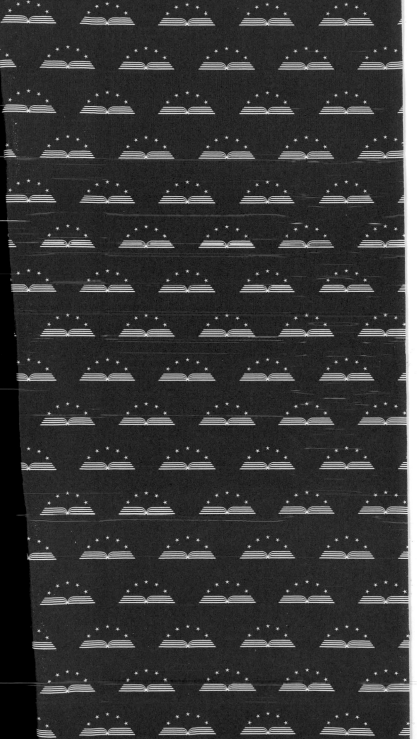

Library of Congress Cataloging-in-Publication Data

Crane, Hart, 1899–1932.
  [Selections. 2006]
  Complete poems and selected letters / Hart Crane.
      p. cm. — (Library of America ; 168)
  Includes index.
  ISBN 1–931082–99–5 (alk. paper)
      I. Title. II. Series.

PS3505.R272   A6   2006
811′.52—dc22   2006040922